ALSO BY STEVEN BRILL

*The Teamsters*

# After

How America Confronted
the September 12 Era

## Steven Brill

Simon & Schuster

NEW YORK · LONDON · TORONTO
SYDNEY · SINGAPORE

SIMON & SCHUSTER
Rockefeller Center
1230 Avenue of the Americas
New York, NY 10020

SIMON & SCHUSTER and colophon are registered trademarks
of Simon & Schuster, Inc.

For information regarding special discounts for bulk purchases,
please contact Simon & Schuster Special Sales at
1-800-456-6798 or business@simonandschuster.com

Designed by Paul Dippolito

Manufactured in the United States of America

1   3   5   7   9   10   8   6   4   2

Library of Congress Cataloging-in-Publication Data is available.

ISBN 0-7432-3709-9

*For Emily, Sophie, Sam—and Cynthia*

# The Main Characters

**John Ashcroft:** United States Attorney General

**James Brosnahan:** Lead defense lawyer for John Walker Lindh

**Michael Cartier:** Business information systems manager at cable television company in New York; co-founder, Give Your Voice; brother of September 11 victim James Cartier, an electrician working in the North Tower

**Larry Cox:** President and CEO, Memphis–Shelby County Airport Authority

**Kenneth Feinberg:** Special Master, Victim Compensation Fund

**Bernadine Healy:** President and CEO, American Red Cross

**Salvatore Iacono:** Proprietor, Continental Shoe Repair (two blocks from Ground Zero)

**Robert Lindemann:** Senior Border Patrol Agent, U.S. Border Patrol (Detroit)

**Brian Lyons:** Recovery Supervisor, Ground Zero, and brother of September 11 victim Michael Lyons, member of New York City Fire Department, Rescue Squad 41

**Sergio Magistri:** President and CEO, InVision Technologies (Silicon Valley)

**Kevin McCabe:** Chief Inspector, Contraband Enforcement Team, United States Customs Service, Port of New York (based in Elizabeth, New Jersey)

**Dean O'Hare:** Chairman and CEO, Chubb Corporation

**Tom Ridge:** Director, White House Office of Homeland Security, and Secretary, Department of Homeland Security

**Anthony Romero:** Executive Director, American Civil Liberties Union

**Gale Rossides:** Associate Undersecretary for Training and Quality Performance, U.S. Transportation Security Administration, Department of Transportation

**Charles Schumer:** Senior senator from New York, and husband of Iris Weinshall

**Larry Silverstein:** President and CEO, Silverstein Properties, real estate developer (New York City)

**Eileen Simon:** Harrington Park, New Jersey, widow of September 11 victim Michael Simon, an energy trader at Cantor Fitzgerald

**Iris Weinshall:** Commissioner, New York City Department of Transportation, and wife of Charles Schumer

**Edmund Woollen:** Vice President, Raytheon Company (Virginia)

## Other Key Figures

**Hollie Bart:** Sal Iacono's pro bono lawyer

**Joshua Bolten:** Assistant to the President and Deputy Chief of Staff, the White House

**Robert Bonner:** Commissioner, U.S. Customs Service

**Michael Byrne:** Senior Director of Response and Recovery, White House Office of Homeland Security

**Andrew Card, Jr.:** Chief of Staff, the White House

**Michael Chertoff:** Assistant Attorney General in charge of the Criminal Division, U.S. Department of Justice

**David Crane:** Senior Policy Advisor to Senator Trent Lott, and then a lobbyist representing real estate interests

**Mitchell Daniels, Jr.:** Director, Office of Management and Budget, the White House

**Mary Delaquis:** Area Service Port Director, U.S. Customs Service (based in Pembina, North Dakota)

**Ali Erikenoglu:** Electrical engineer (Paterson, New Jersey)

**Richard Falkenrath:** Special Assistant to the President and Senior Director of Policy and Plans, White House Office of Homeland Security

**Jennie Farrell:** Co-founder, Give Your Voice, and sister of Michael Cartier and September 11 victim James Cartier, an electrician working in the North Tower

**Joshua Gotbaum:** CEO, September 11th Fund

**Mark Hall:**  Senior Border Patrol Agent, U.S. Border Patrol (Detroit)

**Kip Hawley:**  Director, go teams, Transportation Security Administration, U.S. Department of Transportation

**Mark Isakowitz:**  Washington lobbyist for private airline security companies, and then for the insurance industry

**Michael Jackson:**  Deputy Secretary, U.S. Department of Transportation

**Syed Jaffri:**  Pakistani immigrant, detained in September after dispute with Bronx landlord

**Lee Kreindler:**  Plaintiffs lawyer specializing in representing victims of air disasters

**General Bruce Lawlor:**  Senior Director of Protection and Prevention, White House Office of Homeland Security

**Elaine Lyons:**  Westchester, New York, widow of September 11 victim Michael Lyons, member of New York City Fire Department, Rescue Squad 41

**David McLaughlin:**  Chairman, American Red Cross

**Norman Mineta:**  Secretary, U.S. Department of Transportation

**Sohail Mohammed:**  Attorney and Muslim community leader, Paterson, New Jersey (represented Ali Erikenoglu)

**Barry Ostrager:**  Lead lawyer representing Swiss Reinsurance Company in suit against Larry Silverstein

**Hugo Poza:**  Vice President, Homeland Security, Raytheon Company (Virginia)

**Eliot Spitzer:**  New York State Attorney General

**Herbert Wachtell:**  Lead lawyer representing Larry Silverstein

# Prologue: September 11, 2001

**Kevin McCabe**'s office in Elizabeth, New Jersey, was drab, even by government standards. Except for the view. It had a heart-stopping vista of the New York skyline. McCabe ran the squad of seventy U.S. Customs Service inspectors who checked all the cargo that comes into the port of New York, which includes piers in Elizabeth in New Jersey and Staten Island and Brooklyn in New York. From his window in Elizabeth, it looked as if he could throw a football across to lower Manhattan.

September 11 was McCabe's first day as the chief inspector of the Contraband Enforcement Team. He'd been acting chief for a year, and his official promotion had come through late in the afternoon the day before.

McCabe, a stocky, perennially cheerful forty-two-year-old veteran of the endless Customs war on drugs, got to the office at about 8:00 and sheepishly took the congratulatory handshakes from the staff for his long-awaited change in title. He was sipping coffee and talking on the phone at 8:46 when he saw the first plane hit the World Trade Center. Because he had seen how big the plane was, he thought it might be an attack.* He flipped on the television, then called the Customs office in New York, which was at the Trade Center, to find out what was going on. Eighteen minutes later, while still on the phone, he heard a CNN reporter say another plane had hit. He whirled around in his chair, looked out the window, and saw the second tower on fire. Now he knew for sure.

McCabe got up and looked out not only at the two towers engulfed in black smoke, but at the acres of piers and staging areas right below him. There were perhaps a thousand cars just shipped in from Japan and Korea, ready to be trucked out. There were 7,000 or more trailer-truck-sized cargo containers—holding everything from furniture to fabric to computers to

---

*Unless otherwise noted, any thought attributed to anyone in this narrative is based on the author having talked to that person. A full explanation of sources can be found in the Source Notes in the back of the book.

lemons and limes—that had arrived from all over the world in just the last twenty-four hours.

"I figured," McCabe remembers, "that we were under attack, probably from some group in the Middle East, and I had no way of knowing for sure what was in any of those containers."

McCabe and everyone else at Customs quickly sealed the port. Nothing was allowed in or out. All land entrances were patrolled. The Coast Guard was called in to close off the water entrances.

Then McCabe and his troops began their own exercise in racial profiling. Every one of those forty-foot-long containers that had originated in or stopped at ports in the Middle East or North Africa was identified and moved to one side of the port—some 600 containers in all, each destined to be hoisted onto a tractor trailer truck and dispersed across the East Coast. Over the next week, each container would get the treatment that Customs usually reserved for only a fraction of the cargo coming in from the drug-exporting countries of South America. They'd be scanned by a giant X-ray-like machine and, if need be, searched by hand after that.

It was, McCabe would readily admit, "as much an emotional reaction as a practical one. We felt we had to do something."

It was not something he could keep doing for long. There was no way they could search more than 2 or 3 percent of the 7,000 to 9,000 containers coming in every day without so delaying these shipments that commerce all over the world would be paralyzed. Worse, these searches didn't deal with the real problem—which was that the same kinds of people who had flown the planes into the buildings could ship a nuclear or biological device into the port, and, as McCabe now figured, it wouldn't be like drugs where nailing a big stash on the docks occasioned high-fives all around. If this stuff even got to the docks, it would be a catastrophe.

What are we going to do, McCabe thought that afternoon as he looked across those thousands of containers at the smoke where the towers had been.

In Pembina, North Dakota, at the edge of the Canadian border, Customs area service port director **Mary Delaquis** knew exactly what she wanted to do. Delaquis, forty-four, was in charge of inspecting any goods that come into the United States over 570 miles of border stretching from Duluth, Minnesota, to eastern Montana. (The Immigration and Naturalization Service, or INS, is in charge of *people* entering the U.S.) On September 11, Delaquis had 103 agents, along with a small contingent from INS, to cover twenty-four official crossings, called ports of entry. Delaquis was now going to make sure that every car and truck coming through the Pembina sector of this Customs region (which averaged about 1,000 tractor trailer trucks and 3,000 cars a day) was inspected for bombs, weapons, and other terrorist threats. Usually, 3 to 5 percent of incoming vehicles were inspected. A proud, patriotic eighteen-year Customs veteran and mother of two who is married to a Canadian customs inspector, Delaquis immediately told her staff, "Whatever the next threat is, it is not coming through me." *

It was an admirable sentiment. But on September 11 Customs work up north was done in part on the honor system: At sixteen of Delaquis's twenty-four ports of entry, her inspectors went home at 10:00 every night, and put an orange traffic cone in the road along with a notice telling people to come back for inspection at 9:00 the next morning. By the afternoon of September 11 Delaquis told her deputy that two agents would have to replace those orange cones all night at all sixteen crossings.

"How, Mary, how," he kept asking. "Where will I get the people?"


**Eileen Simon** was finishing up the breakfast dishes in her kitchen in Harrington Park, New Jersey. A radiant, thirty-five-year old blonde, she was about to get dressed to take her five-year-old son to a play date when the phone rang.

"Did Michael go to work today?" her friend asked, without even bothering to say hello.

"Of course, why not," Eileen answered.

"Is he already in the office?"

"He's a trader," she answered. "He's chained to his desk from seven o'clock on. You know that."

Her friend told Eileen that a plane had hit the North Tower of the World Trade Center, the place where she knew Eileen's husband, Michael, worked.

---

* All quotations of conversations held between others that were not heard by the author are contained within quotation marks if one or more of the people involved in the conversation spoke with the author about it. However, it should be remembered that even in those situations a person's recollection of a conversation may not be exact. If the person or people in a conversation did not seem to the author to have an exact recollection of the conversation, it is paraphrased and not put within quotation marks. In some instances conversations are italicized because they were long, and, although the participants seemed to have a good recollection of what was said, italics are used to indicate that the printed words are unlikely to be exactly what was said in every respect.

"Turn on the television. I'll be right over," she added.

Eileen's five-year-old son, Tyler, was playing in the kitchen. He looked up at the TV and recognized the famous building where his father had taken him to his office on the 105th floor.

"Isn't that Daddy's building?" he asked.

"Yes it is, honey."

"Is Daddy okay, Mommy?"

Recalling her answer months later, Eileen is still surprised at what she blurted out: "No, Tyler, I think Daddy's just been killed."

Simon explains that she thought that "the top of the building had been blown off. I couldn't see it through all the smoke."

Eileen called her mother, who lived nearby. "Mom, you'd better come over. Michael's been killed."

But then, for a while, the black smoke seemed to clear, and Eileen could see the top of the tower. "I had hope again," she remembers. "That was the worst part. For about an hour, until the buildings came down, I had hope. I tried to call Michael, and someone answered and put me on hold. Like an idiot I hung up and tried to call again, but just got a busy. I paced the house, then went outside and paced. . . . The house started filling up with friends. Everyone knew Michael because he coached four teams here for the kids, three soccer, one baseball. And we're a very close community. There must have been fifteen people here with me when the building finally came down and I knew it was over."

Eileen and her mother ran over to the elementary school, which is about 300 yards up the block. "I could see other parents going there to get their kids," she remembers, "and I panicked because I thought Brittany and MJ [her twelve-year-old daughter and ten-year-old son] would hear about it from someone else. So, I ran over, and got the others to make way for me so I could get to them first. I saw Brit, and told her, 'Daddy's dead,' and she let out a shriek and ran away."

That night, two or three dozen neighbors filled the house, along with some of her sisters, brothers, and in-laws. There was food and lots to drink. The in-laws and some of the neighbors—including one woman who kept telling Eileen that "Michael is going to walk through this door any minute"—insisted that there was hope. Eileen wouldn't even consider the possibility. She and the children mostly stayed upstairs. The kids rummaged through Michael's closet and laundry bag, putting on his clothing, sniffing it, using it to dry their tears. Then they all curled up in Eileen and Michael's bed.

At one point in the middle of the night, Eileen panicked. Although she'd once been an industrial reinsurance broker, she hadn't worked or paid attention to the family finances since Brittany had been born. She remembered that Michael had just switched banks, and she had not yet even gotten the signature cards to be on the account with him. Where was she going to get any money? What bills needed to be paid? Did she even have enough cash for the next few days? How much life insurance did he really have? What was the mortgage?

The children's fear was more basic. In one way or another—sometimes with a murmur, or in five-year-old Tyler's case, with a shriek—through the night they asked their mother if the bad guys were going to come and get them, too.

The man who would soon become responsible for the Simon children's safety watched the initial moments of the Trade Center disaster on a TV set in a hospital room in Erie, Pennsylvania, where his mother was recovering from vascular surgery. Governor **Tom Ridge** quickly went back to the house he still keeps in Erie, the town far off in the northwest corner of Pennsylvania that he had represented as a congressman before winning a long-shot race for governor in 1994. He made a few calls to mobilize the disaster task force he had organized years before to supervise emergency drills, and ordered that a long-standing state emergency plan—involving everything from closing liquor stores to tightening security at the state's five nuclear power plants—be put into effect.

After negotiating with the federal authorities, who had downed all nonmilitary air traffic—authorities whom, it turned out, he would be coordinating less than a month later as the country's first Director of Homeland Security—Ridge was allowed to get a state helicopter to take him back to the capital in Harrisburg. By the time be got there, he knew he had more to do than preside over hypothetical emergency plans. A member of his security detail relayed word that there was a fourth plane down in Shanksville, Pennsylvania. After more negotiations with the feds, another chopper took him to the crash site.

**Sergio Magistri** was jarred out of bed in Silicon Valley at 6:00 by his girlfriend, who was on the phone from Toronto, where she was attending an airline industry conference that included the executives who run most of America's airports. "Turn on your TV," she said, then hung up. For the first three hours, Magistri recalls, he was "completely spaced out in front of the

TV." Then Magistri started to come to grips with the reality of what had happened, and how it affected the company he ran. "I looked up across the [San Francisco Bay] and realized that there were no planes flying into the airport. Then I saw a jumbo jet from one of the Asian airlines coming in—and saw that it was being escorted by F-16s."

Magistri, who was forty-eight and still spoke with a thick, strange accent that reminded anyone who heard him that he was born in Switzerland and raised among people who spoke German and Italian, was the President and CEO of a small Silicon Valley company called InVision Technologies. In-Vision made giant machines that screened passengers' checked baggage at airports. The purpose was to see if the bags were carrying bombs. InVision was the clear leader among only two companies certified by the federal government to make these machines.

Magistri had come to InVision in 1990. Some friends from a company that made CT scan machines for hospitals and doctors had started the company two years before, right after Pan Am 103 had exploded over Lockerbie, Scotland, when a bomb was planted in the checked luggage. "We were a reaction to Lockerbie," says Magistri.

But Lockerbie had not produced the business Magistri and his cohorts had hoped for. Congress had passed a law in 1990 requiring the Federal Aviation Administration (FAA) to get explosive detection equipment in place by the end of 1993, but by 1994 the FAA still hadn't approved standards for the devices, which are the size of a minivan. It had taken until that year for Magistri even to sell his first $1 million machine, and the sale was to an airport in Brussels. The Israelis had also become customers, but few other airports were willing to foot the bill. Magistri's machines were expensive, because they required not only an enormous amount of software to pinpoint the combination of mass and density that suggested explosives, but also a giant, rapidly rotating X-ray chamber that can record multiple images from multiple angles at high speed. By the end of 1996, Magistri had sold only twenty units, mostly to airports in Europe and in the United Kingdom (where by September 11, every piece of checked baggage was screened).

He had sold none in the United States. The American airline industry, concerned about passenger inconvenience and maintenance costs (the federal government would buy the machines), had continually persuaded the FAA to forgo the installation of Magistri's machines. Nonetheless, he had somehow been able to take his company public in the spring of 1996.

When TWA Flight 800 exploded over the Long Island coast in the summer of 1996, it looked like Magistri's shareholders had been in the right place at the right time. The stock nearly doubled, and Magistri was certain that the need for his machines had finally been demonstrated. A presidential commission, headed by Vice President Al Gore, investigated aviation safety and recommended the screening of every checked bag. The federal government quickly ordered fifty machines. It seemed that Magistri and InVision had made it. He began producing and selling ten to fifteen InVision units a month. Legislation was passed mandating 100 percent screening by 2013; then, the deadline was moved up to 2010. Magistri pushed his many suppliers to ramp up, while he hired and leased more space.

However, as the memory of TWA Flight 800 faded (or as it became clear that a fire in the plane's fuel system, not a bomb, had caused the crash), America and its government seemed to lose interest. The FAA and Congress stopped appropriating funds for his machines, and the airlines—who had lobbied against the machines even when the government promised to pay for them, because they feared they would slow down the check-in process—certainly weren't going to ante up on their own.

Magistri's sales stalled out, so much so that by September 10, 2001, he had sold only 140 in the United States (and about 110 abroad) in the seven years that the product had been given FAA certification and put on the market. Magistri had just subleased a chunk of his factory space and completed a round of layoffs that trimmed his workforce 15 percent, down to 180. Morale sagged among those who remained, as the company tried to cut costs by eliminating even little perks, such as the donuts and drinks that had been the staple of most meetings.

In short, Magistri was generally in the soup along with the rest of his Silicon Valley neighbors. His factory was nearly idle, making only one machine every week or two. He had even diversified InVision, developing an imaging product to track faults in logs for the lumber industry. That hadn't helped much: InVision's stock, which had gone public in 1997 at $12 and soared as high as $25, was at $3.11. To Magistri, the stock's rise and fall seemed to track America's dangerously short attention span when it came to security issues.

Now, by noon, or 3:00 Eastern Time, Magistri, who has the optimist gland endemic to any entrepreneur, was sure that everything had changed, this time for real. True, it seemed that the terror attacks had nothing to do with checked baggage, but Magistri's instinct was that September 11 was a seminal event that would result in a swift hardening of all targets in aviation. So he instructed his chief operating officer to think about ramping up again, quickly. "We had reduced ourselves to be a $40 million [in revenues] company," he recalls. "That afternoon, I decided we should at least ramp up to $60 million."

Magistri made two other decisions that afternoon. He instructed every-one in the company not to talk to the press at all, no matter who called. He did not want to seem to be taking advantage of the tragedy. At the same time, he rehired the PR firm he had laid off a few months before, in order, he says, "to prepare to respond to what I knew would be the new demand for coverage of us in the media and in the investment community. We had to get ready."

New York City's Department of Transportation Commissioner **Iris Wein-shall** found herself with lots of quiet time early that morning. She'd left her Brooklyn home at about 6:30 to vote in the city's Democratic primary, then was chauffeured in her government car to City Hall in Manhattan. She thought she had a cabinet meeting with Mayor Rudolph Giuliani, but when she arrived she found that the 7:30 session had been changed to 9:45. So she grabbed some coffee at Starbucks, then proceeded to her office, which was about two blocks from City Hall and four blocks from the Trade Center. She was doing paperwork at her desk and talking on the phone to a business association leader, who was complaining about a water main and sewer proj-ect that was blocking traffic on lower Broadway, when she heard the noise from the first low-flying jet. Weinshall ran to another side of the floor, saw the fire, and was soon in touch with her deputies to make sure they would help clear traffic from the area so the firemen could get easier access. It was only when the second plane hit that she realized this was more than a local traffic problem.

Weinshall had two immediate worries. Her elder daughter, Jessica, was a senior at nearby Stuyvesant High, the elite magnet of the New York City pub-lic school system. And her husband—Senator **Charles Schumer**—was in Washington.

Chuck Schumer was watching TV and reading a newspaper in the House of Representatives gym at ten to nine. The senior senator from New York didn't seem the type who'd still be in the gym that late in the morning. He was a notoriously hard worker, the kind of driven politician who mixes obsessive involvement with the details of any issue with such a drive for publicity that the old joke, "he'd show up at the opening of a phone booth," seemed to have been written about him. But, he says, "I sweat a lot when I exercise. Even if I get to the gym at 7:00 and work out for an hour, it takes me another hour to be able to put my clothes on. So I use the time to read the paper and make some calls." *

After Schumer saw the reports of the first plane, he called some staff people to ask them to get on the phones to get more information. When he saw the second plane hit he called Weinshall.

"Chuck, could these buildings come down?" Weinshall asked her husband.

"Don't be ridiculous, Iris," Schumer answered with characteristic certainty. "These buildings are built to withstand anything." They agreed to try to reach their daughter and talk later.

When the first tower came down, Weinshall, amid what she recalls as mass hysteria in her building, got her husband back on the phone. Schumer reported that Jessica's cell phone had just gotten through to his office in Washington, where she had told a staffer that she was on the ninth floor of Stuyvesant and was about to be evacuated but that all the elevators were out. Weinshall then took out a street map of Manhattan and counted the blocks from the North Tower to Stuyvesant, which was about four blocks from the Trade Center. The transportation commissioner and the senator now tried to calculate how tall the Trade Center tower was, what the length of an average block was, and, therefore, whether it would hit Stuyvesant if it fell over. "I wanted to leave to go find Jessie," Weinshall remembers. "But I couldn't. I was in charge of all these people and we had responsibilities. It was awful."

Weinshall deployed all of her staff—from executives to her own driver—to fan out in the yellow vests they'd all been issued for emergencies, and divert all traffic out of lower Manhattan. Amazingly, Weinshall's driver soon spotted Jessica with her friends running north up West Street. He scooped her up and brought her to Weinshall's office.

When the second tower collapsed, Weinshall's building lost all power and phone service. She and her senior staff, with Jessica in tow, began moving uptown in a caravan toward a Transportation Department depot in upper Manhattan that they would use as a command center. She stayed there until about 11:00 P.M., when she got her driver to take her home to Brooklyn so she could change her soot-laden clothes before attending a midnight emergency command meeting with Mayor Giuliani. As the driver began to go over the Brooklyn Bridge, which like all bridges and tunnels had been closed to the

*In 1996 and 1997, while not working as a journalist covering politics or Schumer, the author contributed to Schumer's first Senate campaign.

public, a police sergeant leaned in and told Weinshall that "we haven't had a chance to check the bridge out yet; the scuba team won't be here until the morning to look for bombs at the base." Weinshall thanked him, then told her driver to "gun it." They hurtled over at 100 miles per hour, she recalls, "as if we were trying to get a good running start in case it blew up."

Meantime, Schumer, whose Senate office had been evacuated, had commandeered a lobbyist's suite on K Street. He began getting his staff focused on what he saw as the twin callings of his job—combining, as he puts it, referring to two predecessors, "Al D'Amato when it comes to bringing home the bacon for New York, and Pat Moynihan when it comes to being serious about policy." The bacon had to do with all the aid New York would need to rebuild. Policy had to do primarily with the law enforcement and national security issues related to terrorism.

Construction engineer **Brian Lyons** was at a meeting in midtown Manhattan, where he was supervising a multimillion-dollar office renovation for a brokerage house, when his and everyone else's cell phone started going off with the news of the first plane hitting the North Tower. He and his colleagues went up to the roof of the building to take a look. When they saw the second plane hit, Lyons, forty-two, started to worry about his kid brother Michael, thirty-two, who was a fireman assigned to one of New York's elite Rescue Squad units.

Lyons called his wife at their home about sixty miles north of Manhattan, and she screamed for him to leave Manhattan, and come home to her and their two daughters. He tried to call Michael at his firehouse, but the phone went dead. He kept trying, but got nothing. So he called Elaine, Michael's wife, who was seven months pregnant with their second daughter, to ask if maybe Michael had not worked today. No such luck. Elaine, a small, striking brunette who'd been Michael's sweetheart since high school, was, she recalls later, "already getting semihysterical." Lyons promised her he'd somehow find out about Michael.

With the subways already shut down, Lyons set out on foot to Michael's firehouse. He walked the 100 blocks up Third Avenue over the bridge to the Bronx, and by about noon made it to where he hoped to find his kid brother.

The firehouse was locked. He peered through the window and saw no trucks, no firemen. He made his way to another firehouse, where a fireman was poring through the teletypes that were emblematic of the New York Fire Department's antiquated communications system, looking for reports of who was safe and who wasn't. The fireman knew and liked Michael, as it seemed everyone did who had ever met the outgoing, fun-loving youngest of the Lyons brothers. Brian got him to check for Michael's squad, and the teletype seemed to say that Michael and his crew had been ordered to advance to a firehouse on 14th Street in Manhattan in case they were needed at the Trade Center. Lyons somehow got through to Elaine and told her that Michael must be okay, that he had not made it down to the Trade Center. Then he hitched a ride to a train station and caught a train north to Elaine's small, two-bedroom house in Westchester to await further word.

When he got there, Elaine still hadn't heard from Michael. Worse, Elaine's sister, whose husband was also a fireman (and who was now accounted for) had called to say that Michael's rig had been seen at the Trade Center. Elaine was hysterical.

Lyons worked the phones through the afternoon, the evening, and into the night but found out nothing. Finally, after trying fruitlessly to take a nap on the couch, he decided that he had to do something. So he went to the basement and found some of Michael's spare fireman's gear and an old badge, and at about 6:00 A.M. he headed out in Elaine's car back to Manhattan. Flashing his brother's old badge to get past the roadblocks, he finally made it onto the FDR Drive, which threads along Manhattan's East Side. He recalls that as he approached downtown "the whole thing was like a dust storm. You could barely see. It was dark, even though it was light out. And no one was there. It was like after a war."

Minutes later he pulled up to about three blocks from where the Trade Center had stood, left the car, and started walking through the debris. The first thing that stunned him was that everything had been reduced to dust. Cement, paper, the thousands of desks and computers from the Trade Center offices, body parts—all had settled in what looked to be six inches of white-gray powder. A block away his heart stopped when he came to Rescue Unit 41, Michael's rig. It was mangled and abandoned under a fallen street sign less than two blocks from what had been the South Tower. "I just started walking around, looking for my brother," he says.

After about an hour, Lyons hit on a strategy that would keep the police from making him leave the scene at the same time that he could make himself useful. He started acting like one of the other firemen, clawing around looking for survivors. "There was no one supervising anyone," he explains. "People were just walking around."

Soon he realized that his skills as a construction engineer could help more, so he whispered to a fire captain who he really was and how he was looking for his brother from Squad 41, and volunteered to advise them on what could be safely moved and what couldn't. Within an hour, he was on a team evaluating which buildings around the site were likely to fall and which ones weren't. All the while, he kept looking for any sign of his brother.

**Bernadine Healy**, the President and CEO of the American Red Cross, was on the phone in her palatial Washington headquarters, talking to her disaster operations center about getting the first Red Cross relief trucks to the Trade Center, when she felt the explosion at the Pentagon. After being assured that the northern Virginia chapter would have people there in a few minutes, she turned her attention to the larger job ahead. Healy, a Harvard-trained cardiologist who had headed the National Institutes of Health, knew immediately that this would be the Red Cross's biggest domestic challenge since World War II. She wondered where the Red Cross—which provided blankets and temporary shelter to victims of 70,000 fires and other disasters annually, ranging from a one-alarmer where a family needs a place to stay overnight to massive earthquakes—would get the money to tend to so many victims all at once in a situation where the devastation would last so long. More than that, she knew that in terms of the Red Cross's disaster relief, as well as its role as the country's leading source of blood supply, she had to think big. She had to prepare for other attacks that might come the next day, the next week, the next year.

The Red Cross is a quasi-government organization, in the sense that the Congress charters it as an officially recognized agency charged with providing aid to disaster victims at home and to soldiers fighting abroad. In fact, several months before, Healy had prepared a six-point plan for how the Red Cross might respond to a major terrorist attack. It included everything from traditional relief, to long-term counseling and economic aid, to stockpiling huge supplies of blood. The plan had also contemplated that the effort would be financed by segregated donations rather than be put into the charity's general relief fund.

At fifty-six Healy exuded a cool toughness. An Irish woman who'd grown up in an Italian neighborhood of Queens in New York City, she has blue eyes so arresting, so laserlike, that they seem to snarl with determination. She knew that night that to get the 200-year-old Red Cross on a footing to meet her ambitious vision she'd have to be tough in a way that belies the Red Cross's benign, open-arms image. She'd have to navigate a bureaucracy and a power structure embedded in various corners of the marble headquarters building and in local chapters across the country. In fact, by late that night she had a hint of the problems to come, when an aide slipped her a note during a meeting, saying that Pentagon officials were complaining that only a handful of Red Cross workers had shown up from a local chapter to help out at that crash site. What she didn't know was that getting donations to finance her projects would not be a problem. Far from it.


**Michael Cartier**, twenty-four, worked as a business information systems manager for a New York company that owns several cable television networks, including Bravo and American Movie Classics. At about 9:00 he got a call at his midtown office from his brother John, telling him about the crash at the Trade Center. Michael and John had another brother, James, working as an electrician in the North Tower, the one that had already been hit. (In fact, James was working on the same floor as Eileen Simon's husband.) They also had a sister, Michelle, working as an executive assistant for Lehman Brothers in the South Tower. All of the Cartiers—seven siblings—were close. In fact, close doesn't begin to describe what bound the Cartiers, and what would steel them in the months ahead. It was as if the close quarters in the three-bedroom house they'd grown up in Queens, across a parkway from La Guardia Airport and thousands of miles in worldview from the yuppies of Manhattan, had almost physically bonded them.

John and Michael decided that John would go down to the Trade Center from where he was working nearby, also as an electrician, while Michael would man the phones. First, John would get Michelle, and then he and Michelle would find James. Meantime, sisters Marie and Jennie and brother Patrick checked in and signed off on the plan, with one of them agreeing to go to their parents' home to be with the elder Cartiers, Carmen and Patrick Sr.

John got there after the plane hit Michelle's tower and just as her building came tumbling down. Wandering through the dust, he bumped into her just outside St. Paul's Church. They hugged. Then they tried to move toward the still standing North Tower to find James. They were kept back by the police and firemen, and stood across the street as that building, with James possibly inside, collapsed. All the Cartiers, unable to communicate because all phones were dead, then walked over the 59th Street Bridge to their parents' house.

"When I got halfway over the bridge," Michael remembers, "I turned around and started walking back to find James. He and I were so close. We'd slept in the same bed growing up. I had to find him. But then I realized when I looked at all that black smoke that he was gone. I turned around and began walking home."

When he got there, the house, he says, "was frantic. We were working the phones. We were watching TV, taking down phone numbers to call. . . . We prepared a flyer with James's picture, so we could go back the next morning and hand it out. We had to find James and bring him home."

When he got the news of the second plane hitting, Attorney General **John Ashcroft** was in a small government Cessna jet on his way to Milwaukee, where he was going to participate in the President's child literacy program by reading to a group of schoolchildren. (His boss, President George W. Bush, was scheduled to read to a different group of children, in Florida, the same morning.) For Ashcroft, a conservative former Missouri senator, the trip, with an entourage of only two aides and two security people, seemed emblematic of a stewardship at Justice that had so far been uneventful and, in fact, had seemed not to have engaged him fully. Indeed, the policy initiative in which he had seemed most engaged—helping to ease immigration restrictions on Mexicans and others, which the President had urged him to seize as a priority—would now become almost perversely irrelevant.

Ashcroft immediately ordered the plane to turn around, only to be told that there wasn't enough fuel to get back to Washington. After refueling in Milwaukee, he had still more trouble making it back to the center of action. The Federal Aviation Administration insisted that his plane be diverted to Richmond, because of an order it had issued to ground everything that wasn't a military plane. "It was a real negotiation," Ashcroft recalls. "I think when we ended up getting back to Washington we were literally the last plane in the air that day."

By about 11:30 Ashcroft was in the Strategic Information and Operations Center (called the SIOC) in the FBI building across from his office, a place where he would spend most of the next two months. Four teams had already been organized to get information about the hijackers of the four planes, and some of the names of the nineteen killers were already posted on an easel. FBI Director Robert Mueller briefed him on computer terminals that had been set up to link each of the bureau's field offices to the SIOC. By late afternoon, the FBI had already gone over to the Immigration and Naturalization Service (INS, a sister agency, also within Ashcroft's Justice Department) to haul away a giant data dump of hundreds of thousands or even millions (no one knew for sure, or could count them) of names and the possible locations of all people from Middle Eastern countries who had entered the United States in the last two years. True to the INS's reputation as the agency most left behind by the information age, the data was not only hopelessly dated but was in hard copy—hundreds of boxes of paper forms. For years, the INS and FBI had fought an internal war within the Justice Department over computer and data systems. As a result of a standoff that no Attorney General had bothered to resolve, their databases did not talk to each other. Nonetheless, FBI agents in the field offices, having been fed the information by fax, were already out in the field questioning those they could find. Informants who'd been used in prior terrorism investigations, of whom there were precious few, were already, as one federal prosecutor put it, "being rousted."

Ashcroft wasn't satisfied. When he'd arrived at the White House late that afternoon, President Bush had taken Ashcroft aside and said, "John, make sure this can't happen again." Yet Mueller's FBI team seemed focused on an investigation of what had already happened. Ashcroft was determined to change that. The FBI's job now was to protect, not gather evidence that would stand up in court for prosecutions. Ashcroft was determined to force that fundamental shift, even if it meant he'd be de facto head of the FBI.

For Ashcroft, the sudden challenge—indeed, the sudden urgency to a job that had not quite captivated him yet—was an elixir of sorts. Associates would soon notice his new focus, the new bounce in his step. Using one of his many sports analogies, he would explain it this way: "Some people don't like to get the ball at the foul line in the last second of the game. I do. I like to get that ball."

Ashcroft's Immigration and Naturalization Service division is headquartered about ten blocks from the FBI in a backwater Washington neighborhood that was emblematic of INS's status. (So was the building's name; it was called the Chester A. Arthur Building, after a President no one had ever nominated for Mount Rushmore.) There, the INS's Border Patrol unit, which has 10,000 agents across the country, also leaped into action following the attacks. A storeroom full of rifles and shotguns was unlocked and weapons were handed out.

But they didn't go out to safeguard Washington's various landmarks and trophy targets. Instead, they fanned out in front of headquarters to prevent an attack on themselves. Every ten feet, rifle- or shotgun-toting Border Patrol agents in their trademark dark green uniforms could be found preparing to repel an assault against the one law enforcement agency the terrorists had the least reason to want to attack: the INS.


Meantime, for **Robert Lindemann**, an ex-Marine and veteran agent with INS's Border Patrol division in Detroit, the morning of September 11 was the culmination of years of frustration. For years, Lindemann and his partner, agent Mark Hall, had been complaining to their supervisors, and then to a congressional committee, that the Border Patrol on the Northern Border with Canada was woefully understaffed and under-equipped to do its job—which was to catch people sneaking over the border at places that are not official ports of entry, such as a riverbank in Detroit, or the woods in North Dakota. So it was no surprise to Lindemann, though it was something of a last straw, that now the first order issued by his supervisors was that he and all the other agents should come into headquarters because it was too dangerous to be out in the field.

**Larry Cox** was one of the few airport executives not stuck in Toronto that morning at the annual airport industry conference. He had come back early to have stitches removed following some minor surgery. Cox, the president and CEO of the Memphis–Shelby County Airport Authority, kept a looseleaf book behind his desk on a shelf next to his thick budget book. It was full of plans for hostage situations, crashes, snowstorms, fires, and floods. But there wasn't a section to help him and his staff prepare for the deluge of aircraft full of Tuesday morning passengers he was about to get when the FAA issued the order to ground everything.

Because Memphis was midway between America's north and south and east and west, by noon Cox and his team ended up with more than 200 planes at an airport that has 100 gates. He had to tend to 20,000 people who had no place to go. His stockpile of 5,000 inflatable mattresses (bought a few years back after passengers were stranded when a snowstorm in Detroit tied up air traffic), diapers, and lunch and dinner rations would surely not have been enough if so many Memphis families and churches hadn't responded by the afternoon to the live local television reports of the thousands stranded at the airport by opening their doors to them.

Cox, fifty-four, had worked at the airport for twenty-seven years, seventeen as the CEO, and had served as the president of a national airport executives' trade association for two years. He was a tall (six foot five), affable Southerner, whose matter-of-fact way of talking about the outside forces that made his job difficult made his candor all the more jarring. He hated bureaucracy, particularly the kind that comes from Washington. Until September 11, the most frustrating experience of Cox's professional life had been the twelve years it had taken him to get approval—amid a maze of local, state, and federal environmental regulations—for a new runway. Now, by the afternoon of September 11, the FAA was spitting new security regulations through his fax machine in what seemed like hourly blitzes. They seemed to have nothing to do with the attacks, but were certain to make his life miserable; for example, one directive immediately banned public parking spots within 300 feet of any terminal, a rule that would eliminate about 550 of his most lucrative spots and inconvenience customers at an airport where customer convenience was a religion.

Cox had no idea when they'd let the planes fly again. Even cargo planes were grounded, which was particularly bad for Cox because Memphis, with its famous Federal Express hub, is the busiest cargo airport in the world, an honor proclaimed in various posters throughout the facility that trumpet its increasing lead over Hong Kong.

Running airports is a high-pressure, low-margin business, and Cox knows the numbers as well as anyone. He knew that with the planes all down, what he now had for the foreseeable future were the same old costs, but none of the parking or concession revenue from the airport's various shops, and none of the crucial landing fees. And he also knew that he had lots of new costs coming from new security requirements the bureaucrats in Washington would ordain, though he didn't yet know how much these costs would skyrocket, or how much his revenues would now decline if passenger traffic collapsed in the months ahead.

**Anthony Romero** was also worried about what would now be coming from Washington. Romero, thirty-six, had recently been chosen to be the executive director of the American Civil Liberties Union. In fact, September 11 marked his debut before the annual Washington conference of the ACLU's leading donors. The group, about seventy-five foundation executives, left-leaning businesspeople, and wealthy individuals, was about to be briefed on Romero's and the ACLU's agenda. Top items included election reform emanating from what the group perceived were the injustices of the 2000 Florida presidential contest, gay rights, abortion rights, and immigration reform.

The group was eager to see Romero in action. Romero was a Stanford-trained lawyer who had run the Ford Foundation's extensive international human rights programs. A Bronx-born Puerto Rican and out-of-the-closet gay, he was, according to ACLU president Nadine Strossen, the product of an intensive affirmative action effort. As such, he was a sharp departure from his predecessor, a longtime executive director who had come out of the same civil rights/civil liberties community as most of those in the room.

Romero's briefing in the hotel ballroom had not even begun when he was called out of the room and told about the planes hitting the towers. He quickly adjourned the meeting and just as quickly convened what became an almost all-day rump session of his top staff in the hotel coffee shop. "We did a list of what we thought they would try to do," he remembers, referring not to the terrorists but to the government.

For ACLU Washington director Laura Murphy, who had worked at the ACLU on and off for seventeen years, the list was easy. "We simply had to remember what they had tried to pass after Oklahoma City but had not gotten away with," she explains. "More wiretapping, more searches, less involvement of judges in warrants."

Then came a list of what the ACLU would try to do immediately to stop the damage they feared—points they would make, allies they would recruit. That, too, produced little disagreement.

But at about 3:00, as they sat in the coffee shop drafting a press release, Romero had a first test of his power. Most of the staff wanted the press release to warn of the new threats to freedom that were certainly on the way. Romero wanted a statement expressing condolences for the victims and pledging to work with Congress and the White House to pass laws that would keep America "Safe and Free."

The ACLU's job was to keep America free, not safe, argued three of the six people at the coffee shop. Safety is the government's job.

"Safety is what Americans care about today," Romero countered. "That and grief. We need to be relevant. When they propose something, then we can hit them. But today we need to be relevant."

The ACLU staff is a strong-willed group, and some had wondered whether their new leader—who was soft-spoken, had a ready smile, and was not the kind of person who instantly dominated a room, much less bullied it— would really be able to lead them. Romero seemed to be passing his first test.

Romero's version of the release prevailed. But relevance is in the eyes of the beholder: The ACLU's hotly debated statement was picked up by not a single television or print news outlet that day or any day thereafter.


Real estate developer **Larry Silverstein** was on his way to a dermatologist on the morning of the 11th, instead of the Trade Center—the multibillion-dollar complex where he had leveraged a $14 million personal investment in a partnership that owned the leasing rights to the buildings into bragging rights as the complex's putative owner. Silverstein would tell the author five months later that he was so shocked and sickened by the destruction and by the loss of four of his employees that morning that he did not think he focused on issues like insurance or finances until "perhaps two weeks later." In fact, according to his own lawyers, by that evening he was on the phone with them worrying whether his effort to shave costs when he'd bought insurance would now come back to hurt him, or whether his insurance policies could be read in a way that would construe the attacks as two separate, insurable incidents rather than one. The difference was roughly $3.55 billion versus $7.1 billion—the kind of gap corporate litigators dream of.

The windows and shelves in **Salvatore Iacono**'s shoe repair shop on lower Broadway shook slightly when the first plane hit. When he saw people across the street staring open-mouthed up at the sky, he went outside and saw the smoking North Tower three blocks away. Then he saw the second plane swoop over and hit the South Tower. That was enough for him. He was about to send his helper and the two shoeshine guys home and lock his tiny store when people in the office building where he is located began storming through the door that leads from the lobby into his store. The regular exit from the building was too crowded, so they had chosen his store as an alternative thoroughfare. It reminded Sal of those pictures he'd seen on TV of people running from the bulls in Spain, only they were all running through his shop, not a street. One of those fleeing stopped and commandeered the phone behind the counter. When he got off, another took it.

Then, the first tower came down and Sal was engulfed in dust and debris. The windows blew out. He was terrified. Stephen Johnson, an executive with the New York City Housing Authority who worked nearby and had become Sal's friend after meeting him over a pair of worn shoes, came in and told him they had to leave. They locked the front door, but not before Sal did what he did every night at closing—said a prayer in front of the picture of the Virgin Mary hanging near the door.

Sal headed uptown with Johnson. Although Johnson was fifty-two and Sal sixty-seven, Johnson had to ask him to slow down. "I'm stronger than I look," Sal would explain months later, flashing a big smile. "But it was really that I was so frightened. It felt like the world was over."

Johnson left Sal at a wholesale leather shop near Chinatown, where they knew Sal and offered him a ride to Brooklyn. From there, Sal hitched a ride to his home in Staten Island, where he told his wife that "I never want to go back there again."

For years, Sal—who looked and sounded meek but was anything but—had eked out a living repairing shoes, briefcases, and pocketbooks, taking in about

$100,000 a year in sales and coming home with maybe $35,000 or $40,000 in profit for himself after paying his one employee and taking a cut from the two shoeshine guys who use his store. His customers loved him; some called him "Sal the Sole Man." And he loved them back, often saying his store, called Continental Shoe Repair, was like another child. Now, he told his wife, he had nothing. No store. Equipment choked in dust and debris. And no customers likely to be back soon.

**Edmund Woollen**, a vice president of Raytheon, the giant military contractor, was running a small meeting on new products for special forces Army troops in his office on the twentieth floor of a chrome tower in Arlington, Virginia, when he heard what he thought was a sonic boom. He looked up and out his picture window and saw the flames and black smoke at the Pentagon, which was about a half mile away. Woollen had spent enough time in Vietnam to know that this was a fuel bomb of some kind. One of Woollen's subordinates, who'd been a three-star general, looked across at the Pentagon, then grabbed for a phone. His wife worked on that side of the Pentagon. When his call to her yielded a dead line, he ran from Woollen's office.

Woollen, fifty-six, who had served three Navy tours in the Vietnam War and had a pilot's license, had assumed an hour before that the first plane going into the Trade Center could not have been an accident, but even after the second plane hit the towers, he had decided to keep to the day's schedule, at least until he knew more. Now, with the attack on the Pentagon just outside his window, he decided that Raytheon's work for the day was over. Who knew what the next target might be?

From his home, Woollen—who was aware that the National Guard rescue troops now on the scene at Ground Zero were equipped with all kinds of Raytheon products (such as their night-vision glasses), as were the forces likely to be deployed to search out and destroy the terrorists overseas (including the surveillance cameras and software being used by U-2 and Predator spy planes)—began to think about Raytheon's possible role in the new world. Woollen and his colleagues didn't talk about it that day, but everyone knew that Raytheon's stock on September 10 (the market did not open on September 11) was at its lowest point in nearly two years. This tragedy might change that. After all, Raytheon's primary "customer" was the American military and national security community, for whom it supplied everything from radar systems, to Sidewinder and Patriot missiles, to the kill vehicles used to shoot down enemy missiles.

Woollen's job, along with 180 other Raytheon product managers and lobbyists in Washington, was to "stay close" to that customer, closer than dozens of equally determined competitors, large and small. It was a role that was about to take on all kinds of new, high-stakes dimensions—one that could make or break Woollen's career.

Chubb Insurance Chairman and CEO **Dean O'Hare**—fifty-nine, perpetually tanned, perfectly coiffed—seemed like the country-club-groomed soul mate of the first President Bush. When O'Hare got the news of the attacks, he left the small airport in New Jersey where he was about to board the company jet for a trip to Pittsburgh and headed back to Chubb's headquarters in Warren, New Jersey, which is about forty miles west of Manhattan. His people were already at work doing computer models that projected potential Chubb losses, which included payouts to clients such as Cantor Fitzgerald, the Wall Street trading house where Eileen Simon's husband worked that would end up losing more than two thirds of its 1,000 American employees. After checking to make sure that none of Chubb's 12,000 employees had been hurt in Manhattan, O'Hare went to work with his team on the computer models. Because they always have information about policies at the ready organized by locations and industries, they calculated that Chubb's maximum exposure—provided the insurance *they* have from reinsurers kicked in—was $200 million. This included some insurance Chubb had sold to Silverstein's World Trade Center, but the bulk of what Chubb would have to pay involved clients ranging from people whose cars had been destroyed at the Trade Center, to those with companies whose businesses had now been interrupted, to large companies who paid Chubb for insurance to compensate workers killed or injured on the job. To reassure investors and the financial markets, that afternoon they put out a press release describing the projected losses.

But already the lawyers in O'Hare's conference room were raising a troubling issue. Because the President and others were calling this an act of war, and because acts of war were excluded from coverage on all insurance, what would Chubb do about the claims? More important, no matter what Chubb did, what would those reinsurers do? In other words, if Chubb wanted to pay the claims but its reinsurers—some of whom were foreign companies—took the position that they wouldn't, Chubb could be on the hook for more than a billion dollars. Maybe they should hold off on the payouts until things become clearer, the lawyers counseled.

We'll deal with that tomorrow, O'Hare decided.

O'Hare, Eileen Simon, Kevin McCabe, and the rest of America went to sleep with lots to deal with the next day, from the personal to the global. Yesterday, Simon had not even needed to worry about writing checks. Now, she didn't know how her family would pay the mortgage, or get the cash for groceries tomorrow, or even how she would find a key so she could retrieve her husband's car at the train station (something she thought of at about 4:00 that morning and then was embarrassed to be worrying about).

How would the Cartier, Lyons, or Simon families get solace? How could Brian Lyons and everyone else at Ground Zero ever recover all the bodies? What would the 60,000 people who lived near the Trade Center do? How would Healy and her Red Cross help them? What would their landlords do about collecting rent on buildings that were not habitable?

What about the shopkeepers like Sal the Sole Man, who had some insurance but not nearly enough and not a clue about how to put in the right claims for it, let alone any way to make up for all the lost customers in a neighborhood that had suddenly become a ghost town, except for the rescue brigades? Could—would—a government run by people who eschewed activist government do something to rescue Sal? Eileen Simon? New York? The overall economy?

In a country already aching for tort reform, how would the legal system deal with tens of thousands of lawsuits seeking billions of dollars? Would this become the ultimate tort claims meltdown? Plane crashes usually involve a few hundred victims at most. This one had thousands more on the ground at the Trade Center and the Pentagon, and the airlines' insurance couldn't possibly cover that. How would the airlines ever fly again? Who would think it was safe enough to get on board at Cox's airport in Memphis, or anyplace else? And where would the airlines get the money to fly the planes, given all that they would lose while traffic was grounded and the billions more they'd lose from the lawsuits?

Would Magistri's InVision now get the business he had dreamed of, and if it did, would he be able to produce the machines on time? Would Woollen and Raytheon be able to beat their competitors in what seemed might become a whole new homeland security industry?

How would Silverstein and everyone else with a stake in what would become of the Trade Center area ever resolve their inevitably competing interests about what and how to rebuild, and who would pay for it? Was the Trade Center wreckage destined to sit there for a decade or two while the lawyers, the zoning activists, the environmentalists, and the real estate moguls fought it out? Could Schumer persuade Washington to help his devastated city?

What about the stock markets and brokerage houses, headquartered only blocks away and now largely without electricity, telephone and data lines, or breathable air? When could they reopen and what would happen to stock prices once they did?

And could a country whose big debate the morning before had been about the sex life of an obscure California congressman (Gary Condit)—and whose President and Attorney General were out that morning reading to schoolchildren—now deal with fundamental issues, such as making it safe to cross a bridge or tunnel, or take in a baseball game, or go to work in an office tower?

Was the President—elected in controversy, and for whom gravitas seemed to be more a challenging vocabulary word than a defining trait—up to it? Was Congress, perpetually gridlocked and seemingly beholden to platoons of lobbyists, up to it? Were their constituents, who seemed to prefer gridlock to action from a government they didn't trust, up to it? Could a country where the book *Bowling Alone* by Robert Putnam had struck such a nerve, because it seemed to express the American people's withdrawal from civic engagement, come back together to help the victims and fight the new enemy?

The terrorists had, indeed, not only achieved a devastating surprise attack, but they also seemed to have gone after a weak enemy that would be unable to respond. "I think they thought we were soft," President Bush later said in several speeches. "I think they figured we would just sue them." The American adults of September 11 weren't, it seemed, the "greatest generation." They were the children of the greatest—a soft-news-fixated generation that, at best, read books and watched TV shows about the greatest generation. And they lived in a country that, depending on your view, had made great strides in protecting the unprotected, or had become gummed up by regulations, interest group paralysis, and bureaucratic inertia. Either way, it was a more complicated world, a place where swift, decisive action seemed impossible. Imagine if Franklin Roosevelt had had to deal with environmental impact statements, equal opportunity requirements, or vendors seeking indemnification from tort suits before anyone lifted a shovel to break ground on a new airplane factory.

How, then, could America deal with the calamity that was September 11, including not only the devastating damage that had closed the stock markets and other commerce, downed the airlines, and put a giant, fiery hole in the nation's greatest city, but had also ripped the facade away from decades of national security policy. Suddenly, the bedrock of America's strategic defense and foreign policy—deterrence—meant nothing, because it had become breathtakingly, we-will-never-be-the-same clear that the country faced a new kind of enemy for whom deterrence meant nothing.

Since the mid-1990s, policy wonks had been talking about this new, coming threat. About how America had lived in relative safety during the Cold War, when the country only had to worry that the leader of a superpower would be mad enough to try to annihilate the world's number one superpower. And about how that equation had changed, as technology combined with globalization had conspired, first, to enable madmen controlling smaller countries to threaten the United States, and, now, to allow madmen who didn't even control any kind of flag to threaten America in a way Hitler had never been able to and Khrushchev had never wanted to.

Those who had sounded that alarm had played to relatively sparse audiences, while everyone else focused on OJ or the dot-coms. Now everyone saw what they saw—that America had no good way to protect itself against an enemy whose method, it was now clear, was to blend in and then commit suicidal acts of terror, be it with nuclear suitcases, airplanes, trucks, or biological weapons, all aimed at scaring the country out of its way of life. Was there any way Ashcroft could root out that kind of enemy within, let alone do it without hacking away at everyone else's rights? How "relevant" could Romero and his ACLU be in this new world?

Could McCabe really protect his port? Would Lindemann and the Border Patrol ever be able to secure America's 7,500 miles of land and water borders? Indeed, could the Immigration and Naturalization Service, for whom Lindemann worked, ever get its act together? The America of September 10 was so open that 1,660,000 people—760,000 citizens and 900,000 foreigners—had entered or exited the country's borders on that *one day*. How could anyone possibly know, let alone control, who they were and what their intentions were? How could the government do any of that without creating a nation of informants, personal databases, security bottlenecks, and identity checks, which would achieve the terrorists' goals for them, by freezing commerce and snuffing out the country's freedoms?

This is the story of how these Americans—some well known, others not known at all—struggled over the next year to stand themselves and their country up to these challenges, the challenges of the September 12 era. On September 11, they were strangers to one another. A year later, many would have crossed paths in a series of surprising alliances and confrontations.

Theirs is a story of patriotism and amazing displays of American grit. But it is also a story of a constant clash of interests—"special interests"—competing in the boisterous, open arena that is America. Indeed, the first year of the September 12 era became a modern, vivid test of a country that has flourished not only on patriotism and strength of spirit, but also because it allows, even encourages, its people and institutions to seek to advance their own interests.

PART ONE · CLIMBING BACK

# September 12, 2001–October 12, 2001

# Wednesday, September 12, 2001

After breakfast, Eileen Simon and her brother-in-law went through the credenza in the living room that Michael Simon used to store bills and his checkbook. They looked for invoices that needed to be paid and for any sign of the life insurance policy that Eileen remembered her husband had gotten from Cantor Fitzgerald, the bond trading firm that had employed him and about 1,000 others working in the North Tower's top floors. More urgent was their search for an extra set of keys to the antique Mercedes that Michael had left at the train station, and the form from the bank that she could use to get her signature onto the checking account. There was no key. Later, she'd find the signature form and try to take it to the bank, but would be told that she couldn't use it because Michael was supposed to have co-signed it. Her brother-in-law had offered to sign it for him, but she had been afraid to do that. So she had no access to her money. A few days later she'd write one of the checks to her brother-in-law anyway, who then gave her cash and successfully deposited it in his bank account. She'd use that system for several weeks.

In the afternoon, Eileen took a large flag that a neighbor had brought over and went to hang it over the front porch, where the kids kept their sports equipment and bicycles. But the children became hysterical. "Mommy," shrieked one of the children. "If you do that, they'll find us and kill us like they killed Daddy." After tearfully calming them down and explaining how important it was to show the flag and not be afraid, she went ahead and hung it.

Unbeknownst to Eileen and her children, her in-laws were not so sure anyone had killed Michael Simon. Sometime that afternoon, her sister-in-law went to a website set up by Cantor Fitzgerald and, after a while, started whispering feverishly to her brother, Scott. Michael was listed there as a survivor who was in a New York hospital, though it did not say which one, she told her brother. Without telling Eileen, Scott Simon set out for New York to find the man whose wife had been so sure, so immediately, that he had perished. Michael Simon's family had hope even if his wife didn't.

---

29

When the sun came up over the Memphis airport on Wednesday, September 12, Larry Cox was sure of one thing: He should have splurged and bought automatic pumps for those 5,000 inflatable mattresses. His staff was bone-tired from pumping them by hand. He was still juggling local media interviews, while scrounging for food and water for the 8,000 people still marooned at his airport. Some refused to leave, despite the willingness of the city's families to take them in for a day or two.

Meantime, Cox's fax machine was still spitting out new security directives from the FAA on issues ranging from new fencing requirements around the airport to the security of the planes parked at ramps. Another directive ordered all airports to prohibit travel accessory stores and other shops inside the checkpoints from selling knives. The order seemed to illustrate to Cox and anyone else who read it how much the world had changed in less than a day. Selling Swiss Army knives to people about to board jetliners now seemed suicidal.

One FAA fax that Cox didn't get that morning, but which made him angry when he heard about it months later, was one the agency sent to the airlines. It was a list of about 300 people who the airlines were told were considered dangerous by the FBI, the CIA, or the FAA. When flights resumed, the directive said, these people were not to be allowed on board.

One top American Airlines executive, who had been up all night helping to get the airline's planes back in the air (plus tending to the human and legal issues beginning to emerge from the fact that two of American's planes had been used by the hijackers), was incredulous. Why had they waited until September 12 to send us that, he wondered. They must have had a list on September 10.

Indeed, they would have had such a list had the FAA simply compiled and sent, as they now had done on September 12, the separate lists that the FBI and the CIA had been sending the FAA for at least the prior six months, naming people who were flight risks. The lists were sent to Lee Longmire, a longtime FAA official, who was Director of Civil Aviation Security Policy. They were on his desk on September 10, Longmire acknowledges, although he would refuse to comment about what he did with them or who was on them. But according to an FAA official and a Justice Department official, two of the hijackers were on those September 10 lists—something that Ashcroft would later say he could not confirm or deny. In fact, says the FAA official, his agency had crossed those names off on September 12 to avoid embarrassment. "We just never got around to setting up a protocol for who would control the list and how we would get the airlines to implement it," says the FAA person.

Among the recriminations to follow in the months after September 11 over who knew what and when that might have prevented the attacks, this failure of the FAA to circulate that no-fly list—unlike other supposed failures to "connect the dots"—seems clearly to have resulted in, or contributed to, at least two of the hijackings. That the airlines never complained about it publicly said a great deal about that industry's symbiotic relationship with its regulators. For years, the airlines—an industry whose product is regulated from Washington like almost no other—and the FAA have had a mutual support relationship. Their personnel regularly switched sides, going from the agency to one of the airlines' large Washington lobbying offices and back again. They attended the same conventions, and, most of all, they thought of themselves more as partners than adversaries, which had its positive side in the sense that overbearing regulators could easily strangle an industry like this. So, the airlines rarely complained publicly about the FAA, and the FAA didn't hassle the airlines about issues like security.

In fact, on September 11, the FAA was two years overdue on delivering new explosive detection baggage screening regulations mandated by Congress, and its lawyers were at an off-site conference that day discussing what to do with a backlog of 10,000 allegations of breaches of security and hazardous materials regulations that it had not yet acted on.

It was an arrangement that airport directors like Cox resented because, in their view, when the FAA wanted to show it was getting tough on safety, it would send inspectors to check on how well Cox was securing his gates or exit doors, rather than check the baggage screeners, who were under the control of the airlines and who generally operated in a way meant not to hassle customers. For example, the screeners, who were employed by private security companies, never quibbled over whether the customer was bringing a razor blade or a knife on board, as long as the knife's blade was less than 4.5 inches long—a bizarre standard whose history no one at the FAA after September 11 could remember, let alone own up to.

At 11:00 on the night of September 12, things changed. The CEOs of the airlines participated in a conference call with Norman Mineta, the Secretary of the Department of Transportation, which oversees the FAA. It was a conversation that signaled a new era in federal regulation. A Republican administration that had eschewed Washington regulatory power—albeit with a former Democratic congressman, Mineta, at the DOT helm—was about to flex Washington's muscles.

Mineta had told President Bush on September 11 that he'd have the planes up the next day, but September 12 had come and gone. Now the airline executives expected Mineta was calling with the good news that things were go for the next morning.

The call was anything but good news. Mineta sat at his conference table with, among others, John Flaherty, his chief of staff and longtime aide, and Deputy Secretary Michael Jackson, a veteran of the first Bush administration and a Republican, who had worked at aerospace giant Lockheed Martin during the Clinton years.

Because of a classic conference call snafu, Mineta, Flaherty, and Jackson knew that the airlines expected to get the go-ahead even before the call officially started, because they could hear them talking among themselves before Mineta activated his own speaker signaling that the Transportation Department people were on the line. Instead, Mineta told the airlines that they weren't going to fly unless and until a whole raft of new regulations were implemented. These included more careful baggage screening, no razor blades or knives of any kind, no curbside check-in, National Guardsmen at the airports, the hand-searching of a large sample of passengers and their carry-on bags even after they had gone through metal detectors, and arrangements made to accommodate as many as 600 new armed sky marshals immediately to ride (in first class) on selected flights.

Deputy Secretary Jackson told the airline executives they ought to be able to do all that by Thursday or Friday. The airline CEOs said that was impossible. Mineta said they had no choice. The airline people protested that they were running out of cash and would need a federal bailout even if they started flying as early as tomorrow. One offered to fax over a tally they'd begun working up of all the losses. Flaherty and Jackson said they'd consider all that once they got the planes up. They should also understand, Mineta added, that a lot more regulations were on the way, from Congress and the White House.


The Red Cross had gotten some of its people and a van to the Trade Center within thirty minutes of when the first plane hit, which was fifteen minutes better than the forty-five minute standard it sets for itself to be on the scene with refreshments and a blanket at each of the 37,000 fires and other disasters it would cover during 2001, including 185 the week of September 10.

This was like none of those other 37,000. By Wednesday morning there were three different lines stretching blocks from the headquarters of the Red Cross's New York Chapter on the West Side of Manhattan, about seven miles north of Ground Zero. One line was for people who wanted to give blood. A second was for volunteers, 2,000 of whom would be trained on that day alone. And the third was for people who wanted to give money. They came with coins, dollar bills, and hundred-dollar bills, some in buckets, some in envelopes.

Those were just the people who waited on line. Others gave more spontaneously. By Wednesday afternoon, New York Chapter president Robert Bender had shuttled back and forth so often to the satellite care centers set up overnight that he had not taken off his Red Cross vest. Now, as he started to walk to a meeting in midtown, he had to remove it because he couldn't make his way. People were crowding him on the street, trying to give money.

Yet such was the estrangement between local chapters like Bender's and national headquarters that while Bender had been in contact with the national operations centers (requesting and receiving volunteers who drove in that night from as far away as Ohio), he and Healy—the organization's national CEO—had not spoken as of Wednesday afternoon.

Meantime, in Washington, the Red Cross website had crashed under the weight of donors and volunteers trying to log on. So much money was pouring into the palatial headquarters that the finance staff there—used to reviewing monthly bank statements, not counting and bundling dollars—didn't know what to do with it all.

Healy did. She wanted to segregate it—to keep it from going into the Red Cross's general disaster fund, where it might be used on all varieties of Red Cross efforts and expenses, and where much of it might also be disbursed to the local chapters. The Red Cross, whose board is controlled by leaders of the local chapters, had a long-standing policy allowing any local unit to claim up to 10 percent of any funds sent to the national Red Cross from donors in their jurisdictions. The rest stayed in a general national fund. In her short tenure Healy and her staff had already begun to refer to that fund as a "leaky bucket," because, in their view, the money was never well accounted for, often wasted, and in some cases stolen.

Healy was a forceful, take-no-prisoners executive, not prone to agonize over decisions. And she arrived at this decision instinctively, indeed on the fly. It crystallized in the midst of a chaotic scene outside Red Cross headquarters that afternoon. Healy was standing on the steps of the imposing marble building a few blocks from the White House, shooting a commercial for donations that her communications staff had said she should get on the air as soon as possible. Around her were hundreds of people lined up on the sidewalk and the steps waiting to give blood. Staffers, many who'd been up all night, scurried about. She had a few minutes to shoot the ad. When it got to the end of the script for the thirty-second spot, Healy heard herself reading the standard language that the Red Cross had always used to allow it to raise millions on the notoriety of a high-profile disaster, such as a hurricane or earthquake, and then use the money not just for the big disaster but also for the garden-variety fires and floods that are the charity's daily work: "The funds raised will be used for this and other disasters," the standard punch line went. But as she stood on the steps looking out at what she viewed as wartime Washington, Healy realized she did not want to say that, because she did not want to commingle this money into the general fund. So, on the spot, she and the staff decided to delete the disclaimer about "other disasters." Healy had no intention of using this money for fires, floods, or hurricanes, and she knew that the corporate CEOs she had already talked to about six- and seven-figure donations didn't expect that she would.

Later that afternoon, Healy drafted new language to put into all future solicitations: The funds raised would be used "for this disaster and emerging needs related to this tragedy," she now said. The related, emerging needs would be the blood reserve drives, other preparations, and, if necessary, aid to the victims of new attacks, all related to the new war on terrorism, and all consistent with what she was telling the big donors she was talking to individually. None of the money would go into the Red Cross's general disaster fund, let alone be siphoned off by local chapters.

A new policy had been made, one whose ramifications for her organization and her own career Healy—who ironically would later be publicly chastised for *not* using all of the September 11 money to help September 11 victims—didn't come close to appreciating as she stood at the center of this M*A*S*H-like scene.

Across town from the Red Cross New York headquarters, two of that city's oldest, most prominent but most different charities occupied different floors of Two Park Avenue. Since the beginning of the twentieth century, the New York Community Trust has been tending to the legacies of wealthy people who had established 1,600 different charitable trusts worth a total of more than $2 billion. The staff of the Community Trust made grants from these funds based on what these individual trusts were set up to do—aid education, support the arts, help the homeless, finance good government, and so on. The United Way of Greater New York, on the other hand, was a repository of employee and corporate giving programs. Unlike the Red Cross, neither actually operated relief programs; rather, they gave grants to organizations that demonstrate that they can.

Beginning the afternoon of September 11 and resuming in earnest the next morning, the leaders and staff of both groups met to talk about combining forces for a charity to help victims of the attacks. They both wanted to do something, and figured they had special capabilities to create a fund that could focus more on the longer-term needs of victims than could the Red Cross, with its historic emphasis on providing shelter, food, and other immediate aid. The United Way had enormous fund-raising credibility, and the Community Trust had great experience finding organizations on the ground that could administer aid targeted at specific needs. What both didn't have was a lot of ego. Unlike the Red Cross, neither group wanted the limelight, let alone an operating role, in doling out what they thought might be millions of dollars to thousands of recipients. So by mid-morning they issued a press release announcing a September 11th Fund that would raise money and funnel it in grants to groups and organizations best able to help victims. The release was carefully and candidly worded to say that this fund would not only try to help the families of those who had died or were injured but "all those affected by the tragedy." By the afternoon, their website, which unlike the Red Cross's, never crashed, was receiving a flood of pledges—one every five to ten seconds. Within two days, the new fund would have more than $66 million.

By midday, Brian Lyons, the construction engineer, was exhausted. Although he still considered himself athletic, the last decade he had spent supervising construction projects from behind a desk, instead of doing the work himself, had taken a toll. He'd developed a paunch, which gave his average size frame a bit of a fireplug look.

Lyons was short of breath, and his hands and arms already hurt. But he kept picking away through the devastation that had already come to be called Ground Zero, helping to figure out which buildings or parts of buildings were about to crash down, while looking for his firefighter brother. Everywhere he looked there was devastation, but not the type one would have expected from the collapse of the giant office towers. Although there must have been 20,000 computer terminals and as many desks in those buildings, he saw none. Months later, the police inspector in overall charge of sifting all the recovered debris would report recovering no terminals, one leg of one desk, and two phone handsets. The inferno ignited by the jumbo jets full of fuel had been such that all Lyons saw were some steel beams. And ash.

Still, the tally wasn't as grim as it might have been. When terrorists had bombed the parking garage of the Trade Center in 1993, it had taken four hours to evacuate the buildings. This time, because of improved stairway lighting, repeated fire drills, and other measures, it had taken forty minutes. As a result, and with the help of the police and firefighters who rushed in, almost all of those working in the towers below where the planes had hit had escaped. An emergency drill at the Pentagon a month before—which had simulated, eerily, a plane crashing into the building—had helped hold down the casualties there, too.*

As evening approached, Lyons parlayed his pickup role on a team evaluating the structural safety of the debris that was still standing (or leaning) into a job directing the first bulldozers that had arrived. Now, he thought, he was really being useful. So useful that he didn't leave. Not for dinner. Not that night. In fact he didn't leave for ten more days. And then he would leave only for a day and come back for seven more weeks, stopping only to sleep a few hours a day in a car, on a boat, in a church, or at the Red Cross tent.


Ed Woollen's boss, Raytheon CEO Dan Burnham, decided to code-name it Project Yankee. On the phone from his Lexington, Massachusetts, office on Wednesday afternoon to Woollen in Arlington, overlooking the wreckage at the Pentagon, Burnham asked Woollen to take over a whole new business development portfolio. It would be devoted to creating and selling products related to what both agreed would now be a new era in American history: the era of homeland security.

They should call their new effort Project Yankee for now, they agreed, rather than something with homeland security in the name, because they did not want to seem as if they were taking advantage of the situation.

It wasn't that they were doing anything wrong or underhanded, they reasoned. But they didn't want people to get the wrong idea. "Our company is in business to give shareholders a return on their risk capital," Burnham says. "But I also believe that we are a national asset and that we can provide comfort and security to the country. I don't want to be sanctimonious about it, but I decided that day that we had not only a good business opportunity but an obligation to the country to start to think about all this."

Read up on all those old studies and commission reports on homeland security, Burnham told Woollen, and then they'd put together a real plan the following week.

---

*Pentagon emergency planners had decided to stage the drill because the Pentagon is so close to Reagan National Airport.

John Ashcroft wasn't waiting for anything to happen next week. He wanted results now. At about the same time that Romero of the ACLU was ordering his staff to cancel a direct mail solicitation planned to go out the next day— focused on "the new anti-liberty era being unveiled by President George Bush" and on how Americans should be "ashamed" of the "new morality" being pushed by, among others, John Ashcroft—the Attorney General had a morning meeting with the President and his national security team. When FBI Director Robert Mueller assured Bush that everything was being done to track down those who had been involved in the attacks, Bush upbraided him. "Our priorities have changed," he said. "We need to focus on preventing the next attack more than worrying about who did this one." Ashcroft was deter-mined to enforce that focus, even if it meant living in the FBI's operations center.

"Focus" was not a good word to describe what the FBI had been doing since the attacks. Activity, yes. But not focus.

True, they had pulled the passenger lists of the four planes and figured out who the hijackers probably were. (This was due in part to phone calls the flight attendants and passengers on the planes had made before the crashes, in which they had identified the hijackers' seat numbers. Also, these were pretty much the only people with Middle Eastern names on the planes, and in several instances they had bought tickets together.) But beyond that, what the FBI had done was to begin running down the tens of thousands of names on those INS immigration lists, go after a handful of prior leads on Middle East-ern terrorists, and otherwise respond to calls.

Thousands of calls.

Just the Newark office of the FBI—whose jurisdiction includes Middle Eastern immigrant enclaves like Paterson, New Jersey, where it was already known that several of the hijackers had lived—received more than 5,000 citi-zen calls between the afternoon of September 11 and the end of the day on September 12. Whether the government should engage in racial or ethnic profiling would be hotly debated in the months ahead. But among Americans sitting in their homes or offices contemplating the horror of September 11 there was no such debate. One by one Americans did their own ad hoc racial profiling. It seemed that anyone who had ever seen a Muslim or suspected a neighbor of being a Muslim called in. Some reported suspicious-smelling food in a neighboring house or apartment; others reported seeing people in Muslim garb whispering. There were so many calls that the lines jammed and the phones had to be kicked over to FBI operators in the Atlanta office. One by one, Newark-based agents, working through the night and helped by local police, ran down each call, a process that would last through Thanksgiving and ultimately include 27,000 face-to-face interviews from September 12 through February.

The agents and their supervisors tried to prioritize. Obviously, a call about suspicious food smells should be attended to after a tip about three men with guns coming in and out of an apartment at all hours of the day. But mostly they went after everything. And for good reason. From his command post in the FBI operations center, Ashcroft told Mueller that any male from eighteen to forty years old from Middle Eastern or North African countries whom the FBI simply learned about was to be questioned and questioned hard. And anyone from these countries whose immigration papers were out of order—anyone—was to be turned over to the INS. Ashcroft then put Michael Chertoff, the head of his Justice Department Criminal Division, in de facto charge of these INS roundups, even though the INS process was supposed to be part of a civil law proceeding, not a criminal prosecution. The goal, Ashcroft and Chertoff told the FBI and INS agents, was to prevent more attacks, not prosecute anyone. And the best way to do that was to round up, question, and hold as many people as possible.

That was not a message, however, that made it to Lindemann, the INS Border Patrol agent in Detroit. It seemed as if it had been forever since the Border Patrol regarded itself as part of the INS, let alone the Justice Department. September 11 hadn't changed that. So now, while the FBI and INS in New Jersey began rounding up people with families who had worked for years at gas stations or pizza parlors, Lindemann and his fellow Border Patrol agents were instructed to keep to business as usual in the north. That meant that what Lindemann had bitterly come to call the Catch and Release Program, or CARP, would continue in the days and weeks after September 11. He and his partner, Mark Hall, would catch people sneaking over the border into Detroit from Canada and then be told by supervisors to release them because the Border Patrol unit only had a $1,000 a week to pay the local jail to hold people.

A significant portion of those Lindemann and Hall had caught and released in recent years—perhaps 25 percent—were Muslim, which was no surprise because the Detroit area has the country's largest Muslim community. And Canada, which had notoriously looser border controls than the United States (people coming in from twenty different countries, such as Saudi Arabia, who needed visas to get into the United States do not need visas to get into Canada), was known as a hotbed of terrorist activity. Everyone Lindemann caught was, by definition, breaking the law and, unlike many of those being rounded up and held in New Jersey, had no roots in the community. But they continued to be released after filling out a form and promising to come back for a deportation hearing, which, of course, they never did. Lindemann's and Hall's repeated protests to the bosses, which now became more vehement than ever, were ignored. "I was getting to the point where I couldn't stand it anymore," Lindemann recalls. "I felt like I had to do something."

Larry Silverstein got a lot of sympathy calls on Wednesday. His buildings had been knocked down and four of his employees (part of an early vanguard of a planned move of his entire company into the Trade Center) were missing. But, according to two people who called him that morning, Silverstein soon changed the subject. He had talked to his lawyers at Wachtell, Lipton, Rosen & Katz—a premier corporate firm that was so well regarded and so leanly structured that for more than a decade it had earned more money per partner than any of its New York competitors—and he had a clear legal strategy mapped out. They were going to prove, Silverstein told one of the callers, that the way his insurance policies were written the two planes crashing into the two towers had been two different "occurrences," not part of the same event. That would give him more than $7 billion to rebuild, instead of the $3.55 billion that his insurance policy said was the maximum for one "occurrence." And rebuild was just what he was going to do, he vowed.

In Nashville, Tennessee, where Silverstein's insurance brokers were stranded at a meeting, there was quite a different perception. On a conference call with colleagues in New York and London, Silverstein's lead insurance broker on the deal told the others that it seemed to him that under the policy as written this was one occurrence.

To be sure, everything was clouded by the fact that no formal documents had been signed; Silverstein had taken over the Trade Center only six weeks before, and the final documents for the insurance had not been finished. But a deal memo using his broker's policy had been circulated and seemingly agreed to.

By mid-morning, Silverstein put the rebuilding process in motion. He called his architect—David Childs of the renowned Skidmore, Owings & Merrill firm, who had recently been retained by Silverstein to plan a refurbishing of the Trade Center. Start sketching out a plan for a whole new place, Silverstein told Childs, who was working at home because his office, just two blocks from the Twin Towers, had been evacuated. Childs would later marvel that in that initial conversation Silverstein was already keenly focused on another legal issue. He told Childs—who, like most good architects, had always thought of the Trade Center as a monstrosity—that he had to plan to build the exact same number of square feet of office space as had been destroyed. The reason, Silverstein explained, was that his lease with the Trade Center required that, in the event of a catastrophe like this, they had to let him build that much space. More important, the lease required that he actually build it. If one side was going to decide not to rebuild two 110-story towers, it wasn't going to be Silverstein. His best legal position was for him to get the Port Authority to blink first.

The lawyers in Dean O'Hare's conference room at Chubb's headquarters in New Jersey had done as much research as they could, looking not only at the case law and what the Chubb policies said, but also at how the White House and others in Washington had described the attack as an act of war. In fact, Silverstein had by now even called a staffer in Senator Schumer's office, urging her (as if she could) to get the President and others to stop calling it war, because it endangered his entire insurance coverage and, therefore, the rebuilding of the Trade Center. (Chubb was one of the many Silverstein insurers, though with a relatively small stake—$100 million or $200 million, depending on how many occurrences it had been. The bulk of the insurance at issue for Chubb involved the hundreds of policies the company had sold to businesses, car owners, and even homeowners in lower Manhattan, all of whom had now suffered tremendous losses.)

According to White House Counsel Alberto Gonzales, President Bush was told about the possible insurance ramifications of calling this an act of war, but he insisted on "calling it what it was." Another White House staffer says that the President declared he was going to call it war, and that they should "work on" the insurance companies.

Thanks to O'Hare, they didn't need to be worked on. At about 3:00 he came into the cavernous, formal conference room where his board meetings were usually held. It was full of lawyers and executives, their papers of cases and authorities strewn about. No one said that coverage should be denied outright. But there were strong arguments either to delay and do nothing until another insurer announced something, or to issue what in the insurance industry is known as a "reservation of rights," which meant that Chubb would say that it might pay now but later seek return of the payments if the facts and law warranted that. Nobody knew if Syria or Iraq was involved, argued one lawyer, which would, indeed, make this an act of war. (Remember, this was just a day after the attacks.) And who knew if this Al Qaeda group, or whatever it was called, wasn't really the Afghans? Besides, what would the reinsurers—who insured Chubb against about $1.5 billion of what by today seemed to have grown to be $2 billion of potential claims against Chubb—do? Could O'Hare risk that?

O'Hare had already called one of his key reinsurers, a company called General Re, controlled by financier Warren Buffett. He knew that Buffett was prepared to do what's called "follow the lead," meaning his reinsurance would follow what the insurer, in this case Chubb, did. But he wasn't so sure about the other reinsurers, nor was he sure what some of the insurers would do. He'd heard of two specific competitors who were talking openly, at least in insurance circles, about reserving their rights. He just wasn't sure.

But O'Hare was sure of one thing, which was that Chubb's history and culture were based on being the company that always was first and most eager to honor its policies. He bragged about that endlessly. So did his employees. When brokers sold policies, they made a point of telling customers that Chubb was the most honorable, the most hassle-free insurer. Now he was presented with a once-in-a-lifetime test of this Chubb credo. "For us to have done anything different now, for us to not have taken the lead," he explains, "would have been bad business. It would have erased everything we have stood for all these years. And it would have been wrong."

Without calling a single board member—this was a management decision, he decided, not a change in policy—O'Hare told the staff to issue a press release the first thing next morning announcing that Chubb was honoring all claims and was going to start writing checks within a day.

When the release came out the next morning, it was not a moment too soon. Just before it was issued, an insurance industry newsletter on the Internet speculated that insurers could invoke the act of war exclusion, and reporters were already calling around to insurance companies asking what they intended to do. The Chubb announcement ended that speculation, because it was soon followed by Chubb's competitors saying they, too, were prepared to honor all claims.

The act of war insurance question, says White House economic policy advisor Larry Lindsey, was an issue that, if left unanswered, could have really caused a panic. "But we deserve no credit for solving it. We hadn't gotten to it yet."

Indeed, on Wednesday afternoon Lindsey had lots of other issues to deal with, especially the suspension of the country's financial markets.

As undersecretary of the treasury for domestic finance, Peter Fisher was the executive branch's man in charge of the United States financial system. A former wunderkind at the Federal Reserve Board and Harvard-trained lawyer,

Fisher was Treasury Secretary Paul O'Neill's point man when it came to policy on markets, interest rates, and the like. His influence was now magnified by the fact that O'Neill was traveling in Japan.

Fisher, forty-five, had been sent home Tuesday evening with a special, secure satellite telephone. It was a bulky contraption, and he felt embarrassed carrying it on the Metro. That night he had talked nonstop—though not on the satellite phone, because he couldn't figure out how to work it—to, among others, Lindsey; Richard Grasso, the Chairman and CEO of the New York Stock Exchange; and Harvey Pitt, the Chairman of the U.S. Securities and Exchange Commission. The four were trying to figure out how to reopen the stock markets, which hadn't even opened Tuesday morning. The President wants them open by Thursday, Lindsey kept repeating. Fisher and Pitt were game. Grasso was dubious.

That may have been because Grasso was closer to the scene, literally. Spreading his small frame on the long couch alongside his desk, Grasso was on the phone all night from his office at Broad and Wall streets, about three blocks from the Trade Center. He had refused to leave, and now he knew that while his own building had been spared, much around him had not.

By 10:00 this morning, Fisher and Pitt were on a train to New York, where Grasso, having been urged to do so by Lindsey, had convened a meeting, at the Bear Stearns brokerage house in midtown, of the CEOs of key Wall Street banks and brokerages.

Fisher, who had a knack for not being too serious about his serious job, would remember the gathering of Wall Street's top thirty or forty moguls as "the quintessential twenty-first-century business meeting. . . . We went around the room listening to all these CEOs, and the guy from Treasury (me), and the SEC chairman. Then we all stopped and turned to the tech guy—the guy from Verizon. He was the most important guy in the room."

The real issues were, indeed, matters of high and low technology. Could the phone and data lines be restored?

That was no small problem. Verizon had a major switching and transmission station (actually a grand, thirty-one-story building that had been built as the headquarters of the old New York Telephone Company) next door to the Trade Center. Much of one side of that building had been sheared off by falling debris from the now collapsed Seven World Trade Center. The rest had been decimated by steel beams harpooning it as the towers had collapsed, and by flooding in the basement that had come when the beams pulverized the water mains underneath. Hundreds of miles of cable for phones and Internet connections had been sliced and diced, and floors full of switching machines had been flooded, smoked, or pierced into junk. As it happened, the phone lines for the New York Stock Exchange itself came from another switching station, but much of its long distance service came via that old telephone company headquarters building; and all of the services for several of the brokerage houses came from there. On top of that, a major Con Edison electric station had been destroyed at the Trade Center, which meant that the phone company's power was out and was not likely to come back before the backup generators were used up.

Yet, as Lawrence Babbio, the president of Verizon's telecommunications, now explained it to the slack-jawed executives, this was one way in which the terrorists had weakened their punch by attacking Manhattan. For Manhattan had a richer telecommunications infrastructure, including more redundancies in equipment, than any place on earth. So while that building would be a near-total loss for months, huge cables could be laid running into and out of the building and along the streets to other facilities, while switches were rebuilt and reworked so that the Stock Exchange and the brokerage houses could be up and running in days.

How many days are we talking about, asked Fisher, playing the bad guy. Three to five, Babbio estimated.

How about they shoot for Saturday for a test run and then get everything ironed out Sunday to open on Monday, Grasso suggested.

We'll try, Babbio said, not really knowing exactly how or if he really could.

The press was waiting outside the meeting, and Fisher now had a choice. He could spend the next ten minutes explaining to Lindsey, who was waiting at the White House to hear from him, why reopening tomorrow, Thursday, was not going to happen. Or he could figure out with Grasso and the others how to frame the announcement as positively as possible, meaning he'd let Lindsey and the others at the White House watch the announcement like everyone else.

Fisher knew from a conference call he'd been in on during the train ride up that the bond markets—which trade in corporate and government IOUs rather than stock ownership—were much closer to being able to open, because so many of them had multiple operations in places outside New York. So, after Fisher checked in on a meeting going on elsewhere among bond market leaders, he and Grasso announced that the bond markets would open for business tomorrow and that the New York Stock Exchange along with the Nasdaq and the American Exchange (which would have to use space at the New York Stock Exchange) would open on Monday. They cited the communications breakdowns, as well as the desire not to have stock exchange workers interfere in the days just after the attacks with rescue and recovery efforts.

As the Verizon workers began stringing cable out the windows of their almost fallen building that afternoon, Michael Cartier, having bicycled from his parents' house in Queens, rode by with his brother John. They were on their way up from the Trade Center, where they had posted pictures of their brother James wherever they could, to check the hospitals. A volunteer at one hospital told them there was a master list at another hospital, so they kept riding. They found no list, so they made the rounds of other hospitals and police precincts. Still no lists. Later that evening they found a list. James wasn't on it.

They rode back that night to their parents' house. It was now flying a flag alongside flags displayed at all the homes bunched onto the block of this working-class Queens neighborhood, a place where one got the sense that the people with Police and Fire Department hats at the corner 7-Eleven hadn't bought them at a souvenir shop. The house, where the six Cartier brothers and sisters and their parents and friends and a priest were gathered, had become command central in the battle to find James Cartier and bring him home, alive or otherwise. As the weeks went by, command central would take on a life of its own. Recovering James would remain the family's obsession. They were not going to let anything—including bulldozers aimed at clearing the place up sooner rather than later—get in their way.

By the end of Wednesday, the calls started coming in to Kevin McCabe and his bosses at Customs, and to their cohorts at the Coast Guard. When were the ports going to reopen? Someone from one of the New England congressional delegations said that his state was about to run out of oil; Logan Airport in Boston was in danger of having no fuel for its planes when the airport reopened; a major retailer needed its furniture; factories up and down the East Coast that used modern just-in-time inventory controls to save money were about to run out of time; and produce shippers were terrified that their lemons and limes from places like Ecuador would start to rot. The downside of a global economy was that it really was a global economy.

At the Northern Border, the order by McCabe colleague Mary Delaquis in North Dakota to inspect everything had stretched the usual ten- to thirty-minute wait to three to five hours. That was nothing compared to what was going on east of Delaquis at the Northern Border in Detroit.

The Ambassador Bridge from Windsor, Ontario, to Detroit was responsible for more foreign trade, in dollar value, per year than the total shipped from all of Japan to the United States. By Wednesday evening the complaints about delay of that merchandise had come straight into the White House, where economy czar Larry Lindsey's office received calls from representatives of the big three auto companies. The bridge hadn't been closed the way McCabe's port in New Jersey had. But just the step up to Level One alert, which meant more careful inspections of more trucks, had caused a thirteen-hour wait on the Canadian side. When Lindsey had received the first complaint, he called Customs, which soon called his office back to report that Lindsey's information was all wrong: There were no delays. It turned out that this was because Canadian police, concerned about pollution and traffic jams in the city of Windsor, had held the line back outside the city, where the Customs people couldn't even see it. "I guess that's what they call the fog of war," Lindsey later joked.

The whole problem was one of the toughest of the September 12 era. "Nothing sits in storage anymore," McCabe liked to say. "It moves. The container is the new warehouse." This meant that more careful inspections weren't just a matter of finding the money and manpower to do the job. As McCabe put it, "Inspecting every container, even if you could, would tie up what comes through here for five days, maybe ten. That would strangle the economy."

In Detroit, even thirteen hours had done that. Several assembly lines on the U.S. side would shut down on Thursday because parts coming from Canada had been delayed on the bridge.

But the converse was also true, and more horrific. The day before, the hijackers had killed several thousand people and shut down the airlines for what would become two or three days. But had a bomb gone off in a container in McCabe's port, or on the Detroit bridge, it could easily have been a nuclear or bioterror device, killing many more. And beyond the damage to life and property, had shipping commerce been shut down as aviation had until someone could provide plausible assurance that all, or most, or even just a large fraction of containers were being inspected, the economic fallout in the United States and around the world would dwarf the hundred billion dollars of economic damage caused by the September 11 attacks.

Somehow, his port was going to have to reopen the next day, McCabe knew. Other than that, he was sure of nothing.


Chuck Schumer had spent Wednesday morning deploying his staff to make two kinds of phone calls. Some canvassed city and state agencies, including

his wife's New York City Transportation Department, to get a fix on what kind
of aid New York needed to rebuild. Others canvassed various House and Senate staffers to see what might be available and what the other members of
Congress were thinking. Schumer's goal was to get every possible type of aid
from whatever pot possible as soon as possible. Because Schumer had
requested a meeting with him when they had spoken on Tuesday soon after
the attacks, the President had asked Schumer and Hillary Clinton, New York's
junior senator, to meet with him the next day. The senior senator from New
York was determined to be prepared, to make this more than a meeting where
the President consoled the New Yorkers. In fact, he wanted to spring a specific
budget request on the President.

Schumer was fixated on one notion that would govern everything he did in
the days ahead. He wanted to get as much as possible for New York now—right
now—rather than wait. He had two fears. One was that if he waited, attention
to the tragedy might fade. The other was that there was likely to be another
attack someplace else that would dilute the priority given to New York.

It seems a selfish perspective at a time of national crisis. But much of what
follows demonstrates that the American system is built on people and, in this
case, their representatives, being free to assert their self-interest, or, as they
would rightly say, fulfill their responsibilities. McCabe of Customs will be
planning to inspect shipments more thoroughly than the shippers who seek
faster service want him to; the families of the victims will be contending with
those who want to clear the Ground Zero site quickly so it can be rebuilt; law
enforcement people will want to issue strong, candid warnings against the
next possible attack, while business leaders will fear spooking the economy;
and even special interest groups that most citizens might barely be aware of,
such as lobbyists representing the country's universities, will seem to act
myopically or selfishly as they try to discourage new restrictions on foreign
student visas. It would all make for a harrowing test of a system in which all
the players in this American symphony square off in a robust, often messy
clash of ideas and special interests that is supposed to produce the public
interest.

In any event, Schumer was all business that day—until the afternoon.
That's when he boarded a plane from Washington to New York, flown by the
Federal Emergency Management Agency (FEMA). Schumer had made the
flight hundreds of times since being elected, to the House as a twenty-nine-
year-old in 1980 and then to the Senate in 2000. Always, he took at least a
moment as he approached the city, first to look down at the vast beach in the
Rockaway section of Queens, which had been part of his mostly Brooklyn

congressional district, then over to Prospect Park in Brooklyn, where his family's apartment was, and finally, up to the skyline of lower Manhattan. Only now, when he looked at that skyline, there was a hole. And he started to sob.

# Thursday, September 13, 2001

At 10:00 A.M. on Thursday, September 13, Sal Iacono, accompanied by one of his sons, who was on the verge of getting an accounting degree, tried to get back to his shoe repair shop. The police stopped him at a barricade just across lower Broadway near Fulton Street. Sal the Sole Man could see beyond the wrecked cars and fire trucks to his store from across the street, and it didn't look good. The door that he had taken pains to lock was smashed, as were the windows. Inside, it looked like the police and firemen were using it as a rest station. He couldn't tell if the cash register or any of his inventory of polishes, umbrellas, and sole insets and heels was there, but he feared the worst.

The police at the barricade weren't the neighborhood cops, a few of whom were loyal customers. Some were even National Guardsmen. None knew him. They just knew they had orders. No one went to the Trade Center side of Broadway. Sal turned and left, tears in his eyes. In his head, he tried to add up what the damage might be. He couldn't even begin to make a guess.

In Washington, Mitchell Daniels, Jr., the Director of the White House Office of Management and Budget, had been trying a similar numbers exercise, though on a different scale and with more success. Since the evening of the 11th (in a process that began with a round of phone calls while the President was addressing the nation), Daniels and his staff—who controlled the budgets that the executive branch sent to Congress for approval, and did so in ways that rarely left any of those executive departments satisfied—had been trying to get a handle on what September 11 was going to cost. That total would quickly have to become a request for the budget year ending in September of 2002. That budget, the first of the Bush administration, had, in fact, already been calculated and mostly locked up, so this would be what was called a supplemental request, an add-on to what had already been asked for and approved by Congress. Daniels, a wiry, former drug company executive and blunt Republican stalwart from Indiana, treasured the hard-nosed, buttoned-down approach he had brought to putting together this year's budget. Now, the picture looked ugly. Daniels's job was to manage the ugliness.

After canvassing the Defense Department to get them to guess at expenditures between now and next September on a war they hadn't even begun to plan, and doing the same at places like the Transportation Department (where new measures would have to be taken to protect air travel and add to what the Coast Guard did to protect the shores) and Justice (where the FBI would obviously be beefed up), Daniels had come up with a back-of-the-envelope guess of about $20 billion needed immediately, with more likely to come in another supplemental request as things developed. By late Wednesday, Daniels's estimate was being talked about on Capitol Hill.

When Schumer's and Clinton's staffs began hearing that number on Wednesday afternoon, they were horrified to find out that the draft legislation authorizing it included not a word about aid to New York. The two senators were in New York at the emergency command center, when both got a call from their staffs alerting them to the problem.

By Thursday morning, Schumer and his staff had begun to think symmetry. If the country needed $20 billion, well then so, too, did New York. Its economy had been crushed. Its transportation system—subway tunnels and stations, bus routes, streets—in lower Manhattan had been pulverized. Its police and fire departments would be swamped with death benefit payments, plus overtime for those who had survived. And New York had just seen more office space demolished than could be found in most mid-sized American cities. Schumer and Clinton's meeting with the President was scheduled for the afternoon, but the first order of business was getting the support for the request from Senate Majority Leader Tom Daschle and from Robert Byrd, the longtime Democratic senator from West Virginia and the chairman of the all-powerful Appropriations Committee. Schumer talked to Daschle, while Clinton agreed to call Byrd. After she had cajoled his support, Schumer insisted that they should go for it at the White House—seize the moment now and try to get the President on the record before his staff had a chance to build up any opposition to it.

It was an audacious, even outrageous reach. Working with figures from a one-page fax from the mayor's office, Schumer's staff hadn't totaled up more than $5 or $7 billion in clearly defined needs apart from the cost of rebuilding the Trade Center itself, which was Silverstein's and his insurer's problem. But Schumer told them to include that and anything else they needed to, just so that he could say he'd seen a $20 billion estimate; he was sure that ultimately the numbers would stretch that high, anyway. Clinton's staff hadn't gotten even that far with their math. Clinton told her staff she was more pessimistic than Schumer because she didn't think Bush liked New York.

As they walked into the Oval Office, Clinton told Schumer he should do the asking, which had been his intention all along.

Schumer and Clinton, along with the two senators from Virginia (Republicans John Warner and George Allen), which was also considered a victim of the terrorists because of the Pentagon attacks (and perhaps because the White House staff wanted some other Republicans in the room), sat down with Bush. They commiserated for a while. Schumer was emotional, telling the President about how he'd been unable to find his daughter, who went to high school near the Trade Center, for nearly four hours, and that his local firehouse in Brooklyn had lost eleven men. Clinton talked about the devastation she and Schumer had seen on their visit to Ground Zero the day before. Then Schumer turned to Bush and said he'd heard that the nation needed $20 billion to recover. "Well, Mr. President, New York needs twenty billion, too," he said, ticking off some key expense items, such as rebuilding the subways.

Bush hesitated. Schumer recalls that he could "literally see the President thinking. . . . He's clearly figuring that New York had not gone for him [in the election], but he needs to bring the country together."

"New York needs twenty billion?" Bush repeated. By now there were tears in Schumer's eyes. "You got it," the President declared. Schumer and the President stood up. Schumer went to hug Bush, then realized he was in the Oval Office with the President, so he simply grasped his shoulders. "There were tears in my eyes and tears in his eyes," Schumer remembers.

Moments later, Schumer and Clinton were in the Cabinet Room with the New York congressional delegation and the news cameras, praising the President for his promise of $20 billion. They wanted to be sure to lock him in.

But even in America $20 billion doesn't come that easily. By that night, Schumer's staff was hearing that the House Appropriations Committee, with the agreement if not the urging of Daniels of the White House budget office, was making changes in the supplemental appropriation. Suddenly, that $20 billion was earmarked vaguely for "recovery expenses," and not for New York (and in small part, Virginia). It was at moments like this—when he felt he was being shortchanged and fooled with—that Schumer was at his best, and worst. He immediately got on the phone with White House Chief of Staff Andrew Card and screamed that with the President scheduled to visit Ground Zero the next day he did not want to have to report to New Yorkers that Bush had taken less than twenty-four hours to go back on his promise. The $20 billion was quickly re-earmarked. From that day on, Schumer became a believer in Bush, or at least in his honor and his ability to appreciate what had happened in New York. In Schumer's eyes, the President then, and in subsequent episodes of staff or congressional opposition, held fast to his promise.

In New York, Schumer's wife, Iris Weinshall, faced a more basic money crunch. Late Thursday morning one of her aides told her that there was a problem with ATM machines in the city, a comment whose first impact was that Weinshall realized that she was out of cash and needed to go get some. You might have trouble, the aide said. It seemed that because traffic was still so bad coming into Manhattan, and, because most of the bridges and tunnels coming in had been closed Tuesday and parts of Wednesday, the armored trucks that the banks used to fill ATMs all over Manhattan had not been deployed. So Weinshall and other city officials now had to arrange with the Federal Reserve and the banks for convoys full of cash to make their way around town, filling ATM machines. What everyone had begun to fear could become a twenty-first-century money panic had been averted.

Meantime, in New Jersey, Chubb Insurance CEO O'Hare did his part to calm parallel fears. He sent a memo to all of Chubb's agents and brokers, saying, "You may have read media reports speculating about whether insurers will try to avoid paying claims by invoking act-of-war exclusions. You know us; we have already begun paying claims." He soon got a slew of letters and e-mails back, thanking him, some even praising his patriotism.

O'Hare's unilateral action, quickly followed by his competitors, to erase doubts about insurers paying what would ultimately become approximately $50 billion in claims related to the attacks, was one of the few fault lines related to the economy that was not already being closely monitored and managed at the White House. There were now so many domestic issues related to the crisis crowding the agenda of the constantly meeting National Security Council that on Thursday, Joshua Bolten, a deputy chief of staff, was made the chair of a rump Domestic Consequences Principals Committee, which would include roughly a dozen senior staffers and key cabinet members.

The items Bolten listed for the group's first meeting the next morning were dominated by the same challenge facing Cox, who still hadn't left his Memphis airport. How could they get the airline industry back to some semblance of normalcy? These included borrowing law enforcement officers from a multitude of federal agencies (such as Treasury's Bureau of Alcohol, Tobacco and Firearms and INS's Border Patrol) to staff the air marshal positions that Transportation Secretary Mineta said he needed before he'd let planes fly again. They also had to figure out how to train them instantly in how to handle their guns on airplanes. The air marshals, started amid fanfare in the 1970s to deter hijackings, had been allowed secretly to dwindle to a grand total of thirty-two by September 11. Mineta wanted 600 immediately.

There was also the issue of how to evaluate what was now becoming the airlines' increasingly panicky call for a federal bailout of some kind. Bolten, a forty-seven-year-old Princeton and Stanford Law graduate who had worked as an investment banker at Goldman Sachs, was no economic neophyte. Yet along with economic policy czar Lindsey and others at the White House, he was stunned to learn that the airlines were claiming that their businesses were so precarious that a few days' disruption and the prospect of weeks of fear-induced reduced ridership could wipe them all out. Equally surprising was the news that planes not flying for just a few days, combined with the prospect of longer-term disruption if bankruptcies really happened, could have a massive ripple effect on the entire American economy. The aviation industry, they were told, not just by the industry itself but by their own staffers and Mineta, was a unique linchpin for much of the rest of the economy.

Beyond that, Bolten's agenda for the next morning included issues he and the group were already tackling, such as figuring out how to ease the Customs clampdown. Somehow, the fuel barges that were being kept out of McCabe's port in New Jersey had to be allowed to unload before New England ran out of oil and gas. Somehow, General Motors had to be able to get its parts into Detroit over the bridge from Canada.

Another big worry was making sure the stock markets stayed on track to open on Monday, and that once they opened a systems failure of some kind wouldn't shut them down again, something that everyone believed would be worse for the economy's nervous system than the markets not opening at all. Lindsey, a free market fanatic, went home that night and told his wife he now understood firsthand how the Kremlin's centralized economic planning had failed so miserably; one of his aides, he told her, had had to spend the day trying to expedite the shipment by air (even though aviation was still shut down) of a temporary generator that needed to be installed near one of the brokerage houses on Wall Street, while simultaneously negotiating to get the generator a temporary waiver of some kind of permit related to air pollution concerns.

Whatever else could be said about whether the ACLU was relevant in the September 12 era, there was no disputing that the group and its staff felt the effects of the terror attacks as much as anyone else. On Thursday, Romero was still stranded in Washington. And had he been able to get back to New York, he could not have gone to work because the office tower about ten blocks from the Trade Center that housed his national headquarters was still closed. Meanwhile, the ACLU Washington office, where he was now encamped, was so close to the Capitol that people there were constantly jolted by the sirens that screeched by responding to bomb scares and other threats.

The distractions were a kind of relief from the frustrating inaction inside. Romero, who had now been on the job at the ACLU for all of ten days, was trying to rein in his new staff. He insisted that no one respond to calls from the media asking for general comment on hypothetical restrictions on civil liberties that were already being talked about. Yes, the prosecutors had an "insatiable appetite" for more power, as Romero's chairman, law professor Nadine Strossen, liked to put it. But, Romero told the staff, "We have to wait till they propose something specific before we comment. We can't be generally critical. When they propose something specific then we'll hit them. Until then, we say nothing."

At mid-morning on Thursday, the man most likely to offer those specifics left the operations center at the FBI and returned to his desk across Pennsylvania Avenue at the Justice Department. It was the first time that John Ashcroft had been there since the attacks. The first thing he did was check in with Viet Dinh, his thirty-three-year-old assistant attorney general in charge of the Office of Legal Policy. On Tuesday, Ashcroft had asked Dinh, a Vietnamese refugee and Harvard Law graduate who was considered a conservative legal superstar, to head a group that would put together an aggressive set of legislative changes that Ashcroft could quickly propose to Congress as necessary to fight the war on terrorism and, in particular, to change the focus from prosecuting crime to preventing it. Dinh told Ashcroft that the package would be ready to be presented to him at a meeting Friday night.

For Dinh and the Justice Department staff, Ashcroft's assignment was a labor of love. As the ACLU staffers had suspected when they huddled just after the planes hit, prosecutors always have a list of changes in the law that they'd like to see that would help them catch the bad guys—changes, such as making it easier to get wiretaps or search warrants, that for the ACLU people are a list of horribles. In fact, the key deputy that Dinh asked to dig in on this project was David Carp, a veteran Justice Department lawyer who had worked on the same list after the Oklahoma City bombing and had seen little of it enacted into an anti-terrorism law passed then. Now he had another chance.

But there was one problem: Carp was an Orthodox Jew and Friday evening was the beginning of the Jewish Sabbath. Working that night would normally be unthinkable for Carp. But this was just days after September 11, and the career prosecutor was being asked to present his wish list to the Attorney General. "If I work it out with my wife, can I stay?" he asked Dinh. "Sure, but don't get me in trouble with God," his boss replied.

Ashcroft was in his office for maybe an hour when an alarm sounded forcing the evacuation of the building. The Department of Justice hadn't been bombed or otherwise attacked; a construction worker involved in a renovation project had jiggled something in one of the walls that tripped the alarm. Nonetheless, Ashcroft went back to the FBI, where he'd remain for three or four weeks running the war at home.

Or so he thought.

Unbeknownst to Ashcroft, Vice President Cheney and two of his top aides—counselor Mary Matalin and chief of staff Lewis "Scooter" Libby— were already talking about creating a job for someone to run the home front war right from the White House.

Although the job, called Director of Homeland Security, would be new, the idea wasn't. In January of 2001, a presidential commission headed by former senators Gary Hart and Warren Rudman predicted that "Americans will likely die on American soil, possibly in large numbers" from terrorist attacks. Arguing that "the security of the American homeland from the threats of the new century should be the primary national security mission of the United States," the commission, whose report and dire predictions had in retrospect not been given nearly the headlines they deserved, proposed that the many government agencies that had something to do with protecting the homeland—such as Customs, INS, and the Federal Emergency Management Agency (FEMA)—be reorganized into a new department, with its secretary added to the President's cabinet.

The Hart-Rudman commission had issued interim reports in September of 1999 and April of 2000. But the Clinton administration's reaction to rejiggering the government so drastically was lukewarm. Although terrorism became an increasingly high agenda item for Clinton National Security Advisor Samuel Berger toward the end of the Clinton presidency, neither he nor Clinton thought it was feasible to reorganize all those government agencies. It was something Congress was unlikely to allow, because representatives and senators wouldn't want to untangle all the oversight or appropriations committee assignments that give them sway over those departments.

In May of 2001, President Bush had asked Cheney to begin a study of how the new administration should deal with the terrorist alarm sounded by the Hart-Rudman report and by two other high-level commissions. At the beginning of the summer, Cheney chief of staff Libby had recruited Steven Abbot, a recently retired admiral with extensive national security experience, to come to the White House after Labor Day and run the Cheney terror threat study. Abbot, along with another Cheney aide—Carol Kuntz, who had worked for Cheney in the Pentagon—spent the summer reviewing the work of the Hart-Rudman commission, as well as that of the two other commissions and several scholarly works in the field. Abbot reported for work on September 10. On the morning of September 11, he was waiting outside Libby's office for their first meeting when the first plane hit.

By Thursday, Abbot, Kuntz, and Libby had concluded that the first thing the Bush administration should do would be *not* to reorganize all those agencies, but to hire a heavyweight to come work in the White House and *coordinate* them, much the way Condoleezza Rice, the National Security Advisor, coordinated the various agencies involved in foreign and defense policy. They could never get all the agencies with some role in domestic security into one department, they reasoned, because so many also did so many other, unrelated jobs. (FEMA, for example, administrates flood insurance in addition to coordinating the federal response to disasters.) The goal should be to coordinate whatever they did related to homeland security, rather than spend a lot of time and money dislodging them from their current departments.

To be sure, that coordinating would be a lot harder than it sounded. Federal agencies are notoriously turf-conscious. Besides, it wasn't only the federal government that was involved in protecting the homeland. There were thousands of state and local police, fire, and other departments that had equally important and often more immediate roles. For example, even as Cheney's people pondered their Washington solution on Thursday, the Oregon Office of Public Health was making urgent phone calls around the state to everyone in the medical field licensed to have large sources of radioactive materials for various procedures (such as radiation therapy for cancer treatment) to verify that the material was being stored and secured properly; and the North Miami Beach police chief was dispatching special patrols to the area's utility and water supply facilities.

By Friday Libby and Matalin would already be discussing ideas with

Cheney about who the coordinator should be. The three would quickly zero in on one name: Tom Ridge, the Republican governor of Pennsylvania. Ridge was a good friend of the President's both from their days as fellow governors and because he had worked with Bush in 1988, when Ridge played a lead role in Pennsylvania promoting the first President Bush's campaign. He reportedly had been a contender for the vice presidential spot on the Bush 2000 ticket, although his pro-choice abortion views had supposedly eliminated him from final consideration. As an ex-Marine with a bronze star, Ridge had passable national security credentials, and as a former congressman, he knew Washington and Capitol Hill. Besides, Ridge—a big, beefy guy—looked the part. Over the weekend Cheney planned to bounce the idea off of White House Chief of Staff Andrew Card and the President.

At Ground Zero, Brian Lyons called the boss at his construction management firm on Thursday morning and told him that he needed to take some vacation days from his job (supervising construction for an investment bank's renovation) so that he could continue to look for his fireman brother. Then he went back to worrying about keeping the bulldozers moving, hoping that as they cleared away the beams, the dust, and whatever stray pieces of anything else that was left he might see some sign of Michael Lyons. Later that morning, he noticed that the bulldozers were loading the debris onto a truck. When he inquired about where it was going, he was told something about Fresh Kills.

Fresh Kills? The name, he found out, was not intended to have any kind of sick double meaning. Rather it was the site of a garbage landfill in Staten Island. Beginning the night before, trucks and boats had begun loading up with debris to be driven (or in the case of the barges, shipped from the West Side docks past the Statue of Liberty and through New York Harbor) to what until recently had been New York's major garbage dump. Fresh Kills had now been reopened. And a group of FBI agents and New York City police were on hand waiting to receive the "evidence" from this "crime scene."

Deputy Police Inspector James Luongo had arrived to take charge of the effort that morning. As he surveyed the 175 acres, some of it still bubbling with leaks from the methane gas produced by the tons of garbage underneath, he had no idea how he was going to handle all the wreckage that was fast arriving in a place so desolate, so spooky that another cop, who was a Vietnam veteran, likened it to a scene out of *Apocalypse Now.* Luongo needed structures for dressing rooms, refreshment centers, and cleanup areas for what he was told would be a crew of hundreds, working for what he assumed would be a year, sifting through it all. Who was going to build all that? Who was going to organize the crews? What about protective equipment? Food? Water? Electricity?

Brian Lyons had a different concern: Were the remains of his brother and everyone else, now being shunted off to a garbage dump, to be lost forever?

# Saturday, September 15, 2001

Iris Weinshall finally got a decent night's sleep on Friday. When she awoke Saturday morning at about 8:30, she left her husband, Senator Charles Schumer, and walked into the kitchen of the apartment they shared with their two daughters to pour herself a cup of coffee. She'd been up late the night before trying to rig up a ferry service to take people from Brooklyn into lower Manhattan, which would alleviate some of the traffic created by all the recovery efforts going on downtown and help replace the subway services knocked out at the Trade Center. She felt good about the progress she was making; it would normally take years for the city's transportation commissioner to get something like this done. If she kept at it today, she was sure she'd have it finished by Monday.

As she walked from the kitchen to sit down in the den of the airy, informal apartment, Weinshall's sense of satisfaction evaporated. She looked out the window off the left of the couch that had always been the family's favorite because they could sit there and look across at the skyline of lower Manhattan. The towers were missing, and in their place was the lingering smoke. Weinshall started to cry. Months later, she and her daughters still wouldn't look out that window.

Ed Woollen was not the kind of person one would expect to spend a weekend at home reading. The Navy veteran was a devoted outdoorsman who loved sailing, skiing, hiking, and swimming. Good-looking, clean-cut, and clear-eyed, with one of those too-firm handshakes, he looked like a retired football star who now made a living giving motivational speeches between workouts in the gym. That is, until you talked to him and you heard the acronym-filled vocabulary of the big-league aerospace business.

Woollen spent most of Saturday and Sunday hitting the books. The

Raytheon vice president paged his way into a world that had, until Tuesday, been the exclusive preserve of the policy wonks and the mostly ignored members of those commissions that since the late 1990s had sounded the alarm about the terrorist threat to America. There was a method to his curiosity. Indeed, at Raytheon, the business development teams like the one Woollen had now been told to quarterback weren't called "capture groups" for nothing. Their job was to go out and trap new business. And so, as Woollen plowed through the twenty or so pounds of reports (he mainly used the more comprehensive Hart-Rudman volumes as his blueprint, once he discovered a surprising coherence and consistency among all three), he was trying to connect the dots between the threats and solutions that they had identified and the products and services Raytheon provided, or could provide if the company went ahead with the Project Yankee homeland security ramp-up. By Sunday evening he had sketched out three broad areas that seemed highly promising.

First, it was clear that controlling the borders would now be a huge issue. That meant building databases of who was entering and leaving the United States, something Woollen knew Raytheon was good at.

Second, there was the overall challenge of providing for the physical security of facilities and events, including not just airports and airplanes but also power plants, stadiums, and ports. Raytheon already did that at military bases around the world.

Third, and most intriguing to Woollen, was the challenge of providing on-the-ground support to local public safety officials—the police, firefighters, and emergency service workers in every community, known as first responders. Raytheon obviously was heavily into equipping soldiers for the battlefield, but now Woollen saw a whole new opportunity—provided that Raytheon could figure out how to reach a new constituency of local police and fire chiefs, mayors, county commissioners, and local health officials. The front-line troops at home, which is now where the war was, Woollen wrote in a note to himself, are local people, not federal. Which meant, he realized, that Raytheon now had to go after a different customer base. "We have to pay attention to Chief Somebody, not General Somebody," he concluded.


While Woollen mulled the shifts Raytheon would have to make to get into those new markets, the people from the United Way and New York Community Trust running the new September 11th Fund were already benefiting from a shift in resources of a different sort. IBM, which was already the

United Way's largest corporate contributor, had volunteered two days before to help the new fund set up a website that could receive any and all inquiries and contributions. And now on Saturday morning the new site—which was actually a refabricated version of the site that IBM had built for the recently completed U.S. Open tennis tournament—was working perfectly. Thirty-five programmers from IBM had worked nearly three days straight to get the job done. IBM's contribution, which would ultimately be worth millions, was only one example of the corporate generosity, backed by employee sweat, which enabled a variety of stunningly quick responses to the events of Tuesday. The September 11th Fund—which, thanks to having its name on contact numbers flashed repeatedly across television screens, had by Saturday collected $100 million in donations—was by now the beneficiary of donated services from Microsoft (database management), Citibank (check processing), and a host of other companies.

Perhaps most significant, McKinsey & Co., a blue-chip management consulting firm, had assigned a team to help the fund figure out how to organize and target its relief efforts. Consultants of the McKinsey breed were not universally known for their speed or even the actual, or at least tangible, value of their services, but in this case the work they began this weekend would end up being crucial to the fund zeroing in on the right goals and achieving them.

Another September 11th Fund volunteer by Saturday was actor George Clooney. Clooney was among many in Hollywood who, as he put it, "just wanted to do something. . . . We were out here and we felt frustrated that we couldn't help." So on Friday, when Clooney got a call from Dreamworks co-founder and native New Yorker Jeffrey Katzenberg, telling him that a group of top Hollywood people was organizing a telethon, he agreed not only to appear but offered to help Katzenberg recruit other stars. On Friday, Katzenberg had met a challenge from the networks by personally recruiting ten of the ten superstars they'd listed as being such a dream team that they'd have to agree to do the show if he could get them. Now, Clooney was working the phones, and similarly getting no refusals. He was also starting to focus on the fact that Katzenberg had said they wanted to broadcast less than a week from now—on Friday, September 21. It seemed impossible, Clooney thought. No one had worked out what the show would be, let alone written anything for it, let alone found a studio or built a set. But if that was the plan, and if the networks had all volunteered to contribute their airtime in unison on that night, then they should go for it. His only constraint in recruiting, he had been told, was that with all four networks supporting and broadcasting the show commercial-free, he should include at least two stars from each network's prime-time shows. From the responses he had already gotten, he knew that would be no problem.

As for where the money would go, an official with one of the networks who had connections to the Red Cross had called that organization earlier in the week and asked whether, if the telethon passed the donations on to the Red Cross, the organization would guarantee that only victims of the September 11 tragedy would receive the proceeds. But the Red Cross person who got the call—a board member not in sync with, or even at that point aware of, Healy's intention to segregate the money—refused. The United Way got the next call, and its September 11th Fund was designated to receive and dispense the money.

Clooney had himself taken pains to get assurances that the money would only go for victims and not, as he feared, "be swallowed up in some bureaucracy." So he figured that everything seemed on track for the big show. Months later, he'd call himself an idiot for thinking it was all going to be that simple.


By Saturday morning, the planes were up at Larry Cox's airport. In fact, by Thursday afternoon his had been among the first airports certified by the FAA as complying with all the new security arrangements, and that afternoon many of his Federal Express flights had taken off. FedEx had not been subject to nearly as many new FAA security restrictions as the passenger airlines, and therefore had an easier time getting ready to resume operations. FedEx was such an unusually big part of the traffic in Memphis—its planes accounted for 40 percent of the takeoffs and landings—that by Friday things seemed almost normal on the runways.

The passenger terminals were a different story. Saturday was the first full day of restored passenger operations at Cox's airport, but business was awful. Anticipating a new fear of flying, combined with an economic swoon stemming from the shock of September 11, the airlines—including Northwest, which has a key hub in Memphis and is by far the dominant carrier there— had grounded about a third of its flights indefinitely in order to bunch the reduced passenger flow onto fewer flights. And today most of the 60 percent left flying were nearly empty. The tally was almost unbelievable: For the whole day of Saturday, September 15, only 7,574 people flew in and out of Memphis. On the same Saturday one year before, 17,175 had. That was a 56 percent drop.

Cox knew those numbers were only going to get worse. If you deducted all the people who flew on Saturday only because they had been stranded en route on September 11, he told his staff, there would have been almost nobody flying. Sure enough, by Monday passenger traffic would be down 64 percent from the same Monday a year before. Cox had lost nearly two thirds of his passengers.

Traffic and passenger load were an airport manager's scorecard, the equivalent of a storekeeper's daily tally of his cash register. Airports like Cox's had basically two sources of revenue—one from the airlines, the other from passengers. The airlines paid rental fees for the gates they used and landing fees for every time they dropped down onto one of Cox's runways. Passengers paid Cox indirectly when they bought a newspaper or magazine at a newsstand, purchased some Elvis memorabilia in the concourse's Graceland gift shop, or rented a car at the airport: The newsstand owner paid the airport roughly 5 percent of his sales, Graceland about 18 percent, and the rent-a-car companies about 20 percent.

Therefore, a decline in flights meant a drop in landing fees, while the dropoff in passengers meant that Cox's income from all those stores and rental agencies would fall off the cliff.

Memphis International Airport had been growing in flights and passengers—and revenue—every year since the economic downturn of the early 1990s. Suddenly, that was all in jeopardy. And it wasn't just Cox who was bound to feel the pain. Indeed, economically he and the Memphis–Shelby County Airport Authority, which owned the airport, were actually protected by the way the airport was set up financially. As with most airports, except those in some of the largest cities, Memphis operated on a nonprofit basis. Every year its revenues had to be geared to equal expenses. And the only revenues that could be controlled were the landing and gate fees paid by the air carriers; Cox, after all, couldn't make people buy gifts at the Graceland store or rent cars. So in a year when those retail revenues are down, the fees paid by the airlines will be adjusted upward in the following year to make up for the gap. If those other fees exceed the expenses, the surplus is applied in the next year so that the fees paid by the air carriers are lowered. In other words, the air carriers had all the risk. To keep control of all that, the airport's fee-setting board consisted of the airlines that used the facility. They voted on how to adjust the fees upward or downward, or on whether to force Cox somehow to cut expenses. The board votes were weighted on the basis of which of the air carriers were the heaviest users, which meant Northwest and FedEx controlled the process in Memphis. So, if revenues fell and they refused to raise these fees, Cox and the county airport authority board of commissioners who oversaw him would have to curtail operations at the airport, or even shut it down if they could not find other ways to cut costs.

In the seventeen years Cox had been running the airport, nothing that dire had ever happened, and it wasn't likely to now. What was more likely was that the air carriers would agree to pay higher fees—meaning that they faced a double whammy: Because business was down (fewer flights, fewer passengers) not only in Memphis but across the country, they would actually have to pay more to use the country's airports.

But Cox also knew that he'd have to figure out how to cut some of his expenses, even as he began the process of asking the air carriers to pay more. He was proud that he ran things efficiently enough and had attracted enough flights and retailers that his landing fees—which were calculated by the weight of each plane and were now about $200 for a Boeing 727 to land—were the same or lower than most airports. (La Guardia's were about three times higher.) This encouraged more airlines to use Memphis, or at least didn't deter them. Those fees would now have to be raised. The question was how much.

Yet on Saturday morning that was a far-off problem compared to what Larry Cox faced on the sidewalks outside his terminal. Although passenger traffic was a fraction of what he could usually expect for a Saturday, the lines waiting to get through security were running out of the terminal and a hundred yards or more onto the sidewalk. The problem was that the screeners up ahead at the walk-through metal detectors and at the X-ray devices that checked for weapons in carry-on baggage were working in slow motion, struggling to adjust to the new set of rules and protocols issued by the FAA— the rules that Transportation Secretary Mineta had laid out to the airline executives in that late-night conference call. Knives were no longer allowed. Nor were nail clippers. And every fourth or fifth passenger was to be singled out, usually at random, for a personal body and baggage hand search. Worse, each person was checked against the watch lists issued by the FAA, lists that Cox discovered were changing and being added to by the hour as the FAA faxed new names to the airlines. It was the worst of both worlds: fewer passengers and longer waits. The FAA was closing the barn door after the horse had escaped, and with a vengeance, Cox thought.

At the same time he was also fuming over his lost parking spaces, the ones within 300 feet of the terminal that one of the first FAA faxes had ordered him to block. Cox hated losing those 550 spots not only because of the revenue they yielded, but also because customer service was his obsession, and having that many spaces so close to the terminal was one of his airport's most customer-friendly features. For Cox, this was another classic example of stupidity from the cover-your-ass Washington bureaucrats, people who attacked whatever problem was in the public consciousness today because it had just happened, but ignored whatever the real, next threat might be. There was no logic or sense of proportion. The new rule was aimed at preventing a bomb from being left in a parked car and destroying the terminal building and the people in it. But what was so special about airport terminals? What about cars that could be parked, for example, not just within 300 feet of a shopping mall, but in the basement of the shopping mall itself? What about parking spaces within 300 feet of a train station? Or a stadium?

It was only four days after September 11 but already Cox had zeroed in on a challenge that would mark the September 12 era: achieving balance and logic in dealing with the various threats of this new age—or rational "risk management," as the policy people called it.

While Cox sweated his sudden budget and customer service problems, the chief financial officers of the nation's leading airlines convened that Saturday morning on a conference call to agonize over the bigger picture. Their CEOs had already started telling Washington that they needed help, lots of it and fast. The question for today was how much. Led by the financial people from American and Delta airlines, they came up with a total of about $24 billion that they would need in some combination of cash or loans—some of it to make up for what they'd lost by not being able to fly at all from Tuesday morning through Friday, and the rest to deal with what they foresaw was about to be a steep dropoff in air travel for at least the next six months.

Later that morning, their CEOs, along with the Washington lobbyists employed by each airline, had another conference call, put together with the help of the staff of the Air Transport Association, the Washington-based trade association that lobbies for all the airlines jointly. They decided that they had to get to Washington fast—Monday morning—so they could start making the rounds on Capitol Hill with whatever numbers the financial people could put together.

As the airline executives talked retrenchment and bailouts, InVision's CEO was plotting expansion. By Friday, Sergio Magistri had seen enough stories in the newspapers and on television about the airlines' lax security. True, the terrorists had not used a bomb in a suitcase, but the whole issue of airliner safety, including suitcase bombs, was now being talked about. He felt sure the age of

100 percent baggage screening that he'd been waiting for since the Lockerbie crash of 1988 was finally coming. So he told his chief operating officer and budget people to begin planning the necessary hiring and purchases from suppliers that would ramp the company up to sell $80 million worth of products per year. This was about double the company's current capacity—capacity that it was not even reaching at September 10 sales levels. Yet because his top-of-the-line machine sold for about $1 million, and thousands would be needed should the government decide to inspect every suitcase, Magistri was sure he was being conservative.

Then again, he'd been just as sure after the explosion of TWA Flight 800 over Long Island in 1996, and on September 10 he had still been digging out of the hole that optimism had gotten him into.

What especially cheered Magistri this time, though, was a report he'd gotten late Friday night from Patrick McCann, his Washington lobbyist. McCann, a former congressional budget staffer whose boutique practice focused on aviation issues, was already making the rounds of congressional staffers and FAA people talking up baggage screening. The head of the Air Transport Association had declared that afternoon that her airline members wanted to be completely out of the business of aviation security. The government should handle it, ATA president Carol Hallet had said. What was so welcome about this was that from the mid-1970s, when the government first mandated metal detector screening of passengers in order to prevent gun-wielding hijackers from taking planes to Cuba, the system in place was that the government told the airlines what to do, who in turn hired private security companies to do the work. In practice this meant, as with all FAA regulatory work, that the FAA would negotiate with the airlines, with the airlines pushing back on anything that cost them money or their passengers time. Although no one now will admit it in so many words, according to records in the archives of the FAA, that in fact is what had resulted in the rule that razors or knives with blades of four and a half inches or less be allowed in carry-on luggage. The airlines feared that a complete ban on knives or razors would require them to hire more screeners, while further inconveniencing and delaying passengers.

Magistri knew only too well that another hassle and expense the airlines had feared was screening of suitcases that were checked by passengers into the plane's cargo bays, which was the business he was in. Although the government was ready to buy the expensive machines and even assume some of the maintenance costs, the airlines would have had to hire people to operate the machines, and the machines would add another potential wait to the check-in and boarding process. So despite the recommendation by a commission headed by Vice President Gore after the 1996 Flight 800 explosion that all baggage be screened, the airlines had successfully lobbied Congress not to appropriate the funds to allow that to happen. Some airports, such as San Francisco's, had seemed to want the machines, and United Airlines also seemed receptive. But as a general matter, Magistri and his little company had found themselves squaring off against all the other airlines, each with a powerful lobbying office in Washington. It was a lopsided fight. "Sergio is an optimist, like all entrepreneurs," recalls his lone lobbyist, McCann. "So when the Gore commission made its report, he congratulated me and told me that we'd won. And I had to tell him that we were nowhere near winning."

Now, by declaring that they no longer would be in the middle between the government and the security process, the airlines would not be in as good a position to block Magistri's machines. Sure, they would keep lobbying quietly, but even McCann now agreed that the dynamic had been changed by their washing their hands of anything having to do with security. This could, indeed, be Magistri's moment.

On Saturday Brian Lyons still wasn't thinking much beyond clearing the next few yards of rubble. Somehow, he just stayed there at Ground Zero, not even reconsidering it day by day. There was just so much to do. He had only that morning remembered that it had been a day since he had checked in with his sister-in-law, Elaine, to tell her that there was still no sign of her husband. And other than a few hours' sleep in the Red Cross tent, the only time Brian Lyons had stopped working in the last two days had been on Friday afternoon, when the Secret Service had cleared a path so that President Bush, with Schumer, among others, in tow, could visit Ground Zero. Lyons was about twenty feet away when the President had grabbed a bullhorn and ignited the crowd of 2,000 recovery workers, as well as the country watching on television, with his proclamation to the workers that "I can hear you. The rest of the world hears you, and the people who knocked these buildings down will hear all of us soon."

But already there were fault lines in the unity at Ground Zero. The firemen were still looking for their missing brothers, while the construction crews were trying to clear away the wreckage. Who was in charge? And what was the priority, given the slim chance that anyone could possibly still be alive? Lyons, the construction supervisor with a missing fireman brother, felt in the middle, though because he obviously cared most about finding his brother, he had by now begun to see himself as the firemen's ambassador to the construction crews. He could speak both languages. He could help head off the fights if someone tried to move the machinery around too quickly to suit the firemen. Or at least he was determined to try, for he feared that ultimately the tensions would get the firemen kicked out of the site altogether once it became clear they would not find anyone alive.

Bernadine Healy thought that things were going reasonably well. Tens of thousands of volunteers from across the country were deployed all over Manhattan. Millions were pouring in. She'd gotten faxes and telegrams from board members praising her work. Her board chairman, David McLaughlin, had told her that segregating the money raised into a designated fund subject to especially stringent auditing procedures was brilliant. A Thursday board meeting had gone well, as had a session on Friday with the President and First Lady.

Healy was oblivious to two different storms heading toward her from outside Washington.

In San Francisco, Pat Kennedy, a longtime Red Cross local leader and a member of the powerful executive committee of the national board, was livid. Her workers had called her Saturday to tell her about a memo that Healy had sent out across the country that morning announcing that all the September 11 donations were being kept in a separate fund. This meant that her chapter and all the other chapters wouldn't get any of it for their good works. To Kennedy, this was a clear and outrageous violation of Red Cross board policy, and an affront to the board that Healy worked for.

Also, the Red Cross simply was not functioning on the ground to provide the kind of aid that the media reports of millions in donations suggested it should be providing. In Ridgewood, New Jersey, Eileen Simon went with her sister to the local Red Cross, because they had heard on television that significant help—such as funds to meet a current mortgage payment, which Simon was, indeed, concerned about—was available. Simon felt funny about taking charity; she wasn't poor, and, besides, as of that morning her own in-laws still thought Michael Simon would be found alive. But her sister had insisted that they at least go to investigate, and with all of her family's money still tied up in the bank accounts that only Michael had had access to, the trip might be worth it. Besides, Michael would have urged her to get whatever she was entitled to.

What Simon got was about an hour wait and then a volunteer who had the temerity to offer her coupons worth about $20 to buy food. She was also told that if she came back there might be some more coupons for the local Kmart, and that some money for a funeral might be available—if the Red Cross was allowed to call the funeral home and push for a discount. Eileen left in a huff.

Later in the afternoon, Scott Simon came to Eileen Simon's house and asked his sister-in-law for Michael's toothbrush and comb. He needed it to bring to the police in New York. They were, he explained, about to begin a massive effort to identify whatever body parts and other remains they were finding by matching them with DNA samples taken from the hair or saliva of those still missing, or if no such samples were available, by seeking a match from a DNA sample of a parent or sibling. With more than 5,000 people feared dead and only about 150 bodies recovered and identified, it seemed that this one tragic attack at the World Trade Center was going to produce more missing victims than the 2,585 Americans missing in action in the entire Vietnam War. New York's police and the coroner's office were gearing up to use the latest in DNA techniques to keep that from happening.

Scott Simon told his sister-in-law that after hearing the call for families to supply the samples, he and the rest of his brother's family had decided that they were now prepared to assume the worst. They had held out hope, he added, because his sister had thought on Wednesday morning that she had seen Michael's name on a Cantor Fitzgerald website listing those who had been found and were in hospitals. It now seemed clear that these early lists had been filled with mistakes. In fact, while searching the Internet from his office, he'd seen Michael's name on another list, of people being treated at a New Jersey hospital. But that had turned out to be a different Michael Simon.

The Cartier family in Queens didn't try going to the Red Cross. They weren't thinking about money; James had been living on his own, supporting only himself. Maybe they'd have to pick up some of his bills and the cost of a funeral, but that was a cost they would have welcomed by Saturday. What they feared most was that James would be left in the dust.

After going to a memorial service near their neighborhood that did not single out James (it was too soon for that) but honored all who had died, James's six siblings spent Saturday, as they had all week, on the telephones in their parents' home, making calls to the various information numbers that had been flashed on the television screens. By now, two of them—Jennie Farrell, a trainer of local college instructors, who was the oldest at forty, and Michael, the youngest at twenty-four—had emerged as the leaders.

What frustrated them most was the lack of information. Some of the numbers, like the Red Cross's, weren't answering. Others gave conflicting answers or no answers at all. Whose DNA sample was best—their father's, their mother's, or some kind of trace from James's hairbrush or his toothbrush? And where should they take it? The confusion was making them increasingly angry, exacerbated by the fact that their father sat fuming in the living room as each call ended in futility. They felt that they had to do something, not just for their brother, but for their parents. Things would get worse the next day, when their father would be told by his Catholic priest that, no, a funeral service would not be possible unless James's body, or some part of it, was found.

## Monday, September 17, 2001

At 7:00 on Monday morning, September 17, the police allowed Sal Iacono back into what was left of his store.

The windows were smashed. The two doors, the one at the front of the fifteen-foot-long store and the brass door leading from the other side into the lobby of the office building that sat on top of the store, lay flat on the floor. That brass door, which to Sal was the one shining piece of elegance in his work life, was black and twisted.

Inside, three firemen were spread out on the floor asleep, two in the middle of the small customer area, one behind the counter. They and their brethren had obviously been using Continental Shoe Repair as a relief station.

And as a bathroom. In a corner, just under where the picture of the Virgin Mary still hung by a nail on the wall near the front window, there was a large plastic bucket filled with liquid and solid excrement. In the other corners were puddles of more urine. The place reeked.

As Sal looked up from the bucket he saw that his walls had been stripped bare, except for some shoe polish. The 200 or 300 sole insets, arch supports, and heel cushions he kept in stock and sold for $5 or $6 apiece were gone. Sal supposed that for firemen and rescue workers to have taken items that might make them a little more comfortable was okay. It was as much a part of the cost of that horrible day as was the damage to his expensive leather-shaping machinery, now sitting behind the counter under a mound of gear-jamming dust and debris. But the bucket of human waste? The urine on the floor?

Well, maybe even that could be explained, he thought. Who knew what these rescue workers had gone through, or if they had had access to any real bathrooms. But then he looked at his cash register. It had been forced open.

(Almost anyone could have done it, because in the hours following the attack all varieties of people, not just police and firefighters, were at Ground Zero.) Because Tuesday was Sal's regular day of the week for taking cash to the bank, there had, he would later say, been $1,400 in there when he'd left on the morning of the 11th. None of it was there. Not even the coins.

Sal was furious. Why did they have to destroy the shop that he had always regarded as another of his children? Why did someone have to take his money? When he got home, he tearfully told his wife that he had lost everything. Franca Iacono, reminding him that he was sixty-seven, told him it was time to retire.

Richard Grasso had a better morning. As he had on the night of September 11, the CEO and Chairman of the New York Stock Exchange had slept on the couch in his office on Sunday night. Despite a successful dress rehearsal, Verizon and his own people had continued testing the communications equipment through the night, and he needed to be there early on Monday to prepare for a reopening that promised to be high on both ceremony and behind-the-scenes drama. Would everything work and stay working? Would there be another attack? Would enough workers be able to get past the security checkpoints aimed at preventing one? And could the Federal Reserve Board's lowering of interest rates before the opening bell, combined with the Fed's generally making credit more easily available, plus a Securities and Exchange Commission relaxation of restrictions on companies buying back their own stock, work to avert a meltdown?

At about 9:25, a Marine sang "God Bless America" on Grasso's trading floor. The audience joined in. At 9:28 there were two minutes of silence. Sobs could be heard. And at 9:30, the stock exchange roared back in a frenzy of volume, not once interrupted by a glitch. A record 2.3 billion shares traded. And although the Dow Jones Industrial Average finished down 685 points, which was a record, the decline of 7 percent was not even close to the worst day ever on Wall Street. The damage was ugly but not as bad as many had feared.

Dean O'Hare's Chubb Insurance suffered even less, closing at about 5 percent below the September 10 price of $66.47.

Sergio Magistri got up early in Silicon Valley to watch what would happen to his stock. For him it was a great day. InVision, which on September 10 had traded at $3.11, soared from the opening bell. By the end of the day, the stock was at $8.25. On paper, Magistri, who owned or had options in 603,591 In-Vision shares, had just made $3.1 million.

Ed Woollen's company also made out well. On September 10 Raytheon had closed at $23.95. It ended today up more than $8, at $32. Meantime, Woollen was already at work trying to make sure that his company met the market's expectation that lots of new business was now on the horizon. Taking his notes of the three areas of opportunity he had extrapolated from all those commission reports on homeland security, he began canvassing Raytheon to see what kinds of products and projects the company already had that could be built up to go after these targets. Because he'd been there for more than seventeen years, Woollen knew people in all the different corners of the giant conglomerate who might be able to tell him what he needed to know. And before long, he'd have leads that were so promising that even he was surprised. What he didn't know was that his two larger competitors, Lockheed Martin and Boeing, were similarly in the hunt.

By Monday morning, Eileen Simon knew she could no longer wait to deal with Michael's car, the antique Mercedes that he had left at the train station Tuesday morning. She couldn't find a key but knew that she couldn't responsibly leave a car that valuable at the train station forever. So she called a local mechanic whom Michael had relied on to service the temperamental convertible. He assured her that he symphatized with her and would take care of it. By the end of the day he came to her house with the car, and a large bill—along with a diatribe on "terrorist immigrants," delivered in his heavily accented East European voice.

As they made their rounds on Capitol Hill, the airline CEOs and their lobbyists were hardly newcomers. Although their fares had been deregulated in the late 1970s, almost everything else about the airlines—schedules, personnel, equipment, safety, even service standards—was still controlled by Washington. The industry had for years responded by making sure that the members of Congress who wrote the laws and appropriated funds for the Federal Aviation Administration were carefully tended to. Each airline had its own lobbying office, which was in turn supported by two floors' worth of staff at their trade group, the Air Transport Association. Beyond that, because most members of Congress typically went home from Washington and back again every weekend, they were among America's most powerful frequent fliers; and the airlines made sure they got the best service possible. Each of the major carriers had a special staff that made reservations for the representatives and senators, putting them off and onto planes as congressional schedules changed on a Thursday or Friday afternoon. Delta, for example, had three people working in a room with chalkboards keeping track of the 250 members who regularly fly the airline.

The airline executives came armed with a white paper to demonstrate to these valued customers just how dire their situation was. Even before September 11, revenue from business travel—by far the most lucrative passenger segment for the airlines—had been down 41 percent. Combined with a rise in fuel prices, this had caused cumulative losses of more than $1 billion prior to September 11. That was small change compared to what they now faced. First, the shutdown from Tuesday through Friday night had cost more than $2 billion. Second, they anticipated a falloff of passengers of approximately 25 to 60 percent, which, the white paper said, meant that "the entire airline industry now faces a severe liquidity crisis." Assuming that passenger declines were 60 percent in September and came down to 25 percent by January and then 15 percent by April, the airlines would need $24 billion in aid by June of 2002. Without it, they would pretty much all be bankrupt, or on their way to bankruptcy.

There was an even worse problem, which the white paper dealt with last: The liability suits resulting from the September 11 crashes would not only likely bankrupt American and United airlines, which had operated the four planes, but just the threat of that risk would cause all of the airlines quickly to lose their insurance. This meant that the financial institutions that lend the airlines money so that they can buy planes would invoke contract clauses to keep the planes from flying because the loans are secured by the planes, just the way a homeowner's mortgage is secured by his house. (In other words, if its loan goes bad the lender gets to take possession of the plane.) With no insurance on the planes, the planes couldn't fly, no matter how much of a bailout the government extended; and if United and American in particular didn't get relief from liability for the September 11 crashes, they would almost certainly be grounded immediately.

It was enough to convince most of the legislators of the need not only to do something but to do it far faster than Congress usually does anything. David Schaffer, forty-eight, was one of the most important people to the airline industry; he was the longtime top aviation staffer for the House Transportation Committee subcommittee on aviation. Schaffer supported the industry; indeed, he routinely referred to air crashes as situations "where one of our planes goes down." But he was also a stickler for legislative procedure, which means hearings and debate, and more hearings and more debate, and drafts and redrafts before anything important is allowed to pass. So he was shocked on Monday when his boss, Congressman Don Young, the burly Alaska Republican who chaired the Transportation Committee, told him that they had to pass a bill within a day or two. When he protested that something this important and unprecedented, not to mention expensive, never moved that fast, Young thundered, "We're at war. We have to do this now."

Even the rock-hard conservatives in the House Republican leadership— Majority Whip Tom DeLay of Texas and Deputy Whip Roy Blunt of Missouri—were convinced. It helped that both represented areas that were home to major airlines; Continental is based in Houston and TWA (recently acquired by American) is based in St. Louis. But the prospect of this kind of government interference in the marketplace did not go down easy for them. When one of the airline lobbyists meeting with Blunt cited the success of the Chrysler bailout, Blunt interrupted, laughed, and told the lobbyist to quit while he was ahead. He'd been against saving Chrysler, Blunt reminded him, but was willing to assume that this situation was different.

The key event in the airlines' lobbying day (which had been easily stocked with meetings, in part because in this week after the attacks no one else was out there lobbying any of the usual issues) was a session with Senate and House leaders in the office of Senate Majority Leader Tom Daschle, the Democrat from South Dakota.

Several of the airlines' proposed solutions listed in the white paper, such as allowing them an antitrust exemption to coordinate routes and a suspension of ticket, fuel, and cargo taxes (called a "holiday") amounting to $7.8 billion, were quickly dismissed as unrealistic. But the airline lobbyists had agreed among themselves that morning that this was likely to happen; they had kept the items in just so that they'd have something to lose. What they really cared about was their request for $5 billion in direct cash aid (to be apportioned among them according to their market share) and another $11.2 billion in loans. There were no strong objections to either provision.

At the White House, where top staffers had received the airline group and promised them aid, President Bush convened a meeting later that day that included Chief of Staff Card, his deputy Bolten, and economic policy czar Lindsey, as well as key people from the Transportation Department. The goal was to figure out what kind of aid made sense. When the President asked the utterly logical question of why the airlines couldn't save money in anticipation of reduced demand by cutting back even more flights than they had announced, Lindsey, who had now studied up on the depressing world of airline economics, explained the trap of the airlines' much vaunted hub-and-spoke system. That's the system that forces passengers to fly through a hub like Atlanta (or, in the case of Northwest Airlines, Larry Cox's Memphis) and change planes to get to a smaller surrounding city (such as Birmingham in the case of Atlanta, or Little Rock in the case of Memphis). The whole system depended on the hub connecting to a certain number of through flights. Cut out too many of them at a given time, and the hub no longer made economic sense and the whole system would collapse. Anything more than about a 40 percent cut in overall flights would drive the whole industry under, Lindsey concluded. They really had no choice but to do the bailout.

On Monday morning, Pat Kennedy, the still enraged Red Cross leader from San Francisco who was worried about a different kind of bailout, began her counterattack. She faxed Red Cross chairman David McLaughlin an angry letter stating it was long-standing policy that funds were never to be designated for any particular disaster, because "efforts to designate would deplete the [general] Disaster Relief Fund . . . Money is raised for very high profile disasters. It is very difficult for the less viable disasters we face on an ongoing basis." But, wrote Kennedy, "It appears that on Saturday [when Healy sent out a memo designating the September 11 donations] Bernadine . . . deliberately decided to violate [board] policy." Kennedy's phone, she said, had been "ringing off the hook" with calls from local chapters concerned about the change. "This is unacceptable," she concluded. "I look forward to hearing from you as to how I should proceed—understanding I have no intention of ignoring this."

McLaughlin, a former president of CBS and Dartmouth College, who as chairman worked part-time supervising CEO Healy, sent the fax on to the Red Cross's acting general counsel and to Healy, with a note asking if "we" had changed board policy with the segregation of the funds.

Kennedy later explained in an interview that to her it was a "sacred" Red Cross principle that no victims of any disaster were to be treated better than others, which meant that the organization should never solicit funds for any particular victims. If a donor made an explicit request that his money go to a particular cause, they would always honor that, but to *ask* a donor to give money for a special cause violated everything the organization stood for. "On September 11, there were 70 other disasters around the country," she said. "Fires, floods, and things like that. The Red Cross is supposed to treat all those victims equally." Beyond the fact that Healy saw the Red Cross general fund as a "leaky bucket" that could never withstand the public scrutiny it would now get if funds for the victims of the September 11 attacks went there, what eluded Kennedy, or what she chose to ignore, was the confusion that would definitely be the result had the Red Cross run ads for donations that, while mentioning at the end that funds would go for "this and other disasters," showed video of the attacks and talked about the attacks. There was no way that people would *not* have seen that as a solicitation for a special cause, the September 11 victims, that was going to go only to them. There was no way that any donor would have thought he was sending a check that might aid a victim of a house fire in Nevada.

When James Sensenbrenner, the powerful Republican chairman of the House Judiciary Committee, had come out of the shower at his home in Wisconsin on Sunday morning, he heard the voice of John Ashcroft on one of the Sunday talk shows saying something about the legislation he was proposing to give his agents and prosecutors more tools to go after terrorists.

What legislation? Neither Ashcroft nor any of his people had told Sensenbrenner a thing about it, and, under usual House rules, it was Sensenbrenner's committee that had to pass on any such new laws related to the criminal code before the full House would consider them. Sensenbrenner suspected some kind of end run. Normally, that would seem unlikely, given that he and Aschroft were of the same party and same conservative persuasion. Yet Sensenbrenner had been puzzled that the Attorney General had rebuffed any effort by Sensenbrenner to discuss legislative matters since the attacks. Hoping to clear up the confusion, Sensenbrenner called House Speaker Dennis Hastert to ask what was happening. Hastert said he, too, knew nothing but would call around.

By that evening Sensenbrenner, still in Wisconsin, was sitting on his porch reading a faxed draft of an entire 100-plus-page piece of legislation. It was the handiwork of Ashcroft's policy assistant Viet Dinh and his staff, who had been cooking it up since Thursday. Sensenbrenner, marking up the document furiously, was astounded. Ashcroft and his people had written a law that was the magna carta of federal agents, freeing them to wiretap, search, arrest, and hold almost at will, with little judicial oversight.

Most shocking was that the bill suspended what was known in the law as habeas corpus—which gave anyone detained on American soil the right to demand a court hearing to challenge the authority of those holding them. Lincoln had suspended habeas corpus for a time during the Civil War. Now Ashcroft was proposing that it just plain be eliminated during this undefined emergency that had no designated end date.* What was going on at Justice, the conservative Republican from Wisconsin wondered.

It was only now, on Monday morning, that Sensenbrenner learned that following Ashcroft's Sunday talk show appearances and a call from Hastert upbraiding him for not telling even his supporters on the Hill in advance about the proposals, Ashcroft had hastily convened a Sunday afternoon briefing for the few congressional leaders who were in Washington. No papers were handed out, nor was the habeas suspension mentioned.

Mid-morning on Monday, Sensenbrenner called Ashcroft and told him how eager he was to produce a good piece of legislation that both Democrats and Republicans could support but that he had been undercut by not being kept in the loop. Ashcroft offered no apology, saying the bill had just been drafted and that this was an emergency. Sensenbrenner said the bill needed a lot of work and that the habeas section was such a nonstarter that he'd better not even include it in the draft he circulated if he wanted anything passed before Christmas. Ashcroft said he'd think about that, but that they needed the bill passed within the week.

As Sensenbrenner stewed about the bill, Romero and his ACLU staff spent the day trying to get a copy of it or at least an outline. The Justice Department said that nothing was available. After more than a dozen congressional staffers from offices of all political stripes said that they, too, had seen nothing, Romero started to believe them.

When Sensenbrenner and Romero would finally get copies of the official proposal on Wednesday, the habeas suspension had been removed. But Sensenbrenner still thought the bill needed a lot of trimming. Romero thought it was Armageddon. Still, he held off saying anything too inflammatory, or so he thought. He waited two days to issue a press release and even then, while saying the proposals "go far beyond any powers conceivably necessary," essentially called only for careful deliberations. "In this time of

---

* Ashcroft said he could not "reconstruct with any accuracy" whether the suspension of habeas corpus was proposed. Dinh would not comment. Sensenbrenner's recollection, as well as that of White House officials who say they saw the draft, seems credible. See Source Notes.

national crisis," Romero said, "the people's representatives must be even more careful and deliberative than usual."

To Ashcroft, being "more deliberative than usual" was exactly what he wanted to avoid. He'd soon be in front of the Senate Judiciary Committee equating such deliberations with aiding the terrorists. Indeed, the day Romero issued his press release, Ashcroft declared that he needed the new bill passed by the end of the week.

In fact, it turned out that Ashcroft had excluded not just Sensenbrenner but an even more influential Republican power center from his deliberative process: the White House.

When one of deputy chief of staff Josh Bolten's aides heard Ashcroft on the talk shows Sunday, she was curious. She hadn't heard anything about his new proposals. On Monday, when she asked someone in the White House counsel's office for a copy, she was told that one was on the way—that they hadn't been directly involved either. That was unusual; the White House counsel and his staff are at the center of executive branch legal policy. When Bolten's aide, who is a former Supreme Court clerk, finally got to read the draft, she immediately warned Bolten that there was a lot of explosive stuff in the document. Equally important, there were a lot of provisions, such as those dealing with money laundering, that other departments in the government, like Treasury, needed to know about.

Bolten had already gotten a complaint the night before from the White House legislative affairs director that Ashcroft had offended the Republicans on the Hill by not consulting them, something he thought odd since Ashcroft had been a senator and knew how the process needed to work. Now, it was clear that the problem was much worse. Ashcroft had apparently taken the President's order to him, to "make sure this never happens again," too personally. Bolten now had to call Ashcroft and tell him that this was not the way it was done, that the bill now had to be recalled, circulated and "scrubbed" by the affected departments and the White House staff, and that the strategy for pushing it in Congress had to run by the White House's congressional liaison people.

Ashcroft came over to the White House and offered what all thought was a graceful apology.

Beyond his predilection to want to control as much as he could, some on his own staff thought that another reason Ashcroft hadn't "scrubbed" the bill beforehand was that he didn't appreciate the significance of the prosecutor-written laundry list he was proposing. Although Ashcroft is a graduate of the highly regarded University of Chicago Law School and a former Missouri state attorney general, even some of his own deputies at Justice were surprised

by how uninterested he was in the niceties of the law. One veteran staffer
recalls that through six different meetings on this bill and on another key legal
initiative, he had never once heard Ashcroft cite a legal case and had watched
him blanch when someone in the room cited a case, as if that person was dis-
courteously speaking another language. Two senators—one a conservative
Republican, the other a moderate Democrat—who spoke with Ashcroft at
about this time were surprised at his lack of command of the basic issues.
Whether it was lack of interest or lack of intellectual firepower, the Attorney
General seemed not to appreciate the complexities of the constitutional issues
he was dealing with.

# Wednesday, September 19, 2001

Lee Ann Ryan, a Chubb insurance examiner, remembers being nervous.
How would they react? Would they be suspicious? Unwilling to talk? Resent-
ful? Ryan was one of three team leaders recruited by Chubb to begin a series
of extraordinary phone calls that had begun the day before and by now were
in full swing. With Chubb CEO Dean O'Hare having given the go-ahead, the
giant insurance company was actually now in the business of calling people to
see if it could send them money.

Those getting the calls were members of families whose loved ones had
worked for companies at the Trade Center that had purchased workers' compensation insurance from Chubb. There seemed to be about a thousand such
people who might be dead—which was extraordinary: In a given year Chubb
pays maybe three or four death benefits under the workers' compensation
law, which insures people only for on-the-job deaths.

Most of the employers, such as Cantor Fitzgerald (a large Chubb client),
had no records of the families' home phone numbers because their offices had
been destroyed, so since Friday the Chubb teams had been searching telephone directories, the Internet, and anywhere else where they might find a
lead. The plan was to call and ask if their loved one had died—death lists were
utterly chaotic—and if so inform them that they were entitled to a death benefit of up to $600 a week until they remarried or died. Those eligible would be
told that Chubb—which this same day was preparing a press release for
tomorrow projecting overall September 11 losses at $500 million to $600 million that would all but wipe out the entire year's earnings—was prepared to
write the check that day for twelve weeks in advance.

No other insurer was trying to make outgoing calls like this, and, in addition to the fact that they obviously weren't obligated to, there were all kinds of good reasons to stop short of this beyond-the-call outreach. What if the person was alive? What if the person was missing but the family held out hope? What if the family thought this was an insurance company trying to negotiate a fast settlement during their time of trauma? (In fact, all workers' compensation benefits are the same and are regulated by state law, but the families wouldn't know that.) "I just felt it was important for us to help them as fast as possible," O'Hare recalls. "For many people with high salaries, workers' comp isn't much money, but it turned out even these families appreciated the call and appreciated getting some cash so fast. In many cases we were the first call they got offering real help. And we were prepared to mail out the checks that day, with no paperwork first."

The Chubb people recruited for the job were told how wrenching it might be, but they all volunteered. "How could I not," Ryan says. "Here we were sitting on the sidelines and this was a chance to help. It turned out to be the most satisfying time of my career."

Months later, Eileen Simon would remember the call from Chubb as if it had happened yesterday: "What a call! It was so great. The Chubb people were fantastic. I still had no access to cash, so their check [made out to her] came in very handy. And they were so nice."

Chubb had had a team of psychologists work with the callers on Friday and Monday, preparing them for the emotional drain and, more important, preparing them to change their telephone habits. Insurance adjusters who work by phone on workers' comp are trained to move the conversation along quickly in order to be cost-effective in dealing with these small policies. Now they were told to listen as long as the client wanted to talk, which resulted in the average call lasting ten to twenty minutes instead of the standard minute or two.

Many shared stories of their husbands or wives with the Chubb team. One caused the Chubb caller to well up with tears when she said her husband's date of birth was September 11. Another said she had recently divorced and wanted to know if she would still get the payments. One husband said that his family had just that week moved into their new home, and now he had no idea where to put the furniture his wife had purchased that had been delivered that morning. Others asked about how to make funeral arrangements when there is no body. Some told them to call back because they were sure their loved one would be found. And one told Ryan that she'd take the check for now because she needed it, but would be returning it in a week or two when "John comes walking through this door."

By Wednesday, George Clooney had become so caught up in the telethon that with two days to go he, too, was worried about phone calls. The network consortium had commandeered a studio, but they hadn't yet hooked up the phones. How were the thousands who were supposed to call all the stars he'd recruited to sit at the phone tables (still not built) going to connect? Worse, there was also a glitch with the website, one that infuriated Clooney, who had a flair for indignation. It seemed that someone in Canada had heard what the telethon was going to be called and immediately bought the corresponding dot-com name. Now he wanted $5,000 for it. Clooney told the network executives working on the problem that he wanted to get a few television news crews and go to the guy's house and present him with a huge check, Ed McMahon/Publishers Clearing House style, in order to humiliate him. Or at least, he wanted to get on the phone himself and threaten the man with it. But the suits told him to cool it, to work on the scripts and the talent while they dealt with the phones and the website (for which they quietly wrote a check to the Canadian).

Meantime, the September 11th Fund, which was going to get the proceeds from the telethon, had already gotten its first checks out to victims. By the end of the previous week, staffers from the New York Community Trust and United Way (the fund's two parents) had met with more than 300 organizations to vet their credentials for being the conduits for dispensing aid. By Monday they had made their first grant. It was for an initial $10 million to an organization called Safe Horizon, which had long been in the business of aiding crime victims and had a large, well-trained staff. Now, Safe Horizon had activated an emergency cash distribution system, opened its aid center to September 11 victims, and was writing checks of up to $1,500 on the spot. The same center also housed Red Cross volunteers, but people who waited on that line got nothing immediately. The confusion there was becoming maddening.

In addition to three commendation plaques, on the wall of Kevin McCabe's office overlooking the New York harbor in Elizabeth, New Jersey, is a framed letter that suggests what kind of public servant he is. Dated 1989, it's from the Customs Commissioner commending McCabe, then an inspector at the Newark Airport international arrivals terminal, for helping an impaired seventy-nine-year-old Norwegian woman. At midnight, hours after clearing her through Customs and as he was leaving to go off shift, McCabe had noticed her sitting alone in the terminal. It seems that she had lost the address of her daughter, and, worse, had no money. McCabe spent an hour locating the daughter, after which he gave the elderly woman $30 out of his wallet to give a cab driver, whom McCabe had carefully briefed on the intended destination.

More than a decade later, Kevin McCabe, forty-two, was still the same wisecracking, gun-holstered, uniformed Customs agent. He took any excuse to talk about his two sons, seven and ten, and his five-year-old daughter, or about his golf game. Only now he was a supervisor with a ton of September 12 era responsibilities that he took seriously but with characteristic good cheer.

His port, which includes Brooklyn and Staten Island in New York and Elizabeth, near Newark in New Jersey, had reopened on Thursday. He and his team of seventy inspectors on the Contraband Enforcement Team had been there since Tuesday with only an occasional break. None asked whether overtime pay, usually carefully appropriated and approved in advance, would be coming. (It ultimately was.) None complained. They just worked, often refusing suggestions to take a break.★

Within eighteen hours they had separated out and inspected some 600 containers that had come into the port prior to the attacks from North Africa, South Asia, and the Middle East. They were proud of an awesome accomplishment. Usually, they inspected no more than 200 of the 7,000 containers arriving daily.

Deciding which ones to check on a typical day was hardly random. They made inspection decisions in part on the country of origin—in the September 10 era that had meant looking for containers from South America or South Asia that might be hiding drugs—but also based on whether they knew the shipper or the entity to whom something was being shipped, or whether the commodity listed as being in the container made sense. For example a shipment of roof tiles from Venezuela had seemed suspicious a few months ago, because that region was not known for its roofing products. Sure enough, they had found drugs.

Much of that information was put into a computer, which weighted the various factors—country of origin, reliability of shipper, reliability of recipient, type of cargo—to produce a score of up to 1,000. Anything over about 400 got checked.

★McCabe, who makes $92,000, didn't qualify for overtime because of his supervisory position.

First it was screened by a truck-sized machine called a VACIS (Vehicle and Cargo Inspection System), which took an X-ray picture of the insides of the entire container. McCabe's VACIS crew then looked for what they called "anomalies," such as one section of the container that looked as if it was holding something of far higher density than the rest of the giant metal crate. If anything looked suspicious, they would unload the entire shipment and inspect it all by hand.

Now, eight days after the attacks, McCabe's team in Elizabeth, aided by programmers at Customs headquarters in Washington, had started punching in new criteria. On September 10, Customs had been mainly in the drug interdiction business; indeed, two press releases issued by the agency from Washington that day had trumpeted a three-ton marijuana seizure in Laredo and a 1,412-pound bust in El Paso. Although the overall heightened border security in the months ahead would actually produce an increase in drug busts, the days when that was the priority were suddenly over. The new points system was a model of practicality if not political correctness. A container that had come from or gone through Afghanistan, for example, was certain to get enough points on that basis alone to merit a VACIS inspection. In fact, an unknown shipper or recipient from any of more than a dozen Middle Eastern, Asian, or North African countries also passed the threshold, with little or nothing else required.

Beyond that, McCabe was already using other intelligence sources to help screen for the new threats. Sometimes those reports were so ominous that he and his men would go check a ship before it even docked. Early Thursday morning, two days after the attacks, that is what they had done with a ship coming in from Saudi Arabia that had stopped at Norfolk, Virginia. Naval Intelligence had notified them the day before that a Navy captain had noticed that as the ship was leaving Norfolk, two Arab-looking men seemed to be up on the deck using a video camera to photograph the Norfolk naval base. One seemed to have a weapon.

As the Saudi ship approached New York harbor, three of McCabe's men boarded a Coast Guard boat to intercept it. Technically, the Coast Guard is responsible for keeping unauthorized ships and enemies from American shores, while Customs is responsible for unauthorized goods entering the ports. But in practice the two agencies worked well together in New York. And since September 11 they had worked virtually in tandem, with the Coast Guard suddenly letting its traditional work of at-sea searches and rescues take a back seat to its new job as a first line of defense against terrorists. In fact, the Coast Guard's mission changed and intensified so drastically, so quickly that within three months its ships would have logged more sea time than would normally be budgeted for the agency for fifteen years.

When the Coast Guard cutter pulled up to the giant freighter, McCabe's three men and two from the Coast Guard boarded, guns drawn. They asked the captain about the report of men on the deck with the video camera. He said he'd seen nothing. One of McCabe's men spotted two guys on an upper deck looking nervous. The team approached them. They spoke no English. Their passports seemed in order, and a radio check to see if they were on any watch lists yielded nothing. The Customs people then inspected the whole crew and all the cargo—for four hours. They found nothing.

False alarm.


Peter Fisher, the Treasury Department undersecretary for domestic finance, who had spearheaded the Bush administration's drive to reopen the stock markets, believes devoutly that industries and companies should live or die in the marketplace on their own, without government interference. So as he sat at a Wednesday meeting with presidential economics aide Larry Lindsey and others in the White House and heard Lindsey say that the President had ordered that they make sure no airlines go bankrupt before Christmas, he couldn't resist a quip. "None?" he asked. "Not even the worst, or the dumbest?"

Lindsey, who often went off on humorous tangents of his own, was dead serious. No airline failures before Christmas. What was coming into focus, he explained, was a program that would provide $5 billion in cash, ostensibly to make up for the losses caused by the temporary grounding of the airlines after September 11 (though, in fact, at most those losses were $1.5 billion, according to the airlines' own internal estimates), and an additional $10 billion in government backing for loans that the airlines could take out to cover their losses during what was likely to be six months to a year of dramatically reduced demand, especially among business travelers.

Transportation Secretary Norman Mineta added that they had to move fast to protect a national asset—the aviation industry—whose demise would be an economic catastrophe. Mineta didn't have to argue too hard. Fisher—who as a top aide at the New York Federal Reserve Bank had been pivotal in the mid-1990s in devising a plan to rescue a huge hedge fund whose demise had threatened a market meltdown—loves to tweak people with his free market doctrine. But he also understands the real world.

By the end of the day, Fisher was working with the Transportation Department and Congress on a program that, by offering the possibility of government guarantees, would do exactly what the President wanted: prevent any credit meltdowns before Christmas. But he would also build a stringent, free market toughness into the program's guidelines for actually extending those guarantees, so that when the airlines came around to ask for them the following spring, only the strongest would get approved. Others, including some of the largest, would face death if they could not push unions and other suppliers to cut their costs dramatically, so that they might become viable businesses.

. The thornier problem was the issue of liability both for future terrorist-caused air crashes that insurers no longer wanted to insure, and for the September 11 crashes, for which United and American did not have enough insurance to cover the thousands of victims on the planes and in the Twin Towers and at the Pentagon.

This was a place where Lindsey's and Fisher's economic theories meshed more easily with the airlines' needs. In their view, a private insurance market can exist only when insurers can measure risk and are willing to charge an affordable price for assuming it. If they perceive the risk as too high and, therefore, won't insure against it, then it is the proper function of government to decide whether the activity in question—in this case, flying passenger airplanes—is worth preserving. If it is, then the government, which can finance risks that insurers can't, should provide the insurance. This is what the government had done with nuclear power plants; a law provides that in the event of a disaster, the government pays off the claims of the victims. So, Lindsey and Fisher decided that any airline bailout bill would provide a backstop of government insurance for any terrorist attacks on planes, meaning that the government would pay off any resulting lawsuits. Deputy Transportation Secretary Michael Jackson, who was in hourly contact now with the airlines, reminded the group that they had to move fast. On Monday the airlines had received letters from the insurers telling them all that their insurance against a terrorist-generated crash was canceled as of next Monday. After that, the planes had to be grounded.

But what about the United and American planes that had already crashed and for whom there were now estimated to be 6,000 dead victims? Air crashes typically result in a payoff of averaging $1.5 million to $2 million per victim, which could mean a $9 billion to $12 billion payout. And that was before all the collateral damage, such as the interruption of thousands of businesses and the destruction of the Twin Towers and surrounding property, was calculated. That amount was estimated to be $50 billion. But the airlines only had insurance of $1.5 billion per crash (an amount that was always enough, given that there are maybe 200 or 300 people on a typical plane). The airlines' solution was that the bailout bill would have a provision simply capping their liability at the amount of their insurance—or a total of $6 billion for the four plane crashes. All those with claims against the airlines (the passengers, the people at the Trade Center, the owners of the Trade Center) would somehow have to split that $6 billion. But the Democrats had resisted that plan when it surfaced earlier in the day, because that would leave the victims without enough money.

Fisher and Lindsey, who were joined in this part of the discussion by budget director Daniels, had a solution to that, too. The bailout law would provide for the government to cover any claims won by the families of those injured or killed in lawsuits that went beyond that $6 billion. (All that other damage to businesses and property would be covered by their owners' own insurance, they reasoned.) Daniels was aghast at the idea of the government paying off the victims. There would be a run on the Treasury, he argued.

But Fisher—who had a Harvard Law degree, though he had never practiced law—had done some legal research. It was unlikely that the airlines would be found to be at fault, he countered. Besides, if they put in the new bailout law that all lawsuits related to the attacks have to be brought in New York federal court under New York law, the government would be protected because New York law does not allow juries to award pain and suffering damages to families in what's called wrongful death cases. The only damage awards have to be for lost wages, and even those can only go to a family member if he or she would have shared in those lost wages. Thus, in theory a family like the Cartiers, who had lost a brother and son who was not providing any of them with his earnings, could recover nothing. They could not collect for their pain and suffering (such as emotional distress) due to his death, and they could not claim any lost wages. And even a widow could only claim lost earnings, not any pain and suffering. The $6 billion in insurance was likely to cover most if not all of that.

This was one case where knowing a little law can hurt. Had these White House Republicans had a street-smart plaintiffs lawyer in the room, they'd have known that juries even in New York typically ignore the law when faced with an emotionally distressing case and award widows far more than lost earnings. Smart plaintiffs lawyers in air crash cases often came up with a value in the hundreds of thousands of dollars just for the loss of the deceased father's child-rearing skills. And though a case like the Cartiers' would be tougher, even that one posed enough of a threat of pulling on a jury's heartstrings that insurers typically settle for something in six figures, even seven figures.

On Capitol Hill, the Republicans were not nearly as naive about the potential for the plaintiffs' suits. There was no way that people like House Majority

Whip Tom DeLay or Senate Minority Leader Trent Lott—Republicans from two states, Texas and Mississippi, where plaintiffs lawyers had enjoyed some of their greatest success at the expense of the two Republicans' prime business constituents—were going to allow the trial lawyers to get the run of the federal Treasury with a law like that. Lott, whose close hometown friend and brother-in-law was one of the country's richest plaintiffs lawyers and who was wise to their ways, was aghast when he heard about the White House plan to be the insurer of last resort for September 11. There was no way we can do this, he told his staff. We have to think of something else.

It was a three-party stalemate. The Democrats wanted the victims fully taken care of. Plus, they were talking about including an aid package in any industry bailout for the airlines' 100,000 laid-off workers. The White House wanted to wrap things up the simple way, with a government backstop to all claims. And the Republicans in Congress were worried about a trial lawyers' run on the Treasury. Lott insisted that there had to be a way out.

At about 4:00 Wednesday, David Crane—Lott's thirty-six-year-old senior policy advisor, who had been wrestling with the issue since the afternoon before—got an idea that he began to doodle on a pad. Why not set up some kind of federal victims compensation fund, run by a Special Master who would act as a one-man judge and jury? Anyone who promised not to sue in a real court could come to the fund and automatically get a payment for whatever economic losses and pain and suffering they could demonstrate in a simple, uncontested hearing. No victim would have to prove it was the airlines' or anyone else's fault.

The Special Master could establish guidelines for the awards in advance so that the victims would have a pretty good idea of what they would get. Attorneys would be allowed, but they wouldn't be necessary and their usual contingency fees of 33 to 40 percent wouldn't make sense, because the whole process would be uncontested. Thus, there would be more money for the victims. Punitive damages—money juries award to punish and deter a defendant's bad conduct—would not be allowed because the "defendant" here would be the government. Victims would be enticed into the fund because if they didn't go in and sued instead, they would have to prove that the airlines, or the World Trade Center, or some other entity was at fault (a dicey proposition), and because even if they won a suit they'd have to worry that the $6 billion, insurance-related limit that the law was going to put on the airlines' total liability would not be enough to pay them, given the prospect that the Trade Center and others were also likely to sue the airlines.

Lott told Crane he loved the idea and ordered him to type it up on a single piece of paper. Show it to other key people on Capitol Hill, Lott told him. But don't show it to anyone at the White House—yet. First, Lott would sell it on the Hill, then present it to the White House people as a fait accompli.


Robert Lindemann thought he had not done anything wrong. When a reporter from the *Detroit Free Press* had called on Monday, she had said that Lindemann's boss at the Border Patrol station in Detroit had given her his name and that of his partner, Mark Hall. So he and Hall figured they could talk to her and made a date for breakfast on Tuesday. Lindemann and Hall, after all, were the union leaders of the Border Patrol agents in the Detroit Sector, so why shouldn't they speak for the men about the challenges they faced in the aftermath of the attacks?

The resulting front-page story this morning shocked Lindemann's bosses, sector chief George Geoghegan and his deputy, John France.

Under the headline, "Release of Pakistani Wanted for Questioning Illustrates Border Problems," the piece by Tamar Audi and David Zeman began by recounting an incident on June 4 when Hall and Lindemann had "captured a Pakistani man trying to sneak into the United States aboard a freight train from Canada."

The story continued: "They questioned him, and with nowhere to detain him, sent him back to Canada. Monday, the arresting agent saw a name that matched the Pakistani's on a list of 200 people wanted for questioning in connection with last week's attacks on the World Trade Center and Pentagon.

" 'When I saw that name I almost got sick,' said Mark Hall. Hall said that he would have been able to question the man and his associates more thoroughly if his office had facilities to detain suspects."

The article—citing Hall and Lindemann's report that only twenty-eight agents are there to cover 804 miles of border, and that they have only one working boat and one remote surveillance camera that has been out of service for six months—quoted Lindemann as saying, "The stuff is falling apart. We're putting it together with duct tape."

"It's dangerous and it's scary," Hall added. "The Northern Border has been basically abandoned by the government."

Lindemann and Hall maintain that they were simply sounding the call to protect their country. To get to know either one of them was to believe them. Sure, they were officers in the Border Patrol's local union, something that Geoghegan's deputy would later assert means "they are paid to complain and bitch about little things." But unions in federal law enforcement agencies had strictly limited rights that Lindemann and Hall readily accepted. They could not strike and never had threatened to. They didn't bargain over wages, which were set in civil service tables across many agencies. And in Hall's and Lindemann's case they didn't get paid for their union posts; in fact, they didn't even get their dues waived. About all the union did was negotiate work rules on matters such as transfers or notices to be posted for promotions, and act as a forum for workplace grievances. Raymond Kelly, the current New York police commissioner who was commissioner of the Customs Service in the 1990s and dealt with a union there that operated similarly to the Border Patrol's, says that although negotiating over issues like work rules and transfers is bothersome and often impedes good management, "Federal law enforcement unions are nothing like local police unions. There is typically little of the adversarial relationship and no bargaining or posturing over big issues like money."

"I'm a Marine from a family of Marines," says Lindemann. "I love this country, and when I spoke to the paper, if anything, I thought I was helping the bosses here by helping to get them the resources they need. Everything I did, I did to strengthen my country."

Geoghegan and France didn't see it that way. Almost immediately after they read the article, they took steps to fire Lindemann and Hall, a move initially backed by the INS regional director, who told Geoghegan and France that he considered Lindemann's and Hall's comments in the article to be "treason." But in Washington slightly cooler heads prevailed.

On Saturday at about 6:00 P.M. France would show up at Lindemann's and Hall's desks (everyone was working seven-day weeks) and serve them each with a letter declaring that because they had breached national security with their unauthorized interview they were being put on day shifts (they had always worked nights, which allowed Lindemann to take his two small children to school, while his wife worked), would no longer be partnered together (they had been partners for eleven years), and that it was being recommended to headquarters that they be suspended for ninety days. The fact that they had provided the same account of the sector's lack of resources in public congressional testimony two years before, or that a supervisor had been quoted in the same newspaper in March of 2000 saying her unit was understaffed, was ignored.

As he read the letter, a knot formed in Lindemann's stomach that was so painful that the buff thirty-nine-year-old thought he might be having a heart attack.

By Wednesday, Ed Woollen had called around Raytheon and discovered that the company was so big that even he hadn't appreciated how well positioned it was to take advantage of those three areas of opportunity he had identified. When it came to securing facilities, such as airports and their planes, it turned out that Raytheon already had a contract to install InVision's explosive detection machines in airports around the country. True, this was part of the slow-motion, September 10 era program—scheduled to be completed in 2010—that had stalled out so badly that only about 150 machines were deployed at maybe fifteen airports. But it was a start, and more than anyone else had done. Moreover, Raytheon was already working with a company called Visionics to experiment with its facial recognition machines at airports and other facilities. These machines mapped a person's face and compared the live image to a database of other mapped faces. Thus, a fugitive walking by one of Visionic's video cameras would be recognized from the database and an alarm would sound.

As for using its database expertise for border protection, Raytheon had already done work for INS on its Ident system. Ident allowed Border Patrol agents to take the thumbprints of anyone it caught, put them into a machine, and see instantly if there was a match to the prints of anyone on the patrol's database of repeat border jumpers. There were all kinds of problems with the system, chiefly that this database didn't match up with a more important FBI data bank of wanted criminals and known terrorists, and it wasn't deployed at many Border Patrol posts. But Woollen didn't know that. This, too, was a foothold.

Then there was that big target of local police and other first responders, the people who would be on the front lines of any homeland attacks and needed all kinds of command and control equipment. Woollen found that one Raytheon unit had a small contract to provide emergency communications equipment to the California city of Barstow. It included gadgets to allow different local agencies that operated on different radio frequencies to connect to each other at a disaster site, something those commission reports had identified as a major problem (and which, unknown to Woollen, would be revealed a few months later to have been a critical failure at Ground Zero). Barstow wasn't much, but it, too, was something.

Project Yankee was now more than a name.

Sergio Magistri of InVision was also thinking big. In Washington and around the country, the talk in the media about aviation security—encouraged by his newly rehired PR people, although not much encouragement was needed—by now almost always mentioned the threat of bombs hidden in checked baggage. Magistri, his sales staff, and his lobbyist, McCann, now agreed that they should no longer worry about their one competitor, L-3. Nor should they worry about L-3's key lobbyist—Linda Daschle, the wife of Senate Majority Leader Tom Daschle. If anything, Daschle could help things now, Magistri reasoned, because the question wasn't what share of the market either company got, but how large the market would be. After all, if the country decided on anything remotely approaching a system of screening all checked luggage, neither company had anything near the ability to produce all those machines anytime soon.

This alignment, unspoken though it was, was quite a switch. Just two years before, L-3 had suddenly come to represent an enormous threat. It wasn't as though the L-3 machines were better or its sales force more potent. In fact, although L-3 was a much larger company than InVision, with multiple products, its explosive detection machines were generally regarded as inferior, because they produced more false alarms and often broke down; and its market share was minimal. But L-3's lobbying prowess, led by the firm where Linda Daschle was a key player, was something else. In the fall of 2000, congressional appropriators had inserted into a law covering the federal transportation budget for the fiscal year October 2000 through September 2001 a provision requiring that the FAA purchase one L-3 machine for every InVision machine it purchased. Magistri and McCann had been taken completely by surprise; the provision had been inserted by the House of Representatives and agreed to by the Senate at the last minute during a late-night negotiating session between the two chambers. The ostensible purpose was to encourage competition, but Magistri was devastated. The government was buying so slowly that the market was maybe $40 million a year. Now, half of it had been yanked away by law. To be sure, because the Transportation Department's inspector general later reported that the L-3 machines didn't work well, Magistri had not lost quite that much, but the threat was still there, especially once L-3 improved its machines, which, by the summer of 2001, is what Magistri was hearing had happened.

In the September 12 era, the math changed. It would take 2,000, 3,000, maybe 4,000 detectors, costing as much as $1 million each, to cover every airport, meaning a market in the billions. The challenge was going to be making that market a reality—and then ramping up to get even half of it before others jumped in. So Magistri began instructing his PR people to talk about explosive detection generically and not to worry about touting his machines over L-3's. He told McCann the same thing.

———

Michael Cartier called ahead on Wednesday morning to a Red Cross center to say that his father was coming down to inquire about getting aid to pay for any bills that James Cartier might have left behind. Patrick Cartier, Sr., who like James had also been an electrician, was sixty-seven and had a heart condition. But he insisted to Michael that he wanted to make the trip alone. Can they make sure he doesn't have to wait long and that he's treated well, Cartier asked the Red Cross person, after waiting on hold about half an hour. We'll do our best, the Red Cross worker promised.

Patrick Cartier really didn't feel the need for the cash as much as he felt he just wanted to get out of the house and do something related to the tragedy by going somewhere to get some of the help the television people were all talking about. So after lunch he made his way into Manhattan and over to the Red Cross center on the Hudson River piers. Two hours later, he walked out, empty-handed—after being shunted to various lines and then asked for his son's birth certificate, which no one had told Michael he would need and which the family had no idea of how to locate.

"There is no question that at the beginning we did not provide consistency of service," Red Cross New York chapter chief Robert Bender concedes. "Like everyone else, we had never handled anything like this, and we were trying to train more than 30,000 volunteers. We also were trying to make sure we had some controls on the funds our donors had given to us, so that they went to the right people."


Tom Ridge was in the governor's mansion at about 1:30 on Wednesday when his secretary said that Andrew Card, the White House chief of staff, was calling. Ridge immediately took the call.

Card wanted to know if Ridge could come down to Washington from Harrisburg to talk about a new job they were thinking about involving homeland security. It turned out that Ridge was already supposed to be in Washington the next day to testify at the International Trade Commission in support of his state's steel industry. Stopping by for a chat would be no problem, he told Card.

Ridge aides recall that he seemed preoccupied after the call, but that he kept mum.

About an hour later, the staff became more curious when the secretary put through a second call from Card. After they chatted for a few minutes, Card said, "someone else wants to talk to you," and Vice President Cheney got on the phone.

Cheney told Ridge he was delighted that he was coming to talk about the job, that it was a job that Cheney and his staff had been focusing on in the last few days, and that he was hoping Ridge was prepared to give it serious consideration. Ridge was surprised that things had gotten far enough that the Vice President was already involved.

At about 4:15 Ridge left in the state plane for a funeral in Meadville, Pennsylvania. When the plane returned to Harrisburg, Ridge was greeted by an aide as the door opened. The President had been trying to reach him.

Ridge went quickly to the governor's mansion where he could take the call from the privacy of his bedroom. The President was also glad Ridge was coming to town so quickly, he said, because this was a really important job.

As he finished the call, Ridge's wife, Michele, came in, surprised to see him at home. "I took one look at his face," Michele Ridge recalls, "and stopped. I knew something was going on."

"We have to talk," Ridge said. "Right now."

"Is it your mother?" Michele asked. Ridge's seventy-eight-year-old mother had recently been in the hospital for surgery.

"No," he replied. "Let's talk."

"I'm an Army brat," says Michele Ridge, "and was used to getting told we were moving. And Tom was drafted, too. So for some reason, without him saying it, this seemed to me like the time he'd been drafted—which it kind of was."

As Ridge's aides speculated about all the calls, Michele told him she knew he had to take the job. But they also discussed another problem: With Ridge needing to rent an apartment in Washington and the family needing to move out of the governor's mansion and find a home in Harrisburg at least until the end of the school year, Michele was going to have to go back to work. There was no way they could suddenly assume all those new housing costs, plus keep the kids in private school, on his White House salary (which he later found out was $140,000). Plus, she'd have to buy a car (they had not needed one of their own in the seven years he had been governor), and figure out how to pack up their files and furniture with none of the usual transition costs budgeted by the state for this kind of sudden move.

The Ridges decided that they could not tell anyone, including their children—son, Tommy, fourteen, and daughter, Lesley, fifteen—until the next evening, because, as Michele remembers, "the kids are so networked on the computer that they were bound to let the word out."

At 6:45 the next morning, Thursday, September 20, Ridge flew to Washington for his testimony. By 9:30 he was in Card's office at the White House. Soon Cheney joined them, then the President. The meeting had all the urgency of a wartime conference. They outlined the coordinator's role. Bush promised his friend that he'd have his full backing to shake things up. But they needed an answer now because the President wanted to make the announcement of a new homeland security chief in his address to Congress scheduled for that evening. Ridge shook the President's hand and said yes.

Tom and Michele Ridge talked to Tommy and Lesley on Thursday afternoon, just before Ridge left to go back to Washington to be there for the President's announcement. It helped that the kids knew and liked the Bushes. They'd spent weekends with them in Kennebunkport, Maine (at the Bush family compound), when their father and Bush had been fellow governors. And this past summer they'd stayed at the White House during a July 4th celebration. Bush had also stayed with them a few times at the Pennsylvania governor's mansion. But this was quite a shock. Would he really leave Harrisburg and the governorship? What would this job be? What about the kids' schools?

Ridge said that Washington was only about a two-hour drive and that he'd commute on weekends, at least until the school year ended. Then they'd see how things were going.

Ridge would later say that, although he loved being governor, the decision was not that hard, and was made easier by his longtime friendship with Bush. "The President wasn't asking me to run into a burning 110-story building like those firemen did," is the way he put it. "This sacrifice, if it was one, was the least I could do."

Nonetheless, it was an extraordinary decision, and one that was emblematic of the time—that brief, probably too brief, period of weeks following September 11 when for most Americans the unprecedented urgency of the moment was such that no sacrifice, no disruption of normal life, seemed too much. In the space of about twenty-one hours, the seven-year governor of Pennsylvania had quit his job. He had forced his family to find a new home. (Ridge's successor, Lieutenant Governor Mark Schweiker, soon decided to let the Ridges stay in the mansion until December 31.) He had left his family. His wife would have to go from being a first lady with a staff of five involved in a variety of community service projects to a working mom. And he had gone from being a chief executive to a staff position that was, at best, ill defined, and would soon be challenged and belittled.

# Friday, September 21, 2001

If one day best presented a snapshot of America in the September 12 era—its strengths, its weaknesses, its challenges, its foibles, its glories—that day was September 21, 2001.

At about 2:00 A.M., the airline lobbyists were still pouring drinks for Tom DeLay in his Majority Whip's office at the Capitol. They had stayed since Thursday night to make sure the congressional staff didn't screw anything up in their write-up of the airline bailout bill.*

Among those there was Will Ris, American Airlines's man in Washington. American's political action committee (to which Ris personally donated $5,000 annually in recent years) had been a steady contributor to DeLay's campaigns and to DeLay's own political action committee, a fund he was known to use obsessively to promote the conservative Republican cause and to keep control over his House colleagues by doling out money to their campaigns as long as they follow his lead.

The PAC of Continental Airlines, which was represented that early morning by its top lobbyist, Rebecca Cox, was also a DeLay contributor. Cox, however, had another ticket to the room: She was the wife of Christopher Cox, a Republican House colleague of DeLay's.

In fact, except for D. Scott Yohe from Delta Air Lines, everyone else in the Majority Whip's office, including two staffers from the Air Transport Association and one lobbyist from United Airlines, were direct or indirect contributors to DeLay. But the man with the best connection was Continental lobbyist Steven Hart, the senior partner at Williams & Jensen, one of Washington's two or three most connected lobbying firms. Hart was DeLay's personal lawyer. And he liked to tell clients (and was not ashamed to tell a reporter) that he did DeLay's personal legal work (as well as that of several other congressmen) for free as a "loss leader." †

By 3:00 in the morning, the group was wondering where the draft was. Then the phone rang. It was a Republican staffer reporting that there was a

---

*DeLay declined to be interviewed. His communications director, Stuart Roy, who was not there, confirms that DeLay was in his office with a group of lobbyists but does not know whether he was drinking, although he concedes that "it is possible he had a glass or two of red wine."

†DeLay communications director Roy promised to check with DeLay about whether Hart does free legal work for him, but then did not call back or return subsequent calls.

problem. It seemed that Senators Fritz Hollings of South Carolina and Robert Byrd of West Virginia were insisting that as a condition of the bailout, the airlines had to be kept from reducing service on any routes. Hollings, the chairman of the Transportation Committee, and Byrd, the chairman of the Appropriations Committee, were key players; and because they came from small states that had no major airline hubs, the issue of reduced service had long been a priority they shared. Everyone thought the issue had already been worked out with some language in the bill requiring the Secretary of Transportation to review any proposed reductions carefully, or some such thing. Now, the two Democrats were insisting on something with teeth. The whole bill was in jeopardy, and with the airlines' insurance set to expire Monday without a bill, something had to be signed this weekend—which at 3:00 A.M. on Friday was fast approaching.

"You've got to do something, Tom," Hart said to his pro bono client.

"Please, Tom, go up there and shut them down," added one of the others, referring to the deadlocked staffers in a conference room a floor above.

DeLay smiled. "Shut them down, huh? Okay." Whereupon he put his drink down, got up, went upstairs to the conference room, flung open the door, and said, "Gentlemen, this meeting is over. Tell your boss," he added, looking at the top staffer for Hollings, "that this is the bill. Now get out of here. Now!"

Minutes later he was back downstairs with his drinking buddies. "Okay, what's next," he asked with a grin.

That settled, a group of other staffers drafting the more essential elements of the airline bailout bill—the financial conditions and the provisions for a fund to compensate the victims of the September 11 attacks—began preparing it for a final vote by both chambers a few hours later, when the House would vote for it 356–54 and the Senate 96–1.

The quality of the document they were completing and the speed with which it had been created adds perspective to this tawdry scene of the liquor-plying lobbyists having their way with the House Majority Whip. However threatening to the public interest this mix of money and schmoozing may be generally, DeLay and the airlines were right that the Hollings-Byrd restrictions were pork barrel provisions that had no place in this bill. More important, the overall bailout bill was a model, albeit messily put together, of what representative democracy—of which lobbying by informed and intensely interested parties is a part—can produce at its best.

The loan provisions of the bailout had been tightened considerably. The requirement that loans only go to airlines that presented long-term, viable business plans all but guaranteed that any airlines that were on their way down before September 11—and there were quite a few—would not now benefit from September 11. Only those experiencing relatively short-term September 11–related problems were likely to qualify. Moreover, a provision insisted on by Republican Senator Peter Fitzgerald of Illinois and Democrat Jon Corzine of New Jersey (a former investment banker) allowed the board deciding on the loans to seek an option to buy shares in the airlines as part of the deal. That way, the taxpayers could share not only in the risk but the upside.

Most important, the staff on the Senate Judiciary Committee, helped by a lawyer on Hillary Clinton's staff, had done a good job running with the idea that Crane had first presented to Lott for a victims fund. The lawyers on the committee had soon realized that Crane's out-of-court fund looked a lot like one established by private companies for victims of Agent Orange, a defoliant whose use during the Vietnam War had produced thousands of injuries, and lawsuits. Using the Agent Orange setup as a framework, they had developed a fund mechanism that really seemed to be a solution to getting the airlines off the hook of liability beyond what they were insured for, while still offering victims a fair, and relatively fast, payout.

Interestingly, no one seemed to spend a lot of time worrying about an obvious constitutional issue: By capping the airlines' liability for damages to an amount equal to their insurance, wasn't Congress unlawfully taking from the victims a right they had—to sue the airlines for whatever a court and jury would allow? The staff lawyers talked about what would seem to be an unconstitutional taking of property (in this case the right to sue the airlines without a limit on their liability), but decided that no appeals court, especially the United States Supreme Court, was likely to veto this kind of congressional emergency action. But it did make them especially determined to make sure that the compensation fund—where the victims would have to choose to go instead of a court—would be regarded as a desirable, fair alternative.

What was also interesting about this solution was that it did not come from the White House. The Bush administration, it should be remembered, had been willing to settle for the government simply providing a backstop to the airlines' insurance coverage and stepping in and paying off all the verdicts people won in court that exceeded the airlines' coverage. It was a simple solution, but one that captured the worst of two worlds. It didn't offer the prospect of limiting the long court process or trial lawyers' large contingent fees. Yet it risked either being much more expensive because juries, not a Special Master, would be dispensing the taxpayers' money, or being of no help to the victims, because jurors would decide that only the terrorists, not the airlines or anyone else, were at fault. The fund seemed to be a much better solution.

Earlier the night before, however, it had been far from a sure thing that the fund, and therefore the whole bailout, was going to happen.

Immediately after President Bush's extraordinarily successful Thursday evening speech, which was followed by those memorable hugs he had given to Speaker Dennis Hastert and Majority Leader Tom Daschle, Hastert and Daschle convened a meeting of all the congressional leaders in Hastert's Capitol conference room to talk about the bill. With the loan and aid provisions largely having been agreed to, the main issue was the victims fund. The debate, which began at about 10:00 Thursday night, lasted nearly three hours.

Deputy Senate Republican Leader Don Nickles of Oklahoma, supported by DeLay and Deputy Majority Whip Roy Blunt from Missouri, was adamantly against the fund. *Why should these people get a federal fund, when the victims of terrorism in Oklahoma City hadn't?* Nickles asked. *What kind of precedent were we setting? Were we going to do this for the next terrorist attack? And the next one?*★

*We didn't take away the ability of Oklahoma City victims to sue the way we are doing here by capping the airlines' liability,* said House Minority Leader Richard Gephardt. (True, but those victims had had no one to sue, except bomber Timothy McVeigh; a few suits against the companies that produced the fertilizer he used for his bomb had, appropriately, been fruitless.) *By bailing out the airlines with this liability cap, we're taking something away from the victims. We have to give it back,* Gephardt added.

*Maybe, but why do it so fast,* countered Nickles, who considers himself a careful legislator who likes to craft well-considered bills. *We are creating this giant open-ended fund and we have no idea what the rules will be* [the draft law said the fund's Special Master would promulgate rules], *or what it will cost. We're hearing estimates like $6 billion to fund this, but no one really knows. First we heard the recovery was going to cost $20 billion. Then Schumer and New York come along and they get another $20 billion. Now we have this fund and we don't know if it'll cost $6 billion or $20 billion. My whole state spends $5 billion a year on its entire budget. . . . We just heard the idea yesterday. Shouldn't we hold hearings and get some experts in here to help us? And the way I read this, this Special Master we are creating will have unlimited power to write checks for whatever amount he*

---

★The portions that are italicized here are what these speakers or others in the room say they said. But because no one kept notes, because the conversation was so long, and because their recollections came months after the event, these can only be considered approximations of the actual conversation. Thus, the use of italics instead of quotation marks.

*wants. No one has ever had that power in this government. We're creating a king! This is crazy,* he thundered.

Nickles was right. Daniels of the White House budget office, who was in the room, had originally wanted to limit any awards to $250,000 per victim, the amount paid by the government to public safety officers killed in the line of duty. But the Democrats had argued that that was not nearly enough to make up for what they could get in court. Not wanting to push what at the time seemed the politically suicidal and downright heartless cause of short-changing the victims, Daniels had relented, and a compromise had been struck on Thursday. The Democrat-controlled Senate would give up the right to approve the Special Master, who would decide the awards. In return the Special Master would not have to operate under any cap on those awards. Nickles, nonetheless, was shocked by the idea that there were no limits on this giveaway. And he didn't feel any better when the *New York Times* reported the morning after the bill passed that "experts said claims could easily rise to $18 billion."

*Well then, we are not going to pass an airline bailout,* said Daschle, *because if we don't do this now, you guys are never going to do it and the victims will be out of luck. Tell me how we go to the American people,* he added, *and explain to them that we've protected the airlines but not the victims.*

As if that wasn't enough, Gephardt now chimed in with a renewed argument to help the other victims—all those laid-off flight attendants, baggage carriers, and ticket clerks. That got DeLay back into the fray, saying they, too, could be dealt with later if at all. *The job tonight,* DeLay said, *is to save the airlines, not dispense money to the victims or the laid-off workers.*

*We're making this new foray into a completely uncharted area of law with this fund and doing it at midnight just to get something else done, the bailout, that we have to do,* added Blunt. *That's just wrong.*

*Then we're going to do nothing,* said Daschle, who presumably could deliver on the threat because the Democrats controlled the Senate.

At about 1:00 A.M., from the front of the room, Speaker Hastert, who had been opposed to the fund but, characteristically, had been the quietest of the Republican leaders, signaled Daschle and Gephardt to come talk to him. They went off to a corner. "We're going to do this," Hastert whispered. "Now. A fund, but no aid for the laid-off workers."

As the two Democrats went back to their seats, the Speaker announced that he thought the debate was over. He was going to ask the House to move ahead with the fund. Later that morning the bill passed and was sent to the White House for the President's signature. In less than two days from the inception of the idea, the United States had enacted the largest single corporate bailout bill in history and the largest public entitlement program—the victims fund—in decades. And a single, unelected person, the Special Master, had been given unprecedented, unchecked power to write checks from the Treasury for whatever amounts he wanted.

However rushed and heated the process, and however breathtaking the stakes, those in that meeting would later be unanimous about one thing. This was exactly the kind of debate that there had been too little of in Congress in recent years. The principals, not their staffs, were really deciding the nitty-gritty. They were arguing on the merits, openly and forcefully, without name calling or personalizing the issues. And in the end, they actually did something.

"Here we were sitting there in that room in the Capitol, with planes and helicopters buzzing around in the night sky providing protection from some other airplane bombing us," one key staffer would remember. "And I had two emotions. First, I wished we could get the hell out before another attack came. And second, I was really, really proud. This was the way the process was supposed to work."

Even the lobbyists, who remained outside the room but nearby in DeLay's office, had played an important role, this leadership staffer would add. "I have to admit that there is a lot we didn't understand about the industry. Even the guys on the staff whose specialty is the airlines don't really understand economics, because they typically deal with regulations related to stuff like safety. One of them didn't know the difference between load factors, which only has to do with percentage of seats filled, and revenue, which has to do with, well, revenue. If you cut back flights and fill a lot of seats with people on discounts who are not business travelers, which is what was happening, then your load factors stay okay but your revenues drop. The meeting went a lot better because the lobbyists had walked us through all that."

"It was," says budget director Daniels, who didn't like the open-ended victims fund, "an extraordinary night, where everyone did their jobs."


Extraordinary or not, Chuck Schumer was not allowed into the meeting, not even after pleading with Daschle that as home to the most victims, New York deserved to be represented by its senior senator. Schumer may have been the senior of New York's two senators (he'd been elected two years before Hillary Clinton), but as a three-year veteran of the exclusive club, he had nowhere near the stripes to get into the room. Besides, according to a Schumer aide,

Daschle knew that DeLay detested Schumer, and the sight of him pushing for his New York victims when Nickles's Oklahoma City constituents had gotten nothing would be like waving a red flag in front of Nickles.

Daschle promised Schumer that he'd make sure the victims were taken care of, but being left out of the action like this drove him crazy. Besides, Schumer had another constituent he wanted taken care of—Larry Silverstein, the real estate mogul whose partnership had bought all the leases at the Trade Center and had taken over management of the buildings six weeks before the attacks. Silverstein was just as worried as the airlines about liability from the crashes and perhaps had better reason to be; after all, Trade Center personnel (it was not clear if they were his employees or Port Authority police) had actually told people in the South Tower to stay put after the first plane hit the North Tower. And as had happened after the 1993 terrorist bombing of the Trade Center, which had resulted in dozens of lawsuits that had not yet been resolved, there were all kinds of issues related to safety and evacuation procedures that could at least get a plaintiffs lawyer into court. Worse, the collapse of the towers had resulted in lots of damage and even some death on the sidelines, and suits against the person responsible for these buildings seemed definite. Now Silverstein, having heard that the airlines were about to have their liability capped at the amount they were insured for, wanted the same thing.

Silverstein had contributed to Schumer in the past, and in October he and his wife would make an additional $2,000 contribution to his next election, which was three years away. Schumer was known in the Senate as a voracious fund-raiser, and Silverstein was only one of thousands of his contributors, just as the airline lobbyists—who also gave heavily to Democrats, it should be noted—represented only a fraction of the money taken in by DeLay and his Republican colleagues. Nonetheless, Schumer had almost computer-like personal recall of his contributors, which means that Silverstein was, at the least, a special constituent.

Silverstein also had a compelling argument related to Schumer's larger constituency. If all of his money, including the billions he stood to get from his insurance companies, were tied up fighting and paying off lawsuits, Silverstein would have no money to rebuild Ground Zero. Besides, if a fund was now being established to compensate the victims, why discourage them from going into the fund by allowing them to sue Silverstein instead?

The argument made sense. But Schumer, calling from outside the Hastert conference room, had to report to Silverstein that they were not going to get a liability cap added onto this bill. Daschle had said that loading the bill down with anything else was impossible.

They'd have plenty of other opportunities, the New York senator added. Don't worry.

As the Hastert meeting was breaking up at about 3:00 A.M., Ali Erikenoglu was still trying to get to sleep. He had not yet calmed down from the visitors who had left just after midnight.

At about 11:00 P.M., he had heard rustling in the bushes below the bedroom window in the small three-family house he owns in Paterson, New Jersey. Leaving his wife, he got up, leaned out the window, and saw four men in suits with flashlights rifling through his backyard and garbage. After asking the men what they wanted, they identified themselves as the FBI and asked to come in.

As the four agents entered his second-floor apartment, Erikenoglu turned and asked, "Gentlemen, would you mind terribly removing your shoes?" There was silence for about ten seconds, and then one of them stared at him and said, "That's not gonna happen." They came into his living room and onto a carpet that, in deference to Erikenoglu's Muslim tradition, had not been walked on with shoes in the ten years he had occupied the home and prayed on it.

"I felt violated," Erikenoglu remembers. "I even reminded them that President Bush had taken his shoes off when he had visited a mosque a few days before. But there was just silence. That's when things turned hostile."

Change his name to Al Erikson and Erikenoglu's story of that night becomes hard to fathom. A graduate of Rutgers University, he was a forty-year-old industrial electrician. He was born in the United States (his parents were born in Turkey), went to the local Catholic high school, and married an Irishwoman. Soft spoken, with dark hair and glasses, he looked like the quintessential average American. Except for a speeding ticket when he was a teenager, Erikenoglu says, he had never before even had a conversation with a police officer, let alone been in trouble with the law.

This was not a pleasant conversation. While two agents roamed the apartment, examining books and videos on his shelves, looking at papers on his dining room table, the two more senior-looking agents made him produce his license, his passport, and his wife's passport (she was still in bed), then asked a series of questions about his political beliefs, how often he prayed, what tourist sites he had visited, and how often he had traveled abroad. They demanded to know "what kind of American are you" and "what is it about your religion that allows people like these terrorists to do what they did." (To which he answered, "Assuming you gentlemen are all Christian, what is it about your religion that allowed Timothy McVeigh to do what he did?")

The agents finally told Erikenoglu that they were there because someone from "one of the places where you work" had called and said that after American naval officers on the USS *Cole* had been killed by a terrorist bomb, he had expressed sympathy for the terrorists. They wouldn't say who had called, or even if the person had given his name to them.

Erikenoglu told them that that was ridiculous, that he had never said anything like that. At that point his mouth went dry. He was scared.

The agents asked him whom he had voted for in the last election. He complained that this was like McCarthyism. Some anonymous person had called, or maybe he didn't call and maybe it was just because he had a Middle Eastern name. Then there's the knock on the door, asking whom you voted for.

After taking down all of Erikenoglu's answers (if you care, he voted for Ralph Nader, which he says elicited an "Oh" from his interrogators) and collecting his home, office, and cell phone numbers, the agents left. On the way out, one of them promised that they would be back to take him in if any of his answers turned out to be untruthful, or if the phone numbers turned up any calls to or from terrorists.

They never came back.

But by Friday afternoon, this rousting of an American citizen—scary and outrageous though it was—was on its way to being turned into something more positive. Erikenoglu, who was active in establishing the local mosque, is well known and respected in Paterson's large Muslim community. So the story of his FBI interrogation spread quickly, and the resulting resentment got back to the FBI officials in Newark, who checked with the agents and found that Erikengolu's account was completely true.

Although the agents had simply been carrying out Attorney General Ashcroft's dragnet, what happened next would have surprised Ashcroft had he known about it. The Newark FBI officials, who had worked hard in recent years to build bridges to the large Muslim community in their area, were quietly appalled by the orders coming from Ashcroft in Washington to treat every call about a Muslim like a smoking gun. Even their field agents didn't like what they were doing. Now they had all seen one of the results. Indeed, one of the field agents would later say that he had felt awful walking across Erikenoglu's carpet and asking him all those political questions, and he felt worse once he came to appreciate the significance of the carpet and that his suspect was "as law-abiding an American citizen as I am. . . . I'm an educated person, not some bigoted Southern sheriff from the 1960s."

Within days, the FBI brass in Newark would be talking with Sohail Mohammed—a Paterson lawyer who was a friend of Erikenoglu's and had complained publicly when he learned the story of his interrogation—about setting up sensitivity training sessions for their agents so that these kinds of incidents could not happen again, and that, if anything, the law-abiding Muslim community would cooperate in the search for terrorists.

By Friday afternoon, the volunteer management consultants from McKinsey working on the September 11th Fund were ready to present what they said was a tentative sketch of the issues that the United Way and New York Community Trust would have to face now that they were over the first hurdle of dispensing some of their money. Actually, it was a long, savvy analysis of the decisions that lay ahead, one that prepared the fund to think in a way that would consistently elude the Red Cross. Everything from continuing with some forms of emergency disaster relief to the immediate victims, to supporting the economic recovery of workers displaced by the attacks, to providing long-term psychological aid to the victims, to helping other nonprofit organizations continue with their work, to "monitoring and mitigating the environmental impacts of the disaster" was bullet-pointed and matched with a staff team that would be responsible for that area, as well as with a list of organizations that might receive grants to achieve those goals.

Later that evening George Clooney, who had been sleeping in the September 11th Fund telethon studio for two nights while he helped to build the set, write cue cards, and otherwise get ready for the 9:00 P.M. broadcast, was under a desk trying to help hook up the phones. At about five to nine, only the connection to Whoopi Goldberg's phone was working. The phones for the other stars arrayed at the celebrity table were still dead. (They would be fixed within a half hour.) "If they're not working when we go on, pick them up and fake it for a few minutes," Clooney told the actors. "The calls will still come into the call center and we'll get the money, only there won't be anyone reaching you guys for a while."

"Fake it?" Kurt Russell asked. "How can I do that?"

"You're a fucking actor," Clooney whispered. "Figure it out, for Christ's sake!"

Bill O'Reilly, the host of Fox News's phenomenally successful prime-time talk show *The O'Reilly Factor*, was often accosted by neighbors, pushing him to pursue some common man's claim that the powers that be are screwing up. O'Reilly took pride in the fact that he listened, and that much of what he heard made it onto his show.

By midweek two of those neighbors in the town on Long Island where he lives—which, he says, was home to twenty-nine September 11 victims—had told O'Reilly that they were September 11 widows and were having trouble with the Red Cross and all those other funds that had sprung up. The charities were raising millions, they told him, but so far they were getting nothing but a runaround when they called seeking help. They pleaded with him to do something on his show about it.

So at 8:00 Friday night O'Reilly went on the air with a segment about where the money was going. He introduced the topic by noting that *America: A Tribute to Heroes*—the telethon that Clooney and the September 11th Fund were involved in—was airing later that evening. Declaring that he trusted the Red Cross, because "they know how to handle that money," O'Reilly said that he was worried about other groups such as the one running the telethon. "They're going to have all this money pour in," he intoned, "and there's really nobody watching the money." Somebody needs to watch all those charities to make sure they are honest, responsive, and coordinated, he concluded.

"I saw that show, and realized that O'Reilly was the only person speaking for us," Michael Cartier recalls.

It was the beginning of a crusade.

## Saturday, September 22, 2001

The 11:00 memorial service for Michael Simon at St. Mary's Roman Catholic Church in Closter, New Jersey, featured seven eulogies, two scripture readers, five gift bearers, and no empty seats. Simon, who had celebrated his fortieth birthday in late July, had coached four different teams for the local kids in just the fall season. Many of them and their parents were there, along with hundreds of neighbors and friends. His brother eulogized Michael as hotly competitive when it came to his own athletics—he'd been a star hockey and lacrosse player and had a 100-mile-an-hour tennis serve—but also praised him as the coach who instructed, and played, every kid equally. Everyone else seemed to be whispering a variation on the same theme. It was what you usually heard at funerals, only this time the passion was unusual: Michael Simon—doting father, manic athlete, caring coach, up-and-coming

Cantor Fitzgerald trader, outgoing community do-gooder, and the perfect match for Eileen's always-on sense of humor—was a really great guy. The recessional hymns were "America the Beautiful" and "God Bless America." Almost all of the 1,200 mourners left sobbing.

Although it was eleven days since the attacks, some of Eileen Simon's friends had told her that she was having the service too soon, that she should hold out hope for a miracle. Eileen had lost hope within minutes of the plane having hit Michael's office tower. When her husband's family had resigned themselves to Michael's fate the weekend before, they had agreed to hold the service today.

Among other September 11 families, that kind of consensus was harder to come by. There were many families where the wife wanted a service and the in-laws insisted on waiting, or vice versa. In one instance, involving a widow with five children, who lived near Eileen and would become one of her best friends in the months to come, the wife refused for nearly two months to acknowledge her husband's death. And when she finally agreed to have a memorial service, she stood at the doorway afterward and told friends consoling her that she didn't understand why they were even having the service, because her husband was surely still alive.

Eileen Simon didn't have to suffer through that kind of family tension, but she did have a huge problem at home: the state of her children. As far as she knew, Eileen was not one of the many Cantor Fitzgerald widows whose husbands, tortured by the fire baking under them, had jumped from the North Tower in groups, holding hands. At least she hadn't heard about Michael doing so from any of the others who had been in phone contact with their husbands just before they died. In any event, she preferred not to think about that. Certain that her husband's body was now not likely to be found, she decided to frame a story of Michael's death for her children that was as unhorrible as possible, and that would explain the absence of a body in a positive way. Their father had instantly suffocated from the fumes, then turned into ash from the exploding fire, she had told them. And the ash had floated up to heaven. There was no body to be found—and no pain for their father.

Nonetheless, all three of the children—Brittany, twelve; Michael Jr., or MJ, ten; and Tyler, five—were still in awful shape. They had been comforted by the hundreds of cards they had received, and by the constant visits from friends who had flocked to the house every day. "It was so good having them there," Brittany recalls. But they all still insisted on sleeping in Eileen's bed, where they often awoke with nightmares. They continued to be so eager to clutch, smell, or wear their father's unlaundered shirts that Eileen had been unable to empty his hamper. As for Eileen, she hadn't slept more than an hour straight since the 11th. She was afraid to fall asleep and dream about the jet hitting the tower.

After the service, the Simons' favorite local restaurant—an Italian place about a quarter of a mile from their house that had been converted from a large home—hosted a reception. The owner refused to charge Eileen a penny. It was one of many meals to which Simon and her family would be treated. Beginning earlier in the week, a woman who lived next door to Eileen had come over to tell her that a few friends in the neighborhood had formed a group that wanted to ease her burden. So, they were going to take turns for a while bringing her and the kids a home-cooked, hot dinner every other night. What Simon didn't know was that the group would soon become a network of sixty-six women throughout the area. She'd be getting those dinners delivered from one of their kitchens by 6:00 every other night until May, when she finally asked them to stop.

Chuck Schumer tells a story from his days as a freshman at Harvard that he says explains how he ended up going into politics. The son of a Brooklyn exterminator, Schumer had started college thinking he was going to be a scientist. One night he was working late in a Harvard lab trying to complete a chemistry experiment. He kept concocting different mixes in the test tube, but nothing happened. Finally, at about 3:00 or 4:00 in the morning he got it right, and whatever it was in the test tube turned the magic color. Schumer was thrilled; this was a real breakthrough. Except that when he looked around to show someone what he had accomplished, there was no one there. That moment, looking around that empty chem lab for someone's—anyone's— approval, was an epiphany. He realized that he wanted to get attention when he succeeded, that the loneliness of winning in the lab wasn't for him. It was just not rewarding enough. And because he had grown up with a father who had been so tormented by his work that Schumer's abiding memory is of his dad pacing the floor at 4:00 A.M. worrying about making the rent, Schumer was determined to build a life doing something he really liked. That, he says, is when he began to think about politics.

Colleagues in the House and Senate would not be surprised to hear that Schumer liked the attention that political life offered. After all, then Senate Republican Leader Bob Dole was famously quoted as having said that the most dangerous place in Washington is between Schumer and a television camera.

In that sense, it should have been no surprise that Schumer's account of the battle to pass the victims compensation bill the day before, in a press release issued by his office Saturday, September 22, began: "Families of the World Trade Center attacks will not be forgotten by the federal government, U.S. Senator Charles E. Schumer said today after inserting a provision in the airline bailout bill just passed by the Senate that guarantees full financial compensation to the families of the victims of the attacks."

Of course, the victims fund didn't guarantee "full financial compensation," whatever that means, to anyone. Nor, of course, had Schumer, who had been kept out of the key bargaining session, created the fund, much less inserted it into the legislation. To be sure, the rest of the press release backtracked a bit and gave credit to other, more senior senators such as Daschle. And Schumer, as well as Hillary Clinton, had certainly played a pivotal role making sure the Democrats had not wavered on the fund. But the overheated language of the press release said a lot about Schumer: Even when he did a good job and played a key role, he seemed unable to resist the kind of overreaching for credit that offended those whose help he needed. How well he would hold that urge in check would determine how effective he would be in the months ahead.

By Saturday morning, most of the 9,000 residents of the buildings in Battery Park City—a complex of apartment houses separated from Ground Zero by a now cratered six-lane roadway called West Street—had returned home. Some picked up whatever belongings they could carry, and left, never to come back. Others stayed and tried to put their homes back together, hoping that vacuum cleaners, mops, and other conventional household cleaning tools would somehow erase the dust—if that's what one could call the ash produced by the incineration of two 110-story skyscrapers, all of their interior walls, ceiling tiles, and carpeting, plus 40,000 or 50,000 computer screens, hard drives, desks, chairs, telephones, and whatever else was across the street, not to mention a reported 5,000 or 6,000 people. Depending on how close each Battery Park City building was to the Trade Center, and on whether the residents had left a window open that morning to catch the breeze off the lower Hudson (or on whether some projectile from the Trade Center had pierced a window or a wall), the fine-grained debris was a quarter-inch to several inches thick. No apartment, no matter how tightly the windows were shut or how far away, was spared.

Who knew what was in that dust? How toxic it was? And what about the air that lingered over wreckage across West Street that was still on fire, and, in fact, would be burning on and off into December?

Whether people stayed or not depended not simply on the actual damage, but on their overall outlook. Some, even in the most battered buildings, wanted to dig in and reclaim their homes. Others, whose apartments were dusted the least, were so horrified to be anywhere near Ground Zero that they never looked back. Sure, circumstances played a role; the mother of two who had seen an arm land near her in her toddler's playground was a goner, even if her apartment was far less damaged than that of the freelance writer who'd already gone to work that morning. But some of the differences were so personal, so emotional that they were unexplainable and surely not debatable as being right or wrong, courageous or weak-kneed.

All of which made the attendant legal issues a nightmare, or a feast, for the lawyers. Basic landlord-tenant law says you can stop paying your rent (and move and get your rent deposit back) if your apartment becomes uninhabitable. That's clear enough if the building burns down. But what if you think it's unlivable because you get nightmares being there? Or because the transportation system that you relied on to get to and from work has been knocked out? Or because you're afraid the air outside is unsafe, even though it's been checked and declared safe by government authorities (whom you don't trust)? Or because there's so much noise and light from the cleanup going on day and night across the way? Or because so many of your friends, including the ones with kids who played with your kids, moved out? Or because there's no longer anyplace to buy groceries?

The manager of one of the Battery Park properties explains, "We gave people rent abatements until we could clean up their apartments and assure them that the air was okay. But we did not see it as our responsibility to let people out of their leases because the neighborhood was no longer as good as it was. It's a lousy thing, but why should we be on the hook for that? Something terrible happened. But does that mean you sue your landlord, or break your lease?"

Yet the urge to get someone, preferably someone like a landlord with a presumably deep pocket, on the hook for all the collateral damage of September 11 seemed like it would be unstoppable—and likely to eat away at any sense of common cause that the country needed. By September 10, America had become a place where it seemed that no crime, no accident, even no piece of simple bad luck was not accompanied by an effort by the luckless to sue someone. And so by Saturday, the print and online legal trade publications in New York and around the country were full of stories about how everybody was likely to be suing everybody in the September 12 era, as all kinds of unprecedented legal questions got fought out. "The Tort Lawyers: Preparing for Years of Litigation," proclaimed the *New York Law Journal* earlier in the week.

The landlord-tenant issues in Battery Park City were illustrative and particularly poignant; these were, after all, people's homes. But they were hardly the center of the legal action or the big money. The real speculation about litigation centered on who would be able to collect for death, injury, physical destruction, and business losses estimated to be over $50 billion from a cast of defendants that included the airlines; the owners, managers, architects, and designers of the World Trade Center; the companies that provide the people who screen passengers getting onto planes; the Port Authority, whose police had supposedly told people they were safe in the second Trade Center tower just before it got hit; the federal government agencies that had allowed the hijackers into the country; Boeing, which had made airlines with cockpit doors that apparently were not secure enough; and the terrorists, or the countries that might have financed the terrorists. Then there was the question of who—besides the passengers and property owners who were directly damaged—could sue. Surely, businesses near the Trade Center had a great case for damages, but what about a hotel in San Francisco, hurt by the decline in air travel? Or a restaurant near the Washington Monument, whose business was hurt because tourists were afraid to go there? In a country where fat people can find a lawyer to sue McDonald's (or maybe it's the lawyer who finds the fat people), why would any of these suits be far-fetched?

Saturday morning, as he caught up on his newspapers while listening to opera and puffing a cigar in the acoustically wallpapered music room of his Bethesda, Maryland, home, Kenneth Feinberg had a special reason to be intrigued by the prospect of the September 12 era becoming the ultimate litigation meltdown. In the perennial debate over America's standing as the world's litigation capital—that it helps deter wrongdoing and repay those wronged, or that it is a cynical attempt to put blame where it doesn't belong while providing a bonanza for lawyers—Feinberg had established himself as the practitioner of a third way. Since the mid-1980s, Feinberg, who had been bald for at least a decade but otherwise looked younger than his fifty-five years, had been mediating cases that would otherwise be decided by juries. He was good at it, so good, in fact, that in 1993 he'd started his own law firm in Washington that did nothing but mediate and arbitrate—a specialty called alternative dispute resolution.

Now, as Feinberg read his *Washington Post* and *New York Times,* he noticed something that he hadn't heard about. When Congress had passed that airline bailout bill early Friday morning (boy, those airline lobbyists are good, the former Senate staffer marveled), they'd inserted a provision calling for a compensation fund for all the victims, along with a Special Master to administer it. He read on. This Special Master would have unlimited power to make fair rewards to all the victims. He'd first have to write rules and regulations that would be a roadmap for the awards. Victims could then opt into the fund, or decide instead to try their luck in court.

That job was made for him, Feinberg thought. It would be the culmination of everything he had done. He, more than anyone, understood the awful calculus involved in putting a price on human suffering. He, more than anyone, understood the competing dynamics of treating victims individually and with compassion, yet still dealing with the limits of resources and the problem of putting a higher price on one person's suffering over another's. Who better to fashion the rules of this trailblazing new fund and administer them? This was the ultimate in alternative dispute resolution. Plus it was a chance to do something related to September 11. A chance to make history. To be in on the action.

He had to get that job.

Lots of people have employment fantasies when reading about some new power post in the newspaper. Feinberg had more going for him than the average guy. He had gotten into the business of alternative dispute resolution in 1984, when a federal judge gave him the job of mediating the cases having to do with Agent Orange, the defoliant used in Vietnam. Feinberg's challenge was to figure out a way to settle thousands of cases of soldiers who were suing the manufacturers of the defoliant. (As Feinberg contemplated the September 11 victims fund legislation on Saturday morning, he had no idea that the Agent Orange settlement fund had been used the day before by congressional staffers as the template for that legislation.) Feinberg had finished his Agent Orange assignment in less than two months, and both sides thought he had done a great job.

One of the people with whom he worked on Agent Orange was a Veterans Administration official named Chuck Hagel, a Vietnam veteran. Feinberg and Hagel had since become good friends. And Hagel was now the senior Republican senator from Nebraska.

Feinberg figured it was worth a call.

"Chuck, I've been reading about this Special Master," Feinberg said. "I would be perfect for it."

"I know, I was just thinking the same thing," Hagel replied.

Feinberg was his typical breathless, immodest self—reminding Hagel, who

did not need to be reminded, that he'd done settlements not only in Agent
Orange, but in asbestos, the Dalkon Shield, breast implants, the fight over the
Zapruder film of the Kennedy assassination. "I'll do this for free. I just want
to do it."

"Leave it to me," Hagel said, cutting him off. "I'll call Ashcroft."

Then the two friends turned to the problem they knew they would have
with Ashcroft and the White House. It was a huge problem.

Feinberg wasn't just some lawyer who had done some good mediating and
was liked by the veterans. He was a Democrat. And he wasn't just any Democrat. He was a Kennedy man, as in Edward M. Kennedy, the senior Massachusetts senator and liberal warhorse. Before going out to practice law (and
ending up doing cases like Agent Orange), Feinberg had worked for Kennedy
on Capitol Hill for five years when Kennedy had chaired the Senate Judiciary
Committee. It was not a perfunctory attachment: Feinberg's job was a senior,
high-profile position, and he is still friends with Kennedy. He even has a
Massachusetts accent from his childhood growing up as the son of a tire
salesman in Brockton.

"I'll tell him about Kennedy," Hagel said, meaning that he would warn
Ashcroft and reassure him about Feinberg's Kennedy connection. "You just
make sure Teddy knows. . . . And make sure Hatch is on board," Feinberg's
new Republican rabbi added, referring to the Senate Judiciary Committee's
senior Republican, Orrin Hatch, whom Feinberg had also befriended when
he had worked for Kennedy.

Feinberg called Kennedy. He couldn't reach Hatch, so he faxed him a
note. And then he waited and told his wife, Diane, what he was trying to
pull off.


Sal Iacono also spent Saturday thinking about his future.

Sal's wife, Franca, and his two sons and daughter, had wanted him to
retire after they'd seen how he looked when he had returned home to Staten
Island on Monday from his nearly demolished shoe repair shop. He was in tears
and so furious over the destruction and the theft from the cash register that they
feared he'd have a heart attack and die right in front of them. Going back to that
place to see all that again and trying to deal with it just didn't seem worth it.

Sal resisted. He wanted to go back, he had said. You don't just quit something after twenty-five years.

But while he talked about going back, he didn't behave like a man who still
had the fight in him, far from it. When he came home that Monday, he was a

different person, nothing like the bouncy, gleam-in-the-eye craftsman whose shop was like an old-style politician's clubhouse, where he delighted his customers with promises to perform magic on their leather goods. He stayed in bed late, then moped around the house, saying little. His friend Stephen Johnson (the man who had fled with him from the store on the 11th) had never heard Sal sound the way he sounded when he had telephoned to check on him a few times that week. The cheerful, confident Sole Man seemed depressed, almost suicidal.

Sal remembers his stomach tightening that week as he had visions again and again of the buildings crashing around him and people running through his store "like they were running from the bulls." He remembers being scared, afraid to go back, and knowing that he had nothing to go back to. He felt, he says, "like a beaten dog."

Yet now, two Saturday mornings after the attack, something seemed to change. "I guess I just got tired of being sad," is the way Sal would explain it months later. "And tired of hanging around. It just wasn't like me. I don't like to quit."

Saturday afternoon, Sal told Johnson he was thinking about trying to reopen, and that he'd even done some calculations of what he would need. Johnson told him maybe there would be some government aid, and surely some insurance. Sal said he knew he had some insurance but wasn't sure how much, or what it would cover, but that he was prepared to take $20,000 out of a savings account.

"I'm too young to retire," Sal, who was sixty-seven, told his wife. "And I just don't want to quit. I want to try to go back. You just don't quit without a fight." Sal decided that next week he'd return to the store and start getting estimates for rebuilding.


Herbert Wachtell was two years older than Sal, but he never had to be coaxed into the next battle. Wachtell was the senior partner of a group of about 180 lawyers called Wachtell, Lipton, Rosen & Katz, which had long been numbered first among *The American Lawyer* magazine's ranking of the richest law businesses.*

By Saturday, Wachtell and the three younger partners and ten associates he already had working on Larry Silverstein's case against the insurance com-

---

*Wachtell's firm has represented the author, successfully, in the past, and Wachtell's partner Martin Lipton is a close friend of the author.

panies (soon he'd have more than thirty lawyers working on it) had digested all the bad news in the various documents related to how Silverstein and his company had bought insurance for the Trade Center. To be sure, everything was clouded by the fact that no formal documents had been signed; Silverstein had taken over the Trade Center only six weeks before, and the final documents for the insurance had not been finished. But a deal memo using his broker's policy had been circulated and seemingly agreed to. The wording of that policy, referred to in the deal memo, was a huge problem.

The group of insurance companies that had seemingly agreed in the deal memo to insure the Trade Center (no insurer ever insured something this big by itself) used a definition of occurrence drafted by Silverstein's own broker, which read as follows:

> *"Occurrence" shall mean all losses or damages that are attributable directly or indirectly to one cause or to one series of similar causes. All such losses will be added together and the total amount of such losses will be treated as one occurrence irrespective of the period of time or area over which such losses occur.*

The reason the person buying the insurance—in this case, Silverstein through his broker—would normally have wanted occurrence defined so broadly is understandable to anyone who has ever bought insurance and had the insurance company invoke the deductible when there is a loss covered by the policy. Suppose you have theft insurance and it has a $500 deductible. If your house is broken into and $3,000 worth of stereo equipment is taken, the insurance company would pay $2,500, because it would deduct $500 (the deductible) from the $3,000 claim. But suppose on his way out, the thief also breaks into your garage and takes a $500 bicycle. If the insurance company can call the garage theft a separate "occurrence," then you still end up with just the $2,500, because you have $3,500 worth of loss but two separate $500 deductibles. But if it's one "occurrence" (after all, it's the same burglar and the same premises), then you get $3,000, because the $500 is only deducted once.

In Silverstein's case the deductible was a cool $1 million, so his broker had fought for as broad a definition of occurrence as possible. After all, who thought the Trade Center could ever be completely destroyed? What was more likely was a flood or fire that would not come anywhere near the $3.55 billion total loss limit. In that case, it would be critically important that only one deductible (of $1 million) be applied. Now, however, all of that logic threatened to kill Silverstein's claim that the destruction of the Trade Center was two occurrences and, therefore, worth two payouts.

But there was a sliver of good news, something that at least gave Wachtell and his team an argument that the two planes hitting the two buildings could be counted as two occurrences. If it worked, Silverstein could get two times the $3.55 billion per occurrence limit on the policy. It turned out that one of the insurers among the group of companies insuring Silverstein—Travelers—had come into the deal at the last minute, in late July of 2001. And documents that Wachtell and his team found showed that Travelers had pushed to have its own insurance form apply to the deal, not the form used by the Silverstein brokers—and *its* form did not define occurrence at all. With no definition, whether the September 11 attacks had been one or two occurrences was open to dispute.

It wasn't a slam dunk for Silverstein, far from it. In fact, precedents from prior case law, in which there had been this kind of dispute over an occurrence clause where occurrence had not been defined, seemed to give Wachtell maybe a 40 percent chance of prevailing. After all, this had been one plot hatched by one group, against a Trade Center that had two towers but one common electrical and air-conditioning system and one common insurance policy. Also, the policy called for a $3.55 billion payout in the event of a total loss. How could someone collect twice on a total loss of the same insured property?

What was more important, though, was that Silverstein's own brokers had not yet agreed to the Travelers form for even the Travelers portion of the insurance, much less agreed or even had a discussion about the Travelers form being used for the rest of the insurance. Travelers, after all, was a relatively minor player among the Trade Center insurers; its last-minute entrance into the group had only been for an amount covering about 3 percent of the overall insurance.

But at least the Travelers form gave Wachtell an argument. So all during the week, lawyers at Wachtell's firm had pushed Silverstein's insurance people to call Travelers, and get them to issue their policy formally to Silverstein.

Miraculously, before the Travelers lawyers knew what had happened, the lower-level Travelers people normally in charge of writing up policies had fallen into the trap. So now there was one policy that didn't have that broad definition of occurrence—albeit a policy formally issued after the Trade Center's collapse and covering only 3 percent of the $3.55 billion in insurance.

This slender thread—using the Travelers policy to attempt to reject the Silverstein broker's own broad definition of occurrence as supplied to and negotiated with all the other insurers—was strengthened by the fact that, again, because the deal by which Silverstein had purchased the right to lease all the space and manage the Trade Center had only closed in late July, the formal insurance contracts had not been signed by the rest of the insurers. Instead, these insurers and Silverstein's broker had exchanged e-mail or verbal messages signaling their agreement to those less formal deal memos, called binders. But attached to, or referred to, in the binders was the Silverstein broker's policy form, which had that elaborate definition of occurrence that clearly made September 11 one occurrence. Industry custom was that these binders were binding (that's how they got the name) until a formal insurance contract was written and signed. Therefore, this should have made that broader definition of occurrence binding.

Still, it wasn't a formal, signed contract.

We can argue that nothing was clear, Wachtell assured Silverstein. Ignoring the Silverstein broker's own insurance policy occurrence definition, they'd simply frame the issue as a confused situation, with Travelers's policy going one way and some of the others arguably going the other way. That makes this the kind of case that should be settled, they would conclude, maybe for something between $3.55 billion (one occurrence) and $7.1 billion (two occurrences).

If pushing for an extra $3.55 billion this way in the face of a clear definition that said that September 11 was one occurrence seems preposterous, it wasn't to Herb Wachtell. He was not only a genius when it came to pouring everything possible into an argument, he was also a genius at doing it with feeling—with all the indignation of someone who's been unconscionably wronged by the guy on the other side. Two of the lawyers on his side would later agree that with Wachtell, a leprechaun-looking man who still had his red hair, it was too good an act to be an act. In certain cases, and this was clearly one, he transformed himself into someone who really believed, so much so that within two weeks he bought expensive photos of the old New York skyline with the old Trade Center to hang in his team's conference rooms as a reminder of their mission.

It was a mission that Silverstein was ready to lead. By now he had already hired New York's premier public relations firm to push the notion that this issue of two occurrences versus one was a brain teaser fit for a law school exam, and as such it should be compromised, especially in the wake of a tragedy like September 11. Silverstein was eagerly telling friends that the combination of Wachtell's team and the PR people was going to get all the billions he needed to give New York the rebuilding of Ground Zero that the city deserved.

For Silverstein, who was seventy, this was a new role. Until his purchase of the Trade Center lease, he had had a reputation as a hard-nosed developer and manager of mostly grade-B buildings. A slight, tense-looking man whose white hair seemed poorly dyed, Silverstein was a man whose pride had until now extended beyond the bottom line only insofar as he had paid enough to have pastels painted of these mostly mundane buildings that made them look marginally better when the halo-like renderings were hung in the conference room at his corporate headquarters (housed in another mundane building on lower Fifth Avenue that he had owned, but recently sold). Now, Silverstein took on the persona of the man who was going to rebuild New York back to its glory, a mission that was not going to be thwarted by a bunch of penny-pinching, between-the-lines-reading insurance companies. Like his friend Wachtell, he, too, seemed to believe it.

Dean O'Hare, the CEO of Chubb insurance (which would end up being one of the companies litigating against Silverstein), had accompanied several other insurance executives to the White House to meet with President Bush on Friday. It had started out as a feel-good session, with the President thanking the insurers for having stepped up to the plate so quickly (O'Hare had been the first) to declare that they would not use the act of war exclusion to avoid paying what now looked to be as much as $50 billion in property damage, workers' compensation, and life insurance claims resulting from the attacks. But the meeting had turned serious when one of the executives explained to the President that while the insurers were paying for this attack, they couldn't afford to pay for the next one. It wasn't that they would welsh on any policies. Rather, it was that they wouldn't and couldn't sell policies any longer that insured against terrorist attacks.

Insurers are the right-lane drivers of the economy. While it seems as if they are insuring everyone else against risk, they actually hate risk and won't knowingly sell insurance if their actuaries—the people with the eyeshades and sharp pencils who quantify risk—can't calculate the actual likelihood of that risk, and the likelihood of a profit on every type of insurance they sell. September 11 had been a wake-up call; they could not calculate the risk of terrorism and, therefore, would no longer insure against it.

In fact, it wasn't a matter of their choice. For *their* reinsurers had already sent them notice that by the end of the year they would no longer insure against terrorism.

Reinsurers are the companies from whom insurers buy policies to spread their own risk. For example, if Chubb insures a building for $200 million, it might buy a $150 million policy on the same building from a reinsurer. But within a few days of the attacks, O'Hare and the other CEOs had told the President at the Friday meeting, the reinsurers had told them they were getting out of the business of reinsuring against something they had no way of quantifying.

If the marketplace can't deal with terrorism insurance, then the federal government somehow has to backstop us on this, the CEOs had told the President. This was not like the airline bailout, they added. The insurance companies were not looking for any kind of bailout. They were paying all the claims, with no complaints. But they were also going to have to get out of the business of insuring against terrorism. The free market can't do it.

So now at the White House on Saturday, deputy chief of staff Bolten and his Domestic Consequences Principals Group were trying to sort out the new problem of terrorism insurance, or its looming disappearance. Again, the key players, in addition to Bolten, were economics czar Lindsey and treasury undersecretary Fisher. All were sympathetic; this seemed to be a classic example of a situation where government had a role because the marketplace couldn't work to calculate costs and prices. And they appreciated that although the problem seemed abstract, almost clinical, it had tangible, frightening repercussions. For example, most office building construction is financed with mortgages. The banks that lend money for those mortgages demand that the buildings be adequately insured so that if something happens to the building the bank holding the mortgage can get the insurance proceeds.

Thus, no terrorism insurance might mean no new buildings. As for buildings already built, if, say, the Sears Tower in Chicago lost its full insurance protection, it might be in default of its mortgage, which might cause the mortgage holder to take the building back from its owners, or, as would be more likely, to raise its interest rates to account for the greater risk, which in turn might cause the building to have to raise rents. If a snack bar near an icon like the White House lost its insurance coverage or got soaked with expensive premiums, it might have to close. It all meant a huge potential drag on the economy—but, as this paragraph illustrates, as threats go it would be hard to articulate and explain to Congress and the American people in a way that would get enough people worked up enough to push the government to fix the problem. After all, who gets excited about insurance?


On Saturday afternoon, Attorney General Ashcroft announced that 352 people had been arrested or otherwise detained in the investigation of the attacks.

It seemed like progress was being made. After all, who knew that among those detained, without a hearing or a lawyer, was someone with a Muslim name and an expired visa who made the mistake of reserving a plane ticket online using a computer at the same Kinko's that one of the hijackers had patronized? Or that another detainee was a Muslim who had had the bad luck to have been on line at the same Florida motor vehicle office where another of the hijackers had gotten a license? (The detainee's license was legitimate, but he was held for having a job while only having a tourist visa.) Like all the immigrants detained, he was not given a lawyer. People held for immigration violations are not entitled to lawyers for free the way criminal defendants are; they can hire one if they can afford it and can find one, and in most cases those held were not given the opportunity to call a lawyer. Moreover, although they would be entitled to hearings in front of an INS judge within four days of their arrest, Ashcroft had directed that these INS judges close all these hearings to everyone except the participants, an unprecedented directive that would keep secret who was being held and why. He could do that because INS judges work for the Justice Department. They are not independent.

It was all part of a dragnet that if it had had a code name fitting its focus, or lack thereof, would have been called "Operation Find and Hold the Muslims." There was little other rhyme or reason to it. If one of the terrorists had gone to Kinko's, then the FBI checked to see if anyone else with a Muslim-sounding name had been there. If a neighbor called about an Arab who appeared to spend a lot of time in his garage, why not check that out—and hold him, too, if there was something wrong with his immigration papers? There was little else the FBI could do. Despite the 1993 bombing of the Trade Center by Muslim terrorists and even arrests and convictions in 1996 in a plot to blow up the Holland Tunnel and other facilities, the bureau, according to a well-placed FBI official, had few undercover informants in the Muslim community in September of 2001.

So if this dragnet seemed harsh or blunderbuss, it was really because the feds had no better alternative. Besides, the mind-set of the people in Washington directing the dragnet needs to be remembered. They were sitting in a city where they knew that either the Capitol or the White House would have been destroyed, along with many of the people in it, by the plane that had crashed in Pennsylvania, but for the fact that it had taken off an hour late and, therefore, its passengers had had time to hear about what the hijackers of the three other planes had done. (This fourth plane was about to be shot down by the Air Force when the passengers acted.) On top of that, Ashcroft had been told by the President himself that he had to prevent another attack. And he and his people all knew that the attack had come from Muslim men who had lived quietly in their communities before unleashing their terror. So without any better leads, why not just question any such men you could, and hold those who it turned out were violating the terms of their visas?

The whole mix seemed like a recipe for a wholesale pullback on traditional American freedoms. After all, because terrorism involves enemies unleashing terrible destruction alone or in small groups after they have blended into communities across the country, it is a more insidious threat than that coming from a foreign power. It was bound to inspire more domestic insecurity—what's my neighbor really doing in that garage?—and more of a recalibration of the balance between individual freedom and collective security.

Many Democrats, especially those like Schumer who served on the Judiciary Committee, might have been inclined to scream about tactics that included holding people in secret and without lawyers—something that Romero and his ACLU staff now expected them to do. But they, too, were spooked by the attacks. Also, they were mollified by Justice Department briefings saying that the reason the men were being held secretly was that their mail, e-mails, and phone calls could be intercepted to see if any terrorists, not knowing they had been arrested, tried to make contact with them in furtherance of some new plot. And without being specific, Ashcroft would soon assure Schumer and the others that some important leads were being developed this way.


Between working on the transition with his Pennsylvania staff and accepting congratulatory calls from around the country, Tom Ridge spent Saturday and Sunday with two thick black looseleaf volumes that had been delivered to the governor's mansion Saturday morning. In less than a day, staffers in his office, working with lawyers at the Pennsylvania firm where his best friend was the senior partner, had assembled the books as a primer for Ridge's new job. The first volume—a tribute to the reach of the Internet and the ability to print pages upon pages of downloads on command—was a compendium of articles on everything having to do with homeland security. It was actually pretty good stuff, some of it deeper and more sophisticated than the commission reports (which Ridge had also been given).

The first piece—co-authored by James Loy, the Coast Guard commandant who would end up a central figure in Ridge's new constellation—was called "Meeting the Homeland Security Challenge," and began as follows: "It wasn't supposed to be this way. The break-up of the Soviet Union and the global failure of expansionist Communism were supposed to usher in the Pax Americana."

The theoretical underpinning of all the various monographs, both in Ridge's looseleaf book and in the commission reports, was that society had gotten more fragile as both technology and globalization advanced. Better technology and a shrinking world had put destructive power that could threaten the United States in the hands of increasingly smaller clusters of people: from the major nation-states of the early and mid–twentieth century, to smaller countries in the latter part of the century, to individuals and groups of individuals—terrorists—in the new century. Because individual behavior is both more varied and more erratic than even that of nation-states run by madmen, the risks had multiplied exponentially, especially for a country that cherishes individual freedom and the right of individuals to be left alone and not spied on or searched.

Ridge's second thick black book was an almanac of the bureaucracies he would somehow have to penetrate to do his job. It was a description of all the government agencies having something to do with homeland security, or that should have something to do with it. Ridge used it to begin discussions that weekend with a kitchen cabinet, convened to help him figure out how to staff and organize his new office. Although he had no idea, as he browsed through it in the governor's mansion that weekend, what a true list of land mines, trap-doors, and black holes it actually was, he could already see that he'd probably want to divide things not just according to the agencies involved—the Coast Guard and INS, for example—but also according to functions, such as prevention on the one hand and response to disasters on the other. After all, the whole idea of his new job was to coordinate these functions among the multiple agencies that each thought they had primary responsibility for them.

# Tuesday, September 25, 2001

Since the 11th, Kevin McCabe had gotten several calls from the Coast Guard or Navy Intelligence people—a few even at night at his New Jersey home—warning of possible threats. The one he got at about 8:00 this morning from a Navy officer was unusually specific. A credible source (the Navy man provided no specifics) had said that a container shipped via Malaysia that had arrived on Monday night in the Red Hook port in Brooklyn (which was part of the overall New York seaport covered by McCabe's Customs inspectors) might be carrying a weapon of mass destruction.

McCabe quickly checked and found that the container had indeed arrived at Red Hook, but had already been sent by barge across to where he was in Elizabeth, New Jersey. It was now sitting among acres of other containers visible below from his window.

McCabe ordered that the container be hoisted onto a tractor trailer and moved to a far corner of the port.

When he and his men approached it, the radiation detectors they carry like cell phones on their holsters went off. McCabe's gut tightened, but he and the men didn't panic. The reading indicated a low radiation level, and McCabe and the men knew that lots of harmless items, including ceramic tiles or even people who've recently been to the dentist, can push the needle to that level, as will a container that had passed near a radiation field or had held materials in the past, such as clay, that had small levels of radiation. Still, it certainly wasn't a good sign. A real nuke hidden in a lead box might set off the detectors at that level, as would what's called a dirty bomb—a conventional bomb laced with small amounts of radioactive material that would be dispersed by the explosion. Was someone waiting somewhere with a remote detonator ready to set it off?

McCabe's men then brought a trace detector over to the container—the kind of machine increasingly seen at airports that checks for signs of explosives by rubbing a surface with a pad and then putting the pad into the machine for analysis. It registered nothing.

Next came a bomb dog, a Labrador that McCabe and his men trust as much as the trace detectors. The Lab didn't react.

Still, McCabe had no idea what was inside the container, and he was not inclined to find out just by opening it. Another piece of the Navy guy's intelligence report, such as it was, had been that the container might be booby-trapped to explode upon opening. So McCabe wanted to X-ray it with one of the giant VACIS machines he and his team used. The problem was that the two VACISes he had in Elizabeth couldn't be moved; the container would have to be moved to them, and they were in crowded sections of the port.

But there was a solution. One of the first new resources McCabe had gotten after September 11 was a mobile VACIS that had been shipped up to Elizabeth to help McCabe keep up with all the extra inspections he was now doing. It was small enough to be moved around on a truck.

The problem was that it was in Red Hook, the Brooklyn part of the port. And it was still rush hour, meaning that to get it from Brooklyn into the tunnel to Manhattan and then into the Holland Tunnel to McCabe in New Jersey could take hours. As it was, the New Jersey state police, who had also been told about the container scare, were thinking about closing the New Jersey Turnpike and Newark Airport because the container was so close to a tangle of high-traffic interchanges and overpasses approaching the airport and the Holland and Lincoln tunnels.

Stopping traffic could cause panic. Not stopping traffic could magnify a disaster. They needed to figure out what was in that container, fast.

McCabe asked the Port Authority police (which has jurisdiction at his port) to call the New York City police. A police escort was organized to move the wide-load truck carrying the mobile VACIS through the streets of Brooklyn and Manhattan and the Brooklyn Battery and Holland tunnels. McCabe was amazed when they got it there twenty-two minutes later.

McCabe had been told the container held textiles (plus whatever weapon might be hidden among them), so he knew he'd get a great VACIS picture because textiles have such uniform, and light, density. Sure enough, the picture was fabulous. There seemed to be nothing but textiles inside and, as one of the men put it, there was "nothing hinky" around the door handles indicating a booby trap.

McCabe still wasn't ready to relax. He told his men to drill holes in the top of the container and put a fiber optic scope inside so that they could have a look at the door before opening it. Only then did they pop the seal and open the container to find textiles. Only textiles.

As his men sounded the all-clear, McCabe looked around and suddenly felt dumb. A large portion of the troops and the entire security leadership of the largest port on the East Coast—Customs, Coast Guard, Port Authority, state police, local police—were standing there and had been there throughout the episode. What if there had been a bomb? Why hadn't anyone thought to establish a backup command center, with lots of the bosses, far off the site? We've got to learn to be smarter about this, he thought. This wasn't like looking for drugs, where finding something bad ended the problem.


At about 10:00 A.M., John Ashcroft took his seat at the witness table of the Senate Judiciary Committee. He was there to talk about the legislation he wanted passed easing restrictions on wiretaps and other investigatory tools— the same legislation that he had declared ten days ago needed to be passed within a week.

Those ten days had been quite a comedown. A week ago Sunday he'd been on the talk shows describing a bill that he hadn't even felt he needed to clear with the White House before proposing. It was as if he could get the staff to write it, chat it up a bit on television, and go to a Rose Garden signing ceremony a few days later. But now it was clear that that was not going to happen. Not only had the White House and congressional Republicans, including House Judiciary Committee Chairman Sensenbrenner, neutered the bill of some of its more ambitious thrusts—such as suspending habeas corpus—but the ACLU, yes the ACLU, had now thrown a monkey wrench into the whole process.

At the end of the prior week, ACLU director Romero and his top Washington lobbyist, Laura Murphy, had forged an alliance with conservative/libertarian Republicans in the House that had derailed Ashcroft's plan for legislation on the fly. Working with such unlikely allies as Bob Barr, the right-wing congressman from Georgia who had been the first member of Congress to call for President Clinton's impeachment, Romero and Murphy had forced Sensenbrenner's House Judiciary Committee to forgo rubber-stamping the Ashcroft bill. They'd gotten Barr and four other conservative Republicans on the Judiciary Committee to send Sensenbrenner a letter listing ten provisions of the bill that needed, the letter said, "significant further public debate." Many of the ten—such as allowing a wiretap to cover any telephone a person used, rather than a single phone number—seemed like commonsense changes meant to catch the law up with technology (in this case, people's use of multiple cell phones). But the conservatives and Romero's group didn't see it that way.

Another set of provisions—seven in all—was "unacceptable as written," the letter said. Among them were those allowing the feds to go to a judge in a specially designated national security court, and, after showing that the targeted person was an operative of a foreign terrorist organization and declaring that "a purpose" of the investigation was to obtain foreign intelligence or intelligence related to foreign terrorist organizations, get permission to break into the person's home and search the premises, without telling the suspect there has been a search. Terrorism was broadly defined. And showing that there was probable cause to believe the person had committed, or would commit, a crime, as is necessary in all other instances where a warrant from a judge is sought, was not necessary.

Another provision would allow the feds to get a court to order a phone company or Internet service provider to turn over the suspect's records. Or, they could secretly get a record of the suspected terrorist's library withdrawals or library Internet activity without any judicial involvement at all.

Other provisions the Barr group found unacceptable allowed the feds to detain noncitizens indefinitely, if they were declared by the Attorney General to be threats to national security, and to seize the assets of an organization suspected of providing financial support to terrorists before even a hearing, let alone a trial. And at any hearing that took place later to contest the seizures, the government would be allowed to use evidence submitted to a judge that the suspect might not be allowed to see.

A special court with looser requirements for warrants related to national security investigations targeting "foreign agents" had been established in 1978. Ashcroft was now proposing a profound expansion of what and whom that court could cover. It was based on the legitimate argument that in the September 12 era, a national security threat no longer meant Russian spies, but could mean people living quietly in their communities, who are not necessarily agents of a foreign country but instruments of a terrorist organization that had some foreign connection.

But to Ashcroft's opponents at the ACLU—and, now, on the Republican right in the Judiciary Committee—it was one thing to have a special court allow a shortcut around the Fourth Amendment's protections against unreasonable search and seizure if the target was a Russian who worked at the United Nations mission and was suspected of being a spy. It was something else to allow that shortcut to target a Muslim American who had worked for the last ten years at a pizza parlor in Paterson, New Jersey. Thus, the provisions that Barr and his colleagues found unacceptable cut to the core of what Ashcroft was trying to do.

By the end of the prior week, Sensenbrenner, although still smarting from Ashcroft's not having consulted him, had been mollified by Ashcroft's having softened the bill a bit before publicly releasing it. And he was enough of a Republican team player that he had been willing to push the bill through, almost on Ashcroft's schedule. His staff and Speaker Hastert's staff had agreed over the weekend that he'd schedule a committee vote on it for today, Tuesday. The Senate, controlled by Democrats, had also not signaled any major opposition and it, too, seemed ready to let a vote go forward, though perhaps, as was typical of the Senate, on a slightly slower track.

But the Barr letter, sent late on Friday, September 21, and mostly drafted by the ACLU, changed all that. As the ACLU people had explained to Sensenbrenner's staff on Monday morning, Sensenbrenner could not even carry the Republicans in his committee, let alone the Democrats, who were more naturally the ACLU's allies and whose committee leader, John Conyers, Jr., had been lobbied feverishly by the ACLU's Murphy. Sensenbrenner was about to be mightily embarrassed, the ACLU people told his staff. So Sensenbrenner had been forced yesterday to agree to postpone action on the bill for at least a week. In fact, he had sat through an ACLU briefing on the bill yesterday afternoon that echoed Barr's letter, and had found himself starting to agree with many of the ACLU's and Barr's arguments.

For Ashcroft, it was an appalling turn of events. The proposed law, which through a clever acronym construction was called the USA Patriot Act (as in Provide Appropriate Tools Required to Intercept and Obstruct Terrorism), was, in Ashcroft's eyes, falling into the business-as-usual legislative hopper. They didn't understand that we were at war, and the President had told him that he was the one who had to stop the next attack. He was still spending most of his waking hours in the FBI operations center running that war. Yet these guys, egged on by the ACLU, wanted to debate the fine points of a law that, plain and simple, was meant to give him the tools he obviously needed to do it. These conservatives were as paranoid about government as the ACLU was. It was crazy.

So Ashcroft had decided that although the Senate really wasn't the key problem, he'd lay the gauntlet down this morning and spring some news on them that would remind them and the world that this was no time to cross the t's and dot the i's. "Give me some tangible example I can use that's new and will make headlines, that illustrates what we're up against," he told an aide involved in preparing his testimony. "We need to put it to them."

"The American people do not have the luxury of unlimited time in erecting the necessary defenses to future terrorist acts," his testimony began. "The danger that darkened the United States of America and the civilized world on September 11 did not pass with the atrocities committed that day. Terrorism is a clear and present danger to Americans today. . . . Today," he added solemnly, "I can report to you that our investigation has uncovered several individuals, including individuals who may have links to the hijackers, who fraudulently have obtained, or attempted to obtain, hazardous material transportation licenses."

Having headlined a new threat, Ashcroft went on to an overview of the Patriot Act, then added, "Every day that passes with outdated statutes and old rules of engagement is a day that terrorists have a competitive advantage. Until Congress makes these changes, we are fighting an unnecessary uphill battle."

One would have expected a sharp exchange, or at least a long one, when Ashcroft stopped to take questions from the senators, especially when it was the Democrats' turn to speak up. Instead there was a fawning contest, as the

Democrats and Republicans, while occasionally seeking clarifications on minor points in the bill, spent the bulk of their time competing with each other to heap praise on Ashcroft. The winner was probably Patrick Leahy, the Democrat from Vermont who chairs the Judiciary Committee and had led the opposition earlier in the year in this same forum to Ashcroft's nomination as Attorney General. "General, frankly, I have been very, very pleased that you've been there," the chairman began. "I'll say publicly what I told you privately as we were walking down the hall the other day at the Justice Department: I'm glad you're there leading this effort."

But while "fawning" may seem a fair word when one reads the transcript of the hearing, it isn't in the context of September 25, a time two weeks after the worst attack ever on America—a time when it made sense for an opposition senator to strain to praise his onetime foe.

Besides, the "clear and present danger," Ashcroft described, indeed, seemed clear and present. He had already announced the arrest of hundreds of suspects in the investigation and talked about cells, crop dusting, and intelligence alerts. Now in less than two weeks they'd found people using fraudulent IDs to haul truckloads of hazardous materials around the country, he reported.

All that Schumer said at the Ashcroft hearing was that he hoped the Attorney General would come back for more questions before a vote on the bill. (Ashcroft promised to, but then canceled two scheduled appearances.) It would become an enduring source of frustration to Anthony Romero that Schumer—a liberal Democrat from Harvard and New York, who could usually be counted on to support the ACLU—was not troubled by Ashcroft's proposals. It did not come as a complete surprise; Schumer, after all, had supported a federal death penalty bill in 1996 as a congressman. But he'd done that as a horse trade for a gun control bill that he was pushing, so it was more understandable.

When Romero saw Schumer at several functions in New York and Washington in the weeks just after September 11, and approached him to talk about Ashcroft and the Patriot Act, he got a polite brush-off. Schumer listened, then offered a promise of "let's get together sometime to talk" that never happened. And Schumer's staff, who were more sympathetic to the ACLU, quietly told the ACLU Washington people that Schumer just wasn't going to be with them on this.

Schumer found Ashcroft's style that morning and in subsequent appearances arrogant and counterproductive. But he basically agreed with him on the Patriot Act.

Schumer had been profoundly affected by the attacks. By the loss of that view from his windows in Brooklyn. By the fact that his daughter had been missing (at least to her parents) for a few hours. By the many people he knew, or whom he met, or who called him who had lost loved ones. By the way his city had been devastated. His eyes teared up often now, something that astonished his staff.

To cynics he might have seemed to be holding his fire so as not to alienate a White House that had promised New York $20 billion. Or perhaps he was just another classic liberal who gets mugged and turns conservative. There was more to it than that. Schumer had been macro-mugged. His whole worldview had been changed by the attacks. He had thought about it a lot and decided that in a world in which individuals or small groups could and would do so much harm, the balance between individual freedom and society's need for security really did have to be recalibrated. He just plain didn't believe the country could be quite as free anymore and still preserve the American way of life. In short, he believed exactly what Romero was adamant about not believing. Romero, in fact, had told his staff repeatedly after the attacks that they had to reject the idea of any kind of so-called recalibration. Romero's new tag line on all ACLU literature was "SAFE AND FREE," meaning that Americans could still have it both ways, and that the government simply had to be smarter about using the tools it already had, not be given all sorts of new tools.

Romero's ears would have been burning had he listened in on a phone call the same morning that Ashcroft testified. It was from William Barr, a former Attorney General, in the administration of the first President Bush, to Timothy Flanigan, the deputy counsel in the White House. Flanigan, who had been one of Barr's assistants when he was Attorney General, listened as Barr reminded him of something they had considered after terrorists had blown up Pan Am Flight 103 over Lockerbie in 1988.

"Remember," said Barr, "how we looked at the idea of not treating people like that as common criminals, but instead treating them as unlawful enemy combatants, who should be tried in a military tribunal of some kind? Well, that's what we should do with [Osama] bin Laden and his group."

Barr's idea would soon be buttressed by calls that George Terwilliger, another former Bush I Justice Department official, would make to other members of the current Bush administration, including two of Ashcroft's top aides. Terwilliger, a former deputy attorney general who frequently can be found on cable news shows holding up the conservative flank, was even more straightforward. It had been just plain silly, he maintained to one top Ashcroft aide, "when [FBI Director] Louis Freeh and his people had gone over the Middle East with a magnifying glass to find evidence to prosecute people after the [USS] *Cole* had been bombed. This is a war. You don't worry about the fine points of evidence. And for sure you don't give these people the same level playing field in our courts, if you catch them, that you'd give to a U.S. citizen. They want to destroy our system. You don't let them use it to destroy us."

Ashcroft had heard about the Barr and Terwilliger calls and was intrigued. He asked for more research. But one aspect of the plan bothered him and would have bothered his criminal division prosecutors had they known about the idea: Military tribunals would be run by the Pentagon, not the Department of Justice. And John Ashcroft and his people hated handing off the ball. Still, Flanigan in the White House counsel's office was pushing it, so Ashcroft would have to deal with the idea somehow.

By Tuesday morning,* Sal Iacono, helped by some men to whom he gave a few hundred dollars in cash, had gotten much of the debris out of his store. Most of the dust had been swept out, too. He had developed a deep, hacking cough, because the air was so awful, but he felt good anyway. His store was starting to look like a store.

That morning he also found what's called a public insurance adjuster. Sal agreed that for 12.5 percent of the proceeds, the adjuster would help Sal make claims for damage and business interruption based on a policy Sal had with the St. Paul insurance company. Twelve and a half percent is a relatively high fee, but Sal didn't know that, nor did he have any idea of how he would go about filing the claims himself.

Workmen whom Sal had found through friends of friends were in the store that morning putting up a door and replacing his windows. He was dickering with others over the cost of replacing the ceiling, the floor, and the counter, and repairing and painting the empty shelves. Sal estimated that the cost of repairing everything would be $15,000 to $20,000. There was one thing, though, that he would not be able to repair, and it made him heartsick. The elegant bronze door that had opened onto the lobby of the office building

---

*Iacono is not certain whether the events described here happened on this day or on Wednesday or Thursday, and no records could be found to ascertain the actual date.

where Continental Shoe was housed couldn't be salvaged, and replacing it would cost thousands. He had to settle on a cheap wood substitute.

Herman Garcia, who had been Sal's helper in the shop for more than ten years, was also there. Sal offered to pay Garcia for the week with some of the wad of cash he had in his pocket, but Garcia refused, telling Sal he needed the money to rebuild.

Sal had no idea what he'd get back in insurance, and, although he didn't tell the adjuster, he was prepared to go ahead without any insurance. He just wanted to be back in business, back fixing anything made of leather that any customer brought in.

But that was the problem. He wasn't ready to reopen, but it seemed that if and when he did there wouldn't be any customers anyway. Sal was in the middle of a frozen zone. No vehicles were allowed anywhere near his store, except those carrying emergency or recovery crews. No pedestrians were allowed either, unless they waited to go through a checkpoint and could show identification that proved they worked there. And few people worked there, because most offices were still closed. It was a ghost town.

Sal's was one of 3,400 small businesses (those with fewer than 500 employees) that were stuck in that frozen zone. Another 707 had been wiped out altogether because they had been in the Trade Center. About 100,000 people had worked in just the buildings that had been destroyed (five in the Trade Center complex, plus several more adjoining it) or damaged so badly that they could not reopen without extensive repairs, if at all. And that wasn't counting the tens or hundreds of thousands more who worked in less-damaged buildings, like the one where Sal's store was, and who were not likely to return to work for weeks or months.

There was cruel irony in the way the Trade Center had now wreaked such havoc on these businesses that surrounded it. These were many of the same merchants who in the 1960s had been the field troops in the widespread opposition to the Port Authority's plan to build the Trade Center. (The opponents also included competing real estate developers and anyone with an appreciation for how the Trade Center was a city planning and architectural fiasco.) In hundreds of cases, they'd been forced to move because the buildings housing the stores they rented were condemned to make way for the new towers and its street-eliminating plaza. And all of them feared that the new complex, with its own giant retail mall—a mall that became the third largest shopping mall in the country—would crush them. (At the time, Sal had not started his own shoe repair shop, but he was working down there at another one.)

For many years they had been right. The Trade Center, with its mall and its disruption of pedestrian and vehicle traffic patterns, had killed their businesses. It had only been in the late 1990s that small retailers and restaurants near the Trade Center had begun to regain their stride, as downtown thrived amid the stock market boom. Now the collapse of the Trade Center complex, whose rise had so badly hurt them, had crushed them, almost literally, again.

Sal's willingness to dip into his pocket to rebuild was one thing. Whether that investment made any sense—whether he'd have a business that could survive—was a whole other question. Once he reopened, rent, the phone, electricity, supplies, plus Garcia's salary—a total of about $5,000 a month—seemed destined to eat away at Sal's remaining savings long before enough customers came back.

Bernadine Healy kept finding in different ways that if she wanted something done at the Red Cross she had to do it herself, or at least have it done by the cadre of outsiders she'd brought on when she'd taken over the place two years before.

Over the weekend, in between writing long, handwritten letters to major corporate donors, she'd found herself working with her staff hand-checking the names of missing people at Aon, an insurance company that had been headquartered at the Trade Center, against a list of people being treated at New York hospitals. The staff at her disaster operations center had dropped the ball on doing that, something she'd only found out about after an Aon board member, who is a friend of a friend, had called her to intercede.

Now, on Tuesday morning, she was editing one more time the form the Red Cross would use for its about-to-be-announced Family Grant Program. Healy had decided to take the hundreds of millions being donated to that now segregated 9/11 fund and use some of it to give every family of every victim three months of living expenses. The Red Cross had never done this before. In the past, when a hurricane generated $10 million or $20 million in donations, people displaced would get vouchers for food or temporary hotels, and the rest of the money would go into the Red Cross's general disaster fund. As of today, more than $200 million had poured into the 9/11 fund, and Healy had decided that this was one of the ways it was going to be used.

To be sure, she intended to spend only about $100 million for this, and use the rest to build up blood supplies and Red Cross counseling services, plus do additional disaster training and otherwise enhance preparation for other terrorist attacks. This was exactly what her disclaimer in those television spots—that the money would be used for this disaster "and emerging needs related to this tragedy"—had said. It was also exactly what she was telling those big donors on her handwritten notes. The one she'd sent to the CEO of Coca-Cola that day, thanking him for $6 million and the soda sent to the relief centers, talked about "creating a frozen blood reserve" and getting the armed forces support team ready for the war, as well as the three-month family grant program.

This diversion away from straight relief to September 11 victims is what would get her in trouble with Fox's Bill O'Reilly and other outside critics. Yet inside the Red Cross it was her insistence on using so much money for the victims through this new Family Grant Program—plus segregating all of the rest of it for terrorism-related needs, rather than putting the money in a general Red Cross fund—that would infuriate the local chapter leaders who control the board.

Internally, Healy had already alienated much of the veteran disaster relief staff, because she'd fired the two longtime leaders of the operations center the week before. The firings came after they had failed to get any Red Cross people or vans to the Pentagon the day or night of the attack. (They cited a rule that the local chapter, alone, always responds in the first twenty-four hours; in this case the Arlington, Virginia, chapter had mustered four volunteers and no vehicles.) Then, they had failed to help companies like Aon and individuals plug into the lists of people being treated at hospitals. Healy is never particularly subtle, and the pressure of the days following the attacks made her less so. So reverberations from the firings and her obvious frustration with many of the Red Cross's veterans were now echoing through the organization's marble headquarters.

Then, when disaster relief staff had produced a long, incomprehensible form for people to fill out to qualify for the Family Grant Program and said that there was no simpler way to do it, an infuriated Healy made a big show of going about doing all the redrafting herself, with only one or two assistants. What they came up with was simple enough: A surviving family member of a victim told the Red Cross what the family's monthly expenses were for rent or a mortgage, utilities, transportation, school tuition, and other fixed costs. (Bills and other evidence of the expenses were supposed to be attached.) That amount was added to a per person formula for food and entertainment to produce an overall monthly expense number, which when multiplied by three would yield a three-month family grant total, to which a caseworker also had discretion to add extraordinary expenses, such as a one-time dental bill or house repair.

By Tuesday afternoon, Healy finished the form and announced the program. It, indeed, seemed simple. But was it fair? After all, richer people, who were also likely to be protected by significant life insurance payouts, would get more money because their rents would be higher, as would their car payments. In fact, the richest, who owned the most expensive homes with the highest mortgages, would get much higher payments than those who rented small apartments.

Healy understood those issues, but in her mind this was the fastest way to get relief out there quickly. She'd already heard too many stories about people coming to Red Cross centers and getting nothing but a voucher for some food or clothing, while the headlines talked about the hundreds of millions she was collecting. A former heart doctor used to making fast decisions, she was not going to agonize about this.

She also stayed firm on another decision. Even as the airlines were announcing tens of thousands of layoffs and the media carried news of the economic devastation in New York, she rejected one staffer's recommendation that they consider another grant program for people who were economic victims of the attacks. That, she decided, would be too complicated and too expensive. Where would they stop? At people whose businesses had been in the Trade Center? In lower Manhattan? In all of New York? In industries, like air travel or car rentals or hotels, that had been hurt? There was no way the Red Cross could get into the middle of that. Helping the direct victims with three months' worth of expenses and using the rest to prepare for future terrorist attacks was what they needed to do.

Brian Lyons decided early Tuesday morning that two weeks without a break was enough. So he left the recovery work he was doing at Ground Zero, got on a train, went home, and spent the day with his wife and daughters, ages three and six, who had been shortchanged by his obsession with finding his kid brother Michael. Brian then set out that evening to go to a memorial service that the town where Elaine and Michael Lyons lived was having for Michael and two other local September 11 victims. After the service, he went back to Elaine's house to talk to her. It was a conversation he had been dreading.

Elaine Lyons, who was seven months pregnant on September 11, recalls that she had been virtually catatonic in the days following the attacks and her husband's disappearance. She avoided reading newspapers or watching the news on television. Unlike the Cartier family, she had no interest in jotting down the telephone numbers flashed on the screen where one could call to get information or charitable help. She just sat around her home in northern Westchester County, where Michael had been planning to build a third bedroom out of some attic space upstairs in anticipation of the birth of their second baby in November. Mostly, she watched soap operas, cried, and waited for the phone to ring. She got all her information from Brian, who was on the scene looking for Michael. And she got all the help she needed from the men her husband had worked with in the fire department.

Indeed, she hadn't had to worry about what charities like the Red Cross were doing, because she had almost instantly gotten a bagful of cash, literally. Before going to Rescue Squad 41 in the Bronx, Michael had worked at a firehouse on the Upper East Side of Manhattan. It was one of New York's richest neighborhoods, where the biggest action for a fireman might be a smoke alarm in a pizza parlor or some yuppie starting a fire in his oven. Most firemen are the opposite of placid civil servants; they hate not having hard work to do. So Michael Lyons, like many before him, had been desperate to get out of that no-action East Side firehouse and into a high-action unit like Squad 41. But he had been there on the East Side long enough that the men in that house thought of him as one of their own. Miraculously, they hadn't lost any of their current firefighters at Ground Zero, so right after September 11 they had hung a picture of Elaine and her daughter outside the firehouse, explaining that this woman's husband and little girl's father had been lost. The families of this super-rich neighborhood coughed up $80,000 in a matter of days—all of which had been delivered in a brown paper bag to Elaine.

For Elaine, that was just the beginning. Under an old statute that had recently been updated, the federal government paid any widow of a policeman or firefighter a $250,000 death benefit, tax free. The city paid one year's salary—about $52,000 on average, plus another $25,000 death benefit as part of the union contract. Elaine was days away from receiving these checks. They also would pay her a pension equal to Michael's average salary and overtime during the last five years—about $60,000—for the rest of her life. If her children went to college in New York, the tuition would be free. Then there was the Twin Towers Fund, organized by Mayor Giuliani to help the families of New York police and firemen killed in the attacks. It would ultimately raise and pay the equivalent of $355,000 per fireman, also tax free. A similar fund organized by the International Association of Firefighters was going to pay $418,000 per family. The union's insurance and the New York Police and Fire Widows and Childrens' Benefit Fund would pay out a total of $293,000. And that was before Elaine applied to that victims compensation fund that had been set up by Congress as part of the airline bailout. Word was that each victim's family would get another $1 million or $2 million, again tax free. This and other funds added up to a likely payout to Elaine Lyons and other fire widows of more than $6 million over their lifetimes, although that might be reduced by a million dollars or more if they remarried soon and lost pension and social security benefits that were based on them remaining single.*

Elaine did have one abiding worry. She wanted a place, someplace, where her daughter and the new baby, who was now about six weeks away, could go to mourn their father. That meant she needed a body, or some portion of a body, to bury in a cemetery. Brian Lyons, who had sworn to her that he would find Michael, was here to tell her that it was not to be. He came into the small living room, sat Elaine down, and pulled out a badge from his pocket. It was an extra badge of Michael's, the one he had found in Elaine's basement the night of September 11 and used to talk his way into Ground Zero the next morning. He gave it to Elaine. "This is all we are going to have," he told her. "There is just not going to be anything else. I'm sorry." They both cried.

Now Elaine knew for real that Michael was gone. Until then, she had kept expecting him to walk through the door, cracking a joke. He had always had a joke for everything. Everyone who knew him talked about his sense of humor, his love of children, even before they had had Caitlyn. How he beguiled kids from the Good Humor truck or the hot dog stand he worked at on weekends.

Michael had had a way with adults, too. When he had initially been told by the captain at the elite Rescue Squad 41 that there was no room, he thanked him and left. But he'd kept coming back, bringing bagels and donuts and wearing the captain and everyone else down by talking about how he wanted this dangerous job and would do anything to get it, all the while telling them jokes and winning them over. When he'd finally joined, he'd become one of the most popular men in the group. Members of the squad traditionally called each other brothers, but Lyons had shortened that to "bro." He called everyone "bro," and soon they called him and each other that, too.

Michael had gotten a medal a few years back for risking his life saving a woman in a Harlem rescue, but, except for scalding a knee when he'd knelt down into some boiling water, he'd never been injured on the job. To Elaine, he had seemed invincible, the man who could deal with anything. If something went wrong, somehow Michael—who had a mechanical engineering degree and did that on the side, even after he became a fireman—always had

---

*Families of police officers would get slightly more than $5 million. For a full account of these payments, see Source Notes under September 25.

an answer, a way to fix it. Now she was sitting in a house where she had no idea how to fix anything.

For fifteen years, since they'd met as high schoolers when she was a hostess and he was a busboy at a diner in Yonkers, Elaine and Michael had been inseparable, a strikingly handsome couple. Now he was gone. Brian, in fact, sometimes now gave her the creeps, not because he wasn't helping but because his voice sounded so much like Michael's. It gave her a lift for an instant until she remembered that he wasn't Michael. And that she was alone, with one baby and a new one on the way. Two sizes of Huggies to buy every week and no one to pick them up for her.

And no prospect of ever having a place to take these babies to mourn their father.

Ken Feinberg, the lawyer who wanted the job as Special Master of that new victims compensation fund, didn't think his job quest was off to a terrific start. He'd reached his friend Ted Kennedy on Monday, and Kennedy had assured him he'd do his best. But both of them knew that when it came to getting John Ashcroft to appoint Feinberg, Kennedy was baggage. As for Orrin Hatch, the senior Republican on the Senate Judiciary Committee, whom Feinberg also considered a friend, he hadn't returned Feinberg's Monday morning call, so Feinberg had ended up faxing him a memo explaining why he had been calling. A staffer had called back and said Hatch would support him. It wasn't as good as if Hatch had talked to him himself.

By Tuesday evening Chuck Hagel—the Republican senator from Nebraska, who was Feinberg's prime booster for the job—called and told Feinberg that he'd spoken to Ashcroft's chief of staff over the weekend and then to Ashcroft himself. Hagel had raved about Feinberg, saying he was the only one who could do a job like this. Ashcroft seemed to hesitate when Hagel mentioned Feinberg's Kennedy pedigree, but softened, Hagel told Feinberg, when he explained to Ashcroft that appointing a Democrat would give him and the Bush White House political cover.

"I told him you'd be a team player," Hagel told Feinberg. "That you're not the kind of guy to resign and go on all the cable news talk shows if you don't like the way some conversation is going."

"That's right," Feinberg answered. "I won't be there to embarrass them. I'll be there to make this thing work."

Hagel then said he had also called Mitch Daniels, the budget director, and Karl Rove, the president's top political aide. In all cases, he'd told them that

Feinberg had to be given a chance to see Ashcroft. That he was the perfect person for the job.

"I told them they had to sit with you and hear you," Hagel told Feinberg. "They understand that this guy could hurt them, but I told them that you won't do that."

No one committed anything to Hagel, he told Feinberg, other than to put his name in the hopper.

"Just wait a few days," Hagel told Feinberg. "Ashcroft's people will call you. This'll all work out."

At the Justice Department, though, Hagel's pitch had not gone over nearly as well as he had thought, or at least as he had told Feinberg it had gone. A top Ashcroft aide recalls that the idea of putting a Ted Kennedy man in charge of the fund, with no checks on power to dole out taxpayer money, was greeted with near hoots of laughter. Ashcroft, in fact, had begun one account of Hagel's phone call with, "You're not gonna believe who Chuck Hagel wants me to put in charge of that fund."

Indeed, as far as Ashcroft's staff was concerned, the Feinberg idea was a nonstarter. They already had a prospective list of big-name judges, former senators, and businesspeople—the kind of graybeards that could front a commission or a board while staff guys did the work. They were all Republicans, and all projected both the gravitas and aura of fiscal responsibility that would give the fund credibility while containing the risks its unchecked power presented.

Meantime, at a Park Avenue law office in Manhattan another group was meeting Tuesday afternoon to talk about the new victims fund and the different kind of risk it presented to them. The law firm of Kreindler & Kreindler mainly did one thing: airplane crashes. Lee Kreindler, seventy-seven, had become a millionaire many times over suing the airlines whenever a plane went down. His clients were the families of dead passengers who paid him 25–40 percent of any settlement or verdict. It was a specialty that Kreindler, who now included his son James, forty-five, as a partner in the firm, had built up so spectacularly over the years that he dominated the legal fallout of any air crash anywhere. He didn't have to chase ambulances. Because of his reputation and referrals from other lawyers (who then got a share of his fee), he almost always ended up with a large contingent of the plaintiffs in any air disaster.

Those plaintiffs got Mayo Clinic–like treatment for their claims. Kreindler's lawyers used engineers and investigators to prove fault. They used accountants and psychologists to establish damages where lesser lawyers might not look— such as putting a dollar value on the parenting guidance a dead father would have provided to a teenaged plaintiff if only the plane had not gone down. Sometimes this all played out in a long trial after years of pretrial skirmishing. More often, the experts were deployed by Kreindler in a series of pretrial negotiations with the airlines or aircraft builder's insurance companies that might also take years, but typically would avoid a trial.

The problem that the Kreindler lawyers—ten partners, led by Lee Kreindler, meeting that morning in a lavish conference room—now faced was that this victims compensation fund seemed likely to make all of their expertise useless. The fund wasn't even going to deal with the issue of fault; if your loved one had died or if you'd been injured in the September 11 attacks, you collected. And some Special Master was going to write rules to deal with the issue of damages—that is, how much you collected. Worse, that Master's decisions were not appealable.

Kreindler and his partners, who even now already had ten September 11 clients, were appalled as they compared that scenario to the world they were used to—where an airline or its insurance company had to weigh the danger of a jury being persuaded to make them pay big because of how careless they'd been and because of how much some widow and her children had suffered. How could they represent clients? How could they ask for up to 40 percent of what the clients got, if getting it was going to be relatively pro forma? And how could they tell if clients should skip the fund and take their chances in court by suing the airlines, if doing so meant that they could not get any money from the fund and might also get nothing from the airlines because Congress had capped the airlines' liability at the $1.5 billion limit per plane on their insurance? Indeed, what was so disturbing to them about the fund was that it might work—that it really might entice people away from taking the traditional route of going to court.

It is easy to chalk up their reaction to selfishness. After all, the fund deprived them of a meal ticket. But most plaintiffs lawyers, especially those as successful as Kreindler and his partners, share an ideology that is convenient because it is consistent with how they make their living but that also seems in most cases to be sincere. They believe—or at least they use the argument so much that it's the same as believing it—that the system of being able to sue big corporations in front of a jury of common people makes corporations behave better because it's the way to hold them accountable for the quality and safety of their goods and services. Anything that erodes that basic right in their minds erodes American justice and democracy.

One of the Kreindlers' younger partners wondered whether they should even represent clients who applied to the fund. Wouldn't that be supporting an alternative dispute resolution system that they didn't believe in? Kreindler said that of course they had to represent them if going to the fund was what was best for them. They'd have plenty of opportunities to affect what they got, even at the fund, he added, explaining that no system could be so purely mechanical that an advocate couldn't help influence the result by making arguments where there were ambiguities.

A week before, when the trade association of plaintiffs lawyers had announced with much fanfare that they would urge members to represent victims of September 11 for free, Kreindler and his partners had quickly decided to ignore the request. Unlike just about everyone else, this was their bread and butter, they reasoned. All air crashes are tragic, but this was how they made a living. Now, the question came up about whether they would be able to charge their usual fees. After all, there was going to be no trial and no debate about fault.

Another partner said they should charge 20 percent, instead of 40 percent. But Kreindler, who, of course, controlled the room, insisted that they limit themselves to 10 percent—and that in instances where they came to believe that they could not make much of a difference, they would advise a client to use a volunteer lawyer, or not use a lawyer at all.

There was also some talk about the difference in the situation of the various victims. As with Elaine Lyons's husband having been the only fireman with a connection to that firehouse in the rich Manhattan neighborhood, where $80,000 in contributions had been so quickly collected, the passengers on United Flight 93 were relatively better off than the other victims. This was the plane that had crashed in Pennsylvania, and it had yielded "only" forty victims. The planes that had crashed into the Trade Center had produced thousands of victims, on the ground as well as in the air. The difference was important to the lawyers. Congress's limit of each airline's liability to the insurance coverage for each flight—$1.5 billion—would be more than enough to compensate forty people for large damage awards, but it wouldn't come close to covering all the victims and all the damages from the Trade Center crashes. So, they concluded, maybe there would be some cases they could bring in court and not in the fund for the Flight 93 people—if they thought they could prove fault.

The biggest decision of the meeting, though, was what Kreindler and his partners—who, again, are the dominant players in airplane crashes—did not do. They didn't vow to fight the fund by challenging the constitutionality of a law that had retroactively restricted the victims' rights to sue (by limiting what they might recover to the airlines' insurance coverage). Nor did they decide to advise clients to avoid the fund and take their chances in court.

"We simply felt boxed in," Kreindler says. "The fund offered a fast payout, so we figured it was up to us to try to do our best to influence how the rules were written to maximize that payout. Besides, winning a case against the airlines was not going to be easy," he notes, adding with a candor he would never show in court, "It's hard to argue that any of these crashes—that what these hijackers did—was foreseeable, which is the benchmark standard for liability."

## Wednesday, September 26, 2001

At about 6:45 A.M., Brian Lyons, having gotten home late the night before because he had first gone to Elaine's house to tell her Michael was not going to be found, was waiting for a commuter train to take him from Carmel, New York (about sixty miles north of the city), into Manhattan. He looked a little strange because he was dressed in the uniform from his September 10 life as a construction manager, a jacket and tie, under the yellow hard hat he now wore at Ground Zero.

The combination caught the eye of one of the other commuters, a Wall Street broker who was the type who enjoyed talking to everyone he met on a train. He'd been taking that train for fifteen years and had never seen Brian Lyons before.

The two men talked about how horrible the attacks had been. Then something else caught the commuter's eye: Brian's last name was written on the hard hat in black letters.

Hey, I'm a Lyons, too, the man said. What's your first name?

After Brian told him, the other man said, "My name's Michael."

Brian's face turned white, and this other Michael Lyons—who had gotten calls from friends and relatives who'd seen some of the early lists of the missing and dead—immediately knew why.

They talked a bit more, and Brian explained that he was now working at Ground Zero, hoping to find his brother. The other Michael was so moved that a few mornings later he went down to Ground Zero himself, stood, and stared as tears rolled down his face.

Bob Lindemann hated being separated from his Border Patrol partner, Mark Hall, and he was angry and worried about the prospect of being suspended

for ninety days, as that letter he'd received last week had promised. He'd consulted a lawyer but was told that without a lot of money for legal fees there was
little chance to fight the disciplinary action. Another lawyer at his union's
headquarters in Washington had offered to help draft a reply, but he held out
little hope that that would work. The suspension was likely to stick.

What he didn't know, although he probably should have assumed it, was
that he was now in far deeper trouble than that. The day before, he and Hall
had been on the local NBC station, talking about how they had been disciplined for having talked to the press about the dangers on the Northern Border. Unlike the first *Detroit Free Press* interview, they did not offer any details
about Border Patrol weaknesses or equipment. Lindemann maintains that he
was only speaking to the press in his capacity as a union official talking about
how his bosses had violated their workers'—in this case, his and Hall's—
rights, but he also concedes that he was "pissed and frustrated" and figured
"this was the right thing to do. Why shouldn't I speak out? Isn't that what
you're supposed to do in this country?"

His supervisors, Geoghegan and France, hadn't heard about this new TV
interview until this morning. They were furious. Lindemann and Hall had
once again violated their bosses' strict edict not to talk to the media, and
had now done it in the face of having already been disciplined. They definitely
had to be fired. France called his regional supervisors, who agreed that they
should proceed quickly with termination. But at the INS nothing happens
quickly. Over the next six weeks, Hall and Lindemann would give six more
interviews, never knowing about the meetings that were going on in Detroit
and Washington to decide their fate.


Of all the problems Manhattan Island had on September 26, traffic did not
seem to be one of them. In fact, the city seemed downright serene in places
north of Ground Zero, as it does on Presidents Day or some major Jewish holiday, when it's open for business but a significant number of people and their
cars stay home.

Transportation Commissioner Iris Weinshall knew better. In fact, at the
now daily emergency task force meeting with Mayor Giuliani,* she shocked
the group by declaring that this was the worst traffic day in the history of New
York. No one, including the mayor, believed it. "I had enormous respect for
Iris," Giuliani recalls. "She was almost always right about any issue. But I
remember asking her, 'Where's the traffic?' "

---

*In 1993 the author contributed to Giuliani's campaign for mayor.

"It's in Brooklyn and Queens and New Jersey because it can't get in [to Manhattan],"Weinshall replied. "It's all gridlocked, waiting to get over one of the bridges or tunnels."

In fact, things were so out of control, she said, that they were getting calls from construction companies saying that because cement mixers were stuck on the roads so long, the cement that was arriving was useless. Traffic had been bad, but never like this, she maintained. The massive recovery work going on at Ground Zero with all the attendant street blockages, combined with the devastation of so many mass transit lines connecting through lower Manhattan, plus the fact that the police were stopping and checking all trucks and vans entering the city, had created the perfect traffic storm.

The mayor still didn't quite believe it. So at about noon, he and Weinshall went up in a police helicopter for a look. When Giuliani saw the cars and trucks stalled tens of miles out from the entrances to Manhattan, Weinshall knew she'd convinced him.

"So what do we do," Giuliani asked.

A few hours later, Weinshall presented three solutions to the mayor and his cabinet. They could allow even-numbered license plates one day and odd numbers the next. They could require that all trucks delivering goods to Manhattan do so at night. Or they could ban all single occupancy vehicles (SOVs)—the classic commuter driving himself to work—from using the bridges and tunnels during rush hours. "There were forty people in the room," Weinshall recalls. "And none of them looked at me. They all looked down. They knew these alternatives would all be bad."

When Giuliani asked which one she recommended, Weinshall said that the single occupancy ban was the most doable of the three. "Mr. Mayor," she added, "you've got to trust me on this."

"Let's do it," Giuliani said.

The next day an SOV ban from 6:00 A.M. to 12:00 P.M. went into effect, and within days the traffic bottlenecks would be eased almost completely.

It was not a big news story at the time, nor should it have been given all else that was going on. Yet this SOV ban looms as one of the enduring metaphors of how New York coped in the September 12 era. It was something that many other cities had already done, and New York mayors had thought about doing it since the 1960s. Yet they had never even gotten to the point of formally proposing it because they knew that in New York it just couldn't happen. Commuters from the suburbs, whose legislators would have to pass a state law allowing it, would never agree. Parking garage owners would fight it. People in Brooklyn, Queens, and Staten Island would fight it, arguing that New York was all one city.

Now, Iris Weinshall and Rudy Giuliani had just done it, with Giuliani declaring that a transit emergency stemming from the cleanup downtown gave him the authority. It was an emergency that the new mayor, Michael Bloomberg, and Weinshall, who would stay on under Bloomberg, would never un-declare in the year following September 11, though they would gradually tailor down the hours (to 10:00 A.M.) and the locations (only downtown bridges and the tunnel from Brooklyn to lower Manhattan).

Sohail Mohammed practiced law on his own from a walk-up office in Clifton, New Jersey. On the wall in the three-seat waiting room are framed press clippings, one showing him as a speaker at a state bar seminar on criminal law, and another in which he was quoted as an expert on radar guns used to trap speeders. Next to the window where his receptionist (in traditional Muslim dress) sat, there were insignias indicating that he accepted Visa and Master-Card, a notice informing visitors that he could no longer provide blank immigration forms, and two handwritten letters from women thanking him for his work on their divorces.

In short, Sohail Mohammed was not someone one would expect to be in the thick of the FBI's terrorist investigation. But he had found himself dragged into it when a friend from his mosque, Ali Erikenoglu, had called after he had been rousted by the FBI in the early morning hours of September 21 and told Mohammed about how he'd been questioned about his political views and his religion.

Maybe it was Mohammed's disarmingly friendly demeanor, even when he was angry, that had caused the FBI brass in Newark to respond that they wanted to make sure they did a better job the next time they questioned someone like Erikenoglu. Maybe it was the local press articles describing Erikenoglu's questioning that Mohammed had encouraged, and that had caused a mini-furor in the large Middle Eastern community in Paterson. Whatever the reason, and it was probably a combination of both, the FBI had invited Mohammed to come to its Newark headquarters this morning to conduct a sensitivity training session.

Mohammed had been told that agents involved in the terrorist field investigation would be there and that he should go over with them some of what he'd already complained about, such as the agents' failure to remove their shoes when entering Erikenoglu's apartment. When he arrived, he was stunned to find himself ushered into what looked like the FBI's war room—a massive, hastily put together open space full of temporary tables, chairs, and computers. There must have been 250 gun-holstered cops there, not only from the FBI but from the INS, Customs, the postal police, even the New Jersey state police. It was standing room only.

The assembled firepower was enough to intimidate Mohammed, who had imagined he'd be doing a gripe session with twenty or thirty people around a table. But there was more: Lining the walls were pictures of the burning Twin Towers with the caption "We Shall Never Forget." And mixed in with those were dartboards with Osama bin Laden's face superimposed over the bull's-eye.

Did these guys really want to hear about falafel, prayer carpets, and headdress?

Apparently they did, not just to improve on their "sensitivity" but to get smarter about knowing the enemy—and to stand a chance of enlisting law-abiding allies in a community where the enemy might be hiding. What followed were two intense hours.

The G-men and women heard that for a Muslim woman not to look a male agent in the eye, or for a Muslim male not to look a female agent in the eye, was not a sign of deception. It was because Muslims were not supposed to look directly at members of the opposite sex unless they were family members. They learned what kinds of food they could serve people they were detaining without violating Muslim dietary laws. (Pizza is always a good bet, as are seafood and vegetables.) Mohammed then ran through a brief explanation of the Muslim religion's rituals, including the saying of prayers five times a day during certain, specified windows of time. He explained that reaching out to shake the hand of a Muslim of the opposite sex will cause embarrassment because they are not supposed to do that, that if a woman takes a long time to open a door it could be because she has to cover herself up and not because she's scooting out the back, that "jihad" actually means "struggle" to law-abiding Muslims, that Muslims will typically have four names, and that shoes are removed because Muslims pray on their carpets and that for the same reason police dogs would be especially offensive in Muslim homes (which typically do not have pets). At the end of his set speech, Mohammed reminded the agents sitting under the Osama dartboards of one more thing: his parents and his friend's parents had come to America because it was a place where they could worship freely and have opportunity. In other words, they were no different from most Americans, only maybe they were more religious and traditional than many.

During his talk and for a half hour after, Mohammed was peppered with questions. Some were practical, such as how might they remove a woman's head covering for a search without offending her. (Answer: politely and apologetically.) Some were theoretical and even a bit hostile, such as whether any particular sect is more likely to commit violence. (His answer was that no real Muslim sect espouses violence and that this was akin to trying to ascertain what kind of Christian Timothy McVeigh had been.)

John Paige, a supervising FBI agent who had helped arrange the session, recalls that "it was a real eye-opener. . . . I grew up in Greenwich Village, so I understand all different kinds of people, but I didn't understand most of this stuff. We have to if we're going to get the information and cooperation we need from these people."

Michael Cartier's sister Jennie Farrell would later explain that some people, including Michael, who had lost a loved one in the September 11 attack found that working following the tragedy was a useful distraction. She wasn't one of those people. She, Michael (who had gone back to work), and the rest of the family still hadn't scheduled a memorial service for James. But that was only because their father, Patrick, had so far refused. The others knew there was no hope. For Jennie, this and the fact that there was no body for a proper funeral, combined with such inconsistent information out there about the recovery effort, was so devastating that she could not concentrate on her job, which was supervising new teachers starting in the state's college system. She'd drive to a school and start to enter a classroom and burst into tears. So she decided that she had to take a leave and spend her time not only grieving and tending to her parents, but also trying to get more information about what they were doing at Ground Zero to find more of the dead.

# Friday, September 28, 2001

At 11:00 A.M., the fifty-plus-person board of governors of the Red Cross had a conference call to go over the organization's response to the attacks. No one listening in on the call or reading the notes of it would have gotten any idea of the tensions that were building.

Chairman David McLaughlin began by thanking Healy for her "extraordinary leadership" and describing the Liberty Fund, in which all September 11 donations were segregated. No one objected. The board was told that $217 million had been raised so far. Expenses for the provision of immediate "relief and respite" (blankets, temporary housing, food and supplies to rescue workers, on-site counseling, and transportation and housing for volunteers) might cost $80 million to $90 million. Another $100 million was being set aside for the Family Grant Program that Healy had announced on Tuesday. The rest of the money raised, including as much as $40 million for blood reserves, would be used to get the Red Cross ready for similar attacks.

There were only two signs of trouble. First, Healy described a dispute she was having with New York State Attorney General Eliot Spitzer, who had proposed that in order to coordinate relief efforts, all the charities should contribute to a common database of clients. That way, people could not receive money for the same needs from two different charities, such as the Salvation Army and the Red Cross. Healy told the board that she had categorically rejected Spitzer's idea, because she considered the Red Cross's client information to be as confidential as doctor-patient information. The board agreed, deciding that the information would only be released and pooled if the clients agreed in advance.

The second trouble spot wasn't really a specific problem but rather an issue that loomed over the discussion of several matters. It had to do with whether, and how, the Red Cross as an organization would benefit from all the funds designated to help victims of September 11. First, the vice president for development briefed the board on how the Red Cross could parlay its contact with new donors, especially first-time large corporate donors, into long-term relationships. That was innocent enough. But it was followed by questions from some of the board members from local chapters about when the locals could begin retaining 10 percent of money donated from their areas to the national September 11 fund. This was an arrangement that had always been in place until Healy had segregated the funds. The board agreed that the chapters would not get that 10 percent from any money raised up through September 30 (two days from now), but that afterward they might, and that perhaps they could use it for "local preparedness activities."

Healy knew she would oppose that. But she figured that fight, if there was to be one, could wait. In fact, she was not as worried about that discussion as she might have been because no one expressed a word of opposition to the funds having been segregated. Pat Kennedy, the board member from San Francisco who had sent that angry fax the weekend before, did not say a word during the meeting that anyone involved, including Kennedy, would later recall.

When the meeting ended, McLaughlin congratulated Healy again and gave her a brief hug. But then something odd happened. As they walked down the hall, he told her that there were "rumblings" among some of the board members about her leadership. Then why hadn't she heard any of that at the meeting, she asked. "Because that's not the way they work," McLaughlin responded. "But don't worry. I'm handling it."


James Loy, the Commandant of the Coast Guard, was highly regarded in Washington as a strong leader and savvy executive. When Loy had heard the President announce the creation of the homeland security office and the appointment of Ridge to create it, he started to think about what the challenges of that job would be, especially for someone like Ridge who had a great résumé and relationship with the President, but lacked executive experience in the federal government. By last Monday, he decided that, as a veteran of Beltway battles with Congress and the White House, perhaps he should try to talk to his fellow Pennsylvanian about what he faced. Besides, because the Coast Guard was one of the agencies with homeland security responsibilities that Ridge would presumably be coordinating, building a relationship with Ridge early was a good career move. So Loy had called Ridge last week and offered to come brief him. Ridge, who, unbeknownst to Loy, had just read Loy's article on homeland security in his briefing book, eagerly invited him to the governor's mansion.

Loy assumed when he arrived in Harrisburg that Ridge expected he was going to whine about how the Coast Guard needed more resources. The admiral quickly disabused him of that. Instead, as he puts it, "I tried to tell him what I'd like to know if I were in his shoes and about to come to the Beltway and be run over by all these cultures."

Ridge lapped it up, blowing off one meeting after another so that he ended up spending three hours with Loy instead of the scheduled forty-five minutes. Loy walked him through various models of similar positions, such as National Security Advisor and White House drug czar, and concluded that the only way for Ridge to give himself flexibility was to make sure he had input into the executive order that was being drafted to establish his job. Specifically, he advised Ridge that he should make sure that the executive order called for him to give the President some kind of strategic plan for homeland security within six or nine months. That way, Ridge would have the forum and the excuse to suggest how his own job might be reconfigured once he arrived and began to understand it.

Ridge readily agreed. Even before talking to Loy, just reading the looseleaf briefing books had given him enough pause about the confusion he was jumping into that he had decided he would love to set some milestone, probably next June or July (just about when he'd have to make a decision about moving the kids to schools in Washington for the next year), that would allow him and the President to take stock of how the job fit the country's needs and Ridge's own expectations. This notion of a strategic report fit perfectly with his sense of uncertainty.

## Saturday, September 29, 2001

Two days ago, Syed Jaffri, a thirty-four-year-old Pakistani with a wife and four children back home, had been arrested by FBI and INS agents. The day before he had had a dispute with his landlord in the Bronx, after which the landlord had made good on a threat to call the authorities about his immigration status. Jaffri was working at a gas station without a work visa.

Jaffri, who had no criminal record, was held at the INS lockup, where, he claims, he was beaten and verbally abused, repeatedly called a terrorist, and never advised of his right to a lawyer.*

This morning, he was taken from the Manhattan lockup to the INS's main detention facility in Brooklyn, where, he says, he was strip-searched and placed in a solitary, windowless cell. He claims that one INS guard told him, "If the FBI arrested you, that's good enough for me," whereupon his face was slammed so hard against a wall that his teeth were jarred loose. It was the first day of six months of solitary confinement in that cell. The lights were on all the time. He was never told what time it was, so he never knew when to pray. For the first two months, he claims, he was given two square pieces of toilet paper a day, and denied soap, a toothbrush or toothpaste, and all reading materials.

Jaffri's detention was by now becoming part of a pattern, though it was

---

*INS officials refused to make any of the agents involved available for comment, though the INS repeatedly denied any improprieties in questioning detainees. The Justice Department's inspector general later began an investigation of the charges in this and similar cases, but by early January 2002 his report, promised for October, had been inexplicably delayed. The events recounted here echo other accusations reported by, among others, Amnesty International. However, because they are from one side's complaint in a lawsuit, they could be exaggerated or even fictional.

invisible because Ashcroft had taken such extraordinary measures, including keeping hearings for people like Jaffri secret, to make sure it all happened out of public sight.

It had all been worked out at a series of meetings Ashcroft had with a small group of aides that included Deputy Attorney General Larry Thompson and Criminal Division chief Michael Chertoff. Nothing was put formally on paper.

The perspective the group started with was simple. The nineteen men who had hijacked the planes could not be the only ones who were living in America quietly waiting to attack. There could be hundreds, even thousands, of others, and their job was to find them. The obvious target was young Muslim men, plain and simple. But they had no informants, really no contact at all, in those communities. So they had to use what they had to check as many of the target population as they could, as fast as they could. Again, the first goal wasn't to prosecute them but to prevent them, which meant that violating the kinds of rules pertaining to searches and interrogation that would get evidence thrown out of court wasn't that important.

There were three ways Muslim men could be identified and checked out: First, if a Muslim name popped up in any context associated with the hijackers, they were immediately sought out. For example, if an Arab name was found in a list of students at one of the hijacker's flight training schools, he would be tracked down. Even having gone to the same state motor vehicle office to obtain a license was connection enough.

The second category of people was those who came to the FBI's attention because citizens (such as Ali Erikenoglu's co-workers in Paterson, or Jaffri's landlord in the Bronx), or state or local police officials, notified the bureau about them. For example, a Missouri man with a Muslim name who had been arrested for outstanding traffic violations was turned over to the FBI in Kansas City when the police noticed that he had a lot of checks in his wallet. Their investigation produced an arrest for writing checks with insufficient funds in his account, a federal crime but one not typically resulting in arrests, let alone prolonged detention.

The third category was just plain names. FBI offices, aided initially by INS and sometimes even local police, who were not busy questioning people in the first two categories, were told to check names in their areas from among the hundreds of thousands provided by the INS of Muslims who had come into the country in the last few years. When these proved mostly useless because INS records are almost always inaccurate or incomplete, they were even told to look in the phone book.

How these people were treated depended on who was questioning them (some FBI offices had more polite agents than others, though the FBI was generally more respectful than the INS agents), and, more so, on how tenuous or direct their connection to the terrorists might have seemed. A professor at a college in Indiana, who thinks his name was simply picked from the phone book, says the agents who questioned him four times were polite and respectful and even seemed embarrassed at the job they'd been given.

People like the professor or Ali Erikenoglu, who seemed to check out after being questioned would be left alone; there was little the feds could do to hold them anyway. But Ashcroft and his small group of deputies carefully mapped out how they could exert maximum pressure on everyone else—which meant all noncitizens and any citizens who seemed the least bit suspicious.

If they were not citizens, the FBI and INS would look for something that they had done wrong in terms of their immigration status. Had they taken jobs, even though they only had tourist visas? Had they overstayed their visas? Such violations usually were easy to find, especially since INS's enforcement of these conditions over the years had been almost nonexistent.

They would then be detained for immigration violations and questioned repeatedly. It didn't matter if the violations were minor transgressions for which immigrants of other nationalities are rarely, if ever, held. Ostensibly, they were being held pending a hearing in which the government would move to deport them for the visa violation. But Chertoff had figured out that these hearings could not only be done in secret, but could also be delayed, and that even after the hearings were held and they were ordered deported, there was nothing in the law that said they absolutely had to be deported immediately. They could be held still longer, until the FBI decided they were of no use. Better yet, because immigration detentions are civil, not criminal proceedings, these people were not entitled to free lawyers. They could hire one if they could afford it, which was not often. Under INS rules, they were entitled to call a lawyer from jail, but the lists the INS provided of available lawyers invariably had phone numbers that were not in service. This was discussed at one of the Ashcroft meetings, and, according to one person who says he was there, someone in the room remarked that the government should not try too hard to make sure these people could contact lawyers. "Let's not make it so they can get Johnnie Cochran on the phone," another lawyer added, according to one of the participants, referring to O. J. Simpson's famed defense lawyer.* They were sure to a certainty that at least some of the

---

*Ashcroft says he does not remember this conversation or any reference to Johnnie Cochran, and that he had directed that all detainees be made aware of lawyers who could assist them.

men they were holding or were about to hold were people bent on killing more Americans if allowed to, or at least knew of people who were planning to do that.

According to two people who attended these meetings, and to INS Commissioner James Ziglar, Chertoff was put in charge of all INS detentions. He and his deputies would make all decisions on who was released and even who was held in solitary. This was unprecedented; Chertoff was the head of the Justice Department's Criminal Division and INS detention proceedings were civil, not criminal, tribunals, held in front of INS judges. As for the detention conditions, no one at INS would be ordered in so many words to treat the inmates harshly. But the word would go out that these were suspected terrorists, or people who knew who the terrorists were—and they needed to be encouraged in any way possible to cooperate.

If the targets were citizens, or their immigration papers were in order, they would be held for minor crimes, such as lying to a federal agent or having fraudulent identification documents. The feds would then offer leniency, or threaten to throw the book at them, depending on how much information about terrorists they provided. In other cases, where not even minor crimes could be established, or where the government was worried that these people were so important that they did not want them to get lawyers quickly (as they would be entitled to if charged with any crime), the targets were held as material witnesses. The government can hold someone as a material witness if prosecutors claim to a judge that the person might have vital evidence in an investigation but might flee before being put before a jury or a grand jury to testify. The new twist Ashcroft's team now decided to add was that they would control when, if ever, that person might be asked to testify— meaning they would seek to hold the person indefinitely so as to coerce him to talk.

Chertoff reasoned that while they were being held they would be discouraged from calling lawyers, and could be questioned without lawyers present because they were not being charged with any crime. The advantage of using this newly expanded material witness classification was that the feds didn't have to prove anything criminal about the person being held, but only that he might have material information about an investigation. And as a practical matter it, too, could be done in secret because these material witnesses were meant to testify before grand juries, and all grand jury proceedings, including any hearings involving the status of a witness, are, by law, required to be secret. With a grand jury in New York empaneled for the foreseeable future to investigate the attacks and any plots for new attacks, these material witnesses could be held indefinitely, Ashcroft and his small team reasoned.

The FBI, though, was another issue. FBI Director Robert Mueller was not comfortable with a dragnet that simply held people on the hope that some might know something simply because they were Muslim men. He didn't quite put it that way to Ashcroft, but he did say on several occasions that his agents were not used to going after people about whom they had no real evidence of criminal conduct. To which Ashcroft replied that that was precisely the point he had been making about how the world had changed—how their job now was to prevent new crimes more than solve old ones. And the way to do that, Ashcroft literally said during one meeting at the FBI operations center, was to round up anyone who fit the profile.

Most of the subsequent analysis in the press and even in court decisions didn't fully appreciate how different Ashcroft's perspective was. He had been given a job no other Attorney General had been given—to prevent crime rather than to prosecute it. Thus, to look at his decisions simply from the perspective of whether the agents under his direction violated defendants' rights misses the point. To Ashcroft and his team these were not defendants in cases where evidence stemming from an improper search or interrogation might be excluded at a trial. They were potential killers who had to be stopped.

The reference librarian of the Paterson Free Public Library thinks that it was September 29 that the three FBI agents came to ask her if she recognized the pictures they flashed of several Arab men. She did, because she'd seen them in all the newspaper stories identifying them as the hijackers. They wanted to know, of course, if she'd seen them at the library. She didn't think she had.

Would she mind if they searched the log-in records for the computers she had connecting library patrons to the Internet? They'd have to get a subpoena, she told them politely. (Getting such a subpoena probably did not have to await the passage of Ashcroft's Patriot Act, since the current law seemed to give the agents sufficient authority, if they could persuade a judge that they were hot on some terrorist's trail.)

The librarian thinks that they returned later that day with the subpoena, after which they made copies of the log-in sheets for the previous three months. Although they were extremely polite and apologetic, they also took two of the library's four computers, which would not be returned until two months later. The librarian did not recall if the subpoena had specifically called for the turning over of those computers, and under the law it seems unlikely that it could have.*

# Monday, October 1, 2001

The story of the saga of the Hawaiian snow bunnies quickly spread far and wide through the Customs Service. On October 1, thirty Customs inspectors from Hawaii arrived at the airport in Grand Forks, North Dakota, to help Customs supervisor Mary Delaquis cover her section of the Northern Border. They rented cars, three or four to a vehicle. Five minutes from the airport, at least half of them were in ditches on the side of the road. October 1 had seen one of Grand Forks's first snowstorms, and the Hawaii contingent just couldn't handle it.

Still, with this group and the ones to follow on thirty-day rotations, Delaquis would pretty much be able to routinize the twenty-four-hour coverage of those border crossings in North Dakota and Minnesota that her deputy had said they would never be able to cover during the night. National Guard troops and INS people had supplemented her staff so that the places that two weeks before had had signs posted telling would-be border-jumpers to come back in the morning for screening were now covered by at least two people each. Of course, anyone really wanting to sneak in could still go around these official ports of entry and walk over through the woods or on a dirt road. But it was a start.

*Although an FBI Newark spokesman, Special Agent William Evania, acknowledged that a search of the library's computers would not have been "out of the ordinary" in terms of "what we were doing at the time," the FBI declined to comment on how or if they obtained any kind of subpoena or search warrant allowing them to seize and search the entire contents of the library's two computers, a seizure that presumably would have allowed them to review the reading habits of anyone using the Paterson library. The librarian's best recollection is that this happened on September 29, almost a month before the Patriot Act was signed. However, under prior law if federal prosecutors claimed to a judge in the special national security court that they were investigating a "foreign agent," they might have gotten a search warrant. But because warrants have to be directed at an investigation of a specific person or persons, the only possibility would seem to be that the bureau named someone, such as one of the hijackers who had lived in Paterson, as the subject of their investigation. Nonetheless, this gave them the ability to check on any and all of the thousands of Muslims living in Paterson who might have gone to the library to use the Internet.

At the same time, by using expanded shifts, more National Guardsmen, and even local police volunteers, Customs had also succeeded in reducing delays at the big border crossings in the north. Customs commissioner Robert Bonner had insisted on establishing an information hotline on the Customs website that provided frequent updates of the waiting time at key crossings. Mirroring an already functioning system set up by the Canadians, his public affairs people had been able to get it going within forty-eight hours of September 11. Not only had this given shippers a heads-up on when to go and when to wait, it had also given Bonner and his staff in Washington constant information, which he did not hesitate to use. "Whenever we started to show any significant delay, I'd get a call from Washington asking what's up," Kevin Weeks, the customs chief at the Ambassador Bridge in Detroit, recalls. "It became a brutal management system."


The September 11th Fund was also making progress. By October 1, the leaders of the United Way and New York Community Trust who jointly ran the fund had decided to hire Joshua Gotbaum, fifty, as the CEO. Gotbaum had served as an assistant secretary in both the Treasury and Defense departments in the Clinton administration, as well as a deputy in the White House Office of Management and Budget. For thirteen years before that, he had been an investment banker, but with a twist: In addition to garden-variety mergers and acquisitions, he'd specialized in advising unions on deals in which, in exchange for wage concessions, they gained part ownership of companies where their members worked. Gotbaum was also well connected in New York's political and union circles. His father is Victor Gotbaum, who was a highly regarded New York municipal union leader in the 1960s and 1970s. Gotbaum agreed to take the job for a year, commuting from his home in Washington.

In talking with Gotbaum about the job, New York United Way president Ralph Dickerson, Jr., quickly found that they agreed that the fund's biggest challenge, and opportunity, was to fill in the gaps that were likely to be left by the billions being provided by the federal government, by insurance the victims might have had, and by the dozens of other charities, such as the Red Cross and the fund set up by Mayor Giuliani to aid families of fallen police and firefighters. Their job was to use the fund strategically, by carefully figuring out where the biggest needs remained. That Gotbaum knew his way around New York's political and nonprofit worlds and had an investment banker's sensitivity for leveraging assets was bound to help.

Also on board was Franklin Thomas, who would be the fund's chairman. Thomas had been the president of the Bedford Stuyvesant Restoration Corporation (organized by Robert Kennedy in the 1960s as a public-private partnership to create jobs and housing in Brooklyn's worst ghetto), and then the president of the Ford Foundation, the giant New York–based charity that funds a dizzying array of social programs around the world. Now semiretired, he'd be a hands-on board chairman at least at the start, lending the effort the gray hair, credibility, and even public relations savvy it would need.

By October 1, the fund had gotten a polling company to conduct an online survey that provided an eye-opening view of how broad its options might be for providing help. A sample of 1,182 people were asked which categories of people should get money from the charities organized to help September 11 victims. In other words, who was a legitimate "victim"? The answers ranged from 83 percent *not* agreeing that those who are afraid to continue to go to work should get help, to 96.7 percent agreeing that the spouses and children of those killed should. The categories in the middle were the most intriguing: 79 percent of those polled believed that people who lost jobs in collapsed or evacuated buildings should get help, and 69 percent believed that those who lost wages as a result of the attacks should be helped. Thus, the fund's leaders were encouraged to continue to think expansively about how they might use their money.

On October 1,* Eileen Simon visited a Red Cross relief center in New York with one of her sisters. She filled out the forms Healy had worked so hard on, and left with a check for approximately $30,000, covering her mortgage and other expenses for three months, plus the cost of a tutor for one of her children. By now she had also put in her claim on the $500,000 life insurance policy Michael had purchased just a few months before.

Although one would assume that a gay Hispanic from the Bronx who had made it through Princeton and Stanford Law School was no pushover, Anthony Romero didn't come off as a tough guy. He was average-sized, had a ready smile, was usually soft-spoken, and looked you in the eye not with a stare but with a smile.

---

* Simon's recollection is that she made the trip to the Red Cross on "about" October 1, but she is not certain.

But he was tough, especially when he got angry. And this morning he was angry. Not at John Ashcroft, but at the ACLU's advertising agency.

In July 2001, the ACLU had signed off on a $2 million ad campaign aimed at recruiting new members and their dues and donations. With a total expense budget for the national organization of only $22 million, spending that kind of money on newspaper ads was obviously a big deal. And with the economy now sagging, Romero was already feeling the pinch from his major donors and foundations, who contributed about $9 million of the ACLU's $22 million in annual revenue. He needed to get as much as he could in smaller checks from the public that the ad campaign was supposed to produce.

The ads Romero had approved in July focused on gay rights and abortion rights as prime ACLU causes. Now Romero, who is openly gay, found himself laughing at the ad agency people who had come, they thought, to meet the new boss and discuss future work.

"Are you nuts," he asked the people working on the ads. "Gay rights? Where have you been in the last month? We're in the middle of a civil liberties crisis." There was certainly an air of a crisis, literally, in Romero's office overlooking New York harbor, a few blocks from Ground Zero. He and his staff, who had only been able to move back in the week before, could smell the fumes from the fires still burning at the Trade Center, and many of them were insisting on wearing surgical masks.

The ad men said that the campaign had already been approved, that they'd worked hard on it, and that he couldn't change it without adding all kinds of extra expense and delay.

"I'm not selling widgets here," he argued. "You can't do what you planned in July just because you planned it in July. The world has changed, and so will the ads."


Larry Cox's numbers for the end of September had barely improved from the week following the attacks. He now knew that in the last week of September, passenger traffic at the Memphis airport was nearly 60 percent below where it had been a year ago. On some days the terminal almost looked abandoned. So Cox now began a crash budgeting exercise, trying to figure out where and how deep he could cut to keep from raising his fees more than he'd have to.


James Sensenbrenner was chairman of what in the years before he had held the post was the most notoriously partisan group of politicians in the country—the House Judiciary Committee. The committee, which had started the impeachment process against President Clinton rolling with its raucous 1998 hearings and vote, had firebrands on the Republican right, matched by a healthy contingent of strident Democrats on the left, led by John Conyers, the Michigan congressman who was the senior Democrat. Yet this afternoon, the committee voted 36–0 to approve a scaled-back version of John Ashcroft's Patriot Act. Sensenbrenner had promised Ashcroft and the White House bipartisan support, and he had delivered, big-time—with a unanimous vote from Congress's most nonunanimous committee.

Romero and his Washington director, Laura Murphy, weren't thrilled, but they were satisfied that the sharpest edges of the Patriot Act had been blunted. This bill did not give Ashcroft the expanded authority he wanted to break into homes and search them secretly, or to detain immigrants indefinitely simply by declaring he had "reason to believe" the person was involved in terrorism. It also narrowed Ashcroft's proposed definition of terrorism, and cut back on the latitude he had sought to monitor e-mail correspondence. Also, all the new wiretapping and monitoring authority given the feds under the act would expire at the end of 2003 unless Congress renewed it—a provision that Sensenbrenner thought critical to preserving Congress's leverage and oversight authority.

Romero and the ACLU staff could now turn their attention to the Senate, which was on a slightly slower track in passing the legislation. Their goal was to get the Senate to want to match the House by putting some of its own limits into the Ashcroft bill. That didn't seem like it would be difficult, since the Senate was controlled by Democrats. Then, they might end up with all of the House and Senate limits in the conference bill that would be worked out by the two chambers, once each passed its own version. It seemed like a good plan.

Romero didn't appreciate how determined Ashcroft was to derail it.

## Tuesday, October 2, 2001

Herb Wachtell, Larry Silverstein's lawyer, had decided it was time to test the waters with the twenty-five companies that had insured Silverstein's interest in the World Trade Center. So he had Willis Limited, Silverstein's insurance broker, notify them of a meeting to be held at 10:00 A.M. on October 2 at the elegant Metropolitan Club on Fifth Avenue in New York. A video phone hookup would be provided at Trinity Square in London for the European invitees.

The letter from the Willis CEO made it all seem routine. The invitation said the "forum" would provide information on "preliminary estimates of the WTC losses, claims procedures, and the next steps to be taken."

Swiss Re's lawyer, Barry Ostrager, knew what was coming.

Ostrager, fifty-four, had been retained the week before by Swiss Re, a London-based insurer that had covered 22 percent of the World Trade Center policy—or about $780 million of the $3.55 billion in insurance. This made Swiss Re the biggest player in the group, and the one with the most to lose, an additional $780 million, if the attacks were somehow ruled to be two occurrences. Swiss Re's call to Ostrager had come after it and the other insurers had received a standard "notice of loss" from Willis regarding the Trade Center. The notice had added, matter-of-factly, that "the relevant Travelers wording" was attached.

*Travelers?* What did their wording have to do with anything?

"Almost immediately after September 11, we started reading quotes from Silverstein in the papers saying he was sure the insurers were going to be gentlemen and pay $7 billion," says Jacques Dubois, the Swiss Re America CEO. "And we knew something was up. Then we got the notice, which casually mentioned Travelers, and we said to ourselves, 'Oh yeah, nice try.' "

Dubois and the other insurers had quickly fired off e-mails and letters to Willis protesting the sudden inclusion of the Travelers form, instead of Willis's own form, which had defined one occurrence as any series of related events. Until the invitation to this Metropolitan Club "forum" had arrived, they had heard nothing back.

Ostrager was a veteran litigator for another Wall Street firm, Simpson Thacher & Bartlett, that was much larger than Wachtell's but not quite as wealthy (though the difference was still small enough to put Ostrager's income somewhere north of $2 million a year). He knew a fight was brewing, and he didn't really mind. Although Ostrager has had his share of big-dollar cases, they typically involved more mundane matters than the high-profile corporate takeover battles that had made Wachtell a true legal superstar. Ostrager was convinced that Wachtell might be brilliant arguing in front of judges, but that he had nothing like Ostrager's flair for communicating with jurors. Ostrager relished the prospect of going against Wachtell in front of a jury in a billion-dollar case involving September 11th.

As about fifty insurance executives and their lawyers settled into the leather armchairs in the Metropolitan Club's lounge, Larry Silverstein began a speech that Wachtell had carefully scripted. Wachtell had told his old friend the goal was to be noncombative, reasonable. The attacks had happened only three weeks before. Starting a fight so soon wouldn't seem right. Besides, this was only the opening round, and maybe it was all that would be needed to get these guys to make a deal.

Silverstein began by talking about the tragedy and how they had all been affected; his company had lost four people in the attacks. As he would in the months ahead in talking to the press about all of this, he affected an air of deep sadness mixed with a sense of high purpose. New York had to rebuild, and it was his obligation, with their help, to lead that effort. However heartfelt Silverstein's tone was, it was also the best way to ask for a few extra billion dollars.

Silverstein said he knew there were differences of opinion in the room about whether there had been one or two occurrences, but he was sure that could be worked out. This was a time when all people needed to work together. The most urgent need, he said, was for the insurers to begin making payments for the business interruption part of his policy—the amount meant to cover the fact that he was no longer collecting rents from the tenants. No one disputed that claim, he pointed out. And he needed it to pay the Port Authority the $10 million a month that he owed them. These were the monthly payments he and his partners had agreed to make as part of the deal they had made last July in return for the right to manage and rent out all the office space in the Trade Center for the next ninety-nine years. Silverstein also needed the money to pay the banks the monthly interest on the $563 million he had borrowed to make an initial cash payment that had also been part of the deal.*

As for the dispute over whether the insurers owed $3.55 billion or $7.1 billion, there was an easy compromise for that, that he was prepared to make if only they could all cooperate. It was not likely to cost $7.1 billion, but maybe just five or six to rebuild the Trade Center, he said. And if we take that from you as we build rather than in an immediate lump sum, the real cost to you—because of the delayed payments—on a current basis will be maybe four or four and a half billion, which will be a good compromise. The details can be worked out, Silverstein continued, but the point is that we shouldn't have to fight and shouldn't want to fight at a time like this.

After listening to that fifteen-minute speech, Ostrager made a big show of

---

*Silverstein's deal, in which in the popular press he had become the man who "owned" the World Trade Center, had in fact been done with just $14 million of his own cash; his partners had put up another $111 million and the banks had put up the rest, $563 million, in loans.

having heard enough. He walked out, telling the Swiss Re people that Silverstein was looking for some fast cash so he could invest it in lawyers and PR agents to wage war against the insurers.

They had to prepare to litigate.

# Wednesday, October 3, 2001

While his subordinates at the Immigration and Naturalization Service continued to discuss how to remove Robert Lindemann from the Border Patrol for talking to the media about resource shortages in Detroit, INS Commissioner James Ziglar told a Senate committee holding hearings on protecting the Northern Border that he had "encouraged our employees at all levels to think outside the box."

Other aspects of Ziglar's performance were equally tragicomic. He began by addressing what he said "appears to be a common misperception about our Northern Border, namely that it is 'unprotected' and 'undefended.' " Whereupon he reported, as if to make his case, that there were "334 Border Patrol agents assigned to the Northern Border." With 4,000 miles of border and at least four agents needed to cover one post (taking into account a twenty-four-hour day, weekends, vacations, and holidays), that amounts to roughly one agent on duty for every fifty miles of border.

What Ziglar didn't talk about at all was what happened on the rare occasion that this small band of troops actually caught someone. According to the INS's own records, between September 11 and this morning, Lindemann and his fellow Border Patrol agents had intercepted forty-two people sneaking over the border from Canada. But they had been told to release all of them on their own recognizance. So, other than Lindemann and his colleagues working longer shifts, it was business as usual on the Northern Border for the Catch and Release Program that Lindemann and his partner Mark Hall had been complaining about since 1999.

Ten of the forty-two people who had been released since September 11 had Middle Eastern names, which was to be expected because the Detroit area has such a high concentration of Middle Eastern immigrants, and because Canada does not require visas for people from countries such as Saudi Arabia to enter. As usual, as they were released into the country they had been trying to sneak into, they had each been given a postcard that they were supposed to mail into the INS when they had established a mailing address in the U.S. That way, the INS could send them a notice of when and where to appear for a deportation hearing. Of course, they rarely if ever sent back the postcards and never showed up for those hearings. In other words, as Ziglar sat testifying this morning, a Saudi wanting to sneak into the United States could get on a plane to Canada with no visa required, then sneak over the American border. His chances of getting caught were infinitesimal, but if he did get caught he'd be released to stay in the U.S. anyway.

Ashcroft had been making headlines by having the INS detain people like Syed Jaffri, the Pakistani who worked at a Bronx gas station and had had a dispute with his landlord. In New Jersey and New York and around the country, Jaffri and others with honest jobs, no criminal records, and often with solid roots in the community were being held because they were Muslims and had done something to violate the provisions of their visas, usually by taking jobs. But in Detroit, Lindemann—who would appear briefly on the *Today* show the next morning saying the INS was "leaving its flank exposed"—was being ordered to release Muslims from the Middle East with no community roots at all who were caught committing an actual crime (sneaking over the border). And because Lindemann was enough of an "outside the box" thinker to believe that the program needed to end, and to tell a reporter about how not having a detention facility to hold people had forced this situation, he was about to be fired.

Ziglar, an affable, intelligent former midlevel Wall Street bond executive with white hair and a chronic back problem, had been a boyhood friend of Mississippi Senator Trent Lott. He had just finished a three-year stint as the Senate sergeant at arms that Lott had gotten for him. The Associated Press story announcing his appointment to run INS had called him "a management expert." That obviously was a stretch. But he had taken the INS job just two months before, so he was hardly the only person to blame for what was happening on the Northern Border or anywhere else at INS.

Indeed, more galling than Ziglar's earnest, even self-effacing attempt at captaining this *Titanic* was the figure that Doris Meissner began to cut soon after September 11 as a speaker at Washington seminars on the subject of how to fix the INS. Meissner was the Clinton administration INS commissioner for seven years, a period during which the INS had atrophied under an organizational structure that allowed the bureaucrats running the various regional sections to be accountable to no one. It had been on her watch that a much promised system to track and match immigrants coming and leaving at the borders never materialized. It was on her watch that the Border Patrol had captured the man known as the Texas railway killer and released him so he could kill again, despite the fact that he was subject to a huge manhunt. The INS agents in Texas hadn't known about, let alone tried to use, a lookout database for which Meissner had spent tens of millions of dollars. Meantime, Meissner's boss, Attorney General Janet Reno, had allowed the Justice Department through the 1990s to spend hundreds of millions of dollars to develop two different types of fingerprint databases, one for the FBI and one for INS, that did not talk to each other.

But there was more to the INS story than individual blame. There had to be for things to have gotten this bad. The real culprit was America's historic ambivalence about immigration. Americans have always thought of themselves as a nation of immigrants, but since 1888, when a law was passed requiring the government to keep "lunatics, criminals, and morons" out of the United States, the country has had various laws and regulations to control who comes in. What it has not had is a clear policy or mission.

In that sense a bumbling INS was the INS the country had wanted, or at least wanted until September 11. INS provided poor service to foreigners who took the trouble to go through the immigration process, but it also didn't enforce the law when it came to keeping out those who didn't play by the rules. This double-edged incompetence was not only tolerable but desirable. America needed the INS not to guard the borders too well, so that the country could get cheap farmworkers and other laborers. And because Americans had always been ambivalent about the number of people who should be allowed to immigrate legally, it made sense to force those trying to follow the rules to run a gauntlet of long lines, rudeness, and years of waiting for the paperwork to get done. Conversely, there was no effective constituency for a good INS; other than foreigners, who cared if the agency was dysfunctional? So Congress didn't fund INS to do a good job, and the White House and Justice Department really didn't care how it was run. In fact, Ziglar's standing as head of INS was such that he reported not to Ashcroft but to an assistant to Ashcroft's deputy.

September 11 should have changed all that. Today's hearing—with Ziglar spouting meaningless numbers, and promising initiatives that sounded so much like the promises of his predecessors that it seemed like an old word processing file had been rejiggered—was a clear signal that nothing had changed.


Bernadine Healy thought the meeting of the executive committee of the Red Cross Board—the ten-member group that really runs the organization—was going fine. She'd taken chairman McLaughlin's hint the week before about "rumblings" among the board members and began by apologizing to the group for having made the decision about segregating the September 11 funds without an official board vote. She now realized that she should have consulted them first, she said. One member quickly interrupted to say that they understood that this had been "done in the heat of battle, and it was the right decision." All was forgiven. The executive committee, which included Pat Kennedy, the woman from San Francisco who had been so angry about what Healy had done, formally voted unanimous approval of the specially designated Liberty Fund.

They moved on to hear Healy's update on the new Family Grant Program and the effort to get volunteers in all the relief centers to provide consistent answers and consistent decisions on grants. That, too, went without a hitch. Everyone praised Healy, warmly.

But at the end of the meeting, a member from Louisiana announced that the committee wanted to take up the question of Israel.

That was shorthand for an issue that the Red Cross had wrestled with for years—the refusal of the International Red Cross to recognize the Israeli Red Shield of David, Israel's disaster relief organization, as a member whose emblem would be recognized under the Geneva Convention as belonging to a humanitarian service agency that deserved protection in war zones. Soon after assuming her $400,000 a year job at the Red Cross in 1999, Healy had taken on the issue. To her it was a simple matter of justice, and perhaps anti-Semitism. She had ultimately caused an international storm by withholding the American Red Cross's $5 million dues from the international agency until the policy was changed. The issue had festered since, because many board members had not liked the way Healy had pushed so hard and offended so many sister organizations around the world.

Now, out of the blue Israel had been raised again by one of the old-guard members who Healy suspected did not like her. Worse, he asked that Healy leave the room. She was stunned when the rest of the members agreed that she should leave, and more stunned when a short time later they adjourned and she found out that they had voted 9–1 to reinstate the dues. Healy protested to those that were there (others had attended the meeting by conference call) as they were leaving. This was the wrong time to do this, she said, her voice quivering. It was the wrong time to send that kind of signal about Israel and, worse, the wrong time to distract the organization from its September 11 work. She was angry, and she let them know it.

Healy prided herself not only on her medical skills but on her business sense and ability to function in tough settings. She'd run the National Institutes of Health before coming to the Red Cross. In her two years at the Red Cross, she'd confronted and made strides in fixing serious deficiencies in the blood bank program. She'd tightened management controls. She'd dealt unflinchingly with a financial scandal at a local chapter in New Jersey, then pushed hard for new audit procedures across the organization. Her blunt style had offended some, yet her mix of toughness and instincts for political infighting had, she thought, been effective and had won over those she con-sidered to be the best people on the staff. But, she recalls, "It was at that moment that I realized that my peripheral vision, which I had always prided myself on having, was totally gone when it came to the board. I simply had not seen what was going on. I should have seen this coming. They couldn't attack me for designating the funds, so they were going to use another issue to get me angry and undercut me."

## Friday, October 5, 2001

On the morning of October 5, three men whom Sal Iacono had never heard of met to talk about a program aimed at saving his store. The three, who are part of one of those New York networks—in this case, people involved in the civic and philanthropic causes—that often makes the city feel like a small town, were Carl Weisbrod, Jack Rosenthal, and Bill Grinker. Weisbrod was the head of the Alliance for Downtown New York. Rosenthal, a former top *Times* edi-tor, was head of the New York Times Foundation. And Grinker ran something called Seedco, a nonprofit corporation whose mission was to provide loans to businesses in low-income neighborhoods that work with Seedco's staff to fashion viable business plans. The three were friends whose career paths had often crossed.

Almost immediately after the attacks, the Times Foundation, whose main activity is the Christmas-based New York Times Neediest Fund, had started a fund for the victims of September 11. By now, $25.9 million had come in, an amount that stunned Rosenthal, whose Neediest Cases Fund had raised $8.3 million in 2000. Now he had to decide what to do with it. A week before, he had sat next to the head of the Ford Foundation, another friend of all three, at a meeting, and she had suggested that Rosenthal call Weisbrod, because Weis-brod had been talking about doing something to help struggling businesses near Ground Zero. Weisbrod, in turn, had suggested to Rosenthal that Grinker be included in their discussions, because he had the organization,

Seedco, which could implement such a program. Within an hour, they quickly reached an agreement for the Times Fund to put up $2.9 million for Seedco to start a program that would make loans and grants to small businesses hurt by the attacks. Weisbrod's organization would help with outreach for applications, which Seedco would screen.

An entirely new charitable program that normally would have required weeks, months, maybe years of meetings, memos, and contracts had been created in about an hour. And when the September 11th Fund—whose board Weisbrod would soon join—heard about it, the Seedco program would be able get much more money. Thanks in large part to that telethon that George Clooney and the other Hollywood people had put together, the September 11th Fund had by now raised more than $200 million.

On paper, at least, it seemed that help was on the way for the small businesses devastated by the attacks.

But there was a gap between a program conceived by a group of sophisticated, big-time grant givers and a shoemaker like Sal Iacono, who had one full-time employee, was paying for repairs to his shop mostly by reaching into his pocket for cash, and had never heard of something called a business plan, let alone contemplated submitting one to get a loan or a grant.


Bill O'Reilly was famously tough on the guests who appear in what he calls the "No Spin Zone" on his prime-time Fox News cable show. But to Bernadine Healy he was a lot easier to deal with than her board. At least he comes at you from the front.

Healy appeared on his show tonight and answered questions directly and not at all defensively. Yet she and O'Reilly seemed to talk past each other. O'Reilly's sole concern was that the families of the victims of September 11, which he seemed to define narrowly as those who had died or were injured, get all of the charity money. Healy was much more on his side than board members like Kennedy wanted her to be, but she nonetheless thought of the September 11 tragedy in broader terms than the dead and injured.

*O'Reilly:* How much money has the Red Cross . . . raised so far to help these families?

*Healy:* . . . Remember, the contributions of the Red Cross cover the wide range of our services. It's to help the victims and their families, to help the rescue workers, it is to—

*O'Reilly:* Well, how much money has come in for this terrorist attack?

*Healy:* For all of our activities.

*O'Reilly:* Yeah.

*Healy:* We have a Liberty Fund that covers the range of Red Cross activities.

*O'Reilly:* Good, good. How much money, Doctor?

*Healy:* Roughly about $290 million.

*O'Reilly:* Just to the Red Cross? Two hundred and ninety million?

*Healy:* . . . Yes.

*O'Reilly:* Well, that should be enough to make everybody fairly comfortable, right?

*Healy:* Well, I don't know. It depends on what your services are. We are a service organization. We don't bring the money in and then pass it out. We are doing it for the services that we routinely provide and in this case—

*O'Reilly:* Sounds like a lot of bureaucracy, Doctor. . . .

*Healy:* No! To the contrary. How many organizations can turn around a family gift program within literally twenty-four hours based on one sheet of paper with no red tape at all? The American Red Cross has done it. Now we had checks in the hands of over a thousand—

*O'Reilly:* All right. Hold it. Wait. Wait. Wait. You've got 5,000 dead people. You've got $290 million, and you have a lot of rescue workers who may need things. It sounds like you've got enough money to make these people comfortable.

Healy then started enumerating the work the Red Cross wanted to do to counsel survivors and get the organization ready for future, similar attacks.

"Get it to the families," O'Reilly said.

Although those families were flooding O'Reilly's switchboard and e-mail, complaining that they were not getting what they needed, from Healy's perspective that problem was being fixed fast. Indeed a widow whom O'Reilly had had on earlier that night and on prior shows complaining that she'd received nothing from the Red Cross, had now told him, and he conceded this to Healy, that she had not been home for several days and that when she had returned home earlier that day she had found a Red Cross check for three months of living expenses.

While O'Reilly's is the most popular cable news talk show, its audience is still smaller than that of any of the broadcast networks. Yet his crusade was beginning to have influence far beyond those numbers, as other news organizations started to pick up on the controversy he was stirring. To O'Reilly and to his audience, the issue was simple: Hundreds of millions were being raised, and the victims weren't getting it fast enough.

# Monday, October 8, 2001

Tom Ridge had arranged to bunk at a friend's house in Annapolis, Maryland. It was an hour's drive, but with one of the men from his new Secret Service detail at the wheel, it was tolerable.

Ridge reported for his first day of work at 7:30 to sit in on the joint briefings from CIA Director George Tenet, Ashcroft, and FBI Director Robert Mueller that had become a fixture on the President's schedule since September 11. Early on, Ridge would be struck by three things in these sessions: how well Mueller and Tenet seemed to get along despite all he'd heard about FBI-CIA friction, how deferential Ashcroft seemed to be to Tenet and everyone else when he was in the Oval Office, and the length of the "threat matrix" briefing they were reviewing. It was either because there were so many threats out there, or because no one wanted to be caught after the fact not having mentioned something, or some combination of both.

Today things were especially tense, for two reasons. With the bombing that began the American War in Afghanistan having started the day before, there was so much worry about an Al Qaeda counterattack that Vice President Cheney had been moved to what would soon become the proverbial "undisclosed location." One of the more specific fears, though the information was not at all specific, was that the enemy might try to unleash some kind of radiation bomb in Washington, a concern that had already prompted the posting of radiation detectors throughout Washington and especially in and around the White House.

On top of that, on Friday, an editor at the *National Enquirer* in Florida had died from what had since been confirmed to be exposure to anthrax. Another *Enquirer* employee had since taken ill, and while no one knew for sure that this was anything other than a freak accident, the FBI was now on the case.

After a swearing-in ceremony, Ridge spent the rest of the day working on organizing his staff, which would be housed in the Old Executive Office

Building across the driveway from the small office he'd been given in the White House.

Two people were already unofficially on board. Steven Abbot, the retired admiral whom the Vice President had hired over the summer to run a homeland security task force (and who had reported for his first meeting the morning of the attacks), seemed like he would be a good fit to be Ridge's top deputy. Cheney was pushing him for the post, and Ridge was amenable. Abbot was a Rhodes Scholar, Naval Academy graduate, and former naval pilot, who had gone on to command an aircraft carrier and then a battle group; his last job in the active military had been as deputy commander in chief of the U.S. European command during the war in Kosovo. Abbot thought of himself as someone who could methodically map out obstacles and overcome them one by one. Whether he'd be tough enough to be Ridge's enforcer when it came to getting various agencies to cooperate was an open question, but he was eager to help Ridge fit all the pieces together.

Richard Falkenrath had been an assistant professor at Harvard's Kennedy School of Government and co-author of the seminal book on the country's need to gear up to fight terrorism (*America's Achilles' Heel*). Just after the attacks, Abbot had happily discovered that Falkenrath had recently taken a job on the White House national security staff. Falkenrath seemed a good candidate to work on budgets and look at how the government's organizational structure might have to be changed. Young (thirty-six) and a touch full of himself, Falkenrath would become one of the few members of Ridge's nose-to-the-grindstone staff who seemed glib enough to be a character in *The West Wing*.

Ridge had already recruited some of his old staffers from Pennsylvania, and his success demonstrated not just their loyalty to him but the same urgent sense of mission that had moved him to leave the governor's mansion so quickly. For example, Mark Holman, who agreed to become another top deputy, had served as Ridge's first campaign manager when he ran for Congress in 1982, and then his chief of staff when he was in Congress and governor. Holman had finally left eleven months ago to take a partnership in a law firm so that he could make a better living. He was loving private practice and had just proposed to the woman who would become his second wife, when he got the call from his old boss. He had quit the firm on Friday and started with Ridge today.

On October 8, Mark Isakowitz started work of a different sort. Isakowitz was a partner in a small lobbying firm, and he had just been recruited to help a coalition of three companies that provided most of the security guards who screened passengers at airport checkpoints. The man who recruited him was Kenneth Quinn, a Washington lawyer and lobbyist, who represented Argenbright Security, the company that had the largest market share, 40 percent, of the three.

Quinn specialized in representing aviation industry clients in Washington, and had the classic résumé to do it. He had been chief counsel to the FAA and counselor to the Secretary of Transportation. So why did he have to retain another lobbyist? Because Isakowitz, who'd been active in Republican politics in Ohio, specialized in Republicans. That was a group Quinn knew he needed a lot of help with.

Amid widespread media reports and public disgust about the low quality of the airport screening force, Quinn had heard that the Senate was considering passing a bill that would require that the government take over airport security by hiring a new force of federal law enforcement agents to screen all passengers and bags. Argenbright's business would be instantly extinguished. Leading the drive for the new law was not only Democrat Ernest Hollings of South Carolina, but Republicans John McCain of Arizona and Kay Bailey Hutchison of Texas. So Quinn needed Republican lobbying help, fast, to head off what seemed like it might be a Senate juggernaut. Failing that, he'd have to get the Republican-controlled House to stop the creation of this giant new federal agency.

On Monday, Isakowitz met with Quinn and executives from Argenbright and the other two, smaller players in the industry. He quickly took the job. "These were not dirt balls," he explains. "You can't survive here working for dirt balls. They were serious businessmen who made the case that the real problem was that the airlines had refused to pay them much more than the minimum wage. So the industry had been in a race to the bottom in terms of quality. . . . If the federal government simply set new standards in terms of training and the quality of the people, they would gladly meet those standards. That was the issue, and that made more sense than creating a whole new federal bureaucracy."

By Monday afternoon, Isakowitz had spoken to David Crane, the senior advisor to Republican leader Trent Lott (and the man who had come up with the idea for the victims compensation fund). But after checking with Lott, Crane said that Senator McCain had already signed off on the bill and was adamant about it. Lott had decided that Isakowitz and his clients had to go see McCain if they wanted any Republican help.

McCain politely told the group that the momentum for the bill was already too strong, that these private security companies, particularly Argenbright, had terrible reputations, and that the public needed to be reassured that things had changed and air travel was safe. They were not going to get help from him.

McCain was right about Argenbright's reputation. Since September 11, various stories in the press had reported that the company and three managers had pled guilty a year before to federal felony charges of having fabricated background checks of screeners at the Philadelphia airport to make it seem as if they met the minimum employment requirements. But Quinn had pointed out that in December of 2000 a large, highly regarded British conglomerate, Securicor, Ltd., had purchased Argenbright, and that he had been working with the newly parented company since the summer to clean up its act when it came to enforcing requirements on background checks for employees.

That was true, but it was only half the story. Despite the Securicor purchase for $185 million, Argenbright was still being run on October 8 by Frank Argenbright, Jr., who had founded the company with $500 and one polygraph machine in Atlanta in 1979. And the terms under which he continued to run the company had given him an enormous incentive to continue to cut quality. According to the purchase contract, depending on how well Frank Argenbright did just during the year 2001 in improving the airport screening company's cash flow above its 2000 level, the purchase price could go up as much as $25 million, or down by as much as $10 million. Based on what the Argenbright public filings indicate was Frank Argenbright's share of the stock, this would mean a personal bonus to him for his shares of more than $12 million on the upside, or a penalty of about $5 million on the downside. On top of that, the board of his old company, the one that had sold the airport screening business, had also agreed to award Frank Argenbright its own bonus of up to $3 million if he achieved that additional purchase price bonus. In short, Frank Argenbright stood to get an extra $15 million personally if he could manage the company so tightly in 2001 that it achieved extra cash flow. In fact, a review of available public documents suggests that he only had to improve cash flow by $3.2 million in that one year over the prior year's $16 million in cash flow to get that entire $15 million bonus, which might be achieved by marginal savings in training or wages, or even background checks. On the other hand, a swing downward of just $1.3 million in cash flow would cost him the entire $5 million penalty.

Of course, profits can go up not just with cost cuts but with increased revenue. But with the airline business so hurt following September 11, and with the long history of the airlines pushing the screeners to lower their fees, any boosts in revenue seemed improbable.

This is not to say that Frank Argenbright—who was apparently so proud of his company that he kept a life-sized, handsomely uniformed replica of an Argenbright guard in the study at the vacation mansion he had built for his family in Sea Island, Georgia—didn't care about public safety more than he cared about adding $10 million or $15 million more to what seemed to be his now sizable fortune.* And it was also true that his company had had to work in a world where the airlines constantly played the competitors off of each other, pushing them to lower costs. Nonetheless, that purchase contract did mean that he now had a compelling incentive in the short term to skimp as much as he could.

In fact, the debate that loomed over whether to federalize the private screeners, juxtaposed against that huge short-term-incentive contract, presented the ultimate face-off of two competing value systems. The goal of private enterprise is to maximize profit for individual owners, who in turn provide incentive to employees and managers, like Argenbright, to maximize their own income by performing well. The goal of government is to maximize something else thought to be of value to society, in this case public safety and the public's perception that they are safe. The theory is that government has to step in to provide certain services or goods that are deemed important, but which the marketplace doesn't seem able to provide, or isn't likely to provide in a way that assures a high-enough level of quality if private profit is part of the equation. For example, Americans wouldn't trust the Secret Service's job to a private company, because they want to assure a certain level of quality no matter what the cost. Argenbright's personal profit-incentive deal was not known to anyone in Washington, but Isakowitz and Quinn had an uphill fight if they were going to convince congressmen and senators, themselves frequent fliers, that any kind of profit-making enterprise should still be part of the equation when it came to protecting the nation's air travelers.


Sergio Magistri had another view of the airline security bill. It might crush Argenbright, but it would propel InVision. Another key provision of the bill that was being talked about would require that all baggage checked into a plane's luggage compartment be screened for explosives. When his lobbyist, McCann, had told him about it, Magistri had thanked him. But McCann modestly replied that in recent days when he'd made his rounds on the Hill talking up InVision's baggage-screening equipment to key staffers, he'd been

*Through the company's public relations firm, Argenbright declined requests for an interview.

told to relax, that he didn't have to worry because everyone wanted a screening requirement.

Argenbright and InVision were hardly the only companies that had hired lobbyists following the attacks. By now Washington was teeming with former everythings—congressmen, senators, congressional staffers, cabinet members, procurement officers, and presidential counselors—plying some September 11–related cause. Former Clinton White House counsel and Al Gore confidant Jack Quinn had been hired by Larry Silverstein to try to get Silverstein's liability for the deaths at the World Trade Center capped the way the airlines had had their liability capped so as not to exceed their insurance coverage. Raytheon was paying its longtime Washington law firm—which includes two former Senate majority leaders (Bob Dole and George Mitchell), former Texas governor Ann Richards, and former presidential counselor Harry McPherson—to scour various homeland-security-related legislative and regulatory proposals calling for spending on new products and services. They would then set up meetings for Ed Woollen at the various government agencies that might be dispensing the funds. Raytheon's competitors were, of course, all doing the same. Rental car companies and the hotel industry were seeking relief, arguing that if the airlines had gotten money for the shutdown of travel following the attacks, they should, too. And the *New York Times* would soon report that the traffic sign industry was pushing for more money for federal road signs to prevent traffic jams after terror attacks, while date growers wanted the Pentagon to put dates in food packages going to Afghanistan.

"For about a week, maybe two, people in my business were kind of afraid to go back out there," said one lobbyist who had the busiest time of his career in the months following September 11. "We felt really self-conscious about it. But that ended pretty quickly."

The attempt by so many in the private sector to claim their share of whatever might be available in Washington was matched, sometimes in comical ways, by the ostensibly less selfish nonprofit sector. There was soon heated competition among medical researchers at various universities for grants to study the mental health damage done to children in New York from watching and hearing so much about the attacks. Others competed for grants to study the affects of pollution at Ground Zero. And the September 11th Fund soon found that among the hundreds of organizations submitting proposals for grants to dispense services to the victims were dozens in which the organization's standard description of its work had obviously been rewritten so that the opening paragraph began with something like, "In the wake of the terror attacks of September 11th . . ."

Even people raising money for completely different causes tried to latch on to the September 11 gravy train. The Glaucoma Foundation sent out invitations to its $1,500-a-plate annual New York gala, scheduled for December 4, with a note saying that "In tribute to New York City," a "portion" of the proceeds would go to September 11 charities. Months later the charity conceded that only $17,500, or 2.7 percent of its proceeds, had been donated, all of it to a fund for Cantor Fitzgerald families.

These displays of self-interest in the face of tragedy may seem grubby. Some were. But many of those involved viewed them as inevitable and even healthy, in the sense that the system—American democracy and the American free marketplace—is based on people pushing the policies or the products that are in their interest to push, and competing with others who do the same. As one of the lobbyists for an aerospace company put it, "Suppose after September 11 we all stopped doing this, because we felt guilty. I happen to think that one of my clients' products really could help the FBI keep track of people they need to keep track of. Sure, they'll make money selling it, and, sure, I use my contacts to help them and they pay me to do that. But would we be better off if I didn't?"

# Tuesday, October 9, 2001

Stuyvesant High School, which was about five blocks from Ground Zero, reopened this morning, following what New York City Board of Education officials said was an exhaustive cleanup of the whole building and a full retrofitting of its air filtration system. Many parents weren't convinced that Stuyvesant was safe, which was not unreasonable given that the fires were still burning, the neighborhood still smelled, and no one really knew what was in the air down there.

But like most students, Jessica Schumer was glad to return. She'd been forced to go to Brooklyn Tech the last three weeks, and although Tech, too, was considered an elite magnet school, she hated it. This was an awful way to spend the critical fall term of senior year—a time when she and her classmates had to worry about applying to college and showing the best possible grades and extracurricular achievements on those college applications.

Her father and mother had talked to various officials involved in the cleanup and in the testing of the air, and they had been assured that Stuyvesant was now safe. They were convinced that these people would not lie to them about their daughter's well-being. Besides, Chuck Schumer thought it important that New York move ahead with its recovery as soon as possible.

So although the senator made a rule of not dragging either of his daughters into anything that might involve publicity, and although he usually spent Tuesdays in Washington, he decided that he ought to take Jessica to reopening day. It would help reassure the other parents that there was no danger.

## Thursday, October 11, 2001

As Eileen Simon began to try to create some kind of new routine in her life, she began to feel guilty about not having seen Ground Zero. Before September 11, she regularly came to the city; without traffic on the George Washington Bridge it was thirty or forty minutes to the site of her husband's office. Now she figured she ought to go see it. So she arranged to meet her sister and walk over to a spot near the cleanup.

She lasted there for about a minute. Tears running down her face, she ran up the block in the opposite direction, her sister trailing behind. More than anything else it was the smell that was too much.

Brian Lyons, who was working as a supervisor in the pit just under where Simon had stood, had never had a job that was more fulfilling. Every morning he and the other field bosses met at about 6:00 and mapped out the ground they would try to cover through the day and until about midnight. They'd list all the problems and issues they faced, such as a fire still burning in one spot, or a loose wall in another. Then, with Lyons typically acting as the jack-of-all-trades troubleshooter, they'd go out and join their troops in tackling it. They would reconvene for a similar meeting late in the afternoon, then go out again for the night. The best part was that unlike the usual construction job, there would rarely be union hassles, slow-downs for rest breaks, or guys just plain goofing off. Invariably they'd get further than they had planned in the morning.

All that was satisfying enough. On top of that, there was the possibility that Lyons might find his brother, and the certainty that he was doing everything he could, right there in the trenches, to keep the firemen and construction crews working together to balance speed with respect for the remains scattered in the rubble.

The problem was that Lyons's boss at the desk job he had had on September 11 managing construction projects was getting restless. He understood Lyons's anguish, but it was now a month after September 11. He wanted Lyons to come back, or to quit.

Lyons felt he wasn't in shape to make any kind of career decision. So he had devised what he thought might be a midway solution. He'd get the construction company that was now employing him at Ground Zero to agree instead to reimburse his old employer for his "consulting" services. That way, he'd be working for his old company, and, he told his boss, might be able to get them some additional work down there. But he'd also be doing the new work he wanted to do. He'd be making about a third less than his old $100,000 salary, but at least he wouldn't be cutting off his line to the old job. The other day he had even brought his boss from his real job down to Ground Zero to meet his supervisor, so that they might work it out.

But today, his boss told him that he wasn't going to agree with this loan-out deal. Lyons had to make a decision.

He quit and took the job at Ground Zero.


Following bipartisan floor speeches attacking the private screening companies and declaring that Americans demanded that the nation's airways be made safe again, the Senate passed its Airline Security bill this afternoon, requiring all screening to be done "as soon as practicable" by a new force of federal agents. The vote was 100–0. As Quinn and Isakowitz had feared, they now had to turn to the House if they were going to save Argenbright and the other airport security companies.

The bill also required that all checked baggage be screened for explosives with the kind of detection equipment made by InVision and its one competitor. No actual deadline was set for getting all the equipment in place at the airports, but the FAA was required to submit a schedule for the implementation of the program within sixty days. By the next day InVision's stock was up to $12.95. It had more than quadrupled in the month since the attacks.

Press accounts of the Senate's unanimous action estimated that 28,000 new federal employees would have to be hired and that the cost would be $1.2 billion to $2 billion. This 28,000 number became part of every description of the new law in the weeks that followed, as if it were an immutable truth.

In fact, 28,000 was more of a placeholder than a real number. It had been created by Senator Hollings's staffer on aviation issues, Samuel Whitehorn, who in the frantic hours before the bill was written and passed had called the airport and airline trade groups asking how many baggage screeners were now employed around the country. According to Whitehorn, no one had a "good fix" on a real number, but "28,000 seemed to be somewhere in the middle of the estimates" that came out of these informal conversations. So that was the number that Whitehorn and other staffers fed to their bosses and to the press.

Yet Whitehorn had forgotten about the additional corps of screeners it would take to staff all that new equipment that was going to scan for explosives in luggage being checked into the cargo compartment. He simply hadn't asked about that. Nor had he taken into account that the staffing levels for the current corps of screeners for passengers and carry-on bags was unanimously thought to be grossly inadequate.

The Senate had just passed a law calling for what was probably the birth of the biggest new government agency in history, and no one really knew how big it might be.

## Friday, October 12, 2001

The time stamp on the new House version of the Patriot Act sitting on the fax machine at the ACLU's Washington office said 3:45 A.M. October 12. When Laura Murphy, the ACLU's Washington director, later reconstructed the events of October 11 and 12, she would remember that this was the first clue of what had happened to her plan for a softened-up version of the law.

Murphy had gone to bed on the night of the 11th disappointed that just before midnight the Senate had passed a version of the Patriot Act that had almost none of the modifications that staffers for Senator Patrick Leahy, the Vermont Democrat who chairs the Judiciary Committee, had assured her they would fight for. Instead, the Senate Democrats had basically caved in to Ashcroft, accepting most of what he had proposed. They had decided they were not going to oppose Ashcroft and the White House on a national security issue. In fact, when Russell Feingold of Wisconsin had stood to explain why he was casting the one dissenting vote, Democratic Majority Leader Tom Daschle countered, "We've got a job to do. The clock is ticking." Schumer, a Harvard-trained lawyer and member of the Judiciary Committee, voted yes and did not participate in the abbreviated debate, except to ask for clarification on some clause in the money laundering section that his Wall Street constituents were worried about. Unlike many Democrats who opposed the bill but feared taking on Ashcroft and the White House, or considered a fight to be fruitless, Schumer actually supported the bill as necessary for providing the new tools the government now needed.

Still, Murphy, Romero, and the other ACLU people held out some hope. Senator Leahy's people had assured Murphy that he and Daschle would appoint sympathetic members to the conference committee that would negotiate with the House over a final version of the bill. That way, they might get senators who were more inclined to support the more tolerable House version of the bill, for which Sensenbrenner and Conyers, his Democratic counterpart, had produced that 36–0 vote following the ACLU's successful effort to get Barr and other conservative Republicans on the committee to oppose Ashcroft's original proposal.

But by the morning of the 12th, Murphy knew that was not to be. Amazingly, the more moderate Sensenbrenner bill that the ACLU had helped to orchestrate had been scuttled. The version of the bill with the 3:45 time stamp was a substitute that House Speaker Dennis Hastert had negotiated with Ashcroft the night before, and it was almost identical to the Senate bill. It had stripped out almost all of the softenings of the original Ashcroft proposal that Sensenbrenner's committee had voted for. The only key feature left from Sensenbrenner's Judiciary Committee bill was a watered-down version of the sunset provision that now allowed Congress to end the relaxed surveillance guidelines after five years, instead of Sensenbrenner's two years.

Sometime after midnight, Hastert had agreed to Ashcroft's plea that the Sensenbrenner bill be scrapped in favor of this new bill, and that the new version would be the only one coming up in the House for a vote. "The Speaker said to me that we had to do this for the sake of the country, so I reluctantly agreed," Sensenbrenner would later explain. With the House and Senate bills now almost identical on the key provisions, there would be no real issues for either side to debate in a conference that would meld the two versions together.

By 8:30, Murphy and other ACLU staffers were on the phone to their friends who were staffers on the Hill, screaming about a betrayal. They even reached some members of Congress. Most were sympathetic, but some screamed back that the ACLU people simply didn't understand what was going on—what the atmosphere was like, what the fear was like. Helicopters and jet fighters were still patrolling the skies over the Capitol. There were bomb scares. Ashcroft was announcing new threats almost every day.

Later that morning, the House voted 337–79 to pass the bill. The outraged dissenters complained that no one could possibly have had the time to read the enormously complex 342-page law that amended fifteen different federal statutes and that had been printed out only hours before. Others pointed out that the House had never passed any bill related to criminal procedure and the Constitution that had not been cleared through the Judiciary Committee.

Because the House and Senate bills were not totally identical, it would be another two weeks before a final bill was sent to the White House for the President's signature, but with this House vote the drama was over.

The ACLU effort was dead.

Ashcroft now had the tools he needed.

For example, consider the situation of Ali Erikenoglu—the American citizen from Paterson who had been questioned so harshly by FBI agents in September after they supposedly got a call reporting that he had expressed support for the terrorists who had blown up the USS *Cole*. Suppose Erikenoglu had kicked the agents out of his apartment when they refused not to walk on his carpet, which was his right. Or suppose the agents had decided that they hadn't liked some of his answers, no matter how polite he had been. With no more than a statement to a judge in that special national security court that they had gotten credible information that Erikenoglu might be involved in terrorism or supporting terrorists, they could now have all his phone records searched to see whom he had called or what phone numbers had called him. They could check his library and credit card records. Records of the websites he had logged on to from his modem could be obtained. And all of this could happen without him knowing it.

If these searches yielded any further "evidence" (such as him having called a phone number that had also once been called by a terror suspect, or him having read a book about Osama bin Laden), they could then proceed to break into his apartment and search it, or put a tap on any phone line he used or they thought he might use. In fact, although one hopes the feds would want more than a phone tip to proceed like this, they probably could do it all even without their initial efforts yielding further apparent connections.

If all that didn't produce enough evidence to charge him with being involved in a terrorist plot or of aiding terrorists (under a now more loosely defined definition of "aiding" and of "terrorism"), he wasn't yet out of the woods. For if the wiretaps or the search of his apartment produced evidence of some minor crime, such as marijuana possession or having obtained a fraudulent identification card for an underage nephew who wanted to use it to buy drinks at a bar, they could now get him for that. Under the new law, as long as "foreign intelligence," including a possible foreign terrorist plot, had been "a significant purpose" of the investigation, the results of any search could now be used in a common criminal case. Then, they could squeeze him more by giving him the choice of cooperating by naming terrorists or having the book thrown at him for that minor charge.

And if all that didn't produce any evidence of any type of crime, he could always be held as a material witness, if some connection to the ongoing terror investigation could be asserted.

Jaffri, the Palestinian held in solitary by the INS after a dispute with his landlord, faced all this and more. Under the Patriot Act, an immigrant being held for a visa violation could be detained with no hearing for a maximum of seven days. And, because of new internal rules Ashcroft had ordered written for the INS, that hearing could then be held in secret. After that, the new law provided that even if he was ordered deported by the INS judge, Ashcroft could still hold him indefinitely if he deemed him a threat to national security.

For the ACLU and other civil libertarians, and for an honest citizen like Erikenoglu, whose sole offense was having a Muslim name and perhaps having a co-worker who had made a phone call about him, Ashcroft's new tools presented a whole new version of American justice. But for people living in sleeper cells—waiting to attack, yet not committing any overt crimes or revealing any other explicit evidence for which the old rules of search and seizure had applied—the feds' new latitude presented a whole new set of vulnerabilities. Indeed, the idea of being in a sleeper cell was to live quietly and obey all the rules until the moment came to act. So to Ashcroft and everyone else trying in those frantic early weeks following September 11 to find those who lay waiting to attack, the new law was well named. To them, this was Congress at its patriotic best.

On the same morning that the Patriot Act was being pushed through the House by a lopsided vote after having been supported 96–1 in the Senate, and on the day after the Senate passed the aviation security bill 100–0, the executive committee of the national board of the ACLU convened in Washington—where one of the first issues up for debate was whether the ACLU should continue to oppose metal detectors at airports. Since 1973, the official ACLU policy had been that the organization was against the screening of airline passengers for guns and other weapons because it violated Fourth Amendment protections against unreasonable searches.

Amazingly, the ACLU position had never changed, despite attempts over the years by some members of the board to get it amended. Now, Romero was determined to get the policy expunged before he started reading about it in the press.

After about an hour of discussion, the executive committee voted unanimously to repeal it. But when the full eighty-four-person national board, which includes representatives from the fifty states, would meet two days later, things didn't move that quickly. After a debate that lasted much of the morning, the repeal resolution passed by a voice vote, but not at all unanimously.

Among those who wanted to keep the ACLU on record against screening all passengers for guns and knives was Arthur Heyderman, the delegate from Iowa. "We should not cave in to the pressure of the moment," he argued. "The government should do a better job of figuring out who has to go through a metal detector. They should have probable cause before making someone go through it."

How are they supposed to check every passenger for probable cause, one of the other board members asked. "That's their job, not ours," Heyderman replied. "We have to stop worrying about how they do their jobs. Why can't they just put an air marshal on every plane," he added. "Then they wouldn't have to worry about searching people or finding probable cause. If that's the price we have to pay not to violate our right not to be searched, we should pay it."

Heyderman, who also argued that we should not be bombing Afghanistan "any more than we should have bombed Chicago because Al Capone lived there," is part of what Romero calls "an old-guard faction at the ACLU, which has a lot of respect in the organization but which does not always prevail." Yes, they make his job more difficult in the September 12 era, he says, but they also "help us keep to our principles."

Beyond the metal detector issue (which Romero did succeed in disposing of without any publicity), the ACLU's three-day policy meeting featured what Heyderman would later call "debates over efforts we have to make to reach out to people to get them to slow down. Ashcroft wanted to scare people to death, and we had to figure out how to stop that."

For Tom Ridge, the bad news the first week on the job was that the federal government budget process for the budget year that would not begin until *next* October 1 was about 90 percent over. That meant that all the agencies he was supposed to coordinate, such as Customs, INS, FEMA, or the Coast Guard, had not only already submitted their budget requests, but had had them vetted by Mitch Daniels's Office of Management and Budget. Daniels and the agencies were still negotiating some details, but most of the work had been done.

As a former congressman, Ridge had some sense of the process, but the exact timing was a surprise. How was he supposed to have any effect on these agencies if he couldn't put his stamp on what they would be spending for another two years, he asked chief of staff Card and the President.

The good news was that Card and Bush responded by stopping the process in its tracks. They told Daniels to meet with Ridge and let him review and if necessary redo everything. More important, they asked Daniels to assign members of his staff to Ridge to help him move the dollars around. Their deadline to do it was extended through December.

"The President told me to become Tom Ridge's budget director and to make my staff his staff," Daniels explains. "He wanted to be sure Ridge had an immediate impact and immediate credibility, and giving him my power over the budget was the way to do that." It was one of those bureaucratic shuffles that do not make news and mean little to people outside government, but it was an extraordinary power shift. Instead of Ridge and his new Office of Homeland Security negotiating with Daniels for money the way all government agencies do, Ridge basically took over the other side of the table. At least in this context, the President had delivered on his promise that his friend would have the power he needed.

That would have made for an okay first week for Ridge—if not for anthrax.

By Friday, an apparent bioterror attack using letters laced with anthrax was starting to take over Ridge's life. The news today was that an assistant to NBC's Tom Brokaw had developed anthrax after opening a letter, and that the New York Times newsroom had been evacuated after another letter (which would turn out to be a hoax) had been received there.

On paper, this was a classic job for the new homeland security coordinator. Agencies ranging from the Centers for Disease Control, to the FBI, to the Post Office, to the Environmental Protection Agency were involved. They needed someone to coordinate them and, equally important, to get them to communicate consistently with an increasingly fearful public. The problem was that no one—not the supposed experts, and certainly not Ridge—had much of an idea of what to do, much less what to say.

Ridge had known that his efforts to pull together the government's homeland security efforts could be derailed by daily emergencies. Going to the Oval Office threat matrix meeting every morning was enough to remind him of that. But he hadn't thought he'd be knocked off stride so quickly and so completely by a threat that no one seemed to have a handle on.

PART TWO · NEW ROUTINES, NEW SYSTEMS
# October 15, 2001–December 31, 2001

## Monday, October 15, 2001

At 7:00 A.M. Sal Iacono—having laid out $19,000 for equipment repairs, new doors, a new ceiling and floor, and new locks—reopened Continental Shoe Repair. With the streets around him still blocked to anything but emergency or recovery vehicles, and with pedestrians in the area still required to show identification before getting through police barricades, he took in $45. On an average day customers would have spent $400 to $500.

That same morning in Silicon Valley, InVision Technologies greeted thirty new employees, who had arrived to join a staff that had been depleted down to about 180 on September 10. Magistri's people had begun recruiting in late September, and with just about every other high-tech company continuing to spiral downward following the bursting of the dot-com bubble, InVision had no trouble finding new talent. By mid-morning, many would already be in their blue smocks getting an introduction to the software circuit boards that InVision assembled in a clean room. Others would be learning the finer points of assembling the car-sized chambers where the luggage was examined, or the conveyor belts that carried the bags through the chambers.

For Magistri, this was an initial round of what he expected would be a larger recruitment effort later in the year, once he knew for sure that the government was going to go ahead quickly with deploying explosive detectors at all airports. His goal for now was to mount a holding action. He would gear up to start producing two machines a week instead of the one every week or two that his factory was now turning out. If everything in Washington happened the way he now expected it to, he'd need to produce two or three machines a day, maybe more. He would not only need to hire lots more people, but he'd also have to make a deal with another company to produce his machines at its factory, an outsourcing arrangement that he'd often dreamed of and that he and his staff were already negotiating.

Magistri loved the idea that his cavernous Silicon Valley facility, which during the summer had seemed so depressingly quiet because of all the

181

layoffs, was humming again with stepped-up activity and the enthusiasm of all the new recruits. Entrepreneurs live for days like this.

Red Cross chairman David McLaughlin, calling from his home in New Hampshire, began a phone conversation this afternoon with Bernadine Healy by saying he had something to tell her that would seem "ridiculous."

Several members of the executive committee, he continued, had told him that they wanted Healy out. So at the executive board's insistence McLaughlin had called a meeting of the entire fifty-person Red Cross board next week. He would get this problem behind them by asking the whole group for an up or down vote on whether they had confidence in Healy's leadership.

Healy was flabbergasted. She'd been working on a memo for an upcoming management retreat covering her progress on ten key Red Cross issues. Why not present it to them?

McLaughlin told her to give him a copy and he would present it at the meeting, but that she shouldn't go to the meeting.

Should she call any of them?

"No, that's not necessary," McLaughlin replied. "Just leave it to me. Believe me, this is nothing."

The next day, when McLaughlin came to town to be on hand for a thank-you visit to headquarters from President Bush, he took Healy aside in the hall as the President was leaving. Putting a hand on each of her shoulders, he looked her in the eye and assured her, again, not to worry. "Bernadine, these people are crazy," is how Healy remembers him putting it. "This whole thing is absurd and I'm going to clean them out of here. Just leave it to me." *

Perhaps it was because, except for not having succeeded when she ran for the Senate from Ohio in 1994, Healy had never been rejected for anything no matter how high she reached—Vassar, Harvard Medical School, a Johns Hopkins residency, head of cardiac care at the famed Cleveland Clinic, head of the National Institutes of Health. Maybe it was because after leaving the NIH she'd survived a brain tumor that the doctors had initially said might kill her in a matter of months. Or maybe it was because these days, when she walked the halls of the Red Cross, people stopped her to tell her how proud they were of everything they, and she, were doing in the aftermath of the attacks—a sentiment that belied the unspoken resentment many others on the staff felt toward Healy, but which was reflected in her fan mail and even

---

* McLaughlin, while confirming the basics of this conversation, says he does not remember calling the board members "crazy."

her recent meetings with the President. Whatever the reason, Healy was in denial. She couldn't imagine that this board or any board, no matter how slighted some may have felt by her mistakes of style and protocol, was going to reject her.

She took McLaughlin's advice. She left it to him.

## Tuesday, October 16, 2001

Mark Isakowitz knew after Thursday's 100–0 vote in the Senate to federalize airport security that preventing the private airport security companies from suffering the same fate in the House was not going to be easy. Today it got harder.

The FAA and the Inspector General's Office of the Department of Transportation released a review they had done beginning last Friday of Argenbright Security's current system of employee background checks. Among their findings, which would make headlines tomorrow, were that screeners at some airports had prior criminal records that should have disqualified them from the job, that others were immigrants working illegally, and that seven of twenty Argenbright screeners who were tested during a spot check "were not able to pass the skills tests required as a condition of employment."

## Thursday, October 18, 2001

Tom Ridge took over a large, ceremonial hall in the Executive Office Building this morning to brief the press on the anthrax scare. His goal was to demonstrate to the country that all the agencies of the government were working well together and were now speaking with one voice. So he had the Attorney General, the Postmaster General, the Surgeon General, the FBI Director, the head of the Centers for Disease Control, and several other men leading various aspects of the effort assemble on one podium to explain what they were doing about the anthrax attacks, and what they knew so far.

Ridge, who was taller and beefier than any of the others, seemed to tower over them, physically and bureaucratically. At one point he was asked by a reporter if he was in charge, and he responded by saying he was like the conductor of an orchestra. "The music doesn't start until he taps the baton."

Perhaps sensing the unease of some on the podium with that metaphor, particularly Ashcroft, a few minutes later, Ridge, who had been on the job ten days, stepped back from that a bit. He volunteered that he didn't have "tactical or operational authority" and that his real job was to look at the "forty-six-plus agencies" that had some role in domestic security and "create a comprehensive national plan to deal with homeland security," while also making sure that any response to an immediate threat is "coordinated so that it is quick and . . . aggressive." If in that process "I find some gaps," he added, then he had all the access he needed to the President to suggest changes.

However skittish Ridge may have been that morning about his ill-defined authority, the press sure thought he was a welcome addition. The *New York Times* would report the next day, "Mr. Ridge, the former governor of Pennsylvania and a combat veteran of Vietnam . . . became a brisk, self-assured moderator of a live, televised update on the anthrax scares, featuring some of the powerful officials whose heads it may well become his job to knock." The paper then reported that in a roundtable session with reporters later "Ridge himself took note of questions about his previously low profile. 'My kids used to ask me to read the book *Where's Waldo?*,' he said by way of explaining his debut. 'Where's the Gov? I thought it was the appropriate time to come out.' " The *Times* story also pointed out that "John McCain, a frequent critic of the Bush White House, said he considered Mr. Ridge's appearance 'very important because it's the first time we're getting an authoritative source rather than a chorus.' "

While the press might have liked the show, Ridge didn't. At about 9:00 that night he convened a meeting of many of those who had been on the podium, including Ashcroft, as well as Health and Human Services Secretary Tommy Thompson. Ridge, who has a universal reputation as a true "nice guy," rarely displays anger. "Few people ever leave his office feeling worse than when they came in," says one longtime aide. But tonight he was angry and although he did not depart so much from character that he raised his voice or berated anyone in so many words, he let it show. His tone was sharp, his questioning persistent.

In Ridge's mind, the press conference had papered over a huge problem of interagency coordination, a problem that had continued after the conference was over, when the various agencies continued to say different things publicly about the nature of the anthrax threat. What made him particularly angry was the continuing speculation that the anthrax had been "weaponized," meaning that the anthrax had been ground so fine and perhaps even coated with some kind of additional substance that deadly inhalation became more likely. This was not a scientific term, but it was certainly scary, especially because soon after it had become part of the lexicon earlier in the week, some in the government had then speculated publicly that "weaponizing anthrax" was so difficult that this could mean the attack had come from a foreign country rather than someone working alone.

At the morning press conference, Ridge had made sure that the people on the podium downplayed the possibility of the anthrax being an especially lethal strain when a question about that had come up. But hours later he was getting reports of officials at Justice and the Centers for Disease Control (which Secretary Thompson oversees) speculating once again about "weaponization."

Beyond that, there was the overall problem of getting information. So far, it seemed that everyone Ridge and his still tiny staff had asked all week about anthrax—how hard it was to make, how one could or could not get sick from it, whether it would escape from a common envelope—had a different answer. Or, in some cases, they were too busy to be bothered with his staff's questions.

So, after dealing much of the afternoon with a threat that had been picked up concerning a possible air attack on the Three Mile Island nuclear power plant in his home state, at 9:00 Tom Ridge, in his own quiet but clearly seething way, read his version of the riot act to about twenty-five top government officials in the Roosevelt Room across from the Oval Office. No one would talk to the press about anthrax without clearing it through here. When he brought up the "weaponization" speculation, the FBI and science people in the room interrupted to say they had an update: The strains of anthrax sent in the various letters all seemed to be from the same source and none of it seemed to be in particles small enough or coated in a way to facilitate wider dispersal that would suggest so-called weaponization. "Good," said Ridge, crisply. "That's what we'll tell people at the news conference tomorrow. We have to end that debate."

That was the easy part of the meeting. The harder part was the realization that no one in the room really knew much about anthrax. There was no list of facilities in the United States that made the stuff, let alone a list of employees who worked there, or had worked there. There was no good information on what it took to be exposed to a lethal dose. There was also nothing about how much it was going to cost, or how long it was going to take to get enough of the antibiotic Cipro to protect everyone. That at least was a problem that could be solved; Ridge pushed Thompson to keep negotiating hard with the drug company, Bayer, which held the Cipro patent, to get the price down. He also asked Ashcroft to have some of his lawyers take a look at what they might do to force the issue. (Within a week, Bayer would capitulate.) But on all the other issues related to how the threat could be contained, one person who was at the meeting recalls that "what we really found out over about three hours were that the shelves were awfully dusty when it came to the information our government had about anthrax." And what made Ridge still more frustrated was that it took so long to pry that out of people. "No one in that room wanted to say they didn't know something," another participant recalls. "So we all just tried to fake it, which made Ridge nuts."

# Monday, October 22, 2001

Barry Ostrager, the lawyer for insurer Swiss Re, had gotten tired of playing defense. Last week, Larry Silverstein's brokers from Willis had sent letters, drafted by Silverstein's lawyers, to each of the insurance companies, including Swiss Re, enclosing the full text of the Travelers policy—the one policy form that had not defined occurrence. The letters declared, as if it were obvious, that this was the policy that governed their loss claims for the destruction of the World Trade Center. Now many were busily preparing their own letters disputing that.

Ostrager wanted to seize the initiative. So this morning he filed a suit in federal court in New York demanding that the policy form distributed prior to September 11 to Swiss Re by Silverstein's own brokers at Willis—which was Willis's own form and which defined occurrence as a series of related events—be declared the relevant form and that, therefore, the destruction of the Trade Center be declared one occurrence.

The suit surprised Silverstein and his lawyer, Herb Wachtell, but their side recovered quickly enough so that a rebuttal was distributed by Silverstein's high-powered PR man, Howard Rubenstein, in the same news cycle. As a result, the *New York Times* story the next morning gave equal space to both sides of the argument, and included this attack from Rubenstein: "The suit is absolutely without merit. It is brought by only one of twenty-two insurance companies. It was an attempt to evade their obligation. Mr. Silverstein is surprised that they are doing this at the same time the insurance industry is going to Congress and is representing that they will live up to their obligation as a predicate to getting a bailout."

Of course, the other insurance companies quickly joined Swiss Re in the suit, and from their perspective they weren't seeking to evade an obligation but to get it defined the way the policy they had agreed to seemed to define it. Nor were they seeking a "bailout" in Washington, as much as they were telling the government that the government needed to step into their place to protect not them but their clients when it came to providing insurance against future terrorist attacks.

## Tuesday, October 23, 2001

Not only was Bernadine Healy not invited to the meeting at which the Red Cross board was to vote on her fate, she couldn't even hover near it to get a sense of what was happening. McLaughlin had decided that although most of the fifty members would attend by conference call, he would nonetheless go to a hotel to conduct the session.

Under its congressional charter, the President appoints eight of the Red Cross's fifty board members, including the chairman, McLaughlin. (President Bush had appointed him in May of 2001.) The other seven are representatives from government agencies, such as the Pentagon, that have strong ties to the organization. These seven typically do not participate actively in the organization, and today was no exception. The lead roles at the meeting were played, as usual, by the thirty members elected by the local chapters—such as Pat Kennedy, the San Franciscan who had been so angry when Healy had set up the specially designated fund. (There are also twelve at-large members, mostly from the corporate or academic sectors, chosen, says Kennedy, to "fill in some gaps and provide national perspective.") In fact, it seemed as if several of the local chapter members had developed a script for the meeting, with one criticizing Healy's performance in one area, then yielding the floor (or the phone) to another for a critique of something else.

At about 4:00 McLaughlin called Healy from his car as he was coming back from the meeting.

"How did it go?" Healy asked.

"Not well. I'm coming back to see you."

A few minutes later, McLaughlin came into Healy's office with Harold Decker, the Red Cross's general counsel. They had voted no confidence, he reported, adding that it was "ugly."

It had been "a cabal," he continued, according to Healy. "They had the votes going in." *

---

*McLaughlin says he does not remember using the word "cabal" and doubts that he ever would have.

The board wanted her to resign, McLaughlin concluded, and had named Decker to be the interim CEO.

Healy said that there was no way she was going to resign, that they'd have to fire her. But she also hadn't given up. "Why can't I meet with them and go through the memo with them," she added, referring to the ten-point issues review she had done for McLaughlin the day before. "Did you show them the memo?"

McLaughlin said that he had, but that the meeting was more about her leadership than what was in the memo.

"Well, why can't I meet with them," she continued. "We can discuss my style if they want, and we can also discuss substance and what we've done. This is crazy."

"We're past that," McLaughlin told her, whereupon he and Decker explained that following the no-confidence vote, a member of the group opposing her had pushed through a second motion that referred all future issues related to Healy's tenure and departure to the executive committee, which, Healy says McLaughlin told her, "is controlled by the cabal."

When the two men left, Healy called her husband, Dr. Floyd Loop, who runs the Cleveland Clinic Foundation. She had told him about the upcoming vote the week before, but had minimized it. They had both laughed a real laugh when she'd remarked, "Who knows, maybe next week I'll be out of a job."

Loop was shocked. "Just get out of there right now and come home," he told her, referring to the apartment they kept in Washington at the Watergate.

That night, Loop called a close friend who is a lawyer, and said that Bernadine needed help with her severance package.

The next morning a series of negotiations began over the amount of her severance, whether she would officially resign or have to be fired, and whether she would agree that in return for the severance she would promise not to criticize the Red Cross or any of its officials publicly.

Healy insisted that she would never agree to any kind of gag clause. The lawyer said that she wouldn't get her severance without it. She said it didn't matter. Ultimately, she got the severance without the no-criticism clause, though she did agree not to sue for sex discrimination. (She told the lawyer she'd never do that anyway.)

One issue was not resolved—what they'd say about whether she'd been fired or was resigning. They simply agreed to try to handle that in a spirit of "goodwill."

"We thought we would simply wish each other well and leave it at that," McLaughlin recalls.

# Wednesday, October 24, 2001

The President and Tom Ridge convened a meeting this morning of the chairmen and senior minority party members of the various congressional committees and subcommittees that have oversight of the federal agencies within Ridge's homeland security portfolio. Actually, they had to have two meetings, because leaders from forty-four committees and subcommittees had to be invited. Looking around at the crowd, a few in the group, particularly Senator Joseph Lieberman of Connecticut, suggested that it was evidence that the agencies that Ridge was supposed to coordinate needed to be consolidated into one super-agency charged with protecting the homeland. The President said he did not think that was necessary or advisable, but Ridge allowed as how "somewhere down the line" he might recommend some kind of realignment.

Later that night, Ridge found himself in another of those tense Roosevelt Room sessions talking about anthrax. This time the issue was why Washington area postal workers had not gotten the immediate testing and antibiotics that congressional staffers had. Workers at the Brentwood postal facility had taken ill, and there was a growing public furor over this apparent disparity in the treatment of blue-collar versus white-collar federal employees. Behind the scenes, Ridge had used his budget authority to get the Postal Service an instant grant of $175 million to improve the safety of postal facilities. What the public saw, however, was that their homeland security czar was presiding over still more confusion and helplessness.

In fact, as bad as the anthrax situation now seemed, the crisis was beginning to ease, though not as a result of anything Ridge or the others had done. Rather, it was because whoever had sent the letters had stopped, perhaps because he had only been trying to send some kind of crazed wake-up call about the dangers of bioterrorism. In fact, some involved in the crisis would come to believe that the few deaths that had resulted might have only come because the nut who had sent the letters didn't realize that the anthrax could seep out of the envelopes. "When you send a letter saying, 'This is anthrax, and you'd better take penicillin or you'll die,' " says one top administration official, referring to the hand-scrawled text of the letters, "that's not a terrorist attack. That's a warning. The problem is that we were totally defenseless had it been a real attack."

# Friday, October 26, 2001

The President signed the USA Patriot Act this morning, declaring that "the changes effective today will help counter a threat like no other our nation has ever faced."

Meanwhile, a small group of Ashcroft's closest aides, including two from his old Senate staff who worried about helping him avoid political traps, were starting to see a big trap in that victims compensation fund. The law setting it up had stipulated that it be housed in Ashcroft's Justice Department, and that Ashcroft appoint its Special Master. It was during this week that chief of staff David Ayers and counselor David Israelite began to sense the hot potato they'd been handed. The law establishing the fund required that any "collateral sources" of financial aid that had been given to someone like Eileen Simon had to be tallied and deducted from the award that might otherwise be due to her under whatever rules the Special Master promulgated. In other words, suppose under the Special Master's criteria Simon might be entitled to $1.7 million. If she had collected $500,000 in life insurance, that amount would be deducted from the $1.7 million. The statute had in fact specified life insurance as an example of a collateral source. But the law also seemed to require that *all* collateral sources would be deducted; its exact words were "all collateral sources, including life insurance, pension funds, death benefit programs, and payments by Federal, State, or local governments related to the terrorist-related aircraft crashes." Did that mean that money Simon and the others got from charities like the Red Cross would also be deducted?

"When we were writing the bill [on the night of September 21] we didn't put charities in the examples only because no one thought of that, because that was before anyone knew all that money would be pouring into them," one congressional staffer recalls. "But we would have, if we had known. Our intention was clear. The taxpayers were not going to give people a windfall."

By now, the Justice aides were getting inquiries from some reporters—at least one of whom had been given the tip by someone at the firm run by Kreindler, the air crash plaintiffs lawyer—about the looming question of whether the charity money would be deducted. They had begun to see the dilemma this posed: This would mean that if someone had donated $1,000 to the Red Cross that had gone to a victim, the donor was actually making a gift to the federal government, because that was $1,000 less that the federal government would have to give to that victim.

The law seemed clear. But the political implications were scary. Ashcroft, already being spoofed on the late night talk shows as the Grim Reaper of the Bush administration, would be rendering meaningless the most generous outpouring of charity in the history of the country.

On top of that, the preliminary thinking Ashcroft's people were now doing about the fund had surfaced lots of other difficult issues, not the least of which was how a government agency, as opposed to a jury doing it case by case, was going to put different price tags on the lives of thousands of individuals. Maybe they needed to think more about who the Special Master should be, Ashcroft's staff thought. This was not going to be an easy, ceremonial job. Maybe it made sense at least to talk to that Ted Kennedy guy that Chuck Hagel, the senator from Nebraska, was still pestering them about.

Anthony Romero thinks of himself as, in his words, a "fanatical patriot" with a classic American bootstraps story—Bronx-born Puerto Rican son of poor hotel worker goes to Princeton and Stanford Law, then becomes head of major national public policy organization. So he had actually believed he'd get in to see his Attorney General. But although the ACLU executive director had tried repeatedly to get a meeting with Ashcroft, he kept getting the brush-off. So today he took sloppy seconds. FBI Director Robert Mueller, who is not nearly as hard-line as Ashcroft, agreed to meet with him.

As the group of eight (three other ACLU people and three other FBI officials) sat down, Romero tried to connect by chatting about the two things he and Mueller had in common. They'd both gone to Princeton and both had started their jobs officially on September 4. That broke the ice a bit, but not much.

Romero's main subject was the immigrant detainees. There were now reports circulating in the press that several hundred were being held, but no one knew for sure. It would later be revealed that approximately 1,200 people had been arrested or detained in the first six months of the investigation, of whom about 800 were immigrants. Romero asked Mueller how many were, in fact, being detained.

Mueller politely said he couldn't answer that. In fact, he might not have known because his men had not made all the arrests. INS and others had made some. Besides, the FBI had nothing to do with whether the INS held those arrested, or for how long. That was all being handled by Chertoff's Criminal Division at Justice.

Romero said that his organization was getting reports of people being held without access to lawyers and then being abused in jail. Mueller said nothing, other than that if they knew of any specific instances of FBI abuse they should tell him so that he could investigate. Romero countered that for the ACLU or any other group to play that role they had to have basic information about who the detainees were and access to interview them. Mueller said he couldn't help with that.

After a half hour, as Romero got up to go, he told Mueller that he felt he should give him a heads-up that the ACLU was going to sue the government in about a week under the Freedom of Information Act in order to obtain the kind of information they had been talking about. The FBI Director thanked him for the courtesy, handshakes were exchanged, and everyone left.

When it comes to the kind of messy New York fights that are likely to make their way not only into the business pages of the *New York Times* and *Wall Street Journal,* but also into the tabloids and onto the nightly television newscasts, it was hard to match Howard Rubenstein's PR firm. Rubenstein seemed to represent everyone—from New York Yankees boss George Steinbrenner, to tax-cheating former hotel queen Leona Helmsley, to Rockefeller Center, to the *New York Post* and its owner, Rupert Murdoch.

Rubenstein had been involved from the beginning in Silverstein's battle with the insurers. Today, Rubenstein and his people performed master work for him. They distributed to the press a three-quarter-inch-thick binder with the following title on the cover: "Swiss Re's Lawsuit Is a Frivolous and Transparent Attempt to Evade Its Promise to Pay for the Rebuilding of the World Trade Center in the Event of a Catastrophe and Shift Its Obligations to City, State, and Federal Government."

The next three pages featured eleven bullet points (drafted by lawyer Herb Wachtell and his team, then translated into plain English by Rubenstein's people) putting Silverstein's best legal foot forward. Behind the bullet points were six "exhibits," which were excerpts from various documents. One was the entire Travelers policy form. Another, which the Silverstein team seemed to trumpet the most, was a copy of the Swiss Re binder (the informal memo that is exchanged by the two parties and is binding pending the agreement and issuing of an actual policy) that contained handwritten notes along the side from a Swiss Re official saying "to be agreed" next to various paragraphs. This was meant to demonstrate that the two sides hadn't really agreed on the details of the policy—which meant that the definition of occurrence was a toss-up. What the bullet point for that one didn't point out, however, was that this "to be agreed" notation was nowhere to be found next to the paragraph referring to "occurrence."

The next exhibit was something that Rubenstein would try to sell to the press as its smoking gun; it was an e-mail, dated July 23, 2001, from an assistant at Silverstein's broker to someone at Swiss Re that attached not only the binder but also the Travelers policy form, which was the policy form that did *not* define occurrence explicitly. This meant that the Travelers form had been sent to Swiss Re last July and had therefore bound Swiss Re to it last July, Rubenstein would argue. Yet the text of the e-mail didn't identify the attachment as a Travelers form, and nowhere in Rubenstein's exhibits was there any document indicating anyone at Swiss Re had acknowledged opening or reading the attachment, much less agreed to use it to change the entire insurance policy that had been negotiated for months without even having a conversation about it.

Other exhibits, such as a blank form that seemed to be from another insurance company, were actually meaningless in terms of the issues in dispute.

However meaningless or incomplete, it all looked extremely official. In fact, it was a dream for a busy reporter, especially one who might not be enthralled with disputes over the wording of insurance policies. Everything was laid out clearly in one bound document, full of quotable quotes in those short bullet points and then the official documents to back them up.

It worked. Not in the sense that it produced stories the next day headlining how Silverstein and New York were being robbed by the big bad insurance company, but in the sense that—despite the overwhelming case against Silverstein's claim for an extra $3.55 billion—over the weeks and months that followed the litigation would be covered as the classic "on the one hand, on the other hand" dispute. More often than not, it would be simplified into being a matter of how a judge or jury was supposed to decide whether the attacks had been one occurrence or two, which was posed as a fascinating legal debate. Of course, while describing the case this way might have intrigued readers, to do so completely ignored the insurers' main, and strongest, argument—that the policy with which they had insured the Trade Center had clearly defined occurrence in a way that turned what might otherwise have been a fanciful law school exam question into a matter of simply reading a contract.

A year later, Bernadine Healy would still be calling this "the press conference from hell." Early in the morning she had delivered a resignation speech to about 200 Red Cross staff people and volunteers.

"I have just decided that it's time for me to resign," she told them.

"The script we had finally worked out," Red Cross chairman McLaughlin later explained, "was that Bernadine would say that she felt it was time for her to leave, and I would praise her and wish her well."

Maybe because her audience of Red Cross people was so stunned, it worked with them. She left the auditorium without anyone asking her why.

But when she got out into the hall, where the Red Cross PR people had assembled the press, the script, in McLaughlin's words, "fell apart."

A reporter asked McLaughlin if Healy's resignation "at a time of crisis for the country was the best thing for the Red Cross."

"I don't say it's the best thing for the Red Cross," he replied. "But I think it may be the judgment of Dr. Healy that it may be the best thing for her at this time in her career."

Healy was asked the same question. According to the report in the *New York Times* the next day, "Dr. Healy fell mute and tears welled up. Mr. McLaughlin tried to end the news conference and Dr. Healy walked away, but she was followed by several reporters. She stopped and said of the board, 'They didn't have any confidence in me.' "

Healy cited the Israel issue as one source of contention with the board, but cut herself short, saying "I really can't talk about it." Then she hurried away from the reporters.


# Monday, October 29, 2001

When he got to work this morning, John France, the Detroit Border Patrol deputy sector chief, who was Lindemann's supervisor, had an e-mail waiting for him from an INS labor relations specialist. It was a draft of a second disciplinary letter for Lindemann and his partner, Mark Hall. Both letters declared that they were being removed from the Border Patrol. The plan was to send the letter next week, after the drafts got cleared at the regional level.


The threat matrix discussed in the Oval Office these past few mornings suggested that terrorists might be planning some kind of new air attack, this time on nuclear power plants using a chartered plane. So Tom Ridge spent the morning coordinating the initiation of air patrols over these 103 facilities and making sure his growing staff was working on some kind of plan to make private air travel more secure. That was easier said than done; everyone with a day's worth of involvement in homeland security quickly came to understand that private planes are a major security gap.

Ridge also agreed that Ashcroft should publicly issue yet another of the threat alerts that had been coming from the White House or Justice Department. He knew that the warning wouldn't mean much; by now the press and public reaction to these vague pronouncements was nothing short of derisive. But Ridge figured they had to issue the warning anyway, especially since the intelligence people insisted that they actually might make a difference in getting the terrorists to put off whatever plans they had.

If Ridge was not already convinced that he had to figure out some kind of new system, the press reaction to this threat alert definitely put him over the top. "Agency Offers No Information About Threats," was the *New York Times* headline. Local police openly expressed frustration to reporters that they hadn't been informed until they'd heard it on the news or been called to comment. Governors, who'd been informed of the news alert on a conference call with Ridge, expressed similar frustration about how vague it all was.

# Tuesday, October 30, 2001

Chubb Insurance announced that for the first time in eight years it would sustain a quarterly loss, because of the September 11 attacks. The announcement said that Chubb would pay out an estimated $3 billion in claims. After reinsurance companies reimbursed Chubb, its own cost for those claims would be about $645 million. The company also said that it had carried the workers' compensation insurance for one third of all the victims of the attack. The announcement, which was a standard press release directed at the investment community, did not mention that Chubb had called the families that would get these workers' compensation checks within days of the attacks, rather than waiting for them to put in a claim.

Quinn and Isakowitz had lobbied the Republicans in the House all last week to persuade them to take a stand against creating the giant new government agency that would be necessary if the baggage screeners were federalized. The leaders—Speaker Dennis Hastert, Majority Leader Dick Armey, and Whip Tom DeLay—were on board, as were other conservatives who instinctively viewed any kind of growth in government as bad. The President seemed in sync, too. The White House Press Office said that the Senate bill requiring federalization was inflexible and that, like the House leaders, Bush wanted to preserve the option of letting the FAA supervise private companies under new, strict guidelines. The issue was whether more moderate Republicans would bow to what seemed a firestorm of public sentiment that the only way to deal with airport security seriously was to put federal agents on the case. It didn't help that all forty-nine Republicans in the Senate had expressed the same sentiment when they had voted to federalize.

That inspector general's report about continued screw-ups in Argenbright's screening of its employees also hurt, as did the continuing flow of news articles detailing other lapses. On top of that, because members of Congress fly so much, it seemed that each one whom the lobbyists approached had a story about one of the people from Argenbright or the other companies doing something stupid at a checkpoint. There was even some occasional racism directed at the heavily minority, low-wage screeners, with more than one congressman telling them that he didn't exactly feel reassured when he and his briefcase were inspected at a gate by someone who couldn't speak English or was wearing a turban.

Nonetheless, by the end of the week, the lobbyists thought they were making progress. Hastert and DeLay's whip operation, the system aimed at counting votes and keeping members in line, was in high gear and seemed to be holding most Republicans. Their arguments—that hiring a whole new workforce would take longer than getting the private screeners to clean up their act, that other countries with the best aviation security outsourced their screeners, too, and that no good Republican should want to create a new force of 28,000 federal workers, let alone workers who might be unionized—was gaining traction.

But on Sunday morning, the air had seemed to come out of the balloon. Appearing on NBC's *Meet the Press,* White House chief of staff Andrew Card reiterated the President's preference for keeping the screeners private. But when Tim Russert pressed on, Card conceded that the President would sign, not veto, the Senate version that federalized everyone, if that was the bill that ended up on his desk.

Without a veto threat, the supporters of the House version had felt undermined and abandoned.

Yet today they staged an upset. With DeLay's whip operation never more effective, they won a 218–214 vote in the House. Only eight Republicans strayed to the other side, and their votes were offset by six Democrats who went the other way.

Isakowitz and Quinn were amazed. They figured they could now at least win a compromise in the conference of senators and congressmen that would have to meet to try to reconcile the Senate and House bills. Maybe the law could set up a pilot project of some federalized airports, while most other airports kept a corps of new and improved private screeners. Or maybe now they'd even get the Republicans in the Senate to see that they had acted too hastily. At least they now had real leverage to save their clients' businesses.

Herman Garcia had worked as Sal Iacono's only employee for seventeen years, and he had never seen the shop so empty. The store had been reopened now for two weeks, yet Sal was still taking in maybe $50 or $75 a day. How could he possibly afford to pay Garcia his $250 a week salary?

Garcia told Sal that maybe for a while he should work for free, just until things got a little better. Sal refused. He wouldn't consider it. But he did agree to let Garcia work part-time for a while. "It'll get better," he assured Garcia, and himself.

To Sal, things could have been a lot worse. Life had certainly been tougher thirty-seven years ago, when he had come to America to live with his in-laws. He had been a shoe designer in Italy and had dreams of doing the same here, so he made the rounds of shoe manufacturers in New York's garment center. No one needed a designer, except for one company, where the boss looked at his designs, loved them, and offered him a job—if he would take English lessons for a few months so the boss could communicate with him. He even offered to pay for the lessons. Speaking to him through an interpreter, Sal replied that his wife and baby son thought he had gone to America to make money, not get an education. "They don't want to hear that Daddy's getting an education," he told his would-be employer. "They need food. I need money."

After Sal went several weeks without work, a manager at another manufacturer who did speak Italian but had no jobs told Sal that he needed to start thinking realistically. "Forget design," he told him. "You want money, get a job as a shoemaker."

Sal bought an Italian language newspaper and scoured the want ads. At 8:00 the next morning he was on a subway for an appointment at a busy repair shop in central Brooklyn. But he got lost and didn't get there until 1:00 P.M. "Be patient with me," he begged the owner, who luckily was also Italian.

"What experience do you have?" the man asked.

"None, but be patient," Sal repeated.

Sal remembers that the first few days he fumbled around trying to mimic a co-worker who had been fixing heels and soles for eighteen years. Within weeks, he says, he had more than gotten the hang of it; he was far better than the eighteen-year veteran. And he was in love with leather.

Sal had stayed there for three years, sending money home the whole time to his wife, while living with her parents and gradually learning English.

There is something else important about this classic American immigrant story: During those three years, Sal was in exactly the same legal situation as Syed Jaffri, the Pakistani who had been arrested and detained by the FBI and INS in September, after they found him working in the Bronx even though he only had a tourist visa. For those three years, Sal Iacono, like Jaffri and so many millions of immigrants before and after him, was working in the United States illegally, too.

After perfecting his shoemaker's art for three years, Sal returned to Sicily, telling his wife that he had now saved enough money to start his own design company there. Before long, he realized that he had no prayer of starting a business in Italy. He didn't have enough money, and the prospects for a new shoe design company were nil. Worse, he and his wife couldn't find a good place to live with what they had and with Sal now having no income.

Sal was at a loss for what to do, when out of the blue a letter came informing him that the INS had approved his long overdue application to immigrate to the United States as a worker and to bring his family. He still remembers the day he received that letter—a letter he would never have gotten had the INS thrown the book at him for working while on a tourist visa—as the best day of his life.

So Sal and Franca Iacono and their son made their way back to the United States, where he took a job at a shoe repair shop in lower Manhattan. He worked there for ten years, before opening his own store in 1977. He remembers that the first day he had three customers.

To Sal, these tough times at Ground Zero were like opening the store all over again. He was prepared to tough it out.


Michael Chertoff, the head of Ashcroft's Criminal Division, was concerned that lawyers who got a chance to meet with terrorism suspects could be used to pass messages to the outside that could generate or aid new attacks. So Ashcroft approved a change in prison regulations that allowed federal agents to eavesdrop on a defendant's conversation with his lawyer.

Described just like that, it sounds like an egregious violation of the attorney-client privilege. In fact, it was more benign. Under the procedure that Chertoff's people had drafted, the agents who listened in were not allowed to be the same people who might be handling the defendant's case, nor were they allowed to communicate what they heard to any of those prosecutors, nor could anything they heard ever be used in court against the defendant. Also, the client and his lawyer had to be notified in advance of any such eavesdropping. Nonetheless, when this new prison rule would become public in about two weeks, it would generate howls of protest that this would chill lawyer-client conversations, and that Ashcroft was, as the ACLU's press release on the subject put it, "insatiable" when it came to wanting to trim back the Bill of Rights.


If Ashcroft needed any further evidence, though, that Americans agreed that they were living in newly dangerous times, he could have come to Yankee Stadium tonight for the first game in New York of the World Series. Everyone had to pass through metal detectors, which they did cheerfully. Then, as it got closer to game time, the crowd stirred, awaiting the arrival of President Bush. A Marine helicopter swooped down from behind right field, landing in a park behind the left field wall. The crowd cheered. But then another helicopter did the same thing. Then another. The Secret Service was obviously using decoys. As everyone tried to guess which one might be carrying the President, many in the stands nudged each other nervously and pointed up over center field. A menacing, giant white cloud had formed and was now swirling down.

Was it anthrax, or just the dust from all those helicopters kicking up a dry Bronx sandlot?

As the dust settled, there was a roar when the President suddenly appeared and strode to the pitcher's mound to throw out the first ball. He didn't say anything. He didn't have to. Having the guts to be there was enough—and that night there was no debate among those in the stands that it really took guts for him to be there. Everyone sensed that this was a dangerous place. It was just a ball game, but tonight descendants of World War II's "Greatest Generation" got a small taste of what it was like to feel at risk.


# Wednesday, October 31, 2001

Bill O'Reilly locked on to a new target tonight—the celebrities, like George Clooney, who had raised money for the telethon that benefited the September 11th Fund. O'Reilly had reported earlier that the fund wasn't giving money to victims, but rather was funneling it to other organizations that supposedly were aiding victims, but were also funding other programs that were not meant for the families of the dead and injured. (This, of course, was exactly what the fund's original press release and website said it was going to do.) In fact, only $35 million of the $230 million it had raised so far had ended up getting to those whom O'Reilly—and, from his standpoint, the donors—defined as victims.

"Where are the Hollywood celebrities who raised money for disaster relief," he began. "Now that we know the donated money will not be going to the grieving families, what do they think?"

He listed every movie star he had attempted to contact for comment and detailed the brush-offs he'd gotten. ("Mike Myers's flack says he needs to pass. Does he have a gallstone? Lucy Liu's flack says she cannot be reached to make a statement. We have alerted the FBI.")

Clooney, who would keep the O'Reilly controversy going in the national press by writing him a nasty open letter the following week, was livid. "Who were we supposed to be giving all the money to at that point," he'd later argue. "There were supposedly 5,000 dead people, but no one knew for sure. You can't just write checks. . . . We knew the government was going to give the victims' families a lot of money with the victims fund, so why didn't it make sense to hold back and help the waiter who worked on the 103rd floor at the restaurant, who was out of work? This was about long-term needs, not some families winning the lottery and getting checks for millions of dollars."

Michael Byrne joined Tom Ridge's staff today as the director of Response and Recovery, meaning that he was supposed to coordinate how the country deals with an attack once the rest of Ridge's office fails to prevent it. Byrne, forty-seven, was a New York City fireman for twenty years. He retired as a captain, worked in New York's Office of Emergency Management, and then became the New York regional director of the Federal Emergency Management Agency (FEMA). From September 11 until today he was the federal official in charge of cleanup and recovery at Ground Zero. Like Ridge, Byrne had just left his family to come to Washington.

One of the items high on Byrne's to-do list was interoperability, an issue that Woollen of Raytheon had started to zero in on. Interoperability has to do with getting first responders from different agencies to be able to speak to each other at a disaster site even though they use different radios with different frequencies. As a fireman, Byrne answered the call for the first bombing of the World Trade Center in 1993—and a communications snafu sent him thirty-four floors up to rescue people in Tower One, when they were in Tower Two. Byrne also had several friends from the Fire Department who were lost on September 11, because they never got word to leave the building. A redhead who still had the easy people skills of someone who'd always been popular in the firehouse, Byrne was anxious to help unleash what he assumed was the eagerness of federal bureaucrats across the government to put aside old rivalries and provide quick solutions to problems like those.

The other key job that Ridge had filled by the time Byrne arrived was the director of Protection and Prevention. The man with that title—which sounded encompassing enough to be the one Ridge ought to have had—was Army General Bruce Lawlor, fifty-four. A Vietnam combat veteran, Lawlor had held a variety of battalion and brigade staff positions in intelligence and operations, and had also worked for the CIA in Vietnam. Then, in an unusual career shift, he'd become a country lawyer in Vermont and had even run unsuccessfully as a Democrat for attorney general before rejoining the army. Until two weeks ago Lawlor had been the first commander of a standing Pentagon task force assigned to help the country respond to a domestic attack. Lawlor appeared so quiet and formal to those who met him for the first time that it was hard to believe he'd ever tried to be a politician. Yet he was also tough-minded and not afraid to push his own views, though always in the context of respecting the chain of command. Indeed, above all else Lawlor was used to a clear chain of command. That seemed, he thought, likely to make this job a new kind of challenge.

By now, Ridge and his people had started to focus on priorities, which was difficult since everything associated with homeland security seemed, in these fearful days, like it should be a priority. They had tentatively decided on four areas: bioterrorism, airport and border security, better sharing of information and intelligence among federal agencies, and providing aid to local first responders (including dealing with issues such as interoperability). If these choices seemed logical, they were not easy, for they excluded giving priority to such vulnerabilities as rail, highway, and bridge transportation or cybersecurity. It wasn't that these were unimportant or to be ignored, just that choices had to be made about which needs had to get the most attention first. To have more than a few priorities was to have no priorities.

Picking them even this quickly was not a theoretical exercise. The choices had instant, tangible ramifications in the conference rooms in the Executive Office Building, where Ridge's staff was now huddled in grueling daily sessions with Daniels's people from the Office of Management and Budget.

Hearing that the budget deadlines had gotten a reprieve to allow Ridge to put his stamp on things, every agency in the government had come back with some special pleading for new funds related to homeland security. The Ridge and Daniels budget mavens now had to ignore those that were outside the range of those four priorities and even chop previous requests that had already been approved. At the same time, they surprised some agency heads by boosting allocations in those four priority areas beyond even what the agency heads had requested.

The amount to be spent sometimes wasn't as important or controversial as who was going to spend it. Almost immediately, Byrne—the former fireman whose last job had been as a FEMA regional disaster response director— decided that new funds to equip and train first responders, such as fire departments, should be administered through FEMA, which would review the plans for those seeking the grants to make sure the money was going for the right projects and equipment. But across the country, police and fire departments had become accustomed to applying for grants from something called the Office of Justice Programs, which was run by the Justice Department. They wanted these new funds put there, where they were used to dealing with the people making the grants. Of course, Justice (run by an Attorney General who loved "to get the ball") wanted the extra funding and power, too. Convinced that FEMA had the expertise for overseeing first responder efforts, Byrne insisted that Justice not get the new money. Falkenrath, the Kennedy School of Government assistant professor now overseeing these kinds of budget issues for Ridge, sided with him. Both assumed that this relatively trivial issue—the kind of issue that no one outside the Beltway ever hears about, and which, they thought, defined the bureaucratic turf warfare of the September 10 era—was settled in that conference room when they decided it.

# Friday, November 2, 2001

Anthony Romero, having scuttled a mass direct mail solicitation the day after the attacks, had rewritten the letters to deal with the challenges presented by September 11. ("The ACLU is determined that our nation will not fall into the trap of sacrificing the values that define us for some understandable, but misguided, notions of national security.") The new packages had gone out in mid-October. By today, enough returns were in to make the results clear:

Romero had a big winner on his hands. In recent years, the ACLU's fall mailing had produced an average of 56,000 new members. Today he was on his way to getting 75,000.

The response was consistent with a phenomenon of American interest group politics: When one side is in power, the other side has an easier time sounding the call and attracting support and money. It's as if the American system is so geared to pulling everything to the center that there's even some kind of automatic ballast built into the dynamics of fund-raising among groups on either edge of a spectrum or an issue.

On the day that Brian Lyons's sister-in-law, Elaine, gave birth to Michael Lyons's baby girl, Brian found himself in the middle of a Ground Zero fight between New York City's Finest and Bravest. Several days earlier, Mayor Rudolph Giuliani had announced that he was cutting back on the number of firemen assigned to Ground Zero. Some would stay to assist in the continuing effort to find remains, but their number would be sharply reduced in order to allow for a faster cleanup. One unnamed official was even quoted explaining that Ground Zero was now more a construction site than a recovery site.

This had infuriated the firemen, and on Friday hundreds had gone to Ground Zero, then to City Hall to protest. Fistfights broke out when the police tried to block them. "Bring our brothers home," they demanded, referring to the 200-plus firemen still missing. Seven firemen were arrested.

To Lyons, it was the ugliest, most depressing day down there since he'd arrived.

# Saturday, November 3, 2001

Michael Cartier, his sister Jennie Farrell, and the four other Cartier siblings sat in their parents' living room last night watching news reports of the police-fire confrontation. Not being able to get day-to-day information about what was going on at Ground Zero was bad enough. But this was their worst fear come true. The city was now giving up on recovering the victims. They'd never have any remains, and never have a proper funeral for James.

They went home shaken and angry, and agreed to come back the next morning to talk about what they could do.

When they reassembled in their parents' living room this morning, with many of James's young nieces and nephews in tow, Michael had a fierce look in his eye. He had stayed up much of the night thinking about their situation. So had most of the others.

We need to start a group, he said. Given his computer skills (he was a tech manager in the business unit of a cable programming company), he could get a website up that day, if necessary. Someone has to speak for the families. Someone had to force the city to give them information and then distribute that information to the families. Someone had to make sure the recovery efforts continued.

The whole point of what we're doing, Jennie said, was to give James a voice. To speak for him and for his recovery. Everyone else—the police's and firefighters' families, the politicians, the real estate people—had a voice. All those people making decisions need to hear James's voice, and our voice.

They decided to call the group Give Your Voice.

Quickly, they took a huge photo collage of James that they had sitting in the dining room, and turned it into two posters proclaiming the start of Give Your Voice.

They called a few other September 11 families that they'd befriended who lived nearby, including one whose son had been an electrician working with James, and told them what they were up to. They agreed to join.

By that evening, Michael had gotten the website up.

Sunday afternoon, they were supposed to go to a memorial mass in Queens that had been organized to honor the September 11 victims. They decided that they'd use the event to launch their organization.

They got some tape, string, and a folding table. Then, they took everything and went off to the service, where they knew there would be hundreds of other September 11 families from Queens and Long Island. Toward the end of the mass, as communion began, the devout Cartier siblings sneaked out two different sides of the church. On one side they used the table to mount the posters, showing James and proclaiming Give Your Voice. As mourners left the church, they began asking for sign-ups with e-mail addresses. Outside the second door they used John Cartier's motorcycle to hang the other poster. Jennie stood there signing people up.

By Sunday night, Michael was e-mailing more than 100 members, stressing that the group wanted no donations of any kind. They just wanted a voice.

# Sunday, November 4, 2001

Some clients have a way of making life difficult. Members of the Senate and the House Democrats were still holding strong on federalizing baggage screeners, but lobbyists Quinn and Isakowitz thought they were making progress getting a compromise that would keep the private airport security companies alive when a final bill emerged from the House-Senate conference in about a week. But this morning newspapers around the country carried stories about how Argenbright had supposedly allowed someone at O'Hare Airport in Chicago to get several knives, a stun gun, and tear gas through a checkpoint.

Isakowitz knew they had to do something to get this story behind them. And by Monday he would have his solution. Their best argument was that Argenbright was under new management, because it had been purchased by that big, respectable British company, Securicor. Well, why not prove it and at the same time give the House Republicans, who were fighting his fight, some cover? So Isakowitz decided he'd urge the man leading the fight, Republican Whip DeLay, to write a letter to Securicor's CEO saying that Argenbright's performance continued to be so awful that the only way in good conscience that DeLay could continue to support private security at the airports was if the Argenbright CEO, Frank Argenbright, was immediately fired.

As soon as Securicor got the letter, Frank Argenbright was let go.

# Monday, November 5, 2001

Larry Cox began the first workweek in November hoping that things would start to improve. How could they not? October passenger traffic at the Memphis airport had improved from the weeks just after September 11, but it had still been about 45 percent off what it was the prior year.

Cox now knew he was going to have to act fast to make up for the resulting revenue gaps by asking the airlines for big increases in the rental fees they paid for their gates. But before he did that, he wanted to have every possible nickel of his costs under control. So he instructed his staff, which was already coping with a hiring freeze, to look for savings everywhere—from reduced wattage in lightbulbs, to cutting back on heat or air-conditioning, to skimping on cleaning services.

Meantime, he was considering hiring a consultant who could do a study that he could give the FAA that would prove that with some alterations to his parking garage he could reopen those parking spots near the terminal, because a bomb left in a car there wouldn't do the damage the FAA feared it would.

# Tuesday, November 6, 2001

A hiccup developed in the plan by the Border Patrol in Detroit to fire Lindemann and Hall for talking to the press. At another meeting among the bosses, someone mentioned that Hall had told him in the morning that he needed to take a day off next week because he had been invited to testify at a Senate hearing.

The hearing, about Northern Border security, was to be conducted by Carl Levin, the senior senator and Democrat from Michigan. Hall had contacted Levin's staff in mid-October, about what he thought the problems were on the border, and about how his bosses wanted to punish him and Lindemann for talking about it. Since then, Levin's people had been monitoring the controversy about Hall and Lindemann having been disciplined after talking to the *Detroit Free Press*. In fact, yesterday Lindemann appeared with Senator Levin on a local Fox news program.

At today's meeting of Border Patrol officials, a special assistant to the regional director declared that he thought Lindemann and Hall had "provided aid and comfort to the enemy." However, after discussing Hall's impending testimony, they decided that they'd better table a decision about whether to fire him and his partner. They might have become too hot to jettison that easily.

Ken Feinberg, the man craving to be the Special Master of the victims compensation fund, finally got a chance to audition. It came at just the right moment.

By the time he arrived for his job interview with three of Ashcroft's top aides, each of whom was nearly a generation younger than he was, they were all aware of how the fund was already generating controversy, even without the Special Master having been appointed or its regulations having been written. People were writing to the Justice Department website, demanding that same sex partners be treated like spouses, that no one's life be valued at more than anyone else's, and that victims of other tragedies be included. And a front-page story this morning in the *New York Times*, by David Barstow and Diana B. Henriques, had deftly smoked out the potentially hottest issue of all—whether all the donations to charity would be for naught because the Special Master would simply deduct whatever the victims had received from the charities from what he would award them.

The Ashcroft aides were running up against a deadline of December 21, when the law required that a first draft of the regulations governing the fund had to be written by the Special Master and made public. That, they now understood, would be a massive undertaking in itself.

"Feinberg bowled us over," one of those in the meeting remembers. "He came in with a plan and a determination to make this work."

But wouldn't a Kennedy Democrat give the store away? "He made it very clear to us that for the plan to be seen as a success, which is what he wanted, he had to keep within a budget."

Yet no specific budget figure was talked about, because there wasn't one. Also, it would have been seen as a crippling blow to the Special Master's independence if those appointing him held him to a number in advance, especially when no one knew at that point how many victims there really were. Six to twenty billion dollars had been talked about in the press. Around the halls at Justice, $6 billion was the most common estimate. But by all accounts no one brought it up. In that sense, the conversation was akin to an interview with a Supreme Court justice nominee. No one is supposed to ask him to pledge how he'll vote on a specific case, but those appointing him want to have a real good sense of his outlook on hot-button issues, such as abortion.

"Feinberg made it clear to us," one of the Ashcroft staffers says, "that he was committed to making this succeed, which to him meant that he would be mindful of the Treasury's limits and mindful that if this turned into a partisan fight it would be a failure. More than that, he just seemed able to do it, and eager to do it. He even volunteered to work for free. . . . He completely turned us around from the idea that we wanted to pick some Republican gray hair to be the Special Master. He showed the value of someone who knew this stuff and would be hands-on."


One would have thought that after her "press conference from hell," Bernadine Healy would have taken her husband's advice and just gone home. But Healy had agreed to stay on at the Red Cross until January 1. This morning, she found herself in front of a House of Representatives committee defending the organization for not giving enough to the victims of September 11, which she thought ironic since she'd incurred the wrath of her board for giving them too much.

The hearing of the House Subcommittee on Oversight and Investigations—an all-purpose forum for subcommittee members who want to jump into any hot issue, whether it's the Red Cross or Martha Stewart—was chaired by Billy Tauzin, an irrepressible Louisiana Republican. It began with testimony from Russa Steiner, a September 11 widow, and her lawyer. They recounted in detail how Steiner had gone from assistance center to assistance center in October filling out form after form. She received a grand total of $1,244 from the Red Cross and $1,500 from the September 11th Fund.

Next up was New York State Attorney General Eliot Spitzer.

Spitzer, forty-two, was one of those public officials in slightly below-the-radar offices who seem eager to leverage their job into something bigger. He was smart, articulate, effective, and wealthy—the kind of politician who everyone agrees has a big future. His twenty-fourth-floor office on lower Broadway was no more than a few hundred feet from Ground Zero, and on the morning of September 11 he had a bird's-eye view of the Twin Towers burning and collapsing. He says that as he evacuated, he thought to himself that all his ambitious plans for making his mark over the next year would have to be put on hold, because the terrorist attacks would now overshadow the types of issues that his office handled, such as consumer protection. That the state's highest law enforcement official, whose office was almost next door to the Trade Center, would think that he was about to become irrelevant following the worst crime in the history of the state may have been ironic, but it was a reflection of the fact that the New York attorney general has limited duties. What Spitzer didn't focus on that day was that one of those duties was regulating charities that solicit in New York.

Within forty-eight hours, he was hot on the issue.* This morning, he pressed his two major points. First, all the charities had to be open about where their money was going and had to make sure it went where they told donors it would go. Second, they all should work together using some kind of common database. That way, people like Mrs. Steiner wouldn't have to fill out multiple forms, and others would not be able to double-dip by getting more than one charity to pay for the same needs. The Red Cross had initially

---

*In fact, the September 11 charities would not be the only high-profile issue that Spitzer would successfully seize; within the next few months he would gain national prominence for his investigations of Wall Street brokers and their stock analysts.

resisted pooling its claims information with that of other groups, but Healy had by now relented, agreeing to provide the data for any of its claimants who signed a waiver allowing their information to be shared.

When Healy took the witness chair, she conceded that the Red Cross had "failed Mrs. Steiner," but reported that hours before the hearing Steiner had been given a check for $27,000. That apparent last-minute attempt at damage control didn't impress anyone. The congressmen demanded to know where all the Red Cross money was going. If the aid to victims and support of relief workers at Ground Zero and the Pentagon was going to cost $300 million, as Healy now asserted, what was going to happen to the rest of the $547 million the Red Cross had by now raised, plus the hundreds of millions more it was bound to get in the next few weeks?

Healy tried to outline her long-term, terrorism-related programs involving blood reserves, training, and other preparedness for similar future disasters. Those were exactly the "emerging needs related to this tragedy" that all of her solicitations had mentioned, though clearly not prominently enough to inform donors fully.

That was when Spitzer broke in, and the fireworks started. "I see these funds being sequestered into long-term plans for an organization, not being spent on the victims," he said. "I hear words like continuity of operations, reserves, reprogramming, and we have . . . victims here at this table who haven't received the money they need. That is anathema to what the American public expects. When people were writing their checks for $100, $200, and $10,000 and sending them in response to the [ads] the Red Cross was running, they believed victims were going to get that money."

Chairman Tauzin joined in, saying that he found it strange that "only three fifths of the money [$300 million of $547 million] was going to be used for these families and these families are telling us they're not getting the help that was intended for them."

Amid repeated questioning from Tauzin about "a disconnect" between what the Red Cross had said it was doing and was actually doing, Healy tried to explain that it took time to get the families what they needed and that that was now happening. She also stressed the need for those longer term terrorism-related programs and that the solicitations had, in her view, made it clear that the money would go for them, too.

If these needs were so important and so much an intended part of the solicitation, then why, Tauzin asked, had the Red Cross announced the other day that it was closing the special September 11 fund because it no longer needed donations? "I didn't make the decision," she responded, not adding that the real answer, of course, was that the board had wanted to get rid of the precedent of a specially designated fund as soon as it could.

"Red Cross Grilled," "Red Cross Quizzed," "Red Cross Defends" were the typical headlines the next morning. More stories soon followed about other instances showing, as the *Washington Post* would headline it on November 19, the Red Cross's "Pattern of Diverting Donations" from high-profile disasters, such as the 1989 San Francisco earthquake, to its general fund.

# Wednesday, November 7, 2001

Larry Silverstein's countersuit was no surprise. But the rhetorical flourish in the papers Herb Wachtell drafted showed a great lawyer at his best when he has no case:

"Swiss Re's attempt in its lawsuit to portray what the whole world saw on September 11—two hijacked airplanes separately crashing into two Towers resulting in separate fires in each of two buildings, which caused each building separately to collapse . . . —as if it were somehow only one occurrence is at odds with controlling New York authorities and seeks to place in jeopardy the very rebuilding effort necessitated by these tragic events. . . . The World Trade Center site today is a sixteen acre scar in the middle of the financial capital of the world. It must be rebuilt promptly to assure the financial health of . . . New York . . . and indeed the country. It must be rebuilt promptly, together with an appropriate memorial honoring the thousands of victims— to show the world that America will not succumb to terrorism."

David McLaughlin stopped by Healy's office looking shell-shocked from this morning's headlines about the brutal congressional hearing the day before. "We've decided to do something that you're not going to like," he told her.

Were they going to fire her again, she responded, laughing.

What the executive board had decided in a morning meeting, McLaughlin explained, was to "spend it all on the victims. We have to put all this bad publicity behind us. It's the only way."

This meant that Healy's Family Grant Program allotting three months of living expenses to the families would be extended to as long as a year. Also, they'd develop another program to aid the economic victims of the attacks— people who'd been thrown out of work or even had their incomes slashed in the aftermath of September 11. This was an idea that Healy had opposed because there would be no way to define or limit who could get that money, and because it took the Red Cross so far from its basic mission that they would never be able to administer a program like that effectively. Worse, it was the ultimate violation of the principle that board members like Pat Kennedy had insisted on in opposing Healy's segregation of the donations in the first place, for this was the ultimate in treating victims of different disasters un-equally. So Healy now found herself arguing Kennedy's and the board's prin-ciple, because they had abandoned it.

McLaughlin said the decision was final.

"I didn't like it, but we didn't have any choice," Kennedy later said, refer-ring to her board's reversal, for which she had voted. "We had to get out from under the bad press."

Disgusted by the policy shift, and watching her staff that same day being fired around her, Healy began packing her boxes. She left for good that night.

## Thursday, November 8, 2001

Robert Lindemann remembers this as "the worst day of my life." He had already been starting to feel desperate because his wife had used up all her sick days and vacation time to take the children to and from school. Linde-mann could no longer do that, because as part of his punishment he had been moved to day shifts. Now, when he got to work a new letter was waiting for him from Deputy Chief France. Citing "Failure to Follow Supervisory Instructions" and "Using Poor Judgment," France rescinded his prior letter suspending Lindemann for ninety days, and said he was not only going to be suspended for ninety days, but was also going to be demoted to agent from senior agent, for one year. The drop would reduce his $58,000 salary by about $13,000.

In the letter, which had been drafted and vetted by at least a dozen INS officials, France wrote that he was "profoundly troubled that at a time of unprecedented crisis that this country is now experiencing . . . you would . . . provide sensitive information and improper comments to the media. Your statements as a representative of this country are an embarrassment to the Border Patrol but more importantly to the United States and to Canada. . . . It is likely that your comments will . . . cause ill will amongst the public and possibly unnecessary paranoia in the country when it is our job to protect the borders and instill confidence in the public. . . . Furthermore, you may well have put the national security . . . in jeopardy."

Lindemann didn't know that the letter was the softer alternative to the outright dismissal that had initially been planned for him and his partner, Hall (who received the same letter).

He was given ten days to appeal the decision. He called a member of Senator Levin's staff to tell him what had happened.

The bill that the House had passed mandating new standards for airport security guards (but not federalizing them) had also included a specific deadline for equipment to be in place to screen checked luggage for bombs. The deadline was December 31, 2003, about twenty-six months from now. For Sergio Magistri, this was a little too much of a good thing. He sensed a new problem. There was no chance he could make anywhere near the 3,000 or 4,000 units in two years that that kind of universal screening would require. His factory was barely up to producing two a week now, and at best he might get up to one or two a day, but only once he knew for sure that any bill that came out of the Senate-House compromise also had a deadline. Yet if the deadline were that soon, new competitors—big ones from big companies— might try to jump into what would look like a gold-rush market. And what if the government, frantic to get the stuff in place, certified their products as acceptable? He'd suddenly have the opposite of the problem he'd had since he'd started the company—too much demand, which could extinguish his lead position in the marketplace.

What Magistri didn't know was that this morning his nightmare was starting to play out, but not with a competitor in explosive detectors emerging. Instead, a different, competing technology was trying to get in on the action.

A lobbyist for a company called Barringer brought the company's CEO and some of his aides up to Capitol Hill this morning for separate appointments with the two most important staffers involved in aviation industry legislation: David Schaffer, who worked for the Republican chairman of the House Transportation Committee, and Samuel Whitehorn, who handled aviation for Fritz Hollings in the Senate. The lobbyist was a partner at one of Washington's most connected law firms, Patton, Boggs & Blow, and he'd been working for Barringer for several years. Barringer made machines called trace detectors, which work as follows: A security agent takes a cotton swab and brushes it against a suitcase or even inserts it inside the suitcase. He then tests the cloth for a trace of explosives by inserting it into a slot or holder in the Barringer device's computer console. The swabbing and inserting process takes a lot longer than running a bag through one of Magistri's giant machines, and there is considerable debate about which method is more reliable. But the trace detection machines made by Barringer and two other large competitors are much smaller (and therefore easier to place in airports), cheaper ($35,000 to $45,000 versus $600,000 to $1.2 million for Magistri's machines), and, most important, relatively easy to produce in large numbers. So the Barringer team's argument to Whitehorn and Schaffer was that they needn't worry about a tight deadline, because their machines could be in place as fast as was necessary.

Whitehorn and Schaffer—both of whom had met with the Barringer lobbyists before, and were by now also being besieged for meetings by the other trace detector companies—said they appreciated the briefing.

## Friday, November 9, 2001

John Ashcroft issued and released to the public an order that formalized what had been going on ad hoc since September 11. Federal prosecutors and FBI officers around the country were to "interview" 5,100 men between the ages of eighteen and thirty-three who had entered the country on visas from countries suspected of harboring terrorists.

Critics howled that this was racial profiling at its worst. But perhaps because Mueller and the FBI had pushed back when Justice Department Criminal Division chief Chertoff had first suggested the order, arguing that if done sensitively the interviews might yield real cooperation, Ashcroft's directive outlined a more benign protocol for the interviews than people like Ali Erikenoglu had experienced in Paterson, New Jersey, last September. There were to be no questions about religious beliefs or practices, and nothing about political views. All the questioning was to be voluntary and, where possible, by appointment. A lawyer could be present, if the interviewee wanted one.

Senator Levin of Michigan sent a letter to INS Commissioner James Ziglar demanding that his Subcommittee on Investigations be immediately given documents related to personnel actions related to Lindemann's partner, Hall, who was scheduled to testify before Levin's committee the following Tuesday. When Lindemann was faxed a copy of the letter, he began to feel a little more hopeful. At the same time, this raising of the profile of his fight made him more nervous. Maybe he was going to get some help. Or maybe this would only make things worse.

## Saturday, November 10, 2001

Sal Iacono's Continental Shoe Repair had been reopened for nearly a month, and business was still so awful that Sal did not know how he was going to survive. He was dipping deeper into savings that had already been nearly depleted by all the repairs he'd paid for. How was he going to keep paying rent, the electric bill, and the reduced weekly salary he was giving Herman Garcia for part-time work? He knew he had some insurance to cover the cost of the repairs, but he was getting nowhere figuring out what was covered or how to make the claim.

So, this morning, he made his way from his home on Staten Island to a center near his store that had been set up by the various charities trying to aid the September 11 victims. He'd heard he might be able to get some kind of loan. When his turn came, he approached a woman sitting at a bridge table, dropped a folder of assorted papers in front of her, and said, "Please help me."

Sal had just caught his first break.

The woman sitting at the table was Hollie Bart, forty-six, who was a partner in the New York office of the Chicago-based law firm of Ross & Hardies. Bart, along with hundreds of other lawyers who typically worked for large corporate clients, had volunteered to help the victims of September 11.

In another context, Bart might have been the kind of lawyer people hate. She was blunt, tough, and relentless to the point of manic. She was always on, in the sense that she was always worrying about her case and her cause. She suffered fools, or even people who just didn't agree with her, terribly. But when it came to her September 11 work, all of that would translate into her firm helping fourteen clients for free at a cost of about $153,000 in terms of the firm's usual billable hours. These pro bono clients included one whom Bart recruited by striking up a conversation in an elevator. And now there was Sal Iacono, for whom Bart's firm would end up spending more than $40,000 worth of lawyer-time.

For starters, Bart got Sal $1,500 on the spot that morning just for making a loan application. Then she made a date to meet with him the following week to get going on a variety of other fronts.

# Monday, November 12, 2001

Chuck Schumer was in Buffalo making a round of constituent stops and speeches when he got word that an American Airlines plane bound for the Dominican Republic had crashed moments after takeoff from Kennedy Airport into the Rockaway peninsula in Queens, an area that had been part of his congressional district. Schumer was sure that terrorists had attacked again, and he had to find some place to be alone because he was so hysterical. After composing himself he made arrangements to fly to Newburgh, New York, which is about seventy miles north of the city and was the closest airport that had not been shut down in response to what was seen as a new emergency. By the time he and his staff finally made it to Rockaway, news reports said that the crash was probably an accident. The scene was horrific nonetheless. One of Schumer's aides had to be helped away after she watched someone recover a severed foot from the burning debris.

What was amazing, though, and a source of inspiration to many at the scene, was that New York's firemen, as they had on September 11, once again answered the call so fast—and in many cases, again, even though they were off duty. The fire was quickly contained.

What was not as easily contained was the new wave of fear the crash generated, accident or not.

In Washington, Congressman John Mica, a Florida Republican who chairs the aviation subcommittee and had been a stalwart in the fight not to yield to the Senate's bill to federalize airport security people, knew that the battle was over. There was now no way that the public would tolerate the deadlock he and his fellow Republicans in the House had forced. They had to pass a bill, and it was going to have to be the Senate's bill, or something close to it.

Everyone at the White House quickly came to the same view. Many of the President's closest advisors thought that it had been crazy for the conservatives in the House to draw this kind of line in the sand around what they saw as a gut issue for Americans who were worried about air safety. What was the principle, other than opposing any expansion of government, behind having federal law enforcement agents in the national parks, or guarding the borders, but not guarding the nation's aviation system? The White House had gone along with the House Republicans, but, in fact, many in the administration—including Mineta, the Transportation Secretary, and Chief of Staff Card, who had been the transportation secretary in the first Bush administration—favored some type of federalization, because they thought aviation safety was now too important to be outsourced. Now, the conservatives knew they had to acquiesce.

Schumer, of course, had voted with the rest of the Senate to federalize the screeners. And as he watched the Republicans in the House fight it, with the White House seemingly in the middle, he came to view the situation as emblematic of a larger issue for President Bush and his party. In his view, the House Republicans just plain hated and distrusted government. Thus, any increase in the size of government, let alone the creation of a giant new agency, was to be resisted at all costs. But a President, even a Republican President, sitting in the White House in a time of a public safety crisis saw firsthand that not all government is bad—that sometimes the country needed government to protect the people. The new age of terrorism, Schumer believed, required a big government response. And any ideology based on the principle that government is always bad was destined to become irrelevant in this new age.

# Tuesday, November 13, 2001

Chubb CEO Dean O'Hare considered himself a rock-ribbed Republican. He supported both Bush presidential campaigns, and was friendly with the first President Bush. But his kind of Republican was the financier, country-club type, which may be why he assumed that good Republicans were sophisticated about business and finance. It is also why he was not prepared for Trent Lott, the Mississippian who was the Republican Senate Leader.

O'Hare came to Washington to talk with Lott and Lott's aide, David Crane, about the need for federal terrorism insurance. He explained that he was not looking for a handout like the one the airlines got to cover September 11. He was there to talk about the future. No insurer was going to take the risk of fully insuring any buildings, stadiums, or amusement parks or anything else that might be a future terrorist target. At least in the short term, the market could not work to provide that coverage, because no one could measure the risk. The government had to step in to provide a backstop, just as it had when Congress passed a law providing federal insurance for nuclear power plants against catastrophic losses, because the country needed nuclear power.

Lott listened politely, then said, "That may be a problem in New York or Los Angeles or Washington and at places like Disney World, but I just don't think it's a problem for the country."

O'Hare couldn't believe it. "Why wouldn't shopping malls be targets, or colleges, or other such places anywhere in the country?" he asked. "I'm telling you that we are just not prepared to extend that kind of coverage."

"I just don't see it as a national problem," Lott repeated. "If those places that are so-called icons are in trouble, that doesn't mean the whole country is."

"The man is an idiot," O'Hare seethed to an aide as he left in a huff. "How can he be our leader?"

Elsewhere that morning in the Senate, spectators in a hearing room at the Dirksen Office Building were treated to what many would have agreed was a more frustrating display of American tax dollars in action. Carl Levin, the Senate Democrat from Michigan, called to order a hearing entitled, "Review of INS Policy on Releasing Illegal Aliens Pending Deportation."

After noting that his witnesses this morning would include INS officials as well as Border Patrol agents on the scene in the Northern Border, Levin declared, "The vast majority of people arrested by the Border Patrol while attempting to enter the country illegally in the Detroit Sector . . . are released on their own recognizance and do not show up for their removal hearings. And, to add insult to injury, the INS has told us that if a person does not appear at the hearing, little or no effort is made to find them."

The first witness was Michael Pearson, who had the title of executive associate commissioner for field operations. As if he had no idea what the subject of the hearing was, and as if reading from a statement prepared on September 10, when illegal entries from Mexico were the country's major border crossing concern, Pearson declared that the Border Patrol was "concentrating resources in the highest area of illegal activity, the Southwest Border." He went on to offer an incomprehensible description of INS's procedures for processing border jumpers. He literally never talked about people being released on their own recognizance and not returning. "As you can see," he concluded, "INS has established standardized procedures for processing persons arrested for illegal entry into the United States."

Even by INS standards, this was an amazing performance.

Levin lit into him. Did he have statistics for how many of the 4,400 people caught by the Border Patrol in the north last year were released on their own recognizance?

No, he didn't have those with him.

Did anyone at INS have that data?

Pearson said he didn't "believe so."

He had, however, gotten some data for just the Detroit Sector. There, it seemed that 315 people had been released on their own recognizance.

How many of those had then disappeared, rather than show up for a hearing?

Pearson didn't have that data either.

Levin wanted to know if everyone released on their own recognizance is required to be checked first with the FBI database to see if they are wanted for a crime or on a lookout list.

"No sir."

"Does that trouble you?" Levin asked.

"The concept troubles me, Senator," Pearson answered. "When you get out in the field, as a practical matter, when you are talking [about] the over a million people we arrest, we have to rely on the individual agent's judgment and the time it takes to do these things," he explained, ignoring the fact that agents like Lindemann and Hall didn't have access to the FBI database no matter what "judgment" they made. Pearson also explained that the Border Patrol was budgeted to pay local jails for only 19,700 prisoner-days per year, or about sixty detainees per day across the country, which meant they could not afford to detain lots of people.

Isn't everybody who is seeking to enter the country illegally a flight risk? Levin continued.

Not necessarily, Pearson said.

After lots more back and forth, Levin, who clearly had had enough, angrily summarized the situation: "Here is a guy sneaking in here illegally, but he is given a piece of paper saying, 'Here, we will notify you when the date and time of a removal hearing is, at the address above,' and there is not even an address. . . . What in Heaven's name is going on? How is it possible, with all these other gaps and holes, that this is a guy who is arrested by Border Patrol, who previously had used false documents, [and that] he is released on his own recognizance? Are you amazed at this or not?"

"Absolutely," Pearson conceded. "It amazed the chief patrol agent when I spoke with him about it, too. . . ."

"Do you think it is real rare?" Levin persisted.

"I do not know how rare it is."

Lindemann's partner, Hall, who was the next witness, knew that it wasn't rare at all. He estimated that 50 percent of those caught were being released on their own recognizance, with most of the rest simply being sent back to Canada, which is the procedure if they are Canadian citizens.

Hall reminded the senators that the Canadian government allowed people from fifty countries to enter without visas, including those from twenty countries from which the United States requires visas. He then noted that the Criminal Intelligence Service of Canada has stated that "many illegal aliens use Canada as a transit point on their way to the United States." Yet, Hall declared, an alien trying to sneak into the United States "risks little chance of apprehension by one of the 334 Border Patrol agents who patrol the border with Canada." If somehow they do get caught, he continued, the Border Patrol agents have to rely on them to provide honest information about their names before they can do any kind of cursory check of them, because they do not have access to machines that can send the arrestee's fingerprints to the FBI for checking. And then, with no checks being done, he testified, they are "usually" allowed to leave on their own recognizance. That is what happened, Hall said, with Abu Mezer, who was caught "not once but three times entering the United States in Blaine, Washington, in 1996. Several months later," Hall continued, "Mezer was shot by New York City police just hours before his planned attack on the New York subway system."

Then Hall added a personal note. "Rather than recognize and address any shortcomings, our local managers' response has been to threaten those who speak out," whereupon he described his recent suspension letter.

Levin closed the hearing by calling it "a wake-up call" that is "so loud that we can expect the INS and Congress to respond, and we are going to do just that."

The name of John Ashcroft—the cabinet official who ran INS, which is a division of the Justice Department—never came up during the two and a half hours of hearings.


*New York Times* conservative columnist Bill Safire called it "Seizing Dictatorial Power." Laura Murphy of the ACLU's Washington office called it "deeply disturbing." The *Washington Post* said it was an "end run" around the Bill of Rights.

But President Bush, in issuing an executive order establishing "military commissions" so that terrorists could be tried outside the confines of the traditional American justice system, called it a necessary tool, because he had determined that "an extraordinary emergency exists."

White House Counsel Alberto Gonzales would later explain that the executive order hadn't included many specifics about how these new tribunals would operate because "we wanted to leave ourselves lots of flexibility." Perhaps, but the vagueness of the order left a lot to the critics' imagination.

Standards for conviction and sentencing were set at "a minimum" of two thirds of the members of the commissions (whose qualifications were not described). Did that mean that two thirds could convict and sentence someone to death, or would a unanimous verdict be required, as it is in conventional criminal cases? The order said Defense Secretary Donald Rumsfeld would promulgate rules deciding that. Other gaps included leaving it to Rumsfeld to decide who the defense lawyers would be, and how open the trials would be to the press, a gap that caused the *New York Times* to write that they would be "largely secret."

In fact, while the order did have the virtue of flexibility, its gaps were more the result of a sloppy, rushed process. Few people were consulted on this monumentally important issue outside the White House counsel's office, where Gonzales's deputy, Timothy Flanigan, and his staff did most of the drafting. The Office of Legal Counsel in Ashcroft's Justice Department, which usually does the government's key work when it comes to rendering legal opinions, was involved in supplying research and attended some meetings, but this was mostly a White House counsel's office product. Ashcroft just wasn't that interested, in large part because he saw the commissions as having to do with people the Army might catch overseas. Terwilliger and Barr—the two Justice Department lawyers from the first Bush administration who had suggested the idea to Flanigan—never attended a meeting and had only brief conversations with people in the White House about it.

As for the Pentagon, neither its lawyers nor Rumsfeld were involved in any discussions with anyone about the executive order, even though they would be the ones charged with refining the rules for the tribunals and conducting them. That, according to one former top lawyer in the first George Bush administration, "was an amazing exclusion. There are lawyers at the Pentagon who really know these issues and who could have helped them avoid all kinds of real and public relations traps."

Military commissions have been used in wartime to try prisoners of war or to prosecute others, known as "unlawful combatants," involved in a war. Mostly, the trials have taken place overseas and involved people caught overseas. But a precedent of sorts was set during World War II, when President Roosevelt used a military commission to prosecute, and execute, a group of Germans caught sneaking into the United States with plans to set off bombs here. The Supreme Court upheld the constitutionality of the tribunals—which set lower standards of evidence and lacked other traditional constitutional safeguards, including a public trial. But critics of the Bush plan cited one difference: Congress had legislated the tribunals that the High Court had allowed, whereas Bush was setting these up by executive order.

The other difference, of course, was that whatever the war against terrorism and Al Qaeda was, it was not a conventional war against a foreign country, much less a congressionally declared war. A terrorist operating in a cell, albeit supported by an international network such as Al Qaeda, falls somewhere in the middle of the spectrum between a conventional domestic criminal (a man mugging a woman in the street) and a foreign enemy attacking with uniformed soldiers. Until now, while acknowledging that terrorists were something more than common street criminals, the government had always tried them in the criminal courts. Thus, the Al Qaeda members accused of bombing two U.S. embassies in 1998 had been tried and convicted in a New York federal criminal court, as had those accused of the first World Trade Center bombing and of a plot to blow up various bridges and tunnels in New York.

It had been Terwilliger's contention, when he called Flanigan at the White House to suggest the military commissions, that this was crazy, that extending to people who see themselves at war with the United States and its system all of the protections of that system was the ultimate in treating the Constitution as a suicide pact. Should Americans really want to try Osama bin Laden (whose imminent capture seemed possible, if not likely) in an American courtroom, with an American lawyer nitpicking about whether he'd been read his rights sufficiently, or whether a search of his headquarters had been legal? Should they want to put jurors and the judges through the risks of such a public trial? Should they want to subject intelligence sources and methods to public scrutiny? Should they want to turn an event and a person that was so tragic, so evil, into a public spectacle—into yet another American "trial of the century"? Or, as Ashcroft put it, did they really want to create "Osama TV"?

Romero and the ACLU had ready answers. The trials of the embassy bombers had worked fine. If anything, they had demonstrated to the world that the American justice system need not and would not be compromised by a bunch of terrorists. The evidence that involved secret intelligence information had been presented in a closed session; there were all kinds of procedures in place for that. Besides, once these exceptions started, where did they stop? What about someone arrested in an organized crime plot, with the evidence pointing to an international organization based in Sicily or Russia? Aren't mob extortionists and drug dealers "at war" with the system, too? Aren't drug cartels international, and hasn't the government declared "war on drugs" the way it has declared war on terrorism?

"If bin Laden is caught in Pakistan," Romero was asked a few months after the executive order was issued, "you're saying he should be brought to the United States and tried in an American courtroom just like OJ?"

"You bet," he replied.

Most Americans didn't agree. Public opinion polls showed broad support for the tribunals. And even liberals such as Schumer believed that the idea made sense. "It's ludicrous to suggest [bin Laden] should be tried in a federal court on Center Street in Lower Manhattan," he declared during a Senate hearing. But Schumer and others also believed that the details still to be filled in by Rumsfeld and his staff at the Pentagon would be crucial in determining whether a logical idea—meant to deal for the first time with transgressions that were somewhere between crimes and war—became an abuse of power.

The good news about successful entrepreneurs is that they love their products. They lie awake nights thinking about the wonders of whatever it is they are trying to make and sell. Their enthusiasm is beyond all perspective. For them, the product, with all its little intrigues, is the world.

The bad news about entrepreneurs is that because they get so wrapped up in all that, they sometimes forget that they have to make the sale.

Which is what made InVision's sales manager so frustrated about the meeting he and Sergio Magistri had today with Transportation Secretary Norman Mineta and Mineta's deputy, Michael Jackson.

"The meeting went for two hours, until about 7:30, and it was only supposed to be forty-five minutes," the sales manager reported the next morning to McCann, Magistri's lobbyist. "But Sergio forgot to close the sale."

By the time that Magistri, who had been trying for weeks to get in to see Mineta, got the call to come to Washington the week before, Mineta and Jackson had become fully engaged in aviation security, in Jackson's case almost to the exclusion of everything else in their Transportation Department. (Mineta had assigned nonaviation issues to John Flaherty, his chief of staff, who methodically developed a list of critical transportation infrastructure choke points, such as harbors, bridges, and railroad junctions, and then focused on getting federal and local forces to enhance security at the the ten most important, then twenty more, and so on.) For Mineta and Jackson, full engagement meant all the details—including the status of the available technology—having to do with how they might deal with a mandate to screen all checked baggage for explosives that Congress now seemed to be on the verge of enacting.

Jackson in particular was fascinated with how Magistri made his machines. While Mineta, his sleeves rolled up, doodled notes, Jackson asked a series of questions. What was the process? How come it took so long and was so expensive?

He couldn't get enough detail.

Magistri, of course, was thrilled to oblige, although his accent made some of his elaborate explanations even more difficult to understand than they otherwise would have been. The ball bearings that allowed the walls of the huge scanning chamber where the luggage was placed to rotate so rapidly were so delicate and had to perform so perfectly that they took twenty weeks to build and test. The chamber walls took almost as long, and the process couldn't be rushed because the enamel that lined them had to be baked on slowly.

*What about trace detectors,** Jackson asked, referring to the smaller, cheaper devices made by companies like Barringer that took readings from cotton cloths swabbed against suitcases.

*They should be a part of any baggage screening system,* Magistri said. *I've always thought that they could supplement what our machines do. You could use them to check a bag after one of our machines gets a hit and before you go search the bag by hand. Or you could use them at isolated gates or other special areas. But,* he added, *they cannot be a substitute, because they require more people and they take much longer than our machines, where you run the bags through on a belt.*

When Jackson asked whether Magistri could produce enough machines on time to meet what looked likely to be Congress's ambitious deployment plans, the InVision CEO said that the best way to deal with that was to get an order from the government as soon as possible so he could ramp up. But, thrilled as he was to talk shop with Mineta and Jackson, he neglected to push the issue by asking, as his sales manager had urged him to, for a firm order immediately.

Jackson would not have responded anyway. He was impressed with Magistri, deciding immediately that he knew his stuff and was passionately committed to being part of the government's solution to aviation safety. But Jackson had another motive for the meeting. He wanted to learn as much as he could so that he could figure out a way to get other companies involved in producing machines like Magistri's. It wasn't that he had anything against Magistri or InVision, or that he was trying to cheat them; if anything the meeting made him sympathize with Magistri and his story of being jilted by the government in the past. It was just that he had a broader responsibility. He had to worry about getting that equipment into the airports a lot faster than he knew Magistri could produce it. By understanding Magistri's operation as best he could, he wanted to size up the prospects for helping to create

---

*Italics are used here because this is the participants' approximation of the conversation. Neither had an exact enough memory of it to merit putting the conversation within quotation marks.

new and larger producers of the same types of machines. He asked Magistri why the government couldn't do a deal to license his intellectual property—InVision's various patents and software programs—and then let other manufacturers use them to build the machine. The government, or those manufacturers, would then pay InVision a set amount, say 5 or 10 percent of the price of the machine, for each one bought from those new manufacturers.

Magistri said he hadn't ever thought about that, but depending on the license fee, they might be able to do that. He tried to sound cooperative. Actually, he was horrified. License fee or not, the government was talking about killing his position in the market. He had dreams of becoming a $2 or $3 billion company; all it took was selling 2,000 or 3,000 of his million-dollar machines. He made 37 to 40 percent profit on those machines, and could expect to make more on them once they were sold and deployed around the country, because InVision would then do all the high-fee maintenance. Licensing the know-how to a company like Raytheon (a name mentioned at the meeting) for a one-time, 10 percent piece of the action, which would disappear once Raytheon or someone else figured out how to make its own machines, wasn't at all what he had in mind.

Jackson came away convinced that there had to be a way that the government, its wallet opened by virtue of the coming congressional mandate, could go beyond Magistri and his smaller competitor (L-3) to produce machines that would keep bombs off of airplanes.

Mineta was even more impressed by Magistri, and not as skeptical as Jackson that InVision wouldn't be able to meet the demand. About a week after the meeting, Magistri would get a call on his cell phone while traveling in Southern California. It was someone asking about his production capacity, who seemed to know every detail of the throughput capacity of every one of his various models—this unit processed these many bags per hour, that one that many. Although the connection was awful, Magistri soon realized it was Mineta asking him more about production schedules and how InVision could subcontract out some of the work producing components of the machine to others in order to increase capacity. Magistri, who by now had been chided by his sales manager and his chief operating officer for not closing the sale in Washington, was on message this time. He told the Transportation Secretary that InVision already did outsource a lot of the manufacturing of components, but that he couldn't do more of it until he got a firm order, because he couldn't ask those subcontractors to build up their capacity until he could guarantee them business. Mineta took down the details and promised to get back to him.

Hollie Bart, Sal Iacono's new pro bono lawyer, applied for a $1,000 grant for Sal from a city agency charged with helping small businesses recover. But she was told that this particular program's money had run out.

She met with Sal and began work on an application to the Seedco program that had been organized in early October to help Ground Zero businesses. By now the September 11th Fund—the one that had benefited from the Hollywood telethon—had given Seedco an initial grant of more than $9 million.

Meantime, she and other lawyers at her firm were finishing a three-inch-thick looseleaf binder that catalogued all the other programs and legal strategies (how to push for rent, electric bill, or phone bill rebates, for example) that might be available to Sal and the other small businesses they had taken on as clients.

The key lawyer working on the book was Lynn Geerdes, a thirty-four-year-old Iowa-born specialist in business and insurance litigation, based in the firm's Chicago office. Geerdes, who had been an insurance actuary before going to law school, had been working late one night the week before when she noticed an e-mail from Bart to everyone at the firm soliciting volunteers for Ground Zero–related pro bono work. She had never met Bart, had only been to New York once as a tourist eight years before, and she would not end up meeting Sal until June of the following year. But she immediately jumped in, and considered herself lucky for the chance. "Who would not want to do this," she thought.

Like George Clooney or Jeff Katzenberg in Hollywood working on the telethon, it was her way, she says, of "getting involved." She would come to regard her happening on to Bart's e-mail late that night as "a turning point in my career. It opened up a new perspective for me on what lawyering could be. When you do work for big corporations all the time, you lose perspective."

The loose-leaf book Geerdes was working on would soon become obsolete, as new charities and grant programs popped up, or as older ones, like the Red Cross, changed their rules. So consulting the book would gradually give way to a process where Bart would get on the phone with Geerdes and other lawyers and push them to come up with new ideas, anything at all, that might get Sal more help. "There's got to be more than one way to skin a cat," she kept telling Geerdes and the others.

## Wednesday, November 14, 2001

Ken Feinberg met at the Old Executive Office Building across the driveway from the White House with Mitch Daniels, the budget director and the man who, other than Ashcroft, had the most to do with deciding who the Special Master of the victims compensation fund would be.

Daniels had been amazed that he was being asked to consider giving a Ted Kennedy Democrat the checkbook for a fund that was so open-ended that Daniels had been against it in the first place. But Ashcroft's staff sold him on meeting the guy, with two arguments: Feinberg could give them political cover for all the fallout the issues related to the fund were likely to generate, and he really seemed as if he knew what he was doing and was determined to make this thing work.

Feinberg and Daniels were each surprised at how well things went. Daniels is a lot looser and friendlier than his image as Bush's hard-hearted budget director suggests. And Feinberg, a wealthy lawyer who has worked for a variety of corporate clients over the last twenty years, is hardly a flower child. They liked each other, and while, again, they didn't settle on a specific number, Feinberg made it clear that he knew that part of making the fund a success would be limiting its total cost to something akin to the numbers that had been talked about in the press—which he put at about $6 billion.

Daniels called Ashcroft's people afterward and told them he was comfortable with Feinberg's apparent budget sensitivity. He, too, thought this could be the guy.

## Thursday, November 15, 2001

Since Monday, Bob Lindemann had been out of town and unable to monitor firsthand what was going on with his case. He was stuck near Brunswick, Georgia, at the federal government's giant law enforcement training facility, where he was taking a four-week Border Patrol course in boat handling and water interdiction. He'd been pushing to get this extra training for years, and in August the paperwork had finally come through.

His partner, Hall, had told him Monday night how well Senator Levin's hearing had gone, and he already knew about Levin's letter to Ziglar of the INS requesting all the files in his and Hall's disciplinary case. Now, he heard that Levin had sent a second letter expressing concern that Hall and Linde-mann had received that additional disciplinary reprisal after the INS learned that Hall had agreed to testify before Levin's committee.

He also found out that something called the Office of Special Counsel was investigating his and Hall's case. OSC is an obscure federal agency set up in the post-Watergate era to protect government whistle-blowers. A government employee who believes he has been treated adversely because he has revealed government wrongdoing can complain to the agency—which is what Linde-mann's union had done the week before on his behalf.

What Lindemann didn't know was that Ziglar, after getting a follow-up call from Levin, had today agreed to refer Lindemann's and Hall's cases to the inspector general of the Justice Department.

That was a big deal. Even in a country where the adversary process—people and institutions fighting it out in some forum or another—is the hall-mark of the messy way America tries to produce balanced, fair results, the existence of an Office of Inspector General in all key federal agencies seemed a bit over the top. True, the federal government is based on a balance of pow-ers, which checks the power of each of the three branches—executive, legisla-tive, and judicial. But the inspector generals are a check within the executive branch itself; they're independent adversaries within their own departments, charged with investigating and publicly reporting on management ineffi-ciency, waste, fraud, political chicanery, or other misconduct. As with that Office of Special Counsel that investigates personnel actions, the law estab-lishing inspector generals was passed in the aftermath of the Watergate scan-dals. Each inspector general is appointed by the President and confirmed by the Senate. They can be fired only by the President, and he can only do so after delivering an explanation to Congress.

The Justice Department's inspector general was Glenn Fine, forty-five. A Harvard-trained lawyer and former prosecutor appointed in the Clinton administration, Fine had an office in the Justice Department's headquarters on Pennsylvania Avenue. But he and his staff were a world unto themselves. Fine immediately assigned a team of investigators to the Lindemann and Hall case.

If Herb Wachtell and his client, Larry Silverstein, thought that the starting point of any negotiation for a compromise was going to be somewhere between $3.55 billion and $7.1 billion, insurance company lawyer Barry Ostrager had other ideas. He sent a stinging "Dear Herb" letter reminding

Wachtell that under the terms of his insurance policy Silverstein could only get an up-front payment in full from the insurers, as he was now demanding, if he declared that he was *not* going to rebuild the Trade Center. Worse, in that case he would only get the replacement cost stated in his policy—$3.55 billion—*minus* several hundred million dollars to account for the depreciation of the buildings. (In other words, while his insurance policy had said it would cost $3.55 billion to build *new* buildings, the three-decades-old buildings that had been there had to have been worth something less than new ones would be worth.) On the other hand, if, as Silverstein kept saying in speeches and press interviews, he was determined to rebuild, then the policy said that he would only get those payments as he incurred rebuilding expenses. This meant that while he might get $3.55 billion, he'd get it paid out over the five- to ten-year rebuilding process, making it worth a lot less than an immediate check for $3.55 billion.

Ostrager was not simply dinging Silverstein with the threat of ending up with less than $3.55 billion, let alone less than $7.1 billion. He was also hinting at another suspicion that he had—which was that what Silverstein really wanted to do was to take his insurance money and not rebuild but instead realize a bonanza profit.

Ostrager figured it this way: Suppose Silverstein collected $3.55 billion from the insurers. His contract with the Port Authority had been so badly lawyered from the Port Authority side that it seemed to require that the authority—which still owned the Trade Center and had only sold Silverstein a ninety-nine-year lease to operate it—would only get paid $1.5 billion from any insurance proceeds if Silverstein decided not to rebuild and was able to get out of his lease with the Authority. Ostrager also knew that Silverstein's deal with the banks that had loaned him the money to do the Trade Center deal required that they be paid off from the insurance proceeds, too, to the tune of another $560 million. So, if Silverstein could walk away from the Trade Center deal, it seemed that he would end up with more than $1 billion—$3.55 billion in insurance, less these two payments and other expenses. That was a fast $1 billion that Silverstein could keep for himself and his partners, who together had put up only about $125 million in July to do their deal.

But Silverstein had repeatedly declared that he was going to rebuild, not walk away. To Ostrager, though, that only meant that Silverstein was playing chicken with the Port Authority. For Ostrager by now had seen the contract Silverstein had with the Port Authority, and he knew that it had two clauses that all but required both Silverstein and the Port Authority to play an elaborate game of bluff. The first clause required Silverstein to use any insurance proceeds to rebuild in the event the Trade Center was destroyed. But the second clause required the Port Authority to *allow* Silverstein to rebuild the Trade Center exactly as it had been, so that he would be able to rent out the same amount of space. What if, as now seemed to be the case, it became impossible to rebuild the site exactly as it had been? After all, even by November, it was clear that two 110-story towers were not going to be built at that site, nor would anyone want to rent all the space in them if they were built.

Amazingly, the contract said nothing about that, except that in the event that it became impractical to rebuild, the two sides had to negotiate. The way Ostrager figured it, as long as Silverstein acted as if he was prepared to rebuild the same size Trade Center, he could get the Port Authority to blink first and say he couldn't, whereupon he could claim they had breached the contract and walk away from the deal with that $1 billion—or more, if this litigation yielded a good settlement.

Thus, Silverstein's effort to get more than $3.55 billion by claiming two occurrences, Ostrager reasoned, had a simple, selfish goal: Anything he could get above $3.55 billion by claiming $7.1 billion—even, say, an extra $100 million—would be part of the surplus that would flow right to his partners. Moreover, if he demanded $7.1 billion from the insurers and then got less, he could use that in the public relations arena as his excuse for walking away.

All of that might have seemed impossibly complicated to a layperson or even to a reporter covering the dispute, but it wasn't to John Martin, the federal judge handling the case. As a lawyer in a sophisticated private practice he had been involved in complex business litigations earlier in his career.

Although Ostrager didn't know it at the time, the theory that Silverstein intended to get the Trade Center to blink first also was consistent with what Silverstein had told his architect within a day of the attacks—that he had to begin with a design that included the same amount of rentable square feet, even if they all thought they weren't going to end up building something like that.

Silverstein's public position was that any accusation that he didn't want to be at the center of the rebuilding of New York was outrageous. He was in the litigation for one purpose and one purpose only—to get all he could from these insurance companies to rebuild New York. Any suggestion by the insurance companies that he was looking to walk away with a windfall was simply an attempt to poison a jury pool.


Michael Cartier got his television debut on Channel 11, the WB network affiliate in New York. They wanted to know what his new organization Give Your

Voice was all about, and what he thought about the cleanup process. He said it was moving too fast.

After a day of feverish negotiations, the Senate and House finally agreed on an aviation security bill tonight. As expected, the House side caved, and a giant new Transportation Security Administration was created and placed under Mineta's control in the Transportation Department.

The major challenge of the day had been to figure out a graceful way for the House Republicans to capitulate. The solution came after Lott, the Senate Republican Leader, suggested that the law allow for five of the country's 429 airports to choose to participate in a pilot project under which they could use private companies operating under tight guidelines. Also, after a three-year period of federalization, other airports could apply to use private security forces, too. It was hard to imagine why any airport would want to do that, but the provision allowed the Republicans to say they had preserved the principle, if that's what it was, of private screeners at the airports.

# Friday, November 16, 2001

It was after the basic agreement on federalizing the screeners was reached on Thursday that the real action on Capitol Hill started. Beginning sometime after midnight on Friday morning, the members of the House-Senate conference and their staffs—working like college kids crashing a term paper—tried to iron out the most difficult of a slew of additional provisions that had significance far beyond the time and public scrutiny they were given. They were desperate to reconcile the House and Senate versions of the aviation security bill so they could produce a law for the President to sign before the Thanksgiving travel rush began the next afternoon.

First, there was the issue of doing for others what Congress had done for the airlines in September when it had capped their liability for lawsuits stemming from the plane crashes. As their lobbyists congregated outside the conference room, one by one a different entity got its cap. Boeing got one so it didn't have to worry about suits claiming its cockpit doors should have been stronger. Boeing's subcontractors got a cap. Then came the airports from which the planes had departed—Logan, Newark, and Portland, Maine. The Port Authority, which built and owned the Trade Center and had run it until making the deal with Silverstein, got a cap limited to its insurance coverage so that it didn't have to worry about claims that it should have designed the building better to withstand the fire, that it should have not locked the roof doors so that people could have escaped that way, or that an announcement, probably by Port Authority police, telling people it was okay to stay in the South Tower after the North Tower was hit had resulted in unnecessary deaths. There were lots of defenses to these claims (a major one being that the harm involved in an injury has to be foreseeable), but it was a relief not to have to worry about them. The architects and builders of the Trade Center also got covered.

The hardest cap to write in was for New York City, which wanted protection against claims such as whether its communication system had worked well enough, whether the surviving firemen were given the right equipment to protect their lungs, or even whether some racing fire truck had struck someone else's car. The problem was that no one knew how to quantify the city's cap, because the city doesn't have insurance. Frenzied conference committee staffers, as well as Schumer's and Clinton's people, called around trying to figure out a number to set the cap at. The key senate staffer, Samuel Whitehorn, got so disgusted with the delay that he took a nap on a couch. Finally, they all accepted a guess that last year's payouts by the city for all liability suits had been $350 million, and wrote that number in.

New York State was the only potential defendant that did not get a cap—because no state lobbyist showed up, and Clinton's and Schumer's staffs couldn't get anyone from Governor George Pataki's office to focus on the issue.

The conference members did, however, take time out to *remove* one cap that had been part of the provision limiting the airlines' liability. At the bottom of the fifty-page bill, they inserted a note excluding private security companies like Argenbright from any liability caps.

As for Silverstein, he had retained Jack Quinn, the former Clinton White House counsel who had become famous ten months before for helping obtain a pardon for tax evasion fugitive Marc Rich. Quinn had worked closely with Schumer and his staff in the last two weeks to win protection for Silverstein so that any liability he might have for structural or management gaps at the Trade Center (which had all become his responsibility when he took over management of the center in July) would be capped at the approximately $1.5 billion in liability insurance he had.

This liability insurance is different from the property insurance that Silverstein had bought to compensate him for any damage to the Trade Center. It was the property insurance, and whether it was $3.55 billion or $7.1 billion, that was being litigated with Ostrager and the insurance companies. But the two types of insurance did get linked by some in Congress. When Quinn or Schumer broached the question of protecting Silverstein with a cap set at his liability insurance, some members of Congress had expressed concern that Silverstein might take the proceeds he had from his property insurance—the $3.55 billion or $7.1 billion—and run. So, if his management of the Trade Center had resulted in injuries, they complained, why should he be protected and end up with a windfall?

Schumer had a ready answer. Silverstein, who with his wife had contributed the maximum to both the Schumer and Hillary Clinton Senate campaigns and thousands more to various congressional political action committees, had assured Schumer he intended to use his insurance money to rebuild the Trade Center. So Schumer and Quinn offered to draft a provision that would stipulate that Silverstein would get his liability cap but would lose it if he didn't rebuild the Trade Center.

That sounded fair enough. And, in fact it's exactly how Quinn and Schumer both described the provisions to the author after it had been inserted into the law. But the actual language had been written by one of Wachtell's partners, and it had a huge but subtle loophole. Silverstein's protection from liability would only be voided, the Silverstein paragraph in the airline security bill said, "if the Attorney General determines . . . that the person [Silverstein] has willfully defaulted on a contractual obligation to rebuild, or assist in the rebuilding of, the World Trade Center." As anyone reading the contract between Silverstein and the Port Authority would have known, if the Port Authority did not let Silverstein rebuild the Trade Center exactly as it had been on September 10, it would be impossible for Silverstein to be in breach of any obligation he had to rebuild, because his only obligation was to rebuild it exactly as it had been on September 10.

Months later, Schumer would bump into Jacques Dubois, Swiss Re's American CEO at a social function. "You were had," Dubois said, after Schumer had tried to explain how Silverstein had to use the insurance money to rebuild.

The second set of issues the conference members and their staff had to deal with concerned deadlines both for federalizing all the screeners and for installing all the explosive detection equipment.

The Senate had provided that the FAA was to set a schedule for the installation of the explosive detection equipment within sixty days, but it did not say what that schedule had to be. The Republican House bill, however, had mandated that the equipment be in place by the end of 2003, or about twenty-five months from now. Mica, the Republican congressman from Florida who chairs the House aviation subcommittee, had insisted on a deadline because he had grown disgusted with the way the FAA dragged its feet for years, even decades, in promulgating even the simplest regulations.

As for the federalization of the screeners, the Senate had set no deadline, and the House, of course, hadn't voted to federalize them at all in its bill.

But now a new set of dynamics took over: The crash of the plane bound for the Dominican Republic earlier in the week—plus the House Republicans' resentment of the Senate and vice versa, and the onset of the travel-heavy Thanksgiving holiday next week and accompanying media stories about the public being afraid to fly—had combined to encourage an orgy of deadline writing, with each side, and even factions within each side, trying to out-deadline the other.

"Once we got into a discussion of deadlines, no one in the room wanted to be less tough than the next guy," one key staff member explains. "So they just threw dates out, without any regard to what was doable or what we should want to do."

John McCain, the Arizona senator who had led the fight for the Senate bill, recalls it as a "perfect example of how democracies overreact in a crisis."

When the group finished at about 3:45 A.M. their draft said that all airports had to have explosive detection equipment in place to screen checked baggage not by the end of 2003, but by the end of 2002—thirteen and a half months from now! And that date only came as a compromise after one contingent pushed for a sixty-day deadline.

The deadline for having a full force of federal agents replacing all the private screeners was set even earlier—at one year from the date the President would sign the bill, on November 19, 2002. ("We just settled on an aggressive round number," a staffer in the room later recalled.) That meant one year to recruit and train a force that would easily be five times the size of the Secret Service, though, of course, no one knew exactly how large a force would be needed, let alone how they would be recruited, where they would be trained, or how the training would be paid for. By way of comparison, McCabe of Customs knew that it took roughly six months to recruit, do background checks on, and train a Customs inspector at a cost of about $8,500. And that was in an agency that had existed for more than 200 years and had training manuals and a recruiting infrastructure.

Their work seemingly done, the staff set out to edit the bill and get it printed up for their members to vote on later in the morning. That's when the computers crashed. The entire file was lost, leaving the bleary-eyed, angry staff working until daybreak to reconstruct what they had done for, and to, the country's aviation system by cutting and pasting segments from various, older drafts of the law.

Hollie Bart convinced Con Ed to forgive the portion of Sal's electric bill covering the first week after the attacks. She had tried to get them to give him a month or two of electricity for free once he reopened.

She also attempted, fruitlessly, to get the *New York Times* to give him and other small businesses at Ground Zero discounted ads in the paper, never realizing that it was the *Times*'s foundation that had made the original contribution to the Seedco fund that had been set up to aid businesses like Sal's.

Bart had also wanted to push Sal's landlord, the manager of the old-style office building on lower Broadway that housed his shop. But Sal refused. He had negotiated on his own with his landlord for twenty-four years and always thought he had been given a fair deal. In fact, he still remembered that if not for the initial monthly rent he'd been offered by the manager in 1977—$500, when the asking price had been $1,000—he would have never been able to go into business in the first place. He didn't want an aggressive lawyer getting in the way of that relationship. Sal did get a rent break, one that Bart thought was less generous than she could have wrung out of the landlord.

## Saturday, November 17, 2001

The deadline for getting bomb screening equipment into all the airports seemed ridiculous, and likely might entice competitors into his market. But when Sergio Magistri got the details this morning of what Congress had agreed on in passing the aviation security law, he was jubilant. This was the law—the call to arms—that he had been dreaming of since 1990. Finally, the orders from the government would come in by the hundreds. The challenge wouldn't be selling the concept of his machines, or even selling the machines. The challenge would be making them fast enough. That was going to be difficult and create a whole new kind of pressure on him and his organization. But as they say in the business world, this was what is known as a "good" problem.

# Monday, November 19, 2001

Michael Jackson, the deputy transportation secretary, went to the White House for the President's signing of the Aviation and Transportation Security Act that created the Transportation Security Administration (TSA) within the Transportation Department. He didn't hang around long. He had to go back to the office and build what was certain to be, in terms of employees hired in its first year, the largest new government agency in the history of the country.

Someone was going to have to be hired to run the agency, but Jackson had wanted to get moving even before that. So he continued today a series of efforts he had begun more than a month earlier to sidestep the traditional bureaucratic process and engage the private sector in a way that was unprecedented.

Jackson, who favored conservative suits and ties, glasses, short hair, and a carefully trimmed mustache, looked like a standard high-end bureaucrat. His résumé—chief of staff to the Transportation Secretary in Bush I, chief operating officer for a division of Lockheed, researcher at the American Enterprise Institute—read like that of a run-of-the-mill veteran of the revolving door between Washington-centric corporate jobs and Republican administration sub-cabinet posts. But there was more there than met the eye. Jackson was whip smart when it came to budget and operational details, a real manager who everyone seemed to think was destined for bigger things. More important, Jackson, a devout Catholic, was said by friends to have an almost religious determination to meet these new deadlines. When Congress passed the law, he spent little time asking why. He started worrying about how.

One of his first conversations about the TSA had been in September with a Silicon Valley entrepreneur and close friend named Kip Hawley. Hawley, who had worked with Jackson's wife in the Reagan administration, had called Jackson soon after September 11 and told him that if he needed some informal help with what looked to be a huge job in tightening aviation safety, Hawley would be glad to volunteer. "I meant it, but it didn't really mean much," Hawley says, "because I was in California. What could I really do?"

But in mid-October, after talking about it with his family, Hawley decided that he really ought to mean it. He called his friend back and offered to come east and work full-time as a volunteer to get the security effort off the ground. He couldn't really help his country from Pebble Beach, California, Hawley acknowledged.

Jackson took him up on it, and by now Hawley was living at Jackson's Virginia home, where the two sat up nights at the kitchen table, mapping out how they were going to get the Transportation Security Administration up and running. They continued the conversations on the drive to work in the morning.

Hawley knew nothing about aviation security, but, like Jackson, he had a good sense of how to connect strategy with tactics, and then map a plan for operations. What that meant here was that the two developed as an overall strategy the idea that aviation security should be a "system of systems"—a ring, or layers, or protective circles. From the profiling and identifying of the riskiest passengers at the time they buy tickets, to the airport perimeter, to the gate checkpoints, to the checking of baggage, to the marshals on board random flights, the protection should be layered on so that it was all part of one system. Yet customer service also had to be a part of each protection circle; for if the process discouraged people from flying it was a failure, no matter how safe.

Broken out that way, dozens of smaller pieces became obvious, such as redesigning passenger checkpoint lines so that they would move efficiently; figuring out how the new screeners were going to be recruited and then developing a training program for them so they'd be able to spot weapons better when looking at X rays of carry-on bags; finding a better way to use all the data that was out there, which private companies already used for consumer marketing, in order to select the most at-risk passengers for hand searches; and designing systems to use InVision's explosive detection machines and the smaller, cheaper but more time-consuming trace detection machines in tandem.

Casting a shadow over all that now, of course, were those two deadlines—for getting the explosive detection equipment in, and for getting all the screeners federalized. Jackson and Hawley were in lockstep about that, too: They were going to make the deadlines because the deadlines were the law. There would be no excuses. By the time of today's signing ceremony, Hawley had sketched out more than two dozen subjects for which he proposed to Jackson that they recruit "go teams" immediately. Each team would attack a specific problem with specific deadlines. Little pieces of each problem would get their own interim deadlines. Some of the go teams would involve specialists on loan from other government agencies. But what was truly different about the plan was that they would find lots of people like Hawley who could be borrowed from a private employer.* Using a Rolodex built up over years

---

*In an illustration of the adage that "no good deed goes unpunished," one of the toughest hurdles Hawley and Jackson faced was fashioning an arrangement that passed muster with government lawyers, who were afraid that having someone working for the government who was still on a private payroll violated conflict-of-interest laws.

as a congressman from Silicon Valley and then as Commerce Secretary in the Clinton administration, Transportation Secretary Mineta called friends of his who were CEOs at places like Intel, Selectron, FedEx, and Marriott and asked them to loan him one of their best people for a sojourn in public service. The executives would stay on their corporate payrolls, and Mineta and the country would get their talent for free.

In fact, there were already several go teams in place, including one that involved a project—ramping up the federal corps of air marshals who ride undercover on airliners—that preceded the passage of the new law and was considered especially urgent. The marshals' corps had dwindled to thirty-two people on September 10, and Mineta wanted to recruit and train 3,000 as soon as possible, a goal that was made even more urgent by pressure from members of the House and Senate, especially one terrified member of the California delegation, who were calling regularly to complain that they hadn't spotted any air marshals on the planes that they took back and forth to their districts every week.

A shadow Transportation Security Administration was being born and run from Michael Jackson's kitchen table, even before the agency's director or any other officials had been hired.

Zacarias Moussaoui seemed an ideal candidate for the military commissions that the President had established with his executive order. Moussaoui was suspected to have been slated to be the twentieth hijacker. He had been detained on immigration charges in Minnesota in August by FBI agents who were suspicious about him taking flight training classes. While prosecutors had not found anything linking him specifically to the attacks, they did have evidence that he had been in contact with the same Al Qaeda operatives overseas who had been in contact with the hijackers. And he was a French citizen, not an American.

Ashcroft knew that Chertoff was having his Criminal Division prepare an indictment charging Moussaoui as a conspirator in the September 11 attacks. The problem was that Flanigan, the White House deputy counsel who had written the executive order establishing the military tribunals for unlawful enemy combatants, wanted to know why he shouldn't instead be put into a tribunal. Wasn't this exactly what they were for—to try non-Americans accused of terrorist plots? Why have a public trial that would be a circus? Why not instead put him in a procedure where he was almost certain to get the death penalty he deserved?

A series of staff meetings began at Justice to decide whether Moussaoui should be handed over to a military commission. Ashcroft sat in on some, and Chertoff or Deputy Attorney General Larry Thompson ran the others. Actually, there was little debate. Everyone in the room wanted to keep the case; everyone was like Ashcroft when it came to being the kind of player who likes to have the ball when the pressure is on. They began marshaling the arguments they'd make to the White House.

Because the company owned by Warren Buffett, America's second richest man, owns a large reinsurance company, Buffett had taken a keen interest in the issue of terrorism insurance. Today, he laid out his point of view in an op-ed piece in the *Washington Post*. (Buffett sits on the company's board of directors.) Admitting that "I did something very dumb" by allowing his company to provide insurance for "a huge catastrophe loss" that no one could measure, Buffett argued that "a potential loss of almost infinite magnitude can be assumed only by an entity of almost infinite resources. That economic species doesn't exist in the private sector," he continued. "Only the U.S. government fits the bill."

Buffett's idea was different from anything O'Hare of Chubb or anyone else had suggested—and seemingly much more logical. Rather than have insurance companies insure for relatively small amounts of terrorism losses and then have the government backstop larger losses, as was being proposed by the industry, Buffett wanted the industry to get out of the business altogether. Instead, the government would insure all losses due to a terrorist attack much the way the government, through the Federal Deposit Insurance Corporation (FDIC), insures losses to depositors if banks go bad. If a bank loses a depositor's money through fraud or bad investments that cause it to go bankrupt, the government steps in and reimburses the depositor. The funds for the government to do that come from a small percentage fee that banks pay on all their deposits. Buffett wanted a small percentage of all insurance premiums for all types of insurance to go into a new fund that would step in and pay terrorism losses. "The insurance industry would not be permitted to earn a dime from the coverage," he added.

The virtue of this idea, Buffett argued, was that if insurers still sold even a portion of terrorism insurance (say, by collectively insuring against the first $10 billion of losses, as one proposal now had it), they would obviously charge their clients based on their individual risk. This would mean that iconic buildings, or even all buildings in large cities, would pay much more than other clients because they present the most alluring targets to terrorists. This completely logical risk-based pricing would have "anti-social consequences," Buffett argued. "Citizens of our leading cities almost certainly bear above-normal physical risks in the war being waged upon us by terrorists. We should not impose crippling economic costs on them as well."

Something had to be done, quickly, Buffett concluded, because without the government stepping in to provide terrorism insurance, "who would ever build a skyscraper in a major city? Or how could a mom-and-pop deli, bare of insurance, locate next to an iconic office tower?"

The article, by one of the world's most respected businessmen, appearing on one of the two or three most influential op-ed pages in the country, was written as logically and as clearly as Buffett's now celebrated annual reports to shareholders, which have an avid, broad audience. Yet Buffett later said that "I really don't think anyone read it or paid attention to it."

He was right. In the several months of debate over terrorism insurance that would follow, not a single person involved in the issue on any side would know anything about it when asked what they thought of Buffett's idea for an FDIC-like structure. (When it was explained to them, House Republicans immediately dismissed the idea, because it would create another government agency.)

Part of the problem, Buffett noted, was "that it was a mistake to have run [the article] during the week of Thanksgiving, when no one's really around Washington." Nor did Buffett, who said, "I've lobbied maybe two times in my life and felt like I had to take a shower afterward," do much to push it himself. He faxed the article to four senators, including Schumer. None remembered seeing it. He made no phone calls.

This was one instance where it would be hard to argue that rich, influential insiders can get whatever they want in Washington.

The real problem, though, was that terrorism insurance as an op-ed issue or as a legislative issue just wasn't catching on as something anyone other than those directly affected wanted to deal with.

# Tuesday, November 20, 2001

Michael Cartier, his sister Jennie Farrell, and their father watched news reports on television last night in which a construction trade association official had noted that work at Ground Zero was entering a "traditional construction phase." Their new organization, Give Your Voice, was getting lots of new members every day, and even some press, but it seemed that their voice still didn't matter much. No one was responding to their demand that the city or the state appoint an advocate for the families of civilians killed in the attacks, who could provide them the kind of information and liaison that the police and fire unions provided their members' families.

Michael and Jennie had tried repeatedly to reach Mayor Giuliani, but the best they'd done was to talk to a mid-level aide, who told them that all due care was being taken to find their loved one's remains. Alarmed by these new reports about Ground Zero now being a construction site and worried even more about rumors they had heard that the place where debris was being shipped in Staten Island—Fresh Kills—was nothing more than a dump, Michael and Jennie dialed their two senators, Schumer and Clinton. Maybe they would help.

Schumer's office agreed to set up an appointment with the senator; Clinton's office suggested they write a letter.


Donald Rumsfeld had gone to law school for a while but had never made it all the way through. Yet he knew enough about the law to appreciate that he needed help setting up these military commissions that the President had just handed him. He wanted to do it right, and he didn't want any fallout from it to distract him from his real job, which was fighting a war.

So he began to reach out to a group of old Washington hands who knew a lot more about all this than he did, and who he assumed could be counted on to give unvarnished advice. Most were his friends, and they had no personal stake in any of this, and no wish for publicity that could help advance their careers. Many were also not the kind of people, however, that Flanigan, the deputy White House counsel who had drafted the order establishing the commissions, would have suggested or assumed that George Bush's hard-line Defense Secretary would want to consult.

Rumsfeld started with Newton Minow, a longtime friend from Chicago. Minow, a prominent lawyer, is a Democrat best known for his chairmanship of the Federal Communications Commission under John Kennedy, when he famously called television a "vast wasteland." Rumsfeld told his old friend he needed help figuring out the rules for the military commissions and wanted him to be among a group of advisors who would discuss the issues with him and the Pentagon's general counsel informally. It wasn't going to be any kind of formal board or panel that the press or public would know about.

Also included in the group were Lloyd Cutler, a revered Washington lawyer, and Democrat, who had served as White House counsel for Presidents Carter and Clinton, and Griffin Bell, the Attorney General in the Carter administration. In all there were nine members of the group, with an average age of seventy-four, including four Democrats and four moderate Republicans.

# Wednesday, November 21, 2001

Larry Cox spent the Wednesday before Thanksgiving making sure the airlines opened all the checkpoints they could at the Memphis airport in order to shrink what looked to be an hour's waiting time. He got it down to forty-five minutes by midday, which, with all the extra checking still being done, was a lot better than many other airports were doing. In Baltimore, for example, the wait at the checkpoints was two hours. Cox wasn't satisfied. A large chunk of his passenger traffic before September 11 was for short-haul flights to places like Baton Rouge, Little Rock, or Jackson. These were people who preferred the short flight to a three- or four-hour drive. But if they had to wait forty-five minutes—and in fact had to arrive two or three hours early because they couldn't be sure the wait would not be a lot longer—they were going to drive. They already were. By today Cox knew that his short-haul traffic was down more than 50 percent.

Tom Ridge, whose staff had now grown to about forty-five, sat for his first extended interview with the *New York Times*. Midway through, when an aide slipped him a note reporting that an elderly Connecticut woman had died from anthrax, he groaned and said, referring to his least favorite term, that "for her it was weaponized." In writing her story the next day, the *Times*'s Alison Mitchell would pick up on an irony of the Bush White House in the September 12 era—and the dilemma that Schumer believed was paralyzing the Bush presidency at home: "Mr. Ridge, the former governor of Pennsylvania who had campaigned at Mr. Bush's side when the president ran against big government, acknowledged with some self-depreciation the oddity of now advocating a more robust federal government." Mitchell then quoted Ridge as saying, "I think there's a legitimate expectation and anticipation on the part of the public that the federal government will do more."

## Thursday, November 22, 2001

Brian Lyons spent Thanksgiving morning working at Ground Zero. At about 8:00 he was with some construction workers when they found a bunch of identification cards lying in the rubble. One hard hat leaned over and picked up two or three, then tossed them up to Lyons. He grabbed one and flipped it over to read it.

It belonged to a man named Michael Lyons. Another Michael Lyons who was not his brother.

## Friday, November 23, 2001

Ken Feinberg got his meeting with Ashcroft, and he felt sure he had hit another home run. He thought he had handled the budget question well, saying he'd be independent but that his goal was to prove that this system could work—and that if it was perceived as being a giveaway, it would be a failure.

Feinberg at one point made what he thought was his most compelling argument for the job: Ashcroft would be making a huge mistake, he said, if he didn't pick someone as Special Master who would be hands-on, who'd go out and talk to people and try to learn from all sides how he should do this. This was not a ceremonial job, he stressed.

Ashcroft had by now talked not only to Feinberg's senator friends about him, but also to Rudy Giuliani, with whom Feinberg had worked as a young prosecutor in New York, and to the federal judge for whom Feinberg had engineered the Agent Orange settlement. He told Feinberg he wanted the rest of the Thanksgiving weekend to think about it. Based on what Ashcroft's aides said as he was leaving, Feinberg assumed he had the job.

## Monday, November 26, 2001

"You know, once I hire you, I really can't fire you," John Ashcroft told Feinberg, who had been called in to meet with him again.

"You won't want to," Feinberg assured him.

Ashcroft said he didn't think he'd want to either. The job was his.

Feinberg spent the rest of the day and night talking to friends and reporters about how fascinating, and hard, it was going to be. For him, the basic dilemma was what he called the safety net perspective versus the tort law perspective. Thinking of the fund as a safety net would put the emphasis on providing the poorer victims' families with economic security, whereas thinking of the fund as a substitute for a tort trial would tilt toward the families of victims who had earned the most money and therefore in court would have deserved the most for the wages lost when their loved one had been killed. It was the difference, he said that night, between "worrying about the Cantor Fitzgerald widow whose husband made $500,000 a year and worrying about the busboy who worked a few floors up at Windows on the World [the Trade Center's rooftop restaurant]. Somehow, I have to figure out how the government can worry about both. But that puts me in the position of having the government say one life is worth $5 million or $6 million and another is worth a tenth of that. Can the government really ever say that?"

## Wednesday, November 28, 2001

Justice Department Criminal Division head Michael Chertoff defended Ashcroft's conduct of the terrorist investigation before a Senate Judiciary Committee that was offended that Ashcroft himself had not come, and that seemed to be retroactively opposing the same tactics it had approved when passing on the USA Patriot Act. Declaring that "sleepers" have integrated themselves into the local environment in communities around United States, Chertoff noted that "in many ways it is more difficult than trying to find a needle in a haystack, because here the needle is masquerading as a stalk of hay." Chertoff also dismissed the criticism from the ACLU and others over the new policy of monitoring some lawyer-client conversations, where the government believes the lawyer might be being used by terrorist detainees as a conduit for messages to other terrorists. He asserted that "this regulation currently applies to only sixteen of the 158,000 inmates in the federal [prison] system."

## Thursday, November 29, 2001

In the White House Situation Room at 8:55, Michael Jackson got a chance to brag about his go teams to President Bush, albeit vicariously. He accompanied Secretary Mineta to a meeting of the Homeland Security Council, the new sub-group of cabinet members that included Ridge and secretaries such as Mineta, Ashcroft, Rumsfeld, and others with agencies that touched on homeland security issues. Today's agenda was a briefing by Mineta on how the new Transportation Security Administration would fulfill its mission, and meet Congress's deadlines.

The day before, Mineta had told some reporters the obvious—that the deadlines might be impossible to meet. But, amid a firestorm of criticism from Congress and the press, and at Jackson's urging, Mineta would retreat from his fit of candor later today and declare that if Congress had declared that those deadlines were the law, his responsibility was to enforce that law, and he was determined to do so.

Jackson and Hawley—his volunteer go teams coordinator—had put together an elaborate PowerPoint presentation for Mineta to unveil in the Situation Room to the President, Ridge, and the others. Jackson was chairing a "war room core team," Mineta explained, that oversaw a large group of "go teams" that were engaged in elaborate "process mapping." Slide after slide summarized each process, such as reconfiguring airport security checkpoints, or recruiting the new federal screeners. Mineta said that 32,000 was now the operative number of people who had to be hired, but that it was certain to go higher. (The press, based on Senate staffer Whitehorn's guesstimate, had said it was 28,000.) The best private sector recruiting firms were being solicited for contracts so that that part of the job could be outsourced and done quickly. As Mineta explained that the go teams were being run by people borrowed from the private sector, someone in the room marveled at his and Jackson's achievement in getting all that high-priced talent for free while somehow getting around government conflict-of-interest laws.

Mineta outlined how the current force of thirty-two air marshals had been instantly boosted to 600 and how they had commandeered a hotel so that they could house these people, borrowed from other law enforcement agencies, in one place to give them training in firing guns in aircraft. The goal, Mineta explained, was to get the air marshal force up to 3,000. They'd fly in pairs at random on the 20,000 flights departing from American airports every day.

Their goals in the whole effort, Mineta said, were both safety and customer convenience—"no weapons, no waiting," in the words of one PowerPoint page.

President Bush loved it. He got actively engaged in the discussion, delving even into the details of a subject that would have made Magistri's stomach tighten: how Jackson planned to withhold signing a contract to buy InVision's explosive detection machines until the government could also negotiate the intellectual property rights associated with the software and other patents behind the machines so that they could find other, larger companies to produce them.

"And so, Mr. President," Mineta concluded, trying to be dramatic. "We're ready. Let's roll."

The meeting marked the beginning of two parallel worlds when it came to Mineta, Jackson, and their Transportation Security Administration. The people involved thought they were God's gifts to effective, modern management. The press and others watching from the outside, such as Larry Cox in Memphis, would see them as the epitome of the bureaucrats who couldn't fly straight.


While Mark Isakowitz had been trying to defend Argenbright and the other private airport security companies from federalization, he'd also been working on another, larger account—trying to push a terrorism insurance bill on behalf of an insurance industry trade group.

Today he succeeded in the House of Representatives, which given his specialty of working with Republicans, is where he was most likely to succeed.

It was a hollow victory, in several respects. First, because the Republicans were wary of spending money, the bill had been refashioned to provide loans instead of backup insurance, which was almost irrelevant to O'Hare of Chubb and other insurers. It worked this way: In the event of any terrorism catastrophe, the insurance industry could borrow from the government any payout it had to make as a group over $1 billion. That was a bit of help, but it wasn't a loan that the insurance industry needed; rather, it was relief from liability. The industry had plenty of cash. What it didn't have was a willingness to risk that cash, even over a long term cushioned by government loans, to pay out for unknown terrorism risks.

Second, the bill contained the conservative Republicans' favorite laundry list of so-called tort reforms aimed at plaintiffs lawyers. It capped plaintiffs lawyer fees in any suits related to claims involving the government backup loan, and banned punitive damages in trials, which is money awarded by a jury to the plaintiff not to compensate the plaintiff for damages, but to punish the defendant's misconduct and deter others from doing the same thing.

In theory, punitive damages make sense. A building owner whose tenants die in a terrorist attack because the owner did not use the legally required fireproofing ought to be punished. But in practice, claims for huge punitive damage awards have often been abused by plaintiffs lawyers to coerce settlements from defendants who might not have done anything wrong but are afraid of juries that might be unduly sympathetic to victims of accidents and just as unduly hostile to large corporations. Through the 1980s and 1990s some limit on punitive damages—and on the huge fees that give plaintiffs lawyers a fierce incentive to seek them because they usually charge clients a percentage of any award or settlement—had become a hot-button issue among likely defendants, particularly corporations, as well as doctors, who believed that lawyers were cashing in at their expense by turning someone's bad luck in a tragedy into a big-dollar lawsuit. President Bush, in fact, had made tort reform one of his pet issues in Texas, which was one of several states that lawyers referred to as a "plaintiffs' paradise" because lawyers there were so successful in finding sympathetic jurors to award damages out of proportion to actual injuries or fault, or in threatening defendants so credibly that they were forced to settle even nuisance suits for large amounts. The problem was compounded by the fact that in many of those states judges are elected, often on the strength of their populist appeals—which are financed by contributions from plaintiffs lawyers.

Thus, insurance companies and business groups had made tort reform a priority agenda item; in fact, there was even a separate lobbying group established in Washington and supported by other business lobbies, dedicated not only to pushing a tort reform agenda, but looking for any opportunity to get some piece of tort reform inserted into any pending law. Terrorism insurance had now become one of those opportunities, and it was a good one, because here tort reform would be protecting not private parties but the taxpayer from plaintiffs lawyers abuse. After all, this kind of backup on terrorism insurance was to be financed with the taxpayers' money.

Yet these tort law provisions, however reasonable, would be completely unacceptable to Democrats, because, as Schumer liked to tell people, most Democrats (but not him, he maintained) were beholden to plaintiffs trial lawyers for campaign money and support the way Republicans were dependent on the National Rifle Association. Thus, since the Senate was controlled by Democrats, a bill like this one had no chance of passing once it got to the Senate. And, because of the loan provision, if it did pass, its usefulness in ending the looming terrorism insurance crisis was questionable. To Isakowitz, though, it was a place to start.

The debate at the September 11th Fund board meeting this afternoon was so fascinating that some of the board members—a mix of charity executives, public service types, and representatives of victims' families—would have said they enjoyed it were it not for the sheer sadness of what they were talking about. The subject was how to define a victim of September 11, or at least how to define victims who should get help from the fund. It was clear that their definition was broader than Bill O'Reilly's—who still seemed on his TV show to think that if there were 4,000 families who had lost loved ones, and 1,000 people injured, then there were 5,000 victims. The question was how much broader the definition should be.

Because it had been September 11th Fund CEO Josh Gotbaum's strategy to use his money to fill in where other funds were not helping, the consultants from McKinsey had produced a series of tables outlining what the charities and other sources of funding, such as private insurance and the government victims compensation fund, were likely to provide. For example, it seemed clear that several groups, such as a fund put together by Citigroup, were covering college scholarships for the victims' families. More broadly, the federal victims compensation fund seemed likely to provide long-term economic aid to the same families. The Red Cross seemed to be getting its act together to provide short-term economic aid to the families to cover their monthly living expenses for up to a year, and it had just announced a program to offer the same short-term cash to economic victims of the attacks, such as workers who had lost jobs. Nonetheless, the immediate cash grants Gotbaum's fund had begun getting to the families of those who had been killed and to injured victims were still deemed important, in part because, the fund's board reasoned, the Red Cross still couldn't be counted on to deliver aid quickly enough consistently enough, and in part because the September 11th Fund donors surely wanted some of the money to go to these victims. Thus, the board decided today on a two-pronged strategy: They would immediately allocate $130 million for "emergency aid" to be distributed the week before Christmas as follows: $10,000 to every victim's family, and $2,500 to all displaced workers.

But the bulk of the fund's money—nearly $400 million more—would be directed at long-term programs to fill in the gaps left by all the other charities. The question was which gaps for which other victims.

No one seemed to be providing mental health counseling. The fund would. No one seemed to be focusing on providing training for workers who had lost jobs and now needed new skills. The fund would. No one seemed to be focused on providing health insurance to workers who had lost their jobs. The fund would. And no other group seemed focused on the small businesses in lower Manhattan that were struggling to reopen and survive. Indeed, the Red Cross had a policy against giving aid of any kind to a business as opposed to individuals and families. This, too, was a gap that the fund resolved to fill.

But that's where the real soul searching began. How far should they go with this type of aid? Even within the aid categories, the question remained: Who was a "victim"?

The McKinsey consultants had attempted to lay out the contours of some of the debate visually, with charts and maps showing colored concentric circles emanating from Ground Zero. How far out in the band of circles, literally and metaphorically, should they go?

Would retailers (such as Sal) who had stores two blocks from the Trade Center that had been closed for a week or two after the attacks and were still hurting for business, to be considered victims who should get the aid to small businesses the fund now contemplated?

Sure, that seemed obvious.

What about garment factories in Chinatown, which was about twenty blocks away, but where many businesses had been forced to close because traffic had been so tied up by the recovery effort that trucks couldn't get there for pickups and deliveries?

Probably.

What about people who worked at the New York airports, where business was down sharply? Did they deserve the displaced worker's aid, and the job retraining if they hadn't gotten their jobs back?

That seemed a stretch.

How about workers at Reagan National Airport in Washington, which had been closed for twenty-three days?

Well, maybe that made sense.

What about hotel workers in Washington? Perhaps. But hotel workers in San Francisco, or rental car clerks in Nashville, was too much.

As for mental health counseling, of course the deceased victims' children should get it. But what about other New York City children who needed counseling because of everything they'd seen and heard about the attacks?

That probably made sense.

What about children who lived in the Washington metropolitan area?

Yes, them, too.

What about children or adults in the rest of the country?

That was too much.


Hollie Bart faxed a letter to the St. Paul insurance company today, informing them that she now represented Sal Iacono and Continental Shoe Repair, and formally making his claim for $19,000 for repairs and $16,000 for business interruption. The losses for business interruption—eight weeks' worth of what had been his average weekly revenue of about $2,000—was meant to cover the period not only before Sal reopened, which had been four weeks, but the additional four-week period up until about a week ago, when the streets around Sal's store had still been closed to nonemergency vehicles and the sidewalks had been partially barricaded. Bart knew that that part of the claim was going to take a fight.

## Saturday, December 1, 2001

At about 12:30 A.M. Border Patrol agent Bob Lindemann was taken from the Federal Law Enforcement Training Center near Brunswick, Georgia, where he was supposed to be taking an advanced course in boat handling and water interdiction, to the emergency room at the local hospital. He was sure he was having a stroke or heart attack.

Lindemann had been having stomach pains and a burning sensation from his stomach up to his throat since he'd gotten the first disciplinary letter. But now he was also having horrific chest pains. It was as if his whole upper body had been roped up and the noose pulled.

Which was not far from how he felt about what was happening to his career in law enforcement. A few days before, two investigators from the Justice Department Inspector General's Office had come to interview him. He thought the session had gone well. How could it not? He had told the press the truth, and he had a right to do so. But he had become concerned when the inspector general's people had told him that their primary focus was whether the proposed demotions of him and his partner, Hall, had come because Hall had agreed to testify before Senator Levin's committee. That really wasn't the point, Lindemann had responded. "We were disciplined for exercising our First Amendment rights about something that the country needed to know." The investigators said they were going to be considering that, too. It had all left him scared. Maybe he wasn't supposed to speak out. Maybe he really had betrayed his country. Why would they have written that letter demoting him, with all those higher-ups signing off on it, if their charges weren't true. Had he gotten carried away? Had he screwed up?

No, that was crazy, he thought, whenever he stopped and thought about it calmly, or whenever he talked to his wife. Of course, he was right. They really were the bad guys, not he.

That kind of ambivalence—the ambivalence of the whistle-blower who has always been the loyalist straight arrow, the ambivalence of the tough, swaggering ex-Marine who really is scared of the bosses because they control what he gets to bring home to his family—was what had tied his stomach in knots.

But it wasn't a heart attack, the doctors concluded by late Saturday afternoon. Lindemann was released after a battery tests. "You just need to relax," the doctor finally told him.

# Sunday, December 2, 2001

Chuck Schumer had always had a rule for balancing his hard-driving professional life with the time he devoted to Iris and their two daughters: He'd do some work on Friday nights, but Saturdays were sacrosanct. He'd spend all of that day with the family, then work some or much of Sunday, if he had to. Lately, Iris had watched as that rule fell by the wayside. Schumer would come home to the apartment in Brooklyn on Friday nights, his pockets stuffed with papers and phone messages. A CEO he knew wanted to talk about making sure EPA really was testing the air downtown. A real estate broker he had run into at a breakfast speech had a great idea for how to speed the redevelopment of downtown. An old friend from Brooklyn with a store in lower Manhattan was having trouble getting one of those loans from the Small Business Administration, and was going to have to close his shop. Mitch Daniels had a question about part of the federal aid package. A friend of a friend knew a company that could really help fix the FBI's computer systems. Schumer, of course, had a staff that did this kind of follow-up. But if the person in need or with an idea was someone he knew personally, he wanted to make the calls himself.

Schumer was obsessive about dealing with the items on his message list as fast as he could, before new ones piled up. But now the list kept growing. "For the first time in my life," he told Iris sadly one Friday night, "I feel like there is just too much to do. I feel overwhelmed. I just don't have enough hours in the day or days in the week."

So he was now working most Saturdays and pretty much all of Sunday.

Which is why when Michael Cartier, his five siblings, and members of two other families representing Give Your Voice ended up meeting with Schumer and two members of his staff in his midtown Manhattan satellite office at about 9:00 this morning, it seemed to Cartier that it was not the first meeting Schumer had had that day.

The Give Your Voice people's issues were hardly senatorial. The only thing they really wanted was to be a part of the city-run cleanup and recovery process, a process that for them involved the remains of their loved ones. But no one from the mayor's office or any other municipal officials had been willing to meet with them. That was why they were here with the senior senator from New York.

After talking for a while about James, Michael Cartier outlined to Schumer all the rumors he'd heard about what was going on at the Fresh Kills garbage fill in Staten Island.

"We don't want James to end up in a garbage dump," he concluded.

Schumer looked up from the pad he was doodling on. The room was silent for a minute.

Months later, Michael Cartier would recall that as the moment he knew that they had gotten through to someone for the first time.

Schumer remembers it the same way, as his own moment of realization. These people were here simply because they loved their brother and did not want him to be forgotten in a landfill.

Schumer said he didn't think things were happening that way at Fresh Kills, but that he didn't know enough and would find out. More important, he promised to put them in touch with city officials. "I'm going to talk to the mayor about this. I'm going to get you in touch with the right people."

John Walker Lindh, an American from Marin County near San Francisco who had been captured while fleeing with a group of Taliban in Afghanistan and then questioned by the CIA, had become headline news. *Newsweek* released an exclusive report about him that will run in its issue that is out tomorrow. On Saturday, CNN had showed an interview with him, in which he acknowledged that he had fought for the Taliban. Lindh could be seen talking groggily to CNN from a hospital bed in Afghanistan after he'd been captured following an uprising at a prison compound that had resulted in CIA operative Johnny Spann becoming the first American combat casualty in Afghanistan.

In San Francisco, a veteran corporate lawyer named James Brosnahan happened to see the CNN Saturday report. "That kid's in a world of trouble," Brosnahan thought to himself.

This afternoon, Brosnahan took a break from watching a San Francisco 49ers game and called in to the voice mail system at the large San Francisco law firm where he is the senior litigating partner. Although it was Sunday, he did have one message, from someone named Frank Lindh—the American Taliban's father.

James Brosnahan, sixty-seven, was about as establishment as a corporate lawyer can get. His law firm, one of San Francisco's largest and most powerful, had worked over the years for a long list of blue-chip corporations, and Brosnahan had held multiple offices in state and national bar groups.

Frank Lindh was also a corporate lawyer, working in the legal department of the local electric company; so Brosnahan's was a name he knew.

But for Lindh, calling Brosnahan to defend his renegade son was more than a matter of name recognition. There is another side to Brosnahan, a tough, independent, liberal streak that Bay Area lawyers know about. Brosnahan is avuncular, but with an edge. Lawyers there still tell the story of how in 1986, when William Rehnquist was nominated to be Chief Justice of the Supreme Court, Brosnahan came forward to testify that as a young civil rights lawyer working on a voter registration project in Arizona in the 1960s he had seen Rehnquist with a group of other Republicans at a polling place allegedly attempting to intimidate Hispanics who wanted to vote. There was no chance that Brosnahan's testimony was going to derail Rehnquist, who vigorously denied the charge. But Brosnahan had come forward anyway. That was not something a corporate lawyer who ran a litigation department that represented clients in front of the Supreme Court normally did.

Brosnahan spent about a half hour on the phone with Frank Lindh, who knew nothing more about his son's whereabouts than what he had seen on television. He and his wife, who were divorced, had thought John was studying Islam in Afghanistan or Pakistan. They knew he had developed strong, even extreme, religious views, but they could not believe he'd become mixed up in terrorism or in fighting Americans for the Taliban.

"John is a really nice, gentle kid," his father kept repeating, as only a father could.

Before agreeing to accept the case, Brosnahan established one condition. He was not going to get involved in a show trial. He would defend Lindh's son, but not Al Qaeda, the Muslim religion, or any other cause. Frank Lindh said he assumed his son would agree with that, but couldn't promise anything until they talked to him.

"That," said Brosnahan, "is our first priority. We have to talk to John."

Brosnahan agreed to arrange immediately for them to go see Lindh in Afghanistan, or wherever else he might be being held. He'd fax a letter to the relevant people at the Justice Department or Pentagon, tell them that Lindh now had a lawyer, and make the standard demand that his client no longer be questioned without Brosnahan present. That night he drafted such a letter, addressing it, just to be sure he didn't miss any potential interrogators, to the secretaries of Defense and State, the Director and general counsel of the CIA, and Ashcroft. After asking that arrangements be made for him to meet with his new client, Brosnahan added, "Because he is wounded, and, based upon press reports, went for three days without food, I would ask that any further interrogation be stopped. Especially if there is any intent to use it in any subsequent legal proceedings.

"I appreciate your cooperation," Brosnahan concluded.

Brosnahan was about to find out that the rules he believed in and had worked under all his adult life had changed.

# Monday, December 3, 2001

Nicholas Roumel, a lawyer in Ann Arbor, Michigan, typically handled petty crimes and landlord-tenant disputes for University of Michigan students under a prepaid legal services plan entitling them to his services. Today,* he sat in on two of the thirteen voluntary interviews that the FBI conducted with his clients, who are Middle Eastern students, as part of Ashcroft's announced plan to interview 6,000 young males from targeted countries. The agents were unfailingly polite, even cracking jokes about one student's passport photo and another's high grades. They worked their way through twenty-one questions taken from the script contained in Ashcroft's original memo ordering the interviews. "Do you know anyone who might know anything about the attacks? Who acted strangely after the attacks? Who might advocate violence against the United States? Who might know how to make a bomb or anthrax?"

Other questions were more personal, such as whether they had ever participated in any armed conflict, what courses they had taken, where else in the United States they had visited, and whether they would be willing to provide information in the future. Roumel let his clients answer all of them. The only place he drew the line was a question about whether they knew of any illegal activity of any kind whatsoever, whether related to terrorism or not. He feared that if they didn't inform on someone who might have used a false identification to buy liquor, they'd be accused of lying to a federal agent.

---

*Roumel was not certain that he participated in these interviews on December 3, but did believe that they happened during the first week in December.

Roumel says that his clients seemed uncomfortable by the questioning, but were nonetheless eager to cooperate. All had responded willingly to a letter from the United States attorney in Detroit—a man praised even by leaders in that metropolitan area's large Arab-American community for his sensitivity—"inviting" them to make appointments for the interviews.

Referring to the initial protests about the questioning, Roumel recalls that "all of us had a role to play here. They play the role of pushing as hard as they can. Lawyers like me and the community play the role of pushing them back. So the questions become more reasonable, they stop making overt threats, and they got some cooperation."

"I came away surprised by the cooperation, and surprised by what solid members of the community these people are," says one FBI agent involved in the Detroit questioning. "Once we went from thinking of these people as suspects to them as people who might help us, it changed."

Not everyone agreed. As one marketing manager living in New Jersey who was interviewed at about the same time, put it, "They were very polite, but you still feel violated by having someone from the FBI knock at your door. . . . You submit, because you figure they'll be watching you if you don't. But it isn't pleasant."

Of course, from Ashcroft's standpoint people being blown to bits in office towers wasn't pleasant either, and this didn't seem too high a price to pay for the FBI to establish contacts—and, yes, a list of those who had refused to cooperate—in communities where they had known almost no one prior to September 11, and from which the sleeper cells that had launched the attacks had sprung.


It turned out that Schumer had been so moved by his meeting with the Cartiers that he had called Mayor Giuliani Sunday night to urge him to see the family. There was no reason to fight with these people, Schumer told him. In fact, they should be your allies. So, this afternoon, the Cartiers got a meeting with the mayor's head of emergency management, Richard Shierer, and other city staff people.

Shierer explained that the rubble being moved to Fresh Kills was being carefully sifted for remains, a process that could not be done at Ground Zero because there simply wasn't room.

"We'd like to go have a look," Michael Cartier said, "because we've heard that there are some bad things going on there. We want to see it."

Shierer said that because Fresh Kills was also a crime scene, where the FBI was sifting for evidence, that would be impossible. He also defended the speed of the work at Ground Zero, maintaining that every effort was being made there to look for (though not by the kind of careful sifting being done at Fresh Kills) and respect the remains that might be there.

The Cartiers asked him to get the mayor to appoint someone who would meet with the victims' families regularly. They also wanted to be able to have one of their representatives have access to Ground Zero so that they could get reports from him or her on what is going on.

That wouldn't be possible, he said.

The Give Your Voice people were not satisfied, and when a member of Schumer's staff called Michael's sister Jennie a day later to find out what had happened, she told him so.

# Wednesday, December 5, 2001

On Tuesday, after James Brosnahan had heard nothing back from the government after his fax Monday morning declaring that he was representing John Walker Lindh, he had sent a second letter to the Defense Department general counsel, William Haynes II. He had also helped Frank Lindh send a handwritten note to his son through the Red Cross. Then he had tried to call Haynes.

Having now not gotten the call returned, and knowing that Haynes had been a partner at another large law firm, where he presumed that the usual good manners were taught, he faxed him a note asking him at least to extend the courtesy of a return phone call. He got no response.

Still, Brosnahan held out some hope that the government would treat his client with compassion, which was reflected in his letter to Haynes describing Lindh as a "scholarly and religiously motivated" twenty-year-old who had converted to Islam at age sixteen. It was a hope that had been buttressed yesterday, when President Bush observed that he regarded Lindh as a "poor fellow" who had been "misled" and had gotten himself into more trouble than he had bargained for.

That certainly was not a sentiment shared by the editors of the *New York Post*. Its front-page headline this morning declared, "Looks Like a Rat, Talks Like a Rat, Smells Like a Rat, Hides Like a Rat—It Is a Rat."

What Brosnahan didn't know, but would later find out when he got access to the government's notes and files in the case (which defense lawyers are entitled to in criminal trials), was that since Saturday, his client had pretty much been treated like a rat. While still suffering from an untreated bullet wound in his leg sustained during the uprising in the holding area where the CIA man had been killed, Lindh was being questioned aggressively by Army intelligence agents.

According to Lindh's later accounts to Brosnahan—which the government did not dispute—the questioning was brutal. Deprived of sleep and all but minimal food, his hands tightly bound, he was taunted with profanities ("shit bag," "shit head") while repeatedly interrogated in sessions that lasted several hours at a time. The government would later not dispute that during these rounds of questioning by Army intelligence people he was never told of his right to remain silent or to retain a lawyer, because this was questioning in battlefield conditions by Army men seeking information about the enemy.

Hollie Bart, the pro bono lawyer working for Sal Iacono, sent a paralegal from her firm down to a Red Cross assistance center this morning to get help for Sal's one employee, Herman Garcia.

Garcia, who has six children, had been forced to work part-time for Sal, and his salary of $250 a week had been cut in half. On top of that, he hadn't worked for Sal at all during the month the store had been closed, and he had also lost another night job he had had downtown at a small business that never reopened. Bart was so taken with his plight that she had actually given him some cash herself and was about to buy one of his kids a bicycle for Christmas.

Within two weeks, Garcia would get a Red Cross check for $5,000.

When Eileen Simon returned home this afternoon, her children told her that two local police officers had been by twice to talk to her. She called the number they had left, and they said they would be over in a few minutes.

When they got there, Eileen stood at the front door, her kids hovering behind her. They explained that they were the officers assigned to notify the next of kin of victims of the Trade Center attacks if their loved one's remains were found. Her husband's remains had now been found, they gravely informed her.

"Mom, I thought you said there was no body," one of her children yelled.

Eileen told the kids to stand back and invited the officers in.

So where is the body, she asked.

They told her that she needed to have her funeral director go to the New York medical examiner's office in Manhattan.

Could they tell her what shape the remains are in, she asked, trying unsuccessfully to whisper so that the kids, standing a few feet behind, wouldn't hear.

They didn't have any of that information.

After the officers left and Eileen alerted the funeral director, Brittany shrieked, "You told us Daddy had been burned and gone up to heaven, that there was no body."

Eileen begged her daughter to wait until they heard more from the man from the funeral home about what had been found.

The wait took until 9:00 that night, with the interim filled with phone calls to and from all of Michael's family. With the phones ringing and the relatives asking if they should come see her, it was like September 11 all over again.

When the funeral director called from the medical examiner's office he reported that there wasn't really a body—just a part of Michael's skull, about three inches long and maybe an inch wide. It turned out that Michael's was among the first seventy remains to be identified by the New York medical examiner's now intensifying DNA-matching efforts. But they may find more of Michael, the funeral director added, so she should probably not have a funeral just yet.

Eileen told the kids that just a small bone that must have been left in their father's ashes had been found. "Don't you dare try to make us go through another funeral for that; we're not doing that again," Brittany demanded, referring to the painful September memorial service.

Eileen assured Brittany that she didn't want a funeral either. But she really wasn't sure. Then she called her relatives and told them it was just a skull fragment and that for now at least there would be no funeral.

Suddenly, she was living in September all over again—the phone calls, the tears, the flowers (after the newspapers reported the find the next morning). Only now that she had some physical fragment of Michael she was horrified in a much more tangible way at the violence done to him. Also, she became curious in a way that she hadn't been, or had blocked before, about what had really happened to her husband. In the next few weeks, as she and the kids were treated to all kinds of holiday events that Cantor Fitzgerald and other groups put on for the September 11 families, she found herself asking other Cantor widows what they thought had happened to Michael and their husbands. Had they jumped? Had they melted? Had they crashed when the building crashed? The others, of course, had long since tried to leave those questions behind, and months later she'd recall "what an idiot I must have made of myself asking those questions while we were waiting on line with our kids for a Disney Christmas event."

# Thursday, December 6, 2001

John Ashcroft was at his best, or worst. In a performance that the *New York Times* called "forceful and unyielding," Ashcroft testified before the Senate Judiciary Committee, fiercely defending his anti-terrorism policies.

"The reasons we cannot [be complacent] are apparent to me every morning," Ashcroft declared. "My day begins with a review of the threats to Americans and American interests that were received in the previous twenty-four hours," he explained, referring to those Oval Office threat matrix briefings he does with Ridge and the CIA and FBI directors. "If ever there were proof of the existence of evil in the world, it is in the pages of these reports. They are a chilling daily chronicle of hatred of America. . . . Terrorist operatives infiltrate our communities—plotting, planning and waiting to kill again. They enjoy the benefits of our free society even as they commit themselves to our destruction. They exploit our openness—not randomly or haphazardly—but by deliberate, premeditated design."

With that introduction, he proceeded to display an Al Qaeda training manual seized in Afghanistan, and used it as a primer in why this enemy was so different and needed such a different law enforcement approach.

Ashcroft, who had been sued the day before by Romero's ACLU for keeping information about the detainees secret and not allowing lawyers in to inspect the conditions under which they were being held, pointed out that one part of the manual instructed captured terrorists "to concoct stories of torture or mistreatment at the hand of our officials." Obviously alluding to the controversy over the monitoring of lawyer conversations, he pointed out another instruction to "take advantage of any contact with the outside world to, quote, 'communicate with brothers outside prison.' "

After elaborating on other steps he had taken to fight this new war, Ashcroft laid down a gauntlet to groups like the ACLU and those who would support them. "To those who . . . scare peace-loving people with phantoms of lost liberty, my message is this: Your tactics only aid terrorists—for they erode our national unity and diminish our resolve. They give ammunition to America's enemies."

Ashcroft ended by casting himself and his Department of Justice as a domestic Pentagon waging war—which meant that he was simply an extension of the commander in chief. Thus, he concluded, "I will continue to consult with Congress so that you may fulfill your constitutional responsibilities. In some areas, however, I cannot and will not consult you. . . . The executive branch is now exercising its core constitutional powers in the interests of saving the lives of Americans. I trust that Congress will respect the proper limits of executive branch consultation that I am duty bound to uphold. I trust . . . that Congress will respect the President's authority to wage war on terrorism and defend our nation and its citizens."

The senators then questioned Ashcroft for more than three hours, and a lot of what he got from the Democrats was hostile. Several questioned the coming military tribunals, and why Congress had not been consulted about them. Ashcroft assured them that the rules would be fair.

Schumer and Senator Richard Durbin, an Illinois Democrat, went after Ashcroft for apparently letting his political biases get in the way of good law enforcement. The issue had to do with why Ashcroft wasn't allowing the FBI access to records of background checks carried out under a handgun control law that Ashcroft had fiercely opposed as a senator, so that the agents could see if any suspected terrorist or other illegal aliens had tried to buy guns.

The law didn't allow the use of those records for that purpose, Ashcroft replied—which to most people who have read the law, including lawyers on Ashcroft's own staff, was simply not true.

Well, assuming that was true, Schumer pressed, why hadn't he asked that the law be changed when he had proposed so many other changes in so many other laws in the Patriot Act?

Ashcroft had no answer.

Would he now support such a change?

The Attorney General said he didn't know.

The Senate Democrats might have thought they had given Ashcroft a rough time, but Ashcroft's reaction to the hearings, as expressed to one aide later in the day, was that they had backed away from challenging him on anything fundamental. He thought the day had been a triumph.

And if Anthony Romero is any barometer, he was right. Romero remembers being "bitterly disappointed" at the Democrats, "because they really didn't go after him on the fundamental idea that he was a wartime general, not the Attorney General. . . . And, when he challenged them about debating him, they backed away. From our standpoint, a time like this is the time you should have the most robust debate, not shut it down."

# Friday, December 7, 2001

John Mica, the chairman of the House Transportation subcommittee on aviation, opened a subcommittee hearing today by declaring that the new deadline for getting explosive detection equipment operating at all airports was "unrealistic," because "some in Congress, the media and the public" had not been "in the mood for extended debate on the issue." Then, one of Magistri's vice presidents testified that, "since September 11, InVision has received more orders from non-U.S. customers than from the federal government." His pitch was that InVision stood ready to help meet the deadlines—if it could only get some orders fast. He also argued that using the less expensive, easier-to-make trace detection machines was not a safe substitute.

Meanwhile, Deputy Transportation Secretary Michael Jackson and his private sector go teams maestro, Kip Hawley, had intensified their efforts to meet the deadlines. In fact, they were putting the finishing touches on a contract they were about to sign with McKinsey—the same consulting company that was helping the September 11th Fund pro bono—to put its consultants to work finding other companies that could make InVision's machines. With that in mind, they had already decided that they weren't going to give InVision any orders until InVision agreed to license the intellectual property necessary to allow others to make the machines.

Jackson and his boss, Mineta—who by now said he was so committed to those deadlines that he said felt as if he had them tattooed on his forehead—had also settled on a choice for the man to run the new Transportation Security Administration. Their pick, first suggested by FEMA chief Joe Allbaugh (who is a close friend of the President's), was John Magaw.

Magaw had run both the Secret Service (where he had also been head of the presidential protective detail covering the first President Bush) and the Treasury Department's Bureau of Alcohol, Tobacco and Firearms—an agency he had taken over and reformed after the disastrous Branch Davidian shootout in Waco, Texas, in 1993. Magaw had since taken a job as head of a national preparedness unit at Allbaugh's FEMA.

What Jackson and Mineta liked about Magaw was, first, that his Secret Service background gave him the no-nonsense credentials the public seemed to crave when it came to aviation safety. Second, they had heard that he had been terrific at building a training program and a can-do, proud culture at the beleaguered ATF.

Eileen Simon found herself standing in line at the checkout counter of a local CVS drugstore. Someone poked her, and Eileen shot around to give whoever it was a dirty look. She saw a hunched-over middle-aged woman whose wrinkled face and disheveled hair made her look a lot older.

The woman poked her again. Eileen said, "I'm having a really bad day. Could you please take it easy?"

"You're having a bad day?' " the woman answered. "I have a son with diabetes who has just lost his legs."

"Well, I just lost my husband," Eileen answered.

"So did I," the other woman shot back.

Eileen gave her another look and realized, she says, that "I was at a crossroads. I had two choices. I could wallow in my misery and end up like her, or I could be a survivor."

According to documents later submitted by defense lawyer Brosnahan that were never contested by the government, John Lindh was flown on a cargo plane this afternoon to a Marine base in Afghanistan called Camp Rhino. When he got there, his clothes were removed. He was blindfolded and tied, naked, with duct tape to a stretcher. He was then put in an unheated metal storage container. When he had to urinate, the stretcher was simply propped into an upright position.

It was under these conditions that an Army intelligence officer conducted a new series of interrogation sessions of this American citizen.

Lindh was desperate for a blanket to shield him from the cold, and desperate for sleep because for the prior two days he had been awakened every thirty minutes, made to sit up, and then searched. According to a memo in the government's own files, the military interrogator told a Navy physician that "sleep deprivation, cold and hunger might be employed" during Lindh's questioning.

Meantime, Brosnahan had heard nothing from the government about his request to see his client.

But it wasn't that the Lindh case was being ignored in Washington. At the Justice Department, Ashcroft had approved a plan to have someone from the FBI interrogate Lindh as soon as possible. And today, a Justice Department lawyer sent an e-mail* to a colleague expressing concern about that. Having

---

*The internal Justice Department e-mails discussed here were first revealed by *Newsweek*'s Michael Isikoff in June of 2002.

consulted with a senior legal advisor in the department's ethics office, the lawyer wrote to counterterrorism prosecutor John De Pue that, "The FBI wanted to interview American Taliban member John Walker [Lindh★] some time next week. Walker's [Lindh's] father retained counsel for him. . . . We don't think you can have the FBI agent question Walker [Lindh]. It would be a preindictment custodial interview, which is not authorized by law. However," the e-mail continued, "the FBI agent can say something to . . . the effect of: 'We understand that your father has retained counsel for you. Do you want this lawyer to represent you?' Given that Walker's [Lindh's] parents think he was brainwashed, maybe he doesn't want a lawyer of their choosing."

# Sunday, December 9, 2001

Sally Quinn, the well-known Washington journalist, wrote an essay in the *Washington Post* that seemed to capture the spirit of American frustration with Ridge and the homeland security effort.

"Heeding a series of warnings," Quinn began, "about 'credible threats' that the administration has issued over the past three months, and the new alert put out on Monday by Tom Ridge's Office of Homeland Security, I tried to find out what the average citizen should do to prepare. And in the process I found, like Alice after she passed through the looking glass, a lot of jabberwocky."

Chuck Schumer liked to hold a press conference in New York about something every other Sunday. He knew it was a slow news day, which made it an ideal way for him to keep himself in the headlines—or as he would put it, to highlight important issues—every other Monday morning.

His subject today was security at the ports, and he set up shop in front of the assembled reporters and camera crews by using the dramatic backdrop of Kevin McCabe's container-filled port in Elizabeth, New Jersey.

Noting that Customs now inspects just 2 percent of containers arriving at the port, Schumer declared that this means that terrorists have a "98 percent chance" of bringing in weapons of mass destruction. His solution was a bill that he said he was going to support to provide funding for 1,500 new Cus-

★The government had originally used John Walker Lindh's middle name as his last name.

toms inspectors and $100 million for grants to improve port security infrastructure.

The idea was a good one, and a version of the law soon passed. But his rhetoric was wildly overstated. As McCabe would have told Schumer, had he been asked, the fact that 2 percent of containers got inspected did not leave terrorists with anything like a 98 percent chance of success, because of Customs steadily improving system of targeting containers for inspection based on the risks they posed.

By the next morning, McCabe and his co-workers were mightily frustrated by the headlines Schumer had made.

A big part of it was that since September 11 they had seen themselves unfairly grouped with INS as the terribly mismanaged, hapless nonprotectors of the borders. In fact, Customs had become a pretty good agency in recent years, with much of the progress attributable to Raymond Kelly.

Kelly, who by 2002 would become the New York City police commissioner, had been the assistant treasury secretary for enforcement in 1998. Beset by the challenge of improving Customs, which he oversaw, he did something rarely done in Washington: He demoted himself and took the lower-rung job of running the agency. He moved aggressively to centralize an organization—"I had to grab them by their throats," is the way he puts it— that, like the INS, had been run by regional and local fiefdoms that were so powerful that they bought their own vehicles and painted them however they wanted to, operated under their own procedural guidelines, and even had their own policies on racial profiling. Kelly had fixed all that and more, giving Customs renewed pride and professionalism. When a Middle Eastern man was caught in Washington State attempting to sneak into the United States with explosive material that he planned to use for a millennium bomb plot at the Los Angeles Airport, Kelly had used that as an opening to pour new resources into protecting the Northern Border—a thrust that Congress soon blunted by refusing to fund the extra troops.

So from McCabe's standpoint, while Schumer's press conference had been useful in calling attention to the resources he needed, it could have been handled a lot more responsibly had Schumer or his staff come to visit with them first and been willing to sacrifice a catchy headline for substantive accuracy.

FBI agent Christopher Reimann, who had been stationed in Pakistan, arrived at Camp Rhino in Afghanistan to question Lindh. Lindh was dressed in hospital garb and brought into a tent, still blindfolded. According to papers filed by Lindh's lawyers, which the government never disputed in subsequent motions and hearings, when Reimann began reading Lindh a statement about his right to a lawyer, he interjected that "Of course, there are no lawyers here." Lindh was not told that his father had retained Brosnahan, who was eager to see him, nor was he given the Red Cross note from his father telling him about Brosnahan, which had been faxed to Camp Rhino. After he'd been read those rights, Lindh asked when he could see an attorney, and Reimann repeated that there were no attorneys there. Lindh later told his lawyers that it was only then, when faced with the prospect of going back into the cold, light-less metal container, naked on the stretcher, if he did not proceed, that he signed the form waiving his rights.

Reimann's account of what Lindh said in this interrogation would later form the basis of Lindh's indictment. Reimann would claim that Lindh had conceded that he had knowingly trained with and fought for the Taliban, and knowingly done so in support of Al Qaeda after the September 11 attacks

The Supreme Court has ruled that once someone asks for a lawyer, as Lindh claims he did, any questioning without one has to stop unless the defendant makes an independent, subsequent decision to change his mind. While the High Court has also ruled that police don't have to tell a suspect that his lawyer wants to see him, it is not clear whether they can deceive a suspect into waiving his right to a lawyer by telling him, or implying, that a lawyer is not available, or that the lawyer he'd get is whatever legal aid lawyer they might find in Afghanistan, not the hotshot counsel retained by his parents. Nor is it clear that if Lindh was under the influence of painkillers that he could have, as the High Court has required, "knowingly and intelligently" waived his right to counsel.

In short, Brosnahan had an argument that the circumstances of Lindh's confinement in that container, or the government's refusal to let Brosnahan contact him—or both—made his confession, assuming there was one, not admissible in a trial. The fact that Lindh was apprehended in a combat environment might explain the government's urgent, harsh treatment in interrogating him. However, Brosnahan could argue that that does not allow the government to use the fruits of that treatment in an American courtroom where standard constitutional protections apply.

Brosnahan could argue all of that, if he could ever get to his client.


At least some Justice Department lawyers appreciated the problems with Reimann's interrogation. The same one who had sent the first e-mail warning that the FBI could not interview Lindh sent another e-mail to the same terrorism prosecutor saying she had just heard that an agent had interviewed Lindh over the weekend. "The interview may have to be sealed or only used for national security purposes," she said.*

# Monday, December 10, 2001

Ken Feinberg was a glutton for punishment. He had a deadline of December 21 for issuing the regulations under which he would make his awards as Special Master of the victims compensation fund, and one would have thought that he'd go about the process by having lawyers at his own firm and the Justice Department do the research and come up with a draft. He was having all that background work done. But rather than sit back and wait for it, he had been relentless about meeting with all varieties of people, including those who were likely to tell him how much they despised even the idea of the fund. In fact, Feinberg had gotten so wrapped up in the work that he had just backed out of a lucrative assignment he recently won for his firm to mediate a group of antitrust suits brought by private companies against Microsoft.

Today, he blitzed New York, doing a round of meetings with law professors, charity leaders like Gotbaum of the September 11th Fund, and, most important, the hostile plaintiffs lawyers, including Lee Kreindler, the dean of the aviation disaster bar.

"I thought he was funny, gracious, and very smart," Kreindler recalls. "And he was genuinely interested in our input."

In small groups like this, Feinberg was a skilled Boston pol. He had a way of convincing people that he thought they were especially insightful and that he was confiding in them, and them alone. He could break the ice when the conversation got tough by mimicking someone the rest of the group didn't like. He was brash and blustery, often prone to overstatement, but never boring. And he was openly enthralled with the challenge he faced, and eager to engage the people he met with in long discussions of the heavy legal, political, even philosophical issues involved.

In all the meetings, he quickly won points by dispatching one issue. In the rules he was going to write, he was not going to deduct the money the victims

---

*As with the first of these e-mails, credit for bringing this e-mail to light goes to *Newsweek*'s Michael Isikoff.

got from private charities, he confided. Even if the law probably meant for it to be deducted, he wasn't going to be dumb enough to get caught in that ambush.

Other issues were not as simple.

"How am I supposed to do this?" he kept asking. "You guys are the ones who can help me. You guys wrestle with this all the time. Can I really give a waiter $400,000 and a stockbroker $4 million?"

"Of course you can," Kreindler replied. "You have to."

"I think I have to figure out some middle way," Feinberg countered. "Where I am is in the middle between providing a safety net for everyone, even the low wage earners, which is the government's traditional function in an aid program, and providing a way for all people to have the lifestyle they would have had, which is what damages in a tort system are supposed to do."

The plaintiffs lawyers, of course, only saw the tort system side of it. But they did appreciate how much he was reaching out.


As Donald Rumsfeld and his lawyers at the Pentagon continued their round of informal discussions with the group dubbed the "wise men," who were advising them on how to set up the military commissions, the commissions lost their first and most logical defendant. Ashcroft, having worn down White House Counsel Alberto Gonzales and his deputy, Timothy Flanigan, announced that the alleged "twentieth hijacker" Zacarias Moussaoui would be tried in a conventional federal court on charges of conspiring with the other hijackers. Ashcroft had used two arguments on the White House lawyers: The first was that because they had decided to charge Moussaoui in a court in northern Virginia—rather than in New York, where a grand jury investigating the terrorism plot had been convened and where, obviously, most of the crime had taken place—they had a good shot at the death penalty, because that jurisdiction was reputed to have conservative judges and juries. Second, because Moussaoui was already being held in the United States, there was a better possibility that a defense lawyer could petition an American court challenging the constitutionality of the tribunals than would be the case for a prisoner not being held in the United States. So why risk having the whole thing challenged just for him? Waiting to use the tribunals for someone being held outside the United States was cleaner and less risky.

Romero of the ACLU was jubilant. They had protested and galvanized the opposition and succeeded in pushing Ashcroft back, he thought.

But to Terwilliger, the former Justice official who had suggested the tribunals to the Bush White House, the decision made no sense. If the logic behind having tribunals was that someone who wanted to make war on our system would not get the benefits of the system, then why reward those enemies who actually got so close to succeeding that they had already made it into the country? It was like giving the most dangerous enemies the best break.

Mayor Giuliani had scheduled a half hour at the end of the day to meet the Cartier family and other members of Give Your Voice before going to a Chanukah candle-lighting service. He ended up blowing off the service and staying for what he says was at least two and a half hours.

The meeting began badly. Giuliani usually does not suffer critics easily, and the Cartiers and the others did not pull their punches. But, recalls Giuliani, "I knew they were angry and decided that I had to let them vent." The complaints were the same, simple ones. No information. No input. No access to city officials. No access to the site. ("You have no idea how much it hurts, Mr. Mayor, when you and everyone else refer to the place where our brother is resting as a cleanup site," Jennie Farrell said.) And no access to see what was going on at Fresh Kills.

In fact, the horrible stories they were hearing about Fresh Kills were now punctuated by a report that the eldest Cartier brother, Patrick, offered of what he called his "undercover" trip there. Patrick, who among the siblings has a singular tendency to exaggerate, said he knew that the sifting was not being done carefully, that some people there lacked the proper equipment, and that personal effects were strewn all over the place rather than being catalogued and stored. And he had heard that manpower had been sharply reduced recently.

Giuliani and his staff denied all that. Patrick hadn't seen enough to appreciate the operation they had there and the dedication of the people who were there, Giuliani said.

Then let us in and give us a full tour, Michael countered.

As the session went on, Giuliani, rather than being the bully the press often made him out to be, seemed to melt. The more the Cartiers and the others pushed, even as their rhetoric grew more bitter, the more Giuliani seemed to want to connect, to make them understand that he was on their side.

It ended with tearful hugs all around, and with the mayor promising to arrange a liaison to meet regularly with a committee of victims' families, and to arrange for them to get a full tour of Ground Zero and Fresh Kills. "It was probably because in many ways I was still as angry as they were," Giuliani later explained. "Besides, it was impossible not to be moved by this family."

# Tuesday, December 11, 2001

On the three-month anniversary of their father's murder, Eileen Simon's two oldest children, Brittany, twelve, and MJ, ten, stopped sleeping in her bed. But not five-year-old Tyler. By now, Eileen had settled into a routine, all of it framed in the context of her family's grief. She tried to keep the kids from watching television reports that talked about Ground Zero, and she herself read little of the newspapers. She even asked the school library not to display weekly magazines quite so prominently, after she found out that MJ was hanging out there to read more about the attacks and Osama bin Laden.

Meantime, simply because her name and status as a September 11 widow had appeared in a few local newspaper articles (and on various Internet lists of victims), she'd get one or two letters a week with checks or gift certificates of $50 or $100, along with heartfelt handwritten notes from people all over the country. She signed up with the Red Cross, whose payments and services she now considered to be terrific. Health insurance was not a problem, because Cantor Fitzgerald had promised to cover all of its victims' families for ten years. Local high school kids had organized to tutor her children in any subjects in which they might need help, plus keep them involved athletically. The local mothers continued to keep those hot dinners coming every other night.

And although cash was not in any way an immediate problem because of the $500,000 life insurance payout, Eileen had begun to talk to her sister, who was a lawyer at a large New York firm, about getting advice concerning if and how she should go into that victims compensation fund. She was also starting to hear about help she and the family could get of a more personal nature: Local community groups were organizing group counseling and therapy sessions for widows and children. Maybe she'd try that after New Year's.

## Wednesday, December 12, 2001

Larry Cox had tallied up all the numbers. They looked awful. Passenger traffic was down so much that his income from the various vendors at the Memphis airport was running at a pace that would put him $8 million in the hole when his fiscal year ended next July 1. He could borrow money in the short term and wait until then to raise his gate rental fees by an amount he estimated would be 60 percent. Or he could try to raise the rates sooner, which would make the increases less steep. He decided to act now, and talked with representatives from Northwest Airlines and FedEx, which so dominated traffic in Memphis that they controlled the votes of his rate oversight board. The number of flights coming in and out had stayed basically the same, since FedEx's business had actually improved because the Post Office, beset by anthrax troubles, was losing business. That meant he had little justification for raising the landing fees. Instead, after outlining all the cost savings he had imposed, Cox proposed raising the rental fees for the terminal gates 39 percent, effective January 1. Northwest and FedEx quickly agreed.

Cox had now precisely measured Osama bin Laden's cost to his airport: 39 percent in gate fees to be paid by the beleaguered airlines.

For the airlines, that was only the beginning. In Washington, their lobbyists were already pushing TSA and Congress to reimburse them for a variety of new costs related to security—which they argued should be the country's national security responsibilities, not the responsibility of their shareholders. New requirements such as securing the meals prepared by the plane's caterers, reserving more first-class seats for air marshals (who needed to fly near the cockpit), or posting extra employees at the airports to take checked bags over to the new explosive detection machines, added up, they said, to an extra $300 million.

When the Aviation and Transportation Security Act had been passed, the airlines had been required to pay the government an amount equal to what they were going to save by not paying for the passenger screeners (who would now be federalized). But with these other added costs, they were deeper in the hole at a time when their businesses were hemorrhaging losses. Their fight to recover these costs would last months, and remain unresolved through the end of the year, because TSA said they were overstating these costs, and Congress said it couldn't afford to help anyway. In fact, one proposed congressional solution to address this issue and the mounting costs of the TSA effort that would crop up in the spring would be an additional tax on all flights, something that the industry frantically repelled, arguing, accurately, that air travel was already taxed at a higher percentage than tobacco by the federal government. Unlike smoking, air travel was something that was supposed to be encouraged.

Because Patrick Cartier, Sr., had been wondering about the victims compensation fund, which seemed to be set up to allow him and his wife to file a claim for James's death, and because Michael had been getting questions about the fund during some of his media interviews, the Cartier children arranged tonight for a volunteer from the New York State Trial Lawyers Association to meet with the whole family at their parents' home in Queens.

The neighborhood full of attached brick and shingle houses was festooned with the season's usual Christmas lights. Only this year all the homes displayed large American flags, too. It is a neighborhood of people who are utterly typical of those who live under that flag—police and firefighter families, civil servants, office support workers, and workers in the various trades, such as electrical work, which accounted for three Cartiers (their father, brother John, and the missing James).

As the family waited for the lawyer to arrive, they sat in a small living room next to a memorial collage of James in the dining area. The house seemed as if it must have been impossibly close quarters for a family of nine, until one understands how close the family was.

Patrick Cartier, Sr., who was in failing health, kept one eye on the television, where the local cable news station was reporting from Ground Zero. He seemed angry in a resigned, long-term way. That was not just because of his son's murder, but also because this morning he had had to bring another cotton swab of his saliva to the medical examiner's office. When he had called the day before to check on any DNA matchups, he had been told that they'd lost the first sample that he had given them two months before.

"We just want to give James a Christian funeral," he said, explaining why tonight's meeting was something he had put off and wasn't all that interested in. "This meeting with the lawyer really doesn't mean much. I just thought we should talk about our options, but what we care about is finding James."

As an interview with a Muslim protesting something about John Ashcroft flashed on the TV screen, the Cartier patriarch lunged to shut it off. "We should just level them," he muttered disgustedly.

When Jennie Farrell mentioned that George Clooney and the September 11th Fund had announced today that everyone was going to get a cash grant for Christmas, her father chimed in that "that's the way it should be. Everyone should get the same amount."

"They're only doing that because of O'Reilly," John, the ponytailed electrician, added. "Clooney and his gang don't care about us."

Did Patrick Cartier think that Feinberg and his government fund should do the same thing—give everyone the same amount?

"You're damn right. We should all get the same slice of cheese," he responded, his hand banging weakly on the dining room table off to his left. "No one wants $5,000 for the janitor and $5 million for a stockbroker. That's not America."

The lawyer from the state bar group arrived and started talking about the fund and whether they might want to go into it. Quickly it became clear to the only other law-trained person in the room (the author) that this was one volunteer program that may have meant well but was likely only to produce confusion. She explained that because her job was to provide preliminary guidance about whether to retain a lawyer to sue or go into the fund, her bar group had decided to avoid conflicts by not allowing lawyers who actually handle personal injury suits to work with people like the Cartiers at this stage. Otherwise, the lawyers with actual experience in the field might be tempted to sign them up as clients. In other words, she had no experience in what she was advising them about. It showed. Feinberg had not yet issued his regulations, yet she seemed eager to opine that any charity money they had received would be discounted out of his awards, which was, of course, wrong.

When John, the most boisterous of the group, asked about whether he could sue the INS, which had allowed the terrorists into the country, for emotional distress stemming from his brother's death, she said he might have a case. Which was doubly wrong: The INS was almost certainly invulnerable to such a suit for a variety of reasons, and New York state law did not allow someone to collect damages for emotional distress caused by a brother's death. Besides, as a brother, John's decisions to sue had nothing to do with the fund. He would not have been a beneficiary of the fund anyway; only his parents would be.

The well-intentioned malpractice continued for an hour, with all varieties of theoretical defendants put in the dock and none ruled out.

The session seemed only to draw out the bitterness the family felt about James's murder and scatter it in all directions. Which was understandable. Here was a family, all eight, who worked hard and played by all the rules. Their government had failed to protect them, and they were angry. Their reaction—that someone ought to pay—was simply the legacy of living in a country where bad luck had come to mean that someone is usually blamed and asked to pay up in court.

But it didn't last long. By the next morning, Michael Cartier would freely concede that the whole thing had been "a waste of time. We all felt kind of sheepish about it." He elaborated with an observation that would apply to much of the controversy the family would be swept up in over the next few months: "We're all sad and angry. And the only thing it seemed last night that we could channel it into was lawsuits, and complaints about the fund the government set up. If the government had said we'd all get $10 million, we'd be complaining about that, too. But it looks terrible to people out there who read about us. My father doesn't care about the money. What's he gonna do with it?"

# Thursday, December 13, 2001

A week after Ashcroft had come to Detroit to announce the assignment of new Border Patrol agents and a temporary posting of additional National Guard troops there, Tom Ridge announced an agreement with Canada to work together to tighten the Northern Border.

Meantime, Lindemann and Hall, while still worrying about what was going to happen with their proposed disciplinary action, were starting to feel a bit better. They'd been allowed to resume their night shifts, which freed Lindemann's wife to go back to work. And with both the inspector general and the Office of Special Counsel (the agency that is supposed to protect whistleblowers) actively investigating their case, they had begun to sense that the bosses were easing up on them a bit.

It also seemed that something was going on with the old Catch and Release Program. A different division of INS was now taking custody of anyone they apprehended and bringing them to a station where their identities could be checked against watch lists. Lindemann, Hall, and their fellow agents were told that unless those they caught posted real bail and proved some connection to someone in the United States, they were not being released. Lindemann and Hall didn't quite believe that. But even checking them out first before releasing them was an improvement, as was the arrival of additional manpower, even if it was a fraction of what they really needed.

# Friday, December 14, 2001

James Brosnahan finally got a response from the government to all of his letters requesting to see John Walker Lindh and that Lindh not be questioned.
Paul Cobb, Jr., a deputy general counsel at the Pentagon, faxed a one-
paragraph letter that said, "I can inform you that John Walker Lindh is currently in the control of the United States armed forces and is being held
aboard USS *PELELIU* in the theater of operations. Our forces have provided
him with appropriate medical attention and will continue to treat him
humanely, consistent with the Geneva Convention protections for prisoners
of war."

The letter, of course, ignored Brosnahan's requests, but did hold out some
hope. If Lindh was being treated as a prisoner of war, Brosnahan thought,
maybe all the press speculation of what crimes he would be charged with was
unfounded.

But he still wanted to see his client.


Herb Wachtell came to court to stress that his case on behalf of Larry Silverstein against the insurance companies was such an urgent prerequisite for the
rebuilding of New York that the usual schedules for pretrial discovery—examining the other side's documents and witnesses—had to be thrown by the
wayside. He thought discovery ought to involve only two witnesses and take
no more than two weeks.

Barry Ostrager, who represents Swiss Re, argued that a $3.55 billion case
required careful discovery of many witnesses, including more than a dozen
who had been involved in negotiating the policy form. It was no surprise that
Wachtell would be eager to put the case in front of a jury before all the facts
were discovered, Ostrager asserted.

Wachtell's push for this hearing to argue for a fast-moving case, which
Rubenstein had told the press about the day before, was, if nothing else,
another savvy public relations strategy. It drew both on the public's general
distaste for the slowness of the legal system and its sense of urgency about all
things related to September 11. However, Judge Martin was not likely to be
an ideal audience for what Wachtell and Rubenstein were attempting. Martin
is self-confident and easily on an intellectual par with the two main lawyers
who'd be arguing in front of him.

Ostrager pointed out what Martin and anyone else involved in real estate or government in New York knew—that "nothing is going to be rebuilt at the World Trade Center for five to seven years, and precisely what it is that is going to be rebuilt and when it is going to be rebuilt are issues that are going to take a very long time to resolve. . . . Mr. Wachtell has invited every member of the press other than the Discovery Channel here because he is trying to effect some type of emergency that doesn't exist."

Judge Martin ruled from the bench that discovery would take four months, and that after that Ostrager could come back for more time if he needed it.

By Friday night, Ken Feinberg had pretty much finished writing his regulations, all seventy-six pages' worth. He'd even reviewed them with Daniels of the White House budget office and some lawyers at the Justice Department. They seemed on board, though Daniels wanted to have another discussion early the following week once his staff checked a few of Feinberg's assumptions. Neither Daniels nor even Ashcroft could veto them without firing Feinberg; but Feinberg had promised to be a team player and intended to keep the promise.

When he would meet with Ashcroft four days from now, the Attorney General's one comment would be that "the cost will be whatever the cost is; I just want you to make sure you add a mechanism so that people can get some part of what they ultimately get very fast." So, Feinberg added a provision allowing for a check within two weeks for $50,000 as a down payment for anyone who filed an application.

The way the system was set up, a representative of the victim (typically the legally designated next of kin) would file on behalf of that victim. Then, any money would be distributed according to the victim's will, or if there was no will, divided up among the next of kin as that is defined by the state in which the victim had resided. (Most states, for example, give a spouse half of an estate and divide the other half among children. If there are no children, the spouse gets it all. If there is no spouse or children and no will, as in the case of James Cartier, then the parents get the estate.) Ashcroft, however, would ask for one additional protection: If there was a will, but it designated that the money go to some weird recipient, such as a pet cemetery, he wanted Feinberg to keep the discretion to give it out differently, such as to a brother or parent.

These were small details compared to the array of more important issues that Feinberg had to deal with, all of which might seem technical to outsiders but were tough calls that would mean everything to those affected by them. Gay partners would not be beneficiaries unless the relevant state allowed them to claim next-of-kin status. (How could he go against what a state legislature had decided, Feinberg reasoned, when it came to basic trust and estate law.) To qualify for status as a victim with an injury, a claimant had to have sought treatment within twelve hours or within forty-eight hours if he was a rescue worker. And the injury had to be physical. (Feinberg didn't want to be in the business of handing out taxpayer dollars to people who said they were traumatized by watching televised reports of the attacks.)

More important, Feinberg had decided not to try to distinguish between degrees of pain and suffering, or what the law calls "noneconomic" damages. Everyone would get $250,000 for that, plus $50,000 per spouse or child. (What if a widow said, "I was married to him for thirty-five years, so I deserve more than someone married six months," or "I talked to my husband four times from the 103rd floor just before he died, so I had more emotional distress than the average person"? Feinberg decided that he just couldn't deal with making those distinctions, even though judges and juries have to do that all the time.)

But even these decisions paled against the basic overlay of what Feinberg had done in terms of the economic damages he would award on top of this standard pain and suffering award. He knew that people on all sides would be screaming about it.

He had decided to expose this contentious issue in its most candid, rawest form by including in the regulations a chart—not simply text, but a chart—showing what various types of victims' families would be presumed to be entitled to, unless they demonstrated special circumstances to him that made the case for a higher payout.

Thus, the chart would show the family of a thirty-year-old stockbroker earning $225,000 with a wife and two children getting $3.8 million.

The family of a sixty-year-old janitor with a wife and one child would get $525,000.

The heirs to a twenty-six-year-old unmarried, childless electrician—such as James Cartier—would get $950,000.

In short, while all men (and women) may be created equal, Ken Feinberg was going to publish a United States government chart, destined to be reprinted in newspapers around the world, saying that their lives aren't worth anything near the same.

Of course, there was a logic to it that any lawyer would understand. The numbers were based on the amount of years each victim was presumed (by government actuarial charts) to have left in the workforce, their salaries, and an assumption (based on still more government data) of how much the salaries would increase over the years, plus that base amount in standard pain and suffering of $250,000, plus $50,000 for each spouse and child. However logical, it was not a chart destined to win Feinberg any popularity contests.

One of the other decisions he had made that was bound to infuriate a high-end plaintiffs lawyer like Kreindler, who had won as much as $15 million for air crash victims in other cases, was to stop the charts at someone earning $231,000, where the maximum award for the youngest person earning that much would be $4.3 million. Feinberg had picked $231,000 because that was the 98th percentile of earnings. For someone to claim lost earnings on the basis of more than that would take a special pleading to Feinberg. Rather than simply picking a higher number off the chart, they'd have to come in and show exceptional circumstances to get a larger award. It wasn't that he wasn't ever going to award more than that, but he was going to make it unlikely and difficult. Put simply, he did not intend to help the wealthiest of the wealthy maintain their prior lifestyle.

It was his way of narrowing the gaps, but he certainly wasn't narrowing them enough to suit people like Patrick Cartier, Sr., who thought everyone should get "the same slice of cheese."

That night, Feinberg spoke to his friend Ted Kennedy, and the two concluded that everyone from Congress west of the Hudson would attack the plan as an outrageous giveaway, while those from New York and New Jersey would say it was outrageously stingy. "Tell me when you're going to announce it," Kennedy said, "so I can arrange to be on Pluto and unavailable for comment."


New York State Attorney General Eliot Spitzer finally achieved the coordination of the charities that he'd been pushing for. Something called the 9/11 United Services Group was announced as an umbrella organization that would pool data from all the major charities—including the September 11th Fund, the Red Cross, and the Salvation Army. Better yet, it would provide a one-stop phone number and aid center where people could come (or phone in) and get a counselor who would help them apply for the menu of services offered by these and smaller funds, such as the Citigroup scholarship fund. Gotbaum of the September 11th Fund had been instrumental along with Spitzer and Senator Hillary Clinton in pushing the idea, and together they had helped recruit a prominent investment banker, Robert Hurst, who would run the effort, pro bono, with a small staff paid by separately raised funds. It would be three months before the database was actually useful, which was, of course, too late to prevent the double-dipping on the one hand and, more important, the confusion on the other hand that had so plagued the charities' efforts so far. But it was a good way to channel long-term relief efforts, as well as a template for responses to future disasters.

Michael Cartier, his brother John, and another member of their group who had lost his wife in the attacks got the full tour, courtesy of Rudy Giuliani.

An official of the mayor's Office of Emergency Management picked them up in a van this morning and began with a visit to the medical examiner's office, where they got a briefing on the elaborate procedures set up there to coordinate DNA matches. They saw the storage facilities for the samples their families had provided, inspected the refrigerated area where remains were kept, and met the doctors in charge and talked about how they were trying to work with even the smallest fragments to make identifications.

"It was like there was a whole world there of dedicated doctors and others working night and day to find James that I just didn't know about before," Cartier recalls.

Then it was on to Fresh Kills, the Staten Island dump. FBI special agent Richard Marx and New York police inspector James Luongo, the men in charge, let them see everything.

Cartier remembers thinking as the van drove up to the vast, movie-set-ugly expanse of debris that it literally looked like hell. He left three hours later thinking that everything he had thought and heard about Fresh Kills was "almost exactly the opposite" of what it really was—starting with Marx and Luongo, who seemed no less obsessed than he did about identifying and dig-nifying the victims.

Cartier spent a half hour with the team of cops and FBI agents—focused, silent, in white coats and masks—sifting through debris arrayed on slow-moving conveyor belts, picking a tooth out here, a fingernail there, or, at one point, a fragment of what looked to be an arm or leg bone. There were 1,000 of them working there every day. It seemed that such a large group of men and women could not possibly have ever worked so silently and so intently for so long. In a picture dictionary, this was the scene the authors would use for "painstaking."

Cartier inspected the property room, where rings, watches, scarves, or anything else possibly of value were carefully stored. He toured the crew's dressing rooms, showers, and a rest center, called the Hilltop Café—facilities that Luongo and Marx had built from scratch, often using their own men who had carpentry or other skills when the city's own building crews couldn't arrive fast enough.

John Cartier asked about a rumor that Luongo's men had lined up firemen's boots with feet still in them and let them sit around for days. Luongo said he'd heard that one, too, and that it was probably because one day they had ordered new boots for the crew and had lined them up for them to pick up. Maybe someone saw that and thought the worst, he said.

To demonstrate the horrific nature of the inferno at the Trade Center, Luongo and Marx opened a small shed and showed the group the only parts of the two jumbo jets that had been recovered. The melted remnants of two engines, some landing gear, and a spare tire looked like they could have fit into the back of an SUV.

Walking the 175 acres of ground that was still bubbling from the methane gas of the garbage that had been stored years before under their feet, Luongo showed Michael Cartier how when a barge arrived with another 650 tons of wreckage, they offloaded it onto a pile, then separated it into large, medium, and small particles, each going through a different conveyor belt system. But before each of the fifteen barges a day was allowed to leave, two or three FBI agents or cops used small dust brushes to brush out the corners of the container so that every last particle was captured.

Cartier was overwhelmed. He had come to yet another world, this one seemingly almost on another planet, where everyone was focused on his brother. When he finished the tour and was standing in the trailer that Luongo used for his office, he pulled a picture of James from his pocket and told Luongo he wanted him to have it.

Eight months later, Luongo and his men would finish the sifting three months ahead of schedule and 50 percent under budget, after finding 4,700 different pieces of remains. In the last days, they would scour even the grounds of the dump with those small brushes looking for any leftover particles. And on the final day, as he packed up his trailer, the picture of James would be the last thing Luongo took off the wall. "I kept it there to keep us going," he says.

The final part of the tour was the pit at Ground Zero. Among those who showed Michael and John Cartier and their friend around was Brian Lyons. John Cartier had been adamant in the meeting with the mayor's people that if the construction crews were scaled back, there would be room at Ground Zero to do much more sifting, rather than having to do most of it at Fresh

Kills. But having now seen what was really going on at Fresh Kills, not even he pushed that idea. Nonetheless, Lyons and the others giving this part of the tour explained why they needed all the people and equipment that they had down there, and why the team approach they were using—firemen and construction workers—seemed to have ironed itself out.

Michael Cartier warmed to Lyons when he identified himself as the brother of a fallen fireman. "I got the idea that he was a kind of double agent, someone who would look out for the victims, and I thought that was really good."

Cartier went home that night to the apartment he shares with his wife and baby daughter and started pounding away at his website, telling his members about the tour. Within a few days, the Give Your Voice site had elaborate information not only about the Fresh Kills and Ground Zero operations (including an explanation of how a loved one's personal property could be recovered, and how tours could be arranged) but a detailed explanation of the DNA process at the medical examiner's office that would have been mind-numbing if you weren't reading it to find out how your brother or husband or daughter might end up getting a proper funeral.

# Tuesday, December 18, 2001

Chuck Schumer may have come up as a liberal, post-Watergate Democrat from Brooklyn, but he has become a great representative of another key New York constituency—the financial community. The cynical explanation would be that he's a relentless fund-raiser, and that's where the money is. Indeed, the top nine sources of his contributions since 1997—totaling $1,357,000—were the employees or political action committees of nine investment banks or brokerage houses. The other explanation is that to represent New York, and, indeed, to represent the middle class who depend on having jobs in New York, a good senator has to help Wall Street whenever he can.

Today, Schumer was at his feverish best, pushing Senate Democrats in a caucus to do something about terrorism insurance before Congress adjourned in a few days for Christmas.

Schumer and a few other senators, most notably Chris Dodd from insurance-industry-based Connecticut, echoed Washington's insurance industry trade group in warning that something had to be done by December 31. After that, most insurance contracts that covered terrorism would expire. If that happened, they said, construction projects might be stopped, stadiums and airports might be closed, and banks might even foreclose on office buildings because the loans they had on these buildings required that the buildings have full insurance protection. Schumer was convinced this was a crisis, albeit a quiet one that was still under the radar.

The problem was that the terrorism insurance bill that had passed the Republican-controlled House had included that favorite Republican agenda item—tort reform. The Republicans had reasoned that if the taxpayers were going to back up insurance companies in compensating for terror attacks, then the least the lawmakers could do was to make sure that the same taxpayers didn't get stuck paying for the abuses perpetrated in court by trial lawyers, who sought exorbitant contingency fees and ridiculously high punitive damages, often against defendants who had not done anything wrong. So they had included in the law a cap on contingent fees and a ban on punitive damages in terrorism-related claims that the government would be responsible for.

The Senate, though, was controlled by Democrats. As Schumer knew, most Democrats were—by dint of campaign contributions, if not the ideology of wanting the little guy always to have free rein to sue deep-pocket corporations and let a jury decide what was fair—in lockstep with the plaintiffs lawyers on opposing such tort reform. So, Tom Daschle, the Senate Majority Leader, was not going to let any bill out of the Senate that included even an iota of tort reform. Like the National Rifle Association, which typically held Republicans to the position that even the most innocent-looking firearms control was the beginning of the end, Daschle's premise was that any tort reform, even if it would save taxpayers and not corporations, would start the country down a slippery slope of taking away the little guy's full access to the courts. His members were mostly willing to go along.

Lobbyists for the insurance industry, which usually loved tort reform, were horrified that this bill had been loaded down with this extra baggage. But Washington, indeed America, is a place where special interests are called that because they worry only about their own interests. Thus, seemingly natural allies can often splinter away as their narrow interests diverge. While the insurance industry, which had heartily supported the tort reform lobby, might now have a higher priority, those who were singly dedicated to the cause certainly didn't. "We try to achieve tort reform anywhere we can," explains Victor Schwartz, a Washington lawyer who is counsel to Americans for Tort Reform. "We encourage our Republican allies to attach it to any bill they can, and the more important the bill is to other interests, the better off we are, because people who want the bill to pass will have to accept our reforms with it."

Schumer tried to persuade the Republicans in the Senate that their supporters in the business community needed terrorism insurance more than they needed this kind of tort reform—which Schumer argued was essentially irrelevant, anyway, since the prospect of punitive damages against anyone other than the terrorists in a terror attack was so remote. But Republican Leader Lott, who had had that stormy session with O'Hare of Chubb, wasn't convinced that there really was a crisis, let alone a crisis worthy of throwing over the principle that taxpayers shouldn't have to risk the perils of the trial lawyers' abuse.

On this score, Schumer found that the insurance lobby had failed miserably. They should have been able to convince all of their big business allies to lean on Lott and the Republicans to come up with some compromise. But they simply hadn't made the issue urgent enough by making it clear that this was more about protecting the economy than about protecting them.

Thus, the tort reform tail wagged the terrorism insurance dog because, except for some members of Congress like Schumer and Dodd, with constituents in the insurance or financial communities, this was a crisis that simply did not captivate Capitol Hill. And when that happens, gridlock prevails.

"As we came down to the wire at Christmas," one insurance industry lobbyist recalls, "it became clear that although we represented some of the biggest money interests in America—the insurers and the banks and builders they insure—we had no juice, because we just had no way of convincing Congress that they wanted to go home for the Christmas recess bragging about what they'd done for terrorism insurance. We all assumed either Daschle or Lott would budge, but they didn't. It was just so stupid . . . the elites of the issue wanted it, but there was just no feel for the issue out there. It just wasn't a hot issue, the way the airline security bill was. That was something their constituents could understand."

Nor did Schumer get much help at the White House. Sure, they favored a bill, but the President was nowhere to be found when it came to getting people on the phone and pushing it.

Schumer and his staff were bitterly disappointed this afternoon when it became clear that nothing was going to happen. The Senate was going to let the year-end deadline pass without doing anything.


Sal Iacono was waiting for Hollie Bart in the lobby of an office building on lower Broadway just across from his shop. They were going to attend a workshop aimed at helping them put together a business plan so that Sal could get a grant from Seedco—the organization set up to aid small businesses near Ground Zero that had received much of its funding from the September 11th Fund, which, in turn, had received about $128 million from the Hollywood telethon.

Sal had thought this was more trouble than he could handle, but Hollie had insisted it would be a snap. They just had to go to this one meeting.

Across the street and to the west a block, the last smoldering fires from the World Trade Center were being doused. They'd be out by the next morning.

When Hollie approached Sal, walking her usually frantic walk through the hard-floored halls of the ornate old building, the Sole Man looked up. "I don't like the sound of your shoes," he said. "Let me see them."

Hollie removed her shoes.

"Just like I thought. You need heels," Sal pronounced. "I'll do it after the meeting."

## Thursday, December 20, 2001

John Magaw, the former Secret Service and ATF head picked to run the Transportation Security Administration, testified at his Senate confirmation hearing that he would meet the agency's seemingly impossible deadlines. "You will not hear me say 'can't,'" the former Michigan state trooper and career Secret Service man assured the senators, his dull-suited, bulky frame and never-crack-a-smile demeanor reinforcing the pledge.

When he finished his testimony, confident that he would be confirmed, Magaw turned to the job of staffing his new department. One of the first calls he made was to Gale Rossides, who ran the training and quality performance programs at ATF.

Gale Rossides's résumé read career bureaucrat. Between the lines it read nepotism, too. Her first job at the ATF was right out of Wheaton College, in 1978, when she took a position as an administrative assistant as a way to earn some extra cash before she was scheduled to enter Georgetown Law School that fall. She got the post because her father had been an assistant treasury secretary overseeing ATF earlier in the 1970s.

But Rossides—forty-six, blond, with a ready smile, childless and married to a Treasury agent—didn't fit any stereotype, including the one usually (and wrongly) associated with career civil servants. Anonymous as she may have been, holding down acronym-laden jobs though she did, she was an incurable workaholic. At ATF, she was not only widely liked, but also viewed as one person who would run over, or cleverly sidestep, almost any obstacle to get to the goal.

Rossides ended up never enrolling at Georgetown. She liked ATF so much, and they liked her so much, that they asked her to stay, much to her father's regret. And every time she thought about leaving to go to law school, they promoted her, until by the time Magaw arrived in 1993 she was director of administration. When Magaw asked around for names of people who could help him remake the organization, hers was mentioned by everyone. She became part of a small group that completely reorganized the place, then became the assistant director for training, a new job at ATF and the first time any woman had held any significant post at the agency.

Now, Magaw wanted Rossides to come join him and build TSA from the ground up. He didn't mention that there were go teams already plotting out much of what she'd be handling, probably because he didn't yet know the extent of the shadow organization of private sector volunteers Deputy Secretary Jackson had pulled together.

Rossides wasn't surprised by the call. Her husband and friends had said she was sure to get it the moment they'd heard Magaw had been offered the TSA job. But she was hesitant about leaving the place she'd help build for twenty-three years, a place where she had so many friends.

She told Magaw she'd have to think about it over the Christmas holiday.


Ken Feinberg formally issued his regulations, and tonight Michael Cartier became a media star of sorts. Because his name had been in the press as leading a group of victims' families, he was asked to come on various television shows, including Tom Brokaw's *NBC Nightly News*. He also talked to several print reporters about the fund. By the next morning, he'd realize he had made a mistake. His issue was making sure the families were informed about, and had a voice in, the recovery of remains and the cleanup. Now he found himself talking about money. He had pretty much taken his father's line, which was that the fund shouldn't be making such drastic distinctions among rich and poor wage earners, and that the whole setup was a way, as his father liked to say, to "bribe" people into not suing. But he didn't like the idea that he'd been so tempted to go on television that he'd neglected his real cause, or maybe had even undercut it.


Schumer had been briefed by Feinberg earlier in the week on what the regulations would be, including that charitable gifts would not be deducted from awards. He told Feinberg that he thought he had come up with a good plan and would not criticize him, but that for his own protection he would also try to avoid comment altogether.

Other politicians leaped at the chance to go after Feinberg. Spitzer, the New York attorney general, was quoted in the *New York Daily News* (whose page-one headline blared, "HOW MUCH FOR A LIFE?") as "blasting" Feinberg's charts as being "far less than the payments of $5 million and up typically awarded in aviation disasters." Of course, "$5 million and up" was hardly a typical payment anywhere, much less in New York, where the law allows damages only for lost wages, not pain and suffering. More-over, any $5 million award "typically" takes five or ten years to collect, and when it is collected, 33 to 40 percent typically has to go to a plaintiffs lawyer.

In the same article, a Long Island widow who calculated her award from Feinberg at $1.5 million called it a "sick joke," while a plaintiffs lawyer called it "a betrayal."

Talking to a reporter from his Florida vacation home, Kreindler, the dean of aviation disaster plaintiffs lawyers, called it "a disaster." Referring to one of the wealthy widows he had already signed up, Kreindler added, "He is taking people like my client . . . and is forcing a change in their lifestyle, which is exactly what the law is supposed to prevent. . . . It's nonsense."

Under the law, these were Feinberg's "draft interim" regulations. He now had three months to listen to comments like these and others and revise the regulations, although in Washington that was rarely a process that anyone took seriously. Feinberg took it completely seriously. Within a week, he'd be responding to one key complaint by telling the press that he planned to revise the guidelines concerning offsets so that every family—even those with large life insurance policies, or the firemen and policemen with generous death benefits—got something. Feinberg's goal, after all, was to make sure people came into his plan instead of going to court. He couldn't just put something out there and let them take it or leave it.

Tonight he began making plans for a new round of meetings so he could once again hear everyone out.

In fact, he could have begun the process immediately, if he were more handy with his computer. For the website his staff had set up was already get-ting comments by the hundreds over the Internet, complaining about every-thing from his not recognizing same sex partners, to his not giving everyone the same amount, to his shortchanging the wealthy.

CEO Dean O'Hare announced how much Osama bin Laden had affected Christmas at Chubb. He sent a memo to all of his employees saying that because of losses related to the September 11 attacks (plus claims related to Chubb having insured some Enron bonds), there would be no bonuses this year for any mid- or senior-level executives. In recent years, these bonuses have represented one third to half of the executives' annual incomes. In O'Hare's case, his bonus in 2000 of $800,000 had been nearly 45 percent of his income. That was now gone. In all, a total of $65 million in budgeted bonuses was eliminated, while a small pool of $15 million was left in place for lower level employees.

# Friday, December 21, 2001

James Brosnahan is nothing if not polite, and it continued to rankle him that no one was responding to his letters and phone calls, other than that one, nonresponsive letter from a deputy general counsel at the Pentagon reporting that his client was on a Navy boat being treated like a prisoner of war. But he finally found the kind of courteous adversary he was used to, in the White House.

White House Counsel Alberto Gonzales returned his call and told him his client was safe and being given the medical attention he needed. He would not say where he was, but did assure Brosnahan that Lindh's whereabouts would be known soon, and that at the right time Brosnahan would be able to see him.

Richard Falkenrath, Tom Ridge's policy guru from the Kennedy School, had written what he thought was a killer memo. No one could read it and not see the inescapable logic of combining INS, the Coast Guard, and Customs into one border protection agency. Ridge and most of his staff agreed. This was a no-brainer, and also the only way to get the hapless INS fixed. In James Loy, the head of the Coast Guard, and Robert Bonner, the Customs chief, they also had a great team that could put this all together, and then maybe add some other agencies along the way.

Falkenrath had long been obsessed by what he thought was the country's dangerously unprotected borders. "The failure of the U.S. to put drug smugglers out of business," he had written in his 1998 book, *America's Achilles' Heel*, "is a good measure of the difficulty of reliable border control. If the risks of detection at the border appear too high, an attacker can manage them in a number of different ways. For example, an attacker could smuggle a weapon or its components into any of a large number of uncontrolled harbors by boat. . . . The chance of being caught would be small." Then to zing the Customs Service a bit, Falkenrath, who was dismissive of constant Customs press releases trumpeting their busts, had added the following footnote: "In another recent example, a Florida businessman was arrested for smuggling 180 tons of freon refrigerant into the United States from Russia. The arrest would be evidence of good border security if the man hadn't smuggled 4,000 tons of the chemical into the U.S. in the previous three years."

Falkenrath's memo promoting the consolidation of the three agencies was only a slightly toned-down version of his book's indictment of the country's border protection posture.

So with the President's agreement that Ridge test the Falkenrath plan, Ridge convened a meeting of what was called the Principals Committee— which is all the heads of cabinet agencies with any homeland security responsibilities: State, Justice, Transportation, Treasury (where Customs was housed), Health and Human Services, plus the FBI, EPA, and even Agriculture (which worried about food safety).

Ridge distributed Falkenrath's memo and walked them through it. One problem became apparent quickly. Falkenrath's cynicism about the performance of the border control agencies overseen by various people in the room wasn't going over well. Falkenrath had thought he was outlining historic and structural weaknesses, not the performance of those who had so recently taken over these jobs. He didn't understand that cabinet members who have been on the job only a year or even less had quickly come to regard the institution they run as their own.

One by one, every cabinet member proceeded to shoot the idea down. The ones not directly affected said Congress, with its obsession for preserving committee jurisdictions, would never accept this juggling of turf, and that it was not worth the fight. Mineta of Transportation, who would lose the Coast Guard, said it was a terrible idea. The Coast Guard's problem wasn't coordination, he said. It was resources. Shuffling the boxes around on an organization chart was no substitute for providing the resources he needed. Ashcroft, however much he always seemed to want to distance himself from his forlorn INS, said he would fight it, that INS was an integral part of the Justice Department. He didn't want to have to negotiate with some other agency head when he wanted the INS to hold someone detained in "my" terrorism investigation, he noted. He, too, argued that the INS's problem was resources, not coordination.

There was one exception. Treasury Secretary Paul O'Neill, already seen as a kind of odd duck in the Bush administration, said the plan was fine with him and that, if anything, it didn't go far enough. He had a lot of other things to worry about. He didn't need to hold on to Customs.

O'Neill's outlook was the exception that proved the rule. This became as open a revolt as ever occurred in the collegial Bush administration. After one member said he would fight the plan as hard as he could, that his department just wouldn't tolerate it, others chimed in that they, too, would go to the President to fight it.

Ridge listened and nodded his head slightly as he often does when he's tense but trying to seem agreeable. Finally, he said something to the effect that he guessed he'd have to rethink it.

The meeting adjourned with everyone trying to lighten things a bit by wishing all a good holiday. The no-brainer was dead.

Card later reported to the President that "Tom tried to sell his plan to them, and the response was classic Washington: 'Don't take anything away from us, just give us more money.' " Bush was not surprised.

Ridge immediately caucused with Falkenrath, who was seething, and with other senior members of his staff. An idea that had been championed by Democrats and Republicans alike in Congress and in various commissions had just been rejected by the entire cabinet, Falkenrath pointed out.

"Don't worry," Ridge told them, still nodding his head slightly. "We'll fight this fight another day."

If we can't get this done, what *can* we do, Falkenrath wanted to know.

Don't worry, Ridge repeated. We'll get it done. "This is just the beginning. We're just getting started. We have a lot more bites left to the apple."

Still, he wasn't oblivious to the obstacles in front of him. In fact, earlier in the week he'd been surprised, and depressed, to hear that the seemingly trivial plan to put the grants for local first responders into the FEMA budget, rather than in the Justice Department budget where different kinds of grants to police departments had always been housed, was running aground. Ashcroft's staff had apparently alerted members of the congressional committees that oversaw that part of the Justice budget about the plan, and they were kicking up a storm. The Justice people had also told various police and sheriff's organizations about it, and they were writing Congress and the White House to complain. Mike Byrne, the Ridge aide and former fire captain who'd directed FEMA's recovery effort at Ground Zero, was reporting that some congressional staffers whom he'd gone to talk to about it had questioned what he knew about first responders and their needs.

Ridge had joked to Byrne that he had probably preferred running into burning buildings as a fireman over going up to Capitol Hill. To Ridge, the whole thing was a ridiculous argument, intolerable at a time of crisis. Yet as Ridge prepared to go home for Christmas, he was more determined than he was discouraged. When he first ran for governor of Pennsylvania in 1994 against five opponents, from a backwater congressional district no less, the front-runner had made fun of him by sending him a birthday cake with eleven candles, signifying where he was in the polls—11 percent. Ridge had kept plugging away, barnstorming the state and quietly raising a war chest so that in the final weeks of the campaign he swamped everyone else with television ads. Ridge's career, and persona, seemed filled with situations like that— instances where to everyone else he seemed down and out, but he kept plugging away, as if he was oblivious to what seemed to be his fate, or just didn't care. Ridge really did believe that he had a lot more "bites left to the apple" when it came to getting this job anchored the right way, so that he and his staff could begin to have real impact.

"If he was disheartened," recalls Michele Ridge, "Tom certainly didn't show it. Tom is really the kind of person," she added, "who defines relentless. He just doesn't get discouraged. You don't run for governor of Pennsylvania from the northwestern corner of the state like he did, without just keeping at it. . . . He'd been to Washington before as a member of the minority party in Congress, and he knows you just don't show up there and govern by fiat."

# Saturday, December 22, 2001

Richard Reid, an English citizen of Jamaican descent, was arrested in Boston after passengers stopped him from setting off a shoe bomb on a flight from Paris to Miami. To Ashcroft it was a defining moment in the fight against terrorism. Vigilant citizens had acted to protect themselves.

Reid's connections, via e-mails, to Al Qaeda were quickly established. He was, noted one member of Ridge's staff familiar with the intelligence file on him, "a dim, forty-watt bulb of Al Qaeda's, probably sent over as cannon fodder just to prove they were still out there, and to scare us."

Yet Reid's case would ultimately contribute to the confusion about what the government's legal policy was when it came to prosecuting terrorists. For it was unclear why he was immediately indicted and held for prosecution in a Boston federal court, rather than put into a military tribunal as an enemy combatant. The answer, though, was clear to anyone working with Ashcroft: If Ashcroft's people got someone, they intended to keep him. Thus, no one at Justice even consulted the White House, let alone the Pentagon, before bringing charges against Reid.

# Tuesday, December 25, 2001

Ken Feinberg was happy to get away with his family to Jamaica for Christmas, figuring it would be his last escape for a while from all the sadness he was somehow supposed to compensate. He didn't get to escape completely. On Sunday his three college-age kids got into a good-natured argument with a New York football fan. The Feinberg kids favored the Redskins, and this guy, a New Yorker, liked the Giants. Somehow, the New Yorker figured out from the kids who their father was, and now, on Christmas morning, Feinberg found himself meeting with Michael Barasch, an ambitious forty-six-year-old plaintiffs lawyer with an office in lower Manhattan, who specialized in bringing suits on behalf of firemen.

Barasch, who featured a "World Trade Center Legal Update," on his website, told Feinberg he had now amassed nearly 1,000 cases involving what he called "the real silent secret"—firemen who had sustained lung injuries during the rescue and recovery effort at Ground Zero. The injuries ranged from the relatively minor to complete inability to do the basics of life, such as walking upstairs or lifting a child. Barasch figured the damages ranged from $50,000 into the millions.

Barasch explained that as the law required, earlier in the month, he had filed notices of his intention to sue the city, because the men had been placed in harm's way and not given the proper protective masks. He even had one of the notices with him; it cited "contact with dangerous levels of toxins, PCB's, benzene, lead, chromium, copper, asbestos, sulfur dioxide, fiberglass, and other toxic and carcinogenic chemicals." But now, Barasch continued as Feinberg listened patiently, he was thinking that the victims fund might be a better alternative. Which of course it would be, because the city's liability for everything involving September 11 had been capped at $350 million. Also the city was known as a tough litigant.

What did Feinberg think?

Make an appointment and show me some sample cases, Feinberg replied.

With the death count from September 11 having steadily dropped in the

last two months to about 3,000 from the 5,000 or 6,000 that had been estimated when the victims compensation law had been passed, Feinberg had
been sure he'd be able to come in well under the $6 billion ceiling that he
and budget director Daniels had danced around in their initial conversation.
And serious injuries (also covered by the fund) were always thought to be limited to a handful. Now, this plaintiffs lawyer was saying there might be a thousand cases he'd never thought about, cases involving hero firemen, no less,
who could not be easily denied. Was he right? Could there be more categories
of victims like this?

## Monday, December 31, 2001

Kevin McCabe's Customs people loaned the New York City Police Department 100 of its personal radiation detectors so that cops could use them in
patrolling the Times Square New Year's celebration tonight.

Eileen Simon had wanted to spend New Year's Eve at home, alone with her
three children. But the kids insisted that they go to the party at a neighbor's
house that they had always gone to. Everything was okay, if muted, until one
of the kids there who was about the same age as MJ, ten, remarked to him that
he'd heard that his daddy's body had been found all smashed up at the Trade
Center. MJ started to cry; then the rest of the family broke down when he
came and told them about it. Between that and the way they were treated so
delicately by everyone else, for Eileen it was a perfectly agonizing end to an
agonizing year.

PART THREE
SHORT-TERM PAIN AND GAIN,
LONG-TERM PLANS

# January 2, 2002–June 10, 2002

## Wednesday, January 2, 2002

Chuck Schumer had been pestered last month by a friend and supporter who is an executive at a major New York real estate brokerage. His was one of those phone messages on the never-ending list that Schumer carried around with him. When he had finally returned the call, the real estate executive, Barry Gosin, promised Schumer that he had an idea for redeveloping the Trade Center site that would blow him away.

Gosin came in with charts, graphs, and pictures showing that the United Nations headquarters in midtown was in total disrepair and so overcrowded that the U.N. had spilled over into office buildings in the area. They were desperately looking for a solution, he told Schumer. His idea was simple: Swap the Trade Center property for the U.N. property. The U.N. could then build a vast new headquarters at Ground Zero. Embassies and consulates from the member countries, now scattered around the East Side, would follow, creating a wonderful new international community of office buildings and residences, while also becoming the ideal site for a fitting memorial to the victims and a monument to world peace. Conversely, the Port Authority, with or without Silverstein, could take over the U.N. property in midtown along the East River, and build office buildings there that would be much more rentable than the more remote downtown space.

It would be the perfect win-win, as salesmen like to put it.

Schumer, who loves big ideas, loved this one.

## Friday, January 4, 2002

Trent Lott mentioned to one of his staff members that "it's January fourth and the sky hasn't fallen in." He was referring to the warnings from the insurance industry and people like Schumer that the Senate absolutely had to act on terrorism insurance before New Year's, or construction would stop, buildings would be declared in default of their financing, stadiums would close, and the economy generally would suffer a body blow.

Lott was right—but only because the insurance lobbyists and their supporters had overplayed their hand in warning of a New Year's meltdown. What was actually happening was more like a snowball slowly gathering mass. Some insurers, in fact, had decided to go ahead and provide terrorism coverage, but in a way that segregated it as a category and that cost their clients more and did not give them the protection they needed. For example, in Georgia, Gwinnett County, which had paid $305,000 in 2001 for insurance to cover damage of up to $300 million on all county buildings, now had to pay $390,000. The new policy provided the same $300 million in standard coverage but only $50 million to cover terror attacks.

Insurance brokers for key, iconic skyscrapers said that they were paying what amounted to an extra $2 to $6 per square foot for limited coverage in buildings that rented for $40 to $60 per foot. When those costs were ultimately passed on to tenants they could amount to a 5 to 10 percent "terrorism tax" on their rents. Yet it would still not cover the building fully in the event of a catastrophe.

Meantime, many construction projects really were being put on hold because the banks didn't want to finance buildings that could not get full coverage. (Without full coverage, the banks would be left with only the lesser amount of the insurance if the building was destroyed and the builder, therefore, defaulted on the loan.) And many facilities and businesses that were already up and running couldn't get coverage at all, at any price. This included the upcoming Olympics, which had decided it would have to go "naked."

Larry Cox was also naked. His insurance policy for the new year excluded terrorism. As he put it, "If our building is bombed, I'll just have to call my board together and say, 'Gentlemen, you either come up with $250 million, or we're over.' "

For his part, Schumer had been so sure that he'd move the Senate to stop worrying about the side issue of tort reform that had been inserted into the terrorism insurance proposals that he hadn't really developed a Plan B. His friends in the banking and real estate industries were asking what went wrong. His only answer was that his own party was a captive of the trial lawyers, but that he would get it done in this new session.

Having heard nothing more from the government about what was going to happen to his client, James Brosnahan faxed a letter to Ashcroft citing "press reports" that "the government is close to recommending that John [Lindh] be transferred to civilian law enforcement authorities," and asking that he get the opportunity to discuss Lindh's case with Justice Department prosecutors.

He received no answer.

# Saturday, January 5, 2002

At a converted naval air base sandwiched between a bunch of strip malls in Glynco, Georgia, near Brunswick, something happened this morning that promised to make Kevin McCabe's life a bit easier and the country's ports safer, sooner. It was one of those shifts in the inner gears of government that those involved think is seismic but the rest of the country never knows about. For the first time since it was established in 1970, the Federal Law Enforcement Training Center (FLETC) went on a six-day schedule, meaning that classes and training exercises for new Customs recruits (as well all other federal agents, except the FBI, which has its own facility) began promptly at 8:00.

The step-up to Saturday classes could not have come too soon for McCabe, who had heard about it in November, when he began anxiously asking when the new recruits he'd been promised would actually arrive at the port in Elizabeth. McCabe had gotten a few men reassigned to his Contraband Enforcement Team since September 11, stretching his workforce from seventy to about ninety. But not only did he need more, he was also worried about these men going back to their home bases and not getting others to rotate in replacing them.

In Pembina, North Dakota, Mary Delaquis had exactly the same concern at the vehicle ports of entry that she supervised for Customs. The Hawaiians who had gotten stuck in the snow on their first day north had rotated out after a month, and been replaced by others. But she, too, knew that the only real solution was to hire new people.

In November, Congress, in a bill supported by Schumer, had appropriated money for Customs to do just that immediately. But things didn't happen immediately. Government, particularly law enforcement, is more complicated than that. First, the men and women had to be recruited. Then they had to undergo background checks, which even now could take a month or two. After that, there was a fifty-five-day training course at FLETC in Georgia, an elaborate process that cost the government about $8,500 per trainee. The recruits take courses in everything from the laws of search and seizure, to narcotics, to marksmanship (they had to learn to shoot so they could hit the lethal body area of a target from three to twenty-five yards 70 percent of the time—with either hand), to filling out tariff forms, to surveillance, to the art of stopping and arresting someone. (Local actors, playing bad guys, talk trash and physically resist the students, as they practice getting them to lie down and put their hands behind their backs for handcuffing.)

These fifty-five days had always translated into eleven weeks. But that was one part of the equation that could be changed to meet the new threat, and as of today it was. The six-day-a-week schedule meant it would now take nine weeks, including an extra course in anti-terrorism. With new instructors added so that double the recruits could be taught at one time, FLETC expected to move 1,200 new inspectors through the center this year, as compared to 450 in 2001.

## Sunday, January 6, 2002

Four New York congressmen held a news conference to protest Ken Feinberg's proposed payout plan as being too stingy. Several victims' family members were in a cheering section.

The Cartiers stayed away. That night Michael Cartier sat in the living room of the apartment in Astoria, Queens, that he shares with his wife, Michele, and their now five-month-old daughter, hunched over one of his computers, a picture of James taped to the monitor. The more he read, the more upset he got. The mailbox for his Give Your Voice website was stuffed. So many of the e-mails were hostile, or worse, that he had to create a separate folder, called "bad mail."

His website, set up to give the victims' families a voice, was now hearing from other voices. They called him greedy, hungry for publicity, ungrateful. There were dozens of them. Soon there would be hundreds.

They were also weighing in on the website set up by Feinberg's staff to receive comments on his interim regulations. "The American taxpayer did not fly the planes into the buildings," wrote one e-mailer. "When this first happened, I was all for helping out the people left behind. But thanks to the whining of some pathetic widows, I now say _ _ _ _ them. Go on like anyone else would have to that lost their husband in a car accident—do it on the life insurance, etc. Get jobs, but most of all—get lost!! Most of them have already gotten money from the salvation army, etc. They just want to turn this

into a chance to get rich and stay home. They should be ashamed of themselves!!"


Eileen Simon didn't go to the rallies and she wasn't whining. But by now, she
had had her first meeting with a lawyer at her sister's old firm, plus gotten
some material from Cantor Fitzgerald, and she, too, was concerned about the
fund.

Based on Michael's earnings, it appeared from the charts that she might
be entitled to about $1.7 million. If that seemed surprisingly far down from
the top of the charts for a forty-one-year-old Cantor trader, it was because
Michael had only recently started at Cantor, after he and Eileen had decided
to move back from a job he had had in London. Also, he hadn't worked for
several months during that period, and Feinberg's formula called for averaging three prior years of income.

But what shocked Eileen was that this $1.7 million might end up being
zero, because of the offsets that were to be deducted from it. First, there was
the $500,000 in life insurance. That was clear. But what was more of a sur-
prise as she started doing her own calculations and asking her lawyers about
them was that it seemed that the value of the standard, and seemingly small,
Social Security and workers' compensation payouts that she and her children
were entitled to over the rest of their lives—and which seemed from the rules
Feinberg had issued also had to be computed and deducted—looked like they
added up to another $1.2 million. For example, each child was entitled to
$657 a month from Social Security until he or she reached age eighteen,
which added up to just over $200,000. The Social Security benefits she would
be entitled to over her lifetime could amount to another $450,000. Her and
the kids' workers' compensation looked like it was worth another $500,000 to
$550,000.

If all that was deducted along with the $500,000 in life insurance, she'd get
nothing. A fund that Congress had set up on that night back in September to
make up for a law that prevented her from suing the airlines (because that law
capped their liability) was actually going to pay her nothing.

Like many widows, Simon had by now become increasingly angry when
she read newspaper stories or heard TV reports that referred to an "average"
payout of $1.6 million. Feinberg, in fact, repeatedly used the $1.6 million figure himself, which was accurate if one looked at the charts, but wildly inaccurate if the deductions for workers' compensation and Social Security—two
benefits that almost everyone had—were calculated. Even to someone like

Simon, an optimist who was anything but cynical about her country, the whole thing, including Feinberg's crowing about a $1.6 million average payment, was beginning to look like a cruel government hoax.

What Simon didn't know was that Feinberg, too, was now starting to hear talk about how these standard benefits would force drastic deductions from so many of his awards. He was as surprised as she was.


Gale Rossides came home from her first day as the new something—no one had any titles yet—at the Transportation Security Administration and told her husband it had been twelve hours of "indescribable chaos." No one had desks, chairs, phones, or computers, let alone any idea of their responsibilities. She bounced around from meeting to meeting, although these were more conversations or encounters than meetings, since they happened spontaneously around a vacant desk or in the tenth-floor hallway of the Transportation Department's white-box, ugly building. Only Magaw seemed to have an office. Sitting outside it in a converted closet was Stephen McHale, who was supposed to be TSA head Magaw's deputy and whom Rossides knew from ATF, where he'd been Magaw's general counsel.

For someone who had spent every day of the twenty-three years of her working life in the same government agency, this might have been Rossides's way of explaining to her spouse why she thought she had made a terrible mistake. But Rossides had loved it. Everything about it gave her the feeling of having been swept away into a group of warriors fighting on an important front in the new home front war.

Even the groups of seemingly know-it-all private sector hotshots, who were running all those go teams she heard about only after she arrived ("who are the guys with all the laptops," she wondered), didn't bother her. The charts full of deadlines and milestones they'd taped along the walls of a conference room that they'd converted into their war room, and all their lists, and lists of lists, made it seem like these guys had everything so well under control that they didn't need her. They cheerfully disabused her of that, welcoming her, clearing a desk for her in the war room, and pushing her to join the fray. They needed help and really didn't have anything solved yet. If it looked like they'd been working here for years, that was only because "TSA time," one of them told her, was something akin to dog years only more so: In terms of how fast they had to move, a day was like a month and a month was like a year. In fact, most of them had started only a few weeks ago.

Rossides had jumped into a budget meeting, agreed to join an organizational structure committee, and begun working with the go team that was a week or two ahead of her on trying to figure out how to recruit and train all those new federal baggage screeners.

By the end of the day, she felt like she'd been there a week or two. The go team guy was right about TSA time and dog years.


# Tuesday, January 8, 2002

The group that gathered in a conference room at the Old Executive Office Building today was exactly what Vice President Cheney had in mind when he first talked to Tom Ridge about becoming the homeland security coordinator.

The subject was cargo container security, which had to do with what Kevin McCabe worried about every day at his port in Elizabeth. Ridge's office had gathered representatives from every conceivable government agency that had anything to do with the subject so they could come up with a plan.

There were representatives from Customs, the National Security Council, the Pentagon, INS, the Defense Department's National Defense University (which, among other things, studies security technology), the Department of Agriculture (which worries about certain food shipments), the Transportation Department (which houses the Coast Guard), and even the CIA, whose technology people had once been consulted by someone on McCabe's staff about methods for breaking into cargo containers without the break-in being discovered.

The meeting was happening because one of McCabe's veteran inspectors, a mechanics buff who doubles as McCabe's in-house expert on how cargo container seals can be breached, had heard that the Department of Transportation and its Coast Guard policy people had formed a task force to work on container security. He had passed the word on to McCabe, who passed it up the line, until Customs Commissioner Robert Bonner called Ridge and asked that Customs be included in the group. (Bonner was certain that Customs knew a lot more about cargo containers than the Coast Guard.) So the Transportation Department working group had been asked today to come brief the others on what it was up to.

Chairing the meeting was Brian Peterman, who was a deputy to Lawlor, the general running Ridge's Protection and Prevention division. Peterman, fifty-one, was supposed to handle all issues related to border and port security. On September 11, he was a Coast Guard admiral stationed in Miami, "chasing thugs and drugs," as he puts it. Driving home one evening the week after the attacks, he had heard President Bush announce the creation of the Office of Homeland Security and decided that he wanted to be involved. Figuring, he later recalled, that "I know borders. I know how to protect them, and now there is a much more important reason to protect them," he put in for a job with Ridge, which he got, in part, because he also had worked as a staffer on the National Security Council. Like so many others on Ridge's staff, he had quickly moved up to Washington, and was hoping to get his family relocated there within a few months.

As everyone around the table provided an overview of what they were doing in container security, Peterman was struck by the mix of overlapping activities and efforts unique to each agency that could be put together into a more powerful effort. It was also clear that everyone in the room had been thinking for a long time, but on their own, about the same strategies for improvement—getting foreign countries to do a better job of screening cargo before it leaves their ports, focusing on the busiest ports, refining the criteria for the kind of targeting of high-risk shipments that McCabe now did every day in Elizabeth, developing satellite technology to track containers, and improving intelligence.

The session ended with agreement that the Transportation Department group would be morphed into this interagency working group. Though that didn't thrill the Transportation people, they didn't let on. Everyone else came away happy.

Peterman was encouraged.

*Specialists in one narrow area from disparate federal agencies meeting each other, often for the first time. Bonding over their commitment to the cause. Promising to cooperate. Expressions of goodwill and enthusiasm all around.*

Over the next several weeks Ridge's people would convene groups like this every day, on subjects ranging from office building ventilation, to chemical industry safety, to student visa controls. The first meetings would always end this way. The next meetings would often be another story.


Ken Feinberg suffered his first defeat. Five September 11 widows gave up their chance to go into his victims compensation fund and sued either American Airlines or United Airlines, as well as the private security companies (Argenbright in the case of the American plane and another company for the United flight) that had screened the passengers who boarded the planes their husbands had been on.

The lawyer in each case was Mary Schiavo, a Los Angeles–based plaintiffs attorney who had been the high-profile inspector general of the Transportation Department in the first half of the 1990s. Schiavo alleged negligence, reckless conduct, and "conscious disregard for the rights and safety of the passengers" on the part of the airlines and the screening companies.

The airlines, of course, had the defense that nothing that happened was their fault, let alone foreseeable. There was no evidence that anyone had violated the FAA's security guidelines in letting the hijackers on with box cutters or small knives. Schiavo's contention was that they should have done a better job screening for danger, and that even if FAA regulations didn't make them keep box cutters or small knives off the planes, they should have done so on their own.

Whatever the argument, the airlines couldn't have cared less about the suits. Under the airline bailout law, their liability had been capped to the amount covered by their insurance. And their insurance companies already knew that, except for the flight that had crashed in rural Pennsyvania, whether it was these suits or claims made for the property destroyed in the crashes, they were already destined to pay out the limit on the policy anyway. So who cared if a few victims' families joined in to go after the same limited pot?

The security companies might have cared, because they didn't have a liability cap, but it turns out that their contracts with the airlines provided that the airlines had to indemnify them, meaning the airlines had to pay any claims against them. But that, too, would be covered by the airlines' liability cap. Besides, proving the security companies did anything wrong would seem to be impossible, since they worked under strict guidelines set by the airlines and were not known to have allowed anything on the planes that violated those guidelines.

Feinberg, however, cared a lot. He didn't want this to be the beginning of a trend, in which people discarded his fund, and he was appalled that any lawyer would advise a client in good faith to do so, given what he thought were the slim chances of proving fault, let alone the problems of collecting on a judgment because of the cap that Congress had put on the airlines' liability. Schiavo, on the other hand, maintained that her clients, whom she did not name in her filing, were people who didn't care about the money as much as they cared about finding out what happened and holding the airlines accountable, something that only a full-fledged court proceeding could do.

Yesterday, Hollie Bart completed Sal Iacono's application for a grant from the Seedco program set up in large part with money from the September 11th Fund to help small businesses around Ground Zero get back on their feet.

Today, she showed Sal and the lawyers working with her that there were, as she liked to say, "lots of ways to skin a cat," when it came to helping Continental Shoe Repair. For weeks, she'd been pushing a friend who is a well-connected PR person to get someone to write a story about Sal's struggles (and, of course, her efforts to help him). The first result came this morning, with a front-page piece in the daily *New York Law Journal,* headlined "Good Souls Help 'The Sole Man.' "

The article warmly portrayed Sal's battle to survive, and highlighted how Bart had e-mailed hundreds of lawyer-colleagues asking them to send business to him. True, the piece equally showcased the pro bono efforts of Bart and her firm, which delighted her partners. But within two weeks it would also lead to features on New York's local cable news channel and in the *New York Times* about Sal as the emblematic, struggling Ground Zero shopkeeper. ("A Downtown Cobbler Gets Back on His Insoles," the *Times*'s headline declared.)

The publicity, plus Bart's e-mail campaign, quickly boosted Sal's business 10 or 15 percent from its still dismal levels.

## Monday, January 14, 2002

Michael Cartier turned down an invitation to appear on the Oprah Winfrey show, though enough other victims' family members agreed to come on to complain about the victims fund that two weeks later Ken Feinberg would be offered equal time.

Instead, Cartier met with doctors in the medical examiner's office, so that he could add still more to his website about how their DNA matching process worked.

Syed Jaffri, the Pakistani seized nearly four months ago after his Bronx landlord told the INS about him, had been told that he'd be deported today, which meant that he'd finally get out of solitary in the INS lockup. But no one came for him. When he asked what had happened, the guard who watched his cell said he still needed to be "cleared" by the FBI.

Sergio Magistri finally got a stock analyst to write about his company. For a relatively small company like his that is listed on the Nasdaq exchange, getting

Wall Street to follow the company is always a challenge, and a goal. As investors and the public would come to realize more fully by the middle of this year, analysts usually say good things about a stock, once they cover it. Since the fall, when one would have thought there would have been a lot of Wall Street interest in InVision, Magistri had been in an awkward position. He was interviewing investment bankers to underwrite and manage a new stock offering for InVision, in which he'd raise money to expand by selling more stock to the public. And, as would also become even more apparent later in the year—when investigators like Spitzer, the New York attorney general, would expose conflicts between the banks' efforts to earn underwriting fees and the objectivity of their research departments—banks rarely start coverage of a stock before they get an underwriting assignment. Conversely, they almost never initiate coverage if they don't get the assignment.

Beyond that, it had made sense even for the analysts who might have been more objective to sit on the sidelines until now, while they waited to see what the legislation being talked about in Congress actually would provide in terms of the deployment of Magistri's machines.

The new year brought an end to that limbo. Magistri had chosen his underwriters for the new offering, and, today, one of them, a small outfit called Emerging Growth Equities, issued the first analysts' report on InVision.

Its initial recommendation was, of course, "Buy." And the report said that the stock, which was by now already up to $27.75 (almost nine times its $3.11 price on September 10), had a "price target" of $50, meaning that was what the analyst expected the price to be in twelve to eighteen months.

"Recent government legislation," the analyst wrote, "calls for 100 percent screening of airline passenger checked baggage by certified EDS [explosive detection machines]." Because more than one billion bags per year are checked, the analyst believed that "this could require more than 2000 EDS machines. InVision is currently ramping manufacturing capability from 7–9 machines per month . . . to 50 machines per month at the end of 2002 to meet expected demand from the United States and abroad."

The report helped boost the stock by the close of business to $30.12, or by $2.37. With Magistri owning or having options of 603,000 shares, on paper just today's bump was worth more than $1.4 million to him.


"ACLU Calls Standardized Drivers' Licenses Plan 'De Facto National ID'; Says Licensing Scheme Ineffective, Expensive, Un-American."

So read the press release the ACLU issued, which went on to say that such a plan would create a "national ID through the back door . . . to bolster a surveillance society that was not in line with basic American privacy rights and civil liberties."

The release was a response to a call by the American Association of Motor Vehicle Administrators for nationwide uniformity in the design and content of driver's licenses, which are issued by the various states—which in turn was a response to the fact that by now it was well known that the September 11 hijackers had easily obtained fraudulent but credible identification with which to board their airplanes by going to motor vehicle bureaus in states such as Virginia.

The ACLU was certainly right about one thing. This was, indeed, part of a plan, pushed by Ridge's office, to standardize strict new requirements for the issuance of driver's licenses in a way that would not create a true national identification card but would at least establish one type of card for people in all fifty states (who drive) that would be recognized as reasonably secure.

What was curious, though, was that Ridge or anyone else thought they needed to go through a back door. Even traditional liberals like Schumer, not to mention approximately two thirds of Americans who were polled about it, actually had no problem, post–September 11, with a real, candid national ID system that allowed authorities at various checkpoints to check IDs that were credible. Indeed, it seemed inevitable that as more checkpoints sprang up around the country, where guards wanted to make sure people were who they said they were, some kind of standards for identification would have to be developed by someone. Ridge's staff thought so, but they had been instructed early on by the senior White House aides that the subject of a national ID card was literally never to be discussed. It wasn't because the ACLU didn't like it; if anything, that might have been a recommendation. The real reason was that the consumer wing of the Republican party was so much against it.

So Ridge had pushed his staff to reach out to state motor vehicle officials and their national association. Their goal, just as the ACLU suspected, was to achieve a standard license that could become, de facto, a warmed-over version of the national ID that they weren't allowed to talk about.

To Schumer, some kind of sensible, secure identification system was part of that basic recalibration of the balance between security and individual liberty that simply had to be faced up to, and the fact that the Bush White House avoided even talking about it was still more proof of how they were willing to let a fringe, government-hating element of their own party block them from taking on the issues that needed to be faced in the war against terror.

The White House was working to lock up the President's State of the Union message to Congress, which Bush was to deliver in ten days. As the final budget deliberations were completed on the homeland security elements of the package, the dominance by Ridge and his staff, at least in this corner of his job, was confirmed. Ridge got everything he and his staff requested, amounting to $38 billion of new homeland security expenditures spread across more than forty agencies and concentrated in exactly the four priority areas he had mapped out. Moreover, that battle of the first responder money was resolved just the way Ridge's man Byrne wanted it—with the President proposing that the money be doled out by FEMA, not Ashcroft's Justice Department.

The way this small but bureaucratically significant victory was articulated in the budget report that would accompany the State of the Union message was equally telling in terms of Ridge's style as an infighter. Reading the document, it was almost impossible to tell that Justice had lost control of a program; the shift was literally footnoted in a way that made it impossible to detect unless you were looking for it. Though this victory came at exactly the time that the press and Capitol Hill were beginning to question and even belittle Ridge's influence, Ridge is not someone who gloats, even about winning a fiercely contested bureaucratic trench battle; and he made sure that his staff, tempted though they were, understood that, too.

Another aspect of the State of the Union message that was debated behind the scenes had to do with just what the President was prepared to ask of the country. In the days after the attacks Bush had been eloquent in defining the challenges the country faced. He had convincingly persuaded most Americans that the threat was unprecedented and meeting it was a matter of survival (and that he was the man to lead them in that battle). But beyond asking Americans to be vigilant, he had demanded no sacrifices by ordinary citizens in meeting that threat, other than going about living their lives and even shopping and buying airline tickets to boost the economy. Some on his staff now urged that he consider some kind of mandatory national service, akin to the draft, in which young Americans would have to give a year or two either in the military or in a variety of civilian jobs, ranging from domestic police work, to bioterrorism protection, or even cybersecurity. If we're really in a state of crisis, let's galvanize the country and harness all the patriotic fervor out there, they argued. But Bush and the majority of his advisors rebuffed the idea. Again, at a time when the conservative Republicans in the House were pushing even to end the government's volunteer programs because they smacked of big government, there was no way something like this would fly. Besides,

Bush argued, there is nothing patriotic about citizen participation if it's mandatory.

Another of Bruce Lawlor's Protection and Prevention division staffers chaired a meeting concerning Combat Air Patrols. These are the fighter planes that were dispatched to hover over major cities following the September 11 attacks, so that they could shoot down any aircraft that new hijackers might attempt to use as guided missiles.

Representatives of the FBI, Secret Service, FAA, CIA, Nuclear Regulatory Commission (the fighters also patrolled over nuclear reactors), National Security Council, and the Vice President's office were there. But so were people from the Department of Defense, which was conducting and paying for the flights. So after the group had begun by agreeing that the air patrols were useful in terms of defending against commercial aviation threats, especially in the New York–Washington corridor, and especially against what were euphemistically called "higher risk" foreign airliners, and after they had agreed that the flights added an important psychological dimension to homeland security, the lead Defense Department representative matter-of-factly reported that they would be making their own recommendation about the patrols to Defense Secretary Rumsfeld in a week or two. The recommendation might be to curtail the flights sharply or even eliminate them, the Pentagon man added, firmly.

When Lawlor's man asked for more details, the Pentagon man said they were not at liberty to elaborate until the Secretary had had a chance to review the recommendations.

Lawlor got a report about this stonewalling after the meeting broke, and tried to get more information from contacts he had who worked in the office of the Joint Chiefs of Staff. He, too, was told that no information was available.

So much for coordinating that aspect of homeland security.

# Tuesday, January 15, 2002

By 8:00 A.M., a line of mostly men, many in turbans and most who looked to be foreign-born, stretched nearly three blocks outside a Red Cross relief center on the corner of Canal Street and Seventh Avenue in Manhattan. They were almost all drivers of what are called dial cars, sedans that ferry heavy hitters around New York after a secretary calls and asks a dispatcher to send one so that the boss doesn't have to look for a yellow cab on the street. Having left their cars double- and triple-parked alongside the line, the men were, as one driver from Yemen put it, "waiting here to go in and get a check."

In late November, the Red Cross had vowed to give all the money to September 11 victims. Now they were doing it with a vengeance.

How these drivers came to be here was an only-in-New York, and an only-at-the-Red Cross story. About six weeks before, a dial car driver had been taking a Red Cross official around town. When asked the standard "how's business" question, he complained to his passenger that things had been lousy since September 11. He mentioned that many of the law firms and corporations that had accounts with the car company that dispatched him were located downtown, and that since the attacks, some had not reopened, while others had sharply curtailed their travel.

Trying to keep up his end of the conversation, the passenger mentioned that the Red Cross had a new program aimed at helping people who had lost their jobs because they worked downtown, or who had lost a significant part of their income even if they hadn't lost a job.

Try applying at one of the Red Cross centers, he said as he left the cab. Who knows? You might qualify.

New York cab drivers, especially those who drive dial cars, are a close community, divided into even closer sub-communities depending on their ethnicity. The Russians are always talking to each other, as are the Afghans, the Egyptians, the Pakistanis, and so on.

The driver, who was Russian, went down to the Red Cross center on Canal Street within a few days. Although he actually owns his own business—which should have disqualified him, because all Red Cross programs include a strict rule against helping even the smallest business—he was asked to come back with a letter from the company that he shares revenue with in return for it serving as his dispatcher and processing the fares that get charged by his passengers. The letter simply had to verify that many of the accounts the company's drivers serve were located in lower Manhattan. Once the Russian-born driver produced the letter, he sat down with a volunteer caseworker, who tallied up all of his monthly expenses for rent, food, health care, entertainment, and the like.

A half hour later another volunteer, hunched over a table full of people writing checks from manual checkbooks, handed him a check for several thousand dollars, representing three months of those enumerated living expenses.

Within a week, the volunteers at the center—who were from places as far-flung as Nebraska, Indiana, and Hawaii—were deluged with New York City dial car drivers from Russia.

By December, the word had spread. The Afghans and Epyptians came.

And now it seemed that every dial car driver of every ethnicity had heard about the Red Cross's eager generosity.

This morning, one driver, an Irishman from Staten Island, presented a letter from his company citing two law firms and an investment bank as accounts located near the Trade Center. In fact, all three were still in business and fully staffed. Besides, further checking would reveal the obvious—that the dispatching company had corporate accounts scattered all over Manhattan, whose executives this driver regularly picked up.

The driver then presented printouts of the fares he had been paid for one week in July and for the week of September 17. It appeared as if his income had dropped more than 60 percent since July.

But a closer look at other printouts he had with him, but which the Red Cross volunteer never asked to see, showed that his income had picked up considerably since September. And by today, the driver would later concede, he was back to within 20 percent of what he was making last year—a deficit felt by lots of New Yorkers and other Americans since September 11. (By this standard, Chubb CEO Dean O'Hare and all of his high- and mid-level executives who had lost their bonuses could have come to the Red Cross for their monthly living expenses.) Because the driver owned his house (and therefore paid no rent) but also had no mortgage left to pay on the house, he left with a relatively small check for $5,100, tax free. Six other drivers that day received checks ranging from $6,500 to $11,000, because they had rent bills due or, in one man's case, had a large payment due on home-improvement construction on his house.

The math added up to a mini-bonanza that no Red Cross donor could have had in mind: These drivers had averaged about $4,000 a month in income—before expenses—prior to September 11. If their incomes had been down even 50 percent over the entire three-month period, these *tax free* payments of $5,000 to $12,000 put them well ahead of where they would have been had the September 11 attacks never happened. And, they were told that day that they could come back at the end of three months and get another six months of payments.

One of the few non-dial-car drivers who was at the relief center that morning was a graduate student from Brooklyn. She had been working as a researcher for a company whose office was in the Trade Center. The texts and specialized newsletters she used for her research had all been stored in her office. She'd heard that she might be able to get help from the Red Cross, but was, she said, hesitant to come in because she really didn't need charity. Nonetheless, last week she'd been told by one of the volunteers that she should try to make a list of all the books and other material she had lost, find a catalogue with their prices, and then add it all up and present them with a simple statement of what it had cost. Today she was here with that one-sentence statement, asking for $4,600. She got it within twenty minutes.

After she left, the volunteer who had handled her case was asked why they had not done any checking of the list or the prices, or even tried to verify that she really needed to buy all the materials all over again. More important, why hadn't they inquired if she really needed the aid? Suppose she was Bill Gates's sister?

"Our guidelines," said Cheryl Clark, a volunteer from Reno, Nevada, "are that we don't inquire into someone's financial background too much. We don't want to make it too hard."

Sarah Baden, a sophisticated New Yorker who had done a variety of community service work since graduating from Brown the year before—and who had become so well regarded since showing up to volunteer at the Red Cross the day after the attacks that she had quickly been made a supervisor—put it more bluntly. "We were told to give the money out as fast as we could. . . . It started with a guideline that we'd only give to people who had lost at least 80 percent of their income. But by December we dropped that completely. . . . The volunteers here from around the country," Baden added, "were really getting kind of disillusioned because when they go home, they have so little money to give to people in local disasters."

Baden, too, felt disillusioned. "If someone comes in here who is just homeless, but has nothing to do with 9/11, we have to give them nothing. And these drivers are laughing about what they're getting."

By today, the Red Cross had 54,653 relief workers, 96 percent of them volunteers like Baden. Their dedication was inspiring, a tribute to the country and, indeed, to the organization that had attracted and deployed them. Sure, the sight of these hard-bitten New York cab drivers taking all of these mostly-out-of-towner, idealistic volunteers for a ride seemed like a scene out of a Woody Allen movie. But it was sad, too. None of the drivers were doing anything wrong (though that could not be said for the few hundred nondrivers who, as word spread of the giveaway, showed up with forged letters from the cab companies attesting to their bona fides). Yet they were partaking in generosity that threw the Red Cross's mission completely out of whack. Assuming 4,000 drivers ultimately got an average of $7,500 each, their

$30 million in aid would have nearly matched the $36 million dispensed by the Red Cross since 1998 to all 2.5 million victims of Hurricane Mitch in Central America.

In their hell-bent effort, in board member Kennedy's words, to "get out from under the bad press," the Red Cross's board had gotten out from under any semblance of principle.

For Brian Lyons and his co-workers, this was one of the most successful days ever at Ground Zero, if one defines success as finding remnants of four-month-old dead bodies.

The remains of eleven firefighters and several (no one could tell for sure) civilians were discovered as Lyons and the others began to dismantle a temporary truck roadway leading down into the pit, which was being replaced by a new ramp running over a cleaned-up section in the middle of the site. Lyons and other denizens of the pit had expected that a lot of remains would be found, because that old roadway had been located over what had been the lobby of the South Tower. Their assumption was that many firemen and the people they were attempting to rescue had been packed into the elevators of the South Tower, which had plunged into the lobby when the building collapsed. Still more firemen, who had been waiting in the lobby unaware of the danger of a collapse, must have perished, too.

James Brosnahan had initially assured John Lindh's parents that he would get to meet with prosecutors before they decided on what, if any, crime to charge their son with. Then again, he had also thought the lawyers involved would return his phone calls. And he never dreamed they'd go ahead and question his client once they knew he was on the case. He had lived his professional life in a world where those kinds of courtesies were observed, where lawyers treated adversaries like colleagues.

This morning marked the end of that innocence.

John Ashcroft held a press conference to announce the filing of a criminal complaint against John Walker Lindh for multiple counts of conspiring to kill Americans overseas, aiding Al Qaeda, and providing aid and support to the Taliban. The charges were punishable by sentences up to life imprisonment, although Ashcroft held out the possibility of additional charges of treason that could yield the death penalty.

Ashcroft volunteered that "the charges against Walker [Lindh] are based on voluntary statements made by Walker [Lindh] himself." He added that "prior to being interviewed by the FBI, Walker [Lindh] was informed of his Miranda rights, including his right to speak to counsel. He acknowledged that he understood each of his rights and chose to waive them both verbally and in a signed statement." Ashcroft said nothing about the conditions under which Lindh had been held and questioned.

Asked about complaints by Lindh's father and by Brosnahan that Brosnahan had not been provided access to his client, Ashcroft added, "I think it's important to understand that the subject is entitled to choose his own lawyer and, to our knowledge, he has not chosen a lawyer at this time."

Ashcroft did not mention the letters Lindh's father had sent to his son through the Red Cross telling him Brosnahan had been hired, or that these letters were never forwarded to Lindh by his captors prior to his questioning. Thus, the Attorney General was following the lead of that Justice Department lawyer's e-mail back in December, which had suggested that they deny that Brosnahan was really Lindh's lawyer.

In the same press conference, Ashcroft even took a sideswipe at his President, who had opined that Lindh was a "poor fellow" who had been "misled."

"John Walker [Lindh] chose terrorists," he said. "John Walker [Lindh] chose to fight with the Taliban, chose to train with Al Qaeda, chose to be led by Osama bin Laden. . . . Youth is not absolution for treachery."

Brosnahan was, of course, caught flat-footed by the indictment and the fact that Ashcroft chose to announce it himself in a live press conference, where he virtually promised the American people that Lindh would get life imprisonment and perhaps death if he could add on a treason charge. But even some lawyers in Ashcroft's own department were also surprised by the nature of the charges and the fact that Ashcroft took the podium to announce them. One longtime federal prosecutor, who was indirectly involved in the case, recalls that he and several colleagues had assumed that because Ashcroft had made so much of how their priorities had to change—from prosecution to prevention—that he would use the Lindh case as an example. They assumed that Ashcroft's position would be, and should be, that all of the urgent and harsh questioning of Lindh had been done in wartime conditions to get information that might prevent future attacks or even inform them of current Taliban battle positions—and that, of course, Ashcroft had to know that they could not then use this questioning in any prosecution and, in fact, that it might compromise a prosecution, as well as embarrass the Defense Department, whose initial interrogation could come under scrutiny at a trial. Instead, Ashcroft had decided to try to have his cake and eat it, too. He was trying to prevent *and* prosecute. The government would do the no-holds-barred interrogations that might prevent attacks and then use the fruits of those interrogations to prosecute. It was something these skeptical prosecutors believed would be impossible and was sure to embarrass Ashcroft and the department.

# Wednesday, January 16, 2002

Sal Iacono's voice was quivering with anger, and fear, when Hollie Bart picked up the phone this morning.* Sal said that an adjuster from the insurance company was standing in his store, in front of any customers that happened in, and openly questioning the truthfulness of the expenses he had detailed in his claim. "This doesn't look like a new door," the man claimed. It was embarrassing. What should he tell him?

Bart told Sal to give the insurance adjuster the phone. When he got on the line, she told him that if he didn't leave the store immediately, he and his company were going to be sued, and he'd regret this day for the rest of his life. He took Bart's advice.

Within a week Bart and Lynn Geerdes had worked their way up the ladder of the legal department at the St. Paul insurance company and gotten a new, senior claims executive assigned to Sal's case.

But as good as Bart was, and as much as she was determined to find all ways to skin a cat, by now she was clearly missing a trick. Turned off by her initial attempts to get Red Cross help for Sal in mid-November, she didn't realize what the Yemeni dial car drivers did—that she or even Sal alone could go down to the Red Cross center on Canal Street and get three months, and then maybe another six months, of all his personal family expenses paid. True, he was a business owner and the Red Cross didn't give aid to businesses; Bart had seen that written in black and white when she and Geerdes had catalogued the Red Cross program into their loose-leaf book. But, meticulous lawyer that she is, Bart had taken that too literally. Like the dial car drivers, Sal could easily have presented himself as a self-employed person whose income had dropped. There is simply no way that in mid-January his claim would have been denied.

-------

*Iacono and Bart are not certain this encounter with the insurance adjuster happened today. This is their best guess.

By now, many of the victims' family members who had joined the Cartiers in their first meeting with Mayor Giuliani had splintered off and were leading other groups, in part because the Cartiers were anxious that Give Your Voice keep the recovery of remains as its main priority. It wasn't that they disagreed with families that wanted to focus more on what they believed to be the unfairness of the victims fund, or, in another case, on the need to investigate structural failings in the Trade Center buildings that had allowed them to collapse. It was just a matter of sticking to what really mattered to them.

Tonight, Anthony Gardner, who had come with the Cartiers to the Giuliani meeting and had since started WTC United Families Group, appeared on New York's local cable news channel to talk about a rally he and the other groups had organized for the next night to protest the rules Feinberg had promulgated for the fund. Predicting a large turnout, Gardner charged that "Mr. Feinberg has blatant disregard for the needs of the families."

Earlier that evening, Feinberg had given people like Gardner the ammunition to make that kind of over-the-top charge. It was really a matter of style, not substance—in this case, Feinberg's way of turning himself almost into a parody of a shark lawyer by using insensitive rhetoric to defend positions that would otherwise be defensible. For all his glibness and charm in talking with lawyers in small groups, he had an awful bedside manner in talking to these citizen-victims, perhaps, in fact, because he's spent his whole life negotiating with fellow lawyers.

The scene was a meeting with the leaders of groups such as Give Your Voice and the other organizations, including Gardner's, that had since cropped up.

Jennie Farrell was there representing Give Your Voice, and she had brought her father, Patrick Cartier, Sr.

The elder Cartier stood, holding Feinberg's chart that showed presumed awards matched to the victim's age and income. Trembling with anger, Cartier said that the chart seemed to value his son James's life at $320,000. Since he would probably have worked another forty years, that in turn meant that Feinberg valued his son's work at $8,000 a year. How could Feinberg justify that?

In fact, Cartier had read the chart incorrectly. It had set economic damages for James at about $700,000. And he had also left out the provision for pain and suffering that would add another $250,000, yielding a total of about $950,000 in cash, tax free. Also, Cartier, not being a banker or accountant, hadn't included in his equation that being paid cash now was worth four or five times what it was worth if paid out over forty years.

But instead of simply saying he would be glad to meet with him and look at the numbers, Feinberg had pressed Cartier. Learning that he was the father of a dead victim and, therefore, not a dependent who was relying on James's earnings, Feinberg said, "We could, in fact, start with the question of why you are entitled to any compensation at all." If not for the fund, "you would be entitled to nothing," he continued, adding, "We're the only game in town."

Under the laws of New York state that was true. But it wasn't what Cartier needed to hear, or what Feinberg needed to tell him. Jennie and her father stormed out of the room. The others who stayed booed and then asked still more hostile questions. One police officer, whose wife had been killed, yelled that Feinberg's standard pain and suffering offer—in his case, $350,000 because his wife had left a spouse and one child—"spits at my wife, spits on my son." Under the plan he was also entitled to about a million dollars in economic damages.

# Thursday, January 17, 2002

Today was the first of the new Transportation Security Administration's deadlines. Although there was no quick way to set things up so that every piece of checked luggage could be screened for explosives, Congress had decided that there was one interim measure that could be put in place almost immediately. So as of today, all checked luggage had to be matched with a passenger who boarded a plane. If the passenger didn't end up presenting his boarding card at a gate, then the luggage had to be removed. That way someone couldn't check a bag with a bomb and then leave.

There were two obvious problems with this security measure that made it little more than cosmetic. First, the September 11 hijackers hadn't been worried about their own safety, so, of course, they'd get on board with a bomb in the cargo area.

Second, under the system implemented today, a passenger whose flight stopped anywhere or who had to change planes could still get off. That was because the airlines and airport executives had lobbied TSA relentlessly not to impose a luggage match system for transfers or flights that had stopovers. That would paralyze air travel, they claimed.

Larry Cox, whose Memphis airport is a key hub, was among the leaders in this rebellion. He depended so much on transfers that he openly told anyone who would listen—his trade association, the local press, his congressional delegation, his airline representatives—that he'd be shut down in a matter of hours if a baggage match system including transfers was mandated. The result was a plainly absurd security regulation, the equivalent of closing two of four windows in a parked car.

The only rationale that Mineta, Jackson, and Magaw (the new TSA head) could offer was that by beginning this cursory bag match, they were laying the groundwork for a complete system, including stopovers and transfers.

Meantime, their go teams paid scant attention to this deadline, because they knew it was meaningless. Instead, by now they were worrying about an issue that loomed far larger: Based on their own initial surveys and calculations and on what their McKinsey consultants (who had just signed a $500,000 contract) were starting to report, it looked like the number of new, federalized screeners they were going to have to hire—the number that had been estimated at 28,000 when the legislation had been passed—was going to be larger. A lot larger.

The Southern California branch of Romero's American Civil Liberties Union sued the TSA to challenge a provision in the new law that prohibited noncitizens from being airport security screeners. The citizenship requirement seemed logical—and certainly reflected the sentiments of the congressmen who had complained to the Argenbright lobbyists about seeing men in turbans working at checkpoints. But on closer look, the merits of the restriction weren't nearly as obvious. Legal immigrants who are not citizens are allowed to work as baggage handlers, flight attendants, airline pilots, mechanics, and plane cleaners. More than that, they are allowed to be in the U.S. military.

In fact, one of the ACLU's plaintiffs in the suit was twenty-one-year-old Jeimy Gebin, whose family had fled the civil war in El Salvador when she was five, and who had served in the U.S. Army for three years. Another was a reserve member of the Philippines army and a licensed security guard. A third, also from the Philippines, was a longtime screener who had risen to supervisor and said that in the last two years she had complained to her company that they were making a mistake by allowing people on board with small knives and razor blades.

Although the Justice Department was obligated to defend the constitutionality of any law passed by Congress, no one at TSA was anxious to defend the citizenship requirement. For in cities like San Francisco and Los Angeles (the two airports where the ACLU's plaintiffs worked), 80 percent of the screeners were noncitizens. Most were from communities of Latin American or Philippines immigrants, where the word has spread years ago that there were good jobs to be had at the airports. Due to unionization and other factors at these two airports, wages had become high enough that these screeners were good workers whose turnover was low. This was true, even though many of the gates were manned by Argenbright employees; in these airports the Argenbright people had reputations for doing good work. All of which meant that TSA would have loved to include them in the pool of people they hoped to recruit into the federal force.

Nonetheless, the suit seemed a sure loser, for the courts would almost certainly rule that Congress had the authority, even if used mistakenly, to require that people in such jobs be citizens.

The state-owned Park Avenue Armory, on 64th Street and Park Avenue in New York, has been best known in recent years for its antiques shows and the charity balls attended by its Upper East Side neighbors. But since September 11, the state had used it as a staging area for National Guard units, and tonight Governor Pataki had made it available to the families of the victims for a rally to complain about what had become known as the Feinberg Fund.

Somewhere between 700 and 1,000 people, plus reporters and camera crews from most media outlets, showed up for the 7:00 P.M. protest. Michel "Mitch" Baumeister, an aviation disaster plaintiffs lawyer with offices in New York and New Jersey, was allowed to set up shop at tables in the front, where his assistants handed out information packets that included his "comments" on Feinberg's rules. On the stage were leaders of the now half dozen family groups that by now had been organized, including Jennie Farrell representing Give Your Voice.

Along the wall of the armory, family members stood holding up posters for the TV cameras, such as: "Mr. Feinberg: There Is Only One Special Master, And My Son Is with Him"; "When Did We Start to Penalize People for Paying Insurance?"; or "Try Being Us, Mr. Feinberg."

A representative of Senator Jon Corzine was introduced, who promised that Corzine was going to push legislation to repeal the provision in the law requiring Feinberg to deduct life insurance payments from his awards. Corzine, a sophisticated former investment banker who had run for the Senate as someone above politics, had voted for the bill that required those deductions, and a month before he had told the author that he thought the law establishing the fund had been "well done."

An economist from Newark's Seton Hall University was introduced to complain that the Feinberg calculations for a person's work life were based on old statistics and that Feinberg hadn't included anything for the value of the "services," such as guidance to the children, that the victims had provided, and would have continued to provide, to their families.

But it was when Jennie Farrell introduced Governor Pataki that it was hard not to be embarrassed at this awful American spectacle of panderer and panderees.

"Every person who died was a hero," Pataki began after the standing ovation had died down. "I deeply believe that the draft regulations Mr. Feinberg has put out are terrible," he continued. "Where in America is a family member required to sign away rights before they have any idea of what they'll get," the governor thundered. In fact, Feinberg had made it clear that applicants could come to the fund and get an estimate of their award before formally applying. Besides, the provision that they give up the right to sue once they do formally apply was in the law—voted for by members of Congress in Pataki's party and signed by the Republican President—not in any Feinberg regulation.

"Who in America believes," the governor went on, now getting his rhythm, "that the people who held cookie sales and went door to door intended that money to offset the federal fund?" Hadn't Pataki, or at least someone on his staff, heard that Feinberg had long since specifically ruled, with lots of accompanying headlines, that all money from charities was *not* going to be offset? Even the audience chuckled at that one.

More generally, did Pataki understand that had the airlines not been bailed out from liability, they would almost certainly have gone bankrupt and none of these people could have collected anything in lawsuits against them? Or that proving that the airlines or anyone else other than the hijackers were at fault in such suits would have been a huge risk, and would have involved five or ten years of litigation and contingent fees to lawyers of a third to 40 percent?

"Your courage will never be forgotten," Pataki continued after waiting for another ovation to die down. "You represent the best of America—a commitment to go on with your lives. . . . Thank you for your courage."

Had his staff not told him that, however brave and sympathetic the families were, he was at a rally that was solely about the money they would get?

Next up was Baumeister, the plaintiffs lawyer, who gave what he would later characterize as "a quick and dirty once-over," entitled "The Law, the Lies, and the Facts."

As the Republican governor happily worked the crowd, Baumeister declared that "The heroes of 9/11 are now being treated by the Bush Office of Management and Budget, in the White House, and by Kenneth Feinberg as simply a budgetary problem. A liability. . . . It has intentionally been written that way so that the budget will be met, and the memory of your loved ones will be sacrificed. . . . You are being lied to. Feinberg is making up what's in the law.

"We're not going away," Baumeister continued, putting himself at one with the crowd, although they were the ones with dead relatives and he was the one hoping for contingent fees. "Never again," he concluded to another standing ovation. "Stay strong. Never again."

## Friday, January 18, 2002

Sergio Magistri made it onto NBC's *Today* show, live from his Silicon Valley assembly line, where it was 4:45 A.M. With the press now starting to focus on the new aviation security law's mandate that all baggage be screened for bombs, *Today* did a feature showing Magistri demonstrating how his machine could detect a bomb hidden in a radio that was packed into a suitcase.

Magistri's stock closed today at $34.62. It was now more than ten times what it had traded for on September 10.

## Saturday, January 19, 2002

Eileen Simon and her children drove to a day-long retreat for New Jersey spouses and children of September 11 victims. It was at a school about a half hour away and was run by a program called the Comfort Zone, a Virginia-based group of volunteers whose goal was to help children who have lost a parent.

For Brittany Simon, twelve, and her two brothers, MJ, ten, and Tyler, five, it was their third such Comfort Zone session since November. They were starting to make friends with the children there, who were their age and had something awful in common. A volunteer sat with a half dozen or more kids, grouped by age, and gently prodded them to talk about the loved one they had lost (who was usually a father). By today's session, the group leader didn't have to push much; they had become comfortable discussing what they couldn't really discuss with the kids in school. Plus, they loved the fact that the Comfort Zone's volunteers included a lot of male adults, something they missed badly at home.

Eileen thought the adult part of the Comfort Zone experience was a bit of a chore, especially the "awkward moments when these Virginians thought they could get us jaded New York widows to dance and sing in a circle."

By now, Eileen had pushed ahead with getting her children into weekly groups of September 11 kids, and in the case of the younger Tyler, some personal counseling. Brittany and MJ liked their sessions, which made all the driving Eileen now had to do to shuttle them around seem worth it. But Tyler still seemed just plain spooked. He'd draw pictures during his meetings with a therapist of airplanes crashing into buildings, and at night he'd often say a prayer hoping that "God gets Osama bin Laden and his team of bad guys."

Eileen herself had joined, not one, but two groups of women that each met once a week to talk about everything from helping their children, to the victims fund, to their own loneliness. One included women from a wider geographic and demographic circle, and Eileen hadn't really warmed to it yet. But she already liked the second group, which met every Friday. There were six women, including two Cantor Fitzgerald widows. A third was a fireman's widow, and although ultimately there would be some unspoken but natural jealousy in the group over all the extra charity funds she would be entitled to, the group would soon form such close bonds that Simon would consider them her best friends.

# Monday, January 21, 2002

"Ninety-one thousand?" shouted go teams leader Kip Hawley. "That's insane. How could it be ninety-one thousand?"

After the chaotic two weeks Gale Rossides had now spent in meetings on the fly with the TSA go teams and the steadily growing full-time staff, it would have seemed that nothing could surprise her, or any of them.

This was a surprise. The best estimate from the McKinsey consultants was that to do all the passenger and carry-on baggage screening at the gates and to operate the explosive detection machines for checked baggage would take a force of 91,000 new federal agents.

Ninety-one thousand. That was more than three times as much as the entire FBI, ten times as much as Customs. Eighteen times as much as the Secret Service.

And more than three times as much, and three times as costly, as the 28,000-person, $2 billion estimate provided by Congress when the TSA bill had been passed.

What had gone wrong? For starters, it was going to take 15,000 to 25,000 people to screen all the checked luggage for bombs, with the amount depending on what mix of InVision machines and those smaller, more labor-intensive trace detection machines they used. Beyond that, Hawley's and Deputy Secretary Jackson's circles of protection required all kinds of new people, as did the simple reality that the old, private screeners had done slipshod work in part because they had been severely understaffed.

Since the law had passed in mid-November, all kinds of numbers had been whispered about internally. By now everyone, from Transportation Secretary Mineta and Jackson on down, knew the number was going to be much higher than the 28,000. But this was the first week that anyone surfaced a real number. The reckoning was worse than anyone had imagined. The private sector people were astonished. How could Congress pass a law and underestimate the cost of implementing it by a factor of three, one of the go team guys remarked during one of the meetings quickly called to deal with the number. "Because they can just blame us," Jackson said.

The good news was that eliminating one position in one of those protection circles had an enormous multiplier effect. The math worked this way: There were a total of about 1,750 checkpoints at the nation's 429 airports. Each job at each checkpoint required an average of four people to cover seven days a week, because people only work eight-hour shifts for five days a week, and they take vacations and get sick. Therefore, as one Magaw aide pointed out in one of these early meetings, each position that gets eliminated results in 7,000 jobs ($4 \times 1,750$) eliminated—which is more than the entire staff of the Secret Service.

Jackson, who was so hands-on that he quickly jumped into the fray once he heard the 91,000 number, asked why the person taking a bag from a conveyor belt to the InVision machine for checking needed to be a federal agent. Couldn't we just do a background check on him and keep him as a baggage handler? That was 7,000 jobs right there.

Rossides watched in amazement. They were making personnel decisions that had enormous budget and operational implications, yet they had no way to be sure that what they were doing here in the war room would have any relation to reality once they got out into an airport and tried to see how many people it really would take to do it right without creating the kinds of waiting lines that would kill the industry. She and everyone else knew that. But they also knew that they had to start somewhere, rather than sit there paralyzed by the unknowable. They had to postulate some scenario that made some kind of budget sense, then go out and see if they could make it work. It was scary. And exhilarating.

# Wednesday, January 23, 2002

Ken Feinberg knew that the attacks on his regulations would come from all sides. He'd even joked with Ted Kennedy about it. But deep down, he also thought that reason would prevail and that it would quickly become clear to the victims that his was, indeed, "the only game in town." Yet as of today only 250 people had applied to his fund. It had now been a month since the draft regulations had been issued. The program guaranteed an immediate $50,000 and the rest within 120 days of Feinberg making an award. Still, most weren't biting.

Perhaps because he didn't yet appreciate how the charities had covered so much of the immediate cash needs of so many of the families, while life insurance payouts had provided even more to people like Eileen Simon, Feinberg was surprised that more people weren't signing up faster.

This morning in Ridgewood, New Jersey, he got a firsthand lesson in what was holding them back. His audience of about 150 were mostly well-dressed widows from the New Jersey suburbs, who arrived at a local courthouse in Suburbans, Lexuses, and BMWs. Several sat with babies in their laps.

Feinberg, standing at a lectern in front of the courtroom, ran through the basics of his program. His voice boomed a bit too loud, his words came a little too quickly, and his promise to get to another subject "in a minute" became more annoying the more he repeated the phrase. Yet he seemed to talk to these people like he was trying to help them. He wasn't defensive. He used no legalese.

"You give up your right to sue, before you know what you're going to get," someone complained.

Feinberg answered that although the statute seemed to require that, he had developed three ways around the problem. First, they could look at the presumptive awards on the charts, something they could ask a lawyer or other advisor to help them with. Second, they could watch his website and see what other, similarly situated people got. (To preserve privacy, names and identifying details would not be given on the website, but enough specifics would be provided to give them a good idea.) Third, and most important, they could make an appointment to come see him or a member of his staff and get an estimate of an award calculated in advance. It would not be binding, but "you would be able to trust me."

"Why should we trust you?" someone yelled from the back.

"Because if I don't make good on those estimates, I'm sure you'll hear about it."

When someone asked what would happen to the money if there was no will, Feinberg reported that the estimates he had seen were that only 25 percent of all the families had had wills—which meant that in three quarters of the cases the money would be divided up according to how the state where the deceased person had lived dictated it be divided. (In New Jersey, that meant a spouse gets half and the children split the other half.)

A woman stood up to complain that because she didn't have children and her husband had no will, under her state's law "my mother-in-law will get half, and she didn't suffer at all. I'll get one twentieth of my loss and she'll get twenty times her loss."

Feinberg said maybe he could talk to the mother-in-law for her and get her to be reasonable. She smiled a teary smile and said, "That's not likely."

A baby let out a wail. Her mother, toting a Prada bag, shot up from her seat to take her out into the hall.

Someone asked if she could come to Feinberg's office and provide proof of her husband's real potential for earnings growth, potential that was "way beyond the formula [for assumed income growth over the years] in your charts."

"You could," said Feinberg, "but it'll have to be more than a letter from someone saying he was a star and would have made a lot of money."

It was that kind of truthful but unvarnished response that alienated the group. Feinberg just didn't have any kind of bedside manner.

"You should talk to a lawyer about what kind of proof you can present."

"What if we don't want to hire a lawyer," someone shouted.

"Then talk to an advisor, or come ask me or someone on my staff."

Another baby cried.

One woman asked why she shouldn't be compensated for the value of her husband's lawn mowing and other services, such as cleaning the pool. Feinberg said it was unlikely that he could help her with that.

Someone else stood and talked about her life partner, another woman who had died. What could she recover?

That depended on whether New Jersey changed its law to recognize same sex partners, Feinberg replied.

One woman complained that she had five kids, ages two to nine, to support, but she'd get zero because of the deductions to be made from any award for life insurance policy payouts, which in her case amounted to $2 million. This brought on a barrage of more complaints, even catcalls, about life insurance offsets. The one who complained most adamantly was the woman who was hosting the meeting—Marge Roukema, the longtime Republican congresswoman from this area of New Jersey. She declared that her constituents were being destroyed by this unfair rule.

When Feinberg reminded the group, and the congresswoman, that the insurance offsets were specifically in the law that Congress had passed, Roukema blurted out, "I voted for it, but I didn't understand the full implications of what I voted for." Some laughed at their hapless congresswoman. Others booed. Someone yelled out, "What else didn't you understand? . . . How in blazes could Congress vote and not know about the insurance?"

"This is a travesty," a heavyset man in the far right corner yelled.

Roukema recovered to tell her audience that she was co-sponsoring legislation to repeal the offsets, but Feinberg politely said that it was unrealistic to expect Congress to pass anything like that. "You should see the letters I get attacking the whole program, or asking, 'What about the Oklahoma City victims?' " he added.

As Feinberg looked at his watch and said that he had to leave soon, another heavyset man in the back asked about pensions being offset, and about Social Security. A chorus of "yeahs" followed.

Feinberg, who had by now begun to understand the widespread concern about the Social Security, workers' compensation, and pension offset issues, seemed to welcome the question. "There are pensions and there are pensions," he said. "Many won't be offset. The same is true for workers' compensation and Social Security. We are looking at that right now. I think an argument can be made that no workers' comp should be offset and most Social Security should not be offset. I'm doing my best to make sure no one gets zero because of this. My goal," he continued, adding something that would have surprised Mitch Daniels back at the Office of Management and Budget, "is to deduct as little in the way of offsets as possible. I'm really going to do my best."

This got the attention of a blond woman in the first row, who had had her hand up through most of the question period. Now, she waved it more purposefully.

"Widows only," said Roukema.

"I am a widow, that much I know," the blonde replied with a chuckle. Then she turned to Feinberg.

"Uh, I have to tell you that you're saying you're doing your best is not enough," she said with a smile. "You have to tell us. What are the rules?" Her face now lost its smile. She stood up, and continued. "In the beginning I felt like you were on my side. Then you put out the regulations, and I'm being told I get zero. I have three children and with their Social Security and workers' comp I get zero. I was counting on you, I really was, to do the right thing. You seem like a decent person. But I can't stand watching them rebuild Afghanistan while America turns its back on me. . . . I have had a huge American flag on my porch since September 12. I want to love that flag."

It was Eileen Simon.

Feinberg, in fact, recognized her, because she's not easy to forget and because she had buttonholed him last month at the first Cantor Fitzgerald meeting to ask about the same thing.

But since that first meeting, Simon had learned the details of the workers' comp and Social Security issues cold. She had consulted both a lawyer at Kreindler's firm, referred to her by people at Cantor Fitzgerald, and a lawyer at her sister's old Wall Street law firm. In fact, a week ago she'd gotten those two lawyers and people from the Justice Department who had worked on Feinberg's regulations on a conference call. When she'd rattled off what she said she thought the workers' comp and Social Security payouts to each of her children and to her were worth, everyone else seemed to doubt her. But as the conversation dragged on and reconvened after the person at Justice got off to check Simon's numbers with others in the government, they all soon concluded that she was right.

Now Simon stood in front of Feinberg, reading from her notes the dollar-by-dollar presumed value of what to Feinberg and apparently everyone else in the government had seemed to be minimally relevant benefits. "Under your rules, as you have written them, I get zero; in fact I get less than zero," Simon concluded.

Feinberg would later recall that after Simon stood up and spoke that morning about the problem and seemed so sure about it, he made a note to himself that he had to go back to Washington and nail down how to deal with workers' comp and Social Security. The lawyers at Justice, working with people at the Labor Department, had handled all that. Had they gotten it wrong? Worse, had they sandbagged him into putting out regulations that were budget-friendly but would screw the victims?

"The blonde with all the numbers really got to me," is how he later put it.

## Thursday, January 24, 2002

John Lindh made his first appearance in court to be arraigned on the various charges that Ashcroft had brought against him. Yesterday, he had met Brosnahan for the first time and been reunited with his parents. He gratefully accepted their choice of Brosnahan as his lawyer.

Randy Bellows, a superstar federal prosecutor, who would soon become a Virginia judge, urged that Lindh be held without bail. Brosnahan complained to the magistrate that the government's entire case was based on statements Lindh had allegedly made to an FBI interrogator, but that he had asked for a lawyer a week before he had been questioned by the agent.

Lindh was held without bail. Outside the courtroom, Brosnahan urged reporters and the public not to prejudge this "twenty-year-old young man," and charged that "for fifty-four days, while he was kept incommunicado, officials in the federal government leaked or stated their understanding of the case against him."

Later in the day, Ashcroft responded by declaring, "Walker [Lindh] knowingly and purposefully allied himself with terror. He chose to embrace fanatics, and his allegiance to them never faltered, not with the knowledge that they had murdered thousands of his countrymen, not with the knowledge that they were engaged in a war with the United States, and not, finally, in the prison uprising that took the life of CIA agent Johnny Spann."

## Sunday, January 27, 2002

Many Sunday newspapers featured articles about the September 11 families' unhappiness with the rules Feinberg had laid out for the victims fund. But in a new twist, almost all had some kind of man-in-the-street quote calling the families greedy. Meantime, Michael Cartier, still stewing from a Wednesday *Wall Street Journal* article that he thought unfairly lumped him with other family groups as being on the front lines of the protest against the fund (when he thought he had repeatedly stressed that his priority was concern about the recovery), sat at the computer desk in his living room poring through what were now thousands of entries in the "bad mail" folder.

"I've really screwed this up," he told his wife, Michele. "This website has one page about the damn fund and twenty-six links about the recovery, and look at how we've come off. Thirty thousand hits this month, and most from people who think we're greedy. . . . I see a woman stand up at these meetings with a rock [diamond] on her finger and $3 million or $4 million in life insurance and she wants $2 million more, and I'm just as disgusted as anyone. But you'd never know that."

# Monday, January 28, 2002

The Justice Department's public affairs staff revealed to reporters that as a result of a visit that John Ashcroft had made to Salt Lake City to review security arrangements for the upcoming Winter Olympics, "major changes" were going to be made because Ashcroft had found that some parts of the venue were "not adequately protected."

The resulting headlines infuriated Tom Ridge's staff and surprised everyone at the White House.

One of Ridge's responsibilities was overseeing what are called National Special Security Events. Under a program begun during the Clinton administration, these were high-profile events for which the Secret Service took over the coordination of all security arrangements. Working under the direction of a new staff person borrowed from the Secret Service, Ridge's office was now overseeing all local, state, and federal agencies involved in the Olympics security effort.

Ten days ago, Ridge had gone out to Salt Lake City to review the elaborate security arrangements, after which he made the rounds of the TV news shows, assuring Americans that while nothing could ever be completely safe anymore, the Olympics site would be more secure than any venue of its kind ever. "I'm absolutely convinced that one of the safest places on the face of the earth from February 8 through February 24 will be the Olympic venues," Ridge told CNN's Larry King.

Ridge hadn't even known that a few days after his visit, Ashcroft had stopped by the Olympics while on a skiing holiday with his family. It turned out that during his brief tour, Ashcroft had remarked, offhandedly, that he thought that perhaps there should be more police stationed in some of the open-air parts of the venue. Today his staff, led by two aides in his office who had worked for him when he was a senator, had turned this into the announcement about major changes, which, of course, Ashcroft had absolutely no authority to order—and which were never made.

Some on Ridge's staff laughed it off as the Ashcroft people's effort to rationalize a ski trip. Others were angrier, seeing it as part of the Attorney General's insistence that anything related to the war on terror belonged to him, not to some White House coordinator.

Ridge kept quiet. He never said a word publicly about it. The next time he saw Ashcroft, he said something to the effect that he hadn't known the Attorney General had been out to the Olympics. Ashcroft smiled and said the whole thing was a mix-up, that the mayor of one of the towns in the Olympics venue had asked him to get more agents out there as a show of force, that he must have said something that implied that he agreed, and that his staff must have misinterpreted that. You know how staffs can be, he added.

## Thursday, January 31, 2002

The Red Cross held a press conference at its New York chapter to report on how it had been fulfilling the promise to dispense all the money it had raised as a result of the September 11 attacks only on September 11 victims.

In addition to chairman David McLaughlin and interim CEO Harold Decker, George Mitchell, the former Senate Majority Leader, was on hand. As part of a Red Cross effort to restore public confidence in its handling of September 11 funds, Mitchell had agreed in December to serve as the organization's pro bono independent overseer in charge of the September 11 disaster relief fund.

McLaughlin and Mitchell reported that out of $850 million raised, $490 million had been dispensed. Their plan for the remaining $360 was that $180 million more would go to the families of those killed or injured, $60 million would go to people who had been economically injured, $80 million would go for long-term relief services, such as mental health care and family support services, and $40 million would be spent on other ongoing services, such as meals for disaster workers.

In other words, the plan basically mimicked what the September 11th

Fund was going to do. The difference was that the September 11th Fund was giving grants to other organizations that had been carefully chosen for their experience in administering programs like these. The Red Cross was going to spend the money all on its own, which, as the fiasco with the dial car drivers showed, was a recipe for continued abuses and inefficiencies. The Red Cross had no experience in running these kinds of projects. No one on its staff or board really knew how these hundreds of millions would actually get spent, and, in fact, the only strong sentiment on the board was to get the whole mess over with. The money, after all, was only there because the board had decided it had to "get out from under" the bad publicity by spending it all on September 11 victims—a group of charity recipients whom the board now believed were the least needy people ever to be aided by the Red Cross. Indeed, some Red Cross executive board members bitterly joked among themselves about how they had been boxed into devoting hundreds of millions of dollars to people who needed it far less than any victims in the organization's history.

When one reporter asked if today's announcements meant that it would now be "easier" for people to get aid, McLaughlin said that it simply meant that programs were continuing in a way consistent with his promise in November to spend it all on the victims.

What the press still didn't appreciate was that, as those dial cab drivers knew, it couldn't get any easier.

But by early next week that perception would change. *Newsweek* published an article detailing the dial car drivers' good fortune.* And an article in the *Wall Street Journal* appeared, describing how Red Cross volunteers were going out and ringing doorbells at six- and seven-figure condos in the TriBeCa area near the Trade Center, asking these wealthy people if they wanted charity.

By the middle of that week, the Red Cross would do "a complete 180," according to Sarah Baden, the young New York volunteer who had quickly become a supervisor. "We had a meeting and were told that the limo drivers program was over immediately, as was the TriBeCa outreach." Instead, much of that money, earmarked at the press conference just the week before as aid to economic victims, was quietly shifted to the "long-term needs" category, where no one really knew how it would ultimately be spent.

Asked about those shifts and the controversy a week later, Senator Mitchell had what may have been the most balanced perspective about it all. Sure, there had been mistakes, he said. But the Red Cross, in deploying tens

---

*The author was also the author of that article.

of thousands of volunteers and collecting and dispensing so much aid, had done a great service to the country. That was true, whatever the abuses.

Moreover, Mitchell's view of the organization's lurches one way and then the other—first being too slow with the aid, then being too quick to write checks—applied to much of the overall challenge of the September 12 era. "When I was chairman of the Senate Finance Committee," Mitchell recalled, "people used to want simple tax rules. And they wanted fair tax rules. But I always found that fairness is the enemy of simplicity, and simplicity is the enemy of fairness. . . . Make the tax code simple, and it's unfair, because you don't tax people according to their ability to pay. If you keep the Red Cross process simple, and let people come and get their Red Cross checks quickly, then some of it will be unfair. Some people will steal. Others will get money they wouldn't get if you took the time to make them fill out forms showing their real need. But if you try to make it fair—to give people what they need and no more and no less—then it can't be simple."

It was an analysis that, of course, ignored the Red Cross board's own lack of backbone. It ignored the fact that pre-Mitchell, and even now with the publication of the stories about the dial car drivers and the TriBeCa condo outreach, the board had simply turned tail when the publicity got bad and had thrown a program out, rather than working to fix it. It ignored the fact that back in November, they could have avoided this kind of fiasco by going back, candidly, to the public and saying that they'd collected too much for these particular victims, that they actually had more than they needed, and that they now wanted to use the rest of it for the organization's other, longer-term needs that were not related to these victims—and if any of the donors didn't like that, they could contact the organization and get a quick refund. They could even have done so by going on O'Reilly's show. Whatever else can be said about him, O'Reilly loves to give his targets airtime.

Still, Mitchell's point that fairness and simplicity are usually at war with each other was an insight that others fighting other September 12 battles, such as Feinberg, would soon appreciate.

Bruce Lawlor, the general who is Ridge's Protection and Prevention chief, convened a meeting of representatives of the Justice Department and state and local police chiefs to hear a company called Acxiom talk about how its expertise in something called "data mining" could help secure the homeland. Acxiom had recently entered into a secret contract with the FBI and Justice Department for a pilot project.

Ironically, Acxiom, a publicly held company based in Little Rock, Arkansas, had gotten its introduction to the Justice Department courtesy of a prominent hometown booster whom one would not have expected to have much juice in the Bush administration. Former President Bill Clinton had called Ashcroft to recommend that he meet with them. Clinton, who knew Ashcroft from their days together as state attorneys general and governors, told him that Acxiom offered a shortcut through all the database problems he knew Ashcroft and the FBI had.

When one of Lawlor's people got wind of the fact that Justice was now talking to Acxiom about helping the FBI collect investigative data, he asked for a presentation that would include local law enforcement agencies that had similar needs.

In fact, as a result of this meeting, Lawlor and his people also planned to get Acxiom in to see other federal agencies that badly needed help in this area. TSA, for example, was trying to come up with a new way to profile airline passengers who would be singled out for special hand searches after they had cleared the regular screening process. The current process, called CAPPS (computer-assisted prescreening passenger system), used pathetically simplistic criteria. For example, if you bought a one-way ticket, especially for cash, and did not use a frequent flier program, you were almost certain to be singled out.

Acxiom could do a lot better than that. Private corporations now used Acxiom to burrow through all kinds of data that Acxiom bought and compiled to find people with the characteristics they most wanted. If a company was starting a magazine for wealthy travelers, Acxiom might be able to find a million members of frequent flier clubs who charged more than $1,000 a month to credit cards, and who bought goods at certain high-end luggage and clothing shops. Or, if a bank wanted to solicit people for a premium credit card, Acxiom could find two or three million prospects who had the economic and personal stability it sought, such as having had the same employer, having earned more than $100,000 a year for three years, and having lived at the same address for five years.

Or, if you were the FBI looking for people who moved around a lot, opened multiple bank and charge accounts, used public Internet outlets, and rented cars in lots of different places for different people—in other words if you were looking for people who fit what might be a potential terrorist profile—Acxiom or its competitors could find them, too.

In fact, the proficiency of the Acxioms of the world compared to the kinds of data the FBI or TSA could now gather illustrated a key September 12 era dilemma. FBI guidelines, promulgated after the Watergate and Vietnam era abuses of the 1970s, prohibited agents from even looking at public websites or attending public meetings, let alone, in the absence of a warrant, checking credit or other private records. Yet that data was freely sold in public markets to private companies like Acxiom. In other words, someone who wanted to start a magazine or a clothing store had far more free range to find out about people than the FBI did in its war against terrorists.

In the sense that no Americans wanted the government to become a big-brother storehouse of information about everyone's buying and living habits, that made sense. But did it make sense when it came to using all available tools to identify people who might be part of a terrorist cell, or at least might make it into a high enough risk category to deserve an airport pat-down more than someone who hadn't joined the US Airways frequent flier program?

There was another subtle Ridge strategy at work in this meeting. Ridge, a former governor, felt strongly that state and local police and other agencies had to be part of any real homeland security effort. After all, they vastly out-numbered federal forces and were the real troops on the front lines. Yet the FBI historically hadn't wanted to share information with the CIA, let alone with local yokels. By presenting the possibility of a new kind of information that could be shared across the federal-local network because it was from public sources and not from the FBI, Lawlor was attempting to tee up at least one platform where the feds and the locals could trade information.*

# Friday, February 1, 2002

January turned out not to be as bad a month as Larry Cox had expected. Passenger traffic had started to pick up and was down only 21 percent from the year before. Meantime, cargo was booming. Because FedEx was getting so much extra business from customers who had been using the Post Office, overall cargo handled out of Memphis in January was up 47 percent from the prior year, giving Memphis an even greater lead as the world's number one cargo airport, and giving Cox great revenue results from landing fees, even as his take from passenger-generated concessions and parking continued to lag.

Cox, however, had a new worry—the new Transportation Security

---

*By year-end, however, local police would still be left on their own to get data-mining information. The FBI and Justice Department refused, following this meeting, to proceed with a discussion about sharing the data.

Administration, with its new congressionally mandated deadlines. There seemed to be no way they could meet those deadlines, and, in his mind, their determination to do so threatened what by now had become the relatively smoothed-out, secure operations at his airport. Where would they put those huge explosive detection machines? Would he have to get his floors reinforced? Would he have to displace Graceland or some of the other concessions to make room for them? What was the plan? These feds were going to come in and take over his security operations, but he'd heard nothing from them. And when he'd tried to ask his local FAA representative what was going on, the FAA man said that he, too, knew nothing—that the new TSA had shut out the FAA, too.

What about all the new screeners who had to be hired? Cox had never had any problem with the Argenbright people in Memphis, but he understood the need for the federal government to take over. He had supported that. But, again, what was their roll-out plan? What was their transition plan? Cox would be the one passengers and press would blame if things broke down, but no one would tell him anything. Were these new screeners going to be so careful that they'd once again clog everything up and keep passengers away? Were they going to protect his airport so well that they would destroy it?

A significant source of Cox's unease had been fed in recent days by what he was hearing from his trade association—the American Association of Airport Executives (AAAE)—and what he was reading that they and the airline trade association were saying in the industry trade press. The AAAE and the Air Transport Association had by now developed a savvy whispering campaign aimed at encouraging skepticism about TSA.

Like all effective efforts of this kind it had enough truth, or the ring of truth, to be credible. The industry line, as explained to reporters, members of Congress, and even the staff of Ridge's Office of Homeland Security, went like this: Magaw, the new TSA head, was a Secret Service man. The orientation of the Secret Service was to protect one man, the President, at all costs. That made sense. But it couldn't work in a job where there had to be a balance between protection and customer service, between security and convenience.

Moreover, Secret Service people didn't talk about what they were doing, which was why Cox couldn't get any information. And no one ever questioned their authority, which was why Cox wasn't going to get any input into what happened at his airport.

Speaking tonight to a rapt audience in the auditorium of the New-York Historical Society on the West Side of Manhattan, Chuck Schumer explained to this group of probable liberals how the September 11 attacks had "profoundly changed" his view of "the balance between freedom and security" and the role of the federal government in what he called "this new era."

He used not a single note. It seemed like this was a speech he'd been giving to himself for months.

"September 11 had been a dramatic, world-changing event," he began, "that shows that the very technology that has made our lives so much better allows small groups of terrible people to do great damage to the heartland of America.

"That marks a tectonic change," he continued, "presenting a whole new world," which he compared to the dawn of the Cold War in 1946, when "America also faced a long struggle. . . . Terrorists and terrorism will now dominate our politics, our economy, our way of life for a long, long time.

"So how do we respond?" he asked. "Well, we have to recalibrate many aspects of our society to make our own physical security higher in our value system." That, he continued, meant "more public and private expense, more inconvenience, and a constant reevaluation of the basic balance between our freedom and our security.

"The second thing government is going to have to do," Schumer added, "is get bigger again. . . . The days of government shrinking, which has been going on since Reagan, are over. Only the federal government has the resources and the unity of purpose to fight this fight."

Which meant, Schumer concluded, that "the Tom DeLays of the world will be fighting a rear-guard action. Their moment is over. . . . The question is whether President Bush, whom I happen to like and think is much brighter than people give him credit for, is going to go down with them, or see that he has these responsibilities."

The audience was probably the core demographic target of the ACLU, if not already its card-carrying members. Yet they seemed to love the political journey that Schumer had just taken them on with this simple but not patronizing, impassioned but calm September 12 manifesto.

## Sunday, February 3, 2002

The Super Bowl in New Orleans came off without a hitch (unless you were a St. Louis Rams fan). Designated one of Ridge's National Special Security Events, the game's security was unprecedented, and there were no incidents.

Which was a lucky thing, since the National Football League had been forced to go ahead with the game without any terrorism insurance.

One of the frustrations that Schumer and insurance industry lobbyists now had was that they couldn't get these high-profile entities that were unprotected to talk about it as a way of illustrating the problem. Owners of stadiums, skyscrapers, amusement parks, or airports didn't want to advertise to their banks, let alone to customers, tenants, or even prospective attackers, that they were unprotected.

## Monday, February 4, 2002

Before Hollie Bart took on Sal Iacono, he had signed an agreement with what's known as a public insurance adjuster to have him process Sal's claims with St. Paul insurance for a 12.5 percent fee. Because Bart was taking over the work she convinced the adjuster to reduce the fee to 5 percent, and have it cover only the damage claims related to the forced entry into his store and the destruction and thefts that had taken place, not the business interruption claim. Then she officially filed all the claims with St. Paul.

She also began a pitch to the insurer on an issue that was the mirror image of the one that Silverstein and his insurance companies were now fighting over, though on a more down-to-earth scale. Sal's policies for business interruption and for forced entry and theft each had a $500 deductible, meaning that St. Paul could deduct $500 from what it paid on *each* of the two claims. Unlike Silverstein's, Sal's interests were served by being able to lump everything into one occurrence, which is what insurance clients typically want, because then the deductible is deducted only once. So Bart now asked them to consider only taking one deductible because the events—the damage and his interrupted business—had obviously stemmed from one occurrence. Bart knew that in this case she didn't have the law on her side, because the policies were, in fact, two policies. But she asked the company to consider it anyway in light of Sal's plight and the special nature of the tragedy they were dealing with.

This week she also began working on getting Sal help from a program that New York state had announced in conjunction with the newly formed Lower Manhattan Development Corporation, a state-city entity set up to coordinate the rebuilding around Ground Zero and dispense much of the federal aid that Schumer had worked to hard to win. The program offered cash grants plus payments to help pay rent for businesses that moved into, or committed to stay in, the area. The problem was that as of now, it looked as if the program was not going to apply to businesses that had fewer than ten employees. Bart was determined to change that.

Ken Feinberg traveled to Staten Island tonight to meet with about 300 families of victims. Because Staten Island was home to so many families who work in New York's uniformed services, most were the relatives of police and firemen.

After declaring, "The program is fair, it is just, it is vastly preferable to any kind of litigation," Feinberg said that "it can be made better," and that "the best input I get is from the families themselves."

Given that politicians usually come off as patronizing when they talk about how much they value the little people's input, his audience could be forgiven their cynicism at that remark. But, in fact, all this week Feinberg and his staff had been drilling down on the problem related to workers' comp and Social Security benefit offsets that he had only learned about from talking to people like Eileen Simon.

This audience, though, was not prepared to cut him any slack. And he did a poor job of turning them around.

When people asked about suing, he outlined all the risks and kept repeating that his was "the only game in town."

When he declared that "what keeps me up at 3:00 A.M. is trying to figure out how you make a program fair because you people can't sue," someone interrupted to ask, "Why did they pass a law saying we can't sue?"

"Because the airlines would have gone bankrupt anyway," he replied.

"So what," the crowd roared back in unison.

An ex-wife complained that she was going to get nothing. Why was that fair?

A mother of a thirty-eight-year-old firefighter asked about all the multi-million-dollar awards for other air crashes.

"For every multimillion-dollar award, I can cite you one that is zero," Feinberg shot back. "And if you get a $2 million award, it's not a $2 million award. It's $2 million after you litigate for seven years and give 40 percent to your lawyer. It's apples and oranges. You can't compare this to the civil justice system."

"Can't you speak softly?" a man stood and asked. "You have an arrogance about you that is so painful that you . . . hurt me to the bottom of my feet."

"I'm waiting for an explanation about how these terrorists got in. Why don't we sue INS?" someone else yelled, to loud applause.

"I can't begin to respond to that," Feinberg said, exasperated. "I don't know if you can sue INS. Ask a lawyer."

"You *are* a lawyer," another person screamed.

Others complained about how offsets would limit their awards. They didn't mention that in the case of firefighter or police widows what was being offset (or at least what they feared would be offset) were six-figure death and pension benefits, let alone acknowledge the millions more, tax free and offset free, that the police and fire families were getting from the special charities set up for them by, among others, Mayor Giuliani.

Someone complained about companies cutting off health care.

"I can't worry about that," Feinberg answered, once again forgetting he was talking to grieving families, not a bunch of lawyers in a negotiation.

The low point came when a well-dressed woman stood and asked about the payout for her twenty-six-year-old daughter who had worked as a stock trader. "How dare you pay my daughter so much less than the police and firemen are getting, with all of their extra charity. These firemen and cops knew what they were getting into. They signed up for danger. My daughter didn't sign up for that. She should get more than them, not less."

At least in terms of the numbers, she probably did not know how right she was. By now, the mix of special charities, pension benefits, and prospective Feinberg fund payments made it likely that widows of police officers would ultimately receive an average of slightly more than $5 million, and firefighters' widows would get slightly more than $6 million.* But this was not a roomful of people who appreciated that kind of math.

A young man, whose father presumably had been a firefighter lost during the rescue effort, rose, screaming at the woman, "Twenty-five thousand people got out of that building because of my father." Others chimed in, agreeing with him and jeering at her.

Feinberg tried to help the woman out. "I think what she is saying is that everyone should get more," he said.

She didn't want the help. "No," she said, standing up again. "I'm saying that there's a difference between civilians and police and firemen and the civilians should get more."

As the meeting wound down after about three hours, a man stood for a final comment.

"You've said this is the only game in town," he began as the room fell silent. "Well, this is not a game. You have a way about you that is just so obnox-

---

*For a full explanation of these benefits, see Source Notes for September 25, 2001.

ious. If you could put yourself, Mr. Feinberg, in our place for just one hour, your tone and your mannerisms would be so different."

More applause.

"I don't mean it that way," the Special Master responded. "I apologize. My tone? My mannerisms? I'm just trying as hard as I can to explain the program as best I can."

Feinberg would later remember this as the "worst night of the whole thing."

It certainly was the most depressing in terms of the picture it painted of September 12 America. If the goal of the terrorists had been to split the country apart, you could have watched this meeting and believed they had succeeded.

# Tuesday, February 5, 2002

This was what now passed for an average post–September 11 morning for Kevin McCabe. Twelve huge container cargo ships had arrived the night before or this morning at his New York harbor ports (Elizabeth in New Jersey and Brooklyn and Staten Island on the New York side). They were carrying a total of 8,556 containers.

As a result of new precautions taken since the attacks, Coast Guard troops had boarded five of the twelve freighters, plus all three oil tankers, before they had been allowed into the harbor. The Coast Guard, which had a command center where radar screens monitor all ships of any appreciable size approaching American shores, picked those to be boarded based on the country they came from and the dangerousness of the cargo. (Thus, the selection of all tankers.) The ships had been given a once-over by the Coast Guard crew before being allowed to be driven into the port, not by the ship's crew but by a certified harbor pilot. In the first two months after September 11, all freighters were boarded; now it was still all the oil tankers and some of the other ships. Before September 11, none were boarded, unless there was some kind of special warning.

Shippers have for years been asked by Customs to e-mail a detailed list of the contents, called a manifest, of each container at least two days before a ship arrives. At Customs's request, since September 11, most were sending the manifest three to five days in advance. They knew that if the ship now arrived without the manifest having been sent well in advance, the cargo was going to be held at the port until McCabe and his people could check it carefully.* Or, if the ship was from a high-risk country, Customs and the Coast Guard might even require that it be held at sea until the missing manifests arrive.

Today, McCabe had gotten manifests at least forty-eight hours in advance for all of the containers that had just arrived. The information was then fed into the computer system used by seven of McCabe's men who were assigned to assess the risks of each container. They can check to see how many points each container gets on their computerized risk analysis chart. Beyond that, based on just a current intelligence rumor or maybe even a gut instinct, McCabe's inspectors on the docks can designate additional containers as high-risk.

There were 211 containers singled out today for a closer look.

One of them was a shipment that had gone from Malaysia to Jidda, Saudi Arabia, before arriving here. It supposedly contains cherrywood dining room tables made in Malaysia and bound for a furniture wholesaler in New England, who the computer said was not a frequent recipient of goods from this shipper.

Earlier this morning the container was put through the giant X-ray VACIS. (McCabe had gotten one more of these machines since September 11, bringing his arsenal to three.) When the container was VACISed, McCabe's man who specializes in checking the resulting image on a computer screen noticed what Customs inspectors call an "anomaly."

"Anomalies are us," McCabe loves to say, meaning that Customs is always looking for something out of the ordinary. Here the anomaly was that the material in the middle of the container looked a lot more dense (the image on the screen was much darker) than the material on all sides. If everything in there was the same, why would that be? Was there something hidden among the cartons of dining room tables?

By mid-morning Customs had moved the container into a warehouse at the port, where other inspectors spent two and a half hours fork-lifting all the crates in it out onto the floor. By noon, the tables were spread out in the warehouse, alongside cartons of limes from another container that had come in from Ecuador. The inspectors were slicing the limes open at random, looking for cocaine. ("It happens a lot," McCabe says.)

---

*Of course, holding a container in the port that has not sent a manifest will penalize a conventional shipper, but will not bother a terrorist who has shipped in a weapon of mass destruction that he intends to detonate *at* the port. Thus, in November, Customs Commissioner Bonner would promulgate a regulation requiring that all shippers file manifests twenty-four hours before their goods even arrive at a foreign port on their way to the U.S.

As they surveyed the furniture in the cold, damp warehouse, McCabe's men quickly had their answer. The tables were being shipped with the round tops separated from the legs. And the cartons containing a dozen tops at a time were far heavier—and, therefore, made for a darker VACIS picture—than the cartons containing the legs. The tops had been loaded into the center of the container, while the legs had been placed around the sides. Thus, the difference in density in the middle.

"Now, we're satisfied," McCabe said.

McCabe joined three of his men who had boarded a massive ship just in from Singapore, carrying more than 2,800 containers. With radiation detectors turned on and holstered alongside the Glock automatics on their belts, they fanned out across the ship's decks, which offered an astonishing view of the lower Manhattan skyline (minus the Twin Towers) across the harbor. The crew of twenty-four, who had been at sea for more than a month, stood by, shivering in the wind. Although their names and passport information had been sent to the Coast Guard for clearance (per another new rule) four days before, they were no longer allowed off the boat for brief stops like this one without special INS permission.

Moving up and down the aisles of containers, the inspectors checked the seals on the doors of hundreds of them at random to see if they might have been opened after loading. McCabe knew the seals were far from tamper-proof; and he was encouraged that the bosses in Washington were now working on a whole new strategy for ensuring container security with improved seals that would send alarms via a satellite transponder if the seals were tampered with. They were also working on devices inside the containers that would send alarms if the lighting or air pressure changed, indicating someone had opened one of them without breaking the seal. But for now, these random checks of containers that had not caught the eye of the guys doing the computerized risk assessments were a useful backstop. Three containers with suspicious-looking seals were pulled and sent to the VACIS, where their images were compared with what the manifest said was supposed to be in them.

McCabe knew that he and his men were keeping the odds of a terrorist smuggling in a weapon of mass destruction far lower than Schumer's 98 percent. He believed that they'd been shrinking those odds day by day as they beefed up their computerized risk analysis and added still more people, radiation detectors, and VACIS capacity. But he also knew they had not eliminated the chances, far from it. For example, a group of really dedicated, patient terrorists—and he knew the September 11 terrorists had been dedicated and patient—could plant someone at an auto factory, where he could slip something into the trunk of any of the thousands of cars that arrived here every day from Japan and Korea and left the dock un-inspected. Or they could go to smaller ports, where Customs didn't have his manpower, equipment, and, he believed, the same on-edge sense of the threat. Worse, they could offload whatever it was they were carrying on the high seas onto a smaller pleasure boat ten or twenty miles out. The smaller boat, which was unlikely to be scrutinized, could then bring it into even smaller ports, or to no official port at all.

Worst of all, the bad guys might not even worry about being allowed in. McCabe's worst fear was of a tanker or large freighter approaching the shores and detonating a device before docking. The Coast Guard had attempted to minimize that threat by not allowing any ships past a certain point at sea at least until it knew that the crew was cleared, and then insisting that high-risk ships allow a Coast Guard protection unit to board it before it moved in. But the only real answer was to have all the manifests checked before anything got close to shore, and even mount radiation detectors at key advance points, such as under the Verrazano Narrows Bridge, which crossed the mouth of the harbor between Brooklyn and Staten Island. McCabe had heard that a lot of that was in the works. But it wasn't in place yet.

In four months, they'd made progress, McCabe thought. It wasn't nearly enough.

# Wednesday, February 6, 2002

Yesterday, Brosnahan filed a motion asking the judge to release John Lindh on bail, arguing not only that he was not a flight risk, but that the case against him was untenable because it was all based on alleged confessions he had made that had to be ruled inadmissible due to the "brutal" circumstances under which Lindh had been held, questioned, and denied access to his lawyer. It was the first time Brosnahan had had a forum to detail those circumstances— Lindh taped naked to the stretcher in the metal container, being forced to urinate while still taped to the stretcher, awakened every hour and searched.

What was so notable about the response the government filed this afternoon was that it didn't dispute almost all of Brosnahan's graphic description of Lindh's detention. The prosecutors' memorandum spent much of its time contending that Lindh was a flight risk, which was not surprising, given that

that's what a bail motion is all about. But when it came to rebutting Brosnahan's charges about Lindh's treatment, the prosecutors only denied that Lindh had been deprived of food or medical attention at the time of his questioning by the FBI agent. They said nothing about him not being given sufficient food or medical care when the military intelligence officers had grilled him in the days before that, yet they used what Lindh had supposedly said in those interrogations to buttress their argument that the case against Lindh was so strong that he had to be denied bail. Moreover, Brosnahan's argument was that Lindh had waived his right to a lawyer when the FBI agent came to question him only because he was so afraid of having his treatment revert back to what it had been before the agent arrived—in other words, he feared that if he persisted in demanding a lawyer and did not sign the waiver, he would once again be deprived of food and medical attention and put back into that metal container. Besides, even after the FBI man arrived, the only medical care Lindh got was that his bullet wounds were dressed. The bullet had not been removed and he was under the influence of strong painkillers during the FBI questioning.

Office of Homeland Security Protection and Prevention Chief Bruce Lawlor couldn't believe they had to meet again.

Lawlor thought that what was called the Salt Lake City Air Working Group had resolved all the issues during a series of meetings last week related to which airspace over Utah would be declared off limits to civilian aircraft during the Olympics, so as to prevent any terror attacks by air. He'd pulled together representatives of not only the Pentagon, whose jet fighters would shoot down any suspect plane, and the Secret Service, which was in charge of overall security for the Olympics, but also people from the CIA, FAA, FBI, Department of Transportation, and any other department that conceivably had a role. Initially, the Pentagon folks wanted a wider swath of protected airspace than Transportation or the FAA (which worried about disrupting airline schedules and causing them to spend more on fuel) wanted, or than the Secret Service thought was necessary. But they had all discussed it, and everyone had finally agreed on what areas to carve out, based on where the venues were located on the ground and how long it would take the jet fighters to shoot something down. They had even briefed the President on the specifics of the plan and gotten his approval, and then briefed congressional leaders.

But yesterday Lawlor found out that on Friday the brass at the Pentagon had decided that the designated area wasn't big enough for its fighters to be certain of providing fail-safe coverage. So someone at the Pentagon had somehow persuaded the FAA to issue a new order, one that contradicted the one Lawlor, Ridge, the President, the airlines, and everyone else thought they were operating under. It would cause havoc with air traffic. Besides, why had they had all those meetings with all those people?

Now Lawlor found himself chairing yet another meeting at FAA headquarters with the same group. The problem wasn't that people were hostile, or even that they stated their disagreements directly. It was just the opposite. What Lawlor had found was that when people in groups like this wanted to sidetrack things, they either kept asking questions or saying that something needed further study. Or they left themselves some other way out, such as mumbling something about how whatever the group was supposedly deciding was okay pending someone else's approval. That way, they could go back to the office and ignore what Lawlor thought had been decided. Thus, he listened this morning as the Pentagon people mentioned that while they had always said that they appreciated the input they were getting at those prior meetings, they had also mentioned that they were going to take whatever the decision made at the meeting seemed to be back to higher-ups at the Pentagon for further consideration. And that is what had happened in this case, the top Pentagon representative said, with a straight face. In other words, the homeland security coordinator wasn't coordinating anything as far as they were concerned.

Lawlor, who was by now emerging as perhaps Ridge's savviest, toughest deputy and certainly among the hardest working in a group of workaholics, now flexed his muscles. He stressed that the President himself had signed off on the plan that they had now jettisoned. The Secret Service representative chimed in that he wanted to leave the plan as it had been before the Friday switch. Lawlor said that this was the President's decision and that the FAA had to change the order back to an order consistent with the plan they had all adopted. Finally, the FAA man relented, saying he would change the plan back immediately. The man from Secret Service said that they would continue to review the Pentagon's concerns, which was the nice way one said "game over" in settings like this. The Pentagon official said he would take the issue back to his bosses for further discussion.

Later in the day the FAA did change the plan back to what it had been.

# Thursday, February 7, 2002

Hollie Bart had clearly gotten the insurance company's attention. Today, which was the twenty-fifth anniversary of Sal opening Continental Shoe Repair, she got a fax offering $5,685 for his business interruption claim covering the four weeks his store had been closed. (The number was arrived at by calculating his average weekly revenue—about $2,000—and then deducting the costs he did not incur, such as for materials, because he did no business during that time.) Bart replied that she'd take it, but not as a complete settlement; she still wanted more for the period when Sal had been opened but the area around him had been so blocked off to vehicular and pedestrian traffic that it was almost as if he were closed.

Larry Silverstein told the author that he expected his trial against the insurers to start in September, that the jury would give him his win by October, and that by the following spring of 2003 the appeals would be over and he'd have his check for $7 billion.

By now David Childs, Silverstein's architect at Skidmore, Owings & Merrill, had completed the elaborate design and mock-up of a new World Trade Center complex that Silverstein had asked him to start on the day after the attacks. It included a glorious new transit hub, with what Childs called his "great train room" at the base, surrounded by four office towers of varying sizes. The tallest had a protective sheaf of glass around it that rose above the office building itself (which stopped at about sixty-five floors) to the exact height of the original towers. In the middle of the four buildings was a grass plaza area of about ten acres that would serve as a memorial. Childs had also meant for the glass sheaf as another kind of memorial; it seemed to rise and fade up into the heavens. Or as Childs explained it to Silverstein, it was "a marker in the sky of the memorial down below." In all, it was an ambitious plan, likely to be far more pleasing to architecture critics than anything they might have expected from Larry Silverstein.

But Childs had a trick that made it even better. Two of the four towers could simply be picked up and removed, leaving 60 percent of the old Ground Zero space open.

Silverstein loved the way Childs could yank the two buildings up off the mock-up and produce something that turned a crowded circle of office buildings into an open, beautiful setting for two beautiful towers, a grand transit station, and acres of serene, open space for a memorial and even a museum or some other cultural amenity. For now, however, they had to show the Port Authority the design with the four towers, which provided the same amount of office space that the old Trade Center had had. Taking away two of the towers left about 60 percent of the original office space, which is about what Silverstein expected to negotiate. But because of that contract with the Port Authority that required him to rebuild it all, and them to let him rebuild it all, the crowded design would serve as their prop for a multibillion-dollar game of chicken. They had to wait for the Port Authority to blink first before Silverstein could lift those two towers and reveal Childs's real design.

Chubb Insurance today announced its final financial results for 2001, and it wasn't pretty. Net profit was $112 million, compared to $715 million in 2000. Had the September 11 attacks not happened, profit would have been about $750 million. In other words, the losses had far exceeded the $200 million (after reinsurance kicked in to help Chubb pay claims) that Chubb's computer program had calculated the day of the attacks.

But not all was gloom and doom at Chubb headquarters. In the annual report he would issue to shareholders a few weeks later, CEO O'Hare would bemoan the continued absence of a government solution to the terrorism insurance problem, but then note improving industry conditions on other fronts—such as diminished overall industry competition that provided more opportunities for rate increases, and a flight to "quality" insurers now that risks had become more apparent. This, he said, promised an "up cycle" in the immediate future. Citing what he called Chubb's "superior competitive position" in terms of financial strength and high profit margins, he told his shareholders that Chubb was "among the very best-positioned companies to capitalize on the improving market" and produce "strong growth and solid . . . results."

Chubb's stock closed at $68.72, up about $2.00 over the day. The price was also about $5.50 higher than the day the market opened after the attacks, and actually $2.25 higher than the stock had sold for on September 10.

Tom Ridge was greeted by a *New York Times* headline this morning saying "Ridge Faces Major Doubts on His Ability."

"Four months into his tenure as director of homeland security, Tom Ridge is facing significant doubts about his authority and ability to do the job," the piece began. Two paragraphs later, none other than James Ziglar, the head of the INS, was quoted as saying, "Let's face it, Tom Ridge's office is brand-new. They are still getting organized and they don't have anybody over there who are experts on immigration, customs, border enforcement. That's why they necessarily have to rely on us." Later in the article, Ziglar, who until August had been the Senate sergeant at arms, was quoted as saying, when asked about a border security agreement Ridge had negotiated with Canada, that "the truth is that . . . these were points that were already brewing here."

The piece, which went on to cite Ridge's failed attempt in December to merge INS, Customs, and the Coast Guard as exhibit A of his powerlessness, closed by noting another issue concerning Ridge that was gathering steam. Although Ridge had been appointed as the President's point man on homeland security and had taken credit for putting together the entire homeland security budget request that had been forwarded to Congress, the Bush administration was taking the position that because Ridge was a presidential assistant and not a congressionally confirmed cabinet appointee, he would not testify before Congress about the budget or anything else. As a member of the President's personal staff, White House lawyers argued, Ridge could not be required to do so, because that would violate the separation-of-powers provisions of the Constitution.

Later today, at about the same time that senators Joseph Lieberman, Arlen Specter, and Bob Graham were promoting a bill creating a Department of Homeland Security cabinet post (whose secretary, like all agency heads, would, of course, have to testify on Capitol Hill), Ridge appeared before the National Press Club. Asked about his power or lack thereof, he cited his having gotten White House approval of all of his $38 billion in homeland security budget requests, but allowed as how "we may make some recommendations about the integration or consolidation of some of these departments that will . . . need congressional approval." But he didn't deal with the criticism head-on. He just smiled and took it, just as he chuckled with his staff at Ziglar's quotes in the *Times* article, and never said a word to Ziglar about them.

The *Times* article reflected a consensus that was developing in the Washington political-media establishment: Ridge was a nice guy but he had no juice, and, some even thought, wasn't that bright either.

It seemed hard to fathom how the son of a meat salesman from western Pennsylvania who'd made it to Harvard on a scholarship, had been a combat hero in Vietnam, then won an against-all-odds race for Congress and a big-state governorship despite coming from an obscure corner of the state, could have taken on this aura of haplessness.

Ridge, though, exuded a serenity about it all that amazed those on his staff who were accustomed to high-profile Washington figures worrying about their press clips, especially those that questioned their place in the Beltway pecking order. He was either better than anyone they had seen at faking it, they thought, or he really didn't care because he truly was confident that if he just worried about getting his job done, the rest would fall into place. "The guy has no guile," marveled one of his top aides soon after this article was published. "He just doesn't play those games or worry about that stuff," added the aide, who had not known Ridge until October. "It's hard to believe he won't get mowed down in a town like this."

# Monday, February 11, 2002

Sal Iacono got a check from St. Paul insurance for $15,980 to cover all the repairs from the damage done to his store, plus the theft of his merchandise and the cash from his cash register. It is almost exactly the amount Hollie Bart had claimed, which included repairs for which Sal had paid cash and had no receipts. Bart had persuaded the insurance company to trust them.

With the check came word that Sal's $500 deductible would only be taken once, even though the company could clearly have deducted it twice under Sal's policies.

When Bart rushed down to the store to give Sal the check, he was stunned. "You lawyers are my angels," he said, almost doing a dance.

As Senator Trent Lott's senior policy advisor, it was David Crane who had come up with the outline for the victims compensation fund. He was also on hand when Lott met with Dean O'Hare in November and told the Chubb Insurance CEO that he didn't think terrorism insurance was a national problem. In fact, Crane had advised Lott that he didn't think the country needed a terrorism insurance law.

Today, Crane began organizing a coalition to push for terrorism insurance.

It wasn't that Lott had switched positions, but that Crane had switched jobs. As of last month, he had become a lobbyist, and one of his firm's clients was a real estate industry trade association that wanted a terrorism insurance law badly. This morning Crane signed off on a press release announcing a coalition led by his client that included real estate, insurance, construction, and banking industry groups, as well as entities ranging from the National Football League to the Association of American Railroads. The goal was to broaden the push for a bill far beyond the insurance industry.

Crane had no trouble squaring his new work with his old position. What he and Lott had been against was acting precipitously based on the insurance lobby's claim that the economy would collapse on January 1 if a bill wasn't enacted. They hadn't believed that, and they had been right. But when executives from a group of real estate investment companies, called real estate investment trusts, or REITS, had come to the lobbying firm he had just joined to explain that the lack of full coverage against terror attacks was slowly going to eat away at their industry, that was an argument he could understand. So now he was on their side.

Glenn Fine, the Justice Department's inspector general, issued a report that was not about Border Patrol agent Lindemann's case, but that gave Lindemann a hint that maybe this was someone who was not likely to pull punches when it came to the Northern Border.

Fine had been asked by Congress to do a review of what INS and the Border Patrol had done to improve protection on the Northern Border since Fine's office had issued a blistering report two years ago stating that the Border Patrol was "unable to adequately respond to illegal activity" there.

Now, Fine reported that the agency had made "some improvements," but that "all eight Border Patrol sector chiefs we interviewed described staffing, equipment and intelligence support deficiencies at the northern border sectors," and that "the northern sectors still cannot staff all stations 24 hours a day, 7 days a week." Those who had told this to Fine's staff for inclusion in what they knew would be a public report included, of course, the sector chief who had pushed for Lindemann to be fired for talking to the press about the same deficiencies.

Michael Chertoff, the head of Ashcroft's Criminal Division, gave a breakfast speech to the Association of the Bar of the City of New York in Manhattan. As a veteran New Jersey lawyer and prosecutor, he knew his audience was the New York legal establishment, many of whom worked for corporate America by day and got involved in liberal causes after hours.

Chertoff has a way of being affable even when voicing strong views that the rest of the room disagrees with, and he was at his blunt best today in defense of the anti-terror campaign he and Ashcroft were waging.

"Liberty is not worth having without security," he began, whereupon he explained that the Justice Department had had to adjust what it has done in the past to come out "somewhere between civil justice and military justice," because "neither paradigm fits" when it comes to terrorism.

Had these adjustments, which resulted in steps such as the secret detentions of immigrants and eavesdropping on a few lawyer conversations, been worth it? "It's like sprinkling powder to keep elephants away," Chertoff said. "If no elephants show up, how do you prove it's because of the powder, rather than because there were never any elephants?"

Chertoff's strongest point was that he and Ashcroft were doing what Eliot Ness and the feds had done in the 1930s and what Attorney General Robert Kennedy had done in the 1960s to go after the mob: They had used any laws they could, however minor (such as tax laws to jail Chicago kingpin Al Capone), to go after people they knew were mobsters but couldn't nail on mob-related charges. "No one has a right not to be prosecuted for breaking the law," he explained, "even if the law is rarely enforced."

The audience seemed convinced on that point. None of the 100 or more lawyers in the room asked about the fault line in Chertoff's analogy, which was that those earlier prosecutors had known, or thought they knew, that the mobsters were mobsters. All that Chertoff and Ashcroft knew about the people they were going after was that they were young men from certain targeted Muslim countries. True, these were the same category of people who had been the September 11 hijackers, and maybe one could argue that at a time when terrorists might be quietly living law-abiding lives in Muslim communities waiting for the moment to strike, it was necessary to target all of them. But that was a different argument. There weren't any Al Capones being held in those INS lockups.

After John Lindh pleaded not guilty, federal judge T. S. Ellis III set August 26 for his trial, rejecting a request from one of Brosnahan's partners that it not start until after the September 11 anniversary. The real drama came outside the courtroom, when Lindh's father approached the father of slain CIA agent Johnny Spann. "I am sorry about your son," Frank Lindh said. "My son had nothing to do with it. I am sure you understand." Mr. Spann turned and walked away.

In fact, although Spann's death had been described in the Lindh indictment and Ashcroft had talked about it in most of his many public statements about the case, the government had not actually charged Lindh with having done anything to cause the agent's death.

# Thursday, February 14, 2002

Eileen Simon, the American flag still dominating her front porch, sat in her living room looking at a dozen arrangements of Valentine's Day flowers that had been delivered by noon, half from strangers. On the coffee table were boxes of cookies brought over by the Girl Scouts. On the credenza, where Michael used to keep the family's financial records, were five checks she had received recently, many from strangers, such as the members of a prayer group in Illinois who had gotten her name off a website and sent $100.

On the mantelpiece, next to two unlit candles, there was a small antique box that held the bone from her husband's skull. She had put it there in December, without ever looking at it or telling the kids what it was.

Simon sat on a couch under the mantelpiece trying to explain how much all of the generosity meant to her—the flowers, the letters, the community organization that had paid for a tutor for her daughter, the counseling groups, the kids who played ball with her kids, the random checks that arrived in the mail. The outpouring made her love her country, she said. "Who wouldn't love a country filled with people, even perfect strangers, who are capable of this?" Yet at the same time, she had begun to fear that her government, in the person of Ken Feinberg, was going to disappoint her. Every sentence mixed tears with laughter, as if to broadcast both sides of her at once. This was a woman who loved to laugh, who had resolved not to be bitter. She wanted so much to see the bright side of everything and not be confronted with the opposite that, she said, with that laugh and a tear, she had "liked it much better when I didn't think Michael's death could be anyone's fault but the terrorists. I hated it when I started to hear things like how maybe they could have escaped from the roof, or maybe the buildings weren't designed right. I don't want to hear that."

So, she hated, too, that she couldn't shake the feeling that her government, the government of a country with such generous people, wasn't dealing with her fairly. "If I can even end up with just $500,000, I think I'll be okay," she said. "That and the life insurance [another $500,000] will let us live okay. I'm just counting on him [Feinberg] not to give me zero."

InVision put out a press release announcing that the FAA had ordered $13.7 million worth of equipment for the San Francisco Airport. However, as Sergio Magistri knew, this order was not only minimal, it was a leftover item from the FAA's pre–September 11 go-slow program. It had nothing to do with the TSA's plans to meet the deadlines. In fact, Jackson and a go team that had been assigned to deal with explosive detection systems were holding firm on not giving any orders to InVision until they negotiated a deal to license the company's intellectual property, so that others could also build the machines. So far Magistri wasn't giving in. He hated the idea of licensing away his chance to make it big, in return for the immediate sales orders that he needed so badly.

For Brian Peterman, the admiral who had come up from Florida to do border security under Lawlor and Ridge, the subject of this afternoon's push-the-INS session was how to build what's called an entry-exit system.

Actually, INS had been required by Congress to have had such a system by 1998. But Congress never funded it, and, if the people from INS at today's meeting were any indication, INS wouldn't have known what to do with the money anyway.

The entry-exit concept is simple, deceptively so. Anyone entering the United States hands an INS inspector a form, stating who he is, where he's from, where he will be staying, and how long he'll be staying there. If he has a visa, he must promise to leave when the visa expires. If he is a citizen of a country for which the United States does not require a visa—such as England, France, or Italy—he must leave within six months unless he has special permission to stay longer.

The problem is that INS rarely knows when anyone leaves. At airports, those departing may be required to fill out a departure card, but not at land borders or at most water ports. And even if someone fills out a card and does so with a name that is legible and matches the name he used when he entered, INS usually never gets around to matching it up with the card he handed in when he entered, because both the entry and the exit form are in hard copy and not computer-scannable. Thus, according to INS, some 3.7 million people may come and stay each year who shouldn't, although that number is ridiculously high because it counts everyone for whom they have not matched an entry card with an exit card, even those who have left.

In other words, INS has no idea of whether anyone who comes in ever leaves, let alone whether they leave on time.

The solution is simple—in theory. Anyone arriving would use a form that could be entered into a computer database. Anyone leaving would submit another form that would be entered into the same database and matched up with the entry form.

Ideally, the next step would be that anyone whose exit card didn't hit the database before his deadline for leaving would be singled out as an illegal visitor. And cops making traffic stops or anyone else encountering him and asking for identification (if he applies for a driver's license for example) could nail him. Overstay a visa and you get on a list of wanted people.

The problem is that with more than 30 million foreigners entering the United States every year, this kind of system demands a massive database, and thousands of checkpoints with thousands of terminals to enter the data. There are other problems. For the process to be reliable, a biometric identifier, such as a fingerprint, would need to be submitted along with each entry and exit form. Otherwise, how could INS be sure that Joe Smith who entered really was Joe Smith, and then that he was the same Joe Smith who said he was leaving? That meant issuing visas with biometric identifiers and forcing countries from which the United States did not require visas to put biometric identifiers on their passports. How quickly could that be accomplished? And what identifier would be used that would be "culturally" acceptable in a world in which, to take two examples, the Canadians were said to distrust fingerprints and many Muslim countries were wary of iris scans (another effective, scannable biometric device) because their religion generally prohibits images of living people?

This meeting was meant to begin to deal with some of these issues. But there was a problem. INS was supposed to have drafted a white paper in conjunction with people from the State Department's visa office. This morning INS showed up with the paper but said that they had not had a chance to show it to State. The emissary from State, diplomat to the core, didn't say how angry he was. He didn't have to.

The meeting broke up with the representative from State taking the paper back to the office. He'd soon see that it wasn't much to work with. It outlined a blue-sky, soup-to-nuts description of what was needed, which everyone already knew. The document contained no implementation strategies, no deadlines, no milestones, no budgets. Was there something in the water at INS headquarters that made all the bosses there incompetent?

Before everyone left, Peterman reminded them that they were working on a tight deadline that might get tighter still because Senator Jon Kyl, a Republican from Arizona, was pushing a bill that would speed the entry-exit deadlines up to early next year from the fall 2003 deadline that had been inserted into the USA Patriot Act. As it was, a deadline in a prior law of October 1, 2001, for a system just covering airports and major seaports had long since been missed, as had the USA Patriot Act's January 25 deadline for a report to Congress on the feasibility of using biometric identifiers.

In fact, Ridge had been quietly encouraging Kyl to push his bill, because he thought he would give him additional leverage to force INS to move.


# Sunday, February 17, 2002

At about 10:00 A.M. a car with Canadian license plates pulled up to the curb of Rescue Squad 41 in the Bronx, the elite unit where Brian Lyons's brother Michael had been assigned. A middle-aged man and woman got out with two shopping bags. The man knocked on the firehouse door and told the men he had bagels for them. Since September 11, this kind of spontaneous outpouring of gifts and goodwill had been happening at firehouses all over the city, although this one was a bit out of the ordinary. The couple had looked on the Internet for the location of a firehouse that had lost men, settled for no apparent reason on Squad 41, where six firefighters had been killed, then driven down from Quebec the night before, and bought the bagels this morning on their way over.

The men in the squad thought this was quite a distance to go to deliver a bag of bagels, and one of them said so. Bagels weren't all he had brought, the man from Canada replied.

He then handed the captain a check for $50,000 that he had raised from his neighbors.

By early the next week, the captain, who like all captains in firehouses across the city had become the unofficial trustee of money and other gifts that spontaneously poured in to his squad, had dispensed a sixth of it—$8,333— to Michael Lyons's widow, Elaine, which, when added in with all the other death benefits and charitable funds to which she was now entitled, didn't actually mean that much. After all, the total—most of it tax-free—was about $6 million, including the value of a lifetime pension equal to Michael's annual salary and average overtime of about $60,000 a year.

Elaine Lyons was, of course, grateful. It was as if one constant worry in her life and the life of everyone she had ever known—money—had been magically eliminated. But the magic that had eliminated it was the death of her mate since high school. And she was not shy about saying that it made her feel guilty, that maybe all of the victims just should have gotten the same amount. In fact, she and the two other firefighter widows, who were part of a larger group of widows that now met once a week, found themselves plotting to arrive at the meetings early, so that before the other women arrived they could discuss everything related to their new wealth, from how to invest it to the guilt they shared about it.

Because of another of Congress's airline security deadlines, as of midnight all of the security screeners now worked under the supervision of the new Transportation Security Administration. No, the new force of federal agent screeners hadn't taken over. That deadline was nine months away, on November 19. Rather, the private companies that supplied the private screeners were now under contract to TSA, not the airlines.

The ostensible purpose was that TSA would now supervise them directly and presumably enforce stricter performance standards than the airlines had. The only real, if unintended, difference was money—taxpayer money. Because these private companies knew that they were going out of business next November, they were not inclined to be anything other than hard-nosed in negotiating these new, short-lived contracts with the federal government. Plus for the time being they had huge leverage, because the government couldn't afford to have them bail out now. The result was that whereas the private companies had been getting about $9 per hour per screener, of which they might have given $7.50 to the screeners, they were now getting about $13 per hour, of which they gave $10 to the screeners, hoping that the wage increase would keep them from quitting jobs they knew they were destined to lose anyway by November, unless they could qualify to be hired by TSA.

There was one other wrinkle to the new regime. Because of all the bad publicity about Argenbright, the TSA had decided that it would not do business with that company at all, even for this interim period. Yet Argenbright had accounted for the protection, such as it was, at 40 percent of the country's airport checkpoints. So beginning today, the two other large private security companies that had been Argenbright's competitors simply replaced Argenbright at various airports. But they did it by rehiring the same people Argenbright had employed. Thus, in the lobby of Cox's terminal in Memphis, Argenbright screeners could be seen changing uniforms.

The Potemkin village nature of all this amused Cox more than it bothered him. He had not had problems with Argenbright or its screeners; in fact he still used Argenbright guards in his parking areas. To Cox, this was just another instance of some stupid edict coming out of Washington that had no relation to the real world.

In many ways the period from today's faux federal takeover until months later—when TSA actually would take over the airports and have its new force of federal screeners there—gave Cox, his customers, and passengers across the country the worst of both worlds: The same people who had not measured up to the job, or been trained well enough for it, were now being asked to do their work more intensely. The result would be delays and daily tales of security run amok, mixed with other news stories about security breakdowns. Infants were hand-searched. Terminals were evacuated because someone forgot to search a medic taking a patient through on a stretcher. Mothers were forced to drink their bottled breast milk to verify that it wasn't a liquid bomb. Meantime, undercover reporters sneaked weapons on board and wrote stories about the lapses, blaming the new TSA.

Mineta's team—Jackson, chief of staff John Flaherty, go teams leader Hawley, Magaw, Rossides, and others—all talked about this as a kind of "dip" period, meaning the public, the press, and the aviation industry people were all going to think the worst of them for a few months. But there was nothing they could do about it, they decided, because they had to do the work of building an agency and getting everything in place to meet the deadlines.

Thus, their top priority was to gather enough facts and do enough planning so that they could get the specifications ready to award four huge contracts to private companies. They had figured out that no agency this big could be gotten off the ground with even a hundred go teams, no matter how little they slept. They were going to have to rent platoons of talent from private industry. Accordingly, the linchpin of their roll-out strategy was that they were going to figure out down to the last detail what needed to be done and then hire four companies to swarm the four key jobs necessary to meet the deadlines. These outside contracts, they decided, would be the "four pillars" of their effort to defy all the odds and get the job done. One contractor would be responsible for designing the baggage screening system at each airport and installing the machines. A second would recruit all the screeners. A third would design the setup at each airport to make the checkpoints move efficiently. And a fourth would train all the screeners, once Rossides and her team came up with the curriculum.

That might have made sense, and it was sure appealing to people like Woollen of Raytheon, who already had his eye on snaring the contract to install the bomb detectors. But there was no denying that to America's airline passengers this really was a "dip" period. It was made worse because the TSA's public persona, TSA head Magaw, was anything but a public person. It was as if the former Secret Service chief was still in charge of protecting the President, a job where silence is golden. He didn't do press interviews and didn't bother to reach out either personally or through surrogates to airport directors like Cox, to others in the industry, or to those frequent fliers in Congress to tell them that this was the temporary valley before things got better. Nor did Jackson, the deputy transportation secretary, who was really running the show, encourage him to.

It was a lapse that the airline and airport lobbyists in Washington were happy to exploit; for, in the absence of anyone knowing that there were guys borrowed from places like FedEx, Marriott, or Disney working on customer-service-oriented go teams, it seemed to confirm their thesis that a Secret Service mentality had taken over a customer service business.

"I fly home every week," said House Aviation Subcommittee Chairman John Mica at about this time, "and I am finding that what passengers complain about now is the hassle factor. It's really bad."

Eileen Simon didn't think it was bad at all. Two days ago, she and her children had flown to Florida, which is where Mica lives, because they had accepted a free trip on a cruise ship and were going to board it there. The screeners at Newark Airport had singled her out for one of those invasive hand searches, and she felt great that they were doing it, even after they took her nail clipper and made her remove her shoes.

But Simon's trip had been downhill from there. On the plane, Tyler kept asking how high up in the air they were. When his mother finally asked why he was so curious, the five-year-old said it was because he wanted to know if he was "higher than Daddy was when he fell."

"Was this what every family trip without Michael was going to be like?" Eileen wondered.

# Monday, February 18, 2002

As Ken Feinberg and his staff struggled to digest the comments they were receiving on the draft regulations issued in December so that they could write a final version, Feinberg finally got to the bottom of the Social Security and workers' compensation problems. The two senior partners in his law firm who were working the issue told him that it was now clear that the Labor Department people had screwed up badly. It was an almost incredible mistake, but it was a mistake, not a conspiracy to shortchange the widows. They simply hadn't counted the value of these benefits correctly. The blonde from New Jersey and all the others who had been screaming about this were right. If you added up everything they might be entitled to over their lifetimes and their kids' lifetimes, it reached high into six or seven figures. Even if you discounted it because it would be paid out over a long time, it was still a deduction from any award of $300,000 to $500,000 for a family with three children, which made his oft-proclaimed "average $1.6 million" award that much less.

Feinberg was amazed. None of the hotshot lawyers had spotted this issue, either before or after he'd put out the regulations. It was that New Jersey widow and people like her who'd brought it to light.

But what could he do? How could he get around the law's requirement that these benefits be offset? In a series of meetings with his staff beginning this week, Feinberg came up with a set of solutions.

First, some of these benefits weren't really the kinds of entitlements that had to be offset because they were not certain. Rather they were contingent on other events happening. For example, Eileen Simon's Social Security payments ended if she remarried before age 60. So, taking the view that any contingent benefit could not be counted because its value could not be computed in advance, he would wipe those out of the equation—completely.

Second, the workers' compensation insurance payment wasn't a real benefit at all because the workers' comp law stipulated that the insurance company that paid out the benefits could try to recover what it paid out from any other death benefit Simon had, including the victims fund.

The bottom line after all these legal gymnastics was that Feinberg could change his regulations in the final redraft that was due to be issued in about two weeks in a way that Simon's only deduction from his award, other than the life insurance, would be about $200,000—the amount of her children's Social Security payments, which were not contingent on anything but only lasted until they reached age eighteen. The difference for her was about $800,000 less in offsets.

Better yet, Feinberg had even found a way to avoid offsetting the death benefits of $250,000 paid to police and firefighter widows. One of the partners in Lee Kreindler's firm had taken Feinberg aside during another of Feinberg's meetings with the plaintiffs lawyers. He pointed out that the federal statute establishing the benefit said that it could not be lowered by any other statute. Well, wasn't offsetting it against what Feinberg would award using another statute (the one establishing the victims fund) to lower it? Feinberg readily agreed, just as he also agreed to some similarly legalistic rationale for not deducting the police and fire pensions.

Feinberg wasn't breaking the law that Congress had written requiring that other sources of aid to the victims be deducted from his awards, but he was bending it—a lot. The advantage he had that officials who try the same thing in other contexts rarely have was that no one was going to go into court to challenge what he was doing. Who, after all, was going to sue to get a judge to lower the payments to the widow of a fireman?

While Feinberg focused on putting these issues to rest this week, others on his staff started drafting the actual form that people would fill out to apply to the fund. Here, Senator Mitchell's admonition about simplicity being the enemy of fairness was on vivid display. Feinberg craved simplicity, but the law—and the need to handle the taxpayers' money responsibly—required that he get all kinds of information before he handed out $1 million or $2 million of the taxpayers' money to someone. Thus, the first draft of the form was forty pages, which the staff was already testing on secretaries and others around the office to see which parts needed to be explained more clearly. When Feinberg heard about the forty pages, he asked to get a copy so he could edit it. He knew they would have to do better.

Meantime, the drumbeat of protests from all sides on all issues related to the fund continued. Late this afternoon a couple calling themselves, simply, "Parents," logged on to the Feinberg fund website to write how "outraged" they were "at some fiancés who feel they should be qualified claimants. . . . We parents sacrificed our entire life for our children only to be dealt with . . . pain and suffering that cannot be experienced in any other relationship."


Gale Rossides was starting to settle into a routine at her new job at TSA. She'd work most weekdays from about 7:00 A.M. (she loved to beat the rush-hour commute from Virginia) until about 8:00 P.M., bouncing from one go team meeting to another, while also finding time to edit drafts of a training curriculum or an air marshals handbook. She'd come to the office most Saturdays, but spend Sunday at home, much of it on a laptop.

Today, she began negotiating with the staff of the White House Office of Management and Budget about what she could pay all those passenger checkpoint screeners she now had to hire so quickly. Go team leaders Cliff Hardt (from FedEx) and Randy Null (from Intel) had almost immediately befriended Rossides as a career civil servant who seemed, despite her unflamboyant style, to be more like "one of us," as Hardt put it. Both commiserated with her over the prospect of having to spend all that time trying to wheedle enough money out of OMB.

But Rossides somehow managed to get the bean counters to agree to a pay scale that, while it started at only $23,600, could go up to $35,000 if the applicant had experience. In other words, the recruiters would have real flexibility in their salary offers, something usually unheard of for these types of government positions. The whole package, with government benefits, was probably worth more than double what the previous screeners had been paid.

## Wednesday, February 20, 2002

When Ed Woollen began to hear that TSA was going to put out for bid what was likely to be a multibillion-dollar contract for a company to do the installation of thousands of baggage explosive detection machines, he had reached out to Raytheon's contacts at the FAA. These FAA officials had supervised the smaller contract Raytheon had had, under which the company had installed about 140 machines in the last five years. This new contract might require 2,000 to 3,000 machines to be installed between now and December 31. But it was exactly the same kind of work. Thus, the connection seemed obvious.

A longtime FAA official whom Raytheon had dealt with set up a meeting for Woollen and a more senior Raytheon executive, Hugo Poza, who ran a multibillion-dollar division that had handled the earlier FAA work.

Yet their meeting this morning was not at the FAA, but at the TSA's office in a chaotic makeshift conference room full of hand-scrawled charts and timetables. What was even more curious was that when Raytheon's FAA contact got there he had to introduce himself to the man who was running the meeting for TSA. Still more strange was that the top TSA man, Null, didn't work at TSA. He was an executive at Intel. Woollen and Poza couldn't figure out what was going on.

Null explained to the group that he was on loan from Intel to TSA because

Norman Mineta had called the Intel CEO looking for help. "My job," said Null, "is to get the EDS [explosive detection system] machines into all the airports."

"That's why we're here," said Woollen.

From there it was downhill. Woollen and Poza were stunned to find out that Null didn't even know that Raytheon had ever done this work before. Worse, once he was brought up to speed on what Woollen and Poza thought was their leg-up in getting the big contract, he didn't seem to care.

After trying to establish his clout at Raytheon by outlining the size of the division he ran, Poza said that he knew that TSA had to be concerned about getting all the machines in on time. And the reason they had wanted the meeting was to outline a plan Raytheon had to help them. Poza knew that it was going to take the government a few weeks or months to get the contracts done, plus get the money authorized to buy machines from InVision. Raytheon, Poza continued, had already talked to Sergio Magistri at InVision and knew that he was champing at the bit to ramp up, but couldn't do so without getting a firm purchase order.

Raytheon's solution, Poza explained, was that Raytheon was willing to lay out the cash right now to buy 1,000 InVision machines—nearly a billion-dollar expenditure—so that production could be ramped up while TSA got its ducks in order. "Then you can just buy them from us at our cost," Poza continued. "And if you don't want to buy them, we figure we can sell them in other countries. The point is we're willing to take that risk to get the process started."

"Don't you dare," Null blurted out.

Woollen and Poza were stunned. They figured they had presented the government with the perfect, no-risk plan to jump-start the procurement process. What they didn't know was that Null was in the middle of the negotiations with Magistri of InVision to allow the government to buy and license all the software and patents necessary to let others build the machines. Raytheon coming in and waving a billion dollars at Magistri would surely screw all that up by taking away all government's leverage.

The meeting ended with Null telling Woollen and Poza that TSA would soon be putting out its invitation for companies to bid on the contract—called a request for proposal, or RFP—and that they'd be glad to have Raytheon compete for the deal. But until then Raytheon should do nothing to interfere with TSA's process.

# Thursday, February 21, 2002

At the insistence of Pat Kennedy, the Red Cross executive board member from San Francisco who had been so incensed that the organization had segregated funds for the September 11 victims, the board took a formal vote to reaffirm a long-standing policy. Henceforth, no special solicitations would ever be made for any specific disaster, even in the event of another terror attack. And unless a donor specifically required it, no donations would ever be segregated for any one disaster.

The vote, which was unanimous, was never announced publicly. To be sure, several months from now the organization would announce that its fund-raising appeals would begin to explain to donors more clearly that their money would not be directed at any specific disaster. But the more important point was that the Red Cross was completely abandoning the role Healy had pushed it into in September—that of being the lead charity whenever the next terrorist attack happened. Thus, the board was guaranteeing that the one organization everyone was likely to look to again for private sector relief in the event of another terror attack was not going to be there.

Anthony Romero has been barnstorming the country for the past few weeks, making speeches and bucking up the ACLU's local chapters. He arrived tonight at the Howard Johnson Express Inn in Billings, Montana, to speak at the annual meeting of the Montana ACLU, which has 863 members. A handful of pickets outside held signs. One, carried by a seven-year-old boy standing in the snow with his father, demanded, "ACLU & Romero Go Home." Thinking about the fact that he was going inside to shake hands with a local Hispanic for whom the ACLU had recently won $50,000 in a racial profiling case, and a Native American couple whose voting rights case they were litigating, Romero was tempted to run over to the boy to give him a hug and say, "I am home; there are all kinds of issues right here in Montana that the ACLU is making a difference on." But he thought the better of it and went in to a warm reception among the true believers, many of whom had driven clear across the state to see him talk about the INS detentions and the new threat to civil liberties arising out of the September 11 attacks.

Saying that the Patriot Act "gives a whole new meaning to the word 'misnomer,' " Romero declared, to loud applause, that, "We must not allow the war on terrorism to become an excuse for the government to do whatever the hell it wants."

Romero would later estimate the crowd at "several hundred." Nonetheless, he says he found trips like this exhilarating—"the best part of the job." The next morning he clipped a newspaper photo of the child picket with the "Romero Go Home" sign, and put it in his pocket to show to friends as a badge of honor. He was so moved by the sight of the young boy standing and protesting in the snow that four months later he would end a speech to a national staff conference by telling the story of seeing him out there and concluding, "If we do our job right, that little boy should be an ACLU member in a few short years."

# Saturday, February 23, 2002

Sergio Magistri had had several phone conversations with TSA's Null in the past two weeks, and they hadn't gone well. Null had made it clear that Magistri was getting no orders from TSA until two things happened: He had to agree to license his intellectual property so that others could build his machines; and, to add insult to injury, he had to lower the prices for the machines he got to build—a lot. Magistri had resisted and even tried to circle back to his telephone friend, Mineta, but was told by Mineta's staff that Null was the person he had to deal with. Null had offered to fly out, but only on a weekend, because things were too busy at headquarters to allow for travel during the week.

So this morning, Magistri and several members of his executive team sat down with Null, who had brought just one person, a TSA lawyer.

Null dangled an order of more than 600 machines in front of Magistri. That would mean nearly half a billion dollars in sales for a company that had revenue of about $40 million in all 2001. Magistri complained that licensing away his intellectual property would kill his company over the long term, especially since it would wipe out the profitable follow-on business they did in providing maintenance for their machines.

Both sides needed this deal too much for it to fail. By late afternoon, they had agreed to terms that were painful to Magistri but were better than continuing to wait.

He'd sell his machines at deep discounts. For example, the highest-capacity unit that regularly sold for about $1.2 million would cost the TSA about $950,000. The machines cost Magistri about $720,000 to make. Null could not absolutely guarantee the high volumes he had flashed at the outset, because Congress hadn't authorized that much money yet, but he thought they could start with an order of at least 100 machines almost immediately. Similar orders would follow in the next twelve months totaling 625 machines, he said.

As for the licensing deal, in exchange for Magistri granting the government the rights to all the intellectual property, Null offered to pay Magistri about 8 percent of his regular price for each machine made by another company. But Null agreed that the rights would only last for two years and would not cover InVision's newest and best model. He also agreed that anyone who might be a likely long-term competitor to InVision could not be given the right to build the machines, and that any company that did get the right would have to agree to a five-year no-compete clause. That meant that InVision's concerns about creating a competitor would be eased considerably.

Finally, InVision was given a right to do all the maintenance work on the licensed machines.

They had a deal. And within two weeks, InVision would finally announce its first TSA order—$148 million. In one conversation, Magistri had more than tripled last year's sales, with more presumably to come. It was now time to ramp up.

When the order (but not the licensing deal) would be announced less than two weeks after this Saturday handshake, InVision stock would climb to $42.75, up $1.80 in a day, and up more than twelve times from its September 10 value.

## Tuesday, February 26, 2002

"If you give them the Kentucky Derby, then they'll want Pimlico and the Preakness, the whole Triple Crown," Tom Ridge said from the head of a conference table in the Old Executive Office Building. "Where do we stop?"

The issue Ridge and his senior staff were trying to deal with was how to decide what should be designated a National Special Security Event. These were the high-profile gatherings, such as the Olympics and the Super Bowl, where the federal government had been providing security on steroids. The Kentucky Derby now wanted the nod. "We're getting calls every other day from some member [of Congress] asking that an event in their district be designated," added the head of Ridge's congressional liaison office.

It was only 9:00. But for the twenty men and women assembled for the senior staff meeting, this was mid-morning. Most had been on the job for two or three hours, including Ridge, who started with a 7:00 daily briefing from the directors of the FBI and CIA, then met with the President, as he now did every morning when both were in town.

Three leather chairs down from Ridge, Mike Byrne seemed concerned about watering down the status of these National Special Security Events. The redheaded former New York City fireman told Ridge that the best course was to get the Secret Service positioned to consult with anyone about any event, but to keep the number of fully designated events strictly limited and based on a "matrix of criteria." The Derby probably wouldn't make the grade, but, said Byrne, "We can offer a continuum of help depending on what they need."

"Okay," said Ridge. "But we should see if we can set up a program so that we offer this consulting in some kind of organized way. Let's get the NCAA, NASCAR, the NFL, and the rest in here on a regular basis."

According to Byrne, within two hours he had spoken with the Secret Service special agent who was on loan to his office and to the Secret Service's deputy director, and "we got an organization in the works that will now do this."

On this issue at least, Ridge's Office of Homeland Security seemed to be functioning as intended, perhaps because Paul O'Neill, the Secretary of the Treasury, which oversees the Secret Service, was so determinedly un-turf-conscious that Ridge's staff was able to make the process work.

Ridge's team by now had grown to about eighty, roughly divided into three categories. Those involved in dealing with state and local officials, Congress, and the private sector typically had worked for him in Pennsylvania. Others, like Falkenrath, were WMD (shorthand for weapons of mass destruction) policy wonks. They'd been reading and writing about the threat for years. Now they had the chance of a lifetime to do something about it. Like Byrne and Lawlor, the general who runs Protection and Prevention, everyone else had experience in the trenches, having been recruited from agencies ranging from the Army Corps of Engineers, to the FBI, CIA, and Secret Service, to the departments of Agriculture, Defense, State, and Commerce (to deal with what's called economic consequence management).

What seemed to bond this quickly assembled team was their zeal. Coming to work when it was still dark and leaving after it had become dark again evoked for them what the White House complex and its people must have been like in the weeks after Pearl Harbor.

In fact, in one of the first weeks after he had left his family in New York and arrived in Washington, Byrne found himself staying up one night rereading the sections of Doris Kearns Goodwin's book, *No Ordinary Time,* that deals with America's buildup following Pearl Harbor. "That's the situation we're in," he explained the night of this staff meeting, adding as he walked out of the driveway alongside the White House on his way to the apartment he had sublet, "I look up at those lights in the White House every night when I walk out of here, and it just blows my mind that I'm here with a chance to do all this."

For Byrne and the others, these early weeks of their homeland security mission were a time of adrenaline-filled euphoria. It was what everyone—entrepreneurs like Magistri, or new government appointees—feels when they're in the first stages of a once-in-a-lifetime start-up. No day was too long. No press story questioning their prospects was anything but uninformed. No obstacle seemed like anything other than an exciting challenge that was sure to be overcome.

The bumps in the road, including the rejection by the cabinet in December of their border consolidation "no-brainer," didn't matter. Nor did it matter to Ridge or his people that in Washington, when you parachute a high-profile new agency into the center of the capital's power structure, the knives are bound to come out, the assumption being that whatever power the new guys were going to have would have to come from somewhere—and someone—else. To them, that was all a September 10 way of thinking. Times were different now.

The next topic of the staff meeting was the new alert system the group had been working on. There was stage fright in the room as they contemplated the upcoming announcement, scheduled for about two weeks from now, of a four-color—white, yellow, orange, and red—system aimed at eliminating some of the vagueness of the warnings that had been subject to such derision in the fall. The plan was that Ashcroft, consulting with Ridge and the President, would take the threat information coming in from various intelligence sources and put it into context. Each color would mean that certain criteria—credibility of source, number of sources, specificity of time or place—had been met. More important, as the system was developed and absorbed by various federal, state, and local agencies, they would gear their own protection plans to the colors. For example, the National Parks Service or even the Miami Beach police would have procedures that would be different for an orange alert than for a yellow alert. Further down the road, a different alert status might be declared for, say, bridges and tunnels, or even a particular region of the country, so that the alerts became still more focused.

It all sounded good, but Ridge knew that it could never meet the public's expectations for true specificity. "The key thing here," he told the staff, "is to manage expectations. We know we can't provide the clarity and sense of security that we would like to project."

"We know we can't rehearse the questions we'll get too many times," warned Steve Abbot, the former admiral who was Ridge's deputy. "We still have some issues that we have to wrestle to the deck," Abbot added, referring to some lingering questions that, he said, "folks" in the White House had about the colors.

Those, like Ridge and his staff, who work in the White House and at the Old Executive Office Building across the driveway, see themselves as the ones who come up with the ideas and make them happen, often despite interference from Congress. On Capitol Hill, that view is almost completely inverted. Legislators think they're the ones that develop policies and pass the laws that put the policies into action. The executive branch simply has to carry out those laws.

It is the ritual of the congressional hearing, of which there are dozens in a given week, where the tension between these opposite worldviews plays out. Legislators think they are holding the hearings to get new ideas for new laws, and to see how the executives are executing laws already passed. Members of the executive branch, who testify because they have to, usually view almost any hearing as a distraction from the real work they'd rather be doing back at the office.

This morning, as four of Ridge's Protection and Prevention staffers were plugging away in quiet meetings with Customs and Coast Guard officials on a plan to secure container cargo, Senator Dianne Feinstein, the Democrat from California, convened a hearing on the same subject. The session illustrated the parallel universes that existed at the two ends of Pennsylvania Avenue.

Schumer, who sat on this subcommittee, began by announcing he was introducing legislation to give Customs additional resources. By now, Schumer's staff had heard from Customs officials about how wrong it had been for him to equate 2 percent inspections with a "98 percent chance of success" for a terrorist. Thus, Schumer had gone from advocating inspections of everything, to giving people like McCabe the additional resources they needed to do the whole mix of challenges they faced on the docks—targeting, inspections, perimeter security. As usual, Schumer wasn't shy about dramatizing the issue. He pointed out that someone could take something like "the bomb in Hiroshima" and "put it in a container, send it on a ship, and create huge havoc."

For Schumer, cargo security had become perhaps his highest-priority national security concern. In some ways he was like a kid with a new hobby—talking about it all the time, constantly searching out and falling in love with experts, and becoming fascinated with statistics and threat scenarios that for him were revelations, even if they were old hat to the people he consulted.

The CEO of a shipping company used a metaphor of his own to illustrate the problem that most haunted McCabe—that catching something at the port wasn't good enough anymore the way it was with drugs. Ports were close to central cities, and the detonation of a bomb once it arrived, possibly by a timed or remote detonator, would be catastrophic. "It's a little bit like a ballplayer with a mitt and another guy with a hand grenade," said Robert Quartel, of FreightDesk Technologies. "The game here . . . is to stop the hand grenade before it ever gets lobbed to the port."

Quartel was arguing for a complete, computerized system that would track all material in all containers, from when it leaves a factory to when it arrives at a port. There would also be secure seals in place to assure that the container is not interfered with along the way. As Senator Feinstein and others pointed out, this notion had been advanced most avidly by Stephen Flynn, a former Coast Guard official who now worked at the Council on Foreign Relations, a Park Avenue–based think tank.

Flynn was the classic insider-outsider who played a crucial role on issues like this. He was the expert everyone quoted—the most credible person sounding an alarm that needs to be heard, even if he may be sounding it too loudly. Many in the shipping business saw Flynn as an obsessed alarmist. Others thought he was the first and smartest person to grasp the danger to public safety and the world economy posed by thousands of un-inspected, un-tracked containers arriving at American ports every day. McCabe thought Flynn "knows his stuff, but because he's been around the Coast Guard all his life, he never understood that we [Customs] have more information on the containers than he thinks we do."

Flynn believed fervently that a tightly monitored tracking system had to be established immediately. It is "crazy," he says, that after September 11 the government was willing to spend "$200 million a month on aviation security, and $100 million for a whole year for stupid little security grants to all the ports combined.

"I lie awake at night haunted by this," Flynn adds. "Without a system that we can demonstrate is there, an attack or the threat of one would cause total paralysis. Imagine the newspaper stories, with headlines that the only thing protecting us is a fifty-cent seal that's now on all those containers. The public would demand that everything everywhere would have to be opened and inspected."

Flynn's prescription was simple, if impractical. For $100, every cargo container could be outfitted not only with better seals, but with a satellite transponder that would track its progress to make sure it hadn't been inexplicably and suspiciously delayed in transit somewhere. The container would also have light and pressure sensors that would make sure it hadn't been opened after the seal had been applied.

The problem was that there were already 40 million containers out there that would have to be replaced or retrofitted, and someone in an industry with notoriously low profit margins would have to pay for it all. But Flynn's role was to set the marker for perfect security, and, as the repeated references to him in this hearing illustrated, he did it well.

On the day of the hearings, Flynn was already working closely with Customs Commissioner Robert Bonner to develop a series of pilot projects in which containers would be tracked this way. Flynn would be perpetually frustrated about the pace of the project—as would be expected of a man who had made this his life's work and was right on the money when it came to understanding the awesomeness of the threat. Schumer, too, thought Customs wasn't moving fast enough. But, although no one would have known it from these hearings, which seemed to imply that few in the executive branch appreciated the threat, Flynn had found a kindred spirit of sorts, in Bonner.

Bonner, a former head of the Drug Enforcement Administration and United States attorney in Los Angeles, had been a partner at a prestigious L.A. law firm before taking the Customs job. He had wanted to be Attorney General and settled for Customs as a consolation prize. Now, as Customs became a center of September 12 era action, he was proving to be the right man in the right place. Although he lacked flair and was more a grind than a showboat, he was eagerly working with Ridge and his staff on the interagency container security group, and had by now begun efforts to negotiate agreements with countries that had the leading ports of the world, so that his Customs inspectors would be stationed on the ground in those ports. It was his way of countering that grenade-in-the-catcher's-mitt scenario.

# Wednesday, February 27, 2002

Chuck Schumer came over to Mitch Daniels's office this morning to try to settle things with the White House budget director. For a few weeks, there had been lots of back and forth between them and their allies about whether Daniels and his President really were going to deliver that $20 billion in aid promised in September. Word had leaked out, for example, that Daniels might count money to be paid out by the Feinberg fund, thought to be $6 billion or more, as aid to New York, because so many of the victims lived there. Maybe the money spent to investigate the anthrax letters sent to New York media outlets would be counted, too.

Schumer came prepared to fight. But he didn't have to. Daniels gave him a detailed list of what would count toward the $20 billion. It included everything, such as FEMA recovery aid and money to rebuild the lower Manhattan transit systems, that Schumer thought should be counted, and nothing that he thought shouldn't be. And Schumer was amazed to find that the total added up to $21.4 billion—not $20 billion. Better yet, Schumer succeeded in getting Daniels to agree that any part of the money that FEMA did not have to give the city for its cleanup and recovery costs at Ground Zero could be used by New York for other projects related to restoring lower Manhattan. It was a stunning concession. Schumer knew—and, though he didn't know it, Daniels also knew—that the work down in the pit was proceeding so much ahead of schedule and below budget that this was the equivalent of giving New York billions more in aid. To be sure, much of that $21.4 billion would take years to get to New York. Some would await specific proposals for its use by the state and city governments; some would languish as the state failed to get the word out sufficiently to people and businesses eligible for the various aid programs; and billions more would be in the form of investment tax incentives that might never be worth the amounts specified, because, in a poor economic climate, New Yorkers would be unwilling to take advantage of the investment incentives. But as a general matter, the package was everything Schumer could have hoped for, even a bit more.

If Schumer was amazed at Daniels's flexibility, Daniels was equally amazed at how Schumer conducted himself *after* the meeting. When they had first sat down, Daniels told Schumer he would go through it all in great detail, but wanted Schumer to agree not to reveal it publicly in advance of the White House getting the chance to announce it with him. Schumer had agreed, but Daniels, knowing Schumer's reputation as a publicity hound and realizing that any senator or congressman would want to make this his story, resigned himself to the probability that Schumer would leak it so that whoever got the scoop would make it a Schumer-centric story. Months later Daniels would still marvel at "what a man of his word, Schumer is. The guy resisted all temptation to leak it, when he easily could have."

Schumer had learned to conrol the urge to tout himself that had gotten the better of him when he had put out that September press release overstating his role in setting up the victims compensation fund.

Brian Peterman, the admiral from Miami who is Lawlor's man on border security, held a 2:00 P.M. meeting on student visas. This was a typical INS mess. Students who enroll in schools in the United States can get visas as long as their school has certified their status. That sounds easy enough, until one plumbs the details, such as the fact that the INS had a list somewhere of more than 74,000 schools—from Harvard to a beauticians academy in San Diego—that were authorized to certify students. This seemed to be more than triple the actual number of schools of any kind offering post-high-school education, but no one at the INS had any idea how the list had been compiled. Surely, there were people out there who had set up an easy end run around visa restrictions by creating a phony school and then charging Saudis or anyone else $5,000 or $10,000 tuition to "enroll."

Then, of course, there was the issue of whether those with the visas to study at real schools actually enrolled, or stayed enrolled.

This was not a new problem. Congress had passed a law requiring INS to set up a student visa verification and tracking system in 1998. But amid an avalanche of pressure from the higher education lobby—which was worried about losing the 550,000 foreign students enrolled in the U.S. annually (usually at full tuition), and having to spend millions on the regulatory paperwork—Congress had then not appropriated the funds for INS to implement it. Then-Senator John Ashcroft had been one of those who had urged INS to delay any kind of tracking program. However, when California Democratic Senator Dianne Feinstein had proposed, in the aftermath of September 11, that all foreign students be kept out until a real tracking program could be implemented, the education lobby had gotten scared and eased its stance. They now said they supported a tracking system.

This meeting was the third Peterman had held to figure out a new plan. As usual, the goal was to get everyone from every conceivable agency with a stake in the issue—the National Science Foundation, the Department of

Education, the State Department (which issues visas), and, of course, INS—sitting at the same table.

Peterman seemed stunned when the woman from INS reported, matter-of-factly, that it was going to take until October 1, 2003, to get all colleges and universities online with a database that would allow the government to make sure that those with student visas were actually enrolled as students. "We're still working on getting buy-in from everyone," she said. The low-key Peterman barely showed his frustration. But he hadn't suddenly moved his family up from Florida, and he didn't come to work at 6:00 and leave thirteen or fourteen hours later every day, to preside over business as usual.

He made a note to make sure he got Ridge or his deputy, Abbot, on the case to get that deadline changed.

Then, something still more frustrating happened. Peterman asked the INS woman to share with the group her new draft of the regulations that INS will use to implement the new visa tracking plan. To which she replied, just as matter-of-factly, that she wasn't authorized to do that until she got clearance from the Justice Department.

Peterman had no choice but to let that pass, too.

The discussion shifted to a controversial plan that had started working its way through Ridge's staff in early January. The idea was to prevent foreign students from particular countries from enrolling in certain types of sophisticated, graduate-level science courses. The group seemed eager to outline all the reasons it might not work and shouldn't be tried. Won't singling out students this way be the starkest form of racial profiling imaginable? How can the courses be targeted? (Actually, it turns out the Department of Education already has a system of classifying courses.) What will be the legal authority? (Maybe the education could be deemed an "export"; the government already had the authority to limit security-endangering exports.) How will enforcement work?

What should have been surprising about the bureaucracy's resistance was that they weren't there to decide *whether* this was to be done. Their President had decided that for them, with a presidential directive he had issued on October 30 ordering a program to screen students from high-risk countries from taking sensitive courses.

So Peterman was thinking more about the solution than the reasons why one would be hard to find. He closed the meeting by telling the group they needed to keep plugging away at it. Later that day, he warned Lawlor that this effort was becoming mired, as usual, in INS intransigence, in this case supported by equally reluctant officials from the departments of State and Education.

Meanwhile, Lawlor was getting his own dose of frustration. At a meeting he chaired on "Medical and Public Health Preparedness," he couldn't get agreement on who should receive smallpox vaccinations now that the government had succeeded in getting a huge supply of them in place. It was the same runaround he had dealt with at prior meetings on the subject. Everyone in the room—except the Department of Health and Human Services (HHS) representatives—wanted to go ahead with a program to vaccinate hundreds of thousands of medical workers and emergency first responders, but hold back on a mass program because it was well known that the smallpox antibody was the most dangerous of vaccines. It typically caused one to four deaths for every million people given the shot, and serious illnesses in several more. That meant that a nationwide program would kill hundreds, maybe even a thousand or more. The HHS people were so worried about these collateral casualties that they didn't want to give the vaccine to more than about 10,000 or 15,000 medical workers, and they weren't even sure about that. Their preference seemed to be simply to establish a plan to vaccinate everyone once it became clear that a terrorist had somehow given someone the disease.

Even though the others in the room disagreed, including a staffer from Vice President Cheney's office who said Cheney was heavily interested in getting the issue resolved and a vaccination program in place, the HHS people held firm. But they didn't hold firm by arguing against the other plans. Rather, they kept raising questions, citing all the unknowns that they had to go back and study, many of which they had promised to study after the last meeting. Today, the question they put back on the table had to do with getting a precise read on how effective the government's quarantine plan would be. If we knew that, they argued, then we would know how widely to distribute the vaccine.

But, of course, getting firm numbers on something that speculative was impossible. Lawlor felt they needed to do something now, so that medics and others could respond safely in the event of an attack. The vaccine took six days before anyone knew if it had worked and the immunity was effective. They needed to build into the system an ability to respond to possible victims quickly; they couldn't be in a situation where if there was an attack, they would inoculate people and then wait six days before sending them in to care for the sick. There was just no excuse for more meetings.

But Lawlor's instructions were that consensus was required before they could move ahead on any issue, a requirement that continued to astonish this Army general.

The debate, he decided, had to be bucked up the chain of command, along with a laborious policy options paper, so that someone could make a decision. That someone would have to be the President. But as Lawlor would find out, Bush was more inclined to let his people fight it out than to call the shots on smallpox shots. It would take until the late fall before Bush finally settled on a policy.

At 3:30 Ed Woollen and two other Raytheon executives, along with two lawyers from their well-connected law firm, were ushered into the Vice President's ornate old conference room in the Executive Office Building. There, they met with Peterman from Ridge's office, as well as members of the Vice President's staff and a senior aide in the White House Office of Science and Technology Policy.

The meeting had been arranged by one of Raytheon's lawyers, Larry Levinson, a longtime Washington hand who was a partner at Raytheon's Washington law firm. Levinson, who is friendly with Cheney chief of staff Lewis Libby, had gotten Libby to convene the meeting so that he could bring the Raytheon people in to brief relevant White House officials on what Raytheon thought it could do to help the government get a handle on its immigration problem. Peterman, who by now was knee-deep in trying to figure out how to build the entry-exit system that Congress had mandated, was glad to be there.

Woollen began with his standard spiel about Raytheon's experience at the airports with baggage scanning machines, then gave an overview of his efforts since September to organize Raytheon to meet the challenges of homeland security. From there, he segued into what they wanted to talk about today, which was "visitor management."

Peterman seemed amused by the euphemism.

As Woollen continued, an aide began to set up a PowerPoint presentation. But as invariably happens when a tech company tries to demonstrate its tech prowess, he couldn't boot it up. After a few long minutes and some nervous laughter from the Woollen side of the table, he finally got it to work, and Woollen continued.

Raytheon's great market dominance in spy satellite software, he explained, was because the company was so good at mining billions of bits of data. Now they would bring the same skills and capacity to visitor management by creating a system that would "keep terrorists out, deport the ones who get in, detect illegal overstays, and manage students on visas."

Where do I sign up? Peterman thought.

Woollen continued, outlining the options Raytheon had for biometric identifiers—iris scans, fingerprints, palmprints, and even a new face scan that could be done reliably from twenty feet away, and not only served as an identifier but also detected enough "vascular changes" in a face to make it "a first order of lie detector." Woollen didn't mention that Raytheon actually subcontracted out all that high-tech stuff to smaller companies in the field, whose products Raytheon would buy and assemble into a working system.

To screen people, the data would be mined through a system that Raytheon called Genesis, which, Woollen explained vaguely, could track "certain patterns of behavior" that indicated someone was a threat.

None of that was enough by itself, Woollen added. The real value Raytheon added was that the Raytheon system would be "proactive." Once a visitor arrived here, his data would be constantly updated, so that everything he did would be "tracked during the entire lifetime of the visa." If he got into trouble here and was wanted by the police, or even if new information about his prior activities was developed by Genesis, he'd be placed on a new lookout list so that he could be apprehended.

Depending on your point of view, it was all fascinating, scary, or encouraging. But Peterman and the man from the White House science office also knew that it was wildly expensive. To take one example, how could they pay for the biometric scanners—whether of the iris, the palm, or the face—at every border crossing? And how would someone be apprehended once put on a lookout list? Where would all the checkpoints be?

Nonetheless, these Raytheon guys seemed determined to build a system that, in some form, had to be built, so Peterman gave them the name of the procurement people at INS who were overseeing the development of the entry-exit system, and said they should get a meeting over there. He added the now standard speech that all homeland security staffers had learned—which was that they did not make any purchasing decisions.

If nothing else, the session with Woollen and his colleagues gave Peterman some ammunition if the INS people told him they hadn't been able to find anyone with a vision of how this could be done.

Woollen felt the meeting was a success, because, he explains, "You always have to make the rounds on projects like this. You go from office to office, from the White House to the agencies, to Capitol Hill, laying groundwork, sounding people out, and accumulating information."

# Thursday, February 28, 2002

Detroit Border Patrol agent Bob Lindemann hadn't heard anything about what Justice Department Inspector General Glenn Fine was doing with the inquiry into his and his partner's demotion, but he would have been cheered to see Fine in action today, putting it to INS at a hearing of the House Subcommittee on Immigration.

The topic was something called the visa waiver program, under which the United States allows citizens of twenty-eight friendly countries to come to the United States without first obtaining a visa. Citizens of other countries have to go to a State Department office in their home country, where they are screened (usually not well enough pre–September 11), before getting a visa that allows them to visit the U.S. for a specified period of time and for a specific purpose, such as studying at an American school. Citizens from visa waiver countries, however, can just show up with a passport. It is the visa waiver program that had allowed Richard Reid, the shoe bomber who is a British citizen, to get on a plane to the United States unscreened.

In early 1999, Fine's office had issued a report that found glaring weaknesses in how the INS ran the visa waiver program. For example, for all people coming from visa waiver countries, the INS inspectors at airports were supposed to enter their passport numbers into a computer before they were allowed entrance. That way, they could check to see if they were on a watch list. Fine had found that the inspectors were often not doing this. Moreover, to help deal with a rampant problem of stolen passports in many of the visa waiver countries—millions of blank ones were thought to have been stolen out of the passport offices in Italy, for example—Fine had urged in 1999 that INS set up a central system to get information about passport thefts from the visa waiver countries, and then enter the numbers of all stolen passports into a database. That way, anyone entering with one would be caught when their number was checked.

This morning, Fine declared that INS still had no stolen passport database, and that inspectors at various airports around the country didn't even know about the requirement to check the visa waiver passport numbers against a watch list.

What followed was what always happened when Fine came to Congress and said INS wasn't doing the basics of its job. A senior INS official, in this case Deputy Commissioner Peter Becraft, thanked "Glenn" for his report, said he agreed with it, said he was issuing a new "policy directive," and promised that he and INS head Ziglar were now going to take "a personal hand" in fixing the problem.

There was something else about the hearing that was emblematic, and instructive. Just when it was becoming obvious that clamping down on the visa waiver program, or maybe even ending it altogether, was a no-brainer, someone showed up to spoil the consensus. William Norman, the president of the Travel Industry Association of America, took the witness chair to argue that the visa waiver setup needed to be preserved for the same reason it had been created in 1986, "to encourage and facilitate international travel" so that travelers will continue "to spend $103 billion annually and support over 1 million direct U.S. jobs." Like the university lobbyists who resisted tighter controls on student visas, Norman was, depending on one's perspective, a selfish "special interest" or a participant in a democracy providing balance and perspective.

John Ashcroft was about as angry as his staff had ever seen him. He'd just come back from a hearing of a House appropriations committee, where he'd been hugely embarrassed.* It seems that someone in the Justice Department's budget office had leaked documents to the committee that proved that when the FBI had sent its initial budget and strategic plan to Justice last summer, Ashcroft had taken anti-terrorism off the list of the FBI's seven strategic priorities. He had also cut its budget request in that area by hundreds of millions of dollars. The money would have been used to pay for additional translators, analysts, and counterterrorism agents. It didn't help that all of this could be found in the attachment Ashcroft had sent along with a budget submission to budget director Daniels—on September 10.

Congressman David Obey, an aggressive Wisconsin Democrat, had sandbagged Ashcroft with smoking gun questions about these documents. Ashcroft had made matters worse by refusing to acknowledge what was obvious and could have been dismissed with a quick "We all learned a lot on September 11; let's talk about what we're doing now." Instead, Ashcroft, who could have prepared a statement like that because the *New York Times* had gotten Obey's papers and reported on them that morning, had stonewalled. Apparently, he couldn't bear not to be known as the ultimate anti-terrorist attorney general.

*Ashcroft's public affairs director, Barbara Comstock, later said that the Attorney General "really wasn't particularly bothered" by the committee hearing, an account sharply contradicted on the day of the hearing by two Justice Department officials. See Notes.

Now he was taking his embarrassment out on his staff. He was outraged at the leak to Congress and angrily instructed them that budget meetings, or for that matter any important meetings that involved him, were not to include any career people unless they were absolutely sure they could be trusted.

The President and Ridge convened a meeting of the Homeland Security Council this afternoon in the Situation Room. The council—which consisted of all cabinet secretaries having anything to do with homeland security, the Vice President and his chief of staff, Lewis Libby, White House Counsel Alberto Gonzales, and National Security Advisor Condoleezza Rice—had met twice a week in November, December, and January. But now, the meetings had begun tailing off to once every week, then once every other week. The reason wasn't that there weren't still all kinds of homeland security issues to thrash out, but rather that these meetings usually weren't held to thrash anything out.

It had become clear to most of those involved that while President Bush was capable, they thought, of extraordinary acts of leadership, he only did that if the circumstance was extraordinary. To be fair, the President had a lot more on his plate, particularly the war now raging in Afghanistan. But it was also clear that he was not a habitual buck-stops-here decision maker. His staff typically scheduled three or four thirty- to forty-five-minute sessions a week of what they called "policy time," where the President would be asked to deal with issues about which there was some disagreement among senior members of the administration. With staff chief Card, deputy chief of staff Josh Bolten (who vetted all the "policy time" issues beforehand), presidential counselor Karen Hughes, political director Karl Rove, and press secretary Ari Fleischer standing by to offer advice, the cabinet secretary, or perhaps Ridge, who wanted to air an issue, would get an audience. Even then, Bush often would send them back, saying "You guys decide it," once again exhibiting his preference that the staff and cabinet secretaries thrash things out on their own and bring their consensus decisions to him to approve. It was for this reason that the Homeland Security Council meetings were tailing off. What one top Ridge aide called "the low-hanging fruit"—the issues for which consensus was easy to achieve, such as boosting the federal air marshals program—had largely been exhausted. Thus, this meeting was on another similarly simple subject, a consensus decision to continue the National Guard at the airports until May 1.

# Saturday, March 2, 2002

Ken Feinberg got his first push back from Daniels and the people at Justice charged with overseeing the victims fund. Much to Feinberg's relief, they hadn't objected at all to his maneuvering around the workers' comp, Social Security, and police and firefighter death benefits and pensions. Nor did anyone have a problem with Feinberg extending the time period during which someone claiming a physical injury had to be treated, or adding into the regulations a provision that protected the families of illegal immigrants who made a claim (one of several such changes that Senator Clinton had successfully pushed Feinberg to make).

But after hearing months of protests about the stingy pain and suffering award spelled out in the first draft of the regulations, Feinberg had also decided to sweeten the overall offer for everyone by raising the standard award for pain and suffering per family member from $50,000 to $100,000. This meant an extra $200,000 for someone like Eileen Simon. She would now get the base payment for pain and suffering of $250,000, plus $100,000 for herself and each of her three children, or $650,000 before economic damages were calculated.

Jay Lefkowitz, a savvy lawyer who had been Daniels's general counsel when Feinberg first took the job and had now gone over to the White House to become a key domestic policy aide, was among those who were not happy about upping the ante this way. Lefkowitz, a conservative, had pushed early on just to pay the victims' families the standard $250,000 death benefit paid to law enforcement officers. He was already afraid of the precedent the fund was setting. But for weeks Feinberg had been cleverly covering this base by telling the family members who he thought were most persuasive when they complained to him about the stinginess of Feinberg's plan to contact Lefkowitz at the White House—but not to say that Feinberg had suggested it.

After a half hour discussion with Feinberg, Lefkowitz signed off. Again, Feinberg wasn't required by law to get his or anyone else's approval, but he had promised to be a team player.

Now, Feinberg had to finish off the application form, which he considered the fund's albatross. His staff, helped by a group at the Pricewaterhouse-Coopers accounting firm, had gotten it down to thirty-three pages of questions about wages, taxes, insurance, and family members. They had tested it for readability on various secretaries and others in the office. The trick was to strike a balance between prompting people to provide enough information, without making it all seem so burdensome that they'd give up. It was a challenge exacerbated by the reality that the audience would range from sophisticated lawyers to low-wage earners trying to make the claims on their own, which is what the law had intended. The staff wished they had more time to give the form a real field test, but testing it internally would have to do.

# Monday, March 4, 2002

Sal Iacono, who had by now taped the *New York Law Journal* and *New York Times* articles about him up on the wall of his shop, calculated that in February business had picked up to about 60 percent of what it had been before September 11. The two young Hispanic men who shine shoes at his store (in exchange for giving Sal a share of what they get paid) had returned. Neither had gone to the Red Cross or anywhere else for charity to cover their four months of unemployment because they feared being detected as illegal immigrants. (They had been told, correctly, that the Red Cross never reported such matters to the authorities, but they refused to take the chance.)

Sal's hopes of business continuing to improve depended on when and if three office buildings around the corner from his shop would reopen, and, more generally, on the return to lower Manhattan of all the jobs that had been eliminated after the attacks. The New York State Department of Labor was readying a report for release tomorrow that would find that New York City lost 132,000 jobs in 2001, of which about 125,000 were attributable to the attacks.

As Sal greeted the customers who arrived in a much steadier trickle than they had in November or December, he kept trying to shield them from an insistent cough. "I've had it since I got back here," he explained. "But I'm not a crybaby. It's okay."

Bob Lindemann hadn't heard the good news until a reporter from the *Detroit Free Press* called to get his comment. The inspector general had just made public a report he had sent to the INS saying that he believed that the demotions of Lindemann and his partner, Mark Hall, would not hold up in court because they would be viewed as impermissible retaliations for comments the two had made to the press that were protected by the First Amendment and, in fact, were not much different from public comments about the lack of protection on the Northern Border that higher-level Border Patrol officials had made in the past. Fine's report urged INS Commissioner Ziglar to rescind the demotions.

Better yet, the Office of Special Counsel, the federal agency empowered to protect whistle-blowers, had also issued a report urging Ziglar to rescind the punishments.

When Lindemann reported for work later in the day, none of the bosses said anything to him, nor did he receive anything in writing that his demotion—which had been put on hold pending these investigations—was now being withdrawn. He figured, though, that it was only because they needed a few days to get over the shock.

## Tuesday, March 5, 2002

With the removal of the temporary roadway going down into the pit that had been built over where the South Tower elevator banks and lobby had been, there were now so many remains being recovered at Ground Zero that Brian Lyons had once again begun staying at the site through the night. At 2:00 A.M. he helped uncover the ashes of two police officers. He and the others identified them as fallen cops by finding parts of their hats that had not been completely burned. An hour later, they found some firefighter gear with some bones crumpled inside.

Lyons was determined to be there if his brother's uniform or one of his tools was found. He wanted to make sure that the ash and particles all around would be scooped up and sent for DNA testing. Besides, his role as referee between the construction guys and the firemen had suddenly become a lot more important. Because word had spread about all the remains being discovered, there were now about fifty firemen working there as volunteers in addition to the thirty that were officially assigned. They were not shy about getting in the way of the construction crews to make sure any possible remains were being tended to. They'd separate a small pile of debris, then sift it carefully before allowing a grappler to lift it into a truck to be shipped to Fresh Kills. Several times in the last few days, fights had broken out when the construction crew's huge grapplers had accidentally hit a fireman who looked as if he had stopped sifting but had then reached down for another look. The construction guys understood the sensitivity, indeed, the tragedy, of the situation. But their company was also working on a fixed cost contract, instead of one that was based on how much time they spent; so proceeding efficiently was a constant goal. As with everything related to the September 12 era only more so, resolving these adverse interests was messy and always mixed emotion with dollars and cents. Lyons found himself right in the middle of it.

This morning he had another worry—Elaine, his sister-in-law. Two or three off-duty men from Squad 41 were now always rotating through the pit, helping to look for their six fallen brothers. The one in the squad who had volunteered to be Elaine's liaison to the group and to spend extra time visiting her (all 243 fire widows had a similar guardian) told Brian that he was worried about Elaine. It seemed, he said, as if Michael's death was now first starting to hit her. She seemed depressed, tearful all the time lately.

It was an accurate, if understated, report. Elaine Lyons recalls that she spent the winter months at her home in Hawthorne, New York (about twenty-five miles north of the city), basically doing nothing. She had volunteer help caring for her two baby daughters, including the one born in November. But she still didn't get out much. Someone had given her and other fire widows an all-expense-paid weekend at the exclusive Canyon Ranch spa in Massachusetts, but she hadn't even thought about making a reservation.

The group sessions she attended with other widows helped. But they were only once a week. Most of the time she just watched soap operas, while avoiding all television news or newspapers.

About a week ago, one of the firemen at Ground Zero had found a wedding band that he thought might have been either Michael's or that of one of his buddies. But because it was burned beyond recognition, they had had to take it to a jeweler, who needed to know Michael's ring size. Elaine had no idea, and because on closer look it seemed to be a closer match to the other man's ring, she had let that widow have it. What she really wanted was a body, or the remains of one, so that her daughters would someday have a place to go, where there was a tombstone to honor their father.

Last weekend Brian had gone with Elaine to look at a bigger house up the street, and she had decided to buy it, which she was able to do without worrying about selling her current house first. But when the realtor asked her something about an escrow payment, she said, "That's something Michael would have known about," and burst out crying.

Tom Ridge had met New York's new mayor, Michael Bloomberg, a few weeks before when Bloomberg had opened his East Side townhouse to a fund-raiser for Governor George Pataki hosted by President Bush. (Ridge had publicly sworn off politics and fund-raising when he took the homeland security job, but later explained that he was simply tagging along with Bush so he could get a lift back to Washington that night on *Air Force One*.)

Now, Bloomberg was interrupted by a call from Ridge at a dinner he was hosting at his home for New York's five borough presidents.

Ridge wanted to talk about an article in this week's *Time* magazine that was reverberating through the media echo chamber of cable talk shows and online news sites. It was about how last October federal officials feared an imminent attack with a ten-kiloton nuclear device on New York, but had failed to notify Mayor Giuliani or the police commissioner. Ridge claimed that the *Time* report was overstated, that there was never a consensus among him and his colleagues that the threat was real. But, he added, "I want to promise you that if we do have any information like that in the future we will call you."

Bloomberg thanked Ridge, returned to his guests, the borough presidents, and told them about the conversation. "If I get that kind of call," he asked, "should I tell you?"

Of course, they all replied.

To Bloomberg that illustrated the problem Ridge faced. Yes, he thought the mayor should be told of such a threat. But if the mayor then told another local official, that official was bound to tell others and the private warning would soon be public. In fact, soon after this Bloomberg-Ridge conversation, the FBI had told the New York police that an Al Qaeda suspect being interrogated in Pakistan had mumbled something about plans to bomb the New York bridge that had been destroyed in the Godzilla movie, which was presumed to be the Brooklyn Bridge. Soon, cable news cameras were beaming live shots of extra police on patrol there, which infuriated Bloomberg, who feared that a mini-panic had been fomented over this kind of dubious intelligence. On the other hand, how could the people in Washington not have warned New York about something like that? On the third hand, wouldn't too many warnings that don't turn out to become actual attacks create a "cry wolf" syndrome that would cause the public to ignore all warnings?

Indeed, this tension between sharing information and causing panic or cynicism was the root of the problems associated with the vague public alerts that Ridge was now trying to fix with his color codes. The public alerts had been issued because once state and local police were told about a spike in threat-related intelligence, that word was sure to leak out, and in the highly charged atmosphere of the weeks immediately after September 11, the resulting rumors were bound to create a demand that the White House come clean and make a public announcement. Yet how specific could they be if they didn't have specific information—or if they did but did not want to tip off the terrorists to their sources, or to the fact that they were on the case?

## Wednesday, March 6, 2002

On September 12, Northwest Airlines had eliminated a large group of connecting flights—called a "bank"—that arrived and left its hub at Memphis at the end of each day. The total number of canceled flights, which had arrived beginning at 7:45 P.M. and departed until about 9:30, was seventy-five, or about 25 percent of all of Memphis's traffic. Worse, getting rid of this evening bank made it impossible for a business traveler to arrive and leave Memphis in the same day and still get a day's work done.

For weeks, Larry Cox had been trying to talk Northwest into restoring the bank. He'd met with the CEO, the marketing people, the planning people, arguing that while other Northwest hubs had also lost a bank, they all had had six or seven banks a day, whereas Memphis had had only four. By cutting Memphis to three, he complained, Northwest was making it impossible for his vendors and his passengers. Memphis just won't be a viable hub with three banks.

The Northwest people knew he was right, and now, as they sensed demand for air travel picking up, they told him they were going to announce that his was the first hub where they planned to restore a bank, in early June. But there was a catch. Seventeen fewer flights would be in the restored bank. More important, there would be a much higher percentage of smaller regional jets and turboprops in the mix, meaning that there would be about 30 percent fewer passenger seats in the restored bank. But at least the bank was back, and Memphis would look like a real hub again.

## Thursday, March 7, 2002

Eileen Simon was thrilled when she got word of Ken Feinberg's official announcement of his redrafted regulations. The work-arounds of the offsets related to Social Security and workers' compensation were worth $800,000 to $1,000,000 to her, and the additional $50,000 per surviving family member another $200,000. She now stood to get about $1.2 million from the fund, even after the $500,000 life insurance was deducted. "I was counting on my government to do the right thing, and it looks like they did," she said.

"Feinberg really listened." However, her friend from her group who had the $2 million life insurance policy was not mollified. She still stood to get "only" several hundred thousand dollars, and was livid.

Simon's concern now had to do with media, not money. Monday was the six-month anniversary of the attacks. To commemorate the day, on Sunday night CBS was scheduled to broadcast a documentary that supposedly featured all kinds of gory footage shot by a cameraman who had gone to the Trade Center with some of the first firemen who responded. Simon did not want her kids to see it. She didn't even want them to go to school the next day, when the other kids might be talking about it.

It was one of those meetings only a lawyer could get excited about. In December, New York state's Empire State Development Corporation had announced that it was going to use some of the hundreds of millions of dollars that Schumer had helped procure from the federal government to create a program to encourage businesses to stay or move into the area around the World Trade Center. Businesses that agreed to sign long-term leases would receive $5,000 per employee.

For Hollie Bart, however, the program had a fatal flaw. Only companies with ten or more employees could qualify for the grants. This meant that Sal Iacono's Continental Shoe Repair was out of luck, as were about a half a dozen other small businesses that Bart was also representing pro bono.

So Bart, being Bart, had begun calling the agency, asking for a meeting. She wrote letters. She called some more. Finally, this morning she and two other pro bono lawyers who worked at other New York corporate law firms got an audience with the three staffers at the Empire State Development Corporation who were running the program. She told them she understood why they wanted to focus on larger companies, but that there were thousands of smaller businesses that needed help, too. She pulled out the news clips about Sal.

They said they'd consider her request.

# Monday, March 11, 2002

Although her brother, Michael Cartier, stayed in New York at work, Jennie Farrell drove down to Washington with her husband, Dan, an executive at a Long Island software company, and her son, James, to attend the White House ceremony commemorating the six-month anniversary.

Nine-year-old James Farrell would later describe in a journal he keeps how thrilling it was to go to the White House and meet the President. But as only a child could, on the drive down he openly shared his confusion with his parents about what he was *supposed* to feel. James knew that he was there only because the uncle who shared his name, and to whom he was the closest among all four uncles in this tightly knit family, had died a horrible death.

"We could tell that he wanted to be excited and be proud, but that he felt bad to feel that way," Jennie Farrell recalls. "It was awful. He was confused and felt guilty, like a lot of the adults, only he was willing to talk about it. The only thing that worked was telling him that Uncle James would want him to enjoy this moment. Then he allowed himself to get excited."

Meantime, Michael Cartier was becoming disenchanted with his Give Your Voice activities, because so much of the focus of the victims in the last two months had had to do with money. Besides, he thought that he had achieved his original goal of getting the city to involve them in the recovery effort, and getting information and assurance that the effort was proceeding in a way that respected the victims.

The group's meetings with the new mayor, Michael Bloomberg, had not gone as well as those with Giuliani. "Bloomberg treated us like a staff that he'd like to fire," Cartier recalls. "With him it's all business." But aside from Bloomberg having seemed insensitive in how he discussed the issue of the memorial that should be built at Ground Zero (at one meeting, he had said, offhandedly, that "small is better"), Cartier had no substantive complaints with City Hall. The medical examiner's office and crews at Ground Zero and Fresh Kills were still doing heroic work as far as he was concerned. Besides, he didn't much care about the memorial. What he cared about now was what he had cared about on September 12—finding his brother. So his Give Your Voice work had tailed off, especially during the day. He sensed that his boss's tolerance for the telephone interviews he often seemed to be giving from his desk in the information systems department at the company that owned Bravo and other cable channels was waning. At night, although he still tended to his website from the computer in his living room, he found himself not doing it as much. Instead, after his wife and baby went to sleep, he'd sit on a chair in the room where his daughter's crib was, and think about his brother.

Eileen Simon's kids had made her promise not to take them anywhere for the half-year anniversary, where, as Brittany put it, "we'd have to cry." So after reading reviews of the CBS show over the weekend, but not watching it, she'd allowed them to go to school. They came home to report that nothing had happened to upset them. In fact, her two eldest children said that they'd been cheered that so many people had remembered the attacks and their father today.

After the White House memorial ceremony, Ridge met with the President and the Homeland Security Council to get final sign-off on the color alert system. For several days now there had been a good deal of back and forth on the details of Ridge's plan, which called for four color categories: white, yellow, orange, and red. This meeting was intended to nail it all down.

First, Deputy Chief of Staff Josh Bolten chimed in that he didn't like using white because it didn't show up clearly on the charts being displayed and, therefore, would look bad on television. That was an issue that had come up repeatedly in the last few days. The President sided with Bolten. That raised the question of whether to change white to blue or to green. But Bush suggested that they use both—that a color, green, should be added to the four as the lowest threat level, in order to suggest a base mark goal that they might not ever get to, but should still be there. Blue would then be the second lowest level, and the alerts would now be five colors: green, blue, yellow, orange, and red.

Then came the issue of what level they should start out with when Ridge made the color scheme announcement, scheduled for tomorrow.

Some, including Ashcroft, wanted orange, the second highest level. But Bolten wanted it to be blue, the second lowest. Bolten seemed to be prevailing when Karen Hughes, Bush's counselor, suggested that based on what she knew about the protective measures being taken near her home in Virginia, and the general climate around the country, she thought yellow was more appropriate. She and Ridge also argued strongly against Ashcroft's choice of orange because, they said, if things got more tense but not extremely so, they'd be stuck with having to go to red when they probably wouldn't want to. The Vice President, who had been inclined to go with orange, also came around to yellow for that reason.

Let's do yellow, the President said.

# Tuesday, March 12, 2002

According to a small, hand-lettered sign, the conference room outside Ed Woollen's office in Alexandria, Virginia, was now the "War Room." It was where the Raytheon team Woollen had assembled was going to convene this afternoon once TSA issued its request for proposals related to the baggage explosive detection installation contract. They'd review it here first, then get on the phone with another, larger team waiting at a Raytheon office in Massachusetts to begin writing a description of how they would deploy a group estimated at 1,200 people to procure, configure, and install the systems made by Magistri and his competitor (the company called L-3).

But although the solicitation to Raytheon and seven other companies asking them to bid on the contract had promised that the RFP would go out today, it was never posted on the TSA website. Calls to TSA to find out what had happened were not answered.

What, in fact, was happening would have rocked not only Woollen but Sergio Magistri if either had known about it. Under pressure from Daniels at the budget office and from Jackson and go team director Null, TSA was beginning to realize that it had to inject the cheaper, smaller, more easily built, but slower trace detection machines into the mix. Otherwise, they were going to spend billions more than they should, plus have no chance of making the deadline. So they were thinking of tinkering with the RFP to reflect the fact that the contractor might not have to build any explosive detection machines using Magistri's intellectual property, and in fact wouldn't have to procure and install nearly as many machines as Magistri was now gearing up to make, but would instead have to design elaborate systems to inject trace detectors much more heavily into the mix.

Not only didn't Magistri have any idea this rethinking was going on, Wall Street didn't either. InVision reached its all-time high today—$49.76, about fifteen times what it had been worth on September 10. Magistri's stock and options were now worth nearly $30 million.

CNN reported that the flight school that had trained two of the September 11 hijackers had received notices late last week from the INS saying that the men's application for student visas had been approved.

The news caused an uproar at the White House. President Bush called Ashcroft, who was in Trinidad, and Ridge and demanded to know how this could have happened.

Then, without asking Ridge or anyone else, INS issued a press statement from Ziglar, who was at a management conference in San Francisco, explaining that the notices were issued because the men had applied for the visas during the summer, before anyone knew they were hijackers. The release made the whole thing seem like standard operating procedure. That made Bush and everyone else angrier. The statement didn't even mention that under a program literally forced on INS by Ridge's staff, anyone applying to take flight training was now being specially screened. ("We had crammed it down at a middle-management level at INS, so I bet the management there didn't even know about it," guessed one Ridge staffer.)

Karen Hughes was dispatched with a Ridge communications aide to put together a new statement that was issued the next day calling the whole thing an unacceptable breakdown in operations and announcing the transfer of four INS managers. Those transferred included the hapless Michael Pearson, who had had such a tough time talking about Northern Border security at that hearing held in November by Senator Levin. The administration also went on the offensive by sending a letter to Congress requesting more authority to discipline or terminate officials for acts of negligence or mismanagement. It was a theme—flexibility in managing employees—that would take center stage by the summer.

For a while now, Tom Ridge and his key staff—such as Abbot (his deputy), Lawlor, and Falkenrath—had been worrying about the new Transportation Security Administration. They didn't know much about the go teams, but were focused on three things that bothered them: Congress's crazy deadlines, the fact that the customer-unfriendly Secret Service seemed to be in charge, and the fact that Norman Mineta, who as a young boy had been put in an internment camp for Japanese-Americans, seemed to be dead set against the kind of profiling that made for what Falkenrath called "efficient risk management."

Lawlor and another Ridge aide who is in charge of liaison with the private sector took a shot at ameliorating some of that, by meeting with TSA officials to urge that they implement a "trusted traveler" program. The idea was that frequent fliers could volunteer to be prescreened so that their identity and the fact that they are not security risks could be confirmed. Then, they could get on a separate, faster line at the airports. Ridge had been talking to airline CEOs and industry groups, and they all urged this trusted traveler notion on him as a customer-friendly solution—and as efficient risk management, too.

But Stephen McHale, TSA head Magaw's deputy for operations (who was a former ATF lawyer), resisted. He explained that they were now working on revising the current passenger prescreening system, CAPPS, which was the rudimentary way the airlines picked people for hand searches. The current criteria—such as whether someone was buying a one-way ticket, plus the selection of some people totally at random—were going to be replaced with an elaborate data-mining system, like the one Lawlor had heard about that Acxiom offered. When that happened, those bothersome pat-downs and searches through a frequent flier's carry-on luggage would mostly end; only people truly deserving of suspicion would get that kind of extra attention. The regular security process—carry-ons going through X rays and people walking through metal detectors—obviously had to continue to cover everyone, even the most trusted traveler, he added. But the new corps of TSA screeners was going to make that much more efficient, too.

McHale was right. Given that no one could or should be trusted enough not to have to walk through a metal detector or put his bag through the X ray, a truly good CAPPS system, which presumably would end the pat-down searches of all people who were obviously not high-risk, would seem to make the trusted traveler idea moot. But although Lawlor let the meeting end with McHale only promising to discuss it again after there was a new CAPPS in place, he still felt more could be done, and was certain Ridge felt even more strongly about it. When he discussed it later with Ridge, Ridge's reaction was that they should still try to keep the idea on the table, because even if a better CAPPS system was developed, a trusted traveler card could supplement it by allowing a person who volunteered to go through the screening to have that used as a factor in the CAPPS assessment of what kind of risk he posed, thereby assuring that CAPPS's data mining didn't somehow mistakenly single him out. After all, computers weren't perfect, and this system hadn't even been built, let alone tested.

Lawyers usually discover smoking guns only on television. But one of the lawyers working for Barry Ostrager in defending Swiss Re against Larry Silverstein's claim that the destruction of the Trade Center had been two events actually found one in a box of files late last week. It was a simple cover note to a fax, and this morning Ostrager got to question its author in one of those pretrial depositions that Ostrager had fought in court to get the time to conduct.

The witness was Robert Strachan, who was in charge of insurance at Silverstein's company. The cover note was dated September 12 and was attached to the insurance form from Silverstein's own broker—the one with occurrence defined broadly as including any series of related events. What it revealed was that on September 12, Silverstein's man Strachan had faxed the financial institution that was the lead lender in the Silverstein Trade Center deal the section of the policy form that defined occurrence as a series of related events. On the cover note he had written, "FYI, the 'occurrence' definition and the insuring agreement . . . that we are working with." Again, the date was September 12.

All Strachan could say at his deposition today was that "I don't recall" the circumstances of his having sent that fax, that "I think you're reading a lot into a brief quick note," and that "I had to send her [the woman from the lending institution] something, and I sent her what was available."

That was not the only killer document Ostrager's team had found in going through all the Silverstein insurance files. A week later, Ostrager would cross-examine Strachan about a note he had doodled to himself at a meeting on September 13, saying the Trade Center had been "underinsured. . . . Did we bite off more than we can chew?"

Asked what he had meant by that, Silverstein's insurance manager was forced to concede, "My initial concern was that the loss limit we had bought . . . was not sufficient to cover the disaster."

That notion of not having bought enough insurance was solidified by two more memos that Ostrager's associates found in the Silverstein broker's files. One put the cost of a total loss of the Trade Center at $5.05 billion, meaning that buying only $3.55 billion to insure against a total loss was, indeed, under-insuring. The other revealed that when Silverstein had gotten a price quote back on $5 billion worth of insurance, he had rejected it because it had cost too much. So, the memo explained, he had settled on $3.55 billion and only even that much because his lenders had insisted he have that much protection. When asked about all that, Strachan and other Silverstein witnesses could only say that the amount they had bought constituted the largest property insurance policy ever purchased.

Ostrager, of course, could use all of this to claim that Silverstein had decided to buy only $3.55 billion worth of insurance for a total loss, but was now trying to collect $7.1 billion for it.

When the insurance company lawyers had trolled other files they'd found still more—including notes of that conference call held on September 12 between some of Silverstein's brokers who were stuck at a meeting in Nashville and others from their firm in London. The lead broker on the Trade Center account—the man who had negotiated and bought the insurance for Silverstein—was quoted in the notes as saying during the conference call that he thought the attacks had been one occurrence because of the form that had been used.

As significant as this evidence was for the insurers, the simple fact that these documents still existed and were handed over by Silverstein's lawyers to Ostrager may be more significant to the larger picture of assessing how America worked in the September 12 era. Those who don't understand the American legal system, or who think it's all bad, might not appreciate how this process called pretrial discovery operates: Lawyers are duty-bound to give the other side every relevant document in their client's files, no matter how damaging. Sure, there are exceptions involving crooked or overreaching lawyers. But most lawyers honor the rules. That they did so here as a matter of routine—no one even discussed hiding or destroying them—in a case involving billions of dollars and humongous egos, and where the documents were so destructive to their side, should not go unnoticed, even if the lawyers involved didn't think turning over the documents was anything special. Indeed, the fact that they thought their conduct was routine is what makes it so noteworthy.

# Friday, March 15, 2002

John Lindh's lawyers fired back at the government. In a motion to compel the government to hand over more of its files in its case against Lindh, Brosnahan's partner George Harris asserted, based on files he had already been given, that summaries of Lindh's "alleged statements" to military intelligence officials written in January differed from other notes that were prepared at the time of the interrogations in December. The motion alleged "important inconsistencies," including that the December notes had said, according to the motion, "that Lindh was obviously disillusioned when he learned of the attacks on the World Trade Center and wanted to leave his Taliban unit but could not do so for fear of death." On the other hand, the summaries prepared in mid-January, "when Mr. Lindh's case was the subject of frequent negative public commentary by government officials, intense media coverage and almost daily public opinion polls," the brief said, "omit reference to these statements and attribute other statements to Mr. Lindh that do not appear in the more contemporaneous reports."

Therefore, Lindh's lawyers now demanded additional information, including the names of the military interrogators, so that they could question them themselves about what Lindh had said, and whether it contradicted the mid-January summaries that had been prepared by the FBI and were almost perfectly consistent with what the FBI interrogator claimed Lindh had said to him.

In short, Brosnahan and his partner were starting to build a case that not only were the interrogations not admissible because Lindh's rights had been violated, but that the earlier sessions with the military people contradicted what the FBI claimed Lindh had said to its agent—who, contrary to the FBI's usual procedure, had questioned Lindh alone and had not asked him to sign a statement afterward. The key, however, was going to be whether Brosnahan and his partners could question those military intelligence interrogators.

# Sunday, March 17, 2002

Brian Lyons had stayed at Ground Zero through the night again, because they were still finding so many firemen's uniforms. At about 8:00 this morning his patience was rewarded. As Lyons and some members of Squad 41, who had come down to the pit this morning still hung over from a St. Patrick's Day party the night before, were sifting through some rubble, Lyons discovered a half-melted crowbar. One of the Squad 41 members quickly recognized it as a tool that Michael Lyons had hand-fashioned into his own personal wedge for prying open big doors—like elevator doors, the Squad 41 man theorized.

Standing on top of what must have been twenty-five feet of rubble that represented what was left of the 110-story tower, the men dug down furiously. There were pieces of three firemen's uniforms, including one collar with a melted American flag, and the remnants of three pairs of firemen's metal suspender clips. They found six five-gallon buckets and scooped all the ash they could into them. The larger pieces were spread out on the ground nearby and sifted. There appeared to be something like 300 or 400 bone fragments, none more than an inch long. There were also four teeth. All of it was loaded onto three stretchers. By now about thirty firemen had gathered, and they formed an honor guard as the stretchers and buckets were carried up to be sent to the medical examiner's office.

Lyons knew that Michael had been a bone marrow donor, which meant that he had left a perfect DNA sample behind. Yet he was told that the matching process could still take six months or more. But at least now he was almost sure he had found Michael.

When Lyons called Elaine later that morning, in his excitement he mentioned finding Michael's firemen's jacket. He forgot that in his world that meant a few charred scraps of something that was once a jacket. When she asked if he would bring the jacket home, he had to ruin the whole moment by explaining what it really was.

# Tuesday, March 19, 2002

The Justice Department released an official report on the interviews begun in November of young male Muslim immigrants that were conducted by the FBI and other members of the federal joint terrorism task forces around the country. As with many efforts by the government to say good things about itself, the report got muted press attention.

But the results were good, and certainly demonstrated that the interviews had not produced the kind of mass witch hunts that critics had feared. Of 4,793 prospective interviewees on the original lists provided by INS, about 1,700 could not be located or had, on further checking, left the United States. (This 35 percent error rate was another reminder of the gaps of the INS's record keeping.) Of the remaining three thousand, 2,261 had agreed to be interviewed.

The public version of the report redacted all but the most cursory description of the approximately ten leads that had been developed. But ten leads out of 2,261 interviews in the most important FBI investigation ever undertaken was itself not bad. What was more important, though, was that, according to a federal law enforcement agent and a local terrorism investigator, two of the leads produced information that had been used to identify what by now seemed to be two nascent terror cells that the FBI had begun to watch closely. And what was perhaps more important than that was that in almost every part of the country the local joint terrorism task forces now at least had some people they could call in the Muslim community for information.

# Thursday, March 21, 2002

Donald Rumsfeld's announcement of the rules for the military commissions created by the President's controversial executive order seemed "surprisingly enlightened" to Anthony Romero of the ACLU. While Romero still hated the idea of the tribunals, even he conceded that what Rumsfled produced today contained "a lot more protections than we thought they would." *

Thanking his group of outsider advisors—"the wise men"—who, he said, had been "enormously helpful," Rumsfeld announced a set of rules that would keep the tribunals open to the press unless the presiding officer determined that some part of the proceedings must be closed to protect classified information or the safety of the participants. Moreover, defendants would be presumed innocent; the standard for convictions would be guilt beyond a reasonable doubt; and although a two-thirds majority could convict, only a unanimous jury could impose a death penalty. Defendants would also have access to the government's evidence against them, be able to subpoena witnesses, and be able to get either a military defense lawyer at the government's expense, or their own lawyers (provided they could get a security clearance) at their expense. Perhaps most surprisingly, Rumsfeld, at the urging of several of the wise men, had even added a provision allowing civilians to serve as the judges.

There was, however, one glaring gap in the whole setup, and it had to do with that chasm that terrorism presented between being a common crime and being an act of war. Under questioning by reporters, Pentagon general counsel William Haynes II conceded that it was entirely possible that a defendant could be acquitted by a tribunal but then put right back in the jail in Guantánamo Bay, Cuba, where those captured on the Afghan battlefields were being held. They would still be considered "enemy combatants that we captured on the battlefield seeking to harm U.S. soldiers," Haynes explained, "and they're dangerous people." Yet they would not be considered prisoners of war because the government had already declared that these captives were "unlawful combatants," not POWs who deserve the protections given to POWs under international law.

While the press jousted with Rumsfeld and his staff at the Pentagon, another group of federal and local Washington officials were dealing with the detonation of a bomb on an empty school bus parked on the south side of the Air and Space Museum in downtown Washington. Initial estimates were that there were 15,000 museum visitors and federal workers (at the headquarters of the

*Romero's organization nonetheless put out a press release attacking the rules. "We always have to be there publicly serving as a balance against the other side," Romero explained. "That's our role."

FAA and departments of Education and Health and Human Services) in close proximity to the blast.

That wasn't the worst part. Within twenty minutes after the first emergency responders arrived, radiation was detected in the air. A so-called dirty bomb had been detonated in the nation's capital.

It was all practice—a scenario set up at a workshop conducted by the Center for Strategic and International Studies (CSIS), a Washington think tank specializing in national security issues. Sitting around the table planning a response were people from Ridge's office, other federal agencies such as FEMA and the Office of Personnel Management (which had to make the call about whether to send the city's workforce home and, if so, how to tell them), and local police, fire, and health officials from the District of Columbia and surrounding counties.

The scenario posited that a conventional TNT bomb had been laced with a radioactive material called cesium 137, or Cs 137, a common component found in medical radiation treatment. Although hundreds or even thousands would die from the explosion, only three or four might get cancer from this level of radiation. But the group knew that fear of the radiation would be devastating. Soon the media would be reporting, accurately, that radiation levels in an area covering most of Washington were above, although not by much, the generally accepted minimums—and might stay that way for thirty years. Not allowing people to evacuate because they might carry radiation traces with them to surrounding suburbs might have been the best idea, but no one could figure out a way to keep them from leaving. Nor did anyone have a plan for getting the media to report on the situation without creating a panic.

Thus, a report of the workshop would later conclude, "The scenario presented participants with reports of deserted D.C. streets and hotels, workers refusing to return to work, and parents refusing to send their children back to schools that had conducted field trips to D.C. the day of the attack. These reports were indicative of the deep, long-lasting psychological impact that a radiological attack could have."

That conclusion echoed a hearing held a month earlier by Senate Foreign Relations Committee Chairman Joseph Biden, in which Biden, who invited a stellar list of witnesses, bluntly stated that his purpose was to highlight the problem that the psychological damage from the fear of such a dirty bomb attack would far exceed the actual loss of life.

The president of the Federation of American Scientists presented Biden's committee with a scenario much like the one those at today's exercise dealt with, only he provided real numbers. Suppose, he said, some cesium about the size of a piece recently found, amid much publicity, in North Carolina was mixed in with a conventional bomb and set off in the center of Washington. Unless the area was basically demolished, scrubbed, and rebuilt, people who remained to live or work for forty years in the general vicinity of where the bomb went off would have their chances of getting cancer increased by one in 10,000. Because that cancer risk increase happens to be the threshold for environments requiring a cleanup under the federal Superfund cleanup law, it could be made in media reports to sound really scary. But it really means an extra fifty deaths in an area of 500,000 people. Indeed, since everyone already has a one in twenty chance of dying of cancer anyway, this only increases their chances minimally. So, the newspaper headlines could either say it was a minimal increase—or that everyone in Washington was now living under the equivalent risk of living near a site requiring a Superfund cleanup. Which means that, as the CSIS game playing suggested, much of Washington might be abandoned and tens of billions might have to be spent to destroy everything and rebuild it.

Biden's purpose in holding this hearing was plainly to call attention to the dilemma, because only by having the public understand it could panic-induced decisions likely be avoided. How else, but with advance public dialogue and understanding, could a President propose that the people ignore radiation levels that equaled Superfund limits, and get back to work and live in Washington?

Some on Ridge's staff believed that this was not a subject that should have been left to think tanks like CSIS, or to well-intentioned senators like Biden. It needed more firepower than that. And it was one area where Ridge and his Office of Homeland Security didn't need new authority to be effective. Ridge's office had recently orchestrated the publication of a booklet on how office buildings could secure their ventilation systems from biological attacks. They could have led the charge here with a public information campaign to prepare the public to deal with the psychological fog of a dirty bomb attack. Ridge didn't need Ashcroft's or Rumsfeld's or anyone else's cooperation to mount the bully pulpit on this issue, and even to bring the President with him, so that the public could be prepared in advance to think about an equation like that one-in-10,000 number, and realize that a dirty bomb attack—potentially the most potent destroy-their-way-of-life threat in the terrorists' arsenal—could not succeed as long as everyone was thinking rationally.

Lawlor, in fact, had another of those interagency working groups working on preparing precise damage estimates for all varieties of dirty bombs. But neither Ridge nor anyone in the White House wanted to panic the public by talking about this in advance of something actually happening. The CSIS workshop and the Biden hearings suggested that that was a mistake, that depending on the citizenry to think clearly and calmly after the explosion was dangerously wrong.

"We know we have to deal with this, sooner or later," one of Ridge's senior aides would say more than six months later. "We just haven't given it the attention it needs. At the least, we should be holding background briefings with selected members of the press, or maybe we should mount a full-dress public campaign."

There was a lot of press accompanying the indictment of a Michigan man who received $268,000 in aid from the Red Cross after falsely claiming that his brother had been killed in the September 11 attacks.

What seemed more newsworthy than the fact that out of thousands of claimants he and twenty-two others accused by the Manhattan prosecutor might have fraudulently tried to reach into the charity cookie jar was that the Michigan man could have gotten $268,000 had he been *telling the truth* about a dead brother. If the Red Cross's forms only allowed someone to apply for basic living expenses—food (which was based on a stipulated per-person formula), rent or a mortgage, utilities, education, transportation, and so on—for three months, how could that have added up to $268,000, assuming even that someone could claim the loss of all support when a brother died? (In fact, the man had claimed he was using the money to support his brother's wife and three children.)

Red Cross records indicated that between November and January the Michigan man had collected four checks, including one for $212,000, to reach his $268,000 total. Apparently, he had gotten the largest check by coming back and claiming that he had to make a balloon payment on his brother's mortgage.

Why hadn't the Red Cross asked him to get another mortgage?

"I just don't know," chairman David McLaughlin said, when asked about the case five months later.

"Who, other than a caseworker and a supervisor, had to approve such a large check?"

"I just can't answer that," McLaughlin said. "I know there is a process but I don't know what it is."

Had he tried to find out what happened in this case—who approved the check?

"Our focus was really on the fraud," he said.

Two days ago, Ridge had come to the President at a Homeland Security Council meeting with a new plan for border consolidation. Let's leave the Coast Guard out of it, he suggested, and just put Customs together with INS in the Justice Department. Those were the two agencies that most overlapped, he explained. It's the INS and Customs people that you see almost interchangeably at an airport or border crossing.

As a practical matter, Ridge knew that this plan would fly with the cabinet, because Treasury Secretary O'Neill didn't care about losing Customs, and Ashcroft, who did care about losing an agency, would instead be gaining Customs. In fact, Ridge had already checked with O'Neill and Ashcroft and they supported it, which they now confirmed at the council meeting (and which is why Bolten and Card, who favor giving the President consensus decisions to sign off on, had put the subject on the agenda).

"See if it flies up on the Hill," Bush had told Ridge. "But," he added, "this seems kind of small to me."

By last evening, it had crashed. Every senator and representative with any jurisdiction over Customs—including members of the powerful House Ways and Means Committee, which oversees Customs, because Customs collects tariffs—vowed to fight it.

So this morning Card told Bush that the plan looked like it was dead.

"You know," Bush said, "maybe we should stop getting pecked to death like this. Maybe it's time to think big. When you do something piecemeal, all the interests here come at you one by one and kill you. Let's just make believe we are re-creating the government from scratch and map out what we'd put in a new homeland department and then maybe we'll go for it."

Another advantage of reshuffling the cards this way, the President and his chief of staff acknowledged, was that it would end the increasingly heated fight about Ridge's congressional testimony. They knew they had boxed themselves into a corner by making Ridge both a staff person and the public point man on homeland security. There really was something to Congress's argument that he ought to testify on the administration's budget and strategy, because no one else had his overview and overall responsibilities.

Card told the President that he and Bolten would think some more about it.

# Tuesday, March 26, 2002

TSA's request for proposals for the installation of explosive detection systems finally came out, only now deep into the first paragraph it referred vaguely to "Explosive Detection System/Explosives Trace Detection" as the installations that were required, meaning that the smaller trace detection systems had now officially been added to the mix.

That first paragraph was also the last paragraph. People from Raytheon and their competitors who huddled around their computers reading it were stunned by how short it was—thirty-eight lines in one paragraph—compared to the reams of documents they usually received for much smaller contracts. Although a four-page supplement to the summary paragraph would be distributed by TSA a few days later, and the vendors would be allowed to come in for Q&A sessions, this truly was the "accelerated competition" that the first sentence declared it was. "We made it short, because we wanted them to show us how they would fill in all the blanks," explains one TSA official involved in the procurement.

But as short as it was, as vague as it was (it didn't even say if the vendors were to charge a fixed price or a price based on time and materials, plus a certain percent of that for profit), and as "mission critical" as it proclaimed the job was "in protecting the American people and the guests of this great nation," the RFP still took the trouble to require that the vendor had to agree to subcontract out at least 5 percent of the work to "small disadvantaged businesses," and 5 percent more to women-owned businesses.

A Republican administration enforcing minority quotas for a homeland protection job at a time of national emergency?

"That stuff didn't faze us at all," says Hugo Poza, the Raytheon executive who would be charged with overseeing the job if they got it. "It's legally required. Besides, with all the local subcontractors you need on a job like that, it's easy."

What wasn't going to be easy was writing the proposal itself. "It was so open-ended that you literally had to think of everything," Poza recalls.

Sergio Magistri raised $86 million to ramp up InVision by selling 2.5 million new shares to the public at $36.50 each. This produced about $91 million, out of which $5 million was paid to the investment banks that managed the offering, which were the same ones that now had analysts issuing reports recommending his stock. They included Merrill Lynch and Lehman Brothers.

This may have been a record for an Office of Homeland Security meeting: 150 people. But it worked.

The two-day session, conducted at a think tank facility near the Pentagon, was a "physical infrastructure protection workshop" aimed at developing a master plan to protect important and vulnerable transportation assets—such as bridges, pipelines, airports, harbors, tunnels, or railroad lines, especially those carrying dangerous cargo—scattered across the country. Representatives from what seemed to be every government agency in the D.C. phone book, plus private organizations from the Chlorine Institute, to the World Shipping Council, to the Air Transport Association were there to identify critical assets and the security issues associated with them. The results were going to be incorporated into a monster national master plan that Ridge's people wanted to complete by the end of September. The next two-day session, scheduled for a month from now, was to cover energy, banking and finance, and defense installations. By early October, the draft would be completed, along with a companion Response and Recovery document.

Eileen Simon and Patrick Cartier, Sr. (accompanied by his daughter, Jennie Farrell), made their way to a Marriott hotel in Manhattan today to audition in front of federal prosecutors and the FBI. The government was looking for potential witnesses to testify in the death penalty phase of the upcoming trial of Zacarias Moussaoui, the alleged twentieth hijacker. So they had sent a mass mailing to the family members of all victims asking them to come in for interviews that they were going to conduct in New York and Washington.

When he first heard about the letter (after Michael Cartier had posted it for all to see on his Give Your Voice website), Patrick Cartier had not wanted to participate. He told his children that he feared someone would try to blow up the courthouse, and their mother wouldn't be able to bear another death. But by last week he had changed his mind. Telling his son Patrick Jr. that "it's a great thing that they're going to kill this guy," he decided he was anxious to help. In fact, the senior Cartier had been infuriated when he and Jennie had mistakenly shown up at a special pre-interview briefing set up just for Cantor Fitzgerald families, and, after realizing where they were, assumed that all these rich people in nice clothes were getting special priority in the witness pageant.

So Patrick Cartier, Sr., eagerly appeared at the Marriott. But when the agent asked him, "What did your son mean to you?" he fell silent, then said that, as he had written in an essay he had brought to show the agent, a child "is like a diamond, and when you look at it in the light you see hundreds of different, glorious aspects."

The agent wanted something simpler. "Tell me in a sentence what was most important about him. Give me a moment that highlights your memory of him."

Cartier said he had no way to do that, then trudged out, not really sure if he was angry at the FBI man for the open-ended but obvious question, or himself for not having anticipated it and thought of a better answer.

Eileen Simon had no such trouble. She was her usual exuberant self, full of stories about Michael and the kids, whose pictures she readily showed to the FBI agent and the prosecutor. "I literally begged them to take me," she recalled. "The waiting room was packed, so I knew I had lots of competition, but I really put on a show. I laughed. I cried. I talked about all the trouble the kids were having. . . . But," she said, "I'm probably not going to get picked because there are Cantor families that lost both a son and a husband, or a father and an uncle, and I don't think they want too many Cantor families." Nonetheless, she was thrilled just to be there. "It was one of the best days I'd had since September," she recalled. "Finally, we were going to get one of these guys."

That the prosecutors wanted any families at all at this point for a phase of a trial that came only after a defendant was convicted was hard to fathom. This well-publicized casting call for witnesses for the death penalty phase of the Moussaoui trial seemed like another instance, as with the Lindh case, of Ashcroft over-promising in a way that risked disappointing the victims' loved ones and the population at large, and making them bitter about the criminal justice system if Moussaoui was not executed.

The whole thing was Ashcroft's idea. He'd come into the office one morning several weeks before, and after reading a newspaper story that hinted that progress in the Moussaoui case was slowing, suggested that they prove the opposite by starting to talk up the death penalty phase now.

A month later, Moussaoui would sandbag not only any hope of a real defense but also any hope of a death penalty by seeking to dismiss his court-appointed defense counsel and become his own lawyer—a move that seemed like it might assure that he'd be convicted but spared capital punishment. But even now, the evidence that he had actually had anything to do with the attacks (as opposed to being in the United States to plot other terror crimes) was hardly airtight. Besides, the trial wasn't scheduled until the summer. Wasn't this jumping the gun?

When his partner, Mark Hall, told him, Bob Lindemann asked him to repeat it again, because he didn't believe it. Hall had just learned from John France, their supervisor, that INS intended to go ahead with the demotion of the Border Patrol agents, as planned. They'd considered the inspector general's report and the Office of Special Counsel's report, and decided to proceed anyway.

To be sure, Fine, as the inspector general, only had the power to issue reports. But his recommendations on something like this were almost always followed. And the Office of Special Counsel similarly only had the power to make public recommendations, to Congress and the President, and to have those recommendations be cited by an aggrieved employee in court. But what agency would defy this kind of report that a whistle-blower had been improperly penalized and would probably win a court case alleging that?

Apparently, the INS would. Lindemann, who had been so encouraged when he had learned in early March of the two reports backing him, now felt like quitting. But Hall had a different idea. They'd go back to the two senators, Levin of Michigan and Charles Grassley, an Iowa Republican, who had backed them.

## Friday, March 29, 2002

Prosecutors responded further to the charges about how John Walker Lindh had been treated in captivity by issuing what Watergate reporters Bob Woodward and Carl Bernstein used to call a "non-denial denial." In a new brief, they handled the allegations that Lindh had been strapped naked to a stretcher and put into a metal container this way: Yes, "his ragged clothing was removed, he was searched, and then placed in a large metal container," where he was "initially secured to a stretcher," the brief said. But then it explained all that by adding, "While the Navy physician who was treating him had to sleep on a concrete floor in a sleeping bag in a room with a hole in the wall and a hole in the ceiling, Lindh slept on a stretcher in a container that protected him from the elements."

## Sunday, March 31, 2002

A ninety-person Raytheon TSA contract team worked all weekend at the company's Burlington, Massachusetts, office crashing drafts of as many sections as possible of their proposal for the airports contract, which was due on

April 9. "It's not every day you get two weeks to turn around on a $4 billion contract," Hugo Poza reminded his team.

Poza, an electronics engineer with a Ph.D., ran Raytheon surveillance and reconnaissance businesses with $1.2 billion in revenues and 5,000 employees. He was supremely confident of his prospects. Raytheon was about to announce that they were teaming up with another giant aerospace and defense contractor, Northrop Grumman, to go after the contract rather than compete for it. And the company that was seen by many as their leading competitor, Lockheed Martin, had been, Poza noted, Raytheon's subcontractor for some of the earlier airport work Raytheon had done. The TSA people had to appreciate that, just as they had to appreciate that it was Raytheon that had gotten a baggage screening system set up in forty-five days at the Salt Lake City airport in anticipation of the Olympics. Only Raytheon had a track record of getting this stuff done, and getting it done fast.

Woollen, too, was feeling great about this prong of Raytheon's homeland security effort. "It's ours to lose," he had told Poza and CEO Dan Burnham. "We're clearly the front-runner."

Three days later, Raytheon stock, in part on the strength of Wall Street's similar assumptions about the TSA contract, would reach a fifty-two-week high of $42.89. That was about 80 percent over its low for the last twelve months (on September 10) of $23.95.

It may have been that Poza, Woollen, their team, and the stock market assumed too much. In the drafting sessions, the Raytheon team seemed to be writing to an audience that it believed already knew what it needed to know about Raytheon's superior qualifications. Indeed, the woman who headed the actual writing effort—neither Poza nor top business-hunter Woollen ever actually read the full text of the drafts—was the woman who had managed the prior contracts with the FAA. But it was Null, on loan from Intel, and the go team from TSA that was going to decide who won the bid, and in their view they were only there because the FAA people had failed at airport security all these years. The Raytheon team seemed to be writing to the wrong audience.

# Monday, April 1, 2002

Tom Ridge continued to marvel at how Jim Loy, the Commandant of the Coast Guard, was such a good manager. Two weeks ago, another mini-scandal at INS had erupted when it was discovered that an INS official had improperly allowed nineteen Pakistani crew members of a Russian ship docking in Norfolk to come ashore. Four had never returned. Ashcroft, a self-proclaimed teetotaler, subsequently told *Fox News Sunday* that what had happened in the INS was enough to drive a man to drink.

But now, Loy, at Bruce Lawlor's urging, had looked at the problem and come up with a solution. As of today the Coast Guard captain of the port will prevent any ships with "problematic crew members" (meaning those from high-risk countries) from docking until the ship or its company demonstrates that security precautions will be in place to prevent crew members from jumping ship. The Coast Guard will also get involved if necessary, including posting its own armed forces on any problem ships or ordering the ship to leave port, if the ship's security is found to be inadequate.

In two weeks, Loy had stepped in and fixed something that INS had never been able to deal with.

At the first substantive hearing in the Lindh case, some air started coming out of the government's balloon. Prosecutors backed off the claim that Lindh had actually been involved in the killing of CIA agent Spann, conceding that they had no evidence of that. They also acknowledged, as Brosnahan had argued in court papers submitted in March, that the camp that Lindh said he had attended was used to train regular Taliban armed forces, as well as terrorists. Thus, the fact that Lindh might have admitted training there did not make him a committed terrorist. Then, as they repeated in court their non-denial denial about Lindh's treatment—and as Brosnahan submitted a photo taken by the Army and handed over to him in the pretrial discovery process of Lindh strapped naked to that stretcher—the press started to pick up on the issue of whether Lindh's confession, assuming he had confessed, was coerced.

It was not all easy sledding for the defense. Judge Ellis denied their motion to force the government to spell out more clearly the crimes Lindh was accused of, and at one point when Brosnahan's partner was arguing that Lindh had not gone to Afghanistan to become a terrorist, Ellis blurted out, "Then, what was he doing out there?"

But Ellis quickly withdrew the question. More important, the judge agreed with Brosnahan and ordered the government to allow the defense to question the military intelligence officials who, the defense contended, had written contemporaneous notes of their interrogations with Lindh that were at odds with later summaries prepared by the FBI. Brosnahan's instinct was that this decision might end up being a big help.

New York City Transportation Commissioner Iris Weinshall began using some of the federal money her husband, Chuck Schumer, had helped procure to begin repaving thirty-seven lane-miles of lower Manhattan streets that had been ripped up by the collapse of the Trade Center and the resulting recovery and repair work done by the various utilities. It would be a massive undertaking, and for a while it would clog the sections of Broadway and Barclay Street where Sal Iacono's store was located, causing him to lose still more foot traffic, because pedestrians wanted to avoid the mess. This relatively quick once-over (more fundamental structural repairs would have to be done next year) was one of the first signs that the rebuilding and recovery was really happening. Another sign had come on Friday, when the Brooklyn Battery Tunnel in lower Manhattan, and West Street, the thoroughfare that ran alongside the Trade Center, were reopened to traffic.

For Weinshall, things were returning almost to normal at home, too. Her husband was still immersed in issues like terrorism insurance, and was running around town trying to drum up support for that far-fetched idea to swap the United Nations with the Trade Center. But Schumer had now finally locked down his aid package with Daniels and had settled down enough so that he once again was pretty much observing his no-work rule on Saturdays.

Syed Jaffri, the Pakistani who had been held since September for a visa violation after an argument with his Bronx landlord, was suddenly taken today by INS agents to Kennedy Airport and put on a plane to Canada, where he had been a legal immigrant. He was not given any of his identification papers or the money he had with him when he was arrested.

## Tuesday, April 2, 2002

The *Detroit Free Press* published a report that INS was pressing ahead with demoting Lindemann and Hall "despite two recent government reports that say the agents' speech was protected." The article also noted that two senators, Levin and Grassley, had already written to INS Commissioner Ziglar appealing to him to intercede on behalf of the agents.

The only INS comment to the paper was that "employees have a responsibility to ensure that the safety of private citizens, as well as the service's national security efforts, are not compromised by comments made to the media."

The heat is on the INS, Hall assured his partner. Lindemann wasn't sure. So far, their bosses had demonstrated that they didn't much care about the heat.

Sergio Magistri sold 100,000 shares of InVision Technologies today for $34.50, netting $3.25 million after exercising options he had in the stock at about $2 per share. "Everyone talks about diversification," Magistri explains. "I decided that this was the time, after ten years, to diversify my assets a little and not have everything in that one stock. That's all it meant." At the same time, he also announced another $170 million order from TSA.

# Wednesday, April 3, 2002

The heat apparently worked after all. Lindemann's sector chief called him this morning to say, perfunctorily, that INS was withdrawing its proposed discipline of him and Hall. "We still think what you did was wrong," he added.

The one-day about-face had come when Ziglar, who had known about and approved the decision to go ahead with the discipline because he agreed that his sector chief needed to be supported, changed his mind after getting an angry call from Grassley, a fellow Republican.

Lindemann was ecstatic. He called his wife and said it was finally over. "I'm normally a funny, jovial guy," he says. "But this had been a complete preoccupation, and it had been hard on her. For the first time in months, I felt like we could relax."

INS's public statement, which was not attributed to Ziglar or anyone else, announcing the withdrawal of the "proposed discipline," said, "We did so after reviewing the investigative reports of the Office of Inspector General and the Office of Special Counsel. . . . INS believes that some of the disclosures made by Agents Hall and Lindemann included sensitive information about the Northern Border in a time of national crisis," but that Hall and Lindemann did not have "formal notice of the INS policies affecting their contact with the press."

The statement closed by saying that INS was "in the process of developing an interim policy" regarding media contacts.

By year-end there would still be no such policy, interim or otherwise.

# Thursday, April 4, 2002

Brian Lyons's old boss called to ask if it wasn't now time for him to come back to his real job, behind a desk supervising contractors and making sure they were on time and on budget, not wearing a hard hat and digging through rubble twelve hours a day.

Lyons didn't reject the offer, but he said he wasn't ready to take it either. He was feeling healthier than he'd felt in a long time. He'd lost thirty-five pounds, and every day he could see what he was accomplishing down in the pit, foot by foot, yard by yard. For now, he loved the work. Besides, they were two or three months away from being done down there. This was not the time to walk away.

Michael Byrne, Tom Ridge's director of Response and Recovery, had now been working for five months on his highest priority—solving the problem of first responder radio frequency interoperability. Today, he was asked about a report in the new issue of McGraw-Hill's *Homeland Security & Defense* newsletter, headlined "Justice Department Getting Word Out on Interoperable Communications." The article was about a Justice Department program called AGILE, which was short for Advanced Generation of Interoperability for Law Enforcement. Its director was quoted as saying that his office, which was funded this year with $45 million, "develops and evaluates ways to ease communications among public safety agencies."

Byrne said he had never heard of AGILE. Ridge would say the same thing, when asked about it a month later.

Six months later, AGILE's director would allow as how he had met Byrne two or three times, but "we really have our own program here, as authorized by Congress."

By now, Byrne seemed worn down by all the turf fighting related to issues such as getting the funds in the budget to provide training and equipment grants to first responders out of Justice and into FEMA—which the President had approved but Congress was still fighting. The excitement seemed drained from his voice. He seemed to talk about events or projects he had worked on in January or February as if those were the good old days, before he realized what he was up against.

In part, it was the typical comedown from the euphoria of a start-up. But it was also because the bureaucracy's reflexive rejection of any attempt at outside "coordination" was starting to get to him.

Lawlor, Byrne's counterpart running Protection and Prevention, felt more strongly about it. He knew they were making progress in certain areas, but as a military man, he couldn't understand how his bosses could let so much, such as the need to revamp the atrophying INS, be paralyzed by the desire to achieve consensus.

Byrne and Lawlor knew that the funk they were in was shared by their staffs. They continued to work mind-numbing hours and tried to be cheerful, but the polite brush-offs and nonresponses they got, plus the news stories they kept reading about their boss not having any power and not being allowed to testify on the Hill, were taking an obvious toll.


Norman Mineta and Michael Jackson thought the briefing for the President in the Situation Room about how TSA was going to meet the deadlines for baggage screening equipment and the federalization of the security people was going perfectly. The President loved the chart showing how they had negotiated a price for Magistri's machines that was 20 to 25 percent below what Magistri usually charged, and what other countries were paying for them. And when they handed out flow charts showing how, with the help of people borrowed from Disney and Marriott, they had reconfigured the passenger lines and were designing new signage at the checkpoints at the Baltimore airport (which they had chosen as their design lab) to speed the flow, Bush dove in. Scouring the charts, he asked all kinds of questions about the little figures of guards and passengers shown moving from the curb through the checkpoints and onto their planes.

Then they passed around a complicated, and classified, protocol for how they were going to mix in about 2,200 of the expensive, bulky InVision (and competitor L-3) explosive detection machines with the smaller, cheaper trace detection equipment. The error rates for each were explained, along with a plan to screen a high enough percentage of bags in different ways that would make the mathematical chances of anything slipping through highly remote. The whole thing, Mineta explained, had been worked on carefully with the staff of the Office of Management and Budget.

"Sounds good," the President said. "Blade, do you have anything to add?"

Blade was Bush's nickname for budget director Daniels (as in cutting budgets with a sharp blade). It turned out that Daniels had plenty to add.

He stood up, while an aide projected a PowerPoint presentation onto the screen at the far end of the Sit Room. Soon a whole new plan appeared—one that cut the number of the big InVision machines to 1,100, while adding thousands more trace detectors.

"Mr. President, this is how we think it should be done," Daniels began.

Mineta, Jackson, and TSA director Magaw were shocked. "Mr. President," Mineta piped up. "This is extraordinary. We haven't had a chance to see or review any of this. Can't we review this first with Mr. Daniels, before we discuss it here?"

"Oh, let's let him continue," Bush replied. "Let's see what he's got."

Bush, however, didn't wait around to see. He left for another appointment. But the rest of the group was treated to a detailed analysis of the costs of explosive detection machines versus trace detectors. The difference in the Mineta mix and the Daniels mix was more than $1 billion. Beyond that, Daniels argued, "you'll never get all those machines on time anyway, and if you do, you'll be getting technology that isn't nearly as good as it'll be in a year or two, when you'll be back here asking us to buy all new stuff."

Mineta, Jackson, and Magaw all protested again that they hadn't had time to review Daniels's numbers. Worse, what he had put together didn't account for all the extra time that it would take all the extra personnel to paw through people's bags with the trace detection swab if they used this system. Plus, this added use of trace machines would not be nearly as secure.

But it turned out that Daniels's staff had been buried in recent weeks with information about error rates, times, and personnel costs from lobbyists for the trace detection companies. When these same lobbyists had made their rounds on the Hill, they had successfully urged staffers there to push Daniels's people on the issue. So now Daniels pushed back that the potential delays and extra personnel costs coming from the trace machines were exaggerated. As for security, Daniels's argument was that in terms of balancing risks against dollars—"efficient risk management"—they were already spending too much on aviation as compared to highways, trains, and ships. "It's called the Transportation Security Administration," he reminded them, "not the Aviation Security Administration."

Jackson, Mineta's deputy, would later have follow-up conversations with Daniels, Ridge, and chief of staff Card, for whom Jackson had worked when Card was Transportation Secretary in the first Bush administration. The decision had been made, they told him; the administration wanted to go with Daniels's mix or something close to it. Jackson, who shared Daniels's frustration with the overemphasis on aviation that the law required and knew that some of the people on his go teams shared Daniels's view, said he'd get it done.

# Friday, April 5, 2002

Card came back to the President today with a plan for rethinking the homeland security setup, as he had promised he would after the Customs-INS consolidation plan had been shot down so quickly on Capitol Hill. He wanted to put together a small group that would not include anyone who had an interest in defending the status quo. That ruled out the entire cabinet. Rather he would start with two people from his and Bolten's staff and one from Daniels's management and budget staff, along with Falkenrath and Lawlor from Ridge's office. Card and others in the White House regarded them as two of Ridge's superstars and in Lawlor's case, someone who by now knew firsthand, from all the frustrations he had had trying to coordinate these agencies, just which pieces needed to be put together under one boss. This small group would sit in a room and map out all the options, then present them to Card, Ridge, and other senior aides in a series of meetings that would produce a decision quickly.

Bush agreed, but added that whatever they did, they had to do it in a small group so that they could keep it secret until they were ready to spring the idea. If it leaked out, the President warned, all the special interests would have time to pile on against it before they had had a chance to put the big idea in front of the public.

Later that afternoon, Card called Ridge into his office. "The President," he said, "wants to take a much broader look at all of this. We want to make believe we're starting with a clean slate and see what kind of department we'd create. Nothing," he added, "is off the table." But, Card continued, secrecy was crucial. No one outside the small staff group could know what they were doing, especially the cabinet.

Ridge almost couldn't believe it. Just that day he'd been reading press reports that his latest defeat, the slimmed down INS-Customs proposal, might be the final straw.

When Ridge told Lawlor and Falkenrath early that evening about their new assignments, both were stunned, and, of course, thrilled—Lawlor because he'd now have a chance to create a system with real command and control, and Falkenrath because, well, he'd written the book on why things had to change.

That night Falkenrath began writing his first memo on how they should go about figuring out what should and shouldn't be in the new, super-department.

## Sunday, April 7, 2002

Eileen Simon flew home from a four-day vacation she had taken with her children to a beach in North Carolina. Waiting in the mail was a note saying that two of her new widow friends had been told that their husbands' remains—one a torso, the other a rib—had been found. There was also a package containing a *New York Times* book that was a compilation of all of the short, poignant profiles of victims, including Michael, that had run in the paper. It was all too much of a reintroduction to the world she had just gotten away from at the beach. She threw the note out and gave the book to her mother.

The next day she did something she'd been meaning to do for a while. She replaced the recording on the family's voice mail machine—which was Michael saying hello and asking the caller to leave a message—with one from Brittany saying the same thing.

## Monday, April 8, 2002

The President staged a big event at the White House with business leaders to push for a terrorism insurance bill in the Senate. With economics czar Larry Lindsey now saying that construction was down 20 percent because of the lack of terror insurance coverage, everyone in the White House was engaged. The problem, as it had been since the fall, was that the House Republicans were holding firm on attaching tort reform to any bill, while the Democrats in the Senate were refusing to accept even the slightest compromise in that direction.

The insurers' lobbyists, as well as David Crane, the former Trent Lott aide who was working for real estate clients and had by now clearly succeeded in broadening the bill's proponents far beyond the insurance industry, were still frustrated that some of the higher profile members of the coalition pushing the bill, such as the National Football League and Major League Baseball, still didn't want to talk about it publicly for fear of scaring fans. But at least they were pushing their senators, while Crane, the former Senate staffer, was sketching out all kinds of parliamentary maneuvers and thread-the-needle compromises that might satisfy Senate Democrats (and their trial lawyer patrons) while keeping the Republicans happy.

Michael Cartier got word that the remains of an electrician who had been working up on the 105th floor with James on September 11 had just been identified by the medical examiner. He called his father to tell him this was a good sign, that there was still hope for a funeral.

# Tuesday, April 9, 2002

Falkenrath and Lawlor from Ridge's staff, two assistants to Card and Bolten, and one of Daniels's top aides met for the first time to scope out how they would go about constructing the options for a new Department of Homeland Security that they could present to their bosses. Sitting in a city where the most potent force is always the status quo, five unknown staffers were meeting to piece together the largest new government agency created in fifty years, and the most complex, controversial reshuffling of government ever.

The "small group," as the five would come to call themselves, began with a matrix that Falkenrath had sketched. Running along the horizontal axis to the right was a list of alternatives for a structuring of the various government agencies. Closest in was the current situation, which was total balkanization. A little further down along the right was Ridge's mini-border-consolidation plan. Still further down was the bigger consolidation plan that included the Coast Guard—the plan shot down in December. And furthest down was a total consolidation of everything that was relevant to homeland security—the big plan.

On the vertical line running up and down on the left side of the page were the alternatives for consolidating power in the White House. At the bottom, Falkenrath listed the alternative of putting the homeland security office into the National Security Council—in other words cutting its power and profile. Next up the line was the status quo, the homeland security office as it now was. Further up was an alternative equivalent to the current National Security Council, which meant the office would be given statutory status by legislation passed by Congress. Even further up was statutory status with specific powers of supervision attached to it.

Because Ridge's congressional testimony had become such a highly charged issue, the next factor Falkenrath added (by shading in various areas on the matrix) was which of the alternatives on the two axes would subject whoever held the office to testifying before Congress. Clearly, anything along the horizontal axis did because agency heads had to testify. As for the vertical axis, it was clear that if the office got statutory authority, let alone got authority and specific powers to go with it (the highest point on the axis), whoever had the job had to testify. And Congress, of course, was claiming that even the point on the axis signifying the status quo (Ridge) also had to testify.

The point of the exercise was that almost no matter what they did to strengthen leadership in the homeland security arena—whether at the White House or in reorganizing the agencies—the person who got the job was going to have to testify—which, the group agreed, wasn't unreasonable anyway. So, they might as well move along the axis they felt was best to get the job done. And that, they agreed, was the executive agency axis—a mass consolidation of agencies into one big department.

Besides, they knew that even after the agency was created they would want to keep a homeland security advisor in the White House to advise the President and coordinate that agency with others, such as the Pentagon, EPA, or Justice, that were not going to be consolidated into it, but that were still involved in the homeland security issues. This way, by having a super-department head to deal with Congress, that advisor would be left alone.

They moved on in this meeting, and in regular meetings two or three times a week for the next three weeks, to sketching out what should and should not be in the new department.

Again they used a geometric figure, in this case a pyramid. At the top were those functions that clearly belonged, such as border and transportation security. At the bottom were functions, such as intelligence and law enforcement, that they were least certain about including. The question for the next two months would be where to cut the pyramid.


Raytheon's proposal to the TSA for the big contract was five volumes long. There were three other bidders, TRW, Lockheed Martin, and Boeing. Lockheed Martin, with 2001 revenues of almost $24 billion, was about 50 percent larger than Raytheon. Boeing, with about $60 billion in revenue, was more than three times as large.

The proposal from Boeing—which by now had teamed up with Siemens AG, which had experience installing baggage conveyor systems at airports—had a statement in the first paragraph that caught the eye of everyone who vetted it at TSA. "The Boeing team is reliant on the aviation industry for more than $50 billion in annual revenue," the proposal pointed out, referring to Boeing's core aircraft business. "As such we are the only team with a compelling reason to deliver a successful program for the TSA."

Perhaps, but as the Raytheon proposal pointed out in several places, only Raytheon had actual experience doing the work called for in the contract.

For Woollen and Poza it was now time to wait. TSA's frenzied schedule called for the decision to be made within two weeks, on April 22.

# Thursday, April 11, 2002

"Where are they possibly going to put those things," asked Larry Cox as he walked a visitor through his terminal. "Suppose they want to put it over there," he said, pointing to the Graceland souvenir shop. "Are they going to pay me for the lost revenue?"

Cox was referring to the mini-van-sized InVision explosive detection systems that he knew were coming to his airport, but only because he'd read newspaper articles about the new law requiring them. He also knew that they were supposed to be installed eight and a half months from today, but he hadn't been told how it was going to be done. His local FAA representative said that he hadn't been told anything either. In fact, all he could tell Cox was that when the FAA man in charge of overseeing security in Memphis had inquired about the new TSA position of "federal security director" that was planned for each airport, he'd been told that he would not be eligible to apply. "I guess they're looking for another Secret Service guy," Cox muttered, referring to TSA director Magaw's résumé. "I hear they're only hiring Secret Service types. That'll be just great. . . . Do I have to give that guy an office? Will he have a staff that needs offices? It would be nice to know."

Walking into a back office, Cox displayed a new $35,000 machine that takes fingerprints and turns them into digital files that get sent to an office in Virginia, where they are then forwarded for checking to the FBI. Under the airline security law, between now and December, Cox's staff had to take the prints of all 6,000 airport employees so that their backgrounds could be checked. Anyone with a felony conviction in the last ten years would be dismissed. Cox thought that was fine, but he had another question for Washington: Who was going to pay the $31 per employee that it cost him to process the fingerprint checks through the airport trade association in Virginia that sends them to the FBI?

"We've got the waiting down to ten minutes now," Cox explained as he walked past the main concourse's checkpoints, which had been increased from five to eight to cut the lines. "Are they going to screw that up, when they come in here with their federal people?"

In a sprawling cafeteria that looked like it could feed a mid-sized state college, the tables and chairs had been pushed aside to make room for dozens of airport checkpoints. Off to the side, stacked in a pile, were hundreds of pieces of used suitcases, sent here from an abandoned luggage graveyard. On a table that once held desserts or salads there was a pile of knives, box cutters, mace sprays, and a variety of other potential weapons.

The scene was the FAA's massive training center near the airport in Oklahoma City, where the first group of federalized screeners Gale Rossides had recruited were learning how to read the X-ray machines that screened carry-on bags. They were also practicing how to detect pens that had been hollowed out to conceal knifelike blades, large plastic combs that had removable handles that turned into lethal knives, and box cutters or knives concealed in bandages taped around legs.

Across the campus, another group sat at computers playing a video game that required them to find the weapon on the monitor's X-ray picture. A false yes (that something was a weapon that wasn't) counted just as negatively on the score as a false no.

Across the way, in an auditorium, a third group was getting a lecture in "conflict management" from a consultant hired by Rossides. Try to isolate an irate passenger in "a neutral environment" away from the crowd, she bellowed, cheerfully. "Speak quietly. Ask open-ended questions that encourage long answers, because letting the person talk will calm him down. Paraphrase the answer back to the person, so that he knows you are listening and feels that his concerns have been validated."

After an hour, which included role playing by trainees whom the consultant had chosen at random, she asked the group to do one more exercise. They were to write down their names on one side of a piece of paper, along with one thing they had just learned that they wanted to remember when they went out there to man the gates. Then they were to fold the paper into an airplane and let it fly toward one of the other 300 people in the room.

"Ready, set, let them fly!" she yelled.

There were cheers and laughter. She got several people to stand and read the airmail messages they had received. "It's gonna get hot in the kitchen," said one. "I will listen and try to be more sensitive," said another. More cheers.

The group then divided up and adjourned to classrooms where other trainers—typically a retired police supervisor or Secret Service agent hired as a consultant by Rossides—ran smaller sessions on the different posts the sceeners will be rotated through during their shifts. Rossides had decided that one way to relieve the boredom of the screeners' jobs was to move them around every hour or so. That way, they would be looking at the monitor for a while, then greeting passengers at the front end of the line and telling them to remove cell phones and other metal objects from their pockets, then patting down those selected for personal searches.

This first corps of trainees—who seemed to be a mix of ex-cops or federal agents and white- and blue-collar workers—were actually going to become supervisors within a few months of the rollout. But for now, when they finished boot camp in Oklahoma City they would become a roving SWAT team, moving into airports around the country and taking over the checkpoints while TSA completed the hiring of a local, permanent crew. A few would stay behind to supervise the permanent people, because that was the city where they had chosen to work. The rest would move on to another newly federalized airport.

Rossides had painstakingly supervised the writing of their curriculum to make sure that it encouraged not only a strong law enforcement perspective, but a culture of customer service. When Cox, who received little else in the way of information about what TSA was up to, saw the curriculum, even this skeptic of anything that came from Washington had been impressed. He thought it hit all the right notes for a new, professionalized service. Indeed, whatever else anyone thought of TSA head Magaw and his management abilities, all seemed to agree that he was great at culture. And Rossides, who had been his culture czar at ATF, was now getting to practice on a broad, blank canvas.

As Mayor Michael Bloomberg got up from the shoeshine throne in Sal Iacono's store where he was now an occasional customer, Sal approached him and quietly asked for some help. Probably because of all the street repaving being done around him, his phone service had been knocked out for a week and he couldn't get Verizon to come and fix it. Could the mayor do something?

Two hours later, Sal's phone was working. Which was a lucky thing, because Hollie Bart had been trying to reach him for three days to tell him that he had to go over to Seedco to sign some more papers for his grant request to be complete. The caseworker from Seedco had been e-mailing Bart, warning her that time was running out to get Sal's application in to make the current round of grants.

Mitch Daniels had a surprise for Senator Joseph Lieberman when he showed up to testify on Lieberman's proposed bill to create a homeland security cabinet post. Lieberman had expected an argument, because Ridge and the rest of the Bush administration had repeatedly said that, although they might consider such a department at some later point, for now they favored the coordinator's role that Ridge had. Instead, in a comment carefully scripted by Card, Ridge, and others at the White House, Daniels said that the administration was "open" to considering Lieberman's idea.

Meantime, back at the White House, the small group plowed away at the list of agencies that should or should not be in the new department. They were already on their way to going well past Lieberman's proposal.

Although he was finished issuing his rules and regulations, Ken Feinberg announced still more wrinkles in his interpretation of what would and would not be deducted from his awards. The changes were bound to cheer the families of those wearing uniforms who had died on September 11.

First, he said that he would consider housing and other benefits given to military personnel as part of their salaries. Therefore, in computing the earnings lost by their deaths—the families' economic damages—he would add all that to the equation. This meant an extra $300,000 to $500,000 for most of the families of military people killed at the Pentagon.

Second, he announced that because police and firefighter pensions had been given to them in their contract with New York City in lieu of higher salaries, their value should be considered as salary and not a benefit paid to them on their deaths. The details were more complicated than that, but the bottom line was that the payouts to widows like Brian Lyons's sister-in-law, Elaine, would now be several hundred thousand dollars higher.

## Friday, April 12, 2002

Chuck Schumer had one of his now periodic meetings with the Cartiers. He'd been looking forward to it because he wanted to let them in on his United Nations idea. He'd already tested it on officials at the U.N. including the organization's longtime undersecretary general in charge of management and administration. They had pretty much told Schumer to forget it. Mayor

Bloomberg had also been negative, telling Schumer that he feared that once anyone gave the U.N. the idea of moving, they'd move right out of New York to Switzerland. But the perennially optimistic Schumer, who was hearing great reaction to it from friends in the city's real estate and business communities, figured he could talk those opponents through it. At least he'd be inclined to try, if he could get the survivors' families on board.

Schumer pitched the idea as a great living memorial to the victims and a monument to world peace and understanding: Where the Trade Center had once been, instead of office buildings, there would be a glorious new United Nations.

"No way," Patrick Cartier, Sr., said without a moment's hesitation. "I don't want a flag from Saudi Arabia or Iraq flying over where my son's body is."

Schumer was floored. He'd been working on the idea for more than three months and hadn't thought of that, nor had anyone mentioned it to him. He knew there were lots of logical arguments he could make back, but he also knew that the emotional force of Cartier's sentiment would be overpowering and, in fact, understandable. It was a good thing he had asked.

Michael Cartier didn't say so at the time, but he actually liked the idea. It seemed, as Schumer said, to be a practical solution to a lot of problems and the kind of majestic use of the site that matched its place in history. But he knew, too, that there was no way anyone was going to change his father's mind about it, and that on this score his father spoke for a lot of victims' relatives.

The Army medical doctor on Bruce Lawlor's staff sat in on an exercise conducted in Oklahoma City, in which an outbreak of smallpox was simulated to test how well the state and local authorities were prepared to deal with it. The whole thing was a failure—or a success, if one defines success in these tests by how many problems are identified. All the key issues, such as how a quarantine would be set up, who would be vaccinated, and how emergency workers would respond if they had not been vaccinated, were never resolved. They had no policies in place and neither did the federal government.

When Lawlor heard about it, he was reminded again of how he'd failed in getting the quarantine and vaccination policies decided in Washington, primarily because the Health and Human Services people were stonewalling. The new homeland security department, he resolved, should take over all of this.

# Sunday, April 14, 2002

The DNA identification staff at the New York City medical examiner's office was so dogged that they were still working Sundays. Moreover, when they confirmed this particular DNA match they didn't go through the normal procedure and pass it off to the police for notification on Monday. They wanted to tell the family immediately. This was a family they knew well, a family whose grief they had come to share.

Jennie Farrell got the call at home tonight. Three fragments of a bone from a left hand had been matched to James's DNA. Soon the whole Cartier family was gathered once again at their parents' house, this time to say a prayer of . thanks.

When Michael got the details the next day, he discovered that his brother's remains had been found at Fresh Kills. Inspector Luongo and his people hadn't let him down.

By Tuesday, mayors Giuliani and Bloomberg, Governor Pataki, and Chuck Schumer had called Jennie, Michael, or both to say how glad they were that James had been recovered.

# Monday, April 15, 2002

Because of the heat from the November congressional hearing, Border Patrol agents Bob Lindemann and Mark Hall had been put back on the night shift and allowed to partner together again. And now that the disciplinary action against them had been dropped, they had just begun to feel like they could relax. But tonight they got some action. At about midnight they caught a young Palestinian trying to sneak through the train tunnel from Canada to Detroit. When they were told to hand him over to another INS division for processing, they figured this was the way the bosses were now going to do it. Rather than have Hall or Lindemann release people and blab to the press about it, they'd make them give the detainee to others, who would release him.

The next day, when they heard that the Palestinian had, in fact, been released, and their supervisor refused to tell them what had happened, they were sure that INS was up to its old tricks.

They were wrong. Their prisoner had been checked out through the right databases, then held and only released after his brother, a doctor with a verified address, posted $10,000 in bail to guarantee his return for a deportation hearing, where he was going to plead for asylum as a refugee.

Maybe their whistle-blowing really had stirred some changes, even if they didn't know it, and their bosses didn't want to admit it to them.

# Tuesday, April 16, 2002

The next morning Ridge was in Lindemann's city. His focus wasn't on people sneaking over the border, but on trucks coming in through the bustling Customs facility at the Ambassador Bridge, which connects Windsor, Ontario, to Detroit.

This is the bridge that, beginning with the Customs security crackdown on September 12, was so snarled by delays that manufacturers such as General Motors, which depended on parts shipments, had had to shut their U.S. factories until it could be unclogged. The delays had quickly eased after Customs people had recruited more inspectors so that they could open up more checkpoints. But the four-lane bridge (which itself is privately owned) was still a bottleneck.

Now Ridge and Customs Commissioner Robert Bonner had come to announce an improvement that would not only move the lines faster, but increase security. It was one of those risk management ideas in action.

Under a program called C-TPAT, for Customs-Trade Partnership Against Terrorism, businesses that shipped goods across the border could agree to go through a process to ensure the security of their shipments, including a background screening of their truck drivers and an assessment of how well they guarded their trucks and the containers they carried. Shippers that qualified would be more trusted than others and get to go through a faster line, where they would be subject to fewer inspections.

It was like an EZ Pass for cargo companies. In fact, combined with a program that Bonner already had working for the car parts shippers, C-TPAT trucks could have a transponder on their windshields, allowing electronic pre-filing of the paperwork related to what they were bringing. Then they could pass through checkpoints quickly, with their entry papers and any tariffs owed recorded automatically on their accounts. This would allow Customs to focus on the cargo and the drivers they didn't know anything about.

In September, Ridge and Bonner would announce an expanded version of C-TPAT, at the same time that they proceeded with a program that pre-cleared individuals going to and from Canada, who allowed themselves to be screened in advance so that they also could use an EZ Pass–type lane.

In Bonner, Ridge and his staff had found someone willing to push harder to focus resources on higher-risk targets, while not hassling those that seemed to be low-risk. Of course, there was always the chance that a terrorist could abuse the system and sneak himself and something dangerous in through the fast lanes, causing a public outcry about why they hadn't checked everyone and everything with the same rigor. But that was what risk management was all about. If only, Ridge and his staff kept thinking, they could convince the people at TSA to think like that.

As Lindemann could have told Ridge, the problem with all of this focus on the official ports of entry, such as the bridge, was that smart terrorists no doubt had their own risk management calculus. So they had to know that it was ridiculous to try to come through an official port of entry when they could walk over any of the thousands of miles of the unguarded border, drive across many parts of it, or take a boat in over the rest of it. Thus, not more than a half mile from the Ambassador Bridge, Ridge could have gone to watch small boats docking on the shores of Detroit completely unchallenged.

# Wednesday, April 17, 2002

The big idea Chuck Schumer wanted to float today at a hearing of the Senate Judiciary subcommittee that he chaired is that it should be possible for all the federal law enforcement databases to be combined quickly so that they can talk to one another. One of Schumer's great strengths was that he was smart enough to appreciate that something like this is complicated, but he was smarter still in terms of not being intimidated by all the people who did nothing but talk about those complications rather than the solutions. He had friends high up in the high-tech world, who told him that it could be done, and he believed them.

Which is what made today's hearing, which included the heads of information systems from the FBI, INS, and Department of Justice, so frustrating. They all restated their problems and made promises of progress that everyone had heard before.

To Schumer, it was part of a pattern. He liked Bush, and thought he was doing a good job in the war abroad. But at home, he just wasn't cracking the whip. There just wasn't enough progress at INS, or at the ports, where Schumer seemed obsessed with the prospect of a nuclear weapon being sneaked in and detonated. Aviation seemed to be moving along okay, but what about trains, or the waterways? Ridge was a nice guy, but he lacked power, because Bush really hadn't given him the power. Why hadn't they fired Ziglar at INS, or moved to do something really significant about the borders, or about the fact that INS still wasn't keeping track of immigrants who overstayed visas or came in from countries where visas weren't even required? Didn't they see that this really was an emergency? Was it going to take suicide bombings here, like the ones now terrorizing Israel, before they got serious and started to think big?

Randy Null, who was running the TSA go team in charge of the rollout of the equipment to screen checked baggage for bombs, got the first reports today from the staff that was starting to read the four bid proposals from the defense contractors hoping to get the job of coordinating it all. He was surprised to hear that on first look Raytheon's didn't look like the best one. Their bid looked to be the cheapest because, for much of the work, they were guaranteeing a fixed price rather than proposing a fee based on however much time it took their people and whatever their expenses were to hire subcontractors. (The latter is called a time and materials contract, and it puts the government at maximum risk of cost overruns.) But Raytheon just didn't seem to have explained in enough detail exactly how they would go about this massive undertaking at the nation's 429 airports. Boeing and Lockheed Martin, on the other hand, seemed to have done that impressively.

Null didn't read too much into these early assessments. There was still a long process to go through involving different teams of TSA people (some focused on the budget, some on technology, some on operations), who now had to vet the proposals a lot more carefully. Moreover, with the White House and the Office of Management and Budget now having forced a radically different combination of big machines versus the smaller trace detectors (something no one on the outside knew about yet), it was inevitable that TSA was going to have to call the contractors back in and tell them to redo their proposals based on the new mix.

Inside TSA, Null and the other go team people on loan from the private sector may have thought of themselves and Jackson—the deputy secretary who was their godfather—as sharp managers getting hold of an unmanageable set of challenges. On Capitol Hill, TSA faced a near lynch mob, who branded the agency as the ultimate in incompetent, runaway bureaucracies.

The forum was the House Appropriations Subcommittee on Transportation.

Oversight committees—such as the House Transportation Subcommittee on Aviation—supposedly oversee the performance of an agency in carrying out its duties. But appropriations committees like the one holding this hearing control the agencies' budgets, which means they determine how much money they get to perform their duties and decide whether they are spending money prudently. The overlap is obvious, which is why the oversight committees and the appropriations committees—and their staffs—were perpetually jealous of each other, and competed by trying to one-up each other in giving fat targets like TSA a hard time. That meant that TSA had four committees to contend with, an appropriation committee and an oversight committee for each of the House and Senate.

In the case of transportation, the House appropriations subcommittee was the toughest of the four, because it was chaired by Harold Rogers, an old-style, cigar-smoking Kentucky Republican who relishes being the lord of this turf.

This morning, Rogers began his hearings by decrying the "lack of crisp decision-making . . . by TSA and the administration, which will not be tolerated much longer by this subcommittee." It didn't seem to matter to Rogers that the largest new department in the history of the country had been created by Congress only seven months ago. Or even that under the law creating it, which Rogers had voted for, it had to implement first-generation technologies and deploy a massive new force of federal agents across 429 airports under deadlines that no one thought were rational.

What was Rogers's main concern? "That TSA projects a workforce now estimated at 72,000 [by now the TSA people had killed themselves to whittle away at McKinsey's 91,000 estimate] when the estimate was only 30,000 a few months ago."

That estimate (actually it was 28,000) had, of course, been Congress's when it passed the law, not TSA's. And the staff member who had come up with it had left out not only the extra troops obviously needed to upgrade the screening of passengers at checkpoints, but also the 20,000 to 30,000 new people necessary to fulfill Congress's mandate that all checked luggage be screened for explosives.

Rogers was similarly shocked that the cost of enforcing the law was going to exceed by a factor of six the passenger fees of $2.50 per flight built into the law. But, again, TSA hadn't written that law.

Rogers had invited the Transportation Department's inspector general to testify. He took the witness chair to point out some basic management chores the TSA hadn't undertaken yet, such as making a firm decision about the exact mix of trace detectors and the larger machines like Magistri's. The differences he cited were that on the one hand the large machines cost close to $1 million, while the trace detectors cost only $45,000. On the other hand using 100 percent trace machines would require 50,480 screeners, whereas using 100 percent large machines like InVision's would require 22,670. How come TSA hadn't figure out the right mix yet, Rogers wanted to know.

Jackson, who testified next, said that they were working on it. He did not let on that they were furiously redoing their plans right now because of the push Daniels had made in the Situation Room meeting.

There was one issue that Rogers and other members of his committee were worked up about that was truly legitimate. They complained, as Cox in Memphis had, that TSA had left the airports largely in the dark about their plans. Members of Congress fly every week, and people like Cox had ample opportunity to complain about that. What was curious, though, was that much of the congressmen's wrath on this and other issues was reserved for Magaw, the TSA head, rather than his boss, Jackson. Indeed, everyone seemed to respect Jackson as a terrific, dedicated manager, whereas Magaw, who came off in this, as in other hearings, as wooden and nonresponsive, got the brunt of their harshest criticism.

Yet it was Jackson, a self-proclaimed "control freak," who had told Magaw, Rossides, and others at TSA that they should not tell airport officials anything about their plans until later in the spring, or in the summer, just as they were ready to come into their airports.

"Michael was worried that we'd look bad if we said we were coming in May and didn't get there until June," was how one TSA person put it. "And he didn't want the airport guys sniping at our plans. So his solution was to tell them nothing until a few days before we were to arrive."

This hearing was one of a series of similar sessions that would play out over the next two months, in which the committees with appropriations or oversight jurisdiction over TSA would flay the agency—the senior House Appropriations Committee Democrat, David Obey, would declare the agency "out of control, run amok"—yet generally put most of the blame on Magaw, while continuing to defer to Jackson. "I think Michael is really good, brilliant, a great manager," Obey would say a few weeks later.

# Thursday, April 18, 2002

The President's morning threat matrix briefing was much more tense than usual. The night before, the CIA had passed along to the FBI intelligence suggesting that "suicide operatives" were targeting American financial institutions.* The information seemed credible. FBI Director Mueller, Ashcroft, and Ashcroft's deputy, Larry Thompson, all urged Bush that the nationwide threat alert be raised to orange, and that banks should be specifically warned. Ridge and Deputy Treasury Secretary Kenneth Dam, representing Treasury Secretary O'Neill, didn't agree. They pointed to the near panic that had resulted a few days before when someone—it turned out to be a kid in the Netherlands—had anonymously phoned in a threat to a bank in Washington. More than 150 local banks had closed as a result. Ridge and Dam said they feared another such panic, only this time it would be national.

The President's response was that the group should talk about it more on their own, then come back to him with a decision. Only now, time was important, and no decision was, in fact, a decision not to issue the warning.

Through the day the officials tried to come to a consensus, but failed. That night they tried again on a conference call at about 9:00. But lacking additional information about the threat to tip the argument one way or the other, there was still no agreement, and no decision.

But by 3:00 A.M. the next morning, new information would be logged in by the CIA. A high-ranking Al Qaeda leader being interrogated that day had also talked about a plan to blow up a bank in the eastern part of the United States. Thus, by the time they gathered the next morning in the Oval Office, there would be consensus that something had to be done. But they still wouldn't agree on raising the general alert to orange. Ridge and O'Neill wanted just to have Ashcroft issue a statement warning banks in the East. The President again told them to work it out, but Card, who always knows what the President wants, pushed Ashcroft to back off from the general alert. Later that afternoon, Ashcroft issued the statement warning the banks, and added, at O'Neill's insistence, that he urged banks not to close.

Ridge's notion of an alert system that wasn't vague, but was targeted to a specific threat, yet also wasn't any more alarming to any more people than it needed to be, had finally materialized. In effect, they had put the banks in the East on orange alert while keeping the rest of the country on yellow.

---

* Most of the details of this story were first reported in the *Wall Street Journal* on May 17, 2002. The author confirmed them with three of the people involved.

At about the time that Ridge, Ashcroft, O'Neill, and the others were on their conference call about the terrorist threat to the banks, CNN cut into its regular programming to broadcast a live shot from a Los Angeles helicopter of a car moving down a freeway in Los Angeles. Unlike O. J. Simpson, the lead occupant wasn't a famous football player, nor was he running from the police. He was a former TV actor named Robert Blake, and the car ride had all the real suspense of watching paint dry. He wasn't being chased by a police car. He was in a police car, on his way to be booked after being arrested (with no resistance) for allegedly murdering his wife.

America had gotten back to normal. This was the news the country cared about.

Sure, one could blame CNN and other news organizations for not instead spending tonight uncovering the deadlock over smallpox vaccinations, or ferreting out the problems Mike Byrne was having getting first responders the equipment and training they needed that might save thousands of lives next month, just as one could blame the press for not figuring out last August that Middle Eastern immigrants were taking flight lessons, or that it was a snap to get on an airplane with a box cutter. But the more important point is that most media—especially the ratings-driven television media—try to follow what the public is interested in, rather than attempt to drive that interest.

Americans had largely stopped seeing the September 12 era as an emergency. The positive way to look at that is that if, as the cliché goes, the terrorists win if their targets change their way of life, then by many measures by tonight they had lost. But it also could mean that the country had lost its concentration, its will, to protect itself from a threat that had not abated. In a democracy, if the public loses its concentration and its will, their elected officials soon follow, unless they can figure out how to lead—which may explain why Byrne couldn't get that first responder aid program up and running. Put differently, could anyone imagine that Congress wouldn't have jumped by Tuesday to set up Byrne's plan exactly as he wanted it if a terrorist had attacked on Monday and left first responders in Peoria or Knoxville helpless to save people?

If a democracy depends this way on its people not losing interest, then the threat of terrorism posed a new kind of challenge. Unlike the September 11 attacks, Pearl Harbor was followed by a world war. Holding the nation's attention was easy. The Cold War didn't have a daily stream of news events to keep the public focused, but there were enough Cold War crises, and the constant threat of nuclear annihilation was something no one lost sight of. Besides, the Cold War was the kind of threat that only required that the people building and controlling the nuclear weapons that provided the protection of deterrence always be focused. Terrorism is different. It happens in a burst and then there is nothing, leaving the country's political leaders struggling with the balance between not letting them "win" by alarming the public too much about continuing threats, and galvanizing them to ward off the next threat.

Schumer, of course, thought Bush had gotten the balance wrong between alarming and galvanizing, that he just wasn't pushing hard enough. It was an argument that paralleled the view of those on the President's own staff who had wanted him to call for mandatory public service in the State of the Union address.

Whoever or whatever was to blame, or even if there wasn't any blame to apportion, tonight's newscast of the Blake nonchase car chase did seem to demonstrate that America and Americans had come a long way from the early days of the September 12 era.

# Friday, April 19, 2002

Gale Rossides spent part of the day making sure that the first group of trainees would have hotel rooms when they arrived next week at the Baltimore/Washington Airport to begin preparations for the first takeover of an airport by the federalized screener force. (A few days later, she'd chuckle when she got a report that every one of them had been a "selectee"—that is, they were all chosen for hand searches by the still antiquated computerized passenger screening process—when they'd flown to Baltimore, because the government had only issued them one-way tickets.)

By now her husband had made Rossides promise that she'd get out of this job within a year. Even for her, these work hours had gotten beyond reason. Yet as she prepared for the debut in Baltimore, she seemed more giddy than overwhelmed. No matter what was added to her plate, or what she reached out for to put on it herself, she seemed to take it in stride. Her office had been moved three times, her phone number changed twice. Each time, she had taken her files and the framed picture of Teddy Roosevelt accompanied by an excerpt from his famous "man in the arena" speech that she liked to keep over her desk, and set up shop anew.

The flak TSA was getting on the Hill and in the press got to her when she took the time to think about it. But that wasn't often. Today, in just the period from 3:00 to 6:00, she had meetings with a group of religious leaders to talk about how the screeners should be trained to deal with passengers wearing special religious garb, and a team from the FAA to discuss the integration of FAA staff who were being moved into TSA. Then came a daily senior staff session to review up-to-the-minute progress on the screener recruitment, training, and rollout, followed by a discussion of how TSA would staff the force needed to guard airport perimeters (did they need their own people, or could they use the local authorities already there?), and, finally, a weekly budget meeting.

## Monday, April 22, 2002

Ashcroft's insistence that the Justice Department keep jurisdiction of Zacarias Moussaoui and prosecute him in federal court, instead of sending him off to a Pentagon military commission, began to look a lot worse this morning. At a routine pretrial hearing, Moussaoui stunned everyone, including his own court-appointed defense team, by declaring to the judge that he wanted to represent himself. In a preview of what his performance as his own lawyer might be like, he then made a speech about how he prayed for "the destruction of the Jewish people . . . and the destruction of the United States."

Judge Leonie Brinkema responded that "you appear to know and understand what you are doing. . . . You are very bright." Thus, she ruled that pending a psychiatric examination to make sure he was making a "knowing waiver of counsel," she was inclined to let him proceed as his own lawyer. But she also ruled that his current lawyers would become his "standby" counsel and be available to help him.

"Can they do that?" was Ashcroft's first question to members of his senior staff when he heard about the alleged twentieth hijacker's move. Indeed, the judge could, he was told.

One of the aides pointed out that the trial could now become a circus, with Moussaoui making speeches and proving to the jury that he had to be insane. Worse, he could try to get prosecution documents about his case that would reveal sources that they'd never want to turn over to a terrorist, and they'd likely be caught up in weeks of legal battles as his standby lawyers helped him file those motions.

"The judge'll never let that happen," someone else said. Ashcroft agreed.

Kevin McCabe got a new mobile VACIS machine today, bringing his total arsenal of the giant X rays to four—two stationary ones, and two mobile units. It would allow him not only to do more inspections of more containers, but also to do them with less waiting time.

The machines were being put to better use, with the choices of which containers they examined getting increasingly more sophisticated. McCabe and his inspectors, along with the Customs people in Washington, were continuing to experiment with refinements. Even now they had done enough so that they were no longer inspecting all shipments from countries like Saudi Arabia, as they had done in the months just after the attacks. Rather, using 280 criteria programmed into the software to assess risk, they were passing up the lowest-risk containers from that country and from other countries highest up on the risk list, in favor of inspecting more containers from places that were slighter lower, or even much lower, but which showed, apart from their country of origin, an increasingly sophisticated array of other risk factors. For example, maybe a shipper from a "safe country" was rumored to be in tough financial straits and the cargo was going to a recipient they'd never heard of.

McCabe also began today to look for volunteers to be posted in Rotterdam and possibly China, Italy, and France. His boss, Customs Commissioner Robert Bonner, was apparently making good progress in negotiating agreements for Customs to post its inspectors in the foreign ports that sent the most goods to the United States, so that the borders could be "pushed back." Word had come down that Washington was looking for a few good men, and women, for these unprecedented assignments, and that perhaps McCabe could recommend some.

Bonner and other Customs officials in Washington knew of McCabe by now, not only because they'd met him in Elizabeth, but because he had become a kind of Customs ambassador of sorts. Easygoing, knowledgeable, and discreet enough to be informative without breaching security, he'd been the one that the head of the port had picked initially when a few congressmen had wanted to come by and talk about security. That had worked so well that now, whenever anyone wanted the short tour or long tour of the port, McCabe had become the guy. This included visitors from abroad, as well as a slew of think tank and congressional researchers, and even two people from Treasury's inspector general's office who wanted to know about the efficacy of that computerized risk assessment system.

McCabe enjoyed doing it. He loved to talk to people, knew he knew his stuff, and was proud of what they were doing at Elizabeth. The only problem was that it took so much time, and he loved to be out there on the docks or looking at the VACIS monitor.

Today, he was hosting visitors from the Netherlands. "Do I really have to have lunch with the Dutchmen?" he asked a deputy, half kidding, before answering his own question: "I guess I do. It's all part of the Rotterdam effort."


The first substantive argument in Larry Silverstein's case against the insurance companies finally made it to court. In January, Wachtell had filed a motion on behalf of Silverstein for summary judgment against Travelers Insurance. Summary judgment means that a jury trial isn't necessary because, based just on the facts that are not in dispute, one side or the other (in this case the Silverstein side) has to win as a matter of law.

Travelers was, indeed, the company against whom Wachtell had the best case. It was Travelers, after all, that had sent Silverstein's broker its own version of a policy form because it didn't like the Silverstein broker's form. And unlike the Silverstein broker's form, which defined occurrence as a series of related events, the Travelers form had not defined occurrence at all—which Wachtell said meant, based on prior court decisions, that the destruction of the two towers had to be deemed two occurrences. Again, the case law on that wasn't at all clear, but Travelers was still Wachtell's clearest target, because at least they had tried to use that form.

Travelers, on the other hand, argued that not only didn't prior case law tip Silverstein's way, but that because Silverstein had never agreed to use the Travelers form, the other form that defined occurrence as a series of related events should apply, or that at least there should be no summary judgment because a jury ought to sort out all the facts surrounding the negotiation.

Today, Barry Ostrager—representing Swiss Re and as a practical matter all of the other insurers other than Travelers, who claimed to have been using the Silverstein broker's form all along—entered the fray with a brief arguing against Silverstein's summary judgment motion in the Travelers case. It was his first chance to summarize everything he and the lawyers working for him had found in the weeks of pretrial discovery.

Citing documents such as the note in the Silverstein insurance manager's files that he had thought they had "underinsured" and that the occurrence definition in his own broker's form was "the one we are working with," as well as the notes about the Nashville phone call, where Silverstein's own lead broker had said he thought it was one occurrence, Ostrager argued that "Silver-

stein intended inclusion of the [Silverstein broker's] occurrence definition"
and that the "contention that Travelers is subject to an occurrence definition
Silverstein itself did not want, tried to avoid, and to which it is undisputed
[that] no insurer, including Travelers, ever agreed is simply incredible."

As for any evidence going the other way, Ostrager contended "the 26 depositions conducted and approximately 230 boxes of documentary evidence
exchanged to date have yielded no credible evidence that any of the insurers . . . were party to—much less agreed to be bound by—post closing negotiations with Travelers," and that the contention that other insurers "are
bound by the never complete . . . discussions with Silverstein and Travelers
is a complete post-loss invention for which there is no support in either the
testimonial or documentary record."

If it is true that when lawyers don't have the law on their side, they pound
the table, it may also be true that when PR men don't have the law on their
side they just publish bigger press handouts. Within a day, Silverstein PR representative Howard Rubenstein was circulating a binder that was three times
the size of anything he'd come up with so far. Thick as it was with excerpts
from deposition testimony, none of it, especially when matched up with pages
not included in the excerpts, actually contradicted Ostrager's assertion. Thus,
when one of the lawyers working on the Silverstein side was asked at about
this time what witness or document he had that could prove that anyone had
agreed to be bound by the Travelers definition, he conceded, "We haven't
found one yet."

# Tuesday, April 23, 2002

Justice Department Inspector General Glenn Fine released a new report
today zapping INS. It was yet another "follow-up review," this time of a
report done in 1997 saying that INS was failing to keep track of foreigners
who overstayed their visas. "The INS has made little progress in addressing
the important issue of . . . overstays since we issued our 1997 report," Fine
concluded. This, of course, was the same entry-exit problem that Ridge's
office was pushing INS to work on.

Ziglar was at a conference in Australia today, but his office issued a statement saying INS was aware of the problems and hard at work on a solution.

Meanwhile, the White House press office announced in the afternoon that
the Bush administration had changed its mind and now backed a bill pro-

posed by House Judiciary Committee Chairman James Sensenbrenner to divide INS into an enforcement agency and an immigrant service agency. Ziglar had no idea about the change in the administration's position until someone in his office called him the next day to tell him about the White House announcement.

The "small group" planning the new Department of Homeland Security had their first session with the bosses. Meeting secretly in the Presidential Emergency Operations Center, or PEOC, which is housed in a subbasement deep below the White House, the group presented their work to Ridge, management and budget chief Daniels, White House Counsel Alberto Gonzales, chief of staff Card, and his deputy, Bolten.

First, Falkenrath did a slide show of his matrix, the one that outlined the various alternatives for a super-coordinator in the White House, versus a head of a super-department. Everyone agreed that the super-department was where they had to go, especially in light of the congressional testimony issues the matrix illustrated.

Next came the pyramid, representing how deep down they could choose to go in terms of functions the agency would perform. When someone mentioned the likely congressional opposition to one such annexation, Card interrupted. "Your job is to come up with what you think is right, not worry about the opposition to it, or the politics of it. We'll deal with that later. Let's just create what we really think makes the most sense." It would be a constant refrain.

Before they left, they ratified the principles the small group was using to make its choices in what would now become their almost daily meetings. Any agency whose primary mission was security but that was in a department whose core mission was something else would be extracted and included in the new department. For example, Customs' core mission now was guarding the borders and keeping weapons of mass destruction out, but it was lodged in Treasury, whose core mission was raising and managing money. Second, if an agency had apparently equivalent and intermingled multiple missions but had one that was key to the homeland security portfolio, it, too, would be considered for inclusion, with the test being the balance between what was lost by not including it, versus the headaches gained by including it and gaining all those non-homeland-security missions. The best example was the Coast Guard, which did vital rescue work but was also supposed to keep intruders from the shores. Another example was FEMA (the Federal Emergency Management Agency). It coordinated recovery efforts after hurricanes and even ran a flood insurance program. But it was also the key to the response and recovery efforts associated with any terrorist attack. A third example was the FAA, which controlled the nation's airspace but which also regulated the airlines on issues having nothing to do with security.

Those were difficult issues. Yet the group always came to a decision. This was not a project any of them were going to let languish while they struggled for an unambiguous answer to questions for which there might not be a clear answer.

# Wednesday, April 24, 2002

In a move that came as a surprise to everyone in the industry, but was preordained by Mitch Daniels's ambush in the Situation Room twenty days ago, Norman Mineta announced at a speech to the Chamber of Commerce that TSA would order only 1,100 explosive detection machines—rather than the previously announced target of more than 2,000—to meet the December 31 deadline and use 4,700 trace detectors with them.

By the end of the day, InVision stock had dropped from $34.35 to $27.44—even though on the day before InVision had issued a stellar report for the first quarter, citing a 90 percent jump in revenue over the prior year and more than three times the prior year's meager profit. (The stock had been as high as $42.75 in recent days.)

Sergio Magistri, who had been on a sales trip in Europe, was on a plane from Frankfurt to San Francisco while Mineta made his speech. The day before he had had a conference call with stock analysts to go over the great first-quarter results, and he had, of course, expressed no doubts about TSA's eagerness to plunge ahead, though he had mentioned that much of his sales to TSA were likely to extend over into 2003 no matter how hard TSA tried to meet the deadline. When he got off the plane at midnight, his cell phone showed ten frantic messages from his office.

He went straight there, worked for three hours preparing a statement for Wall Street, got some rest, then held a 6:00 A.M. (Pacific Time) conference call with the same investment analysts he had spoken with the day before. He tried to tell them that this was not really a setback because InVision couldn't have produced many more machines this year anyway. But even one of the analysts that had underwritten his stock, Lehman Brothers, issued a report that day that, while it was entitled a "Rebuttal to a New Revelation by TSA" and recited all the long-term extra personnel costs the alternative trace detector ate up, nonetheless lowered its projected revenues for InVision for 2002 by about 15 percent.

By Friday, the stock would plunge to $23.95. By Monday it would fall to $21.

"Once again, the government killed us," Magistri said. "They didn't warn us. We had no inkling. Our salespeople had been at TSA every day the week before, and those guys told us nothing. Nothing."

For Magistri, it was the "worst day of the whole period. Just terrible, especially because of the conference call the day before."

Magistri's complaint was that Wall Street hated surprises, and this one could not have been more embarrassing, coming as it did on the heels of his upbeat conference call the day before. If Magistri, who had so willingly shared everything about his company in December with the seemingly sympathetic Mineta and Jackson, had been given the courtesy of being told about it in advance, he'd have had time to spin this to the investment community as a good development. He'd have explained that the government's decision to use more trace detectors was an interim measure—which is what he thought this was all about, and how he played it now in his public comments. It simply gave InVision more time to ramp up and produce more machines for sale next year and beyond, while forestalling the possibility that a new, larger company would be encouraged to jump in and produce the machines themselves, using the licenses of InVision's intellectual property that the government had negotiated for. Mineta's out-of-the blue announcement made that kind of after-the-fact explanation seem like a weak attempt at damage control.


At about the same time that Mineta was making his announcement about cutting back on orders to InVision, the top in-house lobbyist for the American Association of Airport Executives was meeting with Harold Rogers, the House Transportation Appropriations Subcommittee chairman, and sticking a knife into TSA from a different angle. The power of the airport executives association—of which Larry Cox was a prominent member and had served as chairman for two years—derived from the fact that its members lived and worked in just about every congressional district. They ran important businesses with lots of employees and with customers (passengers) who were every member of Congress's voters. Plus, they had easy access to the congressmen and senators who moved through their airports twice a week.

The goal of the association was in sync with Cox's sentiments about TSA.

They resented its impending usurpation of power and wanted to weaken it. Thus, their lobbyist walked Rogers and his key staffer through a series of bullet points aimed at pushing TSA back. TSA was going to overpay for its own perimeter guards, when it would serve the security and budget interests of the taxpayers better if they simply reimbursed airports like Cox's for the cost of Cox keeping his own police force on duty. TSA was planning to waste money on a variety of people at the checkpoints who weren't needed. And as a general matter TSA's Secret Service mentality was going to destroy the aviation industry by repelling its customers.

# Friday, April 26, 2002

The boat, about thirty feet long, left the Canadian side of the border at 11:58 A.M. By 12:02 it pulled up to a dock in the Del Ray area of Detroit, a rundown neighborhood of old steel mills and seedy tenements.

Two men stood on the boat. One, who looked to be in his twenties, hopped off carrying a green duffle bag, which he tossed into the back of a waiting pickup truck. The truck drove away, and the man got back in the boat, which returned to Canada. Except for the author, none of the dozens of people milling around in a park area near this shoreline seemed to regard this uninspected border crossing as anything unusual.

Twenty minutes later, another boat arrived about thirty feet down the dock. A man, a woman, and a dog got out. They walked around before sitting down on a bench. Each had a backpack. They hung around for a while, talked to someone in another pickup truck, then got back on the boat and left. They could just as easily have disappeared into the dense slums just across the boulevard about a hundred yards away, a neighborhood teeming with illegal Hispanic and Middle Eastern immigrants.

Since it was daytime, Lindemann wasn't on duty. Six other Border Patrol agents in his sector were, but they were nowhere to be found. The problem was that their sector has 804 miles of border, stretching from Michigan east to Ohio. Even with increases in manpower since September 11, the sector had only forty agents to cover three shifts seven days a week. The bottom line was that at noon today just one of the six agents on duty in the 804-mile sector was out in the field covering the forty miles of border in the Detroit area of the sector. All forty miles were water, yet there was only one working boat, and it could only be used for special situations and could not be used by one agent working alone.

Obviously, more agents were needed. But Lindemann believed that force multipliers—surveillance cameras situated all along the shore that could be monitored remotely, and sensors that could signal when an intruder arrived—were equally important, as was more equipment like better night-vision goggles, radios, and, of course, boats. All of this had been promised. All of it was the focus of the issues that Lindemann and Hall raised in their capacity as union leaders. (In fact, the area where those two boats had docked was one place that they had recommended would be a great location for a camera.) Congress had even appropriated the funds. But none of these supplies had been delivered.

In July, INS chief Ziglar would once again display the INS way of responding to a national emergency. A letter from the Justice Department to House Judiciary Committee Chairman Sensenbrenner would explain that the installation of fifty-five Border Patrol camera surveillance systems, for which Congress had recently appropriated the funds, required "5–7 month environmental assessments . . . prior to disturbing any land where a pole may be placed." Apart from INS showing a sensitivity to environmental issues not previously associated with the Bush administration, this estimate contradicted the written protocols of INS's own "Headquarters Facilities Engineering Branch/Division of Environmental Assessments," which state that these evaluations will be done in three to four months. And apart from all that, it is impossible to imagine how any pole could disturb the environment anywhere near the grim area where those two boats arrived within minutes of each other today.

The letter to Sensenbrenner would go on to explain that after this so-called environmental assessment was completed, it would take eighteen to twenty-four months to complete all the installations.

John France, the deputy sector chief of the Border Patrol in Detroit, was the unit's operations chief and the man who had spearheaded the disciplinary actions against Lindemann and Hall. Later this afternoon, he explained that in his view the dangers on the Northern Border had been "greatly exaggerated" by Lindemann and Hall because they were "union agitators." The Border Patrol's most important mission, France said, was still the "Southern Border and Mexicans."

When he was asked about the fact that thousands of boats come onto shore every day from Canada on the Great Lakes, and whether it wouldn't be easy for a terrorist to smuggle in a weapon of mass destruction by disguising himself as someone out for a pleasure cruise some Saturday afternoon,

France acknowledged that the Great Lakes are not patrolled by his people at all because it "wasn't necessary."

Why not?

"Because no terrorist would take the trouble to take a long trip on the Great Lakes."

Why not?

"They don't need to, because it's so easy for them to cross over at the river [in Detroit], which is a few hundred yards wide."

It was a new paradigm in law enforcement economics, the perfect converse of the Ridge policy wonks' notion of "efficient risk management." Not protecting the easiest points of vulnerability eliminated the need to spend time and money worrying about anyone trying to penetrate the more difficult points.

Was it any wonder that Lindemann, who had enlisted in the Marines when he was eighteen and had wanted to be in law enforcement since he was a schoolkid, was frustrated on the Northern Border?

John Flaherty, who was Norman Mineta's chief of staff at the Department of Transportation and a Democrat, had a friendly game he liked to play with Michael Jackson, Mineta's deputy and a Republican who had worked in the first Bush administration. When an employee was doing well, Flaherty would claim the person was his hire. When the employee's star was fading, he'd tell Jackson the person had been Jackson's hire.

In Flaherty's mind, TSA head John Magaw had now become Jackson's hire. For what seemed like the fourth or fifth time in the last few weeks, Flaherty's beeper went off today, and when he called in to the Transportation Department's command center, he was told that someone had discovered that a screener at some airport checkpoint had kicked the plug of a metal detector out of its socket and, therefore, the thing hadn't been turned on for who-knew-how-long while passengers walked though it. As a result, an entire section of a terminal had to be evacuated, with all of the planes at its gates emptied so that passengers could go back through the detectors. Dozens of flights had been delayed.

These airports hadn't yet been taken over by the federalized screeners, but supervising security there was nonetheless already TSA's responsibility. Why couldn't they just buy some tape to keep the wires from getting tripped over, Flaherty had said to Magaw after it had happened the first time. Mineta had said the same thing the second time. But still it kept happening.

Flaherty had worked for Mineta since his days in Congress, and he knew that Mineta's mantra was accountability and accessibility, which meant that if there was a problem you got down into it and fixed it yourself. Magaw, it seemed, was good at focusing on and building an organization's pride and culture, but he just didn't seem to have that down-in-the-trenches approach. It's what made him seem so aloof in his congressional testimony; he wasn't seeing or relating to the airports the way these frequent fliers were. And it's what made him, Flaherty concluded today, not the type of manager who would visit airports himself after his boss complained about those unplugged detectors to make sure that someone had gone out to the local Staples or Home Depot and bought some damn masking tape.

Something had to change, Flaherty told Jackson. Magaw's operations guy, Stephen McHale, was a lawyer who'd worked for Magaw at ATF. He clearly didn't have those instincts either. Jackson, who with his go teams was building the TSA organization, and Flaherty, who was dealing with its day-to-day crises, couldn't keep covering for Magaw and McHale.


# Saturday, April 27, 2002

Elaine Lyons got a form letter addressed to the victims' families, telling them that the recovery effort at Ground Zero was winding down and that they would soon be invited to a ceremony commemorating the end of the work down there. But, of course, she knew all that, because her brother-in-law, Brian, had been giving her regular reports.

As she sat among some partially packed boxes that signaled her gradual preparations to move up the block into the larger house that she had bought, what she was more concerned about was that she hadn't heard a thing about whether there was a DNA match with the remains Brian had said he found more than a month ago.


# Tuesday, April 30, 2002

Gale Rossides got to the concourse in front of piers A and B at the Baltimore/ Washington Airport at 2:30 this morning to check on preparations for the debut about ninety minutes later of TSA's federalized screening force.

She reached down to pet one of the bomb-sniffing dogs, then, with a big smile, showed her ID so she could go in the exit aisle to get behind the checkpoint. She was relieved when the guard told her, politely, that she still had to go through the metal detector.

"Is it warm, or is it just my nerves?" she asked one of the supervisors.

"Both," he said, laughing, before going back to a checklist.

"Nice," she said to one of the screeners who was practicing on the X-ray machine's monitor, referring to his uniform that included a crisp white shirt with the new TSA seal that Magaw, ever the culture maven, had personally approved. "Thanks," he said, recognizing Rossides from having seen her a few weeks before when he was training in Oklahoma City. "We really like it, too."

"I wish we had more women to do the women pat-downs," Rossides said to a young man in jeans and no tie, who turned out to be one of the go team consultants from McKinsey, who was in charge of today's launch.*

Another supervisor reached into an equipment table, still labeled "Argenbright," for some masking tape. The metal detector's wires had already been taped down once, but he wanted to make sure with a second layer. Then he took out a box of TSA-issue shoehorns to get them ready for the screeners who would be checking people's shoes at random.

Rossides checked out the new signage, emblazoned with the TSA logo, that politely instructed passengers on how to proceed through the lines, then turned around to inspect the glass "corrals" the Marriott people had designed, where people selected for pat-downs and shoe inspections could go and be isolated but still watch their carry-on bags sitting on the conveyor belt.

Coming back out front, Rossides inspected the rope lines (actually they were bands, not ropes) that had been set up on stanchions. Designed primarily by someone from Disney, they could be easily adjusted to snake around more or fewer turns in order to accommodate smaller or larger groups of passengers waiting to approach the checkpoints. She looked at the container in which passengers would place their laptops before they moved through the X-ray machine and remarked, "We're still doing tests to come up with the perfect bin. We've timed how long it takes people to take their laptops out and put them in a bin to go on the belt, and we know that the right size bin makes a difference."

Back on the other side, a supervisor ran through the color-coded chart showing the various posts his screeners would rotate through to keep them

---

*By October, Rossides would have succeeded in recruiting a workforce that was approximately one-third women, more than enough to do same sex pat-downs with no delays.

alert—X-ray monitoring, supervising movement through the magnetometer, wanding (with a handheld metal detector for people who set off the machine), and line monitoring, which means peeling people from the common line to the four metal detectors at this pier, while asking them to remove cell phones and other metal objects from their pockets and put them in their carry-on bags so they would not get lost.

The supervisor reminded the line monitors to remember the two-person rule, by which he meant a plan that the go team had come up with to have two people at a time standing in front of the magnetometer. "We found that the peer pressure of having someone standing behind you makes you want to move through faster," Kurt Krause, on loan from Marriott, explained.

By now all of the go team was there, along with Rossides's staff and others from TSA. Most had been working ten- to fourteen-hour days since January. All, including the 220 screeners, had been here Sunday night, after the airport had closed down, for an all-hands meeting and rehearsal. Yet they seemed anything but put-upon in the terminal this morning. The laughed with each other like the Yankees after a ninth-inning win.

At about 4:15 they faced their first group of real passengers.

The bleary-eyed road warriors arriving for a dawn Southwest Airlines departure were startled right from the start by the cheerfulness of the line monitor. He actually said good morning and please. He called them sir and ma'am. He was more like a maître d' at a family restaurant than a security guard.

"Who are these people?" one briefcase-laden passenger wondered out loud.

"I love this job," said a monitor, James Burnett, during a break. "It's a great chance to serve." Burnett, a twenty-two-year Army veteran who had most recently worked as a salesman, also appreciated the career ladder that Rossides had set up so that screeners would see their work as more than a paycheck until they found something else.

The real test wouldn't come until an hour or two later, when more passengers started to arrive for more flights. Would the lines back up?

By 6:15, pier A had what looked like a long line, but Rossides timed it, and it was still only a three-minute wait. One of her assistants, another young man on loan from a consulting company, reminded her that each lane should be able to process 150 passengers per hour—two and a half per minute, which meant that they should be okay given the counts they'd done of traffic here. But by 6:30 the lines were backing up. Rossides, sitting off to the side on a black bench, was nervous. This was crunch time. Three transcontinental flights were scheduled to leave at about the same time, beginning in forty-five minutes.

At 6:40, another young consultant told Rossides that the line was about nine minutes. She knew. She was timing it, too. Ten minutes was their limit.

Another member of the team approached the consultant and Rossides. The sun coming in through the airport's glass facade was at an angle where the glare was making it hard to read one of the X-ray screens. We have to do something, he said.

"Uh, that's the sun. It's not like we can call someone to tell it to move," the consultant joked.

Three minutes later one of the other members of the team had cut out a big piece of cardboard and taped it over the monitor. TSA now had created the perfect sunscreen.

The diversion had masked a turning point. When they looked up at the line again, they saw it had eased. Rossides's new count was six minutes.

They had done it.

The passengers agreed. "This is different," said one woman on her way to Birmingham, Alabama. "What happened?"

Rossides didn't read the press clips the next day about the Baltimore launch, which were generally the first positive articles written about TSA since its birth. By now she'd become so jaded about media coverage of her work that she had resolved to ignore as much of it as she possibly could. She didn't need any more frustration than she already had trying to do her job. In the weeks ahead, that resolve, to the extent she could hold to it, would serve her well. There was a lot more bad press headed her way, in part because TSA's earliest Baltimore-like rollouts of these impressive, new troops would not take place at airports that the national press frequented, and in part because starting up the largest new government agency in history was bound to involve a slew of screwups that the press would, and should, jump on.


Because Chubb had aggressively assumed and recorded all of its September 11 costs by the end of last year even though it had still not received or paid out many of the claims, Dean O'Hare was able to announce that Chubb's first quarter earnings had improved by 6 percent over the prior year. What was more surprising was that he also announced that he intended to retire by the end of the year. There was no hint that he had been forced out; Chubb watchers on Wall Street accepted the explanation that O'Hare, approaching sixty, had decided that he wanted to retire soon and thought it best to do so at a time when he believed he had successfully gotten Chubb through what had been a bad several years in the insurance industry, capped by the September 11 crisis.

# Wednesday, May 1, 2002

INS's failure to come up with any real entry-exit program to make sure foreign visitors leave when they are supposed to was a huge long-term problem, but Bruce Lawlor, Ridge's director of Protection and Prevention, had been chairing a group that was trying to come up with an interim solution. Until INS could create a system to monitor everyone, perhaps they could set up something that targets people from the highest-risk countries, and requires them to be photographed, fingerprinted, and to have their names and scheduled exit dates entered into a database.

Lawlor chaired a meeting of people from the Justice and State departments, along with representatives of the National Security Council and Vice President Cheney's office, aimed at deciding on a list of those high-risk countries.

It was as if the people from State and Justice were from different planets.

Ashcroft's people insisted that young males from fourteen countries with large Muslim populations should be included, but State said that to do that would jeopardize the cooperation those countries are providing in the war on terrorism. Nothing Lawlor did to try to whittle down the list worked for either side.

They agreed to reconvene in two weeks. Meantime, Justice's Foreign Terrorist Tracking Task Force would sit with staffers from State and the CIA to try to come up with a list that everyone could agree to.

# Thursday, May 2, 2002

Cliff Hardt, the FedEx executive on loan to TSA, had by now replaced Kip Hawley as Jackson's go teams commander. Hardt sat down to discuss the explosive detection equipment rollout contract with Randy Null, the go team leader working on the rollout, and Pat Schambach, who was in charge of TSA's technology and information systems. Hardt, too, had thought Raytheon was the front-runner, but now Null and Schambach told him that although the precise evaluations weren't in, Raytheon's proposal was disappointing, while Lockheed Martin's and Boeing's looked good.

Raytheon had kept harping on its work for the FAA, but that, they said, had been a project that had stalled out. Sure, that was because Congress had not funded it, but Raytheon seemed to think that its slow-motion rollout of about 140 pieces of equipment over several years was all it had to talk about to get this job. Their proposal showed little vision or creativity. Boeing's, on the other hand, was stellar. There was an excruciatingly detailed risk analysis (using a matrix that plotted each risk's likelihood and its consequences) that enumerated everything that could go wrong and then explained how they would change course to fix it. There were contingency plans for contingency plans, and ripple effect analyses of how one slipup in the supply chain could affect everything else, and how they would step in and fix that, too. Forty-eight site assessment teams would load data and their "passenger movement models" for each airport into a website that Boeing and the TSA people could share every day.

Sure, it was all just a lot of promises on paper, but for a small group that had been working at this stuff since January, not knowing how they would meet the deadline but knowing that they had to, the Boeing proposal, and the thousands of people they vowed to put to work behind it, looked awfully appealing.


Meantime, Mineta was up at the Senate, getting another grilling. Some of it was about how he was going to reimburse airports for the new security expenses that were being forced on them, a subject being pressed on the senators by the airport executives' trade association that Cox belonged to. Mineta said he hoped to get money appropriated for this, but could not promise it unless Congress cooperated.

More of the questioning was about the switch to so many trace detection machines that Daniels had forced on him.

By this time a coalition of small high-tech companies in New Mexico had joined the fray. The group, which had been formed in March, had hoped that its members could get subcontracts from InVision to build all or parts of its machines. That had seemed possible when TSA was going to buy 2,000 to 2,500 of them, but with Mineta having reduced the total to 1,100 from both InVision and its competitor, L-3, there was now no chance. So they'd hired a lobbyist who had met with staffers for members of the Senate Appropriations Committee. The senators now had all kinds of questions for Mineta about the extra personnel costs involved in using the smaller machines, about the long lines that might result because the machines supposedly took so much longer than InVision's to screen a suitcase, and about whether the trace detectors were really as reliable.

Mineta handled all of it gamely. He even skirted an on-target question by Senator Patty Murray of Washington, who is the chair of the Appropriations Committee's Subcommittee on Transportation, about whether the switch to the trace detectors hadn't really been the result of "OMB's [Office of Management and Budget] insistence on constraining costs." Mineta acknowledged that the cost of buying so many machines had begun to loom "very very large," but that when they took a second look at a different combination of trace and the large machines, with trace machines being concentrated at the smaller and mid-sized airports, they had discovered that the combination could work. He didn't add that Daniels of OMB had forced that "second look."

But Murray, whose staff had been lobbied not only by the coalition but by InVision's lobbyist—and to whose 2004 campaign Magistri had donated $1,000 earlier in the year—reserved her sharpest questioning for a different, more basic issue. Didn't the use of trace detectors, especially their planned exclusive use at smaller airports, mean that passengers would have to have their bags dumped out on a table in front of everyone else so that the insides could be swabbed with the trace detector cloth?

"Unless we find a dignified way to open all of the passengers' bags at the rural airports I'm really concerned that even fewer passengers are going to fly and airlines are going to abandon these points," she complained.

Mineta assured her that TSA would configure things so that passengers' bags could be opened in a private area. He also pointed out that for the trace detectors to work, the cloth only needed to be swabbed on the contents of the bag once the suitcase was opened; the contents usually did not have to be removed. Moreover, under the protocols that had been designed, which for security reasons he did not want to explain in detail, only a portion of all bags would even be opened. What he meant was that the protocol TSA had come up with called for some bags simply to get a swab from the outside, others to get a swab across the top of the opened suitcase, and the rest a deeper, probing swab through all of the contents. Mineta did concede that with InVision's machines, bags did not have to be opened at all, unless and until the CT-scan detected something that looked dangerous.

With that in mind, what wasn't mentioned, and in fact was rarely ever talked about when the way the InVision machines worked was discussed, was what happened when the InVision machine did spot something untoward.

The best, most efficient use of the giant machines, and the way they were being planned for use in the largest airports, was to have them positioned as part of the overall baggage loading process. In other words, after a passenger checked his suitcase, the airline clerk would put it on the regular conveyor belt, and somewhere in the bowels of the airport, as it rode along that belt, it would go through one of Magistri's machines. That was the fastest way, and the way not to eat up valuable space in the airports' passenger lobbies. But what happened if the person monitoring the computer screen saw something that needed to be checked out? The passenger and his bag had long since been separated, and the suitcase presumably was locked. "They haven't made the suitcase that the security people can't get into, even if the passenger isn't there to give them a key," Magistri's chief operating officer explains.

To be sure, most airports, in the short term, weren't going to get the machines installed that way into the airport's loading system. As with an InVision machine that Cox had installed at a check-in counter at Memphis last year,* passengers at those airports would be able to be with their bags when they went through the InVision unit. But the goal was to build systems that would speed bags through Magistri's detectors only after passengers had checked them, meaning they would be opened by strangers without the passenger being able to monitor the search.

In other words, Senator Murray's concern about preserving a passenger's privacy may have cut both ways.


This morning, Ridge's office proved that when it came to relatively simple issues a White House office could successfully coordinate things. One of Lawlor's staff people got an assistant to the Secretary of the Interior together with the right people from the FAA, which controls the nation's airspace, to deal with a problem concerning the Statue of Liberty. The statue, which is overseen by the Interior Department, was scheduled to reopen for tours for the first time since September 11. Now in addition to the Coast Guard boat that had been stationed in the water adjacent to it since September 11, Interior wanted protection from an air attack by getting the FAA to ban flights over the statue's airspace. The problem was that commercial planes regularly used a path over Lady Liberty on their way to La Guardia. The solution they worked

---

*Cox's airport had been one of the recipients of the FAA's slow rollout program, and this one unit already allowed for a small portion of the checked baggage at Memphis to be screened.

out was that general aviation—charters and private planes, which were a significant security risk because no one screened their passengers—would be banned, while the airliners would be allowed. The man from Interior liked the plan so much that they were now going to talk about applying it to the airspace over all national icons, dams, and other facilities controlled by Interior.

# Friday, May 3, 2002

The analysts for SG Cowen, one of the InVision investment banks, reiterated their "Buy" rating and price target of $50–$55 for InVision today, publishing a bulletin headlined "Senators Raise Issues of Passenger Privacy, Lack of Long Term TSA Planning."

Referring to yesterday's Senate hearing, the report noted three "key points":

"1. DOT [Department of Transportation] Plan to Use Mix of EDS and Trace Detection Driven by Budget and Deadline Constraints.

"2. Transportation Subcommittee Chairman [Murray] Sees Privacy Issue with Open Bag Trace Detection.

"3. Ranking Member [Senator Richard Shelby of Alabama, whose office the New Mexico coalition lobbyist had met with extensively] Notes That Baggage Screening Requires Long-Term Plan, Not Just Deadlines."

The report added that "compliance with the Aviation and Transportation Security Act should require over 2,000 more EDS [InVision] systems," and that "the market opportunity is clearly significant."

Meanwhile, back at the TSA, yesterday was supposed to have been the day that they would announce the big contract to supervise the rollout of the checked baggage screening machines across the country. Instead, TSA formally told all the bidders to redo their plans to account for the new mix of big machines and smaller trace detectors that Mineta had announced a week ago. The delay was frustrating, but Woollen considered this yet another advantage for team Raytheon, because Raytheon had used the trace detectors in tandem with the big units in their successful Salt Lake City/Olympics installation.

"How can the numbers be that bad?"

That was Gale Rossides's first reaction when she heard that the company given the $100 million contract to recruit the baggage screeners was reporting that in Baltimore only 36 percent of the applicants who had been told to report for a day-long assessment test had actually shown up. Equally bad, only a third of those who had reported had then passed the assessment tests.

The screeners who had launched the federalization in Baltimore on Tuesday morning had been members of that roving SWAT team that had trained in Oklahoma City. Now, it looked as if there was going to be a delay in getting the permanent screeners in place at Baltimore to replace them, so they could move on to another airport.

As Rossides probed more, she began to see the problem—which was mainly the low percentage that had shown up for the tests. The SWAT team people had almost all shown up for their assessments, so no one had factored in this kind of drop-off. The difference, Rossides began to find out, was, first, that because the SWAT team members were actually going to end up as supervisors after they finished roving the country inaugurating federalization at each airport, they were likely to be more responsible people reporting for assessments for higher-paying jobs. That, she should have thought of. But the second issue was that the company doing the recruiting—a training and education contractor called NCS Pearson, which is a subsidiary of the British company, Pearson PLC, that owns the *Financial Times*—had done a poor job giving the recruits advance notice about when to appear. Many, in fact, had been called the night before they were supposed to show up for these all-day assessments.

As for the 33 percent pass rate on the assessments themselves, that, too, was lower than it had been for the SWAT team and lower than they had projected, but Rossides could live with that. After all, the battery of interviews and tests—on everything from the ability to reach into a carry-on bag and feel around and detect a weapon, to finding weapons on the computer monitor, to physical dexterity (they had to lift boxes and walk around cones), to a role-playing exercise dealing with a rude passenger—was meant to be an effective filter. Besides, the whole idea of Baltimore was that it was supposed to be a laboratory. The delay of a week or so in getting the SWAT team on to another airport hurt, but it was fixable. And neither the show-up rates nor the pass rates would matter as long as Pearson now worked them into their assumptions and then made sure they did enough to produce a large enough applicant pool to produce the recruits needed at the end of the pipeline.

When the press and Congress heard about the recruiting snafu, they would see it differently—as more evidence that there was no way TSA was going to meet the deadline to federalize all the screeners. It was now May. The law had been passed in November. Yet TSA hadn't yet hired even 1,000 of the 30,000 or more people that they needed by next November.

"Big Vision for Security Post Shrinks Amid Political Drama."

Tom Ridge—and his staff and the rest of official Washington—awoke this morning to read that headline on the front page of the *New York Times*.

"He was the 'true patriot, a trusted friend' chosen by President Bush nine days after September 11 to create a grand strategy for deterring terrorist attacks," the article began. "But instead of becoming the pre-eminent leader of domestic security, Tom Ridge has become a White House adviser with a shrinking mandate, forbidden by the president to testify before Congress to explain his strategy, overruled in White House councils and overshadowed by powerful cabinet members reluctant to cede their turf or their share of the limelight."

This article got to Ridge. He held a staff meeting the following Monday urging everyone to "hang on" and try to ignore all the bad press. Things were going to get better, he promised.

# Tuesday, May 7, 2002

The PEOC group planning the new Department of Homeland Security had another briefing from the small group of staffers who had been plodding through the government, department by department, making tentative yea or nay decisions.

Their audience now had expanded to include not only Ridge, Card, Bolten, Daniels, and White House counsel Gonzales, but National Security Advisor Condoleezza Rice, congressional affairs director Nicholas Calio, and Cheney's chief of staff, Lewis Libby.

Rice immediately blessed the overall idea, explaining to the group that she basically had two departments to coordinate—Defense and State—and that was hard enough. For Ridge to be able to coordinate twenty-plus agencies from the White House was impossible. "When Tom calls a meeting, he has to do it in the State Room," she joked, referring to one of the White House's banquet halls. With a new department holding most of those agencies, a White House homeland security advisor—everyone agreed there still needed to be one even after the department was created—would be able to function. He or she would only have to coordinate that new department along with the work of the few key agencies, such as Defense or Justice, that were involved in homeland security but that would not be part of the new department.

Now came the hard work of reviewing the staff committee's proposals for what should and shouldn't be included. Card, Bolten, and Ridge were generally familiar with what was to come, because they had been given regular updates of the smaller staff group's almost daily meetings; and Card, in turn, had been keeping the President up to speed with almost daily progress reports. These PEOC meetings were meant to give the issues a fuller airing, often involving deep dives into the details of hundreds of splintered functions in dozens of agencies. Yet now that the decision had been made to go with a new, super-department, the rest of the decisions were not the stuff of heated debate. Everyone tried to focus on the functions involved and came, in most cases, to a clear consensus on whether it belonged in the new agency. It was like deciding to go on a long trip and then worrying about what to put in the suitcase.

The framework for the discussion was that pyramid they had drawn showing functions in descending order from what should obviously be included down to what was not at all obvious. Border protection, transportation security, and emergency management were obvious functions, but some of the agencies that had responsibilities in those areas had lots of other responsibilities, too, which made their inclusion not as obvious. Nonetheless, the PEOC group quickly walked through and ratified the small group's proposals that these agencies—such as FEMA, Customs, and the Coast Guard—had to be included.

The border protection function that gave them the most trouble was the issuance of visas, which the State Department does from its embassies and consulates abroad, and for which State had taken lots of criticism at home for allegedly being too "consumer-oriented" at the expense of security. The staff group said it should be taken over by the new department. But Rice was concerned that visas were a constant diplomatic pressure point. State needed to be involved. They tabled that one.

Other, tougher calls involved functions in the middle and at the base of the pyramid—critical infrastructure protection, intelligence gathering, and law enforcement. These discussions moved slowly and in painstaking detail. Alcohol, Tobacco and Firearms—a Treasury agency that collected cigarette and alcohol taxes but also enforced federal gun laws and investigated bombings—should not be included, they decided, because while some of its work was part of the homeland security mission, it wasn't core, while too much of its work was not part of that job at all.

On the other hand, Treasury's Secret Service should be included, because while it enforced counterfeiting laws, its most important functions—protecting the President, Vice President, and other key members of the executive branch, as well as coordinating National Special Security Events, such as the Olympics—were clearly specialized and integral aspects of homeland security.

The PEOC group had now created a mega-agency that far exceeded Senator Lieberman's relatively modest proposal for a Department of Homeland Security, and they weren't finished. The bioterrorism research and vaccine functions at the Department of Health and Human Services' Centers for Disease Control and the National Pharmaceutical Stockpile were put in, too. Lawlor, who had been so frustrated by the effort to forge a smallpox vaccine policy, was the key driver of that decision. Research units devoted to combating weapons of mass destruction, including the Department of Energy's Lawrence Livermore National Laboratory, were also added.

But they decided that the Nuclear Regulatory Commission should stay where it was in the Department of Energy, even though part of its job was regulating atomic power plant safety. However, the new department would be given the authority to take command of the unit of the NRC that deals with responses to nuclear threats whenever those threats were domestic, such as at nuclear power plants, or if there was a terrorist bomb threat involving nuclear materials.

Transportation security was obviously a core mission, so TSA was a no-brainer. But the FAA was still something the staff couldn't decide on. They tabled that, too, for the next session, after asking the staff group to dredge up more detail.


Persuaded by aviation industry CEOs who were lobbying him personally, and pushed by members of the House and Senate who were also being lobbyied, Ridge hadn't let up on the idea that TSA needed to set up some kind of trusted traveler program, so that frequent fliers who volunteer to be pre-screened can be moved through a fast lane at the airports. He believed it was just a matter of common sense, and that Magaw's opposition showed a Secret Service mentality that did not understand rational risk management.

Lawlor felt just as strongly about it. Deputy Transportation Secretary Jackson tried to calm him down this afternoon by giving Lawlor more detail on what is going to be in the next version of CAPPS—the computer-assisted passenger prescreening system.

Jackson regaled Lawlor with how amazed he had been when he'd gone to a briefing given by one of the data-mining companies hoping to get a contract to help build and run CAPPS. When no one on his staff had been willing to offer themselves up as a guinea pig for fear of exposing some embarrassing remnant of their lives, the straitlaced Jackson had cheerfully given them his name and Social Security number. Within seconds, they produced a report that included, among other things, where he lived, where he had lived in the past, who he was married to, how long he had been married, where he had been married, his contributions to various Catholic charities, and who his next-door neighbors were. There were also reams of financial and travel data.

The point of it all, Jackson explained to Lawlor, was to measure people who buy airline tickets on the basis of whether they are "known and settled members of the community." Those who don't score high on that scale (or who set off other alarm bells because they have criminal records) would be the ones chosen as "selectees" to be hand-searched at the airport gates. Others would move more quickly—but they would not be allowed, as the trusted traveler concept seemed to imply, to get on a plane without going through a metal detector and having their carry-on bags X-rayed. Everyone, even the crew, had to go through that minimum check.

Thus, Jackson argued, a great new CAPPS program made a trusted traveler program unnecessary.

Lawlor wasn't so sure, he said, why there still couldn't be a faster line for people who had volunteered to be prescreened. The prescreening could include going through that CAPPS process, obviously, and, yes they would still go through the metal detectors. But they'd be allowed to get on a separate line that would presumably move faster through the metal detectors, because there would be fewer of them than there would be members of the general public.

Jackson was comfortable with that approach. They now had a plan that would satisfy TSA security concerns and Ridge's goal of doing something for frequent fliers and the airline industry. But it would all have to await the new CAPPS.


Getting the White House on record committed to something early on had its advantages. In the more urgent atmosphere of October, Ridge had gotten the President to sign a directive ordering INS to set up a system to keep foreign students from high-risk countries from taking the kinds of advanced science and math courses that might enable them to go home and make weapons of mass destruction. And although through February and March representatives from multiple federal agencies had sat through meetings with Ridge's people explaining why it couldn't and shouldn't be done, Ridge's staff and the staff of the White House Office of Science and Technology Policy had pushed hard enough that the education lobby had been moved to suggest a workable compromise. In April, a coalition of three higher education lobbies wrote to Ridge that the "fundamentally open character of our higher education system may make it impossible to construct a workable system" to keep students from taking certain courses, but that a solution was possible if the government instead concentrated on screening visa applications of students who want to study certain courses. In other words, rather than let them in and then try to control what classes they sat in on, why not keep the high-risk students looking to enroll in high-risk courses out altogether?

The Bush administration announced that program today, including a panel to screen visa applications from students in high-risk countries who want to do advanced study in certain problem areas.

# Wednesday, May 8, 2002

The FBI swarmed thirty-one-year-old, Brooklyn-born American citizen Jose Padilla as he came off a plane tonight from Zurich at Chicago's O'Hare Airport. He was taken to New York, where he was secretly held as a material witness in the terrorism investigation.

Padilla was grabbed because a high-ranking Al Qaeda operative being interrogated by the CIA had said in April that the group hoped to get one of its adherents to set off a dirty bomb in the United States. He hadn't named Padilla, but by pooling other information, the CIA and the FBI—who proved in this case that they had started to work well together—began to focus on him. Padilla is a former Chicago gang member who had done prison time in Florida, had converted to Islam, and had allegedly traveled through Pakistan and Afghanistan. The CIA had information that he had attended an Al Qaeda training camp and received instruction in making explosives. According to the Al Qaeda operative in custody, the man who now seemed to be Padilla had come to higher-ups in the organization to suggest the dirty bomb plan, and he had been encouraged to try to do it.

The CIA had been tracking him, and gave the word to the FBI when he made reservations for the flight to O'Hare. That enabled agents secretly to board the plane with him to make sure he did not try anything during the flight.

The feds' decision to arrest Padilla when he landed was bitterly opposed by some agents in the field. They wanted to follow him in hopes of uncovering a full-fledged cell, plus real evidence against him, and maybe even the bomb materials. But the word came from Washington—no one was sure if Justice or the bureau was really calling the shots—to pick him up immediately. There could have been three reasons. First, it takes about thirty agents to run a truly thorough 24/7 surveillance operation, and the Chicago office was already overworked on terrorism investigations. Second, no surveillance is truly fool-proof, and even the small possibility of him getting away and setting off such a bomb was too much to risk, especially since prevention, not prosecution, was the FBI's new number one priority. Third, by picking him up now, they could grill him and find out who, if anyone, had those bomb materials, rather than wait. That rationale also fit the prevention goal.

When Padilla arrived in New York, he was not allowed to see a lawyer for six days. When he finally did get to see a court-appointed defense counsel, she was not allowed to say anything public about the case or even file public papers urging his release, because, the government argued, he was being held as a material witness in a grand jury investigation, and all grand jury investigations are secret. In other words, the dragnet had advanced to a new stage, beyond the detaining of immigrants or the holding of people captured by soldiers overseas. An American citizen arrested on American soil was being held in secret.

Bruce Lawlor chaired another meeting of the working group that was supposed to come up with a plan for an entry-exit system. The problem was that INS came in with a proposal that went well beyond what the law required and was more like the soup-to-nuts, track-everyone-everywhere system that Woollen and the Raytheon people had been talking about at the late February meeting in the Vice President's conference room. It would cost $2.5 billion to $6 billion when it was completed. The more streamlined first-phase version that the law required—in which people coming and leaving just from airports would have their biometric-identifier-equipped visas scanned—would cost about $300 million. The issue wasn't just money. Rather it was that everyone in the room, except maybe the INS people, knew that INS had never met any congressional deadline to do anything; thus, its proposal now to go way beyond the mandate seemed wildly unrealistic. Indeed, the proposal they brought with them contained no specifics, let alone deadlines and milestone targets, for implementation. Assuming the White House or Congress would fund it—which they wouldn't—INS would simply waste more money, get mired in a bigger project, and not get anything done, including complying with the requirements of phase one in time to meet the law's deadline.

Lawlor and others at the Office of Homeland Security had now begun to see this entry-exit project as another TSA in the making, which to their minds meant a misguided effort to overwhelm an issue with billions of dollars without balancing other priorities. "Asymmetric risk management" was their polite term for it.

But what they didn't know was that INS didn't much care about what this group thought of their plans. Five days ago, without Lawlor or anyone in his office working the issue knowing about it, INS had posted a formal request for proposal in the Federal Register (where agencies post official notices) asking companies like Raytheon to bid on the giant soup-to-nuts entry-exit plan. And Woollen had immediately put a team together to go after it. It would be three weeks before Lawlor would find out about it and convince Ziglar to withdraw the RFP, which he did, much to the confusion of Raytheon and other eager contractors.

## Sunday, May 12, 2002

Chuck Schumer came back to the ports for another of his every-other-Sunday press conferences. Standing in front of the Manhattan cruise lines ship terminal, he formally proposed legislation to give Customs and other authorities the funding to buy sensors to detect nuclear and other mass destruction materials coming into ports or over bridges and through tunnels, as well as purchase 100 of those mobile VACIS machines that Kevin McCabe liked so much.

In McCabe's eyes, this time Schumer—who had had a staff member talk to customs officials about the proposal—got it completely right. No alarmist numbers, like the "98 percent" chance of terrorist success that he'd used last time. Just resources to let him do his job.

Brian Lyons was down in the pit just after noon when the recovery workers discovered what would be the last remains they would find at Ground Zero. Lyons still hadn't heard anything about a DNA match for his brother, but he knew that his work here had only two or three weeks to go. He was looking for other jobs, but for some reason he concentrated his job search around Ground Zero, or around issues related to the attacks. Maybe the hotel down there that was rebuilding needed him. Or maybe someone wanted an engineer who could help with building anti-terror security and evacuation systems into office towers. He still wanted to keep some connection with what he'd been doing the last nine months.

# Tuesday, May 14, 2002

"My guardian angel" was again all Sal Iacono could say when Hollie Bart arrived at his store with a check for $9,696 from the Seedco program for small businesses near Ground Zero that had been largely financed by the September 11th Fund.

"I told you it would be worth all the paperwork," Bart said.

About two weeks later, Sal would get another check, this one for $2,300, because Bart had done the paperwork for what was called a World Trade Center Business Recovery Grant. These were grants dispensed by a state agency with funds that were part of the federal aid package Schumer had helped secure. Bart was frustrated that the check, based on a formula using Sal's annual revenue, was so small. She knew the state agency had a lot more money to give out, and she was determined to try to get the formula changed.

The Justice Department had arranged a meeting room at an office building in downtown San Francisco for Ken Feinberg to talk to families of the September 11 victims.

The mathematics of the law establishing the fund made this a special group. San Francisco victims families were primarily those whose loved ones had been on the flight from Newark bound for San Francisco that had crashed in Pennsylvania. There had been forty passengers, and no one else had been hurt in the crash. On the other hand, upwards of 3,000 people had been hurt or injured in the crashes into the Trade Center, and those crashes had done billions more in property damage. The law bailing out the airlines had limited their liability in each crash to their insurance coverage, which was about $1.5 billion per crash. Thus, the family of a passenger on one of the Trade Center planes had little chance of recovering much even if it could be proven that the crash was somehow the airline's fault, because there was only

$1.5 billion in damages to go around. But for the families of passengers on the Pennsylvania plane—about two dozen of whom were gathered here this morning—there appeared to be no such problem with the pot being too small. That $1.5 billion only had to be split among forty victims.

Plaintiffs lawyer Mitch Baumeister—who had made that fiery speech at the families rally at the Park Avenue Armory back in January—had already gathered about sixty plaintiffs, he said. The ones he considered the most viable candidates for bringing a conventional lawsuit instead of applying to the fund were the families from the San Francisco flight. In fact, Baumeister said he was even talking to the woman who could have been the likeliest plaintiff of all—Lisa Beamer, the New Jersey widow of Todd Beamer.*

Todd Beamer had left his pregnant wife on the 11th for a business trip to San Francisco, and had reportedly told his fellow passengers, "Let's roll," after which they attacked the hijackers and crashed the plane into that field in Pennsylvania. If anyone could appeal to a jury for millions of dollars, it had to be Lisa Beamer, Baumeister reasoned. Her husband was young and a high earner; and he'd left behind the most sympathetic young family imaginable, and become a hero.

Feinberg knew that getting Beamer in would be tough, but he thought he would be able to attract most of the families from the San Francisco flight, and should attract all of them because a lawsuit, even for Lisa Beamer, was such a painful, drawn-out, and iffy proposition.

Feinberg began by thanking a partner of Kreindler's (the leading aviation plaintiffs lawyer) who had flown out to be there with the group. "This is the guy who showed me something in the federal law that allowed me to disregard firemen's and policemen's death benefits in computing offsets," Feinberg said. "He's a great lawyer."

Having paid obeisance to Kreindler, which was sure to be reported back to New York, Feinberg went on with his standard explanation, adding all he had done by now to liberalize various offsets such as Social Security and workers' comp.

The first question was from a woman who had been a flight attendant on United Airlines and whose son had died on the United plane to San Francisco. She didn't want to waive the right to sue, because she was convinced this was the only way to uncover what she said was United's heavy-handed lobbying over the years to minimize security requirements. "If you think a tort suit brought against United Airlines is essential for them to mend their ways,

*This could not be confirmed with Beamer, who declined to comment for this book.

then file a suit," Feinberg replied, once again reverting to his off-putting lawyer-to-lawyer style.


Jose Padilla, the man seized six days ago on a plane coming into O'Hare Airport in Chicago and brought to New York as a material witness, was finally allowed to see a lawyer. His court-appointed counsel, Donna Newman, immediately went to court to get him freed. She cited a terrorism-related case decided just two weeks before in the same federal court, in which a judge had declared it illegal to hold material witnesses in grand jury investigations, even though it was legal to detain witnesses in actual trials. But in a hearing closed to the public and press (which still had no idea about Padilla's arrest), the prosecutors said they were already appealing that decision, and that this case, more than any other, was a matter of crucial national security because it involved the potential explosion of a nuclear device. The magistrate denied Newman's bail motion.

In the next week, Newman would make more oral motions, as she began to talk to her client and hear his claim that he knew nothing. They'd all be denied, but finally the judge would order that she put her motion in writing and that the government respond. Then, he'd hold a more formal hearing.


# Wednesday, May 15, 2002

James Brosnahan filed a barrage of motions to dismiss the various counts of the indictment against John Walker Lindh for reasons ranging from selective prosecution (others, such as an American phone company, had had dealings with the Taliban government in Afghanistan and they hadn't been charged with providing aid to them), to lack of statutory authority (the prosecution had overreached on its interpretation of the law, he claimed), to a violation of Lindh's rights of free association.

None of the motions stood much chance, especially in front of this conservative judge. The real battle would be over whether any of Lindh's alleged confessions of having trained with the Taliban and, worse, having remained with the Taliban to fight for them even after he knew about the September 11 attacks and knew the Taliban were now fighting Americans, would be allowed to be used as evidence against him. That depended in large part, Brosnahan thought, on what he could learn from questioning the Army intelligence

agents who had first interrogated Lindh. Meantime, he had investigators trying to find out anything they could about the FBI agent who had interrogated
Lindh alone and whose report of what Lindh had said was so damaging.


Today's session in the White House PEOC—the Presidential Emergency
Operations Center—on the makeup of the new Department of Homeland
Security dealt with agencies related to the protection of the nation's critical
infrastructure. The group added to their shopping cart one agency each from
the Department of Commerce, the FBI, the Department of Energy, and the
General Services Administration. The logic of this consolidation was apparent just from the names of the agencies added; except for the General Services Administration's Federal Computer Incident Response Center, the
others all had roughly the same names (such as National Infrastructure Sim-
ulation and Analysis Center), and seemed to do the same thing.

Next they ratified a compromise on visas. The new department would
have the authority to set standards for them, but State Department personnel
abroad would still issue them.

The debate on the FAA continued. On the one hand, the FAA controlled
the nation's airspace, a homeland security function that had become even
more critical given the post–September 11 debates over whether flights
should be banned over all varieties of potential targets, from dams, to nuclear
plants, to stadiums. On the other hand, this was the agency that regulated
every aspect of an entire industry—aviation. Did they really want the new
department to become one of Washington's prime regulatory agencies, too?
The compromise solution, proposed by some at the table, was to split off the
FAA's airspace control duties. But Falkenrath argued that the tear line (a new,
favorite phrase of the group) that would come from trying to rip that out of
FAA would be too jagged, that controlling airspace had to do with minute-by-
minute air traffic control, scheduling, even gate slots at the airports—all the
stuff of constant interaction with the airlines, which is what the FAA's core
function was. It couldn't be stripped out. Card, a former Transportation Secretary, agreed. Before long, so did everyone else.

Three big issues were left. First, there was the question of the National
Guard, the reserve units that are under state control unless the President fed-
eralizes them in an emergency. There was strong sentiment and a lot of logic
behind including the Guard. After all, in a true terror emergency, they would
be the front-line troops. But they ultimately decided against it, because cutting the Guard out of the Pentagon, as well as stripping it away from the

nation's fifty governors, was seen as far too radical a step, and one that would create its own coordination problems with the rest of the Pentagon. Do this, remarked one PEOC participant, and they might as well put all the rest of the armed forces in the new department.

Next there was the issue of intelligence analysis. There was obviously a strong case to be made for taking everything the CIA and FBI did to analyze intelligence related to domestic terrorism and putting it into the new department. The CIA and FBI could still gather the intelligence, but the new agency would analyze it. After all, today's headlines were filled with complaints from Congress and editorial writers about the lack of FBI and CIA coordination that might have enabled the September 11 attacks.

Ridge thought consolidation made sense, as did Daniels. But others argued that separating out domestic terrorism intelligence that the CIA might be gathering from foreign terrorism–related intelligence was impossible. If the CIA had a source in Afghanistan telling them about planned terror attacks in Indonesia and in Chicago, should the analysis of the source's credibility be split up? Moreover, it was impossible to separate intelligence gathering and analysis without hurting both; the analysts needed to go back to the agents with questions and follow-ups.

As a compromise, they began to discuss a plan that would not split off analysis at either agency but would build in some redundance, which Ridge acknowledged was a good thing when it came to making sure important threat signals weren't missed. An intelligence analysis office could be established within the new department that would have access to all the information—even raw informant's reports, if necessary—gathered by either the FBI and the CIA, which would also forward their own analysis of it. The small group was sent back to develop more detail.

The last issue was the hardest: law enforcement, which sat at the base of that functions pyramid they had drawn. Should the FBI be brought into the new Homeland Security Department? Ridge wanted to do that. He and Falkenrath said that the federal government is the only place in the United States where the police (the FBI) are in the same department (Justice) as the lawyers who prosecute. The homeland security department's job was prevention and protection, not prosecution. How could they do that without including the nation's preeminent police force, along with the other federal agents (Secret Service, Customs, TSA) that they were subsuming? In other words, although he didn't put it this way, Ridge was arguing not only that Ashcroft should lose INS, but also that he should lose the field troops of the prevention mission the President had given to him and that he had so aggressively assumed—the FBI.

The position had unassailable logic. But Daniels pointed out that the United States had always avoided having a Soviet-style Ministry of the Interior with all that centralized police power. Others chimed in. This was too much. The balance tipped as the group went back to another principle they had adhered to in discarding the FAA idea, which was that they had to be just as cognizant of the functions they did *not* want in the new agency as the ones they wanted. If taking in an agency gave them something that they didn't want and whose negative effects outweighed the advantages of taking in the agency, then they wouldn't take it. Did the Department of Homeland Security really want to be in the business of enforcing laws related to everything from Enron to child pornography to bank robbery? Collecting tariffs was something they could tolerate in taking in a core mission like Customs' border guarding, but this was too much, someone pointed out.

But the FBI had just been reorganized to make domestic terrorism the overwhelming priority, with those other jobs reduced, others argued. How could it not be included?

The meeting ended with no consensus on this one either. The staff group was asked to report back with still more detail on current FBI functions and on whether some of the FBI might be able to be split off.

# Thursday, May 16, 2002

Two members of Lawlor's staff met with the vaccination people at Health and Human Services again, and struck out again. HHS was refusing even to have the smallpox issue put on the agenda of an upcoming meeting of the Principals Committee, the group of cabinet secretaries that Ridge chairs to discuss homeland security issues. They insisted that more options needed to be studied. HHS's opposition once again stalled a decision.

Lawlor's people working the issue were disappointed, but Lawlor was not as bothered. By now he knew that a plan for much crisper decision making was in the works.

Yet the smallpox gridlock suggested something that some on Ridge's staff acknowledged privately and said Ridge had also acknowledged indirectly. The President could have already decided this issue, if he had the sense of urgency that people like Schumer thought he ought to have, and the willingness to make tough calls not just in the exceptional case but on lots of issues. Maybe they wouldn't have needed to move all the boxes around into a giant new department, where most of the people at this smallpox meeting would become subordinates to a new cabinet secretary who could make a decision. Perhaps a White House coordinator could have carried the day, if behind the coordinator was a President willing, even eager, to make as many decisions as it took to deal with homeland security.

On the other hand, there was no denying that it would be a lot easier to get decisions made within one cabinet agency, and that this was much better than Ridge having to trudge into the Oval Office every day to say that this person wasn't playing well with that person. As Condoleezza Rice had pointed out, she had enough trouble coordinating just two departments.

Lawlor got his own personal dose of frustration today on an issue that was among the ones that scared him the most—the security of chemical industry facilities and the transportation of hazardous chemicals. Thousands of shipments of dangerous chemicals were now being moved every day between some 15,000 industry sites, and to Lawlor and anyone else peering across the array of potential terrorist targets, this represented perhaps the most vulnerable threat. Indeed, the military people and rock-ribbed Republicans on Ridge's staff had come to agree that even the liberal environmental interests groups they had met with had expressed concerns that were thoroughly reasonable.

The Environmental Protection Agency had a plan to mandate vulnerability assessments and security audits. But the Department of Labor, which oversees the Occupational Safety and Health Administration—OSHA—said that it was the agency to handle this, and that it was reluctant to push new regulations. Not to be left out, the Department of Energy, which controls certain shipments of fuel-related chemicals, wanted jurisdiction, or at least wanted to make sure that what it was now doing (or, rather, not doing) was not superseded. On top of that the Office of Management and Budget representative said they favored letting the industry enact its own voluntary standards. Lawlor adjourned the meeting after scheduling a smaller working group.

# Friday, May 17, 2002

Gale Rossides's update from Baltimore sounded better. The private company, NCS Pearson, with the contract to do the recruiting and testing of screener candidates had recovered, and enough recruits were now in place. But she and Jackson—who, as deputy transportation secretary, was immersed in issues like this whenever there was trouble—were still not convinced that Pearson was doing enough to get out in advance at the other airports where rollouts were about to happen to ensure that enough candidates would show up for their assessments. The Pearson executives were called in on the carpet. They promised they'd fix everything.

Larry Cox got FedEx and the airlines to approve his new budgets for the fiscal year that starts on July 1. It wasn't hard. Passenger traffic had improved; it was now back to about 80 percent of last year's levels, and that was without the return of the evening bank of flights, scheduled for early June. He'd also gotten a good handle on his costs, including negotiating a pay freeze for all the unionized workers at the airport.

"Larry opened his books to us, and convinced us," says union negotiator Paul Shaffer. "It was done in an amiable way and in a spirit of cooperation, because he had been a straight guy with us for a long time."

The bottom line is that Cox was able to roll back the 39 percent increase in gate rentals he'd put in on January 1 by about 15 percent. He also held the annual increase in landing fees to one penny per thousand pounds of landing weight, or an average of $1.57 instead of $1.56, a rate that kept Memphis in a highly competitive position.

Hugo Poza couldn't believe it. The head of the Raytheon division that had prepared the multibillion-dollar TSA contract proposal got a call and then an e-mail at about 6:00 this evening telling him that the TSA procurement team had decided that only two of four bidders were in the "competitive range" for final consideration. Raytheon was not one of them.

As word spread to Woollen and everyone else who had worked on the project, there was disbelief and anger. Expletives filled the air about this new band of TSA bureaucrats who had replaced the people they had worked with so well at the FAA. Boeing, one of the two still in the running, had no experience in this at all. And Lockheed Martin, the other remaining contender, had been a Raytheon subcontractor on some of the FAA work. How could this have happened?

Raytheon CEO Daniel Burnham had the same question when he spoke to Woollen and Poza. What had gone wrong? They decided that this was too bizarre, too unexplainable. Burnham decided he'd write to Mineta to get to the bottom of it.

# Monday, May 20, 2002

Anyone who thinks a consolidated new Department of Homeland Security will solve all the government's coordination issues should have sat in on the session that one of Lawlor's aides convened with representatives from the FBI and the Pentagon.

The meeting was about something called the Department of Defense Criminal Investigative Policy and Oversight Directorate, which, it turns out, is a detective unit of the Defense Department that conducts counterterrorism investigations. And, the Pentagon representative reported, they have stepped up their activities dramatically since September 11.

Didn't the FBI do that? When the FBI people allowed as how these investigations ought to be coordinated with the FBI and its Joint Terrorism Task Forces that include other federal police agencies, the Defense Department official agreed only to provide written copies of any already existing agreements among the agencies to cooperate. The Pentagon's own investigations, however, would continue apace.

# Tuesday, May 21, 2002

Michael Cartier's computer was again filled with e-mail. The other day he'd been quoted as saying that he thought that at least seven of Ground Zero's sixteen acres should be preserved for a memorial to the victims. That was a lot more than planners for the Port Authority (who were still playing chicken with Silverstein) and the Lower Manhattan Development Corporation (which was also overseeing the rebuilding) had indicated they were contemplating, but it wasn't enough for many of the victims' families, especially those inclined to send angry e-mails. Tonight Cartier had 287 new, unread messages in his mailbox, and from the looks of the ones he had already opened, most were hostile.

As a personal matter Cartier didn't care much about the memorial. They had found his brother's remains, and soon the memorial for James would be a cemetery plot. But he also understood the anguish of those who would never find remains and would have to think of Ground Zero as their loved one's resting place. Then again, his brother had been an electrical worker, and Michael knew he would want the site to be reconstructed, in part to provide jobs for his co-workers. So Cartier came down on the side of a fitting memorial but not that the site be only a memorial.

Tonight the Cartier family was focused on another issue having to do with Ground Zero. They, along with most victims' family members, were outraged that Mayor Bloomberg had set Thursday, May 30, as the day for the memorial service that would close down the site, because work would be finished by then. How dare Bloomberg set it on a weekday, when many would not be able to take off from work, and when business day traffic would crowd the area?

Some of their anger had to do with the fact that the leaders of what were now several family groups didn't like Bloomberg nearly as much as they had come to like Giuliani. It was as much a matter of style as anything else. As Cartier put it, "Most of what he says makes sense. I find myself going home from a meeting with him and replaying what he's said and agreeing. But in the room I get angry because of how he says it." Or, in this case, he was angry because Bloomberg had chosen a Friday over a Saturday or Sunday—even though, Cartier said, "I have absolutely no interest in going to that ceremony no matter when it is."


In the aftermath of the stunning loss of the TSA contract, Ed Woollen faced a previously scheduled review today of Raytheon's progress on the homeland security front with the corporation's outside advisory board, plus top executives, including CEO Daniel Burnham. After Woollen gave a brief autopsy of what he knew about their TSA loss, he reviewed what he thought were the good prospects for the company's entry-exit "visitor management" systems (he did not know that INS's premature request for proposals on the giant contract was about to be put on hold) and the first responder vehicle with its interoperable communications. Someone asked about the overall prospects for the homeland security business. Was this something that was at its peak this year or next and would cycle downward?

A group discussion ensued before Woollen got the chance to answer. The outside advisors seemed split; one remembered the spikes up and then down in interest through the 1990s in the equipment to screen all checked luggage. Another recalled the same kind of cycle after the 1993 World Trade Center bombing. Others, however, said that this was the real thing.

When the group turned to Woollen, he argued strongly that in an open country like the United States, terrorist attacks, not military attacks, would continue to be the nation's highest priority for "a long, long time," and that if

Raytheon was in the defense business that would be where the business was. After more discussion, the room seemed to shift to Woollen's position. Raytheon might have lost the airports contract, but there was a lot more to come. "This is a twenty- to fifty-year problem," someone said. Burnham agreed.

"How are we supposed to do anything when we have to deal with the threat of the day," one homeland security office staffer remarked cynically, referring to a multi-agency meeting the office hurriedly convened to deal with the problem that the Social Security Administration issued cards to immigrants without first verifying that their status permitted them to work. The meeting was held solely because the *New York Times* had done a story yesterday highlighting the issue, and someone from the White House chief of staff's office had sent Ridge a note about it.

The Ridge people's resentment at having another hour added to their already full day just because someone wrote a story about something was understandable. In some cases, like a TV report about manhole cover security, the threat du jour had been less than pressing. But Social Security cards were a bootstrap to other, more credible identity cards. What was so bad about the press highlighting a threat of the day, if it was a real threat? Wasn't that part of how the system was supposed to work?

It worked here. The group quickly came up with a plan to have Social Security check with INS before issuing cards to noncitizens.

The PEOC group planning the new Department of Homeland Security finished off the two key remaining issues—intelligence gathering and whether the FBI should be taken from Justice and put into the new department. They decided on the more modest course for both. A new analysis unit would be set up in the department, but the CIA and FBI would keep their analysts, something Ridge and Falkenrath felt confident could be implemented, in part because a chief information officer Ridge had recently hired from the private sector appeared to have a good plan for data mining across all the intelligence databases. Moreover, several of the agencies coming into the new department—Customs, INS, the Secret Service, TSA, and the Coast Guard—already had their own intelligence operations, which could be consolidated into a new group with significant critical mass.

As for the FBI, it would stay in Justice. The deciding factor was the group's rule about not taking on too much of what the agency should *not* be handling.

Card had talked to the President about this, and he had agreed. When this discussion had finished, one of the participants at the table whispered to another, "We should have done it just so we could see the look on Ashcroft's face."

The group then went over everything they had put into the new department one more time. There were four main divisions: Border and Transportation Security; Emergency Preparedness and Response; Chemical, Biological, Radiological, and Nuclear Countermeasures; and Information Analysis and Infrastructure Protection. Altogether, there would be twenty-two agencies or divisions of agencies totaling 170,000 employees, making for the largest cabinet department in the government, except for the Pentagon, the Post Office, and the Veterans Administration (which staffed a network of VA hospitals). Card said he was ready to take the blueprint to the President for final approval. He planned to go over it with him that night as *Air Force One* flew the President to Europe.

There was still a lot to do. They had to figure out how to turn this into a draft of a law to be proposed to Congress. They had to map out a public relations and lobbying roll-out plan, too.

Also, said Daniels, they had to work on a management structure. They should use this opportunity, he argued passionately, to streamline what he thought were a lot of antiquated civil service rules that deprived whoever ended up running the new agency of the necessary management flexibility. Card heartily agreed. The small group that included one of Daniels's top aides and Falkenrath, who was also a hawk on the management issue, had already begun sketching out those plans. They promised to come back with specifics.

But one aspect of management was not mentioned. Who would run this mega-department? Surprisingly, while Ridge's people had been at the center of the secret plans and while Ridge was the President's incumbent designated heavy hitter on homeland security, there had been little discussion among Card, Bush, and Ridge about whether he would run the new agency if it got created. But there had been one moment that gave Ridge all the confidence he needed. At one point during the days that they were in the process of constructing the department, the President had said privately and offhandedly to Ridge something to the effect that running the department was going to be a tough job. Ridge had replied that they shouldn't worry about who would run it until they actually got it through Congress—a hint of reluctance that was underscored to some of Bush's surprised senior advisors when they heard from one of Ridge's top aides that he was thinking about getting the department through Congress but then bowing out.

In fact, Ridge was of two minds. On the one hand, he hadn't worked in the private sector since his days as a young lawyer. He was now fifty-seven and with his kids approaching college age, and with all the grief he'd taken since coming to Washington, maybe he should help design the new agency, get it enacted into law, and leave in a blaze of glory. On the other hand, he'd been a chief executive in Pennsylvania and had loved it, and he'd spent the past five and a half months learning that "coordination" wasn't nearly as much fun as command and control.

# Wednesday, May 22, 2002

By the close of the stock market this afternoon, InVision had climbed nearly 40 percent from the $18 low it had sunk to after Mineta's April 24 announcement that TSA would only buy 1,100 machines. Morale was high at the Newark, California, headquarters and factory. Workers were pumping out five to seven machines a week, which would easily be sold, even under the government's reduced purchase plan.

Yet simple math suggested that the price of the company's stock was based on the market assuming that next year and beyond InVision would sell machines at an even faster pace. Indeed, the analysts' reports, which had boosted the stock back up since April 24, maintained that in the long run the InVision products provided the superior security solution, and that use of the smaller trace detectors was a temporary budget and deadline accommodation. Thus, whatever the hiccup caused by Mineta's announcement, InVision's market prospects for 2003 and beyond seemed terrific, which is why the stock was back selling at a price that assumed steep advances in sales and earnings well beyond the growth already achieved since September 11.

There was a catch to the argument: Whatever the efficiency and security benefits of the InVision machines seemed to be to the analysts, the customer still had to be prepared to buy those machines.

The government had no such plans. Part of the evidence was obvious: There was nothing in the Bush administration's proposed budget for the next fiscal year to buy them. To the extent that the stock analysts were even asked about that, they brushed it off, saying that the funds could always come in a supplemental budget requested by the administration. Which was true. But what neither they nor anyone else—including Magistri, who estimated to a reporter today that his sales for 2003 and 2004 would be 1,500 per year—knew was that Jackson and Null (the go team leader on the baggage screening rollout) had decided about two weeks ago to cut InVision off almost completely at the end of this year. Beyond completing what was left of the original promise of 625 orders, and perhaps buying a handful of InVision machines to fill in a few gaps, as of today they had come to the conclusion that they were out of the business of buying Magistri's machines, at least for the foreseeable future. Instead, they were going to try to create an international consortium, backed by countries like the United States that put a high priority on aviation security. The consortium would invest in developing better technologies that would improve the speed and accuracy of explosive detection machines and make them less expensive. If Magistri and InVision participated and created the new, winner product, that would be great. If the trace detection companies came up with a way to make their machines faster and more accurate, that would be great, too. But the window had closed on buying these clunky million-dollar, first-generation products. Instead, they'd muddle along with the trace/InVision combinations they were now installing and wait until someone built a better bomb trap.

In short, Daniels's intercession that day last month in the Situation Room might not have merely delayed Magistri's drive to become a billion-dollar company. It might have killed it.

Raytheon's foray into the September 12 era sweepstakes started looking better this morning. The company unveiled the demonstration model of its First Responder vehicle to a group of sheriffs and police and fire chiefs from Arlington, Virginia, and surrounding communities, then took the show to the Pentagon, where it was displayed for officials from various federal agencies, such as Customs, which might want to use it as a command vehicle for senior officials escaping the city. (Raytheon could install its bulletproof glass in those models.) Everyone seemed impressed with the converted white Chevy Suburban, even the most skeptical chiefs. Several whipped their radios out and demanded to be connected to another chief's different radio frequency. "One guy said we'd never be able to do it," Woollen recalls. "And it took us four minutes. He thought he'd bag himself a contractor, but it was nothing for us."

Beyond that, the Suburban came with systems that could be purchased à la carte that could beam up and pull down video signals, complete satellite phone calls, forecast wind movements, detect biological and radiological threats, display maps of any given area, down to individual buildings and their utility lines, show how individual troops were positioned in a given area, and even show what hospitals casualties had been sent to and what their status was. All that and four leather seats for $150,000 to $250,000 in a car the chiefs were all used to driving.

By now Woollen had recruited a new sales team to go after the locals, headed by a former Dallas deputy police chief. They were preparing to fan out across the country with four demo vehicles.

"The First Responder," Raytheon CEO Daniel Burnham says, "speaks to one of our inherent capabilities, which is that we don't have to invent everything in the product. We are willing to use other people's products," he explains, citing as an example the radio-frequency-linking technology in the vehicle that is made by a small North Carolina company. "But we were able to put this together in a matter of months—which I think surprised the hell out of people."

## Thursday, May 23, 2002

Pat McCann, Sergio Magistri's lobbyist, made the rounds of the Appropriations Committee staffs today with a simple request. As they prepared the legislation to fund TSA's decision to use a heavy mix of explosive trace machines with InVision's larger units, could they please put in language saying that this was only an "interim solution." Magistri badly needed something tangible to show Wall Street that TSA's strategy ensured a smoother flow of orders, not an end to them. Any kind of language would be helpful, he said, and from a public policy point of view it was necessary to ensure that the government persisted in implementing the safest, most delay-free protection.

The best he got were assurances that they would try to put something in, if and when an appropriations bill ever passed, that would state that TSA should keep improving its system.

## Friday, May 24, 2002

Raytheon CEO Dan Burnham faxed a two-page letter, along with lots of attachments, to Michael Jackson at the Transportation Department. It was an unusual document, one that sidestepped a formal appeals process that contractors can go through but rarely do for fear of offending their once and future customers. But it pulled no punches. Burnham said that Raytheon executives had attended a formal debriefing process on Wednesday with TSA to go over why they had lost, and that "based on this information, we believe the determination to eliminate Raytheon was premature." He then listed in an appendix all the different areas "where TSA misunderstood the proposal." His biggest complaint was that TSA people had acknowledged in the debriefing that cost had not been a factor and that the evaluation people had said that they "could not consider their personal knowledge of Raytheon's experience" in running the earlier equipment installation program, but "could only consider the information set forth in Raytheon's proposal. . . . We were simply told," Burnham added, " 'Well, it was not a weakness.' "

Jackson went over the letter with Null and others involved in the contract, and heard chapter and verse about how much better the Boeing proposal was. (They didn't talk about Lockheed because he had worked there and was recused from decisions about that company.) He then called Burnham and thanked him for making the bid, but said the decision was final.

With President Bush having now signed off on the Homeland Security Department plan, the PEOC group turned to talking about how to manage the 170,000-employee, $37 billion monster. At the last meeting, Daniels of OMB had warned that these were going to be tough issues, because he was determined that a new agency created in the twenty-first century be able to shed some nineteenth- and twentieth-century management constraints. If they were going to create a new agency to meet new challenges, Daniels argued, they should use the opportunity to give its leaders the modern management tools they needed. Card agreed, adding that from his experience, the restraints, in the form of well-meaning protection of workers from various disciplinary abuses of the early part of the twentieth century, had been piled on over the years in a way that strangled good managers.

Falkenrath, who had been thinking about this for a few weeks, added, with a chuckle, that after the armed forces had been reorganized into the Defense Department in 1947—a government reorganization that was the only one to eclipse this one in size—the first Secretary of Defense had committed suicide. Most in the room knew the Secretary had had a variety of mental health problems before assuming his post, and it was unlikely that he had hurled himself out of his hospital window over frustration with civil service laws. But they got the point. Whoever took the job needed flexibility to shift his people and resources around.

The plan that the small group had come up with was deceptively simple, and—in keeping with the goal of flexibility—vague. Inserted into the proposed law establishing the department would be a clause granting the new

Secretary the authority to consult with the government's Office of Personnel Management to "establish, and from time to time adjust, a human resources management system for all of the organizational units of the Department of Homeland Security, which shall be flexible, contemporary and grounded in the public employment principles of merit and fitness."

That seemed logical enough. But it flew in the face of decades of restrictions that had been put into effect to protect workers against bosses who would discriminate against them based on political considerations or other factors not related to merit.

Three basic issues were involved. One was the ability to pay people based on their performance, rather than simply set salaries according to the rigid pay scales now in place across the government that guaranteed that everyone in the same job category with the same seniority got the same pay. Second was the flexibility to reassign people around the country, just as Army troops or FBI agents could be moved around. Third was the power to remove people based on misconduct or poor performance.

In the departments from which the new agency's workers would be transferred, management's flexibility in all three areas had been restricted by civil service protections that had increased over the years and, in many cases, by negotiations with various unions that had come on the scene beginning in 1962, when President Kennedy signed an executive order allowing federal workers to be unionized. These unions, such as the Border Patrol organization that Hall and Lindemann led in Detroit, still had no right to strike and did not even bargain over wages, which were set by the government pay scale. But they had negotiated procedural safeguards related to disciplinary actions and transfers. These were not management straitjackets, but they did impose important limits: Customs or INS workers could be transferred to other posts, but only after being given ten days' notice and only for thirty days in a year. Moreover, the union had the right to bargain over the rules for those transfers, such as insisting that it be done on the basis of seniority. However, if the President declared a national emergency, the notice and the thirty-day limit could be suspended.

As for firings or demotions, as had happened with Lindemann and Hall, they were, indeed, entitled to thirty days' notice. After that they could submit a complaint to an arbitration committee, which could reinstate them, but which rarely did because the President appointed the arbitrators. (Thus, Lindemann's fear when he had gotten those disciplinary letters.) And again, if a worker's "primary function" was declared by the President to involve national security, the law allowed for the employee to be dismissed without these safeguards.

Whatever the limits on these protections, and however much "management flexibility" seemed an unassailable tool for the war on terror, what this simple clause seemed to allow was a complete abandonment of any protection for the troops from abusive or incompetent bosses. If you were Bob Lindemann, and the bosses you dealt with were the ones that he dealt with—not Tom Ridge, but the Border Patrol supervisors in Detroit who had accused him of treason—it wasn't going to sound good. Your salary could be set lower than your co-workers' based on the boss's subjective decision that you didn't perform as well. You could be transferred. Or, you could be fired.

Daniels had one additional management prerogative in mind that was likely to upset Congress as much as the abandonment of employee protections might rile the workers. He wanted the new Secretary to have the ability to redirect up to 5 percent of the funds budgeted by Congress for any one activity into another activity if he felt he needed to. This was not likely to go over well with members of congressional appropriations committees, who insisted on directing how every cent was spent everywhere, in order to ensure that their home districts or their favorite agencies got exactly what they had socked away for them.

The PEOC group, which by now included White House congressional affairs chief Nicholas Calio, discussed how much opposition these issues were likely to attract. Some thought it would be a good way to distract Congress from all the turf they were reshuffling, which, one person hinted, might not be bad because this management flexibility stuff wasn't all that important and could be given back to seal a deal. But Daniels and others responded that it really was important and that they should fight for it. Calio, who was focused on Congress, allowed as how it had better be important because it could ignite a firestorm of opposition. Yet he stuck by his overall assessment, the one Bush had first voiced, that because this idea was so big and they were planning to spring it so suddenly, it had a better chance of succeeding than a smaller plan.

# Monday, May 27, 2002

Eileen Simon wasn't sure about having the kids watch the community Memorial Day parade, which was a family tradition. But since it came right by her front door, she had no choice. Luckily, Brittany, MJ, and Tyler—who stood outside under the house's big American flag, dressed in their Little League uniforms—seemed to enjoy it more than ever.

Not everything was going that smoothly lately. On Friday, she'd taken eleven-year-old MJ to a regional poetry contest, after he'd been selected by his school for submitting their best entry. The problem was that almost every other kid's poem, though not his, was in some way about September 11. Many, including two from the children of rescue workers, were horrifyingly graphic, talking about body parts, abandoned firemen's boots, ashes, and the like. She couldn't tell who had been more upset sitting through it all, her or MJ.

And last week she'd been angry when she heard that various members of Congress (including Schumer) had proposed that the victims of Oklahoma City, the 1993 World Trade Center bombing, and the embassy bombings in Africa be added to the Feinberg fund. To most, this seemed like appropriate symmetry. But to Simon, who'd become fairly sophisticated about all this, it was wrong, because the Feinberg fund had only been created because Congress, by legislating liability caps, had effectively taken away her right to sue the airlines and others who might be liable. The Oklahoma City families didn't lose their right to sue.* Another, more prominent news event also bothered her—the now incessant suggestions, such as the stories about a memo written by an FBI Minneapolis agent, that the government could have done more to prevent the attacks. She really didn't want to know about that. She preferred thinking that fate, not incompetence, had taken Michael.

Eileen also suffered lately from sudden feelings of fear, approaching panic, whenever she heard an unexpected loud noise. She'd begun to believe she was suffering from some form of post-traumatic stress syndrome. The kids showed a different, more subtle fear. Eileen had begun to notice that they seemed scared whenever she left them, even if it was just to go shopping or to the gym. They'd ask where she was going and exactly when she'd be back. "I could tell," she explains, "that they were terrified of losing their only parent."

Then again, on most days, she was feeling a lot better about things. Last week, she'd finally canceled the neighbors' delivery of those hot dinners, saying it was time to get out of that routine. And she was forming close friendships with the group of widows she met with each Friday. She was even starting to think about going back to school.

Elaine Lyons went with Brian and his family today to a memorial service for her husband, Michael, at the local firehouse in Westchester, where he had

---

*The Bush administration ultimately proposed instead that these victims and future victims of terrorism get the standard $250,000 death benefit paid to public safety officers killed in the line of duty, but Congress never agreed on any plan before adjourning at the end of 2002.

been a volunteer on call during his off hours. The best part about it was that the fire company had set up a small memorial, with a plaque, out on the lawn next to the firehouse. At least her daughters would now have some place to go, even if no DNA match was ever made with the remains that Brian had thought must have been Michael's.

# Wednesday, May 29, 2002

The small group, which had expanded since the basic go decision had been made a week earlier on the Department of Homeland Security, had begun working on a rollout plan—who would be told what, when. So, joining the group of senior advisors in the PEOC were the President's two top message-makers and (along with Andrew Card) his closest aides: counselor Karen Hughes and political director Karl Rove. Both had been told snippets of what was going on by either Card or the President. Now they became fully engaged in spinning it out, aided by Susan Neely, a veteran Republican political operative who was Ridge's communications director, and Cheney counselor Mary Matalin.

Everything was plotted out, including an elaborate timetable for briefings of political leaders and the press. To backstop it, Falkenrath would be responsible for a thick white paper explaining the department in detail. Included would be tangible examples of how the consolidation would produce better homeland security. Beyond the obvious border protection overlaps between INS, Customs, and the Coast Guard, a favorite was what would happen now versus after the department was created if there were an emergency at a nuclear power plant. Now, the distribution of iodine pills, which prevent radiation-induced thyroid cancer, were regulated by the Nuclear Regulatory Commission within ten miles of the plant. Outside the ten-mile radius FEMA regulated who got the pills. But the stockpile of pills was controlled by the Department of Health and Human Services. The new department would have total control over the whole process.

The announcement date was set for either June 3 or June 6.

Larry Cox joined a group of thirty-three airport directors who wrote to Mineta urging that the December 31 deadline for installing all the baggage screening equipment be postponed. If not, travel in January would be seriously disrupted by long delays, because TSA was so far behind in designing the systems for each airport. "They're cops. They've never built anything. They don't know a thing about airports," the Denver airport director was quoted as telling the *New York Times* in explaining the letter.

Cox signed on because he had become convinced, he says, that "we'd have lines back out on the sidewalk if they didn't stop and plan things." In fact, Cox was equally concerned about the November 19 deadline to have all private screeners replaced by a federal force. "They've got five and a half months, and we haven't heard a word about what they intend to do here—how they're going to hire people, what their setup is going to be, or anything. I always hope for the best and expect the worst."


When Sergio Magistri heard about the airports' effort to extend the deadline on baggage screening machines, he realized that he had another avenue to getting the government to restore a mix that included more of his machines and fewer of the trace detectors. He told his lobbyist to try to join forces with the airports lobby, because if the deadline got extended, TSA would have more time to install his machines—and should install them because they provided stronger protection.


The ACLU of New Jersey and other litigants got the news this morning that a federal judge had sided with them completely in their suit to force Ashcroft to end his blanket rule that all detention hearings involving people held as part of the terrorism investigation were to be kept secret. Judge John Bissell said hearings could be closed only on a case-by-case basis if the government specified that national security interests would be endangered. With another judge in Detroit having recently issued a similar ruling, Ashcroft was now zero for two on this issue.


A ceremony was held tonight at Ground Zero for all the recovery workers to commemorate the removal of the final steel girder from the site. Two hundred thousand pounds of steel had now been extracted, along with 1.7 million tons of other debris, without a single serious injury, three months ahead of schedule and about $3 billion under the $6 billion budget.

The girder was cut down, draped in a shroud, and, as bagpipes played, it was rolled up on a tractor trailer as the workers marched alongside it.

Brian Lyons was thrilled to be in the honor guard.

# Thursday, May 30, 2002

Ashcroft announced that Watergate-era rules that restricted the FBI from scouting for information by attending public forums—in this case mosques or websites—would be lifted. The agents would no longer need to have started a formal investigation to go where the public could now go.

Romero of the ACLU quickly approved a statement declaring that Ashcroft's decision "rewards [the FBI's] failure with new powers . . . and threatens core civil liberties." Once again the ACLU cited Ashcroft's "insatiable appetite for new powers that will not make us safer."

What if those powers *would* make the country safer, Romero was asked. Would you support them, or is the argument that they won't make anyone safer just a rhetorical device?

"We would never see something like this as making anyone safer," Romero replied.


James Loy, who had spent forty-two years in the Coast Guard, including the last four as the Commandant, was supposed to retire this spring. But as Mineta and his staff became more disenchanted with Magaw as a manager, they had settled on an idea, strongly supported by Ridge, that Loy, fifty-nine, could be the solution. They didn't want to fire Magaw; with TSA struggling to meet its deadlines, that would look awful. Instead they'd make Loy, whose tenure at the Coast Guard had dazzled everyone from the White House, to the Transportation Department, to Capitol Hill, the deputy head of TSA and its chief operating officer. He'd surely be on the case when someone kicked a metal detector's plug out of an outlet.

Two weeks ago, Mineta had called Magaw in and told him he wanted to make the change. Magaw had bridled at the idea. "You can't fire my guy," he said, referring to Stephen McHale, the former ATF lawyer who was his deputy. "You can do it if we can have two deputies."

Mineta had agreed. But Jackson and Mineta chief of staff John Flaherty were appalled. Subordinates didn't lay out conditions like that to cabinet secretaries. They had decided from that moment that Magaw had to go, only they would control the timing.

Today, Loy's appointment as Mineta's second deputy was announced. He was slated to start in a few weeks after a vacation. Rossides, too, had heard great things about Loy, but she and other Magaw people figured that something more was afoot. Jackson or Flaherty had been inserting themselves into everything all along, but now they were putting their man in to run the department.

Chuck Schumer was scheduled to be on hand at Ground Zero for the ceremony marking the end of the cleanup. He and everyone else had to be in place by 10:29. That was when the bell would start to toll to commemorate the fall of the second tower—10:29 on September 11.

But Schumer had two places he needed to be first. He had a speech at a prominent New York business association breakfast at the Plaza Hotel in Manhattan and then a commencement talk at Queens College. He wanted to do both.

He started out behind schedule. The tunnel into Manhattan from his apartment in Brooklyn had been partially closed because it was so near the Ground Zero ceremony. So Schumer—cursing the traffic all the way, as he returned phone calls, and as his police driver tried to weave through it—got to the business speech about fifteen minutes late. He explained about the traffic to his audience of about 500 in the hotel ballroom, but added that his wife—Transportation Commissioner Iris Weinshall, who was seated at a center table—"doesn't control the tunnel." He added that ever since Giuliani, a Republican, had appointed Weinshall, and she'd publicly thanked the mayor for ignoring the "baggage" she carried, he had thought of himself as "Senator Baggage." The crowd laughed and applauded.

Schumer's stated topic was his "vision for rebuilding lower Manhattan." It was a perfectly pitched performance, mixing substance with idealism, modesty with a subtle reminder of his own vision and achievements, all packaged around a thoughtful, uplifting analysis of what New York was and could be. He touched on terrorism insurance, Bush as a man "who stepped up to the plate," and the continuing role of New York in an "ideas economy." ("If you walk down any street in midtown or even downtown, you'll find someone born in Des Moines and someone born in Delhi, and they are each here for the same reason. They have an idea, and this is the place you come to do something with it.")

He also went over the federal aid package he had won for the city, crediting Hillary Clinton, the whole congressional delegation, the governor, the mayor, and again the President. He even passed up the chance to tout his stellar performance in negotiating with Daniels at OMB to allow the city to spend any money left over from FEMA's cleanup and recovery on other projects. He simply mentioned it in passing and noted that it now gave the city an extra

$3 billion, or a total of $5 billion, to build "a truly grand" transportation terminal downtown.

Then he got to his main subject. When it comes to figuring out how to rebuild downtown, he said, "We should reach and stretch and try to do something grand. Both the horror of the tragedy and the greatness and ascendance of our city demand that we at least try."

He had, he continued, come across and seriously explored "one truly grand concept, and it looks like it will fail, but I thought I'd share it with you." He laid out the U.N. swap idea, crediting his real estate broker friend, and talked about how he'd researched and pushed it for nearly five months. Then, he explained why it would fail: "The U.N. is against it, which is one small problem." The audience laughed.

"The second objection we ran into is equally understandable and just as important," Schumer continued, describing the Cartier family's reaction.

Schumer floated a few other possible "grand ideas" that had not been fully thought out, and also urged that the infrastructure downtown—a new transportation hub, cultural and recreational facilities, and an "apron park" around the area's now shabby shoreline—be part of any grand plan. But the trick of the speech was that he really did succeed in giving the audience a vision of something "grand" based on an idea he had that he readily conceded was not going to happen. They gave him an ovation and pressed him with so many questions that he had trouble leaving the room.

Schumer was so delayed that by now it was 9:50 and his staff told him that there was no way he was going to get to Queens College and back to Ground Zero at 10:29—which was one deadline that was not going to be extended for a habitually late senator. In fact, he might not even get down there in time even without going to the college, unless they hustled.

Since winning an upset race in 1974 for the state assembly as a recent law school graduate (in part by being audacious enough to cajole an endorsement out of one of his law professors, Archibald Cox, the famously fired Watergate prosecutor, who was a godlike figure), Schumer had only run on one speed—fast. And as his car barreled down toward Ground Zero, with Schumer backseat-driving from the front passenger seat so relentlessly that the police driver assigned to him since September 11 began to laugh, Schumer muttered to himself, "I shoulda tried to go to Queens. We coulda made it."

As the car approached the dignitaries' dropoff point, its police light flashing, Schumer seemed almost boyishly thrilled by it all, even surprised that he was waved through each barricade. He still wasn't used to the police car, still wasn't used to being seen as an insider. He was old enough to have a paunch.

He was a senior senator with thoughtful, moderate views on foreign policy, and a leader on nitty-gritty issues such as cargo security. He had a daughter going off to college. But in many ways Schumer was still the shaggy-haired insurgent kid pictured on the state assembly campaign poster that greeted visitors to his Washington senate office. Which, for his constituents, was a good thing. It's what made him try harder, return all those phone calls, do those press conferences every other Sunday, and take a meeting with the Cartier family on a Sunday morning.

The service at Ground Zero had no speeches. The mourners would have been there until the next day if all the officeholders on the podium had been allowed a turn at the microphone. Instead, the audience of family members of victims and recovery workers (or both, in the case of Brian Lyons) stood silently in the already hot sun at the top of the pit. Police bagpipes played for the workers as they marched up and out. When the music stopped, the cheers started.

Michael Cartier and Brian Lyons were among the two dozen people in the honor guard leading the march. Cartier had changed his mind, and decided that he should be there, weekday or not, to honor the people who had looked for his brother.

Lyons brought his two children and his wife. But his sister-in-law, Elaine, still couldn't bear something like this. Instead, she went to a quiet ceremony at her husband's old firehouse.

Later that evening, Cartier appeared on the *NBC Nightly News with Tom Brokaw*. "Today for us as a family," he said, "is almost the equivalent of a judge slamming down the mallet and saying, 'I sentence you, as a family, to live the rest of your lives without your loved one.'"

# Friday, May 31, 2002

Ken Feinberg had said that family members or their lawyers could come talk to him and get a preview of the awards he might give, so that they could decide whether to go forward. Today was the first dry run for the heavy hitters.

Lee Kreindler, the dean of the aviation bar, came in with what he considered one of his best test cases—a twenty-nine-year-old who'd been earning $750,000 a year and had left behind a wife and a baby born after September

11. Clearly, Kreindler's client was far off the charts that Feinberg had written into his regulations, which mapped awards against the deceased's earnings and years left in the workforce, but stopped at an annual salary of $231,000.

Kreindler, who referred to the victim "as a summa cum laude with undisputed great earnings potential," said this was an uncomplicated case. It was easily worth $15 million to $20 million, he told Feinberg, who had said in December that he doubted any but the most extraordinary awards would go above $4 million, because his job was to provide a bridge between a government program that concerned itself with providing a safety net for all, and a tort system that allowed for widely divergent awards based on earnings. For a while they sparred over whether this case, or any case, was really that uncomplicated. Feinberg pointed out, for example, that much of the lost future earnings that Kreindler had brandished were stock options, which were highly speculative. But rather than argue, Feinberg mostly asked questions, and thanked Kreindler profusely for coming in.

Feinberg came away from the session thinking Kreindler was really talking $9 million or $10 million and that he, Feinberg, might be prepared to go to $6 million, maybe $7 million. They'd get to an agreement, he figured. But it would take time.

Everything about the fund—which was supposed to speed past the usual court process—seemed to be taking time. As of today, only 496 people had filed even preliminary claims with the fund, out of a possible 3,000. Only a dozen had formally completed the whole process. Feinberg knew that the families had until December 31 of 2003 to file, and that many were still too grief-stricken to deal with the long, complicated form. Also, by now it was clear that most had been tided over enough by Red Cross or September 11th Fund gifts, or by life insurance or other death benefits, that they didn't feel a pressing need. Others, including most who had lawyers, wanted to wait to see how he came back with tentative awards after dry runs like the one he had just conducted with Kreindler, or after he actually rendered decisions, the basics of which he had promised to post on his website.

Feinberg understood all that, but he was getting restless. He also knew that the service centers he had opened in New York and elsewhere to assist people in making applications were largely empty most days.

## Saturday, June 1, 2002

Almost nine months ago, Ali Erikenoglu had consulted his friend and lawyer, Sohail Mohammed, after being rousted late one night in his Paterson, New Jersey, home by FBI agents investigating a tip that he might be a terrorist sympathizer. Mohammed, in turn, had complained loudly and publicly about how the agents had questioned Erikenoglu, an electrical engineer and American citizen, about his political beliefs, and had insisted on not taking off their shoes in his home. That had resulted in the New Jersey office of the FBI reaching out to the lawyer and asking him to conduct sensitivity training sessions for the FBI and other New Jersey law enforcement agents.

This evening the goodwill that had begun to build last fall blossomed into an extraordinary love fest of sorts: The FBI, Secret Service, INS, Customs, and New Jersey state police joined with Mohammed and other community leaders to stage a job fair at a mosque in northern New Jersey. More than 500 young American citizens with roots in all varieties of Muslim countries showed up to talk to the recruiters. Although the four-year college requirement presented an obstacle to some, each agency got at least twenty sign-ups for additional information and discussion.

## Monday, June 3, 2002

The fact that federal judge John Martin threw out Larry Silverstein's motion for summary judgment against Travelers Insurance today didn't surprise anyone, except maybe his lawyer, Herb Wachtell, assuming he believed his own predictions, made as early as February, that he'd win it.

The decision, nonetheless, was significant. First, if Travelers—the one company that had insisted on a policy form that did not have the Silverstein broker's "series of related events" definition of occurrence in it—could still win a motion like this against Silverstein, that had to say a lot about what the judge thought of the argument by Ostrager's client, Swiss Re, and the other insurers. After all, they had negotiated *only* with that "series of related events" definition on the table, never with the Travelers form.

Second, the judge's opinion against Travelers had stated that the reason not to grant summary judgment in a case like this was that the term "occurrence" was so ambiguous that to decide what it means would require a look at the "evidence concerning the parties' intentions that is available in this case. This includes," the judge added, tellingly, "the specific definition of the term occurrence circulated by the insurance agent for . . . Silverstein, testimony and documents relating to the negotiations prior to September 11 . . . and testimony and documentary evidence concerning statements made after September 11 by those who had been involved in negotiating the insurance contracts, in which they expressed their views on the question of whether there had been one or two occurrences."

Judge Martin had, of course, seen all of that—the broker's policy and all the evidence about the negotiations and about what Silverstein's own people thought occurrence meant after September 11. That material, such as the notes of the Nashville telephone conference, in which the lead Silverstein broker said he thought it was one occurrence, had been highlighted in Ostrager's brief against Silverstein. Thus, it was impossible, perhaps even for Wachtell,* not to recognize that the judge was sending a clear signal that he was going to lose at a trial.

The conservative magazine *National Review* published a cover story on Tom Ridge entitled, "The Impossible Position of Tom Ridge." The sub-headline was, "Color Me Pointless."

# Wednesday, June 5, 2002

The Red Cross held a press conference in which chairman David McLaughlin announced a series of reforms in its fund-raising practices. The organization had spent $100,000 on focus groups, he explained, and had found out that donors didn't fully understand how the Red Cross collects and distributes its money. The key change announced was that from now on donors will be asked to confirm that they know that their donations, unless they

---

*Nonetheless, Wachtell continued to maintain to the author that his case was a "clear winner." With that in mind, in fairness to Wachtell and the reader, it should be pointed out that Wachtell continually cited to the author numerous documents and other supposed evidence uncovered during the discovery phase of the trial that, he said, proved his case. The author reviewed them extensively and decided that they did not come close to matching the evidence on the other side; in fact, most seemed almost comically beside the point.

specifically designate otherwise, will be used for a variety of Red Cross operations.

By now, the Red Cross had received $967 million in contributions related to the September 11 attacks, and still expected to spend all of it, somehow, on its now extended definition of victims.

What was not announced was the policy the organization had adopted in February that it would never again solicit for a particular disaster, which meant that the organization would go from oversoliciting and overspending on this terror attack to being largely on the sidelines for the next one. Then again, given the organization's predilection for overreacting to press criticism, in the event of another attack the policy might well be abandoned following bad publicity about it, and the Red Cross would once again be taking in and spending millions on the fly.

Federal prosecutors demonstrated to James Brosnahan that in the John Walker Lindh case the government can play in his league when it comes to bombarding the other side with paper. In a blizzard of motions contesting all of Brosnahan's arguments to dismiss the charges, the prosecution team claimed Lindh had known of plans for terror attacks "even worse" than those of September 11, and "knew he was in league with a group of individuals dedicated to the murder of Americans." The government even circled back to its concession a month ago that Lindh had not killed the CIA agent, saying, "The fact that we do not have evidence that Lindh wielded the weapon that fired the bullet that killed Spann [the CIA agent] has been taken by the defense as an admission that Lindh was an innocent bystander. He was neither a bystander, nor, in any respect, can he be described as innocent. He was a member of a conspiracy to kill Americans. . . . By well established conspiracy law, the murder of Mr. Spann is attributable to all conspirators."

As for an argument that Brosnahan had made that "government misconduct" related to all of the press statements from Ashcroft and others about Lindh had generated pretrial publicity that made it impossible for Lindh to get a fair trial, the government asserted that Brosnahan had conducted its own "aggressive media campaign," the first priority of which was "to portray Lindh as a gentle, sweet youth . . . and loyal American."

A few days ago, Ridge had been told by Lawlor that he was still unable to get Justice and the State Department to agree on which countries should be included in the stopgap entry-exit program that would select young adult males entering with visas from high-risk countries for fingerprinting and special monitoring. So he took up the issue with the President during policy time in the Oval Office. Bush then made the call, accepting State's recommendation that the countries included would be Iran, Iraq, Syria, Libya, and Sudan. (Ashcroft had wanted to include Pakistan and Saudi Arabia, but they were left out, even though fifteen of the September 11 hijackers had been Saudis.)

Today, the program was announced.

Senator Mitchell's notion, in comparing what he'd seen of the Red Cross's problems to his work writing tax legislation, that "simplicity is the enemy of fairness," played out for Ken Feinberg on the editorial page of the *New York Times*. Noting that people are "not rushing to sign up" for Feinberg's fund, the *Times* wrote that "although Mr. Feinberg has made every possible effort to reach out to the survivors," his thirty-three-page application form "is dauntingly complex. . . . Mr. Feinberg should be able to simplify it."

Tonight, Feinberg, who had spent hours editing and trying to cut the form after his staff had spent days in the same effort, took another crack at it. His goal was twenty pages. But he couldn't cut it down by even a paragraph.

"It has to be what it is," he said a few days later, after returning from a trip to Europe, where he had gone to solicit families of foreign-born victims. "We have to get all this information. We have people filing forms with a crayon. Some answer 'not sure' for how much did he earn. . . . You can't give away millions of dollars of the government's money without getting all this information and getting a way to check it all out. What would the public reaction be, or the reaction in Congress be, if I gave away three million bucks to someone who spent ten minutes filling out a form? If the *Times* is worried about complexity, they ought to try litigation and discovery and depositions and expert economics witnesses. . . . Agent Orange," he added, referring to the mass torts case he had mediated, "was so much easier, because the judge ordered that everyone who qualified as a victim was given the same amount."

All of that might be true, but Feinberg still knew that the *Times* was right that the program was lagging in bringing in families. As he faced the summer, he was worried that by the time the press started writing their September 11 first-year anniversary stories he still wouldn't have given out an award. "We've got to get a bunch of awards in and out the door by Labor Day," he kept telling his staff. "Or we'll look like fools."

Among the many who hadn't filed with Feinberg were Eileen Simon, Elaine Lyons, and the parents of James Cartier.

Simon was certain she was going to file, but her lawyer—from Kreindler's firm—wanted her to hold off until they saw what Feinberg was going to do with some of Kreindler's test cases.

Elaine Lyons just couldn't face dealing with the paperwork yet, and, like Simon, she had no pressing money needs. And Patrick Cartier, Sr., still hadn't resigned himself to submitting to a program that he thought was a bribe to get him not to sue the government and was unfairly favoring the rich. His son Michael figured he'd come around sooner or later, and end up using the money as a college fund for his grandchildren.

Anthony Romero gave a fiery speech at the John F. Kennedy Memorial Library in Boston, declaring that "people in positions of responsibility—in government, in academia, and especially in the media—are today fixated on trading off [the] basic values" that John F. Kennedy had stood for. Attacking an article by *New York Times* op-ed columnist Nicholas Kristof in which, Romero said, Kristof "took civil libertarians to task for their dishonesty in refusing to acknowledge the trade-off between public security and individual freedom," Romero asserted that "the trade-off . . . is not only a false solution but a dangerous one. . . . By diminishing our freedom, we will be doing the terrorists' work for them," he added.

It wasn't an argument that Chuck Schumer bought. This former darling of the ACLU today proposed an actual broadening of the Patriot Act. Schumer announced that he was introducing a bill that would eliminate the requirement that to get those lower-threshold warrants from the special national security court, federal agents had to assert that the target was suspected of being an "agent" of a foreign government or terrorist group. Under Schumer's proposal, co-sponsored by Republican Senator Jon Kyl of Arizona, it would now be necessary only to assert that the target might be a terrorist, which means that he could be a suspected terrorist acting alone or with others about whom the government knew nothing.

One by one, Andrew Card called or met with the cabinet officers who would lose agencies affected by the new Department of Homeland Security. Treasury Secretary O'Neill said he thought it was a great idea. Norman Mineta said that if that was what the President wanted, then he was all for it and would work hard to deliver a great Coast Guard and a great new TSA to the new department whenever the bill took effect.

John Ashcroft looked at Card, as Card explained that he was about to lose INS, paused for a moment, then, according to what Card later told three asso-ciattes, said, "I'm glad you didn't tell me in advance, because I'd have had to fight like hell to stop it." Then he added, "I have three things I'd like to give whoever gets this job and takes over INS: my best wishes, a bottle of whiskey, and a bullet." *

When Ashcroft got back to the office, he told a few of his closest aides, introducing the subject by declaring that the department had "suffered a real blow today." Someone suggested that he go to the President to head it off, but he said that Card had made it clear that the decision was done, adding the shocking footnote that Card had also said something about having at least saved the FBI for him.

# Thursday, June 6, 2002

At 7:30, Ridge gathered his senior staff of twenty in the secure conference room at the Executive Office Building to announce what only five of them already knew—the new department.

"This guy got slam-dunked by the whole cabinet in December"—when Ridge's modest proposal to consolidate INS, Customs, and the Coast Guard was rejected—"and just kept his mouth shut and took it," one aide said to another as they left the meeting. "And six months later, he's slam-dunked all of them. Amazing."

At 8:15, the President's legislative affairs, communications, and press staffs were called into the Roosevelt Room and briefed on the plan by Card, congressional affairs director Calio, counselor Karen Hughes, communica-tions director Dan Bartlett, and Falkenrath.

At 8:45, the President briefed his Homeland Security Council, using talk-ing points and PowerPoint slides prepared by Falkenrath.

At 9:30, press secretary Ari Fleischer called the broadcast network bureau chiefs to request time on their air at 8:00 P.M. for the President to address the nation.

At 9:45, Fleischer held a background briefing for the White House press corps, called a "gaggle," and laid out the basics of the plan, making sure to use certain talking points prepared by Falkenrath—such as the fact that when the

---

* Ashcroft said he would never comment about a conversation with Card, but that "while I don't have a recollection of the meeting, I don't think that's the kind of thing I would say."

President and Ridge had met with congressional committee leaders to talk about homeland security in October, Ridge had said that he might recommend a realignment at some later point, and that this was the largest reorganization of the government since the 1947 reshuffling of the nation's defense and security apparatus.

At 10:00, Card and Calio briefed the Republican House and Senate leaders. The House group was at first upset at having been called down to the White House so urgently, because they were preparing to hold a press conference on another issue that was a world apart from any homeland security emergency—the repeal of the estate tax.

At 10:30, Ridge, Card, and Calio began a series of calls to other key members of the House and Senate, including the Democratic leaders.

At 11:00, Ridge and Falkenrath briefed the heads of Customs, the Secret Service, INS, the Coast Guard, and the Centers for Disease Control.

At noon, communications director Barlett and Ridge's communications director, Susan Neely, briefed the public affairs heads of all cabinet departments and agencies.

At 1:00, Ridge held a conference call with the nation's governors and state homeland security directors. At the same time, political director Karl Rove held a conference call with leaders of conservative interest groups.

At 2:00, Hughes, Bartlett, Fleischer, Neely, and Cheney counselor Mary Matalin began calling the newspaper columnists whom they had been assigned to brief, while Ridge, Bolten, and Falkenrath began a series of calls to members of the various commissions that had studied homeland security in recent years (and had recommended a smaller version of what they were now doing).

At 4:00, Falkenrath and members of his staff called a long list of presidential scholars and policy commentators.

At 5:00, Card and Hughes called the anchors for each of the television networks, while the press office began to release background binders to the press.

At 6:30, Ridge held a detailed background briefing (in which he could be quoted as "a senior administration official"), using talking points and charts to walk the press through the President's speech, the text of which was also distributed but embargoed until 8:00. Asked if he was taking the job, he answered that he had not discussed that yet with the President and that his focus now was on getting Congress to approve this plan.

At 8:00, the President announced the initiative on national television. At the same time, statements of support were distributed by the press offices of each of the affected cabinet members. Other communications materials, such as the background white paper, were distributed nationwide by e-mail, hand delivery, and FedEx.

At 8:30, cabinet officials were made available for interviews on some of the cable news shows, while Ridge and Card were put on television programs with larger audiences, starting with the Fox News channel and ending with ABC's *Nightline*.

# Friday, June 7, 2002

It seemed to have worked. The television reports last night and this morning expressed skepticism that the plan had been cooked up to divert attention from the hearings being held concerning an FBI whistle-blower who asserted that the bureau should have found out more about alleged twentieth hijacker Zacarias Moussaoui before September 11. But they generally focused on the boldness of the plan and the overlap and disorganization it was meant to eliminate. Better yet, there was scarcely a critical sound from Congress, where the Democrats seemed limited to citing Senator Lieberman's similar proposal as a way of saying they had thought of it first.

A CNN–*USA Today*–Gallup poll taken today that would be announced Monday found that Americans supported the plan 72 to 20 percent.

Chuck Schumer generally supported the plan when asked about it. But to him, it really didn't matter much. He saw it in many ways as a distraction from what the President ought to have been doing all along—which was proposing a strong four- or five-point plan dealing with specific threats, such as cargo security, the INS failures, or dirty bombs, and then pushing the people who ran the current departments relentlessly to make these improvements happen fast.

It was her dream job, the one Gale Rossides had wanted for almost as long as she knew it existed. There was an opening for a new head of the Federal Law Enforcement Training Center (FLETC), whose main campus was in Glynco, Georgia (near Brunswick). Top officials at Treasury (which oversaw FLETC, as well as Rossides's former agency, ATF) wanted her to take it. It was a huge operation that trained agents for INS, Customs, ATF, the Secret Service, and every other federal law enforcement agency except the FBI. It involved all the training and culture building that she loved. They'd even let her have her office, a big office, in Washington, rather than move to Georgia, because FLETC was now so big she didn't have to be at any one campus.

Rossides's husband, who is a Treasury agent, said she had to consider it. How could she not, with the situation she was now in? Her leader and mentor had just been undercut by the insertion of a new deputy. And every day she arrived almost at dawn to work in a grim physical setting, where she got shuffled from office to office, and where it seemed that half the time the phones or something else didn't work, and where no matter how many hours she put in it seemed as if she could never catch up, yet was never doing enough, because she was also at the agency that had become the press's and Congress's favorite target.

All that, and more, was true. But today, she turned the FLETC job down, telling her erstwhile boss that she had come to TSA to get a job done that wasn't finished yet.


Larry Cox got his evening bank of Northwest flights back today, which almost brought him back to September 10 in terms of the number of flights coming in and out of Memphis. Within a week, his passenger traffic would be back to about 90 percent of what it had been before the attacks. (Which was good for him, but not as good for the airlines, since the returning passengers were paying much lower fares, because the airlines had been forced to offer large discounts to reattract fliers.)

Cox had just returned from a four-day industry convention in Dallas, where he and other airport directors had met with Jackson, the transportation deputy secretary, and top TSA officials. "They all said nice things, but nothing that gave me much hope," he recalls. "We tried to be blunt and told them three things are going to happen. They won't meet the deadlines, but will say they did. They'll waste billions of dollars. And the January 2003 waiting lines will make what happened right after September 11 seem like child's play. . . . But Jackson keep saying, 'We're gonna make it. We're gonna make it.' "

Had anyone from TSA been to Memphis to look at his airport and design the baggage screening system yet?

"If they were here," Cox replied, "then it was a Navy SEAL team, because I didn't see 'em. They may come tomorrow. They may come on Christmas Day, but they're not telling me," he added, noting, "It would be nice if I could plan my summer vacation knowing when I should be here to meet with them, but no one will tell me."

Donna Newman, the lawyer appointed to represent Jose Padilla—the American citizen who had been seized in Chicago and brought to New York as a "material witness" after the CIA had developed information that he was trying to develop a plan to set off a dirty bomb—finished her brief this week demanding Padilla's release. Much of her argument was based on the decision a month ago (that was now being appealed) by a federal judge that the detention of another material witness was illegal.

The government's lawyers were worried that the judge in this case might rule the same way. The one clear alternative they had—charging Padilla with a crime—was out of the question, because all they had were the vague accounts of two informants being held overseas that Padilla was talking about planning something. Neither witness was considered completely credible. And Padilla, himself, had refused to talk, so he had added nothing to the scant evidence they had.

In Washington, Ashcroft and his Criminal Division head, Chertoff, were struggling for an alternative. They couldn't risk having someone who might be planning this kind of attack cut loose.


TSA formally announced that Boeing had gotten the baggage screening equipment rollout contract, having bested Lockheed in the final round. Raytheon put out a statement saying it regretted the decision, but noting that it was still working at twenty-two airports under its old FAA contract, and stood ready to help the government do more if needed.

Boeing, meanwhile, got its team leaders ready for a meeting the next morning, a Saturday, at TSA headquarters to start the rollout. By Monday, they'd have 150 teams assembled to begin surveying airports across the country, and Null and other TSA people would be connected electronically to the Boeing information system that would track progress at all the airports that needed to get the equipment.


# Monday, June 10, 2002

Standing in front of an eerily dark, blank backdrop from a TV studio in Moscow, where he was meeting with Russian law enforcement officials, John Ashcroft was beamed by satellite back to a press conference in the United States.

"I am pleased to announce today a significant step forward in the war on terrorism," he began. "We have captured a known terrorist who was exploring a plan to build and explode a radiological dispersion device, or 'dirty bomb,' in the United States."

Had Ashcroft and Justice gotten enough evidence to indict Padilla after all? Not exactly.

Ashcroft continued: "Yesterday . . . I recommended that the President of the United States, in his capacity as commander in chief, determine that Abdullah Al Muhajir, born Jose Padilla, is an enemy combatant who poses a serious and continuing threat to the American people and our national security. After the determination, Abdullah Al Muhajir"—for weeks Ashcroft and other Justice officials would insist on referring to Jose Padilla's adopted Muslim name, instead of the name on his American passport—"was transferred from the custody of the Justice Department to the custody of the Defense Department."

In other words, Padilla had been put in an Army brig, which, it was later revealed, was in South Carolina—which turned out to be important because at the hearing in New York, where his lawyer was scheduled to move for his release on Tuesday, the government would argue, among other things, that that court no longer had jurisdiction over him because he was in South Carolina.

What had happened was clear to Newman, Padilla's lawyer, when she heard about it. The government had been afraid to go forward with the hearing and had instead hurriedly spirited Padilla off to the Army brig. Later this morning, she would be told that the government's position now was that neither she nor any other lawyer could talk to Padilla, that he had none of the rights afforded a criminal defendant, and that he could now be held indefinitely because of his combatant status, just the way the prisoners in Guantánamo, Cuba, were being held.

What was also clear was that Ashcroft had now violated a key principle he had used to argue against putting Moussaoui, the alleged twentieth hijacker, into a military tribunal—that because he was already in the federal courts system as a material witness, changing his status would look like the government was simply trying to switch systems to avoid a bad result. Now, he was doing exactly that.

"In apprehending Al Muhajir as he sought entry into the United States," Ashcroft concluded, "we have disrupted an unfolding terrorist plot to attack the United States by exploding a radioactive 'dirty bomb.'"

In six paragraphs of his statement Ashcroft had turned "exploring a plan" (the first paragraph's description of Padilla's activities) into "an unfolding terrorist plot" (the sixth paragraph's description). There was a big difference, because the only evidence the government had was that Padilla had talked about trying to get the materials and develop a plan for such a bombing.

This change in wording had its own backstory. As with Ashcroft's plan in September to propose the Patriot Act, no one at the White House had any idea until about an hour before the press conference that Ashcroft planned to make the Padilla announcement himself from Moscow. When someone in the White House counsel's office heard about it, chief of staff Card's office quickly asked for a draft of the press release. After reading it and talking to Defense Secretary Rumsfeld's office—Rumsfeld, after all, was the person taking custody of Padilla—White House staffers were, as one recalls, "appalled by the alarmist language; this was way over the top." They tried to get Ashcroft to let an aide make the announcement in Washington so as to downplay it, but they were told that that would be impossible, because Justice had already alerted the press that Ashcroft wanted to talk to them from Moscow. Led by communications director Dan Bartlett, they tried even harder to get what he said toned down. They succeeded in the first paragraph, which is why "exploring a plan" was used. But then Ashcroft personally directed that the "unfolding terrorist plot" language be put into that later paragraph, which no one at the White House was told about.

Within hours of the announcement, a jittery stock market started turning down after an early morning gain. (InVision, however, jumped about 10 percent on news of the new threat.) The announcement set off such a furor that White House aides encouraged Deputy Defense Secretary Paul Wolfowitz to play down the threat in talking to reporters.

Wolfowitz didn't need much encouragement. By now, relations between the Pentagon and Justice Department were at a point of almost unbelievable hostility, mostly because Ashcroft and his people seemed to their counterparts in the Pentagon to be relentless about treating the Pentagon as a junior partner in the war on terror at home. First, there had been Justice's insistence on hanging on to the Moussaoui case, which seemed like it was made for a military commission. Then, Ashcroft's staff had complained to the White House and to some conservative columnists that Rumsfeld's rules for the tribunals were too liberal. The Pentagon people also knew that some on Ashcroft's staff seemed eager to tell reporters that the Defense Department's interrogators weren't doing a good enough job getting them information from terrorists they were capturing overseas. Also mixed in was the personal chemistry between these two senior cabinet officials. Rumsfeld, who is compulsively informal and irreverent, saw Ashcroft, who is straitlaced and downright obsequious in front of Bush, as a kind of strange figure.

Wolfowitz's comments about the dirty bomb plot really not being the threat Ashcroft had said it was, infuriated Ashcroft and his staff so much that through June and much of the summer, according to two senior White House officials and two senior officials at the Office of Homeland Security, Ashcroft and Rumsfeld were barely on speaking terms, except to say hello and observe other civilities when the President was in the room.

However much Wolfowitz and White House aides wanted to play down the security threat signified by Padilla's detention, Anthony Romero was in no mood to play down the threat to civil liberties. In his view, "This was totally crossing the line. Now, Ashcroft was saying that an American citizen could be held indefinitely, in secret, with no hearing, and no lawyer to challenge the evidence against him."

In a blistering press release, Romero seized on the inconsistency of Ashcroft's move. "If a non-citizen like Zacarias Moussaoui can be tried in a regular court of law, surely a United States citizen can be afforded the same access to justice," he said.

He was right about the inconsistency. Not only was Moussaoui a non-citizen, so, too, was alleged shoe bomber Richard Reid, over whom Ashcroft had also kept jurisdiction. In fact, the only person Ashcroft had handed over to Rumsfeld was this American citizen—after his prosecutors had tried and failed to get enough evidence against him to indict him and were afraid that he'd be released in the material witness hearing.* (Another American citizen, Yaser Hamdi, was also being held, but he had been captured fighting against Americans overseas.) Asked in an interview with the author about the apparent inconsistency of Reid, captured at an American airport but who was not an American citizen, being given access to the American court system, while Padilla, who was a citizen and was also captured at an airport, was not, Ashcroft's only explanation was that "decisions have to be made regarding the likely value of the individual in terms of a whole range of things." He added, however, that "detaining a person who is an enemy combatant does not preclude subsequent prosecution."

Much of the debate in the press about the detention of the dirty bomber was over whether an enemy combatant who is an American citizen could be

---

*They may have had little to fear on this score. The same judge who was about to hear the petition to release Padilla would soon issue a decision in another case contradicting his colleague's ruling that holding material witnesses in grand jury investigations was not permitted.

detained this way without any rights. But to Romero that seemed beside the point. The real issue was that no one had proved he was a combatant, a bomber, a terrorist, or anything else. No evidence had been presented, even in secret, to any judge in any kind of hearing where the other side could be heard. The government had simply decided he had to be detained, and detained him.

One of Ashcroft's closest aides was asked by the author a few days later what protection any American had if someone like Padilla could be arrested on American soil and held secretly just on the government's say-so.

After first correcting his questioner for not using Padilla's Muslim name, he answered, "Well, I guess his family could speak out if he's missing, and if that creates a political furor, then the President would be accountable at the next election."

Was that the only protection?

"That and the good faith of the people who hold these offices," he replied.

In his own cheerful way, Kevin McCabe grew exasperated with Washington. It wasn't that he was bothered by the just announced proposal that Customs be moved out of Treasury and into the new Department of Homeland Security. That didn't matter much to him. As far as he was concerned, he already worked well with his friends at INS and the Coast Guard. Rather, it was that Customs headquarters in Washington was insisting that he try a new system for deciding on high-risk containers.

This week they wanted him to implement a procedure, whereby his inspectors would check any container that scored over a certain number of points on the risk factors scale. Previously, he had discretion not to. Moreover, a few new factors had been added and given weights that he didn't agree with.

So he was being required to do many more VACIS inspections than he thought necessary, and was constantly on the phone to Washington talking about how the new rules should be applied or adjusted, all of which forced him to cancel a day off he'd scheduled for later in the week, and to give away the cherished ticket he'd gotten to go out to Long Island and watch the U.S. Open golf tournament.

But it was only a temporary problem. Because the Customs bosses had invited one of McCabe's inspectors to Washington to help them evaluate the experiment, by next week he'd have gotten the overweighted factors removed and he'd be comfortable with the revised rule that anything scoring above a certain number of points had to be inspected unless the points evaluator didn't think it should, and articulated a reason for not inspecting it to McCabe. "That's fine," he said. "It's better than what we had been doing, because it makes sure we're on our toes and accountable."

The President met with congressional leaders to discuss the proposal for the giant Department of Homeland Security, and was stunned to hear House Democratic Leader Richard Gephardt say that he thought they should be able to approve the plan in time for the September 11 anniversary. Although he is from the President's own party, House Speaker Dennis Hastert looked ashen. Hastert apparently knew that his members, particularly the turf-conscious chairmen of the various committees, would have wanted a lot more time than that to pick away at the plan.

When Senate Democratic leader Tom Daschle chimed in that he agreed with Gephardt, everyone could quickly see what was happening: The Democrats were doing what they had done with the Patriot Act, refusing to pick a fight with the President on a national security issue. They wanted this homeland security department resolved well before the November congressional elections, so that they could run against the Republicans on domestic issues, like the economy.

All day today, as the President, Ridge, and members of the White House staff took additional soundings on Capitol Hill, they began to discover that the President had been right: A big plan, indeed, looked as if it would be easier to get past Congress than a small one. Four key potential sources of opposition had been scoped out beforehand, and while it was still too early to tell for sure, it looked as if each was going to fall by the wayside with a whimper, not a bang.

First, California's Bill Thomas, the difficult Republican chairman of the House Ways and Means Committee, would be worried about Customs going into the new department because he might lose oversight of the agency—which he had now, because it was in Treasury, and Ways and Means had oversight over all tax collecting agencies. But Thomas was already talking about his own solution—have the new law wall off the tariff-collecting part of Customs from the rest of the agency, so that it could still be overseen by his committee. Sure, we can do that, if asked, the Bush people thought, although they were not going to get into the middle of Capitol Hill jurisdiction fights.

Second, Don Young, the blustery Republican chairman of the House Transportation Committee, loved the Coast Guard and the power he had as the committee chairman overseeing it. And as an Alaskan, what he loved about the Coast Guard most were all the nonsecurity functions it performed, such as ice breaking, rescues, and inspections of ships for environmental controls. At one meeting, Young declared that the Coast Guard had gone from spending 3 percent of its time and resources on border security to 55 percent—which most would have thought a good thing, but which he considered to be "outrageous." The Coast Guard's other functions have to be protected, he thundered. But then, he, too, offered his own solution: Write into the law language that would guarantee that the Coast Guard's traditional safety and environmental work would not be impeded. Sure, they could do that, too.

Third, when Harold Rogers, the Republican Transportation Appropriations Subcommittee chairman who was giving TSA such a hard time, was approached, he said that he couldn't go along with the plan unless he could keep jurisdiction over the whole new department—which was fair, he reasoned, since, after all, TSA was bringing the most employees in the new agency, and since he had expertise related to INS because he used to chair that subcommittee. That's for Congress to decide, the Bush people told him, passing the issue off to Hastert, who promised to handle it.

Fourth, and most important, they had anticipated complaints that intelligence gathering was now so uncoordinated—as illustrated by all the current media stories and hearings about failures to "connect the dots"—that all of it needed to be put into the new department. Lieberman was a principal proponent of this, but when Ridge talked to him and urged that it was a complicated issue in its own right that they could work on after they got this done, he seemed to sense that the senator would ultimately cooperate.

News stories this week would feature people like Young criticizing the proposal, and speculate about its chances. But Ridge and the other White House people pushing it began to get the sense that the press was stoking fires that weren't there, primarily because lots of people on the Hill wanted to let off a little steam publicly before they succumbed to the inevitable. Indeed, they were amazed that, although they knew they had lots of work left hammering out the details of a bill that almost every congressman and senator felt they had a piece of, the President's strategy to overwhelm them with a mega-plan seemed to be working.

PART FOUR

COMING TO TERMS WITH THE NEW ERA

# June 12, 2002–September 11, 2002

# Wednesday, June 12, 2002

"What happened to the flag?" one of Eileen Simon's neighbors asked. "You took it down. Are you upset about something?"

As her friend continued to ask what had happened to the large American flag that had flown over Simon's front porch since September 12, even if maybe what she'd read about the controversy over the victims compensation fund was what was bothering Eileen, Simon realized that the flag had become a symbol around the neighborhood.

She'd only taken it down after Memorial Day because, well, it just seemed like taking it down was part of moving on. Now, she realized she had to put it back up. She didn't want her neighbors to get the wrong idea.


Tom Ridge went from a ceremony where the President signed a bill that Ridge's staff had been working on providing $4.3 billion for bioterrorism protection and water and food security, to a meeting of a new Homeland Security Advisory Council of business and academic leaders, to a session with more than 200 members of the House to brief them on the proposal for the new department. There were lots of questions about specifics, some of them skeptical, but the bottom line, again, seemed to be that the proposal was going to survive pretty much intact. In fact, Ridge found himself in the surprising position of downplaying its prospects. He told reporters that while he was encouraged that House leaders wanted to pass the bill by the anniversary of September 11, he thought that the end of the year was a more achievable target.

All in all, it was one of the best days he'd had since he came to Washington.

In fact, things were going so well that Ridge and his wife had decided to proceed with plans to move the family from Harrisburg to Washington; they were already looking at Catholic schools for their teenage son and daughter. Ridge told those who asked that this didn't necessarily mean he was going to get the Homeland Security cabinet post, but that it did mean that he was likely to be serving the President for the foreseeable future, meaning he'd take that post, or keep the newly defined White House homeland security advisor's job.

# Friday, June 14, 2002

Ali Erikenoglu, the American of Turkish descent who was grilled in his home in Paterson, New Jersey, by a team of FBI agents last September, supposedly because a co-worker had heard him espouse anti-American sentiments, was reported on by another co-worker this week. Erikenoglu, an electrical engineer, has been supervising a job at Giants Stadium in the New Jersey Meadowlands, and apparently an insulator didn't like him. He had called the football stadium security people to say that a "Muslim on the job" was "acting strangely."

Stadium officials called the New Jersey state police, who arrived at the stadium yesterday to question him. Erikenoglu expected the worst. He still remembered the belligerence of the FBI agents, who had refused to remove their shoes before entering his home and had questioned him about his political beliefs. The treatment he received this time was quite the opposite. The investigators were polite, even sympathetic. This morning, the authorities decided that the insulator had fabricated the whole thing and removed him from the job.


Bob Lindemann had been delighted when he'd read about the proposed new Department of Homeland Security, which was going to include the Border Patrol and the rest of INS. Finally, he might get some bosses who weren't idiots, he thought. Ridge seemed like a smart guy.

This morning he got an e-mail from the national office of the Border Patrol union, of which he and his partner, Mark Hall, are the local officers. There might be something in the proposed new law, he was told, that could wipe out the union and all the protections they'd fought for. No one could tell for sure, because the Bush administration had not yet delivered a draft of the actual bill to Congress. But the administration's summary of the proposal (Falkenrath's white paper) that had been distributed noted that it would include a request for "significant flexibility in hiring processes, compensation systems and practices, and performance management."

The union promised more information as soon as it was available.

Maybe this wasn't so good after all, Lindemann thought.

# Monday, June 17, 2002

Customs Commissioner Robert Bonner came to Kevin McCabe's port to get a briefing on everything that had been done in the last few months. When it came time to have someone walk Bonner through a VACIS inspection and show him how the personal radiation detectors worked, McCabe was the one who did it.

"That's really helpful," Bonner said. "I might ask you to do the same thing for the President next week."

After Bonner left, McCabe asked his boss, the Customs port director, what Bonner had meant. She'd heard there was a chance that there might be some kind of event there with President Bush next week, she explained. But so far, it was just a possibility. He shouldn't count on it.

When McCabe got home that night he casually mentioned what Bonner had said to his wife, but added, "It'll never happen." She agreed.

Ashcroft was furious about a *Washington Post* piece this morning, saying that some Bush administration officials feel that his profile is too high. In the words of one unnamed White House aide, "The complaint is that he tends to announce every little thing."

The piece began with an account of Ashcroft's press conference from Russia when he announced the detention of Jose Padilla, the alleged dirty bomb plotter. "Only after Ashcroft's initial statement did Americans learn that . . . Padilla . . . was alleged to be merely in the initial planning stages of a plot and would not be charged with any crime," the *Post* noted, adding that "surprised" White House aides "viewed his remarks as alarmist," and that "Ashcroft's visibility has also fed speculation, denied by his aides, that he is eyeing another run for office."

The article included four pointed but anonymous quotes criticizing Ashcroft that were attributed to members of an administration where that kind of anonymous sniping is rare. One top Ashcroft aide quickly began trying to sell the idea that the story was the handiwork of Defense Secretary Donald Rumsfeld, Ridge, or both, because they were jealous of Ashcroft's prominence and close relationship to the President. The aide said, "Guys like Ridge and even Rumsfeld just don't get it. They get good press, but they don't see what we're up against. Ashcroft understands. He is the only one who is relentless. He doesn't worry about the press or any critics. He knows he is on a mission, a sacred mission, and the President understands that, even if the bureaucrats in this building, or in other buildings, don't."

It was a telling selection of words. In the suite of offices on the fifth floor of the Department of Justice building reserved for Ashcroft and his closest aides (none of whom are career Justice Department lawyers), little business card holders dispense hundreds of quotes from the scriptures for visitors to take home for inspiration. ("O God, thank you for salvation through Jesus Christ. Draw me closer to you, and help me trust you always, especially in times of trouble," reads one of the little cards.) Ashcroft is a deeply religious member of the Assemblies of God, and it now seemed that he had, indeed, become increasingly isolated from the rest of the government as he forged ahead on his "sacred mission." ("I am come a light into the world, that whosoever believeth in me should not abide the darkness," another card reads.)

Conservative Republicans, such as Judiciary Committee Chairman Sensenbrenner, disliked Ashcroft not only for what they considered to be policies that went too far to put government in a position to curb individual freedom, but also because of his refusal to consult with them. Now, even the not-quite-true-believers in the White House apparently saw him as someone to be reined in.

## Tuesday, June 18, 2002

Schumer finally got Senate approval of terrorism insurance. After nearly a week of parliamentary maneuvering, and with former Trent Lott aide-turned-lobbyist David Crane a key figure working behind the scenes, a deal was put together that included some tort reform but not so much that the Democrats couldn't swallow it. The result was a piece of highly complicated legislation. Put simply, the bill would have the government pay out 90 percent of all insurance claims related to a terror attack that cost less than $10 billion and 80 percent of the amount over $10 billion. However, in a concession to the tort reformers, none of the government's money could go to pay for punitive damages.

One aspect of the law that was odd was that in a key respect the Republicans had actually given the insurance companies more than most would have settled for. Many of the companies had offered to pay a premium to the government to get this kind of 80 percent or 90 percent backstop coverage. After all, it was the equivalent of the reinsurance policies they often buy—but had not been able to buy for terrorism coverage after September 11. Yet when Crane and others floated the idea, they found that the Republicans preferred providing the backstop for free, rather than putting the government into the insurance business, which they regarded as another step toward big government.

The other interesting sidelight to all the legislative wrangling was Schumer's bravura performance. One lobbyist with close ties to the Republicans marveled at how Schumer not only had total command over the details of the dozens of iterations of the bill that were floating around in the final days, but that he was an energizing, bipartisan lobbyist for his cause. He'd come off the floor and be greeted by Republican lobbyists representing business groups, huddle with them, then give them marching orders. "Go talk to [Republican Senator Phil] Gramm about that," he'd whisper. Or "Get [Republican leader Trent] Lott up to speed on that."

"Schumer ran it like I'd run a coalition meeting," the lobbyist recalled. "You know, it could have cut negatively. A lot of us don't like to get up in the morning and think we're coming to work to help New York. But he was really effective."

For many sectors of the American business community, the passage of the bill was a great relief. Two weeks ago, Moody's Investor Service had announced that it was reviewing and considering a downgrade of its credit ratings for some $5 billion worth of real estate loans tied to buildings such as New York's Rockefeller Center and the SunAmerica Center in Los Angeles. Meantime, amid continued reports of new construction projects being stalled for lack of insurance, a judge in New York had allowed a suit to go forward by the mortgage holders of a glitzy office tower in Times Square that was headquarters to the Condé Nast magazine empire. The lenders claimed that the building's lack of sufficient insurance put it in default on its loans.

Still, the battle was not over. Far from it. The Senate bill now had to be reconciled with the House bill passed last fall, which had provided loans to the insurers, not backup cash payments in the event of a terror attack. More important, the House, which was the center of conservative Republican power, had written in tougher tort reforms. The Senate Democrats would now appoint members to negotiate with House Republicans to find something that both could live with. That was an iffy proposition at best. In fact, the whole summer would pass with no agreement, as Schumer grew increasingly frustrated with his colleagues.

When Gale Rossides got the news that the just hired federal security director for the Louisville Airport had been recalled to Washington after he'd been caught taking his girlfriend through the protected area without having her screened the way everyone had to be screened—and that the press had picked up on the story—she couldn't help but laugh. "Can it get any worse than this?" she asked.

Larry Cox chortled, too, when he heard over the grapevine about the tarmac tour by the credential-less girlfriend. He loved the story, telling it to anyone who was interested in the TSA. For him the whole issue of these new TSA federal safety directors, who were to take over the airports, was an especially sore point. Cox had been kept in the dark about who was even interviewing for the job in Memphis. He was certain the appointee would be some gruff Secret Service type, who'd show up unannounced one morning, demand lots of office space, rule that Cox's own police force had to be taken off the job immediately, and quickly make a mess of things by emptying the terminals (which would now be the new guy's call, alone, to make) at the hint of even the most trivial security breach. "They probably brought that guy back to Washington from Louisville and tortured him in the basement, then buried him somewhere," Cox joked.

# Wednesday, June 19, 2002

Yesterday, Ridge and the Bush administration delivered their draft of the Department of Homeland Security law to Congress. Most national newspapers this morning emphasized a controversial provision that would require the FBI and CIA to turn over intelligence reports to the new agency, and also noted that House Speaker Dennis Hastert had decided to bypass all the committees that might take potshots at the bill by appointing a nine-person select committee to vet the proposal. That was a significant coup for the administration. Regular committee chairmen, such as Coast Guard devotee Young from Alaska, could file comments with the special committee, but they were not going to do their own vetting.

However, the hometown newspaper of hundreds of thousands of the nation's federal employees—the *Washington Post*—carried an additional story focused on something else. "Separate Personnel System Envisioned for Homeland Security," the headline in the *Post*'s "Federal Diary" page declared.

"The Bush Administration signaled yesterday that it probably would move 170,000 federal employees out of the civil service system once the proposed Department of Homeland Security was up and running," the story began.

The article then quoted the president of the American Federation of Government Employees (Lindemann's parent union) as saying that the proposal would bring back "the spoils system, undermining the nation's long-standing civil service principles that ensure the integrity of the government."

That night Lindemann got an e-mail and press release saying the same thing, and urging him and fellow union members to prepare to do battle.

About three months ago, the TSA go team members noticed one morning that workers were ripping up the carpet in a twenty-foot area around the corner from the Secretary of Transportation's office, on the dreary tenth floor of the Transportation Department headquarters. The next day, they noticed that in that spot the grade C government-issue gray carpeting had become a thicker, beige luxury weave.

The new carpet was just outside TSA director Magaw's office, which they saw, when they peered through the new double doors, had now become a plush, mahogany suite.

It was all part of an elaborate retrofitting Magaw had personally directed. It would have been difficult to understand, until one understood that Magaw was used to the same kind of pomp in the office he had had as director of the Treasury Department's Bureau of Alcohol, Tobacco and Firearms. At ATF, Magaw had decided that making the director's office a symbol of stature was part of his overall effort to boost pride and morale in the sagging organization that he had taken over. He was no less serious about giving TSA the culture of an important agency. In fact, if anything, laying a marker, or carpet, down that declared TSA was a big-league player was even more important to Magaw because TSA was new, and because, under the law, the head of the agency wasn't even a "director" of anything; his formal title was "Undersecretary of Transportation for Security."

At least that was Magaw's stated rationale for all the expense. Others could easily dismiss all that talk of culture and pride as an excuse to spend the taxpayers' money on personal comfort and ego gratification.

That certainly was what the *Washington Post* implied it was all about in an article headlined, "$410,000 Fix-up of TSA Offices Raises Eyebrows." The *Post* article went on to report that Magaw "will be questioned about his management of the agency at a hearing today before the House Appropriations transportation subcommittee. 'We're going to focus on the whole picture,' subcommittee chairman Harold Rogers . . . said yesterday."

Although the subject of the office never came up (Magaw's answer was going to be a mix of the pride and culture rationale, plus an explanation that eight other people were going to be housed in the suite), it was an excruciating morning, just like all of Rogers's other hearings, in which he cited TSA's over-hiring, and its failure to demonstrate that it was going to make the deadlines or to instill good management controls. The Transportation Department inspector general piled on, with complaints about out-of-whack pay scales that were plainly inaccurate or taken out of context, and the low show-up rates for screener recruits at Baltimore, which Rossides had already fixed. Unlike Fine at Justice, this inspector general seemed to feel free to issue reports without first getting comments on accuracy from the people involved.

Through it all, Magaw was wooden, gamely answering with numbers and promises. He never got angry. He never laughed. He just took it, like a Secret Service man standing in a hailstorm.

Back at Transportation headquarters, Rossides became almost completely undone as she began hearing bits and pieces of the various attacks. She and her now close friends in the office knew that much of it, such as the office construction and certainly the misinformation about pay scales, was coming from staff people at the FAA, who were bitterly jealous that TSA even existed. But that wasn't much comfort; if anything, that kind of sideswiping added to her bitterness. Combined with the *Post* article, the flaying her agency and boss were taking at a time when she was working harder than ever and had, she thought, been making more progress than ever, produced what she would later call "the low point of my whole experience here." She even went home that night and told her husband that maybe she'd made a mistake not taking that job running the federal training center.

For Michael Jackson and John Flaherty, the Transportation Department's deputy secretary and chief of staff, the game of whose hire Magaw was now stopped being funny. The hearing and the office suite extravaganza—which, of course, they had known about, though they had foolishly not appreciated that it was a public relations accident waiting to happen—demonstrated that Magaw had lost the one attribute that they had been sure he had when he was hired: impeccable credibility. He had to go.

# Saturday, June 22, 2002

Today was James Cartier's twenty-seventh birthday. Instead of a celebration, his family finally had a funeral for him.

At least thirty motorcycles pulled up at about 9:00 in the morning at Our Lady of Fatima Church in Queens. The members of the motorcycle club of Local 3 of the International Brotherhood of Electrical Workers wanted to serve as ushers for James, who had bought a bike just weeks before his death. They were soon joined by what must have been 1,000 people, white, brown, and black, who filed into the cavernous 1960s church. Some were in suits; others wore jeans and bike jackets. The politicians who had come to know the Cartiers weren't there, although Schumer and Giuliani had each made unannounced visits to the wake yesterday, as had James Luongo, the police inspector who had run the operation at Fresh Kills that had recovered James's remains.

Patrick Cartier, Sr., and his wife, Carmen, seemed to be holding each other up as they took their seats in the front row. Behind them followed their six children. Then came the grandchildren, some in strollers, some walking solemnly behind.

The eulogies were poignant. It was easy to see how James had nearly filled this church. The singing of "Ave Maria" and "Be Not Afraid" was truly beautiful. But there was something else. You could look at that family in the front row, clutching each other, bussing each other on the head, or helping each other wipe tears away, and you could see their love, indeed their inseparability. It was something so intense, even so instinctively physical, that only in that snapshot of them standing in front of the mostly empty casket could one fully appreciate what they had been saying all along about the true depth of their loss, and how anxious they had been to find some trace of James to bury.

# Sunday, June 23, 2002

"Themes? They don't need to give me themes," Kevin McCabe whispered to one of his deputies. "I saw those towers fall. . . . These guys are so nervous. I'm much better if I don't rehearse any of this."

"These guys" were the advance team from the White House, and they were paid to be nervous if every second of a presidential visit was not rehearsed, from themes down to which way the President turned to walk up to a podium.

Since early yesterday, McCabe's weekend has been taken up with preparing for what might be five or six minutes of presidential conversation tomorrow. First, the advance team wanted to go over those themes, then one of them stood in for Bush as McCabe briefed him on how the mobile VACIS machine worked. "The President saw a stationary VACIS on a visit to El Paso," the head of the advance team said. "So what you can show him that's new is the mobile unit, but you might want to remind him that he saw the other one in El Paso." McCabe rehearsed the briefing at least four times, then rehearsed his walk with the President over to meet some of his inspectors.

The advance team was easy, compared to the Secret Service. They had two problems. One was the VACIS machine, which is a giant X ray. They didn't want the President near the machine, for fear that it might malfunction and irradiate him.

McCabe thought they must be kidding. "Uh, it's kind of hard to demonstrate it to him without it being there," he said. "We need our toys."

They relented on that one, but the bigger issue was the Customs inspectors' guns. The Secret Service didn't want any guns, other than their own and those of any local police who were specifically on duty (and had been checked out). McCabe and the other Customs people argued that their guns were part of their uniforms, that it would look weird for them to be seen without them. The problem was solved when someone said that they could brief the President in full uniform, including the guns, but that after that, when Bush moved from the tented-off corner where the briefing was to take place into the open area where the podium was, McCabe and his people would have to remain behind and not be able to see the President's speech.

That solved, they did another run-through. Then another. McCabe came home that night with a bright red burn on his forehead from having spent so many hours on the pier in the sun.

# Monday, June 24, 2002

Since September 12, Mary Delaquis, the Customs border supervisor based in Pembina, North Dakota, had been eating up staff time by maintaining day and night coverage at remote ports of entry that had only been manned until 10:00 P.M. prior to the attacks.

This morning, Lawlor forged an agreement that promised to end this night watchman's duty. He put Customs and INS people in a room and got them to agree that Customs would quickly install motion sensors and surveillance technology at these less-traveled entry points. Signs would warn people not to try to pass through until Customs people got there the next morning. And the INS's Border Patrol would set up rapid response units that would answer any alarms set off by the sensors. In short, at least at these official, though lightly used, entry points, Customs was stepping in to do in the next few months what INS had told Congress it would take eighteen to twenty-four months to accomplish (supposedly because of those environmental assessment requirements)—installing sensors and cameras. And the Border Patrol was going to get to do what Lindemann wanted to do, respond to alarms set off by the high-tech equipment. This didn't solve the problem of people coming over the border between official ports of entry, such as at that dock in Detroit, or in rural areas, such as those around Delaquis's North Dakota ports of entry.* But it was a start.

Lawlor and his staff sensed something at this meeting that was different. The Customs people, who had always been cooperative, now seemed to want to cooperate even more. And the people from INS, who typically acted like schoolkids sent to the principal's office whenever they were summoned to a meeting like this, suddenly seemed much more eager to join the team. It was almost like they were trying to impress Lawlor and his people.

It wasn't hard to figure out why. With the Department of Homeland Security proposal now out there and looking as if it was going to get through Congress, and with Ridge and his staff at the center of that effort—indeed, with Lawlor having been mentioned by now in news articles as one of the members

---

*For example, a familiar cross-over route—on foot or in vehicles on dirt roads—within Delaquis's jurisdiction begins in the Russian-immigrant town of Tolstoi, Canada, and ends up in Lancaster, Minnesota. According to Delaquis, people could often be seen wandering around Tolstoi in broad daylight with maps, looking for the right foot trails or dirt roads through the woods into the United States.

of the small group that had put the guts of the proposal together—people who now came to meetings like this had to believe that they might be sitting across the table from one of their future bosses. The dynamics had changed, even without Congress having cast a vote.

---

"Good luck," Anne Marie McCabe said to her husband as he walked out the door at about 6:00 A.M.

"It's never gonna happen," Kevin McCabe said. "No way he's gonna have the time to stop and talk. Maybe I'll get to shake his hand."

By 7:00 A.M. McCabe was in the parking lot outside the Elizabeth Customs office, watching as crews finished washing the last of the Customs cars and SUVs. His squad, along with Customs inspectors from all around the port, plus INS officers, state police, and local police, were already assembled in their crispest uniforms. Soon, everyone other than McCabe and his briefing party were led about a half mile down the pier and through a tented walkway, then marched through metal detectors (they had not brought their guns), and allowed to enter what had become an outdoor theater of sorts, whose backdrop was the water, about 100 empty cargo containers (all searched and then searched again), and a Coast Guard cutter, below which was the presidential podium. Flags were draped behind the bleachers that had been set up off each side, and bunting and signs welcoming the President were all around. McCabe marveled at the stagecraft, scarcely believing how what was usually a grungy staging area for trucks loading containers had been transformed since Friday night. Then he walked back under a rope to the place off to the side of the podium (which was hidden from the audience's view by side panels of tenting) where his VACIS had been set up, and where he was supposed to meet the President.

By 8:00, the crowd was in place and the music ("Proud to Be an American . . . God Bless the U.S.A.") was playing. Bush wasn't due to speak until 10:45. McCabe did another rehearsal.

By 9:30, the morning clouds had burned off, and it was getting hot. McCabe cursed himself; he'd forgotten to put sunblock on, and the burn he'd gotten yesterday was already flaring.

George W. Bush is rarely late. Today he was early. By 10:25, the President, along with Ridge, Mineta, and Customs Commissioner Bonner, were standing in front of Kevin McCabe.

Bonner introduced McCabe to Bush. As McCabe began to give his spiel about the VACIS, Bush interrupted. "I saw one of these in El Paso," he said. "But this one looks smaller. Can you move it around?"

McCabe felt like kissing him. He wasn't going to have to do the speech. He could just talk, the way he loved to.

Bush asked if the mobile unit produced the same quality pictures, and what McCabe thought about the plan in the works to send inspectors to Rotterdam and other ports. He asked about the computerized points system McCabe used to decide which containers to inspect, and about container seals. When McCabe said he thought seals were not a complete answer, Bush asked about heat and light sensors inside the containers. McCabe was floored that the President seemed to know so much. When he showed the President his personal radiation detector and explained how it worked, Bush took it and asked still more questions. McCabe could now feel his forehead on fire, but he was ecstatic. Bush really cared about this stuff. Ridge and Mineta jumped in with a few questions. Mineta seemed particularly fascinated by the radiation detector. Ridge wanted to know more about what he thought about seals.

It must have been fifteen minutes, maybe more, before the President thanked McCabe and moved on to greet others, then mounted the podium just after 11:00 to give a speech that was a pep rally for the war on terrorism and the new Department of Homeland Security.

Lawlor and others on Ridge's staff might have found recently that the INS executives who came to meetings with them seemed much more eager to please. But in the bowels of the INS bureaucracy, they continued to march to their own drummer. Whatever cutting-edge human resources management plan the President, Daniels, or Ridge had in mind for the new department (which was, of course, to include INS) didn't seem to matter. A "Presolicitation Notice" from INS seeking to buy "Leadership Development Courses for INS Employees" was added this morning to the federal government's website for vendors looking to do business with Uncle Sam. It could not have been what Daniels was thinking of.

Here are, errors and all, excerpts from its seven pages of typical government gibberish:

"Leadership Development Center Dallas, Texas has identified a need to provide training to a variety levels of government employees, leaders, managers, and supporting personnel agency wide effectively. . . . All training dates are established and will not allow flexibility, which regards to changing of dates. . . . Target audience Senior Executive Service A complete and thorough understanding of the executive core qualifications (ECQ) as identified by the Office of Personnel Management and how they relate to the Immigration and Naturalization Service's Senior Executive Service (SES) program. Ability to write to each ECQ when completing an application for membership within the SES ranks. . . . Objectives are to demonstrate understanding of the communication process, recognize and understand available avenues of communication, identify and reduce message interference, eliminate communication roadblocks, recognize when one is not communicating and how to adjust the message and delivery. . . . Contractor shall demonstrate extensive experience writing for a government agency, i.e., position papers, white papers, project papers, letters, memoranda, and other government-related papers, correspondence and stress the adult or participatory learning model group and collaborative learning projects, and experiential learning methods. . . ."

Apparently, when he had gone through that advisory board review last month and been asked about the homeland security business's overall prospects, Ed Woollen made a good case. Hugo Poza, the operations executive who would have overseen the TSA contract that Raytheon had failed to get, was asked by Burnham this morning to leave his post as head of the company's multibillion-dollar Strategic Systems division to run a new Raytheon Homeland Security unit. At the same time, Woollen was appointed the new division's vice president for business development and marketing.

With overall annual sales of nearly $17 billion, Raytheon would not have made the move if CEO Dan Burnham and his strategic planners had not seen homeland security as having the potential to produce revenues in the billions.

# Tuesday, June 25, 2002

When you're litigating a multibillion-dollar case, you can never be too sure. Barry Ostrager, the lawyer for Swiss Re in its fight with Silverstein, was confident he had the facts and law on his side. Yet he was not about to take a victory for granted, especially since the judge, as sympathetic to the insurance companies' side as his ruling denying summary judgment seemed, had said that a jury, not he, would be the one to look at all the evidence.

It seemed certain that Ostrager, who considered himself a master with juries, would be able to persuade a jury with evidence such as that smoking gun September 12 note from Silverstein's own insurance manager that the "series of events" definition of occurrence was the "one we are working with." But there was one thing that was bothering Ostrager, and it had to do with the public relations pitch that Silverstein had been making all along—which was that if Silverstein won, there would be $7.1 billion to help rebuild New York, rather than $3.55 billion. What New York juror wouldn't want to get all that money to help rebuild his terror-shattered city, especially if the funds were going to come from a bunch of anonymous insurance companies, some of which, like his client, weren't even American?

So beginning about three weeks ago, Ostrager had begun staging what's called mock trials, in which an outside research company recruits members of the public who are likely to mirror a real jury and pays them to sit through a trial conducted by Ostrager's partners and associates. The trick is that the lawyers doing this have to be careful not to be so enamored of their own case that they don't put the opposition's best foot forward. Ostrager was so adamant about avoiding this that he even had his number two partner working on the case take over the role of Silverstein's lawyer at key points.

This morning he started getting reports of the verdicts in the first such mock trial, and he was cheered to hear that Swiss Re not only won, but that the jurors in their debriefings said they had been offended by Silverstein's overreach, and that to them this was a case about a contract, not about the future of New York.

With Judge Martin now pushing both sides in the real case to try to reach a settlement, and with Wachtell openly saying that Silverstein wanted a settlement, this hardened Ostrager's position. He wasn't so sure anymore that he'd even offer the full amount to be paid for *one* occurrence in cash, since the policy said that as long as Silverstein said he was rebuilding, rather than walking away, he could only get payouts of the $3.55 billion for one occurrence gradually as he presented bills he was paying for that rebuilding. In fact, Ostrager and his client were now getting so cocky that they prepared a press release of their own for tomorrow calling on Silverstein simply to abandon the litigation.

The ACLU submitted a white paper to the various congressional committees considering the new Department of Homeland Security. It urged that the proposal be changed or rejected in a variety of areas, including its intention to centralize intelligence information gathered by the FBI and CIA, and its plan to keep the Freedom of Information Act from applying to information that private corporations give to the new department in conjunction with projects such as critical infrastructure protection plans. These objections were predictable, indeed emblematic, of what their opponents believed to be the ACLU's continuingly knee-jerk flight from relevancy.

But a more telling objection had to do with the ACLU's attack on the department for proposing that its employees not get any of the protections of the federal whistle-blower act—the law that had precipitated the Office of Special Counsel's investigation that had protected Lindemann and Hall.

In fact, the question of whistle-blowers had never come up in the White House deliberations about management flexibility in the new department. Sure, a hard-nosed businessman like management and budget director Daniels might not be instinctively sympathetic to whistle-blowers, or, more important, to the litigation that can blossom when anyone fired claims whistle-blower status. But the subject just had not come up. And if it had, it is impossible to believe that anyone would have been tin-eared enough to favor proposing an end to whistle-blower protection during the same week that an FBI whistle-blower was getting so much publicity and praise. Yet by inserting the blanket clause that simply allowed the new Secretary and the head of the Office of Personnel Management to come up with a whole new human resources management system, the Bush administration had certainly allowed for the possibility that whistle-blowers might not be protected.

Indeed, the blanket clause had raised all kinds of other red flags. Prodded by the alerts he was now getting from his union, Lindemann thought the Border Patrol would not only be able to fire him instantly for talking to the press, but that they could lower his and everyone else's salary at will. Again, in theory, that blanket clause didn't protect him against any of that.

In other words, by not being specific—by building their own flexibility into their management flexibility clause—the group that had created the Department of Homeland Security in the White House basement had made a big mistake in two respects: First, they were going to scare people like Lindemann about things they needn't have been scared about. Second, they were going to give those with a natural stake in taking them on—the ACLU or the employee unions—the ammunition to do so by allowing them to scare their followers with all kinds of hypotheticals. The blanket clause was going to make them play defense, denying that they were going to do this or do that.

Indeed, just after the ACLU report was released, Ridge was asked about it while testifying before the Senate Judiciary Committee. He tried to put it to rest by saying he had never meant to exempt employees of the new department from whistle-blower protection, and he eagerly agreed to add a clause to the new law that guaranteed that.

Ridge appeared before two different committees, spending the first three of what would be more than twenty hours during June and July testifying about the bill. Not everything was as easy to deal with as the whistle-blower problem. He pushed back on the ACLU's objections to the Freedom of Information exemptions for private industry, arguing that the government was never going to get private companies to cooperate in developing a critical infrastructure inventory or protection plan if they thought someone could then file a Freedom of Information Act request and make all their security information public. And he resisted suggestions that now was the time to put the FBI's and CIA's intelligence-gathering functions under one roof in this new department. But by and large the sessions went well. Ridge accepted general praise for the proposal and deferentially deflected most of the more parochial objections from those who were worried about the plight of this or that favorite agency.

Larry Cox finally heard from the TSA about his rollout, but the communication just added to his frustration. He received a fax from a "program director" at Lockheed Martin, the contractor hired to design and manage TSA's national deployment of the new federalized screeners. The fax didn't exactly speak Cox's language. It described the program as "an overall optimization challenge that addresses schedule, staffing, logistics and performance risk" and promised that "in the next few days, a member of the Lockheed Martin team will contact you to arrange a specific date and time to begin the . . . activities at your airport."

That sounds nice, Cox thought. But I still have no idea what they're planning, much less when they're coming here.

# Wednesday, June 26, 2002

Movie star Ben Affleck apparently didn't work Sundays. So instead of making this one of his Sunday press conferences, Chuck Schumer stood with Affleck in front of the cargo containers piled up at the part of McCabe's port that is in Brooklyn and announced for a second time the proposed Anti Nuclear Terrorism Act of 2002 that he had held a Sunday press conference about in May. Why Affleck? Because he is starring in the hit movie *The Sum of All Fears*, about a terrorist smuggling a nuke into the port in Baltimore.

Schumer had gotten Republican senator John Warner to co-sponsor the bill, which called for money to develop a new generation of sensors to detect nuclear materials or radiological, chemical, or biological agents coming into ports or through tunnels and over bridges, and for funds for Customs to buy 100 new VACIS machines and develop new seals and sensors for containers. But in the coming weeks, the Bush administration did not officially push it, because Daniels's office refused to sign off on it. Yet in Schumer's mind at least it was there, in place, to be pushed in 2003 or perhaps even enacted sooner by being attached as a rider to pending homeland security department legislation. If not, it could always be enacted in a day if an attack of the kind he was worried about took place. Apparently Ben Affleck and a hit movie were not enough yet to drive home the urgency.

# Thursday, June 27, 2002

"When a company that big loses a multibillion-dollar contract, the least you can do is give the CEO a few minutes with the boss," is how one of Tom Ridge's aides explained the meeting scheduled between Ridge and Raytheon CEO Daniel Burnham. "Their Washington people seem like good guys, and maybe this will help them with their boss," she added.

"We're going over to spend an hour with Ridge. We've been asked to give him a full briefing on what we're doing," was how Ed Woollen described the same meeting.

The session lasted about forty minutes, but Ridge, who had more testifying on the Hill scheduled, only dropped in for about half of that, mostly to exchange pleasantries and thank Burnham for all of the company's interest in helping to secure the homeland.

For the rest of the time, Ridge's staff listened to Burnham, Woollen, and Poza describe all of the Raytheon initiatives in border security, intelligence analysis, and even a new one—nonlethal responses, or stun guns. Neither side brought up Raytheon's failed effort to get the TSA contract.

Ridge's people offered to help Woollen connect to an interagency working group being set up to evaluate new technology related to terrorism. What most impressed them, though, was the description of that first responder vehicle, the converted Chevy Suburban with all the equipment enabling varying emergency radio frequencies to communicate. Burnham remembers being surprised that Ridge, who was there for this part of the conversation, seemed conversant with the details of the interoperability problem and intensely interested in the product. Ridge's people promised to pass information about that on to Mike Byrne, the office's head of Response and Recovery.

Woollen saw the meeting as a necessary part of a long process of hundreds of small steps. But it was frustrating that they hadn't made any big break-through yet on all the plans he'd worked on since that weekend after the attacks. Besides, Raytheon stock was taking a beating, not because of anything related to its homeland security efforts—which, even had they all succeeded, would have at this stage been an insignificant part of this giant aerospace and defense contractor's revenues. The stock was down primarily because of issues related to litigation in another division, some jitters about the company's accounting, and general market conditions. Its price was now $37, which was way up from its $23.95 price on September 10, but down from a recent high of $45. Even if the stock decline wasn't his fault, Woollen knew that a big vic-tory in some homeland security initiative might have given the analysts and the market something to get excited about.

# Friday, June 28, 2002

John Ashcroft got an important reprieve from the U.S. Supreme Court this morning. The High Court agreed to take the government's appeal of the April decision by a New Jersey federal judge—in a case brought by the ACLU and a consortium of media entities—that INS could not conduct secret detention hearings without specifying the need for secrecy on a case-by-case basis. The court also issued an order allowing the secret hearings to continue until the case could be heard, which was not likely to happen for months.

Having gone back and forth since February with the insurance company on the question of getting Sal Iacono more of a payout on his business interrup-tion policy for the weeks when his store had been open but behind barricades, Hollie Bart finally got them to agree to cover all but two weeks of the period she was claiming should be covered. The result: a check for $5,395.

Sal was characteristically grateful, and effusively so, promising Bart and Lynn Geerdes (Bart's associate who worked in Chicago) that he wanted to take them to his favorite restaurant, an Italian place in Brooklyn. "I'm going to buy you the best champagne in the house," he told Geerdes, whom he had still never met. By now, Sal had pretty much lost the cough that had been bother-ing him so much in the early months after he had reopened. And his business was back to about 70 percent of what it had been.

Sometimes even Larry Cox is surprised by Washington's arrogance. Late this afternoon he finally got a call from Lockheed Martin to follow up on the fax he'd received Tuesday. It was someone in the project management office informing the Memphis airport CEO that they were sending a team to Memphis Monday morning. They just wanted to be sure that Cox would be there.

He certainly wouldn't, Cox replied. He and his family had travel plans for a long weekend and he would not be back until late Monday. "For months, I've been asking TSA to tell me when someone was coming, so I could plan it," he added.

Then I guess we could wait until Tuesday, the Lockheed man said.

"You bet," Cox replied, and hung up.

## Saturday, June 29, 2002

A September 11th Fund e-mail to all donors detailed how well the fund, co-founded by the New York Community Trust and the United Way of New York City, had delivered on its promises. Thus far, it had raised nearly $500 million—including more than $128 million from the Hollywood telethon the week after the attacks—and had dispersed $284 million, providing cash relief and other services to 45,000 individuals, including 3,800 surviving families and people who were severely injured, 35,000 who lost their jobs, and 6,000 who were displaced from their homes. The remaining $200 million was now being channeled into programs directed at long-term needs in the areas of mental health, health insurance for families who had lost it, legal and financial advice to surviving families, and job training and placement. All of these programs had been selected from the blueprint provided, pro bono, by the McKinsey consultants.

As had been true from the beginning, no money from any donations was being spent on the fund's administrative costs.

"Talk about my lousy sleep patterns. This thing," Anthony Romero recalls, "kept me up several nights straight, thinking about it after we went through it."

Romero and the eight senior ACLU staff people gathered this morning at an off-site conference room for a strange, five-hour encounter session. Led by a political science professor from the University of California at Berkeley who says he conducts multiday "scenario methodology" sessions for large corporations, the group groped for ways to make the ACLU more relevant by role-playing their way through the following disaster:

*It's November 9, 2003, and a low-scale nuclear device has been exploded in the port of Los Angeles. Suicide bombers have struck at the same time in London, New York, Chicago, Paris, and Berlin. There are reports that New York's water supply has been contaminated with a deadly chemical, and that office workers in major American cities have broken out in rashes.*

For the first two hours, the group left the ACLU out of the picture and instead assumed two roles each that were assigned to them by the Berkeley professor, ranging from Ashcroft, to Mineta, to Bill Gates, to Tom Daschle, to AOL chairman Steve Case. They then plotted what these people would do, coming up with possibilities such as a move to cancel the 2004 elections, a coalition (led by Gates, Case, and Mineta) to push for a national identification card, an initiative to implant a tracking chip in every immigrant, and the formation, by Pat Robertson, Ashcroft, and the NAACP, of a Coalition for National Values, whose platform is that multiculturalism is what has endangered national security.

Then, they put their ACLU hats on—and found that there wasn't a whole lot they could do. Even the allies on the right who had stood with them against the USA Patriot Act had fallen away because things were so dire. Romero wanted the group to agree to focus on fighting the election suspension issue politically, while ignoring the immigrant implant battle. We have to pick priorities, he argued.

But he couldn't get any agreement. The litigators on the staff basically wanted to sue to block everything. Romero protested that they'd never win and would waste resources—which were in particularly short supply, because the economy had collapsed in the wake of this multifaceted disaster, and there were few donors on the horizon. He urged that they had to try to pick whatever spots they could to rally supporters and potential allies. The organization, he said, had to stop thinking so much about lawsuits and start thinking more about political organizing—forging alliances wherever they could, even if it meant compromise. Again, there was no agreement.

Romero's main takeaway from the session was that he needed to get out there now and raise money to sock away for a disaster. They had to reach out and make new friends on Wall Street and in the business community, and even in Hollywood and in the media, so that they wouldn't be caught so flat-footed if something like this happened. They needed to stop thinking as if they were doctors in an emergency room, simply responding to whatever the government did by filing a lawsuit or lobbying to block something. They had to be proactive.

Maybe, but his staff mostly didn't see it that way. They thought the whole thing was just depressing or a waste of time. To them, their mission was, and always should be, to be the one organization that would stick to bedrock principles, however bad the environment was. That was their role, no matter what the real or imaginary crisis.

"These were," said their session leader, "smart, devoted people who really care about what they're doing, and who love and respect Anthony. But," he added, "they just didn't have a clue about what they would do, or how they should change."

Brian Lyons started a new job this morning. It was exactly the type of work he had been looking for. The construction company that he'd signed on with to do the cleanup at Ground Zero had landed a big part of a $300 million contract to rebuild the tunnels carrying New Jersey mass transit trains into lower Manhattan—tunnels that had been flooded when the Trade Center collapsed. Because the bosses there had come to consider Lyons's mix of administrative skills and willingness to get down in the trenches with the men indispensable, they had offered him a position as one of two project managers on the contract.

Thus, he was connected to the rebuilding of Ground Zero at the same time that he was supervising some 500 workers at slightly more than his pre–September 11 $100,000 salary. Better yet, it was a type of construction, tunneling, that he'd been fascinated with since he was a kid but had never had a chance to do. Most days, he'd still get to do what he'd come to love since September—go down in the trenches with the hard hats and make things happen, this time as they redug from Ground Zero to New Jersey.

Lyons's office was in a building that was diagonally across the street from where he'd abandoned his sister-in-law's car the morning of September 12, when he'd driven down to Ground Zero in search of his brother. He was back to wearing a tie and acting like a boss, but every morning he'd look across the street to where he'd jumped out of that car into a cloud of ash, and he'd feel a connection to a place and event that he did not want to lose.

# Wednesday, July 3, 2002

James Brosnahan had gotten the judge to agree to get the government to make the Army intelligence officers, guards, and even the doctors who had been with John Walker Lindh in Afghanistan aware that he wanted to interview them. The rules did not require any of them to agree to the interviews, only that they be asked.

Yet prosecutor Randy Bellows, who has a reputation as a straight shooter, had already made it a point to ask all these potential witnesses in an even-handed, matter-of-fact way whether they were willing to cooperate. There was no wink or nod discouraging them. As a result, Brosnahan had been surprised to hear that some fifty of eighty possible interviewees had agreed to meet with him and his team.

On Saturday, two lawyers on Brosnahan's team had interviewed the surgeon who had removed the bullet from Lindh's leg—twenty-five days after he had sustained the wound, and only after the government had finished interrogating him. The surgeon had said that when he operated, the wound had not healed at all since Lindh had been shot. To him, that suggested that Lindh had been malnourished and cold that entire time.

That and other interviews encouraged the Lindh defenders as they prepared for the hearing scheduled for July 15. There, they would seek to have Lindh's statements to all of his interrogators, including the FBI agent, suppressed. Their argument would be that the conditions under which the statements were made, plus the failure to tell him that he had a lawyer waiting to represent him, constituted coercion in violation of Lindh's rights.

A key witness still to be interviewed was the Army intelligence officer who had been the first to interrogate Lindh in Afghanistan back in early December. He was home in Colorado recovering from an injury, and Brosnahan and his partner George Harris had arranged to meet with him at an Air Force base near his home.

Brosnahan and Harris did not know what to expect. All they knew was that the intelligence officer's notes—cabled back to Washington hour by hour as his interview with Lindh progressed—had differed considerably from later summaries written in January. In particular, the summaries had left out the officer's account that Lindh had said that when he heard about the September 11 attacks he became scared and wanted to leave the Taliban.

Brosnahan and Harris were ushered into a room, where they shook hands with the young military man, who was accompanied by an Army lawyer. He did not play games; every answer was just the facts. And just about everything he said—from how polite, fearful and physically weakened Lindh had been, to his absolute confirmation that Lindh had said that when he had found out about the September 11 attacks he had wanted to leave the Taliban—helped their case. The officer didn't know what someone else might have put into some summary, but that's what Lindh had said. Better yet (from Brosnahan's standpoint), he added that Lindh had seemed "forthcoming," "not hiding anything," and like "he really didn't know all that much" except what he had heard from others—all of which had been in his write-up. In fact, the young officer (he had trained to do interrogations for two years, but Lindh had been his first real interrogation) volunteered to Brosnahan and Harris that the role of Army intelligence officers was to solicit anything the detainee might have heard—rumor, speculation, whatever—and that he had told Lindh that. That was why Lindh had told him about rumors he had heard of other planned attacks. But Lindh had made clear, the officer confirmed, that these were all second- or third-hand rumors and that he had heard them only *after* September 11. He had *not* heard any of those stories before while in training, as the FBI agent's report of his interrogation of Lindh had charged.

The FBI summary had said that Lindh had acknowledged training with Al Qaeda, Brosnahan said. Had Lindh ever said that? Had he ever even used the word Al Qaeda?

No, he hadn't, the officer answered, which was crucial to Brosnahan's argument that Lindh had trained to be a Taliban soldier, not a terrorist.

Brosnahan was encouraged and angry. Now he thought he knew why President Bush had on December 4 called Lindh a "poor fellow" who had been "misled." Bush must have gotten reports of those contemporaneous cables coming in about this interview, a hunch that the officer had all but confirmed when he volunteered that he knew his cables had been "sent to the very highest levels of the government."

It was only once the FBI interrogation took place after December 5 that the assessment of Lindh had changed. Then, he became a willing participant in the terrorist plot against his country.

How could the FBI agent have gotten such a different, more incriminating confession from Lindh? Or had he? At the same time that Brosnahan was getting this fix on what the intelligence officer had been told—and what he would now clearly be willing to testify to—another lawyer in Brosnahan's firm, aided by a private investigator, was zeroing in on the FBI agent. And a picture was starting to come into focus of a strange case involving the agent that seemed to suggest that he would have credibility problems as a government witness swearing to the bona fides of a confession that only he had heard.

# Thursday, July 4, 2002

Although he was still a White House coordinator, there was one operational side to Tom Ridge's job. Early on, he decided to set up a coordinating center at a separate location on Nebraska Avenue outside the center of the District of Columbia. The idea was that members of Ridge's staff would be fed information from all the other federal emergency operations centers—those of the FBI, FEMA, TSA, the Centers for Disease Control, among others, as well as state and local emergency coordinators—so that there would be one place where someone had all the information. Since the Nebraska Avenue facility had opened several months ago, it hadn't quite worked out that way yet, because some agencies like the FBI did not feed information into the center in real time.

But today—the Fourth of July, with the country worried about terrorist attacks, and a time when those working at various agencies had to have figured that Ridge might become their new boss when the Department of Homeland Security made its way through Congress—Nebraska Avenue became the closest thing yet to a nerve center for homeland security. A special watch commander was on duty from midnight on July 3 through 6:00 A.M. on July 5, and the Secret Service and the Department of Health and Human Services, which contained the Centers for Disease Control, sent representatives to be on duty during those times. Moreover, the center had logged in forty questionnaires from state homeland security directors detailing July 4th events in their states (ten hadn't responded).

As a result the center had entered 2,081 July 4th celebrations onto its database watch list, including 256 events with 50,000 or more people in attendance. All listed "points of contact" through which the center could coordinate emergency responses. Beyond that, the center and Ridge's office had worked with the Department of the Interior to coordinate protection and response plans for events planned on the Mall in Washington, at the Gateway Arch in St. Louis, and at Mount Rushmore in South Dakota.

Americans watching the cable news channels on July 4 were jolted to attention by the news flash that a gunman had opened fire at the El Al Israel Airline counter at Los Angeles International Airport, murdering two people before El Al security officials killed him. Worse, it was soon revealed that the man was an Egyptian, and Israeli officials were quoted as calling it a terrorist act.

The airport's international terminal was immediately closed down, which made sense until the area's overall security could be rechecked. What did not make sense—but illustrated the degree to which TSA had become everyone's favorite target—was that soon after that, various politicians took to the airwaves and criticized TSA for not having a security plan in place to stop this kind of thing. It was yet another attack on their agency that would make Rossides and everyone else at TSA almost giddy with gallows humor when they returned to work the next day. Why were the public areas at airports, where people went to see passengers off *before* they went through checkpoints to board planes, any more sacrosanct than train terminal waiting rooms, or even city street corners, each of which offered the same number of targets to a gunman? Unless the government was going to have checkpoints wherever more than a few Americans congregated, was there really a way to protect against this, other than doing whatever was possible to keep guns and bombs out of the hands of criminals and the deranged?

## Friday, July 5, 2002

Larry Cox thought that the man from Lockheed Martin who had shown up to direct the initial site survey of the Memphis airport seemed nice enough. He had arrived on Wednesday with a whole squad, which had fanned out around the airport to see how they could redesign passenger checkpoint lanes that Cox thought were working just fine as they were. After the others had left on July 4, the team leader informed Cox that he was staying behind for a while and would need a desk somewhere. Cox cooperated. But when he suggested that they meet every day or two so that he could bring Cox up to speed on what was going on, Cox suggested instead that he just send him e-mails. Cox was busy, and meetings would not be necessary.

## Monday, July 8, 2002

After the September 11 attacks, the Association of Trial Lawyers of America—the politically powerful organization of plaintiffs lawyers—had smartly decided that as a group they should take the high road. When the law establishing the victims compensation fund was passed, they organized a group, called Trial Lawyers Care (TLC), that would represent people making claims to the fund for free. It was hard to dispute the public spiritedness of that gesture, which aviation accident specialists like Kreindler ignored because situations like this were their bread and butter. Nonetheless, Feinberg knew that the group arguably had an institutional stake in seeing his fund fail, in the sense that if it succeeded it might become a model for the resolution of future claims outside the traditional tort system where the organization's members made such a good living.

So, when Trial Lawyers Care scheduled today's meeting with Feinberg to get his dry-run assessment of a sampling of their cases, Feinberg knew that he had better bowl them over with generous tentative awards. Which he did. He ended up spending nine hours in a conference room going through eighteen cases. In fourteen of them, he left them no reason to complain. (In four others, he said he needed more information.) While he refused to budge on the standard pain and suffering award, which was now $250,000 plus $100,000 per dependent, he took a broad enough view of economic damages (the payments for lost income) that almost every case got a tentative nod of over $1 million. One got $6 million. The trial lawyers were stunned. This wasn't what they might get in a full-blown trial; in fact, it was a little less than half of that. But there was no risk, and the awards seemed perfectly calibrated to account for that, as well as the fact that the claimants would not have to pay attorney's fees. Feinberg seemed to have hit the right formula, they told him, adding that they were certain to file officially before long and would hold a press conference declaring how reasonable his approach seemed to be.

Feinberg left the grueling session figuring, for the first time, that he had finally had a good day. He'd hit a home run, he told himself. Over the past few weeks he had set a target of getting fifty to 100 awards out by September 11. If he couldn't do that, he told himself, in his mind the whole thing would be a fiasco. Now, he thought he had a chance.

But one thing still bothered him; in fact, it bothered him more after today's session. The whole idea of the fund was that people would not need lawyers; they could come file a claim with Feinberg on their own and be treated fairly by a public servant serving as Special Master. Yet Feinberg could not avoid the reality that these lawyers were being effective, that he found himself giving more after they made an argument about some aspect of the earnings power of their client's loved one. In one sense, there was nothing wrong with that, especially since they were working for free. That's how the advocacy system was supposed to work. But it also meant that he, and his fund, risked being unfair to those who took the bedrock principle of the fund seriously and did not come in with a lawyer.

# Tuesday, July 9, 2002

Just four days after the Lockheed people had arrived to rearrange his passenger checkpoints, two people from Boeing arrived at Larry Cox's airport to begin planning the installation of the equipment to screen checked luggage for bombs. Cox was surprised at how polite and professional they seemed. They even had airport experience, having worked as architects designing baggage systems for American Airlines at many airports. By the end of the day they told him they were thinking about a plan that would simply put thirty or forty of the smaller trace detection machines behind the check-in counters, where TSA screeners would operate them. Even Cox agreed that, short of spending lots of time and money installing the big InVision machines downstairs to examine bags after they had been checked in, this was the most sensible idea, and would likely not cause delays. These guys seem to know what they're doing, he concluded.

However, they cautioned that the plan was far from finished; they needed to do a lot more work on it, and then it would have to be approved by the bosses in Washington. Still, this had not gone nearly as bad as Cox had feared.

The leading Democrats on the House Appropriations Committee, David Obey of Wisconsin and Henry Waxman of California, delivered a letter to Ridge outlining their objections to the Department of Homeland Security proposal. It was forty-four pages long.

For these Democrats it was really an exercise in venting. They had no chance of stopping the House, controlled by Republicans, from approving the Department of Homeland Security, nor, in fact, did they necessarily want to. They agreed with the general proposition that the department made sense. Rather, this was their way—especially their staff's way—of getting a few headlines by picking the proposal apart and finding some fun anomalies.

To Falkenrath and others on Ridge's staff and at the White House, the letter read like a recap of all the debates they had had. Putting FEMA into the new department would mean that an agency supposedly in charge of homeland security would now be in charge of federal flood insurance, the letter said. They knew that, and had debated it and decided that that shouldn't stop the federal government's only emergency management agency from being included in a department being organized to deal with terrorist attacks. By taking over the Animal and Plant Health Inspection Service from the Department of Agriculture, the new department would inherit responsibility for programs eradicating the boll weevil and citrus canker. They would even be running a website for missing pets. They knew that, too, and knew they'd get grief for it, but had decided that they had to take over the agency dedicated to dealing with terrorist assaults on the food supply.

The letter's chorus of complaints served to give the country, or at least those in the country who cared, the best arguments available against combining all these agencies into one department. In that sense it played an important role, providing yet another illustration of how the system produces, and arguably depends on, competing interests willing to assert themselves. But it also illustrated the bankruptcy of the Democrats' position, insofar as they had one. Their letter did a great job listing the problems—problems that the small White House staff group and then the PEOC group had debated for hours more than the congressional staff writing the letter ever knew. But over forty-four pages, it didn't suggest any solutions, or even stake out a position in opposition. Rather, it concluded limply, saying, "We need to work together to address the concerns raised in this letter."


When Grant Fine, a San Francisco private investigator hired by Brosnahan to work on the John Walker Lindh case, arrived in Tampa, Florida, to see a defense lawyer named Ralph Fernandez, he was hoping the lawyer would talk to him. Fernandez talked his ear off—about Christopher Reimann, the lone FBI agent who had interrogated Lindh in Afghanistan.

Fernandez had represented Rene and Jose Cruz, a son and father who had been indicted in Los Angeles in December of 1995 for a plot to overthrow the Castro government. When Fine had begun his assignment to look into Reimann, his check of news clips had discovered that Reimann had been the lead agent on the Cruz case—and that the case had been suddenly dropped without explanation soon after the indictment. When he had tracked down Rene Cruz, Cruz had said the case had been thrown out because the agent had "not respected my civil rights."

Rene Cruz's list of specifics included his charge that Reimann had supervised an interrogation of him that had lasted several hours and had been conducted at gunpoint in a car, without his Miranda rights having been read, that he had been coerced into taking responsibility for the plot in exchange for leniency for his elderly father, who was handcuffed outside to a chair while Rene was questioned, and that the confession he was forced to sign went beyond what he had actually said.

After hinting that there was even more to the case than that, which would explain why it had been dropped so suddenly, Rene Cruz had told the private eye that he should contact his lawyer, Fernandez. When Fine called Fernandez, he volunteered that he had broad connections to the anti-Castro Cuban-American community, and that he might have a significant story to tell them about Reimann.

So Fine had flown to Tampa to see Fernandez. Now, he heard a bizarre tale that not only had Reimann allegedly supervised the questioning of Rene Cruz at gunpoint without reading him his rights, but that he had also refused Cruz's offer of evidence that there were Cuban spies who had infiltrated the FBI. And supposedly, when Fernandez had threatened to make those spy accusations public, the FBI had dropped the case, releasing Cruz Senior and Junior, firing one of the other agents who had worked the case—and transferring Reimann out of Los Angeles until he had ended up as the FBI attaché in Pakistan.

Brosnahan had already decided to call Rene Cruz as a witness at the July 15 hearing over whether Lindh's confession to Reimann should be suppressed. The goal now was to buttress that testimony by getting Fernandez to let Cruz sign an affidavit that would get all of this in writing. But Fernandez was cagey. He agreed to work with Fine on a draft, but refused to promise that he'd allow it to be submitted as a supplement to Cruz's testimony.

When he got a telephone report of his investigator's discussion with Fernandez, Brosnahan didn't know whether the whole story about the spies was too preposterous to try to put in front of the judge. It needed a lot more vetting, if any could be done, and fast. But even now, he felt he could use some of it to lob a few questions at Reimann, who was scheduled to be the star witness at the Monday hearing. And certainly he'd use the accusation about how Cruz had been questioned and how Reimann had allegedly embellished his confession.

# Wednesday, July 10, 2002

On his way to testify before another Senate committee, Tom Ridge dropped in on a "Homeland Security Small Business" exposition in a banquet hall at one of the Senate office buildings. Ridge had consistently said that private enterprise would have a major role in protecting the homeland, and his staff had helped to make this event happen. In essence it was like a high school science fair, only the exhibitors were businesses, large and small, with products that they wanted to introduce to members of Congress and their staffs, as well as to procurement and policy people from agencies like Customs, INS, the Coast Guard, and the Pentagon.

Ridge made the rounds of the fifty-two exhibitors stuffed into the room, chatting them up and thanking them for getting involved. Although the exposition's organizers screened out the more bizarre companies that had applied to exhibit, the room still featured a range of products that made it a kind of museum of the American entrepreneurial spirit. With Ridge's office budgeted to spend $37 billion this year on homeland security, and with dozens of state and local governments, plus private corporations, slated to spend billions more, there had been a stampede from the private sector to get in on the action. The room offered a vivid sampling of those who had joined the race. There was, for example, the man from Bethesda, Maryland, showing off the "Tooth Phone," whose literature touted it as a "Tooth Actuator Sensor" system that made it the perfect "two-way, hand-free wireless communication system," whose applications included "High Noise Environments" and "Under Bio-Chem Masks."

Another exhibitor was selling a software program that colleges and universities could buy to handle all the paperwork they were going to have to do to comply with the new regulations about student visas that Ridge's office was pushing the INS to complete. Others were promoting sensors that could detect biological, chemical, or radiological weapons; space-walk-like suits to protect first responders from everything imaginable; portable decontamination showers; consulting services that would do security audits and upgrades for offices, factories, and other corporate facilities; a suspender hookup for firefighters that could allow a helicopter to hoist them to safety; and a skin cream that could be rubbed on to protect against anthrax.

One of the larger exhibits belonged to a company called Ion Track. Ridge didn't spend time walking through its archway-like machine that sounded an alarm if it detected traces of explosives. If he had, he'd have been reminded of a whispered-about gap in the current system of airport security. Carry-on bags are X-rayed, and the X-ray picture on the monitor will show both guns and most types of bomb materials, including plastic explosives. But the portals, or metal detectors, Americans now walk through at airport checkpoints only sound an alarm if they detect a gun or any other metal object. That's why people now have to be pulled out of the line at random and hand-searched; a plastic explosive carried in a pocket or strapped to someone's body would not be detected by the metal detector. It's also why Richard Reid was able to get on that American Airlines flight from Paris with a shoe bomb.

In fact, Magistri saw this same security gap at the checkpoints as a potential market for a small InVision type of machine that would use its CAT scan technology, rather than trace detection, to catch passengers trying to carry on explosives.

Neither Magistri nor anyone else from InVision was at the Senate exposition showing off InVision's explosive detectors, probably because their only potential American customer, TSA, was already buying. But the next generation of the competition was there. One of the larger exhibitors was a company called Ancore, which was marketing something called the Ancore Cargo Inspector. It was a truck filled with computer equipment and sensors that used a new technology (called pulsed fast neutron analysis) to do a combination of what the InVision machine did to detect explosives by computing the density and consistency of the materials inside a container, and what those VACIS machines used by McCabe at the port did to check for inconsistencies, or anomalies, in the density of what's inside. The sales materials boasted that it could go anywhere, beam its sensors at any type of truck or container, and get an instant threat assessment. If it was that good, then some smaller version of Ancore's Cargo Inspector could be used to screen luggage much faster than an InVision machine. In fact, Jackson already had a Transportation Department team assessing it for just that purpose. Or, the larger unit could be used to screen dozens of bags grouped together in one cargo container. Thus, after a big push from one of the company's hometown senators, Customs was preparing to test an Ancore truck as a replacement for the VACIS machines in El Paso.

The Ancore man at the exhibit said that the truck-size unit currently sold for a whopping $9 million to $10 million. But if it was as fast and as accurate as the sales material claimed, it could be more cost efficient than InVision's best unit.

Magistri dismissed the Ancore technology as too expensive and too bulky to work at airports, if it worked at all. (Some researchers who have studied it say it doesn't.) The more important point was that in this one room there was more than enough evidence of the continuing challenges Magistri faced—indeed, that any entrepreneur who tries to make his way in the world with superior technology always faces, and what makes any stock analyst's report about his company so iffy. If Ancore wasn't about to become Magistri's next nightmare, maybe it was one of the two trace detection companies over in the next aisle. Or maybe it was that consulting company down near the front that promised to help the government and big business find the most efficient solutions to the most expensive homeland security challenges. Worse, as Magistri knew too well, overlaid against these competitive technology threats was the obstacle course of a different kind he faced as he tried to navigate his way around the rest of this Senate office building and the other offices on Capitol Hill and at TSA and the White House, where his hydra-headed lead customer would decide his fate.


As Ridge proceeded upstairs to testify before another Senate committee, his appearances began to take on a routine that seemed like a ritual tribal dance, in which the executive and legislative branches circled each other solemnly, gave the other side its due, and moved on. Ridge, accompanied by only one or two aides, would make a brief speech saying how pleased he was to be there. The two or three senators out of the dozen or so committee members in the room would then give their own five- or ten-minute speeches outlining some pet concern. Ridge would listen carefully, or at least give the impression of doing so. Then, using no notes, he'd give a detailed summary of what he thought the issue was all about, and conclude by saying, "Senator, you've identified one of the challenges we face, and I look forward to working with you on it." In many cases—as with Senator Jon Corzine's questions about his own effort to write tougher security requirements for chemical industry facilities and shipments into any law establishing the Department of Homeland Security—Ridge really meant it, even if others in the Bush administration still wanted to side with the industry, which maintained that it would do all of that voluntarily. The senator who'd made the speech and asked a few questions would leave, one or two more would arrive, and the process would start over.

Meantime, on the House side of the Capitol, the legislators, especially the Republicans, seemed to be exacting more of a toll. Sensenbrenner's Judiciary Committee, which was anxious to preserve as much power for the Justice Department as possible, because it oversees Justice, voted this afternoon to keep the Secret Service out of the new department and instead move it to the Justice Department. They also voted to put only the Border Patrol and other direct enforcement activities of INS into the proposed new department and leave the rest in Justice. The Ways and Means Committee voted to keep all revenue-collecting activity of Customs in the Treasury Department, and Don Young, the Alaskan who chairs the Transportation and Infrastructure Committee, had engineered a vote in his committee tomorrow to keep both the Coast Guard and FEMA out of the new department.

Ridge's people and the White House congressional liaison office had set up a war room in the Executive Office Building to monitor these developments minute by minute. They had at least two regular meetings a day to keep up to speed. By the time they met late this afternoon, they knew that these votes, which seemed to eviscerate the still unborn department, looked a lot worse than they were. The catch was that Hastert, the House Speaker, had appointed that special committee with full jurisdiction to consider the new department and write the House's version of the law establishing it. That committee, which was chaired by House Majority Leader Dick Armey, was stacked with legislators who were not going to disappoint Bush and Ridge. These other, regular committees could vote all they wanted, but their votes would only serve to "advise" the special committee. The administration's four most senior cabinet members (Rumsfeld, Secretary of State Colin Powell, O'Neill, and Ashcroft) were going up to the Hill to testify tomorrow before the special committee about why all these changes were terrible ideas, and the war room staff was confident that that would provide the cover for Armey and his panel to reject these advisory votes. They were likely to get by with none of those changes, the war room group assured one another.

But they still weren't focused on the real threat to the bill, which materialized in the Senate's basement cafeteria at lunchtime. Standing on line with their lunch trays were two close-cropped muscular men in sunglasses, dressed in suits and ties. They looked like off-duty Secret Service agents.

It was Bob Lindemann and his partner, Mark Hall. Their union had flown them to Washington to lobby Congress to reject the Department of Homeland Security. As Lindemann, taking a plate of meat loaf with gravy, guided his tray through the line, he let another older, white-haired man go ahead of him. The man thanked him so genially in a thick Southern accent that Lindemann made a joke that "us Marines always try to be polite no matter how hungry we are."

"I was a Marine, too," the older Southerner said. They shook hands, while balancing their trays, then moved on to their respective tables.

Had Lindemann been a more experienced lobbyist, he would not have let that opportunity pass. His Marine friend was Zell Miller, the senator from Georgia. Within a few weeks, Miller would become a swing vote in the fight over unions and civil service rules in the new department, when he'd desert fellow Democrats and side with the Republicans against Lindemann's cause.

Sitting at their lunch table, Lindemann and Hall expressed astonishment at the situation that had brought them to Washington. They were both Republicans, as were two thirds of their fellow Border Patrol union members, they guessed. They had voted for President Bush and intended to do so again.

They'd been thrilled by the announcement of the new department. They admired Ridge.

But they were there because as far as they were concerned, if the bill Ridge supported was enacted, they would have to quit. How could they face France (their supervisor) and all those other bosses, who had made their lives miserable even under the current system's protections? France would be able to transfer them, cut their pay, or fire them at will. On top of that, there would be no union. It wasn't that the positions they had as local union officers were some cushy power base. They received no salaries, and didn't even get the money they spent on union activities reimbursed. But they believed in it as a forum to get management to listen. Why wouldn't Ridge want to keep that?

"If this bill passes the way it is," said Lindemann, "how could I stay? I'll go make more money being a cop someplace, like Long Island, where they pay more and the work is a lot easier. My career is over if this passes."

They weren't about to go down without a fight. They had a dozen visits with congressmen and senators scheduled for the next day and a half, as did nearly fifty of their colleagues. More were scheduled to arrive from across the country next week, and the week after.

Meantime, their union website was beating the drum. Scripts were posted for calls union members could make to their representatives in Washington. A cartoon was displayed on the home page of the union lobbying section, picturing a sign outside the new department's headquarters: "Welcome Homeland Security Workers. Forbidden Items: Self-Respect, Dignity, Union Membership."

How could things have come to pass that patriots like Lindemann, who stood for everything Ridge presumably stood for when it came to turning around agencies like INS, would now consider Ridge the enemy? Ridge and his staff had begun to believe that they had made a major mistake in how they had gone about seeking management flexibility. They should never have settled on the blanket flexibility clause, which allowed the unions to conjure up all varieties of hypotheticals. They should have taken the trouble to be specific about what they wanted and didn't want. That part was their fault.

But another part was the Democrats' doing. In the bill that Joseph Lieberman, the Connecticut Democrat, had introduced earlier in the year calling for a smaller version of a homeland security department, he had added a clause putting restrictions on what had been a President's ability since 1962 to declare that certain categories of workers involved in national security functions were not eligible for union membership. To be sure, there was a reason for this seemingly out-of-the-blue slap at presidential power; in January of

2001, Ashcroft had used that authority to strip secretaries working in federal prosecutors' offices across the country of union representation, because the prosecutors now had such important anti-terrorism responsibilities. The Bush administration argued that this was not an anti-union move, but, rather, that it had been required because some prosecutors were talking about a union, and under the law, the government couldn't bar them from unionizing without including their secretaries. The unions responded that the law didn't require that linkage at all. Whatever the merits, it was against this backdrop that Lieberman had inserted into his own homeland security department bill a provision that limited what had been the President's power to strip away union membership. The President now wouldn't be able to do it unless he determined that every job in an agency within the department had become a vital national security function.

With the Bush proposal seeming to strip away all kinds of worker protections, this Lieberman provision, which otherwise might have been negotiable, became something that the unions rallied around. It became part and parcel of their fight against the blanket management flexibility on salaries, promotions, and the like. Not only wouldn't they yield to that, they'd also insist on the Lieberman provision to protect unions.

To Ridge's staff and people like Daniels, the specifics didn't matter as much as the principle. How could they possibly agree to a law establishing the new department that actually gave the President less authority (because of the Lieberman provision on preserving unions) than he had now?

Ridge was becoming increasingly frustrated about the whole thing. For a Republican, he'd gotten along well with the unions in Pennsylvania. And he quickly saw that the people at the Office of Personnel Management who were staffing the issue—after all, this stuff was their core mission—and providing backgrounders to the press were simply making things worse. They kept offering examples of why they needed the new flexibility—such as, what do we do if we find a drunk Border Patrol officer?—that only made tensions worse. Ridge regretted not having worked on this more before they had announced the plan. His intention was to encourage and promote people like Lindemann, whose story he heard about as this debate started to heat up, not drive them from public service, let alone allow an issue like this to stall the establishment of the department.

In that sense, this issue of management flexibility—or employee protection, if you were Lindemann—began to resemble the role that tort reform (or assaults on the people's access to the courts, if you were a plaintiffs lawyer) had taken on in the fight for terrorism insurance. Like the trial lawyers, the unions had a stranglehold on the Democratic party, particularly party leaders such as Lieberman and House and Senate Democratic leaders Gephardt and Daschle who were contemplating seeking their party's nomination for President. Thus, a relatively narrow issue, when strapped to an issue of broader national interest (getting a new homeland security department), dominated the broader issue. The proponents of the narrow issue cared a lot more about it, and were willing to exact more revenge from those who went against them, than the broad cross section of the citizenry cared about the larger issue. Terrorism insurance had been dragged down by a squabble over tort reform, and homeland security was now in danger, real danger, of being dragged down by this employee protection issue.

One Democrat who could, of course, have appreciated the tort reform/terrorism insurance analogy was Chuck Schumer. Yet in part because he did not think the homeland security reorganization was all that important (he preferred concerted White House action on a few priority areas, such as cargo security, to spending all this time on reorganization), and in larger part because he was, like all Democrats, unwilling to risk alienating the unions, he never expressed a word of opposition to the Lieberman-Daschle position. In fact, although on issues he cares about Schumer is always willing to dive into the finest details and legal niceties, he hadn't even bothered to read the exact language of the Lieberman bill, where he would have seen that it actually trimmed the President's authority back from what it now was. He just toed the party line the way his colleagues had when he wanted terrorism insurance.

Lobbyists explain the phenomenon of a narrow-gauge issue dominating a more broadly important issue as a matter of political physics, in which the narrower issue will be controlled by the "elites" of that issue—those who care about it the most, and, accordingly, are willing to spend money on lobbyists. These elites can ram the issue through, or at least deadlock it. Either way, the elites, whether they are the NRA or the unions, will dominate the issue, unless and until something happens, or some proponents are effective enough, so that the public rises up to force the politicians to abandon the elites.

Which is another way of saying that a terrorist attack on Monday would have made the Democrats and Republicans work something out by Tuesday.

That hadn't happened yet. So Lindemann and Hall finished lunch and prepared to walk the halls of Congress, talking about their plight as patriotic whistle-blowers who were about to be robbed of the scant protection they now had.

Ridge, with an increasingly frustrated Falkenrath and longtime staff chief Mark Holman acting as his principal deputies, would try to counter that by working with the House Republicans to agree on the stripped-down specifics of what was meant by management flexibility.

But the rub would come with that Lieberman union protection provision. That was where, as Ridge and his people saw it, this skirmish threatened to escalate out of control. Lieberman and other Democrats like Daschle were stuck, having mollified their union patrons by supporting that union-protecting provision in Lieberman's bill earlier in the year when no one dreamed that any bill had the slightest chance of passage, because the administration then opposed a homeland security department. How could these senators, who would soon likely be contending for crucial union support for a Democratic presidential nomination, now back down on it? They were forced to draw a line in the sand that had them taking the ridiculous position that in the September 12 era the President ought to have less power than he had had on September 10 when it came to managing employees involved in homeland security.

As with all such battles, in which the elites know it cold and are willing to fight to the death over it, the rest of the citizenry would never see it that clearly, nor would they care much. In part, that was because the Democrats simply refused to admit that they were seeking to reduce the President's power. In press interviews and on the Sunday talk shows they just plain denied it. It was also because the Republicans, out of arrogance, laziness, or because they had bigger plans than they admitted, had allowed themselves to fall into a trap by starting out with that blanket "flexible management" clause that allowed for any and all imagined examples of employer abuse. And in part it was because, as with the Silverstein case against the insurers, the press tends to throw up its hands when it comes to deciding the merits of this kind of complex shouting match and err on the side of making it a "he said, she said" kind of story. The result was that to the public this was just another case of Washington being gridlocked again over some complicated and seemingly peripheral issue, where, as usual, each side blamed the other for the stalemate.

Lawyers from nineteen different firms piled into the courtroom of federal judge Lewis Kaplan at 3:00 to talk about a settlement in the Silverstein insurance case. Kaplan had been asked by his bench colleague, John Martin, who was overseeing the case, to convene the informal discussion so that the lawyers would not feel inhibited about discussing a settlement in front of the same judge who would preside over the trial if there had to be one.

While some of the lawyers representing other insurance companies spoke, the lead roles, as usual, were played by Swiss Re's Barry Ostrager and by Silverstein's lawyer—only this time his lawyer wasn't Wachtell, but a partner at Wachtell's firm who revealed that he was in charge of a whole separate team at the firm working on a settlement.

What was also interesting, if predictable, was that the Silverstein lawyer had no trouble suggesting a settlement number—$5 billion—that was about halfway between the $3.55 billion that would be paid out for a total loss on one occurrence and the $7.1 billion that would be paid out for two occurrences. Yet Ostrager and the insurance lawyers had by now hardened their position to a point that they were suggesting that an immediate cash payment for one occurrence would be as much as $2 billion less than $3.55 billion, because, under the policy, the $3.55 billion payment only got doled out over a period of years as Silverstein spent it to rebuild.

Trying to look past that posturing, the judge ordered the two sides to submit to him by August 8 a letter "not to exceed one page" telling him, in the case of Silverstein, the minimum cash payment he would accept, and in the case of the insurance companies, the maximum they would pay. Appended to that, if they wanted, could be a memo of up to ten pages, explaining how they got their number.

# Friday, July 12, 2002

Ken Feinberg was so sure that the victims' survivors would be better off coming into his fund than going to court that he had taken the unusual step of going to a federal judge to ask for his help in discouraging plaintiffs from suing. Because the law capping the airlines' liability and establishing Feinberg's fund required that any suits be brought in the same federal court district in Manhattan, Feinberg went to see the chief judge there and request that he ask any judge who got a September 11 case to add one simple procedure to the usual litigation sequence. He wanted the judge to convene a conference call with Feinberg, the plaintiffs lawyer, and, most important, the plaintiff himself. That way, the judge, by questioning what the plaintiff had been told by the lawyer, could make sure that the lawyer had given the client accurate information about the fund—which the client would now be forsaking if he went ahead with the suit—and about what the client's real chances were in getting a recovery through the court system.

Feinberg had tried to posture this as the judge's idea, but plaintiffs lawyers immediately saw his fingerprints on it, and they were outraged. How could he and a judge interfere this way in the attorney-client relationship? Just the act of the conference would undermine a client's confidence in his lawyer.

Nonetheless, the lawyers had little choice but to comply.

The first such conference came this morning, when a magistrate convened a call with Feinberg and plaintiffs lawyer Mary Schiavo, the former Transportation Department inspector general, who had filed the first tort claims on behalf of five widows. The widows also participated. The Magistrate asked each if they understood that their chances of recovering anything in the suit Schiavo had filed were far from certain, whereas the Feinberg fund was a sure thing. They all said they knew.

Schiavo would later explain that for these plaintiffs, the case was not about money, but was about getting the truth out about the airlines and the security companies. They had all had sufficient life insurance policies (which, of course, would diminish what they could get from Feinberg's fund) and other financial means, so that they were willing, indeed, eager, to take the chance of fighting in court in order to get at the truth.

Feinberg had definitely lost five claimants. By the end of the year, their case would be languishing in court, years away from any decision.


As James Brosnahan and his team were leaving the courtroom in Virginia after another skirmish with the prosecutors over the ground rules for Monday's pivotal hearing over whether John Walker Lindh's supposed confessions would be suppressed, one of the prosecutors approached him and whispered in his ear, "Don't leave the building. We have an offer we want to make to you."*

The two sides had danced around the subject of a plea bargain before. In one instance, a friend of a friend of Brosnahan's had relayed a message from someone in the prosecutor's office that they might be open to something. But nothing had ever even gotten as far as a real discussion, let alone an actual offer. In Brosnahan's mind, the prosecutors were prisoners of the over-the-top public pronouncements that had been made by their boss, Ashcroft, and had no room to acknowledge what the case really was—a violation by Lindh of an executive order signed by President Clinton prohibiting Americans from aiding the Taliban, which had been one of the lesser counts of the indict-

---

*The details of this account were provided by members of the Lindh side. One Justice Department official in a position to know about these discussions said they were "essentially accurate," but declined to offer any details of his own.

ment trumpeted by Ashcroft that also included a conspiracy to kill Americans and engage in terrorist activities.

Brosnahan thought he had good ammunition for the suppression hearing. Indeed, with the interviews with the Army intelligence interrogator, the guards, and the doctors, plus the potential wild card from the Cruz family about agent Reimann, he was feeling more confident about the case than he had since it started. On the other hand, at the court session they had just completed in anticipation of the Monday hearing, the judge had seemed to signal that he was inclined not to exclude Lindh's supposed confession to Reimann. Brosnahan figured he might win that back on an appeal, or that he could still discredit the alleged confession in front of the jury by raising all of the issues he was going to air at the suppression hearing—Lindh being held blindfolded on the stretcher in the metal container, Reimann having questioned Lindh alone contrary to FBI procedures, Reimann's supposed credibility problems, and so forth. But he also knew he was facing a conservative judge, conservative appellate courts, and what had always been reputed to be an exceptionally conservative Virginia jury pool. So he was willing to listen to anything the prosecutors had to say about a deal.

About an hour later, the defense and prosecution teams sat down in a conference room.

The prosecutors outlined their offer. Lindh would have to agree to say that he did not believe anyone in the government had deliberately mistreated him in captivity. And he'd have to agree to tell them anything he knew about the Taliban and Al Qaeda, and agree not to keep any profits from books he might write about his experiences. All of that was nonnegotiable.

To Brosnahan, that was okay so far. "We're listening," Brosnahan said, signaling that he was waiting for the punch line—the charges Lindh would have to plead guilty to.

Lindh, the prosecutors continued, would have to plead guilty to almost all of the charges except conspiracy to murder Americans. This would still yield prison time of forty to sixty years. It wasn't the life sentence he'd be subject to if convicted on all counts at a trial, but it was close.

Brosnahan got up to leave, saying he'd see them on Monday for the suppression hearing, that there was no way Lindh was going to plead guilty to anything involving terrorism, because there was just no evidence of that. "You know, you should check on your star witness," Brosnahan added, referring to FBI agent Reimann. "You've got a problem with him. A big problem."

What did he mean? one prosecutor asked.

"Well, you've got one of the most important criminal cases in the history of the country," Brosnahan continued. "And what do you do? You send in one guy, not two the way you always do. And he comes out with no written statement from the defendant, the way he's supposed to. It's just his word. And it turns out he's got a big, exotic scandal in his past involving the same kind of credibility problem, in a bizarre case that sounds crazy, until you find out that the whole case suddenly got dropped. That sounds like trouble to me. But if you want to litigate that in court, fine."

By then Brosnahan knew that the prosecutors knew there were problems with Reimann, if for no other reason than that a reporter for the *St. Petersburg Times* had just written a small article the day before, outlining how the Cruz case and a local lawyer, Fernandez, might end up playing a role in the Lindh case. Surely the reporter had called them for comment, and they'd seen the article. Plus, they must have checked Reimann's FBI personnel file in anticipation of his Monday testimony. Now they knew that Brosnahan knew about Reimann's possible vulnerabilities, too.*

Brosnahan also knew that they were aware of his successful interviews with the Army interrogator and surgeon, and he had heard that there was continuing tension between the Pentagon and Ashcroft's people over this and other cases. Some in the Pentagon resented how Ashcroft's bringing this case might embarrass the Army because of how Lindh had been treated—treatment that wasn't terrible for an enemy captive from whom intelligence information was sought, but which would be cast quite differently in the context of a criminal defendant being questioned.

At 11:00 P.M. one of the prosecutors called Brosnahan and said they might have a better offer. Brosnahan agreed that they would meet on Saturday, this time in Criminal Division chief Michael Chertoff's Justice Department office across the Potomac. Brosnahan thought things were moving in the right direction.

# Monday, July 15, 2002

At about 1:30 this morning, after the Justice Department had tried and failed through Saturday to get Brosnahan to agree to three other offers, Lindh sat with Brosnahan in his cell and signed an agreement. It called for him to plead

*The Justice Department offered no official comment on the Cruz case or Reimann's role in it. Ashcroft said he had "no recollection" of problems related to the agent's credibility playing any role in the plea bargain.

guilty to one count of aiding the Taliban and one count of using an explosive device (hand grenade) while committing a felony. The two counts added up to twenty years in prison, which could be reduced to seventeen years with good behavior.

The basics of the deal had been hammered out by about 10:00 on Sunday morning, but the two sides then spent hours exchanging faxes that ironed out the details, including a provision that allowed Lindh to go on pilgrimages to Mecca after he was released from prison, and another that allowed the government to detain him as an enemy combatant (apparently Ashcroft was learning to prefer this to criminal trials) if he ever engaged in terrorism again.

The prosecutors declared the deal a victory, but the only government official whose early assessment of Lindh matched the charges for which he had now been held accountable was not Ashcroft, who had called Lindh a terrorist who had conspired to kill Americans, but President Bush. Early on, he had called Lindh a "misled" youth who had gotten into something a lot worse than he had ever anticipated.

The early stages of the case—the fifty-four days when he had been stonewalled by the government while his client was interrogated without a lawyer under almost unimaginable conditions—had been ugly, Brosnahan thought. It had shaken his confidence in the whole system. He still believed that, in his words, "Ashcroft is a dangerous man," and that the government was being allowed to run roughshod over other defendants, such as Jose Padilla, the suspected dirty bomber being held in a brig. Yet in the end, in Lindh's case, the system had been made to work. The line prosecutors had honorably done their duty, and had allowed Brosnahan the ability to question those Army interrogators and others. Those people had played it straight, too. The press even played its rightful role in taking up the issue of Lindh's detention and interrogation treatment, and even in writing that article in the St. Petersburg paper about Reimann and the Cruzes. The bottom line was that Lindh had gotten the punishment he deserved, nothing more.

Larry Cox resented pilgrimages like this, but he was used to it by now. Lugging a $50,000 consultant's plan for cushioning any bomb that might go off in his airport's close-in parking garage, he waited in the lobby of the TSA headquarters in Washington to see a special agent in charge of explosives.

When he was summoned upstairs, Cox laid out all the evidence showing what would happen, and what wouldn't happen, to his terminal if bombs containing from 500 to 4,000 pounds of different explosives were set off from any of the 550 parking spaces that the FAA had ordered closed since

September 11 because they were within 300 feet of the terminal. Cox wasn't the only one who thought this was overkill. Senator Byron Dorgan of North Dakota was on the warpath because the regulation had forced the elimination of every parking spot at the Dickinson, North Dakota, airport. Thus, TSA had begun to consider modifications to the blanket rule, including accepting presentations, like the one Cox was making today, related to the damage that would be done from 300 feet and the changes Cox would make in the outer walls of the parking garage in order to cushion any blast.

After listening for about an hour, the TSA man in charge, whom Cox found to be "affable and really knowledgeable," said that, as he had explained to Cox during several phone conversations in the past few weeks, if Cox agreed to make the construction changes outlined in his proposal, they should be able to have the garage open by September 1.


Glenn Fine, the Justice Department inspector general, announced a new inquiry that could end up focusing on what had happened to people like Syed Jaffri.

Jaffri was the Palestinian seized after his landlord called the INS and held from September to April on charges of having worked while on a tourist visa. He was then suddenly released and put on a plane to Canada. Jaffri was among the detainees held at a special federal lockup in Brooklyn, where many, including Jaffri, were allegedly brutally abused during their stays.

A provision that House Judiciary Committee Chairman James Sensenbrenner inserted into the USA Patriot Act that somehow survived Ashcroft's convincing House Speaker Dennis Hastert to steamroll the Justice Department version through the House, required that Fine give Congress regular reports on its investigation of any complaints of civil rights violations arising out of the Patriot Act.

Fine announced this morning, in an interim report that received scant publicity, that he was not only continuing to review several charges of abuse that his office has been looking at since the fall, but that his office "is going beyond the explicit requirements of [the section of the Patriot Act asking him to investigate] to more fully implement its civil rights and civil liberties responsibilities." In fact, Fine's report declared he was specifically investigating the facility where Jaffri had been held to examine "three primary issues: the detainees' ability to obtain legal counsel; the government's timing for issuance of criminal administrative charges; and the general condition of detention experienced by the detainees, including allegations of physical and verbal abuse, restrictions on visitation, medical care, duration of detention, confinement policies, and housing conditions." Fine promised a final report in October.

In fact, by now the inspector general had deployed a full team to interview those who had been detained at the Brooklyn facility in Canada, Pakistan, or wherever they could find them. They were also interviewing the jail guards and the guards' supervisors, and the supervisors' supervisors. They even planned to interview people in the Attorney General's office, including possibly Ashcroft, Criminal Division head Chertoff, and Deputy Attorney General Larry Thompson.

Conspiring to violate a person's civil rights is a crime. If Fine believed the facts warranted it, he had the power to push the review up to a criminal case and use polygraph tests and even offer jailers immunity from prosecution in return for testimony about higher-ups.

Ashcroft's staff immediately grasped the significance of this, even if they didn't talk much about it outside their tight circle. Fine was taking it upon himself to delve into more than just some isolated instances of poor performance, misconduct, or even policies gone awry—such as he had found with the INS on the Northern Border. Ashcroft's people knew that everything about the detention of people like Jaffri was part of a centralized policy conceived and, in most cases, dictated from the top—the harsh conditions under which they were held, if not the tacit approval of their abuse at the hands of the jailers, as well as their inability to get ready access to counsel (because the phones often didn't work, or the directory of phone numbers for available lawyers was out of date), and certainly the timing of the decisions made about when to have deportation hearings for them, or how long to hold them after deportation. If Fine pursued his inquiry to wherever it led, it would likely lead to them.

# Tuesday, July 16, 2002

The Lower Manhattan Development Corporation—the agency made up of appointees by the governor and mayor that is supposed to oversee the rebuilding of Ground Zero—released six different plans for the reconstruction of Sal Iacono's neighborhood that had been commissioned from various architectural and design firms. Because the LMDC had a close, if wary, relationship with the Port Authority (both of which were ultimately controlled to some degree by Governor Pataki), all of the plans did little more than play out the Port Authority's game of chicken with Larry Silverstein.

Thus, the designers were all told that they had to incorporate into their plans the same 11 million square feet of office space, as well as the same 600,000 square feet of shopping mall space, that had been guaranteed in the original Silverstein deal. The results were worlds away from Schumer's idea of a "grand" plan. Almost nobody liked any of the designs, which looked like little more than a bunch of high-rise office towers squeezed around an undefined memorial plaza. Indeed, they were all simply less attractive versions of the still-under-wraps model conceived by Silverstein's own architect, David Childs, whose plan at least had a glorious transportation terminal at the base and those glass "markers" rising into the sky. Of course, Childs's plan also contemplated the removal from the design board of two of the office towers, because he knew that this game of chicken ultimately had to have a second move.

Community groups—which had held a series of town meetings to debate what should happen at Ground Zero—quickly attacked the plans, as did architecture critics. "What we got was what was there before, only packaged differently," the head of one prominent civic group told the *New York Times*. "These plans are all driven by hard economics. There's no heart in them, and no recognition of what we all had been led to believe would occur, that we would wind up with something wonderful on this site," added another civic leader, who had apparently not read the contract between the Port Authority and Silverstein.

Almost immediately, even those involved in commissioning and unveiling the plans all but conceded that they were not going to fly. The chairman of the LMDC said that they were only a starting point, and that a likely end point was a development with less office space. The Port Authority's executive director chimed in that the authority might look to take over more space beyond the Ground Zero footprint to accommodate the need to give Silverstein more space while lightening the density of Ground Zero.

For Silverstein, whose lawyers tracked the comments on the designs carefully, the negative reaction provided great leverage. Indeed, just the fact that the Port Authority and LMDC were soliciting designs other than one from Silverstein—who had not even officially released Childs's plan—seemed to give him enormous leverage in getting out of his contract. After all, how could anyone but his architect be involved in rebuilding the space whose lease he owned? Now, the Port Authority and LMDC's public statements about scaling back office space almost amounted to them telling him he couldn't rebuild as the contract required them to allow him to. Suggesting that they'd somehow provide other acreage near Ground Zero to get him room to rebuild all the office space was a nice try, but since it wasn't the same space, that would all have to be negotiated. For the time being, he'd stick to the line that he wanted to rebuild it all, and wait for them to come to negotiate.

# Wednesday, July 17, 2002

Larry Cox's lobbyists from the American Association of Airport Executives and Sergio Magistri's InVision lobbyist combined forces with the airline lobby to get a provision inserted into the write-up of the homeland security department law that Special Committee Chairman Dick Armey finished drafting. It would allow for a one-year delay of the deadline for the deployment of baggage bomb detection equipment. Magistri figured this would lessen the necessity for so many easier-to-produce trace machines to be used in favor of his machines. The airlines and airport directors like Cox thought it would reduce the chances of passenger delays beginning January 1, when all the new equipment would otherwise have to be installed.

Actually, by now Cox wasn't that worried about delays at Memphis. The Boeing people had surprised him by suggesting a plan, using those trace detectors, that seemed workable. But he wasn't sure, and, besides, he wanted to support his fellow airport directors. Two of the most adamant airport executives—from Dallas and Las Vegas—who feared the most extensive delays had gotten their Washington representatives (Congresswoman Kay Granger, in the case of Dallas, and Nevada Senator John Ensign in the case of Las Vegas) to sponsor a bill to push back the deadline.

As the administration's war room team had expected, the rest of the Armey draft pretty much followed everything Ridge and the Bush administration wanted. Rather than keep FEMA and the Coast Guard where they were, as Transportation and Infrastructure Committee Chairman Don Young had publicly demanded, "mission statements" meant to preserve those agencies' non-homeland-security functions were included. (This was exactly what Young had privately acceded to.) To mollify Appropriations Committee members, the bill allowed for the Secretary of the new department to shift only 2 percent of budgeted funds internally, rather than 5 percent.

As for management flexibility, the Armey draft did what the White House drafters should have done in the first place. It codified the specific areas of flexibility that would be allowed, giving management discretion on performance-based salaries, dismissals, promotions, and transfers. But it clearly protected whistle-blowers and allowed for legal challenges to personnel actions that were not based on merit, or that violated federal employment discrimination laws. And it kept the President's power to de-certify employees for union representation where it had been under the current law. The question, though, was whether the forces that had now been unleashed in this battle over union protection and management flexibility—specifically, the push behind the clause in Lieberman's bill that actually weakened the executive in this regard—could now somehow be reined in.

## Thursday, July 18, 2002

But for a split-second decision today by federal judge Leonie Brinkema, John Ashcroft might have been rid of the Zacarias Moussaoui case without having to worry about the alleged twentieth hijacker mounting a soapbox to defend himself. This morning, Moussaoui stunned the court by saying he had decided to plead guilty. However, because he only said that he was an Al Qaeda member, but not that he had participated in the planning of the September 11 attacks, as the case against him charged, the judge told him he had until next week to think about his plea some more.

At a hearing next week, Moussaoui would change his mind, and contend that he was not guilty of the charges and wanted to go forward as his own lawyer.

At about 10:30 Gale Rossides was summoned to a special TSA senior staff meeting at Secretary Mineta's office. Although she had often met with Mineta, who, like Jackson, was a determinedly hands-on manager, those meetings had always been scheduled well in advance. She sensed something was up. Thinking of a *Wall Street Journal* article the day before, headlined, "A New Bureaucracy Takes Flight; Air-Safety Agency's First Steps Look Plodding, Inefficient," that had slammed TSA yet again, Rossides thought that maybe Magaw had been fired.

She was right. Mineta told the group that he had accepted Magaw's resignation, and that Loy, the former Coast Guard Commandant who had been inserted as Magaw's deputy, was taking over. He hoped that they would all stay on to complete their mission, Mineta added.

Rossides's first reaction was sympathy for Magaw. She viewed him as a dedicated public servant whose great career had been tarnished by tenure at a job he hadn't sought and hadn't been able to control because of interference from people like Jackson. It was Jackson who had been responsible for limiting what TSA could tell powerful constituencies like the airport directors about their plans. Yet he had somehow managed to be loved on the Hill while her boss got lynched.

About a half hour after Rossides returned to her office, which now was across the street from the Transportation Department building, Jackson strolled in and sat down. He said that he knew she had had other career options and wanted to know if she was going to stay or go. Of course, he was counting on her to stay, he added.

Rossides looked him in the eye. "I came here because John Magaw invited me to come here," she began, then paused before adding, "But I'm going to stay here for the same reason I declined the FLETC [training center] job. We still have to get this done."

Jackson thanked her and went back across the street.

It continued to seem as if the various federal agencies that had once stiff-armed Ridge's office were becoming more cooperative now that they feared that the person chairing a meeting might be their next boss. Lawlor's staff got the INS this afternoon to sign an agreement with the Virginia Department of Motor Vehicles, whereby INS would begin a pilot project to verify the immigration status of anyone applying for a license. At the same time, the State Department agreed to begin a training program for Virginia's motor vehicle personnel to help them recognize fraudulent documents.

Eileen Simon was angry at herself. She'd agreed to let the New York Fox television affiliate come to her house to tape a report they were preparing for the first anniversary of September 11 on how a group of Cantor Fitzgerald widows were doing. Initially, she had a good reason for doing it, she thought. She knew that her friend with the large life insurance policy and the five children, who was still bitter about the Feinberg fund, had agreed to participate. Simon was worried that unless she, too, appeared in the report, all the widows would come off as malcontents. She wanted to speak for the survivors who appreciated everything that was being done for them—by friends, strangers, the charities, the government, and Cantor. She represented the mainstream view, she thought, and wanted that view presented.

But by 4:00, the reporter and camera crew were two hours late. They'd gotten lost, then had stopped to film another widow. Simon was angry. Worse, she'd worked herself into a frenzy of nervous energy. Why had she agreed to relive all of this?

By the time the crew arrived, Brittany had come home from camp. Now, she'd have to relive it, too.

When the reporter finally got there, she asked Brittany if she wanted to be interviewed, too, and before Eileen could stop her, Brittany, who was now thirteen, had agreed. "I just felt like I wanted to do it," recalls Brittany, who already has her father's dark good looks. "I wanted to talk about it."

After Eileen had gone through her paces, recounting that awful morning and then running through all the generosities extended to her and the family, it was Brittany's turn.

Was she going to watch television coverage of the anniversary?

No, but she was glad everyone else was.

The next part of the interview with her daughter stunned Eileen. Brittany told the reporter that until the police had come in December to tell the family that part of her father's body had been recovered, she had not thought he had really been killed. She just hadn't believed it was true.

Now Eileen knew why her children had been so angry on that day in December, why they had screamed at her for telling them that their father's body wasn't going to be found, because it had all turned to ash. Until then, they had quietly held out hope.

# Friday, July 19, 2002

Gale Rossides's confidence had been shaken enough by the events of the last few days—the terrible congressional hearings, the bad press, and, of course, the firing of Magaw—that she half expected to come to the special 11:00 senior staff meeting that the new boss, James Loy, had called and be told that they'd all been fired.

Nothing like that happened. Rossides quickly spotted what others around Washington had seen in the veteran Coast Guard chief. He was the whole package. Articulate. Blunt. But soothing at the same time. A tall, commanding presence. He seemed to be the embodiment of that cliché—"born leader." He looked you right in the eye and told you what was going to happen, and you believed it. And what he said was going to happen was that TSA—everyone in the room—was going to get on with their work and leave Congress to him, while they made those deadlines and delivered the best new government agency imaginable to the new Department of Homeland Security.

Rossides still felt sad for Magaw, but she grudgingly thought that maybe the change had been for the best.

# Saturday, July 20, 2002

Mayor Michael Bloomberg had a theory about what was ultimately going to happen at Ground Zero, a theory perhaps born of his background as a successful businessman, who saw some of the more democratic rituals of democracy as distractions to be tolerated, maybe even celebrated, but not taken too seriously. In Bloomberg's view, the various civic groups would noisily debate the fate of the property for the next year or two. Then, having let them vent, a real leader—in this case Bloomberg—would step into the vacuum and make the decision that needed to be made, so that the city could get beyond these messy debates and actually build something.

The ultimate in the inconclusive "democratic" first stage of the process was played out for three days beginning this morning at the cavernous Javits Convention Center on the West Side of Manhattan. Five thousand people gathered to tell officials of the Lower Manhattan Development Corporation their vision for Ground Zero. Despite the size of the group and their New Yorker's willingness to express themselves, there was one point of consensus. They hated those six plans that the LMDC had commissioned. So, although the Port Authority's chief engineer said that Silverstein "had a right to rebuild," he quickly retreated to allowing as how some of the office towers might not be built immediately. The authority's executive director even said that all of the office space might not ever be rebuilt.

For Silverstein, the Convention Center gabfest—which never discussed his own design for the new Trade Center, because no one had officially asked him for one—was one more sign that the Port Authority was fast losing its leverage.

In fact, by now, even Silverstein's own architect and one of his lawyers* could see a deal shaping up that might take two or three more years to be consummated because of the continued dances everyone would have to go

---

* This lawyer was not Wachtell, who maintained that he was going to win the case.

through. First, Silverstein would continue to lose pretrial battles in his insurance litigation—so much so that losing the trial would be a foregone conclusion. Second, the LMDC and Port Authority would have to throw in the towel and concede what everyone already knew—that they couldn't let Silverstein rebuild the same amount of office space.

That would open the negotiations. Whereupon Silverstein—whose pride really did make him want to be the kind of civic father who would keep a lead role in the rebuilding of New York, rather than take the money and run—would show off his design with those two buildings removed and that glorious open space for a memorial and cultural amenities revealed. Everyone would like it, or some version of it. At the same time, Silverstein—citing his reversals in court and his inability to rebuild the Trade Center as it once was because the Port Authority and civic concerns required that he not—would settle with the insurers and take a payout of something on the order of the original $3.55 billion. (He'd call that a victory because he'd adopt Ostrager's line that without completely rebuilding he was only entitled to an immediate cash payout of a lot less than $3.55 billion.)

Then, he'd negotiate with the Port Authority and his lenders to divide up that $3.55 billion, paying the Port Authority about $1.5 billion, as his contract seemed to dictate, and the lenders and others another $800 million. Thus, he'd end up with more than $1 billion in cash for himself and his partners on an original cash investment of about $125 million. But rather than pocket the profit, he'd negotiate a new deal with the Port Authority to take back only his original $125 million and plow the rest back into building out the office building part of his architect's design. So he and his partners would own those new office towers free and clear of their original cash investment, the Port Authority would have a cash payout from the insurance proceeds of about $1.5 billion to make up for the diminished rent they'd get from Silverstein on a new lease deal for less space, and Bloomberg and everyone else would bless it all as the perfect confluence of business and civic interests.

Everyone would be happy.

# Wednesday, July 24, 2002

The good news for Gale Rossides today was that the federal screeners had finally begun to be deployed at Kennedy Airport in New York. The bad news was that Pearson, the private company under contract to do the recruiting, was reporting terrible results with no-shows at Dulles and Reagan airports in

Washington. The worse news was that the administrative people who had made Rossides's life miserable since she had started at TSA, shuffling her around from office to office, phone number to phone number, had struck again. When she returned this afternoon from a trip to a Midwestern recruiting session, she discovered that her phone number had been switched again and that her old phone now rerouted any and all callers to her private cell phone.

While she waited to get that fixed, she sat down with Cliff Hardt, the executive on loan from FedEx who had taken over for Kip Hawley as the leader of all the rollout go teams. Together, they mapped out a plan to supplement Pearson by mounting a campaign to solicit community groups for recruits, and schedule media appearances that she and others would make on local television stations in cities where they were seeking applicants.

# Thursday, July 25, 2002

Tom Ridge's style of dealing with a disagreement was to talk and talk, and talk some more to those on the other side. But as much as he talked to Senate Democrats they just didn't seem to be taking him seriously on the issue of unions and the President's discretion. The administration was not going to go backward, he said. It was a simple matter of principle. They didn't seem to believe it.

So today, for the first time, the administration had to lay down the gauntlet. Presidential press secretary Ari Fleischer declared that the President would veto a bill that did not give him the necessary management flexibility. Later in the afternoon, Senator Lieberman's committee voted to pass a bill that had Lieberman's original union protection provision included.

On the other hand, they also voted to include every agency Ridge had proposed and not to include intelligence-gathering functions that Ridge had not wanted to be included.

In other words, the battle was now joined—not over what the new department would be, but over management flexibility. As with tort reform and terrorism insurance, the tail was now wagging the dog.

Syed Jaffri might be in Canada, glad to be far from the Brooklyn detention center where the INS had kept him in solitary from September through April 1, but his case was not going away. A class action suit was filed this afternoon by the Center for Constitutional Rights, a leftist legal action group based on lower Broadway. It charged, among others, Ashcroft, FBI Director Mueller, INS head Ziglar, and twenty FBI and INS agents (named as "John Roes") with violating the civil rights of "male non-citizens from the Middle East, South Asia and elsewhere who are Arab or Muslim" and "were arrested or detained on minor immigration violations following the September 11 terrorist attacks." Jaffri—the Palestinian who was seized for a visa violation after a dispute with his Bronx landlord and who had said that his face was smashed against a wall and that he was otherwise abused—was one of seven plaintiffs named as a representative of the class. His alleged mistreatment was recited in detail.

The suit potentially opened the door for the center's lawyers to take depositions and look through the government's files to find evidence of a conspiracy to violate civil rights, plus ultimately win damages at a trial. But that was a long shot that depended on a judge rebuffing the government's various arguments, including having used lawful discretion in its decision making and the need to keep information like that secure. What was not as far-fetched, though, was that the suit provided a road map of specific allegations and witnesses for Fine's staff at the Justice Department's Office of the Inspector General, as they continued to investigate the same charges.

Ken Feinberg finally got his first official awards out the door—to twenty-five of the first claimants. These included only people who had filed on their own—not any of the trial runs he had done with Kreindler or other plaintiffs lawyers, or with the volunteer trial lawyers organization that had been so cheered by his tentative reactions to their cases. The amounts he proposed ranged from $500,000 to $3.5 million. Now each claimant could accept the award, or appeal. Within six days, Feinberg would have his first five acceptances, including one man who had been offered $2.8 million after saying he would not take a penny less than $4 million.

# Friday, July 26, 2002

The House voted to pass Dick Armey's version of the Department of Homeland Security, along with his proposed one-year extension of the baggage screening deadline. That was no surprise. What was unexpected was a provision added at the last minute that capped the liability of two of the three large private checkpoint screening companies for any lawsuits stemming from the September 11 attacks. Not included in the protection was the largest screening company, Argenbright.

The provision protecting the other two companies had been added after lobbying by the industry trade group, which had tried to get the protection for all three, but had given up on Argenbright when House Majority Whip Tom DeLay declared that his members could not swallow that.

The policy argument the lobbyists made, such as it was, was that although the companies were probably protected by the indemnity they had from the airlines for whom they had worked, the protection was appropriate since everyone else involved had gotten it, and it was likely to take some drag out of the companies' stock prices. Besides, it was only fair—and a way to keep plaintiffs lawyers from filing frivolous suits—since the screening companies had not been shown to have done anything in violation of the guidelines the airlines had given them in screening the passengers who had boarded the hijacked planes.

When James Sensenbrenner, the Republican chairman of the House Judiciary Committee, had capitulated in October on most of his proposed amendments to Ashcroft's USA Patriot Act and allowed the Ashcroft version to pass, he had consoled himself that at least his committee would retain oversight over how the Justice Department used the powerful new tools provided for in the law.

Thus, on June 13 Sensenbrenner and John Conyers, the senior Democratic member of the committee, had co-signed a letter to Ashcroft asking a series of fifty questions regarding how the act had been implemented.

Sensenbrenner was stunned by the answers he received this morning. Twenty-two of the questions were not answered at all, and the most important questions—having to do with how many times the FBI had used the new powers provided under the act for activities such as searching library records or conducting surveillance—were brushed off as follows: "The number of times that the Department has obtained authority for 'roving' surveillance . . . is classified but will, in accordance with established procedures and practices . . . be provided to the intelligence committees in an appropriate channel." In other words, Sensenbrenner would not get the information. Ashcroft would send it instead to the House Intelligence Committee, which had not sought the information and had no plan or mechanism to oversee the enforcement of the Patriot Act.

Sensenbrenner was incensed, and vowed to keep seeking answers or, in the alternative, to subpoena Ashcroft. By year's end he would get an agreement to change the House rules so that his committee could share whatever so-called classified information was sent to the Intelligence Committee, but he would still find the answers incomplete. And, as a general matter, he would continue to be dissatisfied with Ashcroft's refusal to consult with him beforehand on any major policy initiatives. In his view, there would still be "no appreciation in the Justice Department of the role that Congress plays under the Constitution in providing oversight."

# Saturday, July 27, 2002

Michael Simon's brother, Scott, was Eileen Simon's kids' favorite relative, plus he was now one of the only adult male figures in their lives. So Eileen eagerly took them to Connecticut for his birthday party. The problem was that his voice and mannerisms so resembled Michael's that Eileen's youngest son, Tyler, spent much of the time with his hands over his ears because he couldn't bear to hear someone who sounded so much like his father. "He makes me think about Daddy, and it hurts too much," Tyler explained.

Tom Ridge was going to have to take his family on their summer vacation without getting his Department of Homeland Security through the Senate. Senate Majority Leader Tom Daschle declared the bill off the table at least until the Senate returned after Labor Day from its summer break. Daschle acted amid continuing insistence by the Democrats that their union protection provision not be negotiated, and a push by Robert Byrd, the veteran and cantankerous Democrat from West Virginia, that the world's oldest deliberative body should not be bullied by the White House into passing such a momentous piece of legislation so quickly.

Ridge still planned to move the family to Washington following the vacation. He'd made a deal to rent the Virginia home being vacated by presidential counselor Karen Hughes, who was moving back to Texas. But having the Homeland Security Department bill—and what had by now become his own much-talked-about status—in limbo when he got back to Washington in September was not at all the way he had planned it. He had expected that by then he'd have the kids set in their new school, and that he'd be poised to take the job running the new department—a job he had now decided he wanted. The Senate wasn't working on his timetable.

"Chubb Commercial Insurance had a banner second quarter, and its turn-around continued to gain momentum," Dean O'Hare's press release said, as he announced an increase of 31 percent in second quarter operating income. O'Hare added, "We see clear evidence in the market of a flight to quality, as businesses switch to insurers who have the financial strength to pay claims [and] a reputation for paying rather than denying or delaying claims."

Sergio Magistri was surprised to find that Michael Jackson was still clinging to the December 31 deadline. Jackson didn't care if the House bill on the Homeland Security Department extended the deadline by a year. Magistri tried to convince him, when they met for an hour in the deputy transportation secretary's office, that the House plan would, as he put it, "be a wonderful security and budget solution." It would allow 75 percent of the airports to be covered this year and the rest to be covered next year with a "rational high speed, secure solution"—his InVision solution, rather than trace detectors—that would be achieved "at lower cost with less passenger inconvenience."

Jackson, who repeatedly cited the continuing threats he heard about in his daily intelligence briefings, didn't buy it. They had to make the deadlines, or come as close as possible with the money Congress was willing to give them.

Jackson, who had the Boeing executives in charge of the rollout with him for the meeting, also griped about InVision's technology. "You need to get the speed up and the false positives down," he said.

"I can do that if you give me some visibility on Wall Street with some more orders now for next year, so that I will have the capital to spend more on R&D [research and development]," Magistri replied. His argument, that the government should spend more now on technology that wasn't good enough so that he could then have the resources to improve it, surely wasn't going to fly.

The real purpose of the meeting, though, was for Jackson and Boeing to make sure that Magistri was now producing enough machines to make the December 31 deadline and to spotlight any problems, such as with InVision's suppliers or subcontractors, that might come up in the final stretch. Magistri told them that in part because he had floated some $180 million to pay suppliers in advance of his having gotten orders from TSA, his production pipeline seemed on track. With a subcontractor now having ramped up to build one unit a day for InVision at its own factory, and with Magistri's facility producing almost one and a half units a day, they were likely to deliver an additional 300 machines by mid-December, which would bring their total for the year up to about 500. With another 350 coming from competitor L-3, it seemed that TSA would have close to the 1,100 units it needed for 2002, counting the approximately 140 that had been in place on September 11. Whether the Boeing people would get them all installed on time was another question.

Jackson and the Boeing people were happy with that. Unlike Magistri, the current year was all they were worried about.


During an afternoon strategy session of the newly formed Raytheon homeland security division, Poza and Woollen resolved to put a team together to explore whether they should attempt to get back into the airport security game by getting involved, maybe with a partner, in developing the next generation of explosive detection devices.

In fact, they were thinking bigger than that. Much like Ancore, the company that had had an exhibit at that Senate homeland security expo, they saw explosive detection not just as something involving luggage, but as an even bigger issue for ports and border security. One major project that they were now preparing a bid on had pushed them to focus on this kind of big picture. Raytheon was working on a proposal to design and implement a multifaceted security system for the 2004 Olympics in Athens, a contract that could be worth between $200 million and $600 million, depending on the options the Greek government chose. The project involved security at dozens of contest venues, the airports, and eight different water ports. Woollen and Poza would know by mid-winter if they had won it, but their initial readings of the prospects made them optimistic.

# Wednesday, July 31, 2002

"Somehow, this meeting was different," said Larry Cox. "For the first time since September 11, I was optimistic that we may end up with a common-sense security approach at the airports."

Cox had come to Washington again with a group of airport directors from around the country to be briefed by Jackson and the new TSA head, James Loy.

As he had with Magistri, Jackson provided an overview of the threat warnings he still received at a daily intelligence briefing. It was a prelude for a pep talk on making the deadlines. They intended to keep going full steam ahead. But he also said that because Congress had continued to impose a 45,000 full-time-employee cap on the agency—something Rogers, the House Transportation Appropriations Subcommittee chairman from Kentucky, had dreamed up—there was almost no way they could make the baggage screening deadline at every one of the airports.*

Perhaps thirty or forty airports would be delayed for a few weeks, while they resolved that, Loy added, which wasn't all bad because it gave them time to plan the systems at those airports better.

Finally, someone is talking sense, Cox thought.

But the November deadline for federalizing all the screeners who checked passengers would be met, Loy added, because they had tens of thousands of recruits that they were about to roll out all over the country.

Loy then introduced Rossides, who briefed the airport directors on the details of how the screeners were being recruited and trained, emphasizing that the poor results they may have been hearing or reading about were being corrected by supplemental media and community outreach campaigns that were starting to attract large numbers of applicants. The private contractor doing the recruiting might have been weak in attracting applicants so far, she added, but they did seem to be doing an excellent job using the materials she and her staff had created to test applicants once they did show up. Rossides also went over in detail the plans in place to have those roving teams of supervisors come to the airports first and work there while the permanent local team, a lot of whom would be picked from the private screeners already there who could pass muster, was recruited, tested, and trained.

Cox was skeptical. He hadn't heard anything yet about anyone trying to recruit in Memphis. However, he thought the woman knew what she was talking about. Her plan seemed to make sense. In fact, everyone at the meeting who spoke—and a lot more people were given the floor than at previous meetings—seemed to be making sense.

---

*In fact, Loy intended to get around the head count limit by hiring 8,000 to 10,000 part-time or provisional employees, who would not be counted even partially against the 45,000 limit. But he knew that he would still not have all the equipment in place by December 31.

For Cox, the best part of the session came at the end, when Cliff Hardt, the go teams leader, took him aside. Because Hardt is a FedEx executive who had been based at headquarters in Memphis until signing on for a year at TSA, he already knew Cox and had heard he was not happy about being kept in the dark about TSA's plans for his airport. "We think the screeners will get to your airport August 19, and we'll let you know as soon as we know if there's any change," Hardt told him.

You plan for the worst and hope for the best, Cox liked to say. Maybe this time he wasn't going to have to deal with the worst. "Loy," Cox recalls thinking, "seems to have this whole thing under control. This may work after all."

Yet Cox's newfound optimism wasn't based on an iota of change in TSA's actual plans or policies. As Jackson had said, they were still going full steam ahead. And at Cox's airport that still meant making both the federalization and baggage screening deadlines, both of which Cox had thought were ridiculously unrealistic only a few weeks ago.

Rossides understood the difference in Cox's attitude. Like Cox, she was wowed by Loy's performance at the meeting, at how attentively he dealt with what she calls "the important stakeholders in what we were trying to do. . . . He laid everything out to them, outlined all the potential problems, and had us explain how we were dealing with them. The substance was no different from Magaw. If anything, he reinforced everything we were doing. It just came out in a different way."


Just as his lawyer had feared, the government asserted in federal court in New York that because Jose Padilla was now being held in a brig in South Carolina his lawyer's habeas corpus petition—arguing that the alleged dirty bomber was being held in violation of his rights—had to be dismissed because this New York court now lacked jurisdiction. But federal judge Michael Mukasey ordered the parties to submit additional briefs to him so that he could consider the issue further, including not just the jurisdictional issue but the merits of whether holding Padilla as a combatant—with no access to lawyers or any other constitutional rights—was legal. "I'd like to decide everything at the same time," the judge told Ashcroft's disappointed prosecutors. "I want all the pieces in the shop before I start putting the machine together."

Thus, for now, moving Padilla to South Carolina hadn't worked to rid Ashcroft and his lawyers of a judge's intrusion. "This was a big win," says Padilla lawyer Donna Newman. "The judge refused to roll over for them."

It was also fortunate for Newman and her client that James Sensenbrenner, the Republican House Judiciary Committee Chairman, had not rolled over when he had been shocked by Ashcroft's initial draft of the USA Patriot Act, which had, according to Sensenbrenner, called for the suspension of the right to the habeas corpus hearing that had just been held.

## Thursday, August 1, 2002

Chuck Schumer had wanted to find an issue where he could get back on the liberal side of things when it came to law enforcement, but without backtracking on the hard line he had taken concerning the need to "recalibrate" the balance between individual liberty and security.

The answer was a proposal for a law, to be co-sponsored by Democratic Senator John Edwards of North Carolina, that would create a commission that would recommend guidelines for what Schumer's press release called "Snoop and Surveil" technology.

"It is 2002," he said in a statement announcing the proposal, "but if we're not careful, it will feel like 1984. With cameras on the National Mall, at the Statue of Liberty, and on the intersection of First and Main streets, it can feel like Big Brother really is watching. . . . No standards have been set for how these cameras should be operated. For example: Can you zoom in and read lips? Can you run every person attending a Yankee game through a database of fugitives and use biometric technology to see if you get any hits? Can you keep tape of every couple that walks hand in hand through Central Park? When my wife and I stroll across the Brooklyn Bridge, I'd like to be sure that some security camera operator won't know what I'm whispering to her, unless, of course, he has reason to think I'm a terrorist. The question isn't whether we should have the cameras. The question is where they should be targeted and how they should be operated. That's one of the areas where this commission will recommend guidelines."

The proposal was Schumer's way of recalibrating thoughtfully, and his press release managed to get Romero thinking Schumer sympathized with the ACLU, even if Schumer hadn't actually answered the questions he had raised in the press statement, much less answered them the way Romero would have.

Brian Lyons, his wife, and their two children began a vacation on Cape Cod with Elaine Lyons and her two young daughters at a house that had been donated to her for the week. To Brian, it seemed that Elaine was finally starting to unwind, laughing a real laugh as she played on the beach with the children.

Brian, too, felt relaxed for the first time in almost a year. He loved his new job, managing the rebuilding of the transit tunnels from Ground Zero to New Jersey. He felt healthier than he had in years. And every morning on his way to work, as he passed the corner where he had left Elaine's car to pick through the rubble in search of his brother, and crossed the street to get to his new office, he felt not just the horror of that day but also the sense of satisfaction that he had gotten in there and helped to clean it all up.


Tom Ridge had been a member of Congress once, and he, too, had once worried about turf. But the supplemental spending bill that Congress passed and the President signed today to augment funds already appropriated in this year's budget was the kind of thing that made him mutter under his breath. Embedded deep into the appropriation was a provision keeping discretion for the lion's share of grants for emergency first responders at the Justice Department, not at FEMA where he and Mike Byrne, his head of Response and Recovery, had wanted it. The bureaucrats in Justice and their allies on the Hill had prevailed. It was the trivial but important issues like these that drove Ridge and his staff crazy.

Yet a happier ending seemed likely. The law creating the new Department of Homeland Security that the House had now passed moved the entire Justice Department unit that would control those funds into the new department.

## Monday, August 5, 2002

Byrne and his Response and Recovery people were seeing progress on lots of other fronts. One issue the former New York fire captain and regional FEMA director had been pushing since he came to Washington in October was the need for various jurisdictions in the same region to have mutual aid agreements in place before a disaster struck. That way, many of the details— reimbursement formulas, insurance, lines of command, and equipment needs and compatibility—could be worked out sensibly in advance rather than have them unresolved or resolved piecemeal at the scene of an emergency. Like the FEMA grant money, this was another of those issues dealt with outside the glare of publicity that could end up being enormously important.

Thus, they helped engineer the signing of a pact among Virginia, Maryland, and the District of Columbia at a regional summit on homeland security convened by Ridge this morning. The agreement even included provisions for joint training exercises and the enlistment of private sector joint infrastructure protection plans, with FEMA serving as a liaison to the eight task forces organized under the pact.

## Wednesday, August 7, 2002

Eileen Simon had wrestled on and off with whether and when she should take the kids to Ground Zero. In December, when they had gone to Manhattan for a Christmas show sponsored by Cantor Fitzgerald, she had consulted no fewer than seven psychiatrists, psychologists, and other counselors before being convinced by one that she shouldn't do it—that the site, the sounds, even the smell of the place would produce an indelibly haunting memory for her children, rather than bring the so-called closure that some of the others had predicted.

Now as she faced the decision of whether to go there for the first anniversary ceremonies barely a month away, she was not so sure. The kids seemed better, even young Tyler, and the event promised to be something they might later regret having missed.

She talked to her children, and they said they wanted to do it. Certainly, it was better than going to school that day, one of them added. Her in-laws agreed. They should all go.

So Eileen and her family decided to do it right. They'd invite forty-eight people—in-laws, nieces, nephews, uncles, aunts, friends—to come to the ceremony, then have lunch in a private room at a top downtown restaurant. Her father called and booked the place with an $1,800 deposit.

## Thursday, August 8, 2002

There were no surprises in the fanciful letters the judge received from Silverstein and Swiss Re (representing the insurers) in which they were to outline how much they would accept for settling the one occurrence/two occurrences case. The lawyer heading Silverstein's special settlement team offered to drop the whole thing for $5.7 billion, which was a bit more than halfway between $3.55 billion (a full payout on one occurrence) and $7.1 billion (a payout on two occurrences). Ostrager said that Swiss Re and the other insurers would settle for $1.8 billion, which was their view of the discount they were entitled to for paying the one-occurrence amount up front in cash, because in a cash payout the wear and tear and other depreciation on the buildings could be discounted, whereas if they doled it out to Silverstein over the years that he actually rebuilt they would pay out $3.55 billion.

The dance was going to continue. There could be no real settlement talk until Silverstein had figured things out with the Port Authority and the Lower Manhattan Development Corporation—and lost a few more rounds in court.

## Friday, August 9, 2002

Although Gale Rossides felt reinvigorated at work because she liked Loy so much and could now see that they actually might get all those screeners in place by November 19, there seemed to be something wrong with her body. Her husband insisted she go to the doctor. When her doctor couldn't immediately figure out why she wasn't feeling well, he told her she needed to take a stress test, which, of course, was the test Rossides thought she'd been taking since January.

So, in between preparing a briefing for Loy on how the air marshals were being trained to use weapons in flight, and dealing with why there were still so many no-shows among screener applicants in New York this week, she was wired up and put on a treadmill.

A half hour later, the doctor told her that her heart was fine, that she was just overworked and needed some rest. She knew that.

## Sunday, August 11, 2002

Like the Lyons family, the Cartiers—parents, siblings, and the grandchildren—spent last week in Cape Cod, enjoying the beach and unwinding for the first time since September 11. To different degrees, Michael, Jennie, and their sisters, brothers, and parents still had an interest in what got rebuilt at Ground Zero, including the size and nature of the memorial. And Michael continued to update the Give Your Voice website with information, mostly DNA match statistics from the medical examiner's office, or news of an upcoming event for survivors. But for them much of the activity surrounding the tragedy of September 11—except their mourning for James—was winding down. Give Your Voice had given voice to the families and helped to spawn other groups of families now pursuing their own agendas. They had made sure the recovery was being conducted the way it should be, and then made sure everyone knew that. Most important, they had found James and given him a proper funeral mass at a service that he'd have been proud of.

From Michael's point of view, although he cared about the memorial because he felt for the families that had not recovered any remains and would have to settle on Ground Zero as their loved ones' resting place, he especially wanted to wind down his September 11 activism. His office was in turmoil, because its parent company, Cablevision Systems, was experiencing financial setbacks and was talking about selling all or part of the unit where he worked. As a result, he and Michele had put off trying to buy their first home, and he was thinking about other job opportunities.

This afternoon, two days after they returned from Cape Cod, the family had a barbecue at the home on Long Island where Jennie lives with her husband and their nine-year-old son. According to Michael, they invited "all the people from all the families groups that we don't dislike." They also invited the staff of the medical examiner's office to thank them one more time.

## Tuesday, August 13, 2002

Just when Larry Cox was beginning to soften on Washington, he was reminded of why he should still plan for the worst and hope for the best. This evening a woman came up to him at a cocktail reception to say that she'd just been hired to work at his airport as an industrial engineer.

Cox was immediately confused. "Really? Who hired you?" he asked.

"The Transportation Security Administration," she said, smiling brightly.

Their bureaucracy just keeps growing, Cox thought.

Cox was still smarting from a call he had gotten the day before from someone at TSA, who told him that they had selected the federal security director for his airport but that they couldn't tell him the person's name just yet, and that the squad of federal screeners would be arriving for their first day in Memphis on August 26, not August 19.

Cox's worries extended beyond his own tarmac. A few days before, US Airways had declared bankruptcy. The airline didn't have many flights at his airport, and his major carrier, Northwest, seemed to be faring better than most of its competitors. Besides, US Air was going to continue operations anyway. But its financial troubles were only the latest sign of what Cox already knew. While his passenger traffic was steadily rising, all the airlines, including Northwest, were struggling under the weight of rising costs, including all kinds of newly mandated security costs, and declining revenues resulting from the deep discounts they were offering. The cash and loan bailout passed in September had only been a stopgap, and not a fully effective one at that, because getting the loans was conditioned on the airlines presenting viable business plans, something US Airways had so far been unable to do. Now he was reading that giant United Airlines was also in trouble.

Cox's business was strapped to an industry whose fundamentals had never been good, but now seemed so bad that they were destined for a major, painful upheaval.

Thank God his biggest carrier was FedEx.


Ashcroft's lawyers encountered their toughest judge yet, in a federal courtroom in Norfolk, Virginia. The case involved Yaser Hamdi, who had allegedly been caught fighting American soldiers in Afghanistan. Like alleged dirty bomber Jose Padilla, Hamdi was an American citizen (of Saudi descent), and the government was holding him as an enemy combatant in a Navy brig in Norfolk. A few weeks ago, Judge Robert Doumar had ruled that Hamdi was entitled to meet with a lawyer, but the federal appeals court had overturned his decision, saying he should reconsider it in light of the deference the judiciary should give to the commander in chief in wartime. When Doumar had taken the case back, he had asked the government to provide more evidence beyond an annexed two-page declaration from a Pentagon official that had simply outlined the circumstances of Hamdi's capture. But Ashcroft had decided that the government should refuse, on national security grounds, to provide any more details.

Now, Judge Doumar took out his frustration on the Justice Department lawyer standing in front of him. Noting that the declaration didn't say how long the government planned to hold Hamdi, the judge, who was appointed by President Ronald Reagan in 1981, asked, "How long does it take to question a man? A year? Two years? Ten years? A lifetime?"

The lawyer said he couldn't answer that.

"Can the military do anything they want with him, without a tribunal?" the judge asked.

"The present detention is lawful," the Justice Department lawyer answered.

Although Doumar did not make a decision from the bench, the hearing did not bode well for the government, not only in this case but also for the Padilla case, in which a New York judge's ruling was pending. If anything, the facts in Padilla's case were more difficult for the government. Padilla, after all, had been arrested at O'Hare Airport, not on a battlefield fighting for the enemy.

# Wednesday, August 14, 2002

Tom Ridge looked on this morning as the President turned up the rhetoric in the fight over the homeland security department. "I can assure you," Bush told a Milwaukee audience, "I will insist that the new department be able to put the right person in the right place at the right time to be able to protect the American people, that we will reject any plan which has got a thick book of bureaucratic rules aimed at protecting special interests."

By now, Lindemann's view from the other side of the fight had hardened, too, illustrating just how confused and out of hand the whole fracas had become. He had no idea that his union's position, and the position of the Democrats in the Senate, would have actually constituted a rollback of the President's power. Instead he was fixated on what he saw in union mailings and on the website about all that might happen to him and his career if the new law passed the way the President wanted it. Rhetoric of the type that the President used today only reinforced those fears. To Lindemann, Bush's "thick book of bureaucratic rules" were the rules that had allowed the inspector general and the Office of Special Counsel to save his job, and that prevented people like France, his supervisor, from running him out of the Border Patrol. "If the bill passed the way it now is, I would have to quit," he reiterated, soon after returning from another Washington lobbying foray.

Yet the bill that had been passed by the House, which Bush now favored, contained the specific provisions for an inspector general and for whistleblower protection by the Office of Special Counsel that had protected him. True, the House bill provided for enhanced management flexibility, though in a narrower fashion than the administration's original, open-ended proposal. There was no denying that it did lessen the hoops that France and Lindemann's other bosses might have to jump through before firing Lindemann. Yet Ridge had said that the basic protections, including a right to appeal a dismissal, would still be there.

In short, although the differences had narrowed since the homeland security department bill had first been proposed, the two sides seemed to have grown further apart.

Bush's Milwaukee appearance was the beginning of what aides in the White House, particularly chief political advisor Karl Rove, thought should now be an all-out political fight. If the Democrats in the Senate were going to hold up a homeland security department over this, then Bush should force them to answer for it in the upcoming congressional elections.

## Thursday, August 15, 2002

A few weeks ago, Michael Cartier had been asked if his family would join in a case to be filed by a well-known plaintiffs lawyer against several Saudi Arabian parties who would be accused of providing the financing for Al Qaeda. The lawyer, who had won hundreds of millions of dollars in cases involving asbestos and tobacco, was going to hold a major press conference, Cartier was told, and the case was sure to rattle all the people who supported the terrorists—and maybe even end up winning everyone a lot of money. The prospect was initially appealing, especially to Michael's father. Yet after talking about it, the family decided they didn't want to be involved again in anything that high-profile having to do with the victims seeking more money. Besides, said Patrick Cartier, Sr., "I'll be long gone and my kids will be long gone, before a suit like that ever gets finished."

So the Cartiers were not on the list of several hundred plaintiffs when the suit was announced at a press conference in the ballroom of a Washington hotel this morning.

## Friday, August 16, 2002

Calling the case of Yaser Hamdi "the first in American jurisprudence where an American citizen has been held incommunicado and subjected to an indefinite detention in the continental United States without charges, without any findings by a military tribunal, and without access to a lawyer," federal judge

Robert Doumar in Norfolk again ordered Ashcroft's lawyers to give him more information about the circumstances of Hamdi's capture in Afghanistan. Ashcroft immediately appealed, and the case was put on hold.

Like so many other setbacks, Ashcroft saw this as another battle between us—the tight circle of close advisors in his office who truly understood the threat they were facing—and them, in this case a Ronald Reagan judicial appointee, who either didn't understand or didn't care. But none of these bumps in the road really bothered Ashcroft, because he believed, and his appellate lawyers seconded that belief, that when he got to the appellate courts and, certainly, when he got to the Supreme Court, there would be a majority on the bench that understood, too.

Robert Lindemann was thrilled to hear the news that INS Commissioner James Ziglar had announced he was leaving in anticipation of INS's move into the Department of Homeland Security. But for Lindemann the prospect of the bosses who had tormented him so much being driven out of the new agency only made him that much more frustrated that something couldn't be done to break the logjam, and get the law passed establishing the department without killing off his union. He didn't know that Ridge was completely comfortable and on record supporting a provision that protected his union unless the President declared that a national security emergency necessitated that the workers not be in a union—which was exactly what the current law said about the Border Patrol union.

# Monday, August 19, 2002

Eileen Simon thought it was an uplifting scene, something she'd never forget. About a dozen children playing on beautiful Long Beach Island on the Jersey shore were all wearing some facsimile of the flag. Some had the red, white, and blue on their bathing suits, others on T-shirts, others on the caps they wore to protect them from the sun. It wasn't like anyone had planned for their outfits to be themed this way. It had just happened. And although they ranged in age from fifteen down to toddlers, they all seemed to get along. The older ones showed none of the expectable teenagers' scorn for the little kids.

What bound them, and what explained their allegiance to the flag, was that they were all children who had lost their fathers on the same morning in the same place. Eileen's Friday group—the other Cantor widow with five children, a fireman's widow, another Cantor widow, and another woman from her area of New Jersey—had become such good friends that they'd decided to take a vacation together. Five women, all of whom could talk about the same things. Only they didn't dwell a lot on the tragedy. They just had a great time—laughs, sun, wine, and lots of talk about the future, as they watched their kids frolic through what seemed to be some of the first carefree, fear-free moments they'd had in a long time.

They resolved to do a trip like this every year.


On Friday, Larry Cox had finally gotten word about the man Washington had chosen to come in and run security operations at his airport. He was a twenty-five-year veteran of the FBI named Wiley Thompson. That, in itself, was anything but comforting; Cox's airport didn't need some bureaucrat-cop gumming up the works.

But Cox had quickly called a friend in the Memphis FBI to ask him to check out Thompson, and the word he got back was that this was a good guy. In fact, if anything, Cox's FBI friend told him, Thompson seemed too much of a heavy-weight for the Memphis job. His FBI résumé—up through the ranks to special agent in charge of the St. Louis office, then assistant director in Washington, where he had redesigned the bureau's inspections and audit processes—was impressive. And since leaving the FBI, he'd been a senior vice president of a well-regarded international private security firm based in Memphis.

When Cox got to the office this morning, Thompson was already there waiting to introduce himself. Sitting over coffee in Cox's office, they not only exchanged welcomes and vows of cooperation—"We both said all the right things," Cox recalls—but seemed genuinely to hit it off. What Cox especially liked was Thompson's explanation for why he had taken this job. He'd been offered the security director post at several much larger airports, he said, but he had insisted on Memphis because he and his family liked the city so much and didn't want to leave.

# Tuesday, August 20, 2002

Chuck Schumer, unshaven for the ten days he had now been out of the country, relaxed at a sidewalk café in Chianti, Italy, with Iris and their two daughters. It had been years since they'd taken a vacation this long, but he and Iris had been determined to do it. With Jessica going off to Harvard in three weeks, they feared she might be unavailable or reluctant to spend that much time with them again anytime soon. Iris was struck by how long it had been since her husband had seemed this relaxed and satisfied. Although some Americans still recognized the New York senator despite the beard, and although he still called in to the office regularly, they had basically been left to themselves.

Since the last time they'd been away on a trip like this, she reminded him, he had been elected senator and gone through September 11. Schumer mused about that for a while, then told her what she already knew—that although he is congenitally upbeat and optimistic, the attacks and all the work he had assumed after that had shaken him. But now he felt better than ever about the job he was doing, because he thought he really had succeeded in getting New York what it needed, and, he thought, he had staked out a leadership position that he was comfortable with on the various security issues that the attacks had highlighted.

Some of the Customs bosses from Washington came to the port at Elizabeth this morning to put Kevin McCabe and his troops through what's called a tabletop drill, in which they sat around a conference table and simulated the decisions they would make in an emergency.

In this case, the emergency was the discovery of a container with a potentially radioactive bomb inside. McCabe had done that exercise at least twice in the last nine months, only not at a table but on the dock, with actual containers that he feared posed that threat.

Still, he found the exercise useful and approached the day with none of the cynicism one might expect from field troops being "instructed" by suits from Washington. "What was really useful," he recalls, "is that we had to come up with a plan for evacuating our own offices and command center, which is something we should have thought of before. Where do you go? Do you get there with personal vehicles or a bus? Who handles traffic and gets everyone else out? Who stays behind? Can you set up remote cameras? We went through all of that, and then they threw us a bunch of other scenarios. This was good stuff."

# Saturday, August 24, 2002

Tom Ridge's information systems and technology guru had sat in on the meeting Ridge had had with the Raytheon people and had told Mike Byrne, the head of Response and Recovery and the man obsessed with getting interoperable communications for first responders, that he ought to try to get a look at the converted Chevy Suburban that Raytheon was touting as a first responder command vehicle. It seemed, he said, as if they might have come up with a simple solution to get different emergency two-way radios to talk to each other.

At a fire chiefs convention in San Francisco this afternoon, Byrne made a point of going to the exhibit areas so that he could check it out. He instantly fell in love.

"It's great," he told his staff when he got back to Washington. "It's so simple. This thing is a winner." Soon, Byrne would be working to assure that the specifications for first responder grants to local police and firefighting agencies included provisions for the purchase of a vehicle matching the Raytheon model.

Neither Woollen nor Poza nor anyone else high up at Raytheon had any idea that the most important person in Washington when it came to launching their First Responder vehicle had just been sold, and that his enthusiasm would be the key to their getting orders from local police and fire chiefs over the next few years. Byrne had simply asked the Raytheon salesman on the exhibit floor for a demonstration without introducing himself.

The Raytheon team would celebrate another, more visible breakthrough on Wednesday, when the *Wall Street Journal* featured the First Responder on the front page of its Markets section. It was a glowing article that quoted a captain in the New York City Fire Department's research and development unit as calling it "the most advanced technology in communications we've seen to date. You touch the police and fire, click enter, and they are linked on the line." The *Journal* added that both the New York official and the Arlington, Virginia, fire chief had recommended that their cities buy a First Responder.

Woollen, who was at Raytheon's Massachusetts headquarters that morning for another review, got congratulations all around. Finally, he was getting some traction. As of today they had only actually sold two vehicles, but it now seemed likely that they were on their way to building a business.

It seemed that everyone in the Simon family was destined to have his or her own special, spontaneous moment of grief. Three weeks ago, Eileen had bought the new Bruce Springsteen album memorializing the September 11 victims and for two days she loved it so much that she couldn't stop playing it and singing along. By the third day, though, she decided she couldn't stand all the sadness it brought back, and she had suddenly thrown it out.

Now, it was Brittany's turn. The family went to a wedding for one of Eileen's younger sisters, and it started out as a beautiful, joyous affair. But when it came time for the bride to dance with her father, Brittany tearfully whispered to Eileen, "Mommy, who's going to dance with me at my wedding?"

# Tuesday, August 27, 2002

John Ashcroft's prosecutors submitted their brief today to New York federal judge Michael Mukasey, arguing not only that he didn't have jurisdiction over Jose Padilla anymore because Padilla was being held in South Carolina, but also that the President had lawfully exercised his authority as commander in chief in holding Padilla. The courts should not, and could not, interfere with that authority, because, the brief argued, "The capture and detention of enemy combatants during wartime falls within the President's core constitutional powers."

The government attached as an exhibit to its brief a declaration from Michael Mobbs, the same Pentagon official who had offered a declaration in the case of the American citizen of Saudi descent who had been caught fighting in Afghanistan. The evidence Mobbs outlined illustrated the ambiguities in a case like this, which relies on sketchy but impossible-to-ignore information coaxed out of informants questioned overseas in wartime conditions. Mobbs wrote that he had reviewed the "records and reports" about Padilla and that two informants had given the government information that Padilla and "an associate" had met with a "senior lieutenant to Osama Bin Laden" to discuss a "proposal to conduct terrorist operations within the United States." Mobbs added that Padilla and the associate had researched radiological bombs, and that they had discussed a plan to build and detonate such a bomb, "possibly in Washington, D.C." Mobbs concluded that "Al Qaeda officials held several meetings with Padilla. It is believed that Al Qaeda members directed Padilla to return to the United States to conduct reconnaissance and/or other attacks on behalf of Al Qaeda."

But Mobbs also included a footnote, saying that the two confidential sources "had not been completely candid about their association with Al Qaeda and their terrorist activities. Much of the information from these sources has, however, been corroborated and proven accurate and reliable. Some information provided by the sources remains uncorroborated and may be part of an effort to mislead or confuse U.S. officials."

The judge said he would take this all under advisement.

The Empire State Development Corporation, bowing to pressure from people like Hollie Bart, announced that it was going to expand its World Trade Center Recovery Grants, so that business owners like Sal Iacono could get grants equivalent to up to twenty-five days' worth of lost revenue instead of the ten days that had been previously awarded.

This was probably worth an extra $6,000 to Sal. But soon Bart would discover a catch. A rule would now be enforced requiring that anyone like Sal who had also received a Small Business Administration loan (Bart had gotten Sal $29,000) would have to use the proceeds from the additional grant to pay down the loan. Bart would now have to go through all the rules and regulations to see if there wasn't some way around that.

# Wednesday, August 28, 2002

It was a good example of why James Loy was a more effective head of TSA than John Magaw. After discussing it briefly and assuring himself that the rule was as stupid as he had always thought it was, Loy scrapped a long derided airport security requirement that ticket counter clerks ask passengers if anyone else had handled their luggage or asked them to carry something on board the flight.

Loy's announcement of the change meant little in the broader scheme of things. Yet it got wide publicity, and marked the first time that the agency— which had suffered through stories of guards (the private ones, not its new federalized team) forcing mothers to drink their own bottled breast milk to prove that it wasn't a liquid bomb—seemed to be making commonsense decisions.

Two Moroccans and one Algerian living in Detroit were charged with being part of "a sleeper operational combat cell" that "operated as a covert underground support unit for terrorist attacks."

John Ashcroft stepped out of character and did not announce the indictments himself. Despite the criticism he had taken lately for having too high a profile, it was an odd choice of a moment to recede into the background, for these indictments were potentially the most tangible justification for the harsh detention policies he had pursued since the attacks.

The three suspects had been in custody since September 17, when their apartment was raided and they were held on minor charges involving allegedly fraudulent passports and identification documents. Federal agents had come to the apartment looking for another man. They had gotten his name from a telephone tip that was much like the tip that agents got during that frenzied time about Ali Erikenoglu, the innocent American citizen who had been rousted in his apartment the same week in Paterson, New Jersey. Only this time, when the agents looked around, they found, according to an affidavit one of them later filed, two identification badges for the Detroit airport, a day planner that had notations about an American military base in Turkey, and sketches, the affidavit said, "of what appeared to be a diagram of an airport flight line." Further searching yielded a videotape that appeared, the indictments said, "to depict surveillance of such U.S. landmarks as Disneyland . . . and the MGM Grand Hotel and Casino in Las Vegas."

As with the more than 1,000 other Muslims whom Ashcroft's people had locked up in the fall, the men had then been held without bail on the minor documents charges, while the federal agents attempted to pressure them to provide more information.

Now, according to the indictments, one of them had broken and agreed to provide information about their plotting—which the indictments said included taking directions in code from another accused plotter in Chicago, and not only plotting to blow up Disneyland or the MGM Grand, but using their identification badges at the Detroit airport to identify security breaches there, providing false documents and money to other terrorists, and plotting to obtain a truck driver's license to transport hazardous materials.

In short, it seemed as if Ashcroft's strategy had worked. By using minor charges to arrest and pressure young Muslim men who had not done anything overtly unlawful except to have allegedly false documents in their apartment, he had, the indictments said, cracked a sleeper cell.

But because by its nature the accusation that someone is part of a sleeper cell means that the person is not doing anything openly that is associated with

terrorism—either because the person is completely innocent and the indictment is false, or because the sleeper is doing his job and keeping out of trouble—the charges illustrated all the pitfalls of cases like this. One of the
defendants' lawyers, who called the case "ridiculous," asserted that the video
was a common tourist video and that his client had an airport identification
because he had worked for a vendor there. His client had made many calls
and sent money abroad, the lawyer maintained, because that's where his family was. He also said that most immigrants have false identification cards,
adding that, in fact, the charges against his own client for that had been
dropped because none of what was found could be linked to him. His client
was "a twenty-one-year-old kid who sold ice cream at the airport," not a terrorist, he argued. Indeed, the indictment pointed to no evidence that any of
those accused had had contact with Al Qaeda or any other terrorist group. It
conceded that the entries in the day planner had been written by someone else
(but charged that the plotters had instructed a "mentally unstable man" to
make the notes in order that they could not be traced to their handwriting).
Moreover, the lawyer pointed out, all of the indictment's accusations about
planning various plots were based on the supposed testimony of the one
defendant who had decided to cooperate. "How was he pressured into telling
the prosecutors all this?" the defense lawyer asked, referring to the informant.
"What kind of deal did he get?"

This kind of indignant challenge to the veracity of an informant is standard in criminal trials. But in this case, where there seemed to be scant additional evidence about the alleged sleepers, the government was likely to have a
particularly difficult time. If the trial, not scheduled until mid 2003 at the earliest, wasn't sidetracked by a plea bargain, it was certain to produce a tough
test of whether Ashcroft could prevent perceived terror threats by interceding
at the earliest possible point, yet still prosecute his targets.

The indictments also raised another question. If these noncitizens really
were part of a cell, why hadn't they been detained as enemy combatants,
rather than put into the civilian justice system? This seemed to add to the
crazy quilt of how Ashcroft had treated cases ranging from the shoe bomber
and the alleged twentieth hijacker (indictments in the courts for noncitizens)
to the alleged dirty bomber (enemy combatant status for a citizen). What,
other than Ashcroft's predilection to take jurisdiction over everything he
could where he thought he had an indictable case, would explain why he had
kept jurisdiction over this alleged terror cell, while handing off an American
citizen, Jose Padilla, to the Pentagon after not being able to get enough evidence on him for an indictment?

# Sunday, September 1, 2002

Larry Cox chuckled when he heard that his airport had been evacuated at 4:00 P.M., causing flight delays of up to two hours, because someone had reported that a ten-year-old had walked around a security checkpoint wearing a backpack. Wiley Thompson, the new federal security director at Memphis, had ordered the evacuation. To Cox, "Learning from his mistake like this was a good baptism of fire. It was worth more than ten hours of me lecturing him. Luckily," Cox adds, "it was the middle of the Labor Day weekend" and there were fewer passengers than usual on the fifty flights affected.

Under the new TSA rules, the TSA security director had the absolute authority to evacuate the airport, and Thompson had used it immediately when he'd heard the report of the boy with the backpack. Everyone had been ordered off all planes and out of the terminal. When it was over, Cox's people took Thompson aside and explained how he could have looked at videotapes of the checkpoints and within a mater of minutes ascertained that the boy's backpack had, in fact, been checked.

"It was a great learning experience," Thompson agrees, adding that he considers Cox and his staff "high-caliber professionals who run a great airport; they were real good about quietly explaining to me how their advanced video system works, and how my staff and I could have handled it."


It seemed that it had to be a misprint. The words "Rave Reviews" were used in the sub-headline of a Sunday feature in the *Dallas Morning News* about TSA. A reporter had surveyed passengers in New York, Chicago, and Boston, where the new federalized airport screeners had just arrived. Quotes like "the difference between night and day," "more courteous," and "they are doing a really good job" filled the page.

By now, TSA checkpoint screeners were in fifty airports and were scheduled to roll out to fifty more this week. Everything was starting to come together. The recruiting problems had been solved by Rossides's media effort and by a successful push by Jackson to get Pearson, the private recruiting contractor, out there early enough and aggressively enough. (Jackson had finally called Pearson's overall CEO in London to get her to intervene.) Sixteen thousand screeners had now been hired or were in training, with 27,000 more about to be put into the pipeline.

Pearson also appeared to be doing an excellent job screening the candidates who were showing up. The contractor doing the training, Lockheed Martin, was reporting that the recruits Pearson selected were generally of high caliber. Most were passing their final battery of written and dexterity tests (including a video game that challenged them to find the weapons on an X-ray monitor) the first time they tried. Lockheed Martin was also the contractor designing the checkpoint configurations, and that was going well, too. Site survey teams were set to arrive Tuesday at twenty-one new airports, bringing the total they had covered to 416. Even Raytheon had gotten back into the act, having been given a contract to help Lockheed by installing upgraded metal detectors at 215 airports.

"It now really and truly looks like we're going to make it," Rossides would say later in the week. "Everything we have been working on is now breaking our way. And I'll tell you," she would add, "it feels absolutely great. It's been an incredible partnership between these private contractors and the private sector go team people and us in the public sector. We've proven that government can do this."

# Monday, September 2, 2002

It was Labor Day in the United States, but not in Rotterdam, where one of Kevin McCabe's men began work as part of a U.S. Customs team now posted permanently at this massive port to help check cargo before it arrived in American ports. By now Customs Commissioner Bonner, sometimes with Ridge's help, had negotiated similar agreements to post his inspectors in countries that had eight of the twenty largest international ports. The top twenty were Bonner's priorities, because they accounted for 68 percent of the containers coming into the United States. He was close to completing agreements with countries, including China, where ten of the others were located. With that critical mass achieved, he would then have the leverage to convince other ports that their shipments were going to be delayed or even excluded if similar pacts were not signed.

The arrangement was that the U.S. Customs inspectors would use their computerized information to get each country's local customs officials to inspect the cargo, with a U.S. Customs person either looking on or confirming that the local authorities were performing according to standards that had been agreed on.

To help McCabe's inspectors make the best use of their new venues, Bonner was also about to promulgate tough new regulations that would require shippers to send Customs their cargo manifests at least twenty-four hours before a ship bound for the United States was loaded *at the foreign port*. This meant that the inspectors in Rotterdam, who would be hooked into the Customs computer network, would have the information they needed before the cargo arrived to do their computerized points assessment of the container's risk.

The seals and sensors necessary to track containers and detect intrusion were still ideas rather than realities, as were the large radiation detectors that McCabe hoped could be mounted in strategic places, such as the Verrazano Narrows Bridge, outside the New York/New Jersey port. But some version of the bill Schumer was co-sponsoring providing the funds for these improvements was now likely to be attached to the Homeland Security Department legislation when that finally passed, or be passed in a companion bill. Meantime, with Bonner succeeding in pushing out the borders to places like Rotterdam, with the risk assessment system for deciding which containers to check having been refined significantly, and with McCabe having about a third more inspectors than he had had on September 11 and twice as many VACIS machines, the ports were not nearly the open targets they had been a year ago. Change had come incrementally, and would continue to come that way. It wasn't nearly fast enough to match a threat that easily surpassed the threat to aviation that had been addressed so quickly. But it was a significant improvement.

## Tuesday, September 3, 2002

Tom Ridge came back from the beach to Washington and moved his family and three yellow Labradors into the Virginia house he was renting from Karen Hughes. It was only a temporary setup until he and Michele found a bigger place, but he made no bones about telling friends that he was definitely staying in Washington for the foreseeable future. In fact, he seemed to people who talked to him about it not to be trying as hard to dismiss as premature any suggestions that he was going to take the job of secretary once the Department of Homeland Security happened.

Maybe it was that the prolonged battle to get the proposal through the Senate had worn down his resistance to engaging in that discussion. Or, it could have been that stories in the press speculating about other people being considered for the job were getting to him. But he definitely projected a confidence about his role in George Bush's Washington that hadn't been seen since the first weeks he had arrived amid fanfare as the White House coordinator last October. Whether by dint of the solicitous, painstaking negotiations with members of the Senate that he resumed on his return, or by winning the battle of public opinion with the President out on the hustings attacking the intransigent Senate, Ridge seemed certain that there was soon going to be a Department of Homeland Security. Moreover, by now it was clear to his own staff and to the people he worked with in the White House that he had decided to take the job—and that Bush was going to offer it to him.

# Wednesday, September 4, 2002

The *Washington Post* published a comprehensive article this morning about what TSA's new computer-assisted passenger prescreening system (CAPPS II) might look like. The story quoted Anthony Romero's Washington legislative counsel as questioning whether it could work. She also said that the system—which would look, among other things, for people who have traveled extensively to high-risk countries and don't have established roots in a community—"challenges core values, such as privacy, the right to travel, and the right to engage in certain activities."

Yet wasn't CAPPS, in fact, exactly the kind of sophisticated screening that the ACLU board member who had opposed making everyone walk through metal detectors at the board's October meeting had argued for?

"We have to make this a big fight," Romero explained. "It's our role to challenge this kind of government intrusion into people's lives. It's a fishing expedition, and the problem is they can build a whole databank of profiles. If we didn't do this, who would? By challenging something like this," he added, "we're at least likely to make it less intrusive or abusive and more accountable."

By the end of this week, the problem that Brian Peterman, who runs the border protection efforts in Ridge's office, had called a meeting to discuss would become obvious. There would be an article in the *Yale Daily News* about foreign students not getting back for the new school term because their visa approvals had been held up. The *New York Times* would do a similar story about Muslims complaining about visa delays. But because Secretary of State Colin Powell had raised the same issue at a National Security Council meeting last week, Peterman was already on it.

It all had to do with a policy quietly put in place in May, requiring that officials in Washington sign off on all visa applicants for males sixteen to forty-five years old from twenty-six different countries with high Muslim populations. As a result, there were now more than 20,000 backlogged applications that the government knew about affecting students, businesspeople, and those traveling on government-sponsored trips. The problem was so bad that even one of chief of staff Andrew Card's assistants came to the meeting. As Peterman went around the table asking representatives of six different agencies to weigh in, what they all discovered was that the logjam seemed to be at the CIA. The agency was now also screening these applications, yet rarely if ever putting a stop on any of them. So, the group decided to cut the CIA out of the process, unless the FBI or INS, which also screened everyone, thought there was a reason to send one to the agency for additional review.

The change was implemented later in the day. Almost immediately the backlog eased.

# Thursday, September 5, 2002

Marsha Evans, a former head of the Girl Scouts whom the American Red Cross board had appointed to replace Bernadine Healy as president, issued a one-year anniversary report of the aid provided to September 11 victims. A total of $1.001 billion had been donated to the victims in the year since the attacks, and $643 million had been distributed. An additional $200 million was expected to be given out by the end of 2002, with the rest slated for "long-term needs, including health care, mental health and family support services."

The report estimated that the 3,000 families of the deceased and seriously injured would end up receiving an average of $115,000.

What was not in the press release was the $37 million that had been set aside for what the Red Cross's financial statement called "Fund Steward-ship." This was an accountants' term for the organization's own overhead and administrative costs. It was an amount that was more than the Red Cross had ever given to the victims of any other disaster, except for Hurricane Andrew and the September 11 attacks.

Having just returned from a last gut check session with the Lockheed Martin team in St. Louis that was overseeing the training of the tens of thousands of recruits still to be moved through the pipeline and out to the airports, Gale Rossides spent two hours on a new issue. Congress seemed to be moving rapidly to allow pilots to carry handguns in their cockpits as a final defense against a hijacker; in fact, the Senate had voted an hour ago, 87–6, to allow the guns, and the House had passed a similar law in July. Rossides was meeting with her staff to get a program in place that would mirror in many ways the elaborate training regimen she had overseen for the ramp-up of the federal air marshals program at a facility in Atlantic City. TSA head Loy had written the Senate that he estimated the start-up cost of training the thousands of pilots at $950 million and annual costs after that of $250 million. It was another illustration of how a seemingly simple, logical idea was enormously complicated and expensive to execute.

# Monday, September 9, 2002

For several weeks, at the early morning threat briefings with the President, Ashcroft and Ridge had occasionally heard CIA Director George Tenet talk about the interrogation in Afghanistan of Omar al-Faruq, thought to be an Al Qaeda operative who had been captured in Indonesia and turned over to American intelligence authorities last June. It seemed that Faruq had finally begun to cooperate, and as he talked it was becoming evident that he might be a bigger fish than had originally been assumed.

This morning, Tenet reported that Faruq was beginning to talk about a variety of plots to attack American facilities throughout Asia, and that he had even implied that the upcoming September 11 anniversary might be a target date.

Ashcroft chimed in to talk about a case he was almost about to announce concerning another terror cell, this one based just outside Buffalo, New York. Unlike the alleged cell recently indicted in Detroit, these young Muslims were American citizens. Also unlike the Detroit defendants, there was solid evidence that the Buffalo suspects had traveled to Pakistan and Afghanistan, and had even been to one of the Al Qaeda training camps.

Twelve hours later the same group that had met in the morning, plus assorted aides (but without the President), was called back to the White House from a September 11 commemorative concert at the Kennedy Center for an urgent meeting on the same subject. The immediate question was whether to recommend to Bush the next morning that they boost the threat alert from yellow to orange, the second highest level.

During the day, information had come in from Faruq's interrogators that he was now being more definitive about car and truck bombings planned for U.S. embassies and other facilities in Asia. Also, the CIA and National Security Agency were reporting more of the "chatter" in their monitoring of suspected terrorists and their financial benefactors of the kind they had found when they went back and looked at intercepts from last September 11. It was nothing specific, just a lot more talk that could be code for something. Layered onto that was Ashcroft's conviction that this Buffalo case was the real thing, and that it demonstrated exactly the extent of what the threat might be out there in dozens of other communities. The suspects, he said, were perfect sleepers; they'd never been in trouble and had even been popular soccer players at the local high school.

Ridge agreed that this was a case where the balance between alarming people and alerting them had to come down on the side of an upgraded alert, although he and others pushed back on one suggestion in the room—that some of the September 11 anniversary events ought to be canceled. There was even agreement with a Secret Service decision to move the Vice President out of Washington to one of his "undisclosed locations" first thing in the morning, after the President had signed off on the Code Orange.

# Tuesday, September 10, 2002

This was the first time the colors had been changed since the advisory alert system had been launched in March, and it meant more than just informing the public. A whole series of steps was now initiated at various government agencies across the country consistent with a Code Orange, ranging from added Interior Department police posted at national monuments to federal air marshals being ordered to forgo their days off.

In Elizabeth, it meant extra shifts for McCabe and his men (which meant that McCabe would not be able to attend the Ground Zero memorial service tomorrow), and extra screening of all incoming boats. As a result, after one ship was double-checked with a new, super-sensitive radiation detector and found to be giving off slightly suspicious signals, it was sent back out to sit offshore until it could be examined further.

At a press conference with Ashcroft announcing the orange alert, Ridge outlined the various security measures that were being taken, but added that "our advice to America. . . . is to continue with your plans. If . . . attendance at a public event is in your plans, we would like you to proceed . . . but be wary and mindful."

Eileen Simon wasn't sure about that advice. When she heard about the upgraded alert just after lunchtime, she called her sister to ask what she thought Eileen should do. By now, Simon's list of guests at the Ground Zero memorial ceremony and the lunch to follow had grown to eighty relatives and friends.

She was frantic that if anything happened she'd be responsible for all of those people. Surely, the ceremony was a likely target, she told her sister and other relatives. How could it not be? Michael had had no warning. But now she did. How could she ignore it?

At 2:00 she decided to cancel. By 4:00 she had changed her mind and decided to go. At 6:00 she canceled again.

By 7:00 she had settled on a compromise. The plan had always been for her and the kids, plus one of her sisters, to stay the night before at the Hyatt in Jersey City, just across the Hudson River from Ground Zero. They were going to gather there with other survivors' families. Then, early in the morning, special ferries for the survivors would take them across to the service. Now, she decided that since she'd paid for the rooms anyway, she would go to the hotel, but stay there that morning with the families, and watch the service on television. It would still make the day kind of special, because the widows from the group were also going to be there with their kids. But she wouldn't go across the river, and she'd tell the rest of her family not to risk it either. The big lunch would be canceled, too.

She loaded the kids in the car and drove to the hotel for the night.

# Wednesday, September 11, 2002

Larry Cox's passenger traffic yesterday was about 94 percent of what it had been a year ago, a near recovery that was reflected in similar statistics across the country for air travel and hotel occupancy. However, discounts on air fares were now so steep that the airlines were struggling mightily even if Cox wasn't.

Waits at airport security checkpoints in Memphis were down to five to ten minutes, and Cox was now so impressed by what he'd been told of TSA's plans for rolling out the federalized screeners—they were now scheduled to arrive in two weeks—that he was confident that things would keep moving as smoothly, only with what he now conceded would be better security. He wasn't so sure about what would happen when TSA tried to implement the bomb screening of checked luggage in time for that December 31 deadline. Yet, based on what he had now seen of TSA's performance and their plans for implementing the program in Memphis, and on the confidence he had in Wiley Thompson, the Memphis federal security director, he was willing to give them the benefit of the doubt on that, too.

Cox's thermostats were still set at 66 degrees for cold weather and 75 degrees for warm weather to save money on heat and air-conditioning. The hiring freeze was still in effect. And he still feared what he knew was going to be a brutal shakeout in the airline industry. But, as he put it, "We were a lot better off down here than I thought we would be last September 12. Back then, I just couldn't see how we were going to get out of this."


Kevin McCabe sat all morning at a meeting at the Coast Guard regional headquarters debating what to do about that ship giving off the weak radiation signals now being held a few miles offshore. He thought it was a bit of overkill, because the signal was so weak and because he knew that traces from lots of material, such as ceramic tile, could be causing it. But the FBI and the Coast Guard wanted to check it some more, and with an orange alert in place, he understood that.

A few hours later a new piece of equipment from the Energy Department was brought in and declared the ship safe.

But McCabe was already on to another type of threat that the bosses in Washington were worried about. They had just found out that last July a team from ABC News, led by highly regarded correspondent Brian Ross, had begun a project to smuggle a fifteen-pound container of what ABC called "depleted uranium" through seven countries, starting in Austria, going through Eastern Europe and into Turkey, and then onto a container on a ship that had arrived in McCabe's port on July 30. Tonight, ABC was going to report, according to its press release, that it had smuggled "the kind of uranium that—if highly enriched—would, by some estimates, provide about half the material required for a crude nuclear device and more than enough for a so called dirty bomb." In fact, ABC had smuggled it right past McCabe and his inspectors. The broadcast, scheduled for an ABC News September 11 prime-time special, would contain an August interview with McCabe. During the interview, McCabe had demonstrated how well his radiation detectors and VACIS machine worked, never having any idea that ABC's Ross was going use it as a setup for his report that in practice McCabe's procedures and equipment didn't work at all.

However, because ABC had also just done an interview with Customs chief Bonner, in which Ross told him about the uranium and then gave him the precise information about the shipment, McCabe and others at Customs were now able to pull the records of what had happened. The version of the story contained in these records was quite different from the one ABC was preparing to tell.

It turned out that the Customs computerized risk analysis system had performed exactly as it was supposed to. Based on the countries it had been in, the fact that the designee was not a name familiar to Customs, and the number of countries it had traveled through, the container in which Ross's suitcase (which was packed in a wood crate) was hiding had, in fact, been targeted as one of only six containers out of 1,139 containers on the ship to be given special attention. Thus, it was selected for a VACIS inspection and radiation detector screening. The radiation detector had signaled nothing—because the uranium had been so depleted that, by ABC's own admission, it had almost no radiation content. In fact, it was less radioactive than what the detector would find in the earth's natural soils, and could certainly not be used to make any kind of bomb. As for the VACIS inspection, the VACIS crew had zeroed in on the container and concluded that it presented no threat, because it showed no unusual density patterns.

When Customs' press relations people argued these points this afternoon to ABC, the network's response was that they had used depleted uranium so as not to endanger anyone, but that had the uranium not been depleted it could have been shielded in a lead container, which would have rendered McCabe's radiation detectors useless. That was perhaps true, but in that case the VACIS machine would have detected the lead, because of its unusual density, and been suspicious of it enough to hand-search the container.* More-

---

*Later, ABC would claim that although Ross had told Bonner that a narrow sleeve holding the depleted uranium was not lead, after further checking, the network had discovered that it had been lead, and the VACIS had failed to detect it. Customs officials still disputed that the sleeve was lead, or asserted that if it was such thin lead that the VACIS did not detect it, then it would also be too thin to have shielded any actual radiation—if the uranium had been radioactive.

over, un-depleted, real uranium simply was not the material that ABC had smuggled in.

Another ABC argument was that even if McCabe had singled out the container, he had only done so after it reached port. By then if it had been a real bomb it could have been detonated. Again, that hadn't been the point of ABC's experiment. Indeed, McCabe and everyone else conceded that the same could be said of any cargo now arriving in the U.S., which was why they were posting inspectors at foreign ports and pushing to develop broad-area radiation detectors that could be mounted on bridges and other places outside the ports. If that had been the point of the story, then why all the footage and talk about the material being allowed to pass through the port and onto a truck that made its way into New York, the Customs people argued.

ABC went ahead with its prime-time broadcast, though it did remove the term "nuclear material" from the script, and did include a rebuttal from Bonner (which ABC countered with the argument that it could have shielded real uranium in lead, and that a terrorist could detonate a device before McCabe had a chance to inspect it). But a Customs press release responding to the broadcast was effective enough that the media pickup of ABC's scoop was relatively muted.

McCabe was cheered by the whole episode, though frustrated by ABC's conduct. Contrary to its claims, the network's report had demonstrated that at least this time he and his team had picked out the proverbial needle from the haystack for extra attention, determined that it was not a threat, and allowed it to proceed.


Like McCabe, Ken Feinberg was too busy to spend the day at memorial services. A week ago he had announced another eighteen awards, bringing the total to fifty-two. There were now 709 applicants on file out of what he estimated were about 3,000 potential claimants. His average award *after* deductions for offsets such as life insurance was now $1,570,000. With only thirteen lawsuits filed (meaning only thirteen suits had disavowed his fund), he knew that everyone else was waiting to see how he was going to rule not only on more of those claims that had already been filed, but on the test runs he had done with key plaintiffs lawyers like Kreindler, who said he had 300 clients.

Feinberg spent much of the day preparing for two more test run sessions. One scheduled for tomorrow was with Michael Barasch, the personal injury lawyer whom Feinberg had met over his Christmas vacation in Jamaica. Barasch had claimed to have 1,000 firemen clients, whose respiratory systems had been damaged by the air at Ground Zero during the cleanup. Feinberg was surprised to find that the documentation on many of the sample cases that Barasch planned to go over with him looked pretty good. This did look like a large number of legitimate extra claims that he would have to deal with.

The paperwork for the second test run, scheduled for Friday, was more disturbing. This was the case of Juan Cruz-Santiago, a supervising account-ant who had been working in the outer ring of the Pentagon a year ago when American Airlines Flight 77 crashed a few feet away from his office. Accord-ing to an article by Jim Oliphant in *Legal Times,* "Cruz-Santiago was burned over 70% of his body. His eyelids were literally seared off. He would endure 30 surgeries and spend twelve weeks in the hospital. His fingers would be amputated. . . . He will never work again. At 52, he will require decades of medical treatment from a team of specialists."

Cruz-Santiago was still in excruciating pain, and had to wear a mask and gloves. His lawyer had submitted a chart showing dollar amounts awarded for pain and suffering in various burn cases almost equivalent to Cruz-Santiago's that ranged from $3 million to $10 million.

The problem for Feinberg with those comparisons with conventional tort cases was the usual one, only it was harder because of this man's obvious suf-fering and need for money. The sad reality was that unlike the cases the lawyer cited, Cruz-Santiago had little hope of using the tort system as an alternative to the fund. Who was he going to sue? From whom could he expect to recover damages? Then again, Cruz-Santiago's plight seemed to be the saddest, most horrifying among all the cases Feinberg had seen. This wasn't a widow and a family negotiating over how much they would need to maintain or exceed their previous lifestyle. This was a survivor with a lifetime of medical bills and pain ahead of him. That assessment would, if anything, become more certain on Friday, when Feinberg would find himself sitting across a table from Cruz-Santiago and his wife, unable to bear looking at him, let alone think about any number that could compensate him.

In the afternoon, Feinberg appeared on a live telecast of a "town meeting" with NBC's Tom Brokaw that was held across the street from Ground Zero. He was, in his words, "mauled by angry victims" who also participated in the show. As he was about to leave, Brokaw whispered to him, off camera, "You deserve a medal."


John Ashcroft went to an early prayer service at the Washington National Cathedral, where he read the names of some of the victims of the attacks. He attended a Pentagon memorial at 9:30.

Ashcroft then went over the case, now planned to be made public with arrests and indictments on Friday or Monday, against those Buffalo-area men who were suspected of being part of a sleeper cell. Ashcroft's frustration was that the only crime they could be charged with was giving "material support" to a designated "terrorist group." This was a violation of a little-used law (but the one that John Walker Lindh had pled guilty to) passed in 1996 following the Oklahoma City bombing. The only evidence they had even of that was that one of the suspects had, under repeated questioning, conceded that during what he said was a religious trip to Pakistan in June of 2001 (three months before the September 11 attacks) he and his friends had accepted an invitation to go to an Al Qaeda training camp. The law had never been tested in court to see if going to a training camp constituted providing "material support." Besides, the defendants—who had no criminal records and were American citizens—seemed certain to claim that they might have been lured to the camp, but did not know its purpose until they got there (this was, after all, *before* the September 11 attacks), then left and never did anything to further anyone's terrorist designs. Again, the problem with charging members of sleeper cells with actual terrorism was that they were sleepers—or were innocent people wrongly accused.

Although when added to the Detroit case, a pattern of progress on sleeper cells could now be asserted, Ashcroft once again decided not to do the announcement himself.

When the case was explained at a Saturday press conference by Ashcroft's deputy, one aspect that would have helped Ashcroft's public image was never made public, for fear of burning an informant. It turns out, according to one Justice Department official involved in the case, that at least some of the initial information calling attention to the Buffalo defendants and their travels had come from those much derided voluntary interviews that the FBI had conducted of young male Muslim immigrants last fall and winter.

Equally important, as more details would surface as a trial approached, it would become clear that the provisions of the USA Patriot Act giving federal agents wide latitude to investigate suspected terrorists had been pivotal in making the case. Almost from the day the law was signed in October, these defendants' phone conversations, financial and travel records, and e-mails had been relentlessly and secretly examined by FBI agents, after they had obtained a warrant from the special national security court. It was probably only because the Patriot Act now allowed the evidence they had obtained to be used in a criminal case that they had been able to prosecute.

Jennie Farrell and Michael Cartier declined many requests from the media to appear on programs marking the anniversary. The Cartier family's day began at an early morning mass, after which they went to James's grave site rather than to Ground Zero for the morning memorial service. Michael did agree to be in an honor guard that met President Bush at Ground Zero in the afternoon. But other than that the family stayed in Queens, together.

Chuck Schumer left the studio at the Fox network local affiliate in New York just as the station switched from his live appearance to the interview with Eileen Simon and her daughter, Brittany, that had been taped in July. As Schumer got into the car and the police driver raced toward Ground Zero for the memorial ceremony, he called Iris. She had decided to skip the memorial and spend the day in her Transportation Department office.

"Look at this city," Schumer exulted after he got off the phone and the car started approaching downtown. "Look at these people. They went through hell a year ago, and look at them now. They look great. The place looks great."

As Schumer's car approached a staging area across from the old Trade Center site, it was hard not to agree. Newly planted trees swayed in the heavy wind. The lobbies and parks around the Battery Park City apartments, which a year ago were so covered in ash and smothered in putrid air that people had wanted to abandon them, seemed completely refurbished and well occupied. A state program, using some of the federal money Schumer had helped obtain to offer rent aid to people who signed residential leases in the area, had obviously worked. The palm-tree-filled atrium lobby looked better than ever at the World Financial Center—which was once again home to corporations, such as American Express, that had returned following a crash rebuilding effort and the implementation of another federal program providing rental supplements.

Across the street at Ground Zero, there was a tent for people like Schumer who were to read the names of the victims at the memorial service. The readers could wait in the tent and watch the service on a television monitor until it came time for their moment on the stage—which in the case of those reading names further down the alphabet could be two hours or more. In every case, a celebrity reader was paired with a noncelebrity who had some connection to the tragedy, typically because he or she had lost a family member.

It was in this tent that the true spirit of the September 12 era recovery became even clearer.

Because there were more than 100 readers, a rule was being enforced not allowing any of the celebrities to enter with their usual posse. Just about everyone complied, shedding their aides or even security guards at the tent's entrance. It had also been requested by those organizing the event that no one leave before the entire ceremony was over, but instead return to the tent after reading their assigned names.

As a result, celebrities were stuck there for nearly three hours with no one to talk to but other celebrities—or to the noncelebrity readers. And the most stunning thing about it was not only that they all stayed, but that they seemed to prefer talking to the strangers among them. Thus, Secretary of State Colin Powell could be seen sitting in a bridge chair chatting with a fire widow, while Hillary Clinton stood, also with no entourage or Secret Service detail, chatting with a fireman and what seemed to be two widows.

Soon Schumer was in an animated conversation with the widow with whom he had been paired to read names. But then he got up and starting moving around the room, feverishly looking for someone in charge, as if he had a complaint. The problem, he explained, as he grabbed for his cell phone to get his staff working on the case with him, was that his new friend had just discovered that her own husband's name had somehow been left off the list. Schumer spent a half hour ignoring everyone in the tent until he performed this urgent piece of constituent service.


Eileen Simon had not slept much, because she was still so unsure about her decision to stay away from the service. By 7:00 A.M., she had changed her mind again. How could they not go across to hear Michael's name read? The other families she'd been with last night at the hotel were all going. Her sister pointed out that they had left their nice clothes at home, because they hadn't expected to venture outside the hotel. Eileen didn't care. The kids, who were in jeans and T-shirts, didn't care either how they looked. The Simons were now unanimous. They had to go.

So they got on the ferry. As they set off with the Trade Center–less skyline looming in front of them, Eileen could feel how unnerved the children were. Each held on to some part of her, tightly. At the other side, they gave the police at Ground Zero Michael's victim identification number, then stood in the crowd reserved for the victims' families and friends. For more than two hours they listened while the names were read, occasionally looking down into the pit, which was now a pristine sixteen acres—a serene clearing amid the clutter of downtown. It looked so clean, so devoid even of dust, let alone debris, that if not for jagged cement edges and pipes still jutting out from the retaining walls surrounding it, it would have seemed impossible that this could have been the scene of a holocaust.

After the final name, Eileen and the children joined a long, slow procession down to the pit, and added their flowers to those placed in a circle by the other mourners. Eileen and the kids took pictures of one another. Then the children frantically searched for something to take home. "We found some rocks and tiles on the ground," MJ Simon recalls. "We were really happy about it." By now, Eileen had bumped into a group of her in-laws. They, too, had decided to come.

The family lingered at the site for a while, staring up at the cement walls and the skyscrapers hovering behind, some adorned with huge flags rippling in the fierce wind. "Every bone in my body hurt," Eileen recalled the next morning. "I just couldn't believe I was standing there. But I felt so glad I had come. I would have been filled with regret for the rest of my life if we hadn't gone. . . . I never thought it would be true," she added, "but when I saw how the kids reacted I began to think that maybe some day we will all think of that as our grave site for Michael. There was just something about the day, and about being there."

After the children had gathered enough mementos, the Simon family walked up from the pit, and found a place where their scaled-down but no less spirited party could enjoy lunch together.

When Eileen, Brittany, MJ, and Tyler got home, there were gift bags from the local high school, eight bouquets of flowers, and a cheesecake lining the front porch. Before they went in, they drove around the neighborhood and saw that candles had been lit in the windows of various homes in memory of Michael Simon. "The kids felt so good that everyone had remembered us," Simon recalled. "They were so happy about that, and so happy they had gone to the site. . . . There was such a good feeling about everything. It gave us all a sense of the right kind of ending to all of this."

# Epilogue: January 2003

Eileen Simon is enrolled in graduate courses in corporate finance (her college major) at a local college. In December, she finally took the flag down from the front porch to make room for Christmas lights. Her children didn't get as many Christmas presents from strangers as they did the year before, but, as Brittany put it, it was "a more normal Christmas."

Soon after the first-year anniversary of the attacks Eileen started dating, though she spent New Year's Eve 2002 at home with six-year-old Tyler while Brittany and MJ went to their own parties.

Because Ken Feinberg has now responded to a wide enough range of claims submitted to his fund by Lee Kreindler, whose law firm represents Simon, she is about to complete her application. She should get $1.3 to $1.5 million after the deduction for her $500,000 life insurance policy. The actual amount will depend on how stringently Feinberg averages her husband's earnings in the period prior to 2001 when he was between jobs. She will have to pay the Kreindler firm 10 percent of that. Her lawyer has advised her to file the claim rather than sue, because as a general matter it seems that Feinberg has been paying out amounts that, while not nearly as much as the lawyers have asked for, are more than enough to outweigh the risk and delay of a lawsuit and the cost of their legal fees to file one.* His

---

*Although Feinberg did not do the calculations this way, a review of many of his decisions seems to yield a pattern, in which the award ends up, before deductions for life insurance, being about one third to 40 percent of what the mid-range of a court award might be expected to be. For example, someone who might end up winning $6 million in court typically got about $2 million to $2.5 million from Feinberg. That seems to be a fair bargain: If the $6 million is discounted by the attorney's fee in a conventional tort case (33 to 40 percent, although some lawyers say they have reduced their fees to as little as 15 to 25 percent for these cases), then further discounted for the extra years a case would take, plus, of course, the risk inherent in proving fault at a trial and then collecting awards, the resulting $2 million to $2.5 million makes sense. The only instances in which this kind of calculation is not likely to produce a satisfactory result for the family are those in which an offset from a large life insurance policy drastically reduces the actual award from the fund.

actual awards so far have averaged about $1.5 million after offsets are deducted.

During the fall, Simon had delayed her application after lawyers for Cantor Fitzgerald distributed a well-publicized memo criticizing various aspects of the fund's legal procedures and standards, which they followed up with a meeting of all the Cantor families, urging them to hold off on formally filing with Feinberg. The basic argument of the Cantor memo—that Feinberg did not have the discretion under the law to award anything other than the full amount of damages someone would have received in a courtroom, even if under the fund they don't have to risk proving fault, wait years to collect, or pay high lawyers' fees—will probably become the basis of a legal challenge to Feinberg's rules by someone in 2003. But no judge is likely to interfere with Feinberg's exercise of discretion.

In fact, many Cantor families have gradually become persuaded by their own lawyers and advisors that the Cantor memo may have overstated or misstated the key issues,★ and that, in any event, the Feinberg fund was their best option.

Some widows and lawyers saw the Cantor Fitzgerald memo as the firm's way of compensating for not supplying each widow with a memo that they say had originally been promised, which was supposed to outline what their loved one would have earned had he lived. Their contention was that Cantor feared raising the expectations of their surviving staff by providing high-end estimates of what these deceased colleagues would have earned. But Cantor general counsel Stephen Merkel says that no such memos were ever promised, and that his firm's continuing involvement and its challenge to Feinberg's decisions is based only on its desire to help the families of their former colleagues by assuring that they get the "full compensation" that, he says, the law establishing the fund says they should get.

On November 19 the Senate voted 90–9 to approve a version of the homeland security bill that was identical to the one the House had passed in July. The new law ran 187 pages, compared to the White House's original thirty-

---

★For example, the Cantor memo criticized Feinberg for deducting presumed income tax from the victim's presumed earnings when making his economic damages award, whereas payments in tort cases for lost earnings do not reduce the earnings by the expected taxes. But because Feinberg's awards were tax free, whereas court awards for lost earnings are taxable, the resulting payout would be roughly the same.

five-page version. The extra space was needed to contain dozens of provisions meant to mollify special interests. One, which Congressman Young of Alaska had written, protected the Coast Guard's pre–September 11 missions. Another, tucked deep into the back of the bill and pushed by Romero and the ACLU's newfound friends on the Republican right, declared that nothing in the law was intended to authorize "the development of a national identification system or card."*

The law gave the new Secretary of the Department of Homeland Security additional management flexibility in areas such as performance-based compensation, but it protected whistle-blowers and otherwise narrowed the range of flexibility that had been included in the President's original plan. Gone was the provision in Senator Lieberman's version that had actually decreased the President's power to suspend union collective bargaining for national security reasons. A scaled-down version of the budget flexibility Daniels and Ridge had sought was included, allowing the Secretary to move up to 2 percent of the money Congress appropriated for one agency to another during any given budget year, to a maximum of $500 million.

The Senate Democrats had been forced to cave following a surprise Republican victory in the November congressional elections. In fact, in at least three states in which the Republicans had scored victories that enabled them to take back the Senate, President Bush had made multiple campaign stops urging voters to give him a Republican Senate that would eliminate the Democrats' ability to block the homeland security legislation. The President repeatedly charged that the Democrats' allegiance to a "special interest" (the civil service unions) was getting in the way of protecting the homeland.

There was strong consensus among the pundits that Bush's appeal on this issue was among the key reasons the Democrats lost the Senate. In other words, Bush turned what had been a narrow, elites' issue—civil service and management rules in the new department—into a broader issue that everyone cared about.

The Democrats accused the Republicans of deliberately creating the pre-election stalemate, so that they would have a campaign issue with which to win the Senate. Beyond the fact that that's akin to arguing that the Republicans took advantage of the other side's slavish, irrational devotion to a special interest, it

---

*Also included in the bill was the provision that the House Republicans had inserted to cap the liability of two of the large private airport security companies—but not Argenbright. This protection, however, was probably meaningless, since these companies had been indemnified by the airlines for whom they worked.

just does not square with the facts. The Bush team, in fact, was not nearly that smart. They stumbled into this fight, not appreciating how their open-ended provision for management flexibility would ignite Democratic opposition.

Tom Ridge's appointment as the first Secretary of the Department of Homeland Security was confirmed 94–0 by the Senate in January. Most of his top White House staff people went with him—including Byrne, the former fire captain, and Lawlor, whom Ridge made chief of staff of the entire department. They and Ridge are working the same hours they did in those first weeks after their arrival in Washington. Although bogged down in details like office space and reporting structures, plus worried about what they will do if Congress doesn't consolidate the dozens of committees and subcommittees that have had jurisdiction over the new department's old agencies, they are starting to get a taste of the command and control that the former governor quickly learned to miss in his White House coordinator's office. However, they are still concerned, particularly Byrne, that the administration must now follow through on the potential of the new department by providing meaningful funding for key initiatives, such as aid to local first responders. Last year they were on budget director Daniels's side of the table, making budgets with him and his staff for the various agencies that are now in their department. This year, they are on the other side, petitioning Daniels while trying to deflect criticism from Democrats that, especially in light of the increased possibility of terrorist attacks stemming from heightened tensions related to Iraq, the Administration is shortchanging the homeland security effort.

Richard Falkenrath, who drew the diagrams that were the building blocks for the new department, decided that he still preferred policy to operations, and remained at the White House Office of Homeland Security, where he became the acting deputy director.

The Ridges are about to move into a larger house in Virginia. Lesley and Tommy Ridge have gradually adjusted to their new school, and Michele Ridge is happily working in Washington for a Massachusetts-based publisher of health and preventive science booklets and community service program guides. It's the same job she began last February from Pennsylvania once she had finished getting her husband's files stored and the family's belongings moved to the temporary home they had occupied in Harrisburg until the move to Washington.


Larry Cox got through the busiest travel day of 2002—the Wednesday before Thanksgiving—with waiting times at the checkpoints that never exceeded six minutes. That was faster than the lines were before the September 11 attacks—meaning that in Memphis, and probably throughout the country, far better security was achieved at the same time that customer service was improved. Cox's revenue from concessions and parking for December was back up to its pre–September 11 levels. Passenger traffic was double what it was in December 2001 and 96 percent of what it was in 2000. Thus, in July 2003, Cox plans another rollback of the fee increases he imposed on the airlines last year.

Cox never spent the money to reconstruct his parking garage to make it more bombproof, because the Transportation Security Administration decided to scrap that rule prohibiting parking spaces within 300 feet of a terminal.

TSA got all of the necessary explosive detection equipment into the Memphis Airport a week before the December 31 deadline. Except for a short-lived snafu involving some passengers arriving on international flights and transferring to domestic flights leaving Memphis, there were none of the delays in early January that Cox had feared.

Cox now believes TSA is "a great improvement over what we had before." He considers his federal security director, Wiley Thompson, "a fine man, who I like a lot." Yet Cox fears that Thompson lacks sufficient authority and was dismayed to hear him say in December that TSA intends to go ahead later in 2003 with a plan (that Cox thought had been shelved) to hire and deploy his own eighty- to ninety-person federal police force to protect the airport perimeter. "They're back at it, trying to federalize everything," Cox says. "But I can't believe Congress will allow it."

Thompson, who says he likes and respects Cox, maintains that the federal force will work with, not supplant, Cox's thirty-person police squad, and that more protection is necessary, especially given new threats from terrorists firing shoulder-mounted missiles at planes.

As planned, Dean O'Hare retired as CEO of Chubb insurance on December 31, 2002.

At the last minute O'Hare had to cancel plans in November to attend a White House ceremony, where President Bush, empowered by the Democrats' loss of control of the Senate, signed a terrorism insurance bill that included a compromise on tort reform. The tort reformers got limits on punitive damages and a provision that such suits must go into federal courts, rather than state courts, which are thought to be more amenable to plaintiffs lawyers abuses. But the more stringent tort reforms sought in the House bill did not survive.

Brian Lyons continues to work on the $300 million tunnel rebuilding project at Ground Zero, supervising 500 workers. He spends about two thirds of his time in the office on the sixth floor of a building on lower Broadway. The rest of the day he is down in the trenches. He loves the work so much that he says he now understands why as a kid he had an obsession with digging tunnels.

Lyons's sister-in-law, Elaine, finally moved into her new, larger home in October. She spends most of her time taking care of her two-year-old and one-year-old, and stopped going to the group session of women from her area in Westchester who lost husbands, because the children take up so much of her day. She continues to get calls and visits from the men of Squad 41.

Elaine has not yet filed with the victims compensation fund, but expects to sometime in the first half of 2003. She and other fire widows were delayed in filing in part because the contract under which their husbands worked was only finally negotiated and approved retroactively in the latter half of 2002; thus, they did not have the numbers with which to compute their husbands' lost earnings. Based on those earnings and her husband's age, Lyons should receive about $1.5 million from the Feinberg fund, counting deductions for union-sponsored life insurance. With all the other government and charitable funds available to firefighters' widows, this would bring her estimated total lifetime compensation to $6,076,000.*

The medical examiner's office still has not reported a DNA match for Michael Lyons among the thousands of remains that have yet to be linked with any of the victims, but Brian and Elaine remain hopeful that one will be discovered in a new round of tests being carried out using a new matching procedure.

Elaine Lyons says she found Christmas 2002 to be, "if anything, worse than last year, because this year the realization settled in that I had lost him."


Larry Silverstein suffered another unsurprising setback in court in October, when Judge Martin ordered summary judgment for three insurance companies whose claim that they had only negotiated using the form defining occurrence as a "related series of events" was even clearer than Swiss Re's claim. Then, in a strong signal that the Silverstein side no longer had any hope of winning, his lawyer, Herb Wachtell, got Judge Martin to postpone the big trial with Swiss Re that had been scheduled for November. Wachtell said he

*For a full accounting of the awards available to Lyons and other firefighters' widows, see Source Notes under September 25, 2001.

wanted the delay while he appealed this summary judgment decision concerning the other insurers.

Swiss Re lawyer Barry Ostrager believes that Wachtell might even win that appeal because summary judgments are supposed to be reserved for cases where the facts don't matter and the case can be decided simply on the basis of the applicable law. After all, Ostrager's whole argument has been that it was the facts—such as the use of that particular definition of occurrence, or the discovery that even Silverstein's own insurance executive sent a fax on September 12 saying this was the applicable definition—that made his case. But all that was beside the point. As Ostrager puts it, "Wachtell has clearly become so scared of a verdict at trial that he postponed a trial where he could in theory win billions of dollars, so that he could appeal a summary judgment in a much smaller case. No one ever does that."

The delay pending the resolution of that appeal is likely to be three to twelve more months—which would give Silverstein time to work out an arrangement with the Port Authority, the Lower Manhattan Development Corporation, the city of New York, and every other interested party to build less office space, at the same time that he figures out a face-saving settlement with the insurance companies. In December, one variation on that scenario began to emerge as Mayor Bloomberg presented his own grand plan for lower Manhattan, making more clear what had been his intention from the start—to end up playing a key role in the future of Ground Zero, perhaps by making a deal to take over the Port Authority's interest in the property and then conduct his own negotiation with Silverstein and the insurance companies.


Chuck Schumer was not invited to the signing of the terrorism insurance bill, although he should have been, because his relentless efforts had been pivotal in getting the law through the Senate.

A week before the terrorism bill was signed, Schumer put out a press release—his 142nd press release since September 11, 2001, related to issues associated with the attacks—announcing that he had inserted a provision into the law establishing the Department of Homeland Security that would allow the FBI to share intelligence information with appropriate local police agencies. Schumer hadn't known about the roadblock Ridge's staff had hit over the last year trying to get the FBI and Justice Department officials to do just that, but one of Ridge's people says that "this provision will give us more leverage than Schumer probably realizes."

The same week a sharply scaled-down version of the bill Schumer co-sponsored giving Customs more resources to develop new sensors and other equipment to protect the ports was passed, as was a bill he co-sponsored to give the ports themselves more resources for security.*

Whatever he achieved last year—$21.44 billion in aid packages for New York and the security-strengthening proposals he pushed as part of his effort to "recalibrate" the balance between individual freedom and security—Schumer is treating the new year almost as if none of that happened. He is lobbying for still more September 11 aid for New York, having announced with Hillary Clinton on the anniversary of the attacks last fall that the $21.4 billion hadn't, in fact, covered all of New York's expenses. Ironically, with a Republican-controlled Senate, Schumer is now more hopeful than he was that his proposal to get rid of the requirement that suspected terrorists be shown to have foreign ties before they can be targeted under the USA Patriot Act will be enacted. He thinks his commission to study "Big Brother" technology will pass, too. More than that, he continues to use many of those Sunday press conferences to highlight the dangers he sees stemming from the "tectonic change" brought on by the attacks that he outlined at the New-York Historical Society speech last February. And, in late January, he was named by the Democrats in the Senate to be their point man in monitoring, and criticizing, Ridge's new department and the administration's willingness to fund it sufficiently.

Schumer also plans to spend 2003 continuing to raise money and lay the groundwork for his 2004 reelection campaign, a contest that current polls suggest he has nothing to worry about—but which, of course, he will worry about until the last vote is counted. Despite—or maybe because of—his accomplishments and growing stature, Schumer has become more modest over the last year. Yet his confidence in the aftermath of September 11 that he has mastered the twin arts of servicing his constituents and staking out leadership positions on the big issues is now such that some of his closest friends say that Hillary Clinton may not be the only New York senator thinking about higher office in 2008.

Anthony Romero just as avidly continues to argue against the need to recalibrate anything. For example, the closer that CAPPS II—the airline passenger screening program that will use data mining to profile the nature of a would-

---

*It should be pointed out that although Schumer was selected as an emblematic legislator for this narrative, many other representatives and senators, Democrats and Republicans, worked on this and other legislation in which Schumer was involved or played a lead role.

be passenger's roots in the community—comes to being a reality, and the more the press writes about it, the more he and his staff have attacked it. The ACLU continues to fight any effort to standardize driver's licenses, claiming it's a backdoor national identification system; Romero continues to attack Ashcroft's refusal to share information about how he has used the various provisions of the USA Patriot Act; and in November, he began a small television advertising campaign attacking Ashcroft and the Patriot Act.

One of Romero's new allies in these fights is recently retired former House Majority Leader Dick Armey, the conservative Texan. Romero has signed Armey up as a consultant to the ACLU on privacy issues.

Romero can't point to any legislative victories. But he has won a federal court ruling that INS detention hearings cannot automatically be closed (the government's Supreme Court appeal is pending), as well as a surprise federal court decision siding with his California chapter that Congress could not ban all noncitizens from TSA screener jobs. (That, too, is on appeal.) More important, it is easy to trace a continuing trail of vital public dialogue to the ACLU—in which an ACLU press release or Romero speech or media appearance on a particular topic becomes the crux of the material used by other political critics, commentators, and news reporters when discussing that issue.

Sounding the alarm seems to have worked in another context. It gets more true believers to respond to those direct mail campaigns. That will enable the ACLU to continue to act as a check against a program like CAPPS II becoming so universally embraced that those who run them do what those in government often do if no one monitors them—abuse their power.

The ACLU's list of current members and contributors has swelled 15 percent to 380,000 since the terrorist attacks made the organization's role in the national dialogue much more bothersome to most—and, even if Americans don't always appreciate it, that much more important to all.


Ed Woollen hunted enough business in the first year of Raytheon's Homeland Security division—getting most of it in the last three months—that the unit recorded sales of about $92 million in 2002. Just six First Responder vehicles were sold, producing an amount totaling about $1.2 million by year end, but Woollen says that eighty-five more orders totaling more than $20 million are already in the pipeline for 2003, with many more to come. In December, the company solidified its hold on that marketplace by negotiating a deal to buy the small North Carolina technology company that produces the equipment Raytheon uses in the First Responders that allows different radio frequencies to connect to each other.

Jobs awarded from the FAA and TSA to supplement the work of the big winners of the TSA contracts amounted to another $25 million, while contracts for domestic telecommunications interception equipment and Internet network security tools brought in another $45 million. With only one competitor still in the running, Raytheon may also be on the verge of winning the Greek Olympics contract (considered part of the Homeland Security unit's work), which could produce $200 million in revenue in 2003 and 2004.

While INS still hasn't bitten on Raytheon's Genesis data-mining and Web-crawling system for "visitor management," Raytheon did recently get the Dallas police department to agree to test the software. The opening came in December, after a Raytheon sales executive had tried in October to use a friend at the Dallas department to get an introduction to the task force running the investigation into the sniper who was terrorizing the Washington, D.C., metropolitan area. Raytheon wanted to show the investigators there how using Genesis could produce leads for them about who the sniper was. The Dallas police official, after relaying a message that his contact in the sniper investigation was too busy to see Woollen and his group, said that he was interested in a system that could cull through data to produce leads for him in big cases. It's just a test in one police department, and, according to a Dallas police spokesman, "we're still in negotiations about buying it." But small steps like these are how businesses get built.

During the summer, Poza (Woollen's boss now running the new Homeland Security unit) had said that even in their start-up year, he expected at least $100 million in sales. Although Raytheon fell short of that, he and Woollen continue to express confidence that their 2002 efforts planted many of the right seeds. They believe that Raytheon has developed enough products like the First Responder and made enough inroads in Washington and among local officials across the country (and perhaps in Athens, with the Olympics), that they are projecting $450 million in sales in 2003, and $3 billion in total sales by the fifth anniversary of the attacks.

Other promising products include a radar system designed to track small planes and boats approaching American shores, which the company successfully demonstrated in Washington and West Palm Beach, Florida, in October.

There continues to be lots of frustration, and even more of the meetings like the one in the Vice President's conference room, or the one with Ridge, that seem uneventful but move the ball slightly forward. There have been no champagne moments; the system doesn't work like that, especially at the start. But they may, indeed, be on their way to building a new business.

"This is a far more chaotic marketplace than the defense industry, where you know what all the procedures are and who's doing what," says Raytheon CEO Burnham. "So you can't throw a lot of money at it, and we haven't. Hugo [Poza] has a small staff; the rest is a virtual staff that he borrows from other divisions. But I'm confident that this is a big business for us in the years ahead."


Daniel Geoghegan and John France, the chief and deputy chief of Robert Lindemann's Border Patrol sector, were transferred in October. Lindemann's new boss is someone, he says, who "has an open door. She's not a pushover, but she listens to us. It's so different."

What's also different is that Lindemann has started seeing some of the equipment arrive that he and partner Mark Hall have been asking for since 1998—radios, boats, night-vision glasses, even some of the remote motion detectors that could serve as force multipliers.

"We're getting stuff like there's no tomorrow," Lindemann says. "They're even coming out here from Washington, and asking us where we want them to put cameras and sensors."

Lindemann's sector has also been given 142 percent more agents since the attacks—having gone from a force of twenty-eight to sixty-eight.

That's impressive, though it is still not enough to provide complete protection for the forty miles of the Detroit area. The sensors still aren't up at most places (such as that docking area where two different boats arrived unchecked within minutes of each other in April 2002). Yet Lindemann says, "For the first time I really do sense an improvement, a real change."

Another change is that Lindemann will soon no longer work for the Justice Department. INS and its Border Patrol division are becoming part of the new Department of Homeland Security. And while Lindemann is still worried about the fate of his union, he now acknowledges that "there were a lot of loud voices on both sides during the fight. Both sides put their spin on it, and it was hard to tell what was really right.

"They've said that they're not going after whistle-blowers," Lindemann adds, "and that they have no more power to go after unions than they had before. So I'm willing to wait. And I have to admit, that so far, it seems all for the good. The tone has changed," he concludes. "We don't feel beaten down."


Except on the worst days that the press and Congress seemed to gang up on her agency, Gale Rossides never felt beaten down as much as overwhelmed. But once TSA made the November 19 deadline—they had a champagne party for that—and even came within forty of 429 airports in getting the bomb detection equipment installed by December 3,* she was ready to jump into the less frantic and more interesting work of building the agency's training and quality control systems for the long term.

But that was not to be. Instead Loy—who was shown on all the television news shows on New Year's Eve declaring victory in meeting the explosive detection deadline with none of the passenger tie-ups that Cox and other airport executives had predicted—decided to promote Rossides to be his deputy in charge of all of TSA's administrative and management functions. That includes finance, training, quality control, technology, and administrative services—and means she supervises, among others, the gremlins who kept moving her office and switching her phone number.

With TSA and its screeners having received such good press reviews, Rossides and others, like Jackson, have become stars of sorts. Jackson, who by December seemed wistful at the prospect of losing TSA to the new Department of Homeland Security, is now being talked about as cabinet material, and Rossides is being asked to give speeches to college and graduate school classes studying public administration. She has quite a story to tell: From a standing start in January, Rossides and her staff supervised the curriculum building, recruiting, and training for the largest new workforce in the history of the government. Over one million applicants were attracted, of whom 100,000 were screened and qualified, with more than 50,000 full- or part-time workers then trained and deployed.

Beyond that, Rossides has heard that the Department of Homeland Security, where she will work when TSA's transition there becomes official in March, is thinking about centralizing much of its administrative, training, and quality control functions as part of its avowed effort to build the right new culture into the new agency. It's something she'd love to be involved in.

By the beginning of the year, Ken Feinberg had received 899 out of what seems to be a universe of about 3,000 possible applications. New ones were coming in at a rate of about twenty-five a week, although a bulk of some 300 cases from that trial lawyers' pro bono group is expected to be filed by Febru-

---

*The remainder of the airports used squadrons of people doing hand searches where equipment wasn't fully available, and were scheduled to have most of the rest of the equipment installed during the first quarter of 2003, although some reconfigurations and more permanent construction will continue through the year.

ary or March. The deadline is not until December 31, 2003. Except for about 600 Cantor Fitzgerald claims, which were still on hold because the company had advised its people to wait a bit longer, the flow of applications began to pick up when, beginning in October, Feinberg rendered a series of tentative decisions on his dry-run cases. These included cases involving the group formed by the pro bono trial lawyers, who, upon seeing the decisions, began the process of filling out their applications. The momentum built in November, after a *New York Times* story quoted critics saying Feinberg was delaying other, bigger-ticket dry-run decisions involving Kreindler and other plaintiffs lawyers working for 10 or 15 percent fees. The article spurred Feinberg, who had been agonizing over these cases, to start turning them around quickly and relatively generously. These included awards of between $5 million and $6 million to two of the Cantor Fitzgerald families that had ignored Cantor Fitzgerald's advice and filed their claims. Another dry-run decision that signaled the generosity of the fund—at the same time that it demonstrated it was not in the business of matching the awards one might hope for in court—was the $6.8 million Feinberg awarded to Juan Cruz-Santiago, the man who had been so badly burned in the Pentagon crash.

Lisa Beamer, the celebrated New Jersey widow of hero Todd Beamer and now best-selling author, still hasn't filed, nor have most of the other thirty-nine passengers on the flight that crashed into the field in Pennsylvania. But three have, and Feinberg is confident that more will. Even Mitch Baumeister, the fiery plaintiffs lawyer—who had called Feinberg a liar and shouted "Never again" at that January 2002 rally of victims' families, and who says he has talked to Beamer about her claim but hasn't yet "told her what we should do"—concedes that most, if not all, of his clients will probably end up depending on Feinberg rather than a jury and the appeals courts "if my negotiations with him go well."

It's a sentiment echoed by Stephen Merkel, the general counsel of Cantor Fitzgerald, which distributed that memo in September challenging some of Feinberg's regulations. Although just fifty of Cantor's 658 victim families have filed so far, "It is inevitable that all of our families will file with the fund before the deadline, no matter how those challenges get resolved," he concedes. "Is the victims fund better than going to court? Of course, it is."

Feinberg has also agreed, at the strong urging of Mayor Michael Bloomberg's administration, to receive applications from Michael Barasch related to the firemen's breathing disorders that Barasch now says are likely to number in "the several hundreds."

Having appointed a group of A-list lawyers to serve as his hearing officers,

Feinberg, who runs the fund for free, has started to spend more time on his private practice. Hs is confident, he says, that he has achieved his goals, of "doing something after September 11 that would help" and demonstrating "that a system like this can work better than the courts in tragedies of this magnitude."

Based on what Feinberg has awarded so far, plus his fund's administrative expenses, the total cost of the federal compensation program is likely to total between $4.5 and $5 billion, which is significantly less than the $6 billion to $12 billion that government officials and many in the press initially estimated it would be.

The victims fund continues to attract critics. Some cite as proof of the fund's failure the fact that more than sixteen months after the attacks only about a third of the potential claimants have filed. That fails to account not only for the typical uncertainties that claimants face in situations like these, but also for the parties' lack of need for immediate cash because the charities were so forthcoming, the time that was necessary to get the regulations in place and for Feinberg to make his intentions clear by making some initial awards, and, of course, the inclination of most plaintiffs lawyers to put the worst possible early spin on the fund in talking about it to clients and the public generally. There is also the more practical dynamic at work, in which the plaintiffs lawyers who are ultimately going to bring their clients into the fund find it strategically beneficial to hold out, hoping to use that as leverage on Feinberg. For they know that they have an extended deadline of December 2003, whereas Feinberg's goal is to demonstrate acceptance by getting them to come in as soon as possible. It is a classic bargaining scenario, and one that suggests that the last few months before the deadline at the end of 2003 will see an avalanche of claims.

Indeed, in terms of time elapsed, the far better measure of the fund's apparent success is that so far only thirteen suits have been filed in which plaintiffs gave up their rights to go into the fund by instead going to court. The tort suit meltdown that everyone in the legal community had feared following the attacks just hasn't happened.

In December, a thoughtful *New York Times Magazine* article criticized the fund for treating September 11 victims better than victims of other tragedies and, more generally, for being an anomaly, rather than a solution that could set a precedent for future attacks. In many respects, that is true. Yet in creating a system that has, indeed, allowed the victims to be compensated, while avoiding the tort claims meltdown that seemed inevitable in the days just after September 11, the program has been a success. And it does seem to have a compelling policy rationale that could be the basis for how the country deals with similar attacks: The fund, and the accompanying impulse by millions of Americans to donate to charities related to the attacks, sent the message that the victims of terrorism will indeed be treated as "special"—because the country wants the terrorists to know that America has the resources and the will to make sure that, at least economically, terrorists will not victimize innocent citizens and destroy their way of life.

Michael Cartier, his sister, Jennie Farrell, and their siblings had thought that by now they would be able to recede from much of their Give Your Voice activities. But a new issue cropped up in the fall, having to do with the 18,000 pieces of human remains that had been collected and were being stored in refrigerated tractor trailers on a blocked-off street adjacent to the New York City medical examiner's office in midtown Manhattan. The Cartiers and other families wanted to know what was going to happen to those remains. As some of the 1,340 victims who as of the end of 2002 were still missing are identified through the ongoing process of DNA matching, their families would probably come to claim them for funerals. But others would never be identified. And some might be identified but would not be claimed by the families, either because they were not interested in burying a few inches of a shinbone, or because they had already buried remains that had been identified earlier. In fact, the Cartiers fell into that last category: Soon after James's funeral, they had been notified of a match of another small piece of bone, but had chosen to leave it at the medical examiner's facility rather than exhume the casket. Their intention was to have those second remains—and any subsequent matches, which they thought were likely—buried at what they anticipated would be the memorial at Ground Zero. "It can't stay on the street in a bunch of trailers under a tent forever," Michael explains.

Thus, the Cartiers have been drawn more intensely back into the issue of what that memorial would be. It now had to do not just with a public monument, but with what kind of burial ground any memorial might become for the unidentified remains, as well for some of their own brother's remains. So far, none of the authorities claiming to be making decisions about Ground Zero—the Port Authority, the Lower Manhattan Development Corporation, or the city—had specified plans for a memorial, although in January the LMDC did declare that the memorial should be a burial ground for the unidentified remains (and, thus, become exactly the cemetery that Mayor Bloomberg had implied earlier in the year should be avoided there).

Moreover, and as Michael's brother John points out, "Because DNA science is constantly developing, I know a lot of the families are going to want the memorial to be built so that if they figure out a way to make matches that they haven't figured out now, they can get into the vaults and reexamine the remains. So, this is going to be a very complicated issue."

Still, as Jennie Farrell puts it, "While we're involved and we go to meetings regularly, it's nothing like it was a year ago. We found our brother, which is what we cared most about."

For the Cartiers that solace made the 2002 Christmas season worse in one respect. "Because last year was so frantic," says Jennie, the second Christmas without James "was really our first year to grieve. Last year we were down at Ground Zero, meeting with the mayor, going on television. We grieved in snippets. Now it's calmer and in many ways it's a lot worse."

Patrick Cartier, Sr., expects to file with the victims compensation fund sometime during the winter. "By then I think maybe I'll be ready emotionally to do the paperwork," he explains. "My wife and I go to the cemetery every Sunday, with as many of the kids as can go," the senior Cartier adds. "We stand there and hold each other up as best we can."

"I have enormous respect for this family," says former Mayor Giuliani. "They helped me and they helped hundreds of other families."

Bernadine Healy is living in Washington and writing health and medical columns for *U.S. News & World Report*. She also serves on several corporate boards.

Healy's successor at the Red Cross, former Girl Scouts president Marsha Evans, announced that as of the beginning of November 2002, the organization had dispensed $656 million of $1.001 billion in September 11 donations. This means that only $13 million more had been spent since the end of August, and that $445 million that the Red Cross collected in September 11 donations had still gone unspent. In mid-December, the organization's chairman, David McLaughlin, told the author that no more funds were likely to be expended by the end of the year, meaning that the Red Cross would fall far short of its promise, in issuing its one-year anniversary report in September, that $200 million more—or a total of $843 million—would be spent by the end of 2002. Put simply, as 2003 began, $445 million of the $1.001 billion donated to the Red Cross to aid the victims of the September 11 attacks was still in Red Cross bank accounts.

According to an audit report, a total of $40 million (up from $37 million in

September 2002) has now been diverted to the account called "Fund Stewardship," which is meant to cover the Red Cross's administrative expenses. The same report said that an additional $5 million is expected to be diverted there in the next year.



Sergio Magistri closed out the year 2002 telling stock analysts that the burst of deliveries of InVision machines to airports in November and December had boosted his revenue for the year to $429 million, which is more than ten times the annual pace of sales prior to the attacks. He expected to record a solid profit of about $15 million. InVision stock ended the year 2002 at $26.36, almost nine times its price on the day before the attacks but about a third lower than where it was the day Mineta announced the switch from Magistri's machines to a richer mix of trace detectors. His stock and stock options, which were worth little before September 11th, are now worth about $10 million, not counting the $3.25 million he made by exercising other options last April.

Magistri is confident that Congress will mandate and provide the money for purchases of InVision equipment in the future, but his optimism in this regard has clearly waned from the days last spring when he anticipated that sales would be enough—more than 1,000 of his $500,000 to $1.2 million units a year—to make InVision a billion-dollar-revenue company. Near year-end, he told stock analysts that he expected revenues to be about $400 million next year. The analysts—who have learned to be more conservative in the wake of scandals related to stock research reports—have even expressed mild skepticism about that. Their target price for InVision stock is generally about $40, rather than their mid-2002 targets of $50 to $55. The conservatism may be warranted. Although Congress may force them to do otherwise, for now Jackson and the TSA still aren't planning to buy more InVision units over the long term unless and until the technology improves.

Still, Magistri will sell several hundred units in 2003 (including about 250 already ordered by TSA in 2002 that are still to be delivered), plus enjoy revenue increases in fees to service the machines now out there. He is also seeing an increase in sales abroad. So he should meet or beat that $400 million target, which means his business will have grown tenfold since the summer of 2001, although it will not have grown at all from 2002 to 2003. He now has 600 employees, compared to 180 prior to the attacks, and is gradually expanding his management ranks to make InVision a more mature enterprise.

Looking beyond 2003, however, unless he develops the next-generation bomb detector that everyone seems to be waiting for, it would seem that Magistri could again ride the roller coaster down as fast as he took the ride up.

But he knows that. And he intends to spend about $25 million in 2003 on research and development to improve his machines' speed and rates of false positives, and make sure that when TSA ultimately moves to the most cost-effective, convenient security solution—completely moving the equipment to screen luggage into the bowels of the airport—he'll have the next generation of products that they'll want to buy. Having spent all those years selling machines one by one, month by month, he has paid his dues and is confident now that this is a business and a technology he knows better than any new-comers, even the giants who might try to compete. He's also looking at the market for some version of his machines at passenger checkpoints, where the TSA still doesn't have equipment to detect many types of explosives in carry-on bags or that people may be concealing in their clothing. And he's consider-ing using some of his cash—he is well financed and has little debt—to diversify with acquisitions in related areas, such as biometric identifiers and even trace detection. As always, Magistri is looking past not only the bruises of the last year, but also the hurdles ahead, confident that if he's come this far, he'll now surely be able to survive and thrive.


Sal Iacono thinks he'll make it, too. Hollie Bart is still trying to get the Empire State Development Corporation to ease up on its rules for additional grants for small businesses. Even without that, the combination of loans and grants from the state and from Seedco, plus the insurance payments Bart negotiated, total $69,550, which, he says, has been enough to keep him going. Sal consid-ers Bart a "friend for life—a truly wonderful person regardless of the fact that she's a lawyer."

Although hundreds of firefighters and other rescue workers still complain of breathing problems, Sal says his cough is "still there a bit, but not much of a problem for me."

His business is now back, he says, to 75 to 80 percent of what it was before the attacks. Like almost everyone else in New York and the country, Sal is not as well off as he was before September 11. Yet thanks to his pro bono lawyer, and to a large cast of benefactors—those who established the government grant programs, people like Schumer who helped get the money to fund them, those who gave to the September 11th Fund telethon, and the actors like George Clooney who made it happen—he's survived.

———————

At his office in Elizabeth, which now not only has that stunning view of lower Manhattan but also a picture of a sunburned McCabe briefing the President last June on the art of a VACIS inspection, Kevin McCabe now receives, or will soon be receiving, reports from U.S. Customs inspectors on the ground in eighteen of the world's twenty largest foreign ports. These include all the major ports in Europe and Asia, except for one in Taiwan and one in Thailand, where Customs Commissioner Bonner expects to sign agreements by February to allow for the posting of customs inspectors. Their work was buttressed by the new rule Bonner promulgated requiring all shippers to send Customs specific information about the contents of a cargo container 24 hours before it is to arrive for loading at the foreign port.

Meantime, McCabe's inspections team, supplemented by new recruits who graduated from the six-day-a-week training camp in Georgia, has grown from seventy on the day of attacks to 110. In November he got another mobile VACIS unit, bringing his total number of inspection machines to five, compared to the two that he had on the morning of the attacks.

By June, Bonner expects many more smaller foreign ports will have Customs people overseeing the inspection of cargo bound for the U.S. At some of these foreign ports, as well as the sea and land ports in the United States, large radiation detectors will have been mounted to provide an additional line of defense. Bonner also plans to have created a "model" cargo container box by then, equipped with new seals and sensors that can use satellite transponders to signal unwanted intrusions. He will then move to get the shippers who have joined the Customs prescreening program in return for expedited shipment to adapt the containers, after which he will push for a regulation requiring all shippers to use them.


In early October, John Ashcroft couldn't resist returning to the podium to announce an indictment against another alleged terrorist cell—this one involving six men in Oregon. He declared that the combination of that indictment, the formal sentencing of John Walker Lindh, and the guilty plea of shoe bomber Richard Reid made this a "defining day in America's war against terrorism."

In each of the terror cell cases (now involving groups in Detroit, Buffalo, and Oregon), Ashcroft faces a difficult challenge of establishing guilt beyond a reasonable doubt against people who, by definition, were sleepers, if they were anything at all, not overt criminals. But by mid-January he had achieved at least partial vindication of his prosecution of one of the cases, when one of the Buffalo defendants agreed to plead guilty and testify against the others.

Besides, whether he wins convictions or not, if the defendants in these cases were sleepers, he certainly has achieved his primary mission of preventing them from carrying out attacks.

Ashcroft also faces a series of tests in the appellate courts, including the Supreme Court, which still have to decide the constitutionality of his having closed the deportation hearings, and of his holding two American citizens as enemy combatants without any rights to a hearing or to counsel. In early January he won the first such appellate ruling, when the 4th U.S. Circuit Court of Appeals overturned the ruling of the federal district judge in Norfolk, Virginia, who had given the government such a hard time. The appeals court declared that Yaser Hamdi, the Saudi-American caught on an Afghan battlefield, could be held, because the judicial branch should defer to the commander in chief on decisions such as this. "The events of September 11 have left their indelible mark," the judges concluded. "It is not wrong even in the dry annals of judicial opinion to mourn those who lost their lives that terrible day. Yet we speak in the end not from sorrow or anger, but from the conviction that separation of powers takes on special significance when the nation itself comes under attack. . . . Judicial review does not disappear during wartime, but the review of battlefield captures in overseas conflicts is a highly deferential one."

Yet Ashcroft lost the first round in the more difficult case of the American citizen captured on American soil, when in December the federal judge in New York—who had decided in August that he would not automatically throw out a challenge to Jose Padilla's detention simply because Padilla had been moved out of his jurisdiction (to a brig in South Carolina)—ruled that Padilla was, indeed, entitled to consult a lawyer, who could then move in court for a hearing to challenge the government's decision to hold him indefinitely.

The judge—who was appointed by the first President Bush—did say that the President had the power to detain unlawful combatants, even if they are American citizens. But the important setback for Ashcroft was his ruling that Padilla is entitled to a hearing, with a lawyer, to determine if he is an unlawful combatant. In other words, the judge did not agree with that declaration to the author by Ashcroft's aide that the only protection someone like Padilla had was the good faith of those in charge at the Justice Department and at the White House. Ashcroft is appealing. Interestingly, the appellate judges who decided in favor of Ashcroft in the case of the Saudi-American caught on the foreign battlefield went out of their way to say that their decision was not necessarily applicable to the situation of Padilla, who was arrested at O'Hare airport.

Then, there's the looming embarrassment of the Zacarias Moussaoui case. It could become a circus, as Moussaoui begins to defend himself at a trial that has now been delayed until at least the spring because of disputes over what government materials Moussaoui will be able to see in order to defend himself. Alternatively, Ashcroft will have to admit a mistake and try to turn the case into one of those military tribunals that the President had established a year ago, but which have yet to see any defendants. That would be an exercise in forum shopping certain to infuriate Ashcroft's critics.

On a less publicized front, Ashcroft also faces the battle to keep other documents from being discovered by that left-wing litigation group that has brought a civil rights class action on behalf of, among others, Syed Jaffri, the Pakistani detained after a dispute with his Bronx landlord.

In mid-December a federal judge in Brooklyn held a hearing to consider a motion by the Justice Department to dismiss the case on the grounds that government officials are permitted wide discretion in enforcing immigration laws, including how long they hold a detainee before deporting him, and that the plaintiffs had not specified in their complaint the personal connection between officials like Ashcroft and whatever abuses of rights might have taken place at the detention centers. But although he did not rule from the bench, Judge John Gleeson, a Clinton appointee and former federal prosecutor, seemed skeptical of some of the Ashcroft lawyers' arguments. He seemed as if he might allow the plaintiffs to go ahead with the case, including taking depositions of officials and seeking discovery of Justice Department documents that could link Jaffri's treatment to top officials at Justice. "How can they [establish a connection] without discovery?" Gleeson asked the government's lawyer. "What if their marching orders were . . . 'Give 'em a rough time,' " he added, alluding to the necessity for a discovery process that could end up making public the details of the harsh dragnet that Ashcroft and Chertoff had directed.

In November Ashcroft had won a major victory on a different front. A special national security appeals court upheld his assertion that the USA Patriot Act allows him to tear down the wall between national security and criminal investigation, so that evidence obtained in searches authorized under the lower standards of proof allowed for foreign intelligence and terrorism investigations may be used in criminal prosecutions.

The other potential problem looming for Ashcroft was the report of the Justice Department's inspector general on how the USA Patriot Act was being enforced, including a promised examination of the circumstances and detention conditions imposed on people like Jaffri at the Brooklyn detention center. Inspector General Fine had promised Congress that he would finish his report in October, but by mid-January there was still no report, and Fine's office declined to offer any explanation for the unusual delay.

Nonetheless, Ashcroft continues to feel comfortable, indeed energized, by what he sees as the mission the President gave him when he demanded that he prevent the next attacks.

In fact, it is hard in one important respect to argue that all of his searches and detentions and the ongoing Patriot Act wiretaps of suspected cell members haven't worked. Chertoff, the head of his Criminal Division, may have told the breakfast audience of New York lawyers that gauging the effectiveness of these efforts was like scattering elephant repellent; if the elephants don't show up it's hard to tell if it's because the repellent worked or because there were no elephants. But Ashcroft knows from the threat matrixes he sees every day, and from all those wiretaps and other intercepts—and, indeed, from the reality of the September 11 attack itself, which was carried out by nineteen sleepers—that there are lots of elephants out there, and that none were able to pull off a new attack in the year after the first strike.

However, the focus, or the test, cannot rest on eliminating terrorist attacks, especially at a time when Americans may be fighting in Iraq, Afghanistan, or other hot spots. That cannot be achieved even in the most rigid police states, let alone in the United States. Ashcroft's and everyone else's effort since September 11 should not instantly be rejudged a failure once there is a new attack, which is inevitable.

Rather, one lesson from the first year of the September 12 era should be that the real challenge is to create a set of *systems* for protection, in which the threat of terrorism is figured into the mix and dealt with in a visible, credible way that gives the public confidence that the possibility of an attack has been minimized, and that if even there is an attack, it does not mean that there is no protection at all from the next one. That, indeed, does mean a recalibration between freedom and security—or convenience and security, if you worry more about waiting on lines than about being questioned when you get to the front of the line.

What was so especially destructive about the September 11 attacks was that they revealed that the system of airport security wasn't a system at all. The screeners were incompetent and weren't even directed to screen for what everyone discovered could be lethal weapons in the hands of hijackers, who could get into cockpits, kill pilots with razor blades, and fly the planes themselves. So the entire aviation industry had to be shut down while the government retooled the system with short-term measures, then went about the business of fixing it for the long term. The real triumph of the Transportation Security Administration isn't that there has not been another hijacking, but that there is now a real system in place: trained screeners, thousands of air marshals, baggage explosive detectors, hardened cockpit doors, and, soon, a better passenger prescreening program. The result is not only an infinitesimal chance of another hijacking, but, more important, that even if one happens, the reaction will be to see what incremental improvements can be made to the system, not panic and a shutdown because there is no system.

This is the key point that Stephen Flynn, the obsessed expert on cargo security, constantly makes—that if one container got into one port and detonated any kind of bomb, the government would have to shut down all the world's trade until it could assure the public that a real protective system was in place.* That is why Customs Commissioner Bonner and the people in Ridge's office and at the Coast Guard deserve credit. They've worked hard to build a system—better risk assessments of cargo, radiation detectors for McCabe and all of his inspectors, agreements to post Customs inspectors in foreign ports to push back the borders, research on better seals and sensors to keep track of containers and who gets into them. They aren't where Flynn wants them to be yet. Indeed, a war game conducted in October by a consulting group for the shipping industry, which simulated dirty bomb attacks in the ports at Los Angeles and Minneapolis, found that shipping would have had to have been paralyzed across the country for eight days, causing $58 billion in losses. But Customs is well on its way to having a real system in place. And new programs for screening trucked cargo have boosted safety at the land borders, too.

Similarly, the procedures for National Special Security Events are a system that is, in fact, being expanded by the Department of Homeland Security, which now houses the Secret Service, which handles such events. Americans have reason to feel safe, rather than lucky, at the Super Bowl.

The same cannot be said for multiple other vulnerabilities. If tomorrow

---

*In November 2002, Flynn served as the project director of a special Council on Foreign Relations task force co-chaired by former senators Gary Hart and Warren Rudman, in which Hart and Rudman reprised their earlier roles as leaders of a presidential commission sounding the alarm regarding America's vulnerability. The task force's report, mostly written by Flynn, was called "America Still Unprepared—America Still in Danger," and reflected Flynn's urgent concern about the lack of protective systems in areas such as cargo security and the protection of bridges, tunnels, and gas pipelines.

morning someone carrying a backpack set off a bomb in a New York City subway, what would New Yorkers and the rest of the country do? There are almost exactly as many entrances to the New York subway system as there are checkpoints at all the airports in the United States. Would the government shut down the subways until they put Rossides and the go teams to work re-creating TSA for the subways? Would they put another TSA to work in office buildings across the country, when—not if, but when—someone sets a bomb off in the lobby of a building like the Sears Tower? Will there be thousands of people on the sidewalks outside every building the next morning waiting on line to get into work? What about train terminals, or large restaurants?

Shouldn't the government begin now to create a system of protection to address this looming problem of security in multiple "soft-target" venues where large numbers of people congregate? One possibility would be a system based on some kind of credible but voluntary nationally accepted identification card, aimed at dealing efficiently with these kinds of threats, while understanding that the vulnerability is so broad that it cannot be swarmed with the kind of troops and money spent on the more concentrated threat to aviation. The identification card need not be a government program. Indeed, because most of the problem involves access to places that are not government facilities, the solution cannot come completely from the government. But the government has to push the debate and encourage and facilitate the creation of a system in the private sector.

Reliable identification cards could be issued by private companies licensed by the federal government, which would strictly regulate the cards' standards and use. (For example, the law could provide criminal penalties for the CEOs of any government-licensed company that even allows the names of card holders to be sold to marketing companies the way magazines allow their subscription lists to be sold.) Anyone who signs up for the card would be checked against government criminal and watch list databases that are constantly updated. Those with certain problems in their backgrounds, as defined by the private sector issuer of the cards—perhaps they have convictions for felonies, are not legal immigrants in the U.S. on valid visas, or are on watch lists—would not get a card. The card would also have a biometric identifier, such as a thumbprint or an iris scan, to verify the identity of those using it and prevent the ultimate identity theft—by a terrorist.

Those with cards could get on a fast, EZ-Pass-like line, swipe their cards through a machine (that would also check the thumbprint or do an iris scan), and move quickly onto a train or into a terminal or office building. Those who do not want to be screened and pay for cards, or who cannot pass the screening required to get a card, would have to wait on line to be checked more thoroughly.

If that sounds wildly inconvenient or expensive, think about how it might sound the morning after a subway bombing, or the day someone sets off a bomb inside Union Station in Washington, at the Rose Bowl, or at the Mall of America. Can there be any doubt that perhaps as a result of hostilities in Iraq or some other flare-up in the world, some crazed individual or group won't attempt something like that next week, next month, or next year?

Similarly, can there be any doubt that if a terrorist hijacked a truck carrying one of those thousands of daily chemical shipments that kept Lawlor awake at night, the shipments wouldn't be suspended amid panic that the nation has no system to protect against this? Is there any doubt that if a dirty bomb were set off in Washington, just the way that tabletop exercise envisioned it could be, that the country's leaders would wish they had prepared its citizens to think calmly and rationally about the real dangers associated with it? Or that if someone pulled a boat up to the shoreline in downtown Detroit with a biological or chemical weapon, Americans wouldn't immediately panic because, people would realize, en masse, as Bob Lindemann has been saying since 1999, that the country has no system in place to protect the Northern Border?

The terrorists' goal is fear, not conquest. If terrorists can convince enough people to be scared because their government hasn't figured out how to deal with any number of threats at the same time, they win. Yet from a political leader's point of view, if he or she alarms people so much by talking about all the threats and making the price of addressing them so onerous in terms of freedom, cost, and inconvenience, the terrorists win that way, too.

Dealing with that dilemma takes an especially skillful, indeed unprecedented, kind of leadership. So far President Bush deserves credit for his patient, successful waging of the war in Afghanistan, and for coming up with the big idea of a homeland security department, rather than continuing to let Ridge's efforts to achieve coordination be "pecked to death." The question is whether he should have, and could have, gone to the country more often with bolder ideas to minimize these threats and the prospect of disruption and panic that could come if another major attack succeeds.

An argument can be made that a choice to tone down the call to action out of fear of scaring Americans, or fear that they wouldn't understand, is a choice that underestimates them—indeed, that a choice not to ask them to pay more in inconvenience, public service, or even taxes for fear of alienating them underestimates them even more, and certainly doesn't match the portraits of the American people we saw step into the breach in the September 12 era. The America of Brian Lyons, Kevin McCabe, Gale Rossides, Bob Lindemann, Ken Feinberg, or Eileen Simon certainly seems willing to be led that way.

If the country really faced, as President Bush said, the greatest threat to its survival since World War II, then the case can be made that he should have, as some of his own aides suggested in January, demanded a program of national service. The case can be made that he should have pushed relentlessly—obsessively and personally—for systems to protect sea cargo, the rails, critical infrastructure, shipments of hazardous chemicals, and the Northern Border, and that he should have insisted on a total overhaul and housecleaning of INS. And the case can be made that he should have made sure that federal aid for first responders and other homeland security expenditures did not get delayed, as it did, in budget wrangles with Congress at the end of 2002—though the real test in this regard will come during the remainder of 2003, when the President will have the chance to demonstrate how serious he is about giving Ridge's new department the resources it needs.

The other side of that argument is that if the country learned anything in the first year of the September 12 era, it should have learned that building these kinds of protective systems is difficult work. Finding more that could have been done in any area is easy, but it all has to be seen in a broader context. Sounding the alarm more, and spending more, at a time when the economy was so fragile had its own risks, especially with a country engaged in one war abroad in Afghanistan and preparing for another one, in Iraq. Besides, who can say that speeding up spending on cargo container security, for example—before the research on new technology for sensors was completed, or before enough foreign ports agreed to take American customs inspectors—wouldn't have simply been a waste of money?

More than that, while it is true that the President did not mobilize the country the way Franklin Roosevelt did following Pearl Harbor, it must be remembered how different and how multifaceted this new threat is. It is one thing to enlist troops and retrofit factories to build armaments to fight a conventional war against an enemy that is visible. It is quite another to protect the homeland against terrorists. In this new war, the complaint that the government is not doing enough will always be true. The inevitable finger-pointing after the next, inevitable attack that this or that vulnerability was not given enough attention will always be impossible to refute. But while the criticism will be classically American and play its usual role in pushing the government to do better, it will also be unfair to the people who have worked so hard since September 11 to make the country more secure. After all, in a country that has 7,500 miles of border, thousands of miles of natural gas pipelines, tens of thousands of facilities storing or shipping dangerous chemicals, infinite entrances to subways, trains, or office building lobbies, and just as many points of vulnerability related to food or water supply or office building ventilation systems, it is impossible to plug all the holes.

Significant progress was made on all of these fronts (even at INS's Border Patrol). To deny that, or to slough it off as "not enough" without acknowledging how difficult this work is, is to ignore what tens of thousands of dedicated people—from Ridge's staff to McCabe's inspectors, to Rossides's recruits, to thousands of local police and other first responders—did in the year after September 11. And while it is true that the only nearly completed *system* of protection achieved in the first year, aviation security, was accomplished over the Bush administration's early opposition to a federalized screening force as a big-government idea that would fail, it is also true that Jackson, Rossides, and the go teams and civil servants at TSA ended up proving—with Bush's support, and in a Republican administration—that big government can work.

If, as Senator McCain said, in explaining the rush to give TSA unrealistic deadlines, that democracy "overreacts in a crisis," we saw, in the stalled attempt to get the homeland security apparatus working at full throttle during the winter and spring of the first year of the September 12 era, that the converse is true. Democracy under-reacts to a real threat that it should be addressing when there is not a perceived crisis to focus attention on it. Thus, as the terrorist emergency seemed to fade from public consciousness—as Americans turned to live telecasts of some actor being arrested—the bureaucracies, or the "elites," took over.

Yet the establishment of the Department of Homeland Security—indeed, even the decision by the President to sponsor it—suggests that the special interest, turf-jealous system that is America ended up curing itself. The Democrats maintained that the homeland security department was their idea, and that Bush only proposed it because their bill (introduced by Lieberman) was gathering steam. Any objective observer who had the chance to watch Ridge's operation, Congress, and the White House from September 11 on knows that the Lieberman bill, which was far weaker than the President's proposal, was going nowhere, and that Bush's view really did evolve by late March into a decision to go for a mega-department. In short, the inertia promoted by all those special interests ultimately was overpowered when the need to act became something the President refused to ignore. It became a crisis of sorts. It didn't happen as quickly as it ideally should have, but it did happen.

That this step forward, and most of the others that have marked the September 12 era so far, came amid partisan and special interest bickering—in other words, that it came in an environment in which everyone assumed their usual roles—should not go unnoticed. Nor should it be regretted.

One of the most poignant moments of the September 12 era came on the night of the attacks, when hundreds of members of the House of Representatives stood together on the steps of the Capitol singing "God Bless America." As the furthest-left liberal Democrats stood arm in arm with the hardest-right conservative Republicans, it was difficult not to appreciate the extraordinary nature of the moment. People who were the bitterest of political enemies had been moved by the tragedy to clutch one another, literally.

Yet as wonderful as that moment was, it had a time and a place that is limited. Only in Saddam Hussein's parliament is that kind of unanimity a constant. The American system depends on its legislators, and everyone else, fighting with one another much of the time, when they think it is in their interest to do so. It's that battle of people who are sympathetic to various "special interests," and who have a vested interest in making the strongest arguments on each side, that often produces the best, most sensible result. If, as we saw with the Red Cross's struggle to pay victims quickly, and the September 11th Fund's more thoughtful effort to define "victims," that "simplicity is the enemy of fairness," it can also be said that simplicity, in the form of one person or interest making a unilateral, uniform decision, is often the enemy of the right result in a complicated society struggling to deal with complicated problems. The right solutions often come only when those with the strongest interests on opposing sides get into the arena and do battle.

Americans should want campaign finance rules and other laws to limit the undue influence of money by business groups, trial lawyers, unions, and other special interests. But they should be glad that the airline lobbyists had the access to prowl the Capitol Hill offices of their Republican allies the week after the attacks so they could present the case for an industry bailout, just as we should be glad that Schumer and others were there to make sure the victims were protected by a compensation fund that stands as a piece of frenzied legislation that worked. Similarly, having Magistri's lobbyist going head-to-head with lobbyists for the trace detection companies undoubtedly helped inform congressional and budget office staffers and produce a workable mix of the two technologies in the nation's airports. Even having travel industry lobbyists urge moderation in the drive to clamp down on visas, or university lobbyists push for more realistic programs to screen foreign students wanting to take advanced technology courses, added perspective to these debates.

Indeed, what we really saw in the first year after the attacks was how resilient a system could be that is built not only on a generosity of spirit in a time of crisis but also on people asserting their selfish interests in an arena full of competitors who do the same thing. Their battles more often than not produced a messy, drawn-out, but good result.

Boeing selfishly wanted that TSA installation contract, went for it, and, after being judged on the merits, won it away from Raytheon and then profited by doing a good job fulfilling it.

Woollen of Raytheon saw that his career interests were best served by working the weekend after the attacks doodling out a plan for Raytheon to get into the homeland security business. And one of his early ideas—a first responder vehicle for local police and fire officials—became the answer to the dreams of Mike Byrne, who ran Response and Recovery for Ridge.

The plaintiffs lawyers pushed Feinberg—whose career dream was an out-of-court victims fund that most would participate in—to make his fund more generous. Which he did, and which is why it has worked to stave off an avalanche of tort claims.

The insurance companies squared off against Silverstein, and the community groups and the city squared off against the Port Authority. The result is likely to be a rebuilt Ground Zero that fairly accounts for the interests of everyone.

The Cartiers, angry that they couldn't get any information about the efforts to recover James's remains, pushed to have a voice. Although they were initially brushed off and shut out, after Schumer and then Giuliani listened, their own brand of advocacy, based on simple family love, became a positive force in giving comfort to other families, while providing officials involved in the cleanup and workers, like Brian Lyons, the credit they deserved.

Ashcroft took the mission the President gave him of protecting his country seriously, too seriously for many lawyers on the other side—such as Romero of the ACLU; Brosnahan, who defended Lindh; Republican Judiciary Committee Chairman Sensenbrenner, who refused to abide a suspension of habeas corpus; Sohail Mohammed, who sounded the alarm when his client was rousted by FBI agents in New Jersey; and Donna Newman, backed by a supporting brief from the ACLU, who fought to get Jose Padilla a hearing in front of a judge so that the government could not decide on its own that an American citizen could be held secretly and indefinitely. The result was a check on Ashcroft's latitude to do whatever he wanted, and the continuing prospect that the courts handling further appeals will check him more. As Nicholas Roumel, a lawyer representing Muslim students at the University of Michigan, put it when the FBI agents came to see his clients during the Ashcroft-initiated interviews of young male, Muslim immigrants, "All of us had a role to play here. They play the role of pushing as hard as they can. Lawyers like me and the community play the role of pushing them back."

Eileen Simon pushed her simple issue of Social Security and workers' compensation offsets. Because Ashcroft—who liked the idea of a Democrat fronting the fund—picked a man to run it who was willing to get out there and listen endlessly to survivors like Simon, that issue got resolved fairly.

Dean O'Hare's quick decision not to let Chubb cite the act of war clause, and instead declare that the insurer was going to pay all claims, was gutsy and public-spirited. But it was also based on the good business instinct that his company's reputation was on the line, and that by going first with the announcement he could look better than his competition.

Because someone like Schumer was willing to hold press conferences, in part for the "selfish" reason of seeing his name in the paper, visibly serving constituents, McCabe got more of the resources he needs to protect his ports, and New York got the money it needed to recover.

Because Lindemann was willing to speak out, and because members of Congress relish holding hearings that can embarrass executive branch officials, like the one they held about the "Catch and Release Program" on the Northern Border, aliens sneaking over the border are no longer let go.

Because Congress so distrusts the executive branch that they have planted adversaries—inspectors general—within executive departments, and because these inspectors general make *their* careers by exposing wrongdoing, whistleblowers like Lindemann were protected, and the INS's continuing failures were exposed to the point that not even Ashcroft could make a case, even had he been asked, for keeping that agency within his control.

Because reporters and editors have a selfish interest in boosting their careers by getting scoops, selling papers, and enticing viewers, the government was pushed to do better on all fronts, from making the INS check on people before they got Social Security numbers, to pushing the charities to be more accountable (it is not Bill O'Reilly's fault that the Red Cross overreacted), to forcing Ziglar out of INS, to keeping the pressure up to federalize airport checkpoint screeners. Sure, the press criticized those who are "in the arena," as Rossides's Teddy Roosevelt quote puts it, often taking potshots at management challenges that are really difficult. (Every large media company, for example, has gone through the same types of agonizing decisions about consolidations and quests for "synergies," not to mention the hiring and quality control snafus associated with expansion, that many of these companies' own reporters lambasted the government for as it tried to gear up after September 11.) Lots of stories were unfair and demoralized people like Rossides. The alternative—no press on the watch—would have been far worse.

In short, the way the system throws people into the arena and encourages them to fight for their "special interests" seems to have served America well.

But there was more than this adversarial system at work. When President Bush said after the attacks that the terrorists must have thought that America was "soft," it was easy to agree not only that the country's enemies had assumed that, but that Americans, too, considered themselves soft, or at least not as tough as the "greatest generation" that had fought off Hitler.

Americans turned out to be anything but soft. Remember Eileen Simon standing up to Ken Feinberg at that crowded meeting, clutching her research about workers' compensation, or her success through the year in helping her children recover. Remember Gale Rossides and the go teams, toughing it out at TSA. Remember Brian Lyons and his co-workers, cleaning up Ground Zero, early and under budget; or Michael Cartier and the relentless teams at the medical examiner's office and at Fresh Kills, who found his brother. Remember Larry Cox reviving his airport, or Sal Iacono summoning the will to start over. Remember James Brosnahan standing up for the American Taliban, the tens of thousands of Red Cross volunteers swarming New York, or that IBM crew pulling all-nighters to hook up the September 11th Fund's website.

Many of those people were heroes—men and women who were inspiringly motivated by more than their own interest. In some cases—Bob Lindemann risking all to speak out about the naked Northern Border, or Hollie Bart working for free to keep Sal's shop afloat—that seems obvious. They and others—such as Lawlor, Byrne, and dozens of other members of Ridge's staff, or Rossides and the thousands of people who joined the TSA, or Romero, who manned what he sees as the barricades of freedom—are patriots in the true sense of the word. But it is hard to argue that nearly everyone involved wasn't moved to some degree by the tragedy of September 11 and by loyalty to his or her country in a way that made them think about both the public and their private interest. More important, it is pointless to try to gauge the mix of "selfish" or "selfless" motivations at work. We live in a society that depends on both. Asking whether Ken Feinberg worked all those hours for free, traveled all those miles, and put up with all those attacks to bolster his professional reputation, or because he wanted to do good for the world, is to ask the unanswerable and ultimately the irrelevant. What counts is that he did it, and that he lives in a country where a mix of public and private motives encourages him to do it.

Similarly, when Sergio Magistri says he cares about people not blowing up in airplane explosions, and when the blue-smocked men and women in his factory say they derive special meaning from their work because it has a special, higher purpose, there is no reason not to believe them. But what counts is that Magistri and his people, motivated undoubtedly by a mix of enterprise and mission, did ramp up and did get those machines out there into the airports. There is every reason to believe that what got Gale Rossides up before dawn most mornings, as she fought to get TSA into all those airports on time, was her commitment to her mission, but what matters most is that she was tough enough to pass her test.

Whatever combination of public and private motivation made people like these, or McCabe, or those TSA go team leaders, or Romero work so hard, or that made Tom Ridge leave his family and his governorship to come to Washington and work his way through all the obstacles thrown in his path, or that kept his staff working day and night, the important thing is that they did.

The results have hardly been perfect. We could all write a happier ending, in which America is completely safe and the enemy, like a disease, has been eradicated. But this threat isn't like that. Although the country might have moved faster with a leader in the White House less afraid of the anti-government wing of his own party, the results are far better than most would have imagined on that morning after the attacks.

We need to remember where America was that morning.

No one knew when the stock markets would be able to reopen, or even whether New York's economy, or the country's, would ever get back on its feet.

Sal Iacono had no idea whether he would ever re-sole a shoe again, and those who lived in the apartments near him at Ground Zero thought they had lost their homes.

Chuck Schumer didn't know whether the President would stiff him when it came to helping New York.

Eileen Simon didn't know how she was going to pay the bills, or when her kids would stop crying as they rummaged through her husband's laundry to sniff his memory.

Michael Cartier didn't think he had a prayer of finding his brother or getting the time of day from the people in charge of finding him.

Larry Cox couldn't imagine how the planes were going to get back in the air.

Sergio Magistri, who had just finished a round of layoffs and was producing fewer than three machines a month, thought he should ramp up production at InVision, but he was scared of once again getting out ahead of demand.

Bernadine Healy and the Red Cross had no idea of how they were going to attract and channel charitable contributions to thousands of victims. Although the Red Cross failed the test of establishing a coherent, accountable policy, other groups, such as the September 11th Fund, stepped into the breach with sensible strategies, sound management, and the creation of a system for pooling information and efforts that provides a template for handling future disasters. And, of course, all the thousands of volunteers and millions of contributors proved that at least in this context Americans were not "bowling alone."

On the morning after the attacks, Ken Feinberg and any other lawyer who'd ever worked the country's tort system couldn't begin to predict how many thousands of lawsuits spanning how many decades were going to tear the country apart, as victims of the tragedy tried to cast blame on everyone except the terrorists who had caused it. The victims fund has proved to be a far better alternative.

And, as Kevin McCabe looked out across his port and was able to do nothing but put aside hundreds of containers based only on the country he thought they had come from, while his colleagues in North Dakota and Detroit strangled trade by holding up trucks at the checkpoints, and while Bob Lindemann was called back from the front by Border Patrol bosses who actually said it was too dangerous to be out there, it was hard not to believe that there really was no way America was ever going to be safe again.

America is still not safe, not in the sense that an attack is not possible or even probable. But the country is much less vulnerable than it was. America has come a long way, making progress fitfully, as democracies must, toward achieving the longer-term changes that will enable the country to protect itself in the September 12 era.

Although American freedoms and the legal system that protects its people have been tested and even changed, Americans are still fundamentally free. Although terrorism, by definition, involves those living quietly in their communities, the country did not constrict freedom at home nearly to the degree it did during World War II, when thousands of its citizens were interned in camps.

A cost—in inconvenience as well as expense—has been added, and will continue to be added, to the nation's commerce. But the country's economic system has not been crippled, far from it.

How Americans live has been indelibly affected. But the country's core values and way of life remain the same.

The American people and the American system have been as resilient as ever. Even as the nation changed, it prevailed, because its people remained fundamentally the same—motivated enough and tough enough to pursue the same mix of self-interest and public interest in the same spirited, open arena that since its beginning has been the source of America's enduring strength.

# Acknowledgments

This was an ambitious book to structure, because I wanted to convey the full array of challenges America faced in the September 12 era, yet also present a coherent narrative. To the extent that I have succeeded, I am grateful for the guidance and encouragement of Alice Mayhew. In thanking her for performing her magic on my first book twenty-four years ago, I called her the ideal editor. It's nice to know that some things don't change.

Also at Simon & Schuster, Anja Schmidt and Mara Lurie, along with copy editor Fred Chase, were indispensable in turning a manuscript into a book—and improving it every step of the way.

This book benefited from the remarkable journalism that immediately followed the September 11 tragedy, particularly in the *New York Times, Washington Post, Wall Street Journal,* and *Los Angeles Times*—whose daily coverage I used consistently, and grew to respect even more, the more I learned about the subjects they were handling under daily deadline pressure. Similarly, *Time* and *Newsweek* rose admirably to the test of September 11, as did the *Detroit Free Press* in its coverage of Northern Border issues. There was also one newsletter that I found indispensable in helping me keep up with the world that I was trying to penetrate—McGraw-Hill's *Homeland Security & Defense.*

I am particularly grateful to my colleagues at *Newsweek* for providing an important, early forum during 2002 for some of what now appears in these pages. National Affairs Editor Tom Watson and Editor Mark Whitaker provided great editorial guidance and friendship at the same time.

Throughout this process I was lucky enough to hire three recent graduates of the journalism class I teach at Yale to work as research assistants. Louise Story worked through the winter and spring of 2002, and was then relieved by Elise Jordan, who worked through the summer. Both were tremendously helpful in a variety of jobs that demonstrated their talent and dedication. Claire Miller joined the project during the summer and stayed on through the completion of all drafting, editing, and fact checking, doing a magnificent job in every respect, while never complaining about the open-ended research assignments I gave her or what seemed to be my constant ability to lose some key document. With that in mind, all my thanks goes to my office assistant, John Elmore, and to my executive assistant, Olga Georgevich, who, in addition to keeping my life in order, made significant research and fact-checking contributions and provided important editorial feedback.

Five friends made the mistake of expressing curiosity about how I was doing—

only to be bombarded by a manuscript that was longer even than the version you are now holding. Floyd Abrams, Roger Altman, Tom Heise, James Warren, and Ed Wasserman made great suggestions.

Last, but most, is my family. Although I guess at some level I was aware that college and high school require some reading, too, it didn't keep me from burying Emily, Sophie, and Sam Brill in the draft. They all read through it (sometimes even cheerfully) and made valuable, if not always subtle, suggestions. And then there is Cynthia Brill, the multitalented, sharp-eyed editor of my life, who read it even more times than any of the kids, and kept pushing me to do better. I am forever grateful for that, and for everything else she means to my life.

# Sources

Listed below are the people who were interviewed for this book. Most were interviewed in person, some by telephone. Many, especially the "main characters," spent more time than they could possibly have anticipated or wanted to, and for that they have my deepest appreciation. Unless otherwise noted, the author personally conducted the interviews of those listed.

All titles and affiliations are as of the date of the interview, or in the case of multiple interviews, the date of the first interview.

Most sources agreed at the author's strong urging either to be quoted directly and on the record, or to have their names listed as sources in the Source Notes section so that the information they imparted about a particular situation or event could be attributed to them (and, often, others) without their having to be concerned about how their specific words might be used in quotations. However, some sources were reluctant to have their names attached at all to the information they provided. These include FBI agents, some senior White House officials, some Justice Department and other agency officials, recovery workers, lawyers, and others. They are cited in the text or in the Source Notes by their titles as precisely as was possible without revealing their identities.

Abbot, Steven — Deputy Director, Office of Homeland Security

Ahmad, Harris — Director, Council on American-Islamic Relations (Michigan)

Alexander, George — Office of Homeland Security

Ashcroft, John — U.S. Attorney General

Atick, Joseph — Chairman and CEO, Visionics Corporation (Union City, New Jersey)

Baden, Sarah — Family Services Coordinator, American Red Cross, New York Chapter

Barasch, Michael — Plaintiffs lawyer, representing firefighters (New York)

Barocas, Edward — Legal Director, American Civil Liberties Union (New Jersey)

Barr, William — former U.S. Attorney General, George H. Bush administration

Bart, Hollie — pro bono lawyer for Salvatore Iacono (New York)

Basham, Richard — adjunct instructor at Ivy Tech State College, community college partner with Vincennes University (Evansville, Indiana) (interviewed by research assistant Claire Miller)

627

Baughman, Bruce — Director, Office of National Preparedness, Federal Emergency
    Management Agency

Baumeister, Michel — plaintiffs lawyer, representing victims (New York and
    New Jersey)

Baxter, Col. John — Commander, Flight Medicine Clinic, the Pentagon

Beane, John — attorney, involved in the Argenbright sale (Atlanta)

Bender, Robert, Jr. — CEO, American Red Cross, New York Chapter

Bennis, R. Adm. Richard — Commander, United States Coast Guard (New York)

Berard, James — staff member, House Committee on Transportation and
    Infrastructure

Berger, Samuel — former National Security Advisor, Clinton administration

Berger, William — Chief, North Miami Beach police (Florida)

Berman, Jeffrey — Judiciary Committee Counsel to Senator Charles Schumer

Berry, Kate — former Executive Vice President and Chief of Staff, American Red
    Cross

Billings, Christopher — Director of Transportation Planning, Disney World

Bloomberg, Michael — Mayor of New York City

Blunt, Roy — U.S. Representative, Missouri

Boies, David — attorney, worked with Kenneth Feinberg for Senator Edward
    Kennedy

Bolten, Joshua — Assistant to the President and White House Deputy Chief of Staff

Bonner, Robert — Commissioner, U.S. Customs Service

Borowski, Patricia — Senior Vice President, National Association of Professional
    Insurance Agents

Brodsky, Jeffrey — President, Related Management Company, LP (owner of
    buildings in Battery Park City)

Brokaw, Tom — anchor, NBC News

Brosnahan, James — attorney, defended John Walker Lindh (San Francisco)

Buchan, Claire — Special Assistant to the President and Deputy Press Secretary

Buckholz, Carl — Special Assistant to the President and Executive Secretary, Office
    of Homeland Security

Buffett, Warren — CEO, Berkshire Hathaway

Burke, Charles — Public Affairs Specialist, Internal Revenue Service

Burnett, James — baggage screener, Transportation Security Administration

Burnham, Daniel — CEO, Raytheon Company

Byrne, Michael — Senior Director of Response and Recovery, Office of Homeland
    Security

Campbell, Duncan — Senior Director, Intergovernmental Affairs, Office of
    Homeland Security

Canfield, Sally — Director of Policy and Plans, Office of Homeland Security

Card, Andrew, Jr. — White House Chief of Staff

Carey, David — Vice President, Information Assurance, Oracle Service Industries, Oracle Corporation

Carroll, Sandra — Special Agent, Federal Bureau of Investigation (New Jersey)

Carter, Ashton — Professor, John F. Kennedy School of Government, Harvard University

Cartier, John — brother of victim James Cartier

Cartier, Michael — brother of victim James Cartier and co-founder, Give Your Voice

Cartier, Michele — sister of victim James Cartier

Cartier, Patrick, Jr. — brother of victim James Cartier

Cartier, Patrick, Sr. — father of victim James Cartier

Chaffee, Barbara — Special Assistant to the President and Public Liaison, Office of Homeland Security

Charles, Fran — Vice President of Administrative Service, United Way of New York City

Chatterjee, Raj — attorney, worked on defense for John Walker Lindh (San Francisco)

Chertoff, Michael — Assistant Attorney General, Criminal Division

Chiames, Christopher — Managing Director of Transportation and Public Affairs, Burson-Marsteller (represented Argenbright)

Childs, David — Consulting Partner, Skidmore, Owings & Merrill (New York)

Chlopak, Robert — Consultant for American Red Cross and Partner, Chlopak, Leonard, Schechter and Associates

Christianson, Scott — President and CEO, Glaucoma Foundation (interviewed by research assistant Claire Miller)

Cilluffo, Frank — Special Assistant to the President and Advisor for External Affairs, Office of Homeland Security

Clabes, John — Public Affairs Officer, Federal Aviation Administration (Norman, Oklahoma)

Clark, Cheryl — volunteer, American Red Cross (from Reno, Nevada, working at New York aid center)

Clarke, Victoria — Assistant Secretary of Defense for Public Affairs, Department of Defense

Clinton, Hillary — U.S. Senator, New York

Clooney, George — actor and organizer of telethon, *America: A Tribute to Heroes,* fund-raiser for the September 11th Fund

Cobb, Paul "Whit," Jr. — Deputy General Counsel, U.S. Department of Defense

Collins, Jeffrey — U.S. Attorney, Eastern District (Michigan)

Comey, James — U.S. Attorney, Southern District (New York)

Comstock, Barbara — Director of Public Affairs, U.S. Department of Justice

Cooper, Steven — Special Assistant to the President, Office of Homeland Security

Corallo, Mark — Press Secretary, U.S. Department of Justice

Corzine, Jon — U.S. Senator, New Jersey

Coty, Thomas — Senior Program Manager, AGILE, U.S. Department of Justice

Cox, Larry — President and CEO, Memphis–Shelby County Airport Authority

Craig, Aubrey — Director, Surveillance and Instrumentation Systems, Raytheon Company

Crane, David — Senior Policy Advisor to Senator Trent Lott; then a lobbyist representing real estate interests

Crisologo, Vizente — passenger screener, San Francisco International Airport

Cronin, Michael — Assistant Commissioner of Inspections, Immigration and Naturalization Service

Cutler, Lloyd, Jr. — attorney and former White House Counsel, Carter and Clinton administrations, and member of Defense Secretary Donald Rumsfeld's informal advisory committee on military commissions

Czesak, Cindy — Director, Paterson, New Jersey, Free Public Library (interviewed by research assistant Claire Miller)

Daniels, Mitchell, Jr. — Director, White House Office of Management and Budget

Daschle, Tom — U.S. Senator, South Dakota

Decker, Harold — General Counsel, American Red Cross

Degnan, John — Vice Chairman, Chubb Corporation

Delaney, Pamela — President, New York City Police Foundation

Delaquis, Mary — Area Service Port Director, U.S. Customs (Pembina, North Dakota)

De Mauro, Joseph — Regional President, National Operations, Verizon

Dickerson, Ralph, Jr. — President, United Way of New York City

Dickson, Edward — Assistant Special Agent in Charge, Federal Bureau of Investigation (Newark, New Jersey)

Dinh, Viet — Assistant Attorney General, Office of Legal Policy, U.S. Department of Justice

Doctoroff, Daniel — Deputy Mayor of New York for Economic Development and Rebuilding

Donaghue, Frank — CEO, American Red Cross, Southeastern Pennsylvania Chapter

Donahue, Thomas, III — Director of Corporate Communications, Delta Air Lines

Doyle, William — member, Give Your Voice, and father of victim

Drake, John — investigator on Finance Committee for Senator Charles Grassley

Dranove, Joel — attorney, representing immigrant-detainee (New York)

Dubois, Jacques — Chairman, CEO, and President, Swiss Re America

Dunn, Karen — Communications Director for Senator Hillary Clinton

Efford, Richard — staff assistant, House Committee on Appropriations

Einzig, Barbara — resident, Battery Park City (interviewed by research assistant Louise Story)

Engola, Aleta — member of tenants committee, Battery Park City

Erikenoglu, Ali — electrical engineer (Paterson, New Jersey)

Ernst, Kevin — attorney, defending alleged Detroit terrorist cell member

Evania, William — Special Agent, Federal Bureau of Investigation (Newark, New Jersey)

Eve, Leecia — Counsel for Senator Hillary Clinton

Falkenrath, Richard — Special Assistant to the President and Senior Director of Policy and Plans, Office of Homeland Security

Farrell, Jennie — sister of victim James Cartier and co-founder, Give Your Voice

Feinberg, Kenneth — Special Master, Victims Compensation Fund

Ferer, Christy — liaison for victims' families for Mayor Michael Bloomberg

Fernandez, Ralph — attorney (Tampa, Florida)

Fidell, Eugene — President, National Institute of Military Justice

Fine, Grant — Private investigator, worked for John Walker Lindh defense (San Francisco)

Fisher, Peter — Undersecretary for Domestic Finance, U.S. Department of the Treasury

Flaherty, John — Chief of Staff, U.S. Department of Transportation

Flynn, Stephen — Senior Fellow for National Security Studies, Council on Foreign Relations

France, John — Deputy Chief Patrol Agent, U.S. Border Patrol, Detroit Sector

Garrett, John — defense security lobbyist, Patton Boggs, LLP (Washington, D.C.)

Geerdes, Lynn — pro bono lawyer for Salvatore Iacono (Chicago)

Gephardt, Richard — U.S. Representative, Missouri

Giuliani, Rudolph — former Mayor of New York City

Goldman, Lloyd — Senior Partner, Silverstein Properties

Gonzales, Alberto — White House Counsel

Goodman, William — attorney, Center for Constitutional Rights (New York)

Gosin, Barry — Vice Chairman and CEO, Newmark and Company

Gotbaum, Joshua — CEO, September 11th Fund/New York Community Trust

Granieri, Marie — sister of victim James Cartier

Grasso, Richard — Chairman and CEO, New York Stock Exchange

Gray, C. Boyden — former White House Counsel, George H. Bush administration, and attorney (Washington, D.C.)

Green, Jeffrey — General Counsel, Port Authority of New York and New Jersey

Green, Joseph — Executive Director, Office of Field Support, Immigration and Naturalization Service

Greenberg, Mark — Senior Vice President and Chief Communications Officer, Chubb Corporation

Greenberg, Maurice — Chairman and CEO, AIG Insurance

Greenspan, Deborah — Partner, Feinberg Group

Gribbon, Francis — Deputy Fire Commissioner, New York City Fire Department

Grinker, William — President and CEO, Seedco

Haage-Gaynor, Kathleen — Area Director, U.S. Customs (New York and New Jersey)

Hagel, Charles — U.S. Senator, Nebraska

Hakensen, David — Vice President, Public Relations, NCS Pearson

Halkias, Rebecca — Deputy Assistant to the President for Legislative Affairs, Office of Homeland Security

Hall, Mark — Senior Border Patrol Agent, U.S. Border Patrol (Detroit)

Haltzel, Michael — staff member, Senate Committee on Foreign Relations

Hardt, Cliff — Senior Advisor, Transportation Security Administration (on loan from FedEx)

Harris, George — attorney, worked on defense for John Walker Lindh (San Francisco)

Harris, Robert — Associate Chief, U.S. Border Patrol (Washington, D.C.)

Hart, Steven — attorney for Representative Tom DeLay, and lobbyist

Hauptli, Todd — Senior Vice President for Legislative Affairs, American Association of Airport Executives

Hawley, Kip — Director, go teams, Transportation Security Administration

Haynes, William, II — General Counsel, U.S. Department of Defense

Healy, Bernadine — former President and CEO, American Red Cross

Hegler, Michael — Supervisory Customs Inspector, U.S. Customs Service (Elizabeth, New Jersey)

Herwig, Roland — Public Affairs Officer, Federal Aviation Administration (Norman, Oklahoma)

Heyderman, Arthur — Board Member, American Civil Liberties Union (Iowa)

Heymsfeld, David — Staff Director, House Committee on Transportation and Infrastructure

Hoechst, Tim — Senior Vice President of Technology, Oracle Corporation

Holman, Mark — Deputy Assistant to the President for Homeland Security

Hughes, Karen — Counselor to the President

Hughes, Kelly — Director of Operations, Comfort Zone Camp

Hurst, Robert — CEO, 9/11 United Services Group

Iacono, Salvatore — proprietor, Continental Shoe Repair

Isakowitz, Mark — lobbyist for private airline security companies, and then for the insurance industry (Washington, D.C.)

Israelite, David — Deputy Chief of Staff and Counselor, U.S. Department of Justice

Jackson, Michael — Deputy Secretary, U.S. Department of Transportation

Johnson, Stephen — close friend of Salvatore Iacono

Jordan, Joanne — Director of Public Relations, Restaurant Associates

Joseph, Jofi — professional staff member, Senate Committee on Foreign Relations

Katzenberg, Jeffrey — Co-founder, Dreamworks SKG

Kelley, Rob — member of tenants committee, Battery Park City

Kelly, Raymond — Police Commissioner, City of New York

Kennedy, Charlene — Manager, Government Affairs, Delta Air Lines

Kennedy, Pat — Board member, American Red Cross (San Francisco)

Kerner, Francine — Chief Counsel, Transportation Security Administration

Klein, John — lobbyist (Washington, D.C.)

Kline, C. Robert — Vice President, Hytec (New Mexico)

Krause, Kurt — Senior Advisor, Transportation Security Administration

Kreindler, James — attorney, representing victims of air disasters

Kreindler, Lee — leading plaintiffs lawyer, representing victims of air disasters, including Eileen Simon

Kroll, Jules — CEO, Kroll Associates (security firm, consulted for Port Authority)

Kuntz, Carol — Director of Homeland Security for the Vice President

Lamparas, Daz — field representative, organizer and trainer of passenger screeners, AFL-CIO

La Roca, Joan — Public Affairs Specialist, National Institute of Justice, U.S. Department of Justice

Lawlor, Gen. Bruce — Senior Director of Protection and Prevention, Office of Homeland Security

Lefkowitz, Jay — Deputy Assistant to the President for Domestic Policy

Lemons, Terry — National Media Relations Chief, Internal Revenue Service

Levine, Edward — professional staff member, Senate Committee on Foreign Relations

Libby, Lewis — Chief of Staff to the Vice President and Assistant for National Security Affairs

Light, Paul — Director, Center for Public Service, Brookings Institute

Lindemann, Robert — Senior Border Patrol Agent, U.S. Border Patrol (Detroit)

Lindsey, Lawrence — Assistant to the President for Economic Policy

Litchfield, Beth — friend and neighbor of Eileen Simon

Longmire, Lee — Director of Office of Aviation Security Policy, Federal Aviation Administration

Loy, Adm. James — Undersecretary of Transportation for Security/Director, Transportation Security Administration

Lungren, Jeffrey — Communications Director, House Committee on the Judiciary

Lunner, Chet — Director of Public Affairs, Office of the Secretary, U.S. Department of Transportation

Luongo, James — Deputy Inspector and Incident Commander, Fresh Kills Landfill

Luzzatto, Tamera — Chief of Staff for Senator Hillary Clinton

Lyons, Brian — Recovery Supervisor, Ground Zero, and brother of victim Michael Lyons

Lyons, Elaine — widow of victim Michael Lyons

Lyons, Michael — commuter who Brian Lyons met at the Carmel, New York, train station

Magaw, John — Undersecretary of Transportation for Security/Director, Transportation Security Administration

Magistri, Sergio — President and CEO, InVision Technologies

Marchand, Mark — Director of Consumer Services and Network Media Relations, Verizon

Margalit, Yotam — Director of Product Management, InVision Technologies

Martin, Robert — Vice President/Operations, Memphis–Shelby County Airport Authority

Marx, Richard — FBI agent in charge of Fresh Kills Landfill

Matalin, Mary — Assistant to the President and Counselor to the Vice President

Mattson, Don — COO, InVision Technologies

McCabe, Kevin — Chief Inspector, Contraband Enforcement Team, U.S. Customs Service, Port of New York (Elizabeth, New Jersey)

McCain, John — U.S. Senator, Arizona

McCann, Patrick — lobbyist for InVision Technologies

McHale, Stephen — Deputy Undersecretary of Transportation for Security, Transportation Security Administration

McKay, John — Head of Customs Training, Federal Law Enforcement Training Center (Glynco, Georgia)

McKelvey, Gerald — Executive Vice President, Rubenstein Associates (public relations representative for Larry Silverstein)

McLaughlin, David — Chairman, American Red Cross

McNally, Edward — Senior Associate Counsel to the President and General Counsel, Office of Homeland Security

Mecey, Michael — Senior Associate, Coltrin and Associates (represents InVision)

Meenan, John — Senior Vice President Industry Policy, Air Transport Association of America

Merkel, Stephen — Executive Managing Director and General Counsel, Cantor Fitzgerald

Merlis, Edward — Senior Vice President Legislative and International Affairs, Air Transport Association of America

Mica, John — U.S. Representative, Florida

Miller, Emily — Communications Director for Representative Tom DeLay

Miller, Pamela — volunteer, Comfort Zone Camp

Miller, Steven — Director, Exempt Organization Division, Internal Revenue Service

Mills, Timothy — attorney and lobbyist, Patton Boggs, LLP (Washington, D.C.)

Mineta, Norman — Secretary, U.S. Department of Transportation

Minow, Newton — Rumsfeld advisor in setting up rules for military commissions and attorney (Chicago)

Miranda, Eleanor — passenger screener, San Francisco International Airport

Mitchell, George — head of special American Red Cross monitoring committee and former U.S. Senator, Maine

Moffitt, William — attorney, represented detained immigrant (Washington, D.C.)

Mohammed, Sohail — Muslim community leader and attorney, represented Ali Erikenoglu (Paterson, New Jersey)

Morrison, Bruce — former U.S. Representative, Connecticut (regarding historical problem of INS)

Murphy, Dennis — Assistant Commissioner, Office of Public Affairs, U.S. Customs

Murphy, Laura — Director of Washington National Office, American Civil Liberties Union

Naccara, R. Adm. George — Commander, U.S. Coast Guard (Boston)

Neely, Susan — Special Assistant to the President and Senior Director of Communications, Office of Homeland Security

Newman, Donna — attorney, representing Jose Padilla (New York)

Nickles, Don — U.S. Senator, Oklahoma

Null, Randy — Associate Undersecretary and Chief Technical Officer, Transportation Security Administration

Oberstar, James — U.S. Representative, Minnesota

Obey, David — U.S. Representative, Wisconsin

O'Connell, Kimberly — spokesperson, St. Paul Companies

O'Connor, Michael — former Chief of Transit Police (New York)

O'Hare, Dean — Chairman and CEO, Chubb Corporation

Olshansky, Barbara — Assistant Legal Director, Center for Constitutional Rights (New York)

O'Reilly, Bill — host, *The O'Reilly Factor*

Ostrager, Barry — Lead Trial Counsel for Swiss Re America

Overpeck, Earl — Senior Technical Examiner, Chubb Corporation

Paige, John — Supervisory Special Agent, Federal Bureau of Investigation (Newark, New Jersey)

Pardo, Raymond — Inspection Specialist, Contraband Enforcement Team, U.S. Customs Service (Elizabeth, New Jersey)

Perez, Carlos — Petty Officer 3rd Class, U.S. Coast Guard (New York)

Perkins, Steven — Senior Vice President, Public Sector Homeland Security, Oracle Corporation

Perlman, Ronald — government contracts lawyer (Washington, D.C.)

Peterman, R. Adm. Brian — Deputy Senior Director for Protection and Prevention, Office of Homeland Security

Phillips, Leslie — Communications Director, Senate Committee on Governmental Affairs, for Senator Joseph Lieberman

Porcari, John — Secretary, Maryland Department of Transportation

Poza, Hugo — Vice President, Homeland Security, Raytheon Company

Pyrek, Steve — Director of Communications and Liaison, Tax Exempt and Government Entities Division, Internal Revenue Service

Quinn, Jack — lobbyist and former White House Counsel, Clinton administration

Quinn, Kenneth — attorney and lobbyist (Washington, D.C.)

Rallonza, Maria Aurora — passenger screener, San Francisco International Airport

Rapaport, Janet — Director of Public Affairs, U.S. Customs (New York)

Ricchiuti, James — stock analyst (for InVision), Needham and Company

Ridge, Michele — wife of Tom Ridge

Ridge, Tom — White House Office of Homeland Security Advisor

Ris, Will — Senior Vice President, Government Affairs, American Airlines

Robinson, Michael — Associate Undersecretary for Aviation Operations, Transportation Security Administration

Rochman, Julie — Senior Vice President, Public Affairs, American Insurance Association

Rogers, Harold — U.S. Representative, Kentucky

Romero, Anthony — Executive Director, American Civil Liberties Union

Rosenzweig, David — Vice President of Network Operations, Northeast, Verizon

Ross, Brian — Senior Correspondent, ABC News

Rossides, Gale — Associate Undersecretary for Training and Quality Performance, Transportation Security Administration

Rothrock, Aubrey, III — lawyer and lobbyist, Patton Boggs, LLP (Washington, D.C.)

Roumel, Nicholas — lawyer, representing University of Michigan students interviewed by FBI agents (Ann Arbor)

Roy, Stuart — Communications Director for Representative Tom DeLay

Ruane, Jack — Deputy Chief Inspector, Contraband Enforcement Team, U.S. Customs Service (Elizabeth, New Jersey)

Rubenstein, Howard — Founder and President, Rubenstein Associates (public relations representative for Larry Silverstein)

Rubin, Robert — former Secretary of the Treasury, Clinton administration

Rutherford, Nancy — American Red Cross (worked in New York in fall 2001)

Rutkin, Amy — Chief of Staff for Representative Jerrold Nadler

Ruvolo, Philip — Captain of Rescue 2, New York City Fire Department

Ryan, Lee Ann — team leader, workers' compensation, Chubb Corporation

Salyer, J. C. — staff attorney, American Civil Liberties Union (New Jersey)

Santo, Leticia — passenger screener, San Francisco International Airport

Schaffer, David — Aviation Staff Director and Senior Counsel, House Committee on Transportation

Schambach, Patrick — Associate Undersecretary and CIO/CTO, Transportation Security Administration

Scheeler, Kate — staff member, Senate Committee on Banking, Housing, and Urban Affairs, for Senator Charles Schumer

Schiavo, Mary — attorney for plaintiffs in September 11 tort cases (Washington, D.C., and Los Angeles)

Schumer, Charles — U.S. Senator, New York

Schwartz, Victor — Counsel, Americans for Tort Reform

Scoppetta, Nicholas — Commissioner, New York City Fire Department

Sensenbrenner, James, Jr. — U.S. Representative, Wisconsin

Shaffer, Paul — Business Manager and Financial Secretary, International Brotherhood of Electrical Workers Union (Memphis)

Shea, David — Director, Media Relations, Raytheon Company

Sheehan, Patrick — Legislative Director for Representative George Gekas

Silberling, Tracy — Special Agent, Federal Bureau of Investigation (Washington, D.C.)

Silverstein, Larry — President and CEO, Silverstein Properties (New York)

Simmons, Roger — attorney (represents Muslim charity in suit with government)

Simon, Brittany — daughter of victim Michael Simon

Simon, Eileen — widow of victim Michael Simon

Simon, M.J. — son of victim Michael Simon

Simon, Scott — brother of victim Michael Simon

Simon, Tyler — son of victim Michael Simon

Singh, Tejinder — dial car driver (New York)

Sirota, David — staff member, House Committee on Appropriations

Slutsky, Lorie — President and Director, New York Community Trust

Smith, Larry — Sheriff, Riverside County Sheriff's Department (Riverside, California)

Sperduto, Tom — photojournalist, Public Affairs, United States Coast Guard (New York)

Sperling, Michael — Senior Public Relations Manager, Oracle Corporation

Speziale, Jerry — Sheriff, Passaic County Sheriff's Office (Passaic, New Jersey)

Spitzer, Arthur — Legal Director, American Civil Liberties Union, Washington, D.C., Chapter

Spitzer, Eliot — New York State Attorney General

Steinhardt, Barry — Associate Director, American Civil Liberties Union

Stephens, Richard — Vice President for Homeland Security and Services, Boeing

Stewart, Larry — President, Trial Lawyers Care

Stover, Maj. Steven — Spokesperson, U.S. Army

Strassberger, William — Press Officer, Immigration and Naturalization Service

Strossen, Nadine — President, American Civil Liberties Union

Swain-Staley, Beverly — Acting Executive Director, Baltimore/Washington International Airport

Terwilliger, George, III — former Deputy U.S. Attorney General, George H. Bush administration, and attorney (Washington, D.C.)

Thompson, Larry — Deputy U.S. Attorney General

Thompson, Wiley, III — Federal Security Director, Memphis International Airport

Trottenberg, Polly — Legislative Director for Senator Charles Schumer

Tucker, Mindy — Director, Office of Public Affairs, U.S. Department of Justice

Tusk, Bradley — Director of Communications for Senator Charles Schumer

Valencia, Linda — passenger screener, San Francisco International Airport

Vivanco, Fernando — Director of Communications, Homeland Security and Services, Boeing

Wachtell, Herbert — attorney, representing Larry Silverstein

Wall, Kenneth — Director of Critical Infrastructure Recovery, Office of Homeland Security

Ward, Rachel — Director of Research, Amnesty International

Weber, Steven — professor, University of California at Berkeley (led encounter session for American Civil Liberties Union)

Wedgwood, Ruth — Rumsfeld advisor in setting up rules for military commissions and Yale Law School professor

Weeks, Kevin — Director of Field Operations, U.S. Customs (Detroit)

Weinshall, Iris — Commissioner, New York City Department of Transportation

Weisbrod, Carl — President, Alliance for Downtown New York

Welch, Robert — Partner, Acquisition Solutions

West, Anthony — attorney, worked on defense for John Walker Lindh (San Francisco)

White, Walter — Director of Operations and Public Safety, Memphis–Shelby County Airport Authority

Whitehorn, Samuel — Democratic Senior Counsel, Senate Committee on Commerce, Science, and Transportation

Williams, Deborah — team leader, workers' compensation, Chubb Corporation

Wilson, Mary — reference librarian, Paterson, New Jersey, Free Public Library (interviewed by research assistants Elise Jordan and Claire Miller)

Wolinsky, Marc — attorney, representing Larry Silverstein

Wood, Kenneth — President, Barringer Instruments (New Jersey)

Woollen, Edmund — Vice President, Raytheon Company

Wright, Edwin — Manager of the Radioactive Materials Licensing Program, Office of Public Health Systems, Oregon Department of Human Services (interviewed by research assistant Claire Miller)

Yohe, D. Scott — Senior Vice President, Government Affairs, Delta Air Lines

Younes, Mohamed — President, American Muslim Union (Paterson, New Jersey)

Young, Don — U.S. Representative, Alaska

Ziglar, James — Commissioner, Immigration and Naturalization Service

Zito, Robert — Executive Vice President, Communications, New York Stock Exchange

Zuckerman, Mortimer — CEO, Boston Properties

# Source Notes

Detailed below are the sources used to assemble this narrative.

Sources are listed by last name; their affiliations can be checked against the source list presented above. Unless otherwise noted, the listing of a name denotes one or more interviews conducted by the author. Most interviews were conducted in person.

Source references are not included for unambiguous statements of fact—such as the closing price of a stock, or noncontroversial statistics related to a particular organization. Nor are references included where the text itself has made the source clear. Statements of facts drawn from obvious public records—such as budget figures, legislative provisions, or campaign finance records—are also not separately referenced.

Similarly, if the text has quotations from a television program, newspaper article, or congressional testimony, the reference is not cited again here if the text makes the forum and date clear. Quotations from court hearings or documents filed in court are taken from transcripts of those hearings or from the actual documents, unless otherwise noted as coming from newspaper reports.

Where multiple sources are cited, the most important source is listed first.

Where the information is significant and in dispute I have signaled those disputes in footnotes in the body of the book.

## Prologue

*McCabe September 11 experience:* McCabe, Haage-Gaynor, Hegler.

*Delaquis September 11 experience:* Delaquis, one of her inspectors.

*Statistics on New York and North Dakota ports:* Haage-Gaynor, Delaquis;
U.S. Customs Service Office of Public Information.

*Simon September 11 experience:* Simon, Litchfield.

*Ridge September 11 experience:* Ridge, Holman, Neely.

*Magistri September 11 experience:* Magistri, Margalit, Mattson.

*InVision and explosive detector historical numbers:* Magistri, Mattson, McCann;
InVision SEC filings; FAA Office of Public Information; multiple stock analysts' reports.

*Weinshall September 11 experience:* Weinshall, Schumer.

*Schumer September 11 experience:* Schumer, Weinshall, Trottenberg, Berman.

*Lyons September 11 experience:* Brian Lyons, Elaine Lyons.

*Healy September 11 experience:* Healy, McLaughlin, Berry.

*Michael Cartier September 11 experience:* All six Cartier siblings and their father.

*Ashcroft September 11 experience:* Ashcroft, Israelite, Larry Thompson, Dinh, Chertoff, Ziglar.

*Ashcroft in FBI SIOC room:* Ashcroft, Chertoff, Ziglar, Larry Thompson, Tucker, and two FBI officials who were present.

*President takes Ashcroft aside:* Ashcroft, Card.

*INS fanned out to guard its own building:* Robert Harris, Strassberger, Ziglar.

*Lindemann September 11 experience:* Lindemann, Hall, France.

*Cox September 11 experience:* Cox, Martin, White.

*Cox background and bio:* Cox; "Airport Chiefs Nationwide Pick Cox; Local Hub's Top Executive Will Head 5,000-Member Association," by Richard Thompson, *Commercial Appeal,* May 21, 2000; "Airport's New Pilot Looking to Next Century with Ambitious Expansion Plans," by Paula Woodruff, *Memphis Business Journal,* June 17, 1985.

*FAA spitting out faxes:* Cox, Ris, Mineta, Jackson.

*Romero September 11 experience:* Romero, Laura Murphy, Strossen, and ACLU donor present at the meeting.

*Silverstein September 11 experience:* Silverstein.

*Silverstein would tell the author:* Interview with author.

*According to his own lawyers he was on the phone:* Wachtell, Wolinsky.

*Structure and money involved in Trade Center deal:* World Trade Center Properties LLC partnership agreement obtained by author; Goldman.

*Iacono September 11 experience:* Iacono, Johnson, Bart, shoeshine man at Continental Shoe Repair.

*Continental Shoe Repair business economics:* Iacono, Bart.

*Woollen September 11 experience:* Woollen, Shea, Poza.

*Woollen bio:* Woollen.

*O'Hare September 11 experience:* O'Hare, Degnan, Mark Greenberg.

## September 12, 2001

*Simon experience:* Eileen Simon, Scott Simon.

*Cox experience:* Cox, Martin, White.

*FAA fax sent to airlines:* Ris, Yohe, Merlis, Lunner, Mineta, Longmire.

*FAA had two hijackers' names on the lists:* Senior FAA official who would have had personal knowledge of the list. Longmire said that "it might have been that some of the hijackers' names were on the list, but I can't comment." Mineta, Lunner, and Flaherty acknowledged that it was "possible," but would neither confirm nor deny that the names were on the list. As a general matter, five officials in the Justice Department and Office of Homeland Security freely acknowledged, when asked, that the CIA and FBI had been forwarding these "no-fly" lists for several months and that they had heard that at least two of the hijackers were on it.

*Names erased before list was faxed:* The same senior FAA official.

*FAA two years overdue:* FAA records, Merlis, Kevin Quinn.

*Cox resented:* Cox.

*FAA 4.5-inch rule:* Longmire, Lunner, Merlis, Kevin Quinn.

*Mineta had told President he'd have planes up:* Mineta, Flaherty.

*Conference call snafu:* Flaherty.

*New security rules:* Cox, Flaherty, Merlis, Jackson.

*Other details of conference call:* Jackson, Merlis, Yohe, Ris.

*The Red Cross had gotten some of its people to the site:* Bender.

*Red Cross handles 37,000 fires and disasters:* McLaughlin, Bender, Red Cross Public Affairs Office.

*Three different lines for people wanting to help:* Bender.

*Bender crowded on the street by donors:* Bender.

*Bender hadn't talked to Healy:* Bender, Healy.

*Red Cross website crashed:* Healy, Decker.

*Healy's decision on donor solicitation:* Healy, Berry, McLaughlin, Decker.

*Red Cross new language:* Red Cross solicitation materials, text of ads.

*New York Community Trust statistics:* Trust's public relations brochure and website.

*September 11th Fund formation:* Dickerson, Slutsky.

*Lyons experience:* Brian Lyons, two fellow workers, Elaine Lyons.

*Months later, the police inspector in charge:* Luongo, Marx.

*Four hours to evacuate Trade Center in 1993:* Kroll (his company consulted with the Port Authority, which owns the Trade Center).

*Emergency drill at Pentagon:* Baxter.

*Reasons for Raytheon code name Project Yankee:* Woollen.

*Woollen-Burnham discussion:* Woollen, Burnham.

*Romero orders staff to cancel direct mailing:* Romero.

*Text of direct mailing:* Copy obtained by author.

*Ashcroft, Mueller, Bush meeting:* Ashcroft, Card.

*FBI activities:* Paige, Ziglar, Chertoff, Comstock, two agents in Newark office, one in Detroit office.

*Specific data on FBI Newark office interviews:* Paige.

*Border Patrol Catch and Release Program:* France, Lindemann, Hall, testimony of Pearson and Hall before Senate committee on November 13, 2001.

*Larry Silverstein's sympathy calls:* Two people who called him.

*Nashville conference call:* From records revealed in discovery process related to subsequent Silverstein–insurance company litigation, obtained by author.

*Insurance deal memo:* From records revealed in discovery process related to subsequent Silverstein–insurance company litigation, obtained by author.

*Silverstein tells Childs to begin plan:* Childs.

*Meeting in Chubb conference room:* O'Hare, Degnan, Mark Greenberg.

*O'Hare call to Buffett:* O'Hare, Buffett.

*Insurance industry newsletter:* Insure.com, September 12 posting.

*Fisher sent home:* Fisher.

*Fisher phone conversations:* Fisher, Lindsey, Grasso.

*Grasso on his couch:* Grasso.

*Fisher activities Wednesday morning:* Fisher, Lindsey.

*Verizon problems at switching center:* Author's personal visit, June 13, 2002; Rosenzweig, De Mauro, Marchand.

*Meeting with financial leaders and Verizon:* Grasso, Fisher, Rosenzweig, De Mauro.

*Fisher knew from a conference call:* Fisher.

*Cartiers look at hospitals:* Michael Cartier, John Cartier.

*Cartier home:* Personal visits.

*Calls to McCabe:* McCabe, Haage-Gaynor, Bennis.

*At the Northern Border:* Delaquis, Dennis Murphy.

*Foreign trade transported over the Ambassador Bridge greater than trade with Japan:* Dennis Murphy.

*Complaints at the Ambassador Bridge:* Weeks, Lindsey, Dennis Murphy, Bonner.

*Schumer activities on Wednesday:* Schumer, Clinton, Trottenberg, Berman.

*Schumer plane ride:* Schumer.

## September 13, 2001

*Sal tries to get back into shop:* Iacono, Bart, Johnson.

*Daniels tries to estimate numbers:* Daniels, Call.

*When Schumer's and Clinton's staffs began hearing that number:* Schumer, Clinton, Trottenberg, Dunn.

*Clinton told her staff:* Dunn.

*Schumer, Clinton meeting in Oval Office:* Schumer, Clinton.

*Problems with the $20 billion that night:* Schumer, Daniels, Trottenberg.

*Weinshall faced a more basic money crunch:* Weinshall.

*Formation of Domestic Consequences Principals Committee and its agenda:* Mineta, Card, Lindsey, Fisher, Jackson.

*ACLU feels the effects:* Romero, Laura Murphy.

*Ashcroft forms group to propose legislative changes:* Ashcroft, Dinh, Comstock, Chertoff.

*Problem with Carp being Orthodox:* Dinh, Corallo.

*Alarm at Justice:* Ashcroft, Comstock.

*Cheney thinking of homeland security advisor:* Libby, Abbot, Kuntz.

*Clinton administration hadn't favored moving the boxes around:* Samuel Berger.

*Oregon checking radiation materials:* Wright (interviewed by research assistant Claire Miller).

*North Miami Beach police checking utility and water supplies:* William Berger.

*Brian Lyons calls boss, finds out about Fresh Kills:* Brian Lyons.

*Luongo had arrived:* Luongo, Marx.

## September 15, 2001

*Weinshall looks out at skyline:* Weinshall.

*Woollen's weekend:* Woollen, Shea, Poza.

*September 11th Fund gets startup aid from big corporations:* Dickerson, Gotbaum.

*Hollywood telethon activities:* Katzenberg, Clooney.

*Red Cross declines telethon money:* Healy, Dickerson, Katzenberg.

*By Saturday morning, planes up at Cox's airport:* Cox.

*Memphis passenger statistics:* Supplied by airport.

*Memphis airport economics:* Cox, airport's annual reports.

*Memphis traffic trends:* Cox, airport's monthly statistics.

*Memphis airport fees:* Cox.

*Lines at the airport:* Cox, Martin, White.

*Airport CEO's and financial officers' conference calls:* Ris, Yohe, Merlis.

*Magistri ramps up:* Magistri, Mattson.

*Magistri gets word from McCann:* McCann, Magistri.

*History of 4.5-inch blade rule:* Longmire, former FAA lawyer.

*Some airports had seemed to want the machines:* McCann.

*Lyons still at Ground Zero:* Brian Lyons, Elaine Lyons.

*Healy thought that things were going well:* Healy, Berry.

*Kennedy was livid:* Pat Kennedy.

*Simon's Ridgewood Red Cross experience:* Simon.

*Scott Simon comes to Eileen's house:* Eileen Simon, Scott Simon.

*Number of MIAs in Vietnam:* The Pentagon.

*Cartier family activities:* Michael Cartier, Farrell.

## September 17, 2001

*Iacono allowed back into store and description:* Iacono, Johnson.

*Grasso has better morning:* Grasso, Zito.

*At about 9:25:* "A Nation Challenged: The Scene; Wall Street Returns to Work, Finding Good in Falling Prices," by Alessandra Stanley with Diana B. Henriques, *New York Times,* September 18, 2001.

*Sergio Magistri got up early:* Magistri.

*Magistri's options:* InVision public filings.

*Woollen begins canvassing:* Woollen.

*Lockheed Martin and Boeing similarly in the hunt:* Stephens of Boeing and a spokesman for Lockheed Martin.

*Simon gets the car:* Simon.

*Background on airline lobbying activities:* Merlis.

*Delta has three people taking care of congressional fliers:* Charlene Kennedy.

*Airline executives' white paper:* Copy obtained by author.

*Schaffer conversation with Young:* Schaffer, Young. However, Young did not recall the conversation in these words, which are presented in the text as Schaffer remembered them.

*Blunt laughed and told the lobbyist to quit while he was ahead:* Blunt.

*Session in Daschle's office:* Ris, Daschle, Crane.

*Airline lobbyists had agreed among themselves:* Three lobbyists.

*White House meeting on airline bailout:* Lindsey, Fisher, Jackson, Mineta.

*Pat Kennedy fax:* Copy obtained by author.

*McLaughlin copy of fax sent to Healy:* Copy obtained by author.

*Healy and aides saw Red Cross fund as "leaky bucket":* Healy, Berry, Decker (who acknowledges that they saw it that way, but does not share their appraisal).

*Sensenbrenner comes out of shower, hears Ashcroft on television:* Sensenbrenner.

*Sensenbrenner reads draft:* Sensenbrenner.

*The draft repealed habeas corpus:* Sensenbrenner. Ashcroft said he could not remember whether the draft repealed habeas corpus. Sensenbrenner's staff subsequently said they no longer could find a copy of this original draft. Two White House aides who read this draft do, however, recall habeas corpus being repealed, and that the draft did this by citing some sort of emergency.

*Sensenbrenner called Ashcroft:* Sensenbrenner.

*Romero's reaction to the bill:* Romero.

*Ashcroft had excluded the White House:* Dinh, official in White House counsel's office, two senior Bush administration policy officials.

*Bolten calls Ashcroft; Ashcroft apologizes:* Two senior White House officials.

*Ashcroft's lack of command of the legal issues:* Two senators, one a Republican, the other a Democrat, one veteran Justice Department senior lawyer.

## September 19, 2001

*Chubb employees' experience in making the calls:* Ryan, Overpeck, and Williams—all service representatives for Chubb.

*Clooney worried about website name:* Clooney, Katzenberg.

*September 11th Fund progress:* Slutsky.

*McCabe's office wall:* McCabe, author's personal visit.

*Account of McCabe helping Norwegian woman:* Letter seen by author, McCabe.

*McCabe salary:* McCabe.

*Customs activities at Elizabeth port since September 12:* McCabe, Ruane, Hegler, Haage-Gaynor.

*Customs points system:* McCabe, Bonner, Dennis Murphy.

*Incident regarding ship from Norfolk:* McCabe, Haage-Gaynor, Hegler.

*Coast Guard mission, budget, and logging fifteen years' worth of sea time:* Bennis.

*Fisher-Lindsey discussion about airline bailout:* Fisher, Lindsey, Mineta, Jackson.

*Airlines' solution for bailout:* Their white paper, obtained by author; Fisher, Merlis, Ris, Berman.

*White House proposed solution:* Fisher, Lindsey, Daniels, Berman, Crane.

*Republicans not nearly as naive about plaintiffs' suits:* Crane, Nickles.

*Crane's idea:* Crane, Berman, Ris, Merlis; Crane's memo summarizing it, obtained by author.

*Geoghegan and France reaction to article in* Detroit Free Press *quoting Lindemann and Hall, and steps they took afterward to discipline them:* France, Lindemann, Hall; report of U.S. Justice Department Office of Inspector General, which documents this sequence of events in detail, based on witnesses interviewed by that office for its report.

*Fact that others had provided the same accounts of sector's lack of resources:* Described in detail in inspector general's report.

*Woollen's survey of Raytheon activities:* Woollen, Shea.

*Magistri now thinking big:* Magistri, Mattson.

*Decision to ally tacitly with L-3:* McCann, Magistri.

*Michael Cartier called ahead to Red Cross center:* Michael Cartier.

*Patrick Cartier, Sr.'s, experience there:* Patrick Cartier, Sr., Michael Cartier.

*Sequence of Ridge hearing about the job and accepting it:* Tom Ridge, Michele Ridge, Ridge's scheduling and phone records, Neely, Holman.


## September 21, 2001

*Scene in DeLay's office:* Ris, Yohe, Hart, Blunt, Roy (although Roy, who was not there, said he does not know whether DeLay was drinking).

*DeLay being poured drinks:* Hart, Ris.

*DeLay shuts down staffers' meeting:* Schaffer, Whitehorn.

*Provision inserted by Corzine and Fitzgerald:* Corzine, Whitehorn, Berman, Crane.

*Staff adaptation of Crane's idea:* Luzatto, Berman, Crane.

*Thursday evening scene in Hastert's conference room:* Daschle, Nickles, Gephardt, Blunt, Crane.

*Daniels wanted to limit awards to $250,000:* Nickles, Daniels.

*Hastert takes Gephardt and Daschle aside:* Daschle, Gephardt.

*Schumer not allowed in:* Daschle, Schumer.

*Schumer efforts on behalf of Silverstein:* Schumer, Jack Quinn, Wolinsky, Schumer staff member.

*Schumer conversation with Silverstein:* Schumer, Jack Quinn.

*Erikenoglu account of FBI questioning:* Erikenoglu, one of the agents who was there, Paige.

*Basics of Erikenoglu biography:* Erikenoglu.

*FBI officials in Newark checked with agents:* Paige.

*FBI agents appalled:* Paige, Dickson.

*FBI officials talk to Sohail Mohammed:* Mohammed, Paige.

*McKinsey analysis:* Copy obtained by author.

*Clooney sleeping in studio, writing cue cards, building sets:* Katzenberg, Clooney.

*Clooney worried about phones, tells Russell to fake it:* Clooney. Russell could not be reached for comment.

*O'Reilly takes pride:* O'Reilly.

*O'Reilly told by neighbors:* O'Reilly.

## September 22, 2001

*Michael Simon memorial service:* Copy of program and text of eulogies obtained by author; Simon, Litchfield.

*Eileen frames story of Michael's death:* Simon.

*Children's condition:* Simon.

*Restaurant where lunch reception held:* Visit by author.

*Network of sixty-six women making dinners for Simon:* Litchfield (she organized the dinner providers).

*Schumer Harvard story:* Schumer.

*Residents of Battery Park City return home:* Brodsky, six residents.

*Manager of one of Battery Park City properties:* Brodsky.

*"The Tort Lawyers: Preparing for Years of Litigation":* by Tom Perrotta, Mark Hamblett, and Dan Wise, *New York Law Journal,* September 17, 2001.

*Feinberg on Saturday morning:* Feinberg.

*Feinberg bio:* Feinberg, two former law partners, one former associate (David Boies) in Senator Kennedy's office. The author has also known Feinberg for many years and wrote a profile of him in *The American Lawyer* entitled "The Washington Explosion" in June 1981. For additional background on Feinberg, see "The Calculator," by Elizabeth Kolbert, *The New Yorker,* November 25, 2002.

*Feinberg-Hagel conversation:* Hagel, Feinberg.

*Iacono thinks about his future:* Iacono, Johnson.

*Wachtell, Lipton one of most profitable firms:* *The American Lawyer* magazine, "AM-LAW 100," July-August special supplement, multiple years.

*Wachtell's personal history and characteristics:* The author has known Wachtell since 1976 and written about him and his firm occasionally since then. His firm has also represented the author.

*Wording of the insurance policy:* Documents produced during discovery phase of subsequent litigation and obtained by author.

*During the week, lawyers at Wachtell's firm push Silverstein's insurance people:* Depositions taken during discovery phase of subsequent litigation, transcripts of which were obtained by author.

*Insurers and Silverstein's broker exchanged e-mail and verbal messages:* Depositions taken during discovery phase of subsequent litigation, transcripts of which were obtained by author; documents produced during discovery, obtained by author.

*We can argue that nothing was clear:* Wolinsky.

*Silverstein eagerly telling friends:* Two friends of Silverstein's involved in the real estate business.

*Silverstein's conference room:* Author's personal observation.

*Insurance executives' meeting at White House:* O'Hare, Rochman, Maurice Greenberg.

*White House Saturday meeting about insurance:* Fisher, Lindsey.

*Man detained for going to the same Kinko's; man detained for going to the same motor vehicle office:* "A Deliberate Strategy of Disruption; Massive, Secretive Detention Effort Aimed Mainly at Preventing More Terror," by Amy Goldstein, *Washington Post,* November 4, 2001.

*Ashcroft had directed that INS judges close hearings:* Memorandum from Chief Immigration Judge Michael Creppy to all immigration judges and court administrators, September 21, 2001.

*Well-placed official says FBI had few undercover informants:* Former senior FBI terrorism investigator, one FBI terrorism investigator in Newark and one in Detroit.

*Justice Department briefings of senators:* Schumer.

*Ridge's Saturday and Sunday:* Ridge, Holman, Buckholz.

*Content of looseleaf books:* Obtained by author.

## September 25, 2001

*McCabe incident with suspicious container:* McCabe, Hegler, Haage-Gaynor.

*ACLU forges alliance with conservative Republicans:* Romero, Laura Murphy, Sensenbrenner, senior staff aide to one of those Republicans.

*Conservative Republicans' letter:* Copy obtained by author.

*Sensenbrenner's and Hastert's staffs had agreed:* Laura Murphy, Lungren.

*Letter was mostly drafted by ACLU:* Copy of ACLU draft version obtained by author.

*ACLU people explained to Sensenbrenner's staff:* Laura Murphy, Sensenbrenner.

*In Ashcroft's eyes debate falling into the business-as-usual legislative hopper:* Israelite.

*"Give me some tangible example I can use":* Aide in Ashcroft's Public Affairs Office.

*Romero frustrated by Schumer:* Romero.

*Schumer basically agreed with Patriot Act, found Ashcroft's style arrogant:* Schumer.

*Schumer profoundly affected by the attacks:* Schumer, Weinshall, two members of his staff.

*Romero had told his staff repeatedly after the attacks:* Romero.

*Barr call to Flanigan:* Barr, Terwilliger, and a former official in the White House counsel's office (Flanigan did not return calls seeking confirmation).

*Terwilliger calls:* Terwilliger, two Justice Department officials, Barr.

*Iacono rebuilds store:* Iacono, Bart.

*Iacono one of 3,400 small businesses in frozen zone and similar statistics:* Taken from Seedco report entitled *Back in Business: The Lower Manhattan Small Business and Workforce Retention Project,* by Tom Seessel, April 2002.

*Story of merchants who had opposed Trade Center:* Seedco report; author's father, who owned a small liquor store where the North Tower was built, was one of those merchants.

*Healy kept finding:* Healy, Berry.

*Handwritten letters:* Copies obtained by author.

*Aon Insurance incident:* Healy, Berry.

*She intended to spend only $100 million:* Healy, Decker.

*Healy had alienated veterans on the staff:* McLaughlin, Healy.

*Healy redrafts the form:* Healy, Berry.

*Healy rejected idea to give aid to workers:* Healy.

*Brian Lyons decided:* Brian Lyons, Elaine Lyons.

*Elaine Lyons's activities:* Elaine Lyons.

*Elaine's husband's squad helped her:* Interview with squad members by research assistant Louise Story.

*Donation from Upper East Side firehouse:* Brian Lyons.

*Statistics on funds for Elaine Lyons:* As a fireman's widow Elaine Lyons became eligible for the following funds:

> Federal public safety officer's benefit: $250,000
>
> New York City one-year salary benefit: $52,000
>
> New York State World Trade Center Relief Fund: $20,000
>
> Social Security: $370,000
>
> Fire Department contractual death benefit: $25,000
>
> Victims Compensation Fund (estimate): $1,530,000
>
> Union life insurance (middle-range estimate): $175,000
>
> Accidental death coverage: $50,000
>
> Fire Department group insurance: $8,500
>
> Pension ($60,000 per year, assumes 40 additional years life expectancy): $2,400,000

Firefighters' 9/11 Fund: $418,000

Twin Towers Fund (Giuliani): $355,000

Red Cross average payouts: $121,000

New York Police and Fire Widows' and Children's Benefit Fund: $118,000

Robin Hood Fund: $5,000

September 11th Fund (average payout): $20,000

Leary Firefighters Foundation: $3,500

Union Widows and Children's Fund: $128,000

New York Stock Exchange Fallen Heroes Fund: $20,000

New York Fire Safety Foundation Fund: $7,000

TOTAL: $6,076,000

Police officers' families are entitled to about $1 million less—about $5 million—because their pensions are calculated differently and there were fewer charities dedicated to them.

*Elaine's one abiding worry:* Elaine Lyons.

*Brian Lyons pulls out badge:* Brian Lyons, Elaine Lyons.

*Background on Michael Lyons:* Elaine Lyons.

*Feinberg-Hagel conversation:* Feinberg, Hagel.

*As far as Ashcroft's staff was concerned:* Israelite, Lefkowitz.

*Meeting at Kreindler law firm:* Lee Kreindler, James Kreindler.


## September 26, 2001

*Lyons's story of encountering a different Michael Lyons:* Brian Lyons, "the other" Michael Lyons (interviewed by research assistant Louise Story).

*Lindemann hated being separated:* Lindemann, Hall.

*Supervisors were furious:* Inspector general's report.

*Weinshall attacks gridlock:* Weinshall.

*Parking garage owners, others would fight it:* "Secret Meetings a Capital Offense," editorial, *New York Daily News,* December 10, 2001; "Lone Rangers . . . can use some bridges and tunnels again, but requiring car pools is much better policy," editorial, *Newsday,* April 22, 2002.

*Mohammed's law office:* Personal visit.

*Mohammed's sensitivity training session experience:* Paige, Mohammed, Dickson, a New Jersey state trooper who was present.

*Details of his answers to questions:* Mohammed, Paige. Also the author watched him conduct a similar session on April 2, 2002. Mohammed says the questions and answers at that session were much the same as they were in this earlier session.

*Farrell decides to take leave from her job:* Farrell.

### September 28, 2001

*Red Cross board meeting:* Minutes of the meeting obtained by the author; McLaughlin, Healy.

*There were "rumblings":* Healy, McLaughlin.

*Loy-Ridge meeting:* Loy, Ridge.

### September 29, 2001

*Jaffri detention:* Taken from account provided by his lawyers in their subsequent civil suit. Therefore, this must be viewed skeptically as presenting only one side of the case.

*Account of Ashcroft strategy on detentions:* This was provided by two of the people who are closest to Ashcroft and were directly involved in these discussions. Their account is consistent with the subsequent actions taken by the FBI, INS, and Justice Department lawyers, and was also confirmed by a White House official familiar with Ashcroft's articulation of the strategy in White House meetings. During his discussions with the author, Ashcroft also confirmed the basic strategy of doing whatever was possible to hold anyone on even minor charges who, he said, "we determined . . . was a serious risk of terrorism." But unlike his colleagues, he maintained that all of the hundreds of Muslims detained—few of whom ever ended up being charged with anything related to terrorism—were, in fact, considered to be serious terrorist threats.

*Professor in Indiana:* Basham (interviewed by research assistant Claire Miller).

*Mueller not comfortable:* Two FBI officials (including the one quoted anonymously in the text) and one White House official familiar with Mueller's thinking. Mueller declined to be interviewed for this book.

*Ashcroft literally said:* One person who was in the room at the time.

*FBI comes to Paterson Free Public Library:* Wilson, Czesak (Wilson interviewed by research assistants Claire Miller and Elise Jordan, Czesak interviewed by Claire Miller).

### October 1, 2001

*Saga of Hawaiian snow bunnies:* Delaquis.

*Delays reduced:* Delaquis, Dennis Murphy, Weeks, data from Customs website.

*Gotbaum hiring by September 11th Fund:* Gotbaum, Dickerson, Slutsky.

*Online survey:* Copy obtained by author.

*Simon visit to Red Cross and life insurance:* Simon.

*ACLU ad campaign:* Romero.

*Cox's numbers and budgeting:* Cox and data provided by Memphis airport.

*ACLU's goal with Senate:* Romero, Laura Murphy.

## October 2, 2001

*Letter inviting insurers to meeting:*  Copy obtained by author.

*Ostrager background:*  Ostrager, Martindale-Hubbell directory of lawyers, two of
   Ostrager's partners.

*Finances of Ostrager's firm and Wachtell's firm:*  *The American Lawyer,* "AM-LAW
   100," July–August special supplement, multiple years.

*Account of meeting:*  Ostrager, Wolinsky, two other lawyers who were present.

## October 3, 2001

*Forty-two people caught sneaking over:*  These records were provided to the author by
   an INS supervisor in the region covering Detroit. When the author attempted to
   authenticate them orally and by e-mail with INS spokesman William Strassberger, he repeatedly promised an answer, then, after five months, declined
   comment.

*Associated Press story announcing Ziglar's appointment:*  "Bush Names Management
   Expert to Head Immigration Agency," Associated Press, April 27, 2001.

*It was on her watch:*  The best account of the Texas railway killer fiasco comes from
   another report issued by the Office of the Inspector General, dated March 20,
   2000.

*Red Cross meeting:*  Healy, McLaughlin, Pat Kennedy; notes of meeting obtained by
   author.

*Healy's view of Israel issue:*  Healy. In addition, two excellent articles about Healy and
   the Red Cross were extremely helpful in framing the narrative's account of this
   issue and of Healy and the Red Cross generally: "Who Brought Bernadine
   Healy Down?" by Deborah Sontag, *New York Times Magazine,* December 23,
   2001, and "Fallout at the Red Cross," by Jane Mayer, *The New Yorker,* December
   24, 2001.

## October 5, 2001

*Meeting to set up Seedco program:*  Described in Seedco report, April 2002; Weisbrod,
   Grinker.

*O'Reilly easier for Healy to deal with than her board:*  Healy.

*Families flooding O'Reilly with calls and e-mails:*  O'Reilly.

## October 8, 2001

*Ridge struck by three things at Oval Office meetings:*  Ridge's account to two of his
   senior aides.

*Fear of radiation bombs in D.C.:*  One senior Ridge aide, one memo obtained by
   author referring to the threat.

*Isakowitz and Kenneth Quinn activities:*  Isakowitz, Kenneth Quinn, Whitehorn,
   Schaffer, Crane.

*McCain meeting:* Isakowitz, McCain, Crane.

*Argenbright background and founding by Frank Argenbright, Jr.:* "The Leader in Airport Security, and in Lapses," by David Firestone, *New York Times,* November 9, 2001; "Detroit Metro Security Firm Faces Scrutiny," by Jeff Plungis, *Detroit News,* September 23, 2001; "Company Pleaded Guilty to Previous Violations," by Tyler Bridges, *Miami Herald,* September 13, 2001.

*Details of Argenbright purchase deal:* Documents obtained by author. Frank Argenbright was unreachable by author, and his former company declined to comment for this book.

*Frank Argenbright's house in Sea Island:* By coincidence the author rented this house for a week during the summer of 2001.

*Magistri view of airline security bill:* Magistri, McCann.

*Silverstein hires Jack Quinn:* Jack Quinn, Wolinsky.

*Raytheon paying prominent law firm:* Levinson.

*Rental car companies and hotel industry seeking relief:* Isakowitz, McCain, Crane, Berman.

New York Times *would soon report:* "A Nation Challenged: The Interests; Since Sept. 11, Lobbyists Put Old Pleas in New Packages," by David E. Rosenbaum, *New York Times,* December 3, 2001.

*Vicious competition among nonprofits for grants:* "Researchers Vie to Study Psyches of Youngest Victims of Sept. 11," by Lucette Lagnado, *Wall Street Journal,* April 26, 2002; grant proposals of various kinds reviewed by author.

*September 11th Fund soon found grant proposals rewritten:* Gotbaum, Weisbrod.

*Glaucoma Foundation:* Christianson (interviewed by research assistant Claire Miller); invitation sent to author.


## October 9, 2001

*Jessica Schumer's return to Stuyvesant:* Weinshall, Charles Schumer.


## October 11, 2001

*Eileen Simon visit to Ground Zero:* Simon.

*Lyons stays at Ground Zero:* Brian Lyons.


## October 12, 2001

*Time stamp:* Seen by author.

*Murphy's activities and assumptions:* Laura Murphy, Romero.

*Schumer's view of Patriot Act:* Schumer, Berman.

*Sometime after midnight Hastert had agreed:* Sensenbrenner, official at Justice Department involved in lobbying the bill.

*Murphy on the phone to staffers:* Laura Murphy, three congressional staffers.

*ACLU executive committee meeting:* Romero.

*ACLU full board meeting:* Romero, Heyderman.

*Ridge and the budget:* Ridge, Daniels, Falkenrath, Canfield.

## October 15, 2001

*Iacono reopens:* Iacono, Bart.

*InVision greets thirty new employees:* Magistri.

*McLaughlin, Healy conversation:* Healy, McLaughlin (Healy described the conversation in detail; McLaughlin confirmed the basics of it, but he does not recall saying that the board was "crazy," and maintains that he would never speak disrespectfully of his board).

## October 18, 2001

*Ridge press conference:* Transcript provided by White House Press Office; description: "A Nation Challenged: The Biological Threat; Bush Officials Step Out in Force in Effort to Calm Anthrax Fears," by Todd S. Purdum and Elizabeth Becker, *New York Times,* October 18, 2001.

*Ridge not satisfied with press conference or coordination:* Ridge, Holman.

*Ridge 9:00 P.M. meeting:* Holman, Ridge, two other people who were there.

## October 22, 2001

*Ostrager tired of playing defense:* Ostrager.

*Suit surprised Silverstein and his lawyers:* Wachtell.

## October 23, 2001

*Red Cross board meeting:* Pat Kennedy, McLaughlin.

*Healy-McLaughlin conversation:* Healy, McLaughlin, although Decker and McLaughlin say they do not remember McLaughlin using the word "cabal" to describe the board group and doubt that he ever would have.

## October 24, 2001

*Meeting with congressional leaders:* "Ridge Carries Message on Anthrax; Homeland Security Director's Role in Federal Response Comes Under Scrutiny," by Mike Allen and Eric Pianin, *Washington Post,* October 25, 2001; Ridge; transcript of White House press secretary Ari Fleischer's "gaggle" with the press on June 6, 2002.

*Anthrax meeting:* Holman, Neely.

*Anthrax situation a warning more than an attack:* Three senior White House officials.

## October 26, 2001

*Small group of Ashcroft aides:* Israelite, and account after the fact by another, as told to author by Ken Feinberg.

*Reporter was given tip by someone in Kreindler's firm:* Reporter for national news organization covering this story.

*Romero-Mueller meeting:* Romero (Mueller's office confirmed the meeting and general discussion but would not comment on the details).

New York Times *article regarding Healy's resignation:* "A Nation Challenged: The Charity; Red Cross President Quits, Saying That the Board Left Her No Other Choice," by Katharine Q. Seelye and Diana B. Henriques, *New York Times,* October 27, 2001.

## October 29, 2001

*France had e-mail waiting for him:* Inspector general's report.

*Threat matrix talked about attack on nuclear plants:* Official in Ridge's office familiar with matrix reports.

*Ridge's view of alerts:* Ridge, Neely.

New York Times *story:* "A Nation Challenged: The Investigation; Agency Offers No Information About Threats," by David Johnston and Philip Shenon, *New York Times,* October 12, 2001.

## October 30, 2001

*Quinn and Isakowitz had lobbied:* Kenneth Quinn, Isakowitz, and three House Republican staff members.

*Each member of Congress had a story:* Kenneth Quinn.

*Iacono conversation with Garcia:* Iacono, Bart.

*Iacono's background:* Iacono.

*Iacono working in U.S. illegally:* Iacono.

*Chertoff concerned:* Chertoff.

*Scene at Yankee Stadium:* Author was there.

## October 31, 2001

*Byrne background:* Byrne, a fireman who worked with him in a Brooklyn firehouse, biographical data provided by Public Affairs Office of the Office of Homeland Security.

*Lawlor background:* Lawlor, information provided by Public Affairs Office of the Office of Homeland Security; *The Phoenix Program,* by Douglas Valentine, New York: William Morrow & Co., 1990.

*Ridge's priorities:* Ridge, Abbot, Falkenrath.

*FEMA issue:* Byrne, Falkenrath.

## November 2, 2001

*ACLU direct mail results:* Romero.

*Fight between firemen and cops:* Brian Lyons; "A Nation Challenged: The
Firefighters; Firefighters in Angry Scuffle with Police at Trade Center," by Dan
Barry and Kevin Flynn, *New York Times,* November 3, 2001; "Firemen, Cops in
WTC Brawl; 12 Bravest Busted at Ground Zero Rally Against Rescue Cuts," by
David Seifman, Douglas Wight, and Philip Messing, *New York Post,* November
3, 2001.

## November 3, 2001

*Cartier family upset:* All six Cartier siblings.

*Michael had fierce look in his eye:* Farrell.

*Give Your Voice website:* Can be found at *www.giveyourvoice.com.*

*More than 100 members by Sunday night:* Michael Cartier.

## November 4, 2001

*Isakowitz decided:* Another lobbyist—not Isakowitz—involved in the effort, public
relations person working for Argenbright. Isakowitz refused to comment on
whether he had initiated DeLay's sending of the letter, but he did acknowledge
knowing about it in advance.

## November 5, 2001

*Memphis traffic numbers:* Provided by Memphis airport.

*Cox activities and decisions:* Cox, Martin.

## November 6, 2001

*Hiccup in plan to fire Lindemann:* Inspector General's report.

*Feinberg interview:* Israelite, Feinberg.

*$6 billion talked about in the halls at Justice Department:* Israelite, Lefkowitz.

*Spitzer thought to himself:* Eliot Spitzer.

## November 7, 2001

*McLaughlin-Healy conversation:* Healy (McLaughlin says he does not remember this
conversation, though it "might have happened").

## November 8, 2001

*Letter to Lindemann:* Copy obtained by author.

*Letter drafted and vetted by at least a dozen INS officials:* Inspector general's report;
discussions with senior INS official in Washington regarding who was involved
from that office.

*Deadlines too much of a good thing for Magistri:* Magistri.

*Barringer lobbying activities:* Rothwax, Wood, Schaffer, Whitehorn.

## November 9, 2001

*Levin letter to Ziglar:* Inspector general's report.

## November 10, 2001

*Iacono's business awful:* Iacono, Bart.

*Iacono meets Bart:* Iacono, Bart.

*Extent of pro bono work by Bart's firm:* Bart, Geerdes.

## November 12, 2001

*Schumer in Buffalo:* Schumer, Schumer's driver.

*Account of visit to crash site:* Schumer.

*Mica's view of whether public would now tolerate a deadlock:* Mica.

*Mineta, Card favored some type of federalization:* A high official involved in these policy issues familiar with both men's views.

*Schumer came to view the situation as emblematic:* Schumer.

## November 13, 2001

*O'Hare meeting with Lott:* O'Hare, one other person who was in the room.

*O'Hare's thoughts about Lott:* O'Hare.

*Characterizations of military commission plans:* "Seizing Dictatorial Power," by William Safire, *New York Times,* November 15, 2001; "End-Running the Bill of Rights," editorial, *Washington Post,* November 16, 2001; "Bush Order on Military Tribunals Is Further Evidence That Government Is Abandoning Democracy's Checks and Balances," statement of Laura Murphy, ACLU press release, November 14, 2001.

*New York Times wrote that the tribunals would be "largely secret":* "A Nation Challenged: The Law; Bush's New Rules to Fight Terror Transform the Legal Landscape," by Matthew Purdy, *New York Times,* November 25, 2001.

*Few people were consulted:* White House official involved in the plan, Terwilliger, Israelite.

*Pentagon not consulted:* Haynes.

*Romero asked if bin Laden should be tried, "just like OJ":* Interview with author.

*Public opinion polls:* For example, a poll conducted by ABC News and the *Washington Post* on November 27, 2001, found 64 percent of adults surveyed in favor of military tribunals and 34 percent in favor of using the U.S. criminal court system.

*Schumer declared in a Senate hearing:* Senate Judiciary Committee hearing, "Preserving Freedoms While Defending Against Terrorism," December 4, 2001.

*Magistri meeting with Mineta and Jackson:* Magistri, McCann, Jackson.

*Mineta calls Magistri:* Magistri, Mineta.

*Bart applies for grant:* Bart.

*Bart and Geerdes activities:* Bart, Geerdes.

## November 14, 2001

*Feinberg-Daniels meeting:* Feinberg, Daniels.

## November 15, 2001

*Lindemann-Hall conversations:* Lindemann, Hall.

*Ziglar had agreed:* Inspector general's report.

*Fine immediately assigned a team:* Inspector general's report.

*Ostrager figured it this way:* Ostrager.

*Silverstein–Port Authority contract:* Copy obtained by author.

## November 16, 2001

*House-Senate conference and staff produce final version of aviation security bill:* Crane, Whitehorn, Schaffer, Kenneth Quinn, Isakowitz, Mica, Berman, Schumer, Merlis, Hauptli.

*Bart efforts for Iacono and effort to convince him about landlord:* Bart, Iacono.

## November 17, 2001

*Magistri jubilant:* Magistri, McCann.

## November 19, 2001

*Jackson and go teams:* Jackson, Hawley, Mineta, Hardt.

*Meetings at Justice Department regarding whether to put Moussaoui into a military commission:* Chertoff, two federal prosecutors involved in the decision.

## November 20, 2001

*Cartiers try to reach public officials:* Michael Cartier, Patrick Cartier, Jr., Farrell.

*Rumsfeld reaches out to group of advisors:* Haynes, Clarke, Cutler, Minow, Cobb.

## November 21, 2001

*Cox spent the day:* Cox.

*Crowds at Baltimore/Washington Airport:* Swain-Staley.

## November 22, 2001

*Lyons at Ground Zero:* Brian Lyons.

**November 23, 2001**

*Feinberg-Ashcroft discussion:* Feinberg, Ashcroft, Israelite.

*Ashcroft called Giuliani:* Ashcroft.

**November 26, 2001**

*Ashcroft-Feinberg conversation:* Feinberg.

*Feinberg activities:* Feinberg, two friends with whom he spoke.

**November 29, 2001**

*White House Situation Room meeting:* Copy of PowerPoint presentation seen by author; Jackson, Mineta, and one other person who attended.

*Separate lobbying group in Washington forever looking for opportunity to get tort reform inserted into any pending law:* Schwartz.

*Debate at September 11th Fund board meeting:* Board briefing book obtained by author; Gotbaum, Weisbrod, Slutsky.

*Bart faxed letter to insurance company:* Bart.

**December 1, 2001**

*Lindemann taken to hospital:* Lindemann.

**December 2, 2001**

*Schumer working on Saturdays, seems overwhelmed:* Weinshall, Schumer.

*Schumer-Cartier meeting:* Michael Cartier, Schumer.

*Brosnahan sees John Walker Lindh on television, calls in to voice mail:* Brosnahan.

*Brosnahan conversation with Frank Lindh:* Brosnahan.

*Brosnahan letter:* Later included as defense exhibit in court filing, obtained by author.

**December 3, 2001**

*FBI interviews of students in Michigan:* Roumel, FBI agent involved in some interviews in the Detroit area.

*Schumer called Giuliani:* Schumer.

*Cartier meeting with Shierer:* Michael Cartier.

Schumer's staff finds out they were not satisfied: Schumer staff member, Farrell.

**December 5, 2001**

*Brosnahan letter and fax:* Later included as defense exhibit in court filing, obtained by author.

*Garcia gets aid from Red Cross:* Bart's paralegal (interviewed by research assistant Louise Story).

*Simon is notified about remains:* Simon.

## December 6, 2001

New York Times *called Ashcroft performance "forceful and unyielding":* "Ashcroft Defends Antiterror Plan and Says Criticism May Aid Foes," by Neil A. Lewis, *New York Times,* December 7, 2001.

*Ashcroft thought Senate had backed away:* Senior Justice Department official.

## December 7, 2001

*Jackson and Hawley had decided they were not going to give InVision orders:* Jackson, Hawley.

*Jackson and Mineta thought about Magaw:* Jackson, Lunner.

*Simon in CVS:* Simon.

*Lindh's condition:* Detailed descriptions later included as defense exhibit in court filing, obtained by author. The extent to which these descriptions were ever contested by the government is discussed in the text.

## December 9, 2001

*Schumer liked to hold Sunday press conferences:* Schumer.

*McCabe and co-workers frustrated:* McCabe, Ruane, Hegler.

## December 10, 2001

*Feinberg activities:* Feinberg.

*Feinberg-Kreindler meeting:* Lee Kreindler, Feinberg.

*Feinberg's general demeanor and performance in these meetings:* Lee Kreindler, three other lawyers who attended such meetings, and author's personal observation (at a different meeting).

*Two arguments used by Ashcroft to keep Moussaoui case:* White House official involved in the decision, prosecutor involved in the decision.

*Romero was jubilant:* Romero.

*Terwilliger reaction:* Terwilliger.

*Cartier-Giuliani meeting:* Michael Cartier, Farrell, Giuliani.

## December 11, 2001

*Simon's family situation:* Simon.

*Gifts to Simon:* Simon, and personal perusal by author.

## December 12, 2001

*Memphis airport revenue and expense numbers:* Provided by Memphis airport officials.

*Airlines' expenses and problems:* Merlis, Yohe, Ris.

*Gathering at Cartier parents' home with lawyer:* Author was there.

**December 13, 2001**

*Something going on with Catch and Release Program:* Lindemann, Hall.

**December 14, 2001**

*Insurance case court hearing:* Transcript obtained by author.

*Feinberg preparing regulations:* Feinberg, Greenspan.

*Feinberg speaks to Kennedy:* Feinberg.

*Formation of 9/11 United Services Group:* Eliot Spitzer, Hurst; materials distributed at press conference.

*Cartiers get full tour:* Michael Cartier, Patrick Cartier, Jr., Luongo, Marx, Brian Lyons.

**December 18, 2001**

*Schumer pushes Senate for insurance reform:* Rochman, Schumer aide, Schumer, Crane.

*Last Ground Zero fires about to go out:* Author was present at site.

*Iacono makes Bart take off her shoes:* Bart, Iacono.

**December 20, 2001**

*Magaw calls Rossides:* Magaw, Rossides.

*Rossides's biography:* Rossides.

*Cartier realizes he made a mistake:* Michael Cartier.

*Schumer had been briefed by Feinberg:* Schumer, Feinberg.

*Talking to a reporter, Kreindler said:* The author was the reporter, doing a column for *Newsweek.*

*Feinberg began making plans:* Feinberg, in conversation with author that night.

*O'Hare memo:* Mark Greenberg, O'Hare.

*O'Hare salary and bonus:* Chubb public filings.

**December 21, 2001**

*It continued to rankle Brosnahan:* Brosnahan.

*Gonzales call:* Brosnahan, and described in subsequent court filings.

*Falkenrath memo:* Seen by author.

*Principals Group meeting turns down Ridge idea:* Falkenrath, Ridge, Mineta, Card.

*Card later reported to the President:* Two senior White House aides.

*Ridge tells Falkenrath not to worry:* Falkenrath, Ridge.

*FEMA problem:* Ridge, Byrne, Neely.

*Ridge Pennsylvania campaign:* Holman.

## December 22, 2001

*To Ashcroft it was a defining moment:* Ashcroft.

*No one at Justice consulted White House on Reid case:* Senior White House official who would have known if consultations had taken place, senior government prosecutor.

## December 25, 2001

*Feinberg meets plaintiffs lawyer on Jamaican vacation:* Barasch, Feinberg.

*Contents of notice of intent to sue:* Copy obtained by author.

## December 31, 2001

*Customs loans NYC radiation detectors:* McCabe, Dennis Murphy.

*Simon's New Year's Eve:* Simon, one of her neighbors.

## January 2, 2002

*Schumer meets with real estate broker:* Schumer, Gosin; copy of presentation prepared by Gosin obtained by author.

## January 4, 2002

*Gwinnett County insurance bill:* "Terrorism Insurance Price Tag: $390,000," by Doug Nurse, *Atlanta Journal and Constitution,* January 1, 2002.

*Insurance brokers for key, iconic skyscrapers:* Three brokers, interviewed by author for column he prepared on this subject for *Newsweek.*

## January 5, 2002

*Saturday training at FLETC:* McCabe.

## January 6, 2002

*Cartier's living room setup:* Visit by author.

*Simon calculates offsets:* Simon (numbers subsequently confirmed by member of Feinberg's staff).

*Feinberg, too, now starting to hear talk about offsets:* Feinberg (conversation with author on this day).

*Gale Rossides's first day:* Rossides, McHale, Hawley.

## January 8, 2002

*Cargo container security meeting:* Peterman, another person who attended the meeting, and notes of meeting obtained by author from one of the participants.

*Feinberg cared a lot about suits being filed:* Feinberg.

*Bart liked to say "lots of ways to skin a cat":* Geerdes.

New York Times *article about Sal:* "Lower Manhattan Journal: A Downtown Cobbler Gets Back on His Insoles," by Andrew Jacobs, *New York Times,* January 20, 2002.

*Publicity boosts Iacono's business:* Iacono, Bart.

## January 14, 2002

*Cartier turns down Oprah invitation:* Farrell (Oprah producers do not confirm or deny invitations that are turned down).

*Jaffri expected to be released but not released:* Subsequent court filings in his suit against the government.

*Ridge's staff instructed by White House officials not to talk about national identification cards:* Two members of Ridge's staff.

*Schumer supported sensible identification system:* Schumer.

*Deliberations over State of the Union:* Four Ridge staff members (budget items), Daniels (budget items), two senior members of White House staff (national service).

*Combat Air Patrols meeting:* Notes of the meeting obtained by author.

## January 15, 2002

*Scene at Red Cross center with dial cab drivers:* Author was there.

*Red Cross official told Russian driver about possibility of aid:* Someone who works in New York City Red Cross chapter who spoke with the Red Cross person who was the passenger, Red Cross volunteer caseworker who spoke with Russian aid applicants.

*Remains of eleven firefighters and several others:* Brian Lyons.

*Some prosecutors in Ashcroft's own department were also surprised by the nature of the charges:* Three United States attorneys in different districts across the country, two prosecutors in Washington.

## January 16, 2002

*Iacono's trouble with the insurance company:* Iacono, Bart, Geerdes.

*Feinberg meeting with families:* Feinberg, Farrell, Patrick Cartier, Sr.

## January 17, 2002

*Details of ACLU suit on baggage screeners and backgrounds of plaintiffs:* ACLU complaint and accompanying affidavits.

*Screener who complained about knives:* Rallonza.

*Families rally at Park Avenue Armory:* Author was there.

*Corzine had told a reporter:* Author interview with Corzine.

**January 19, 2002**

*Simon family goes to Comfort Zone:* Simon; "Youngest Victims Heal Together; Camp Brings Together Kids Who Lost Loved Ones to Terror," by Brian Aberback, the *Record,* January 20, 2002; "A Stairway to Heaven: One More Step to Healing for the Children of Sept. 11," by Peggy O'Crowley, *Star-Ledger,* January 22, 2002; "Children of Sept. 11 Victims Cope," Associated Press, April 28, 2002. In addition, background reporting on the Comfort Zone was done by research assistant Louise Story.

*Dynamics of Simon's widows group:* Simon, one of the other women in the group.

**January 21, 2002**

*Struggle to get employee numbers down at TSA:* Hawley, Rossides, McHale, Jackson.

**January 23, 2002**

*Feinberg not getting enrollment yet:* Feinberg conversation with author on this day.
*New Jersey meeting:* Author was present.
*Simon had learned details of offsets:* Simon.

**January 24, 2002**

*Lindh met with his parents and Brosnahan, accepted Brosnahan:* Brosnahan.

**January 27, 2002**

*Cartier tells wife he "really screwed this up":* Michael Cartier.

**January 28, 2002**

*Ridge staff infuriated by Ashcroft announcement of major changes at Olympics:* Five members of Ridge's staff.
*Ashcroft had remarked offhandedly:* FBI agent involved in Olympics preparation with knowledge of these comments.
*Ashcroft-Ridge conversation:* Two people whom Ridge told about it.

**January 31, 2002**

*Red Cross press conference:* Author attended; handouts distributed at press conference.
*Red Cross members bitterly joked among themselves:* Pat Kennedy and one additional board member.
*But by early next week that perception would change:* "An Excess of Riches," by Steven Brill, *Newsweek,* February 11, 2002; "Red Cross Gives Disaster Relief to Tony Enclave," by Anne Marie Chaker, *Wall Street Journal,* February 7, 2002.
*Data-mining meeting:* Summary of meeting obtained by author.

*Bill Clinton called Ashcroft about Acxiom:* One close friend of Clintons, Hillary Clinton.

*Acxiom's capabilities:* The company's promotional materials, someone who attended the meeting.

*Ridge's staff hoped FBI would share with local police:* Summary of the meeting, obtained by author.

## February 1, 2002

*Memphis airport traffic:* Data supplied by airport authorities.

*Cox's new worry:* Cox.

*Industry line about TSA, as explained to reporters:* Author heard this from three other reporters, and it is the way it was explained to author.

*Schumer at New-York Historical Society:* Author was present.

## February 3, 2002

*NFL lacked terrorism insurance:* Rochman.

*Lobbyists frustrated:* Rochman.

## February 4, 2002

*Bart works on Iacono's insurance:* Bart.

*Feinberg visit to Staten Island:* Author viewed videotape of the meeting; Feinberg, Doyle, four other people who were present.

## February 5, 2002

*Process of Coast Guard boarding ship outside the harbor:* Bennis, Perez, Sperduto. Also, author participated in one such boarding.

*Customs activities at port:* Author was present.

*Explanation of points system:* McCabe.

## February 6, 2002

*Lawlor couldn't believe he had to meet again:* One of Lawlor's senior aides.

*Meeting to discuss Salt Lake City airspace:* Minutes of meeting obtained by author.

## February 7, 2002

*Childs's design:* Shown to author by Childs.

*Silverstein's reaction to it:* Childs.

*For now they had to show the design with the four office towers:* Childs.

## February 11, 2002

*Sal got check:* Iacono, Bart.

*Crane's new position:* Crane.

*Chertoff speech:* Author was present.

*Lindh court appearance and drama outside courtroom:* "In Court, a Not-Guilty Plea; Outside, the Real Drama," by Katherine Q. Seelye, *New York Times,* February 14, 2002; "Lindh Pleads Not Guilty to Terror Aid; Judge in Alexandria Considers August Trial," by Brooke A. Masters, *Washington Post,* February 14, 2002.

## February 14, 2002

*Eileen Simon's home:* Author's personal visit.

*Entry-exit meeting:* Minutes of meeting obtained by author. Background of issue: Cronin, Peterman.

*Ridge had been quietly encouraging Kyl:* This was mentioned at a Ridge staff meeting later in the month that author attended.

## February 17, 2002

*Canadians come to Squad 41:* Brian Lyons, Elaine Lyons; members of Squad 41 (interviewed by research assistant Louise Story).

*Elaine Lyons goes to meetings early:* Elaine Lyons.

*Position of private security companies:* Kenneth Quinn, McHale, Kerner.

*Argenbright people change uniforms in Memphis:* Cox.

*The "dip" period, "four pillars" strategy, etc:* Jackson, Lunner, Hawley, Flaherty.

*Simon family trip to Florida:* Eileen Simon, Brittany Simon.

## February 18, 2002

*Feinberg and staff realize mistake on offsets:* Feinberg, Greenspan.

*First draft was forty pages:* Greenspan.

*Rossides's routine:* Rossides.

*Hardt and Null befriend her:* Hardt, Null, Rossides.

*Rossides negotiates pay scale with OMB:* Rossides and Transportation Security Administration public documents, including recruiting documents.

## February 20, 2002

*Woollen reached out to old FAA contacts:* Woollen, Poza.

*Meeting between Raytheon and TSA/FAA officials:* Null, Poza, Woollen.

## February 21, 2002

*Red Cross formal vote:* McLaughlin, Pat Kennedy (Red Cross Public Affairs Office supplied actual date of the meeting).

*Romero in Montana:* Romero; "Risk to Liberty Feared" and "Protest Held at Meeting," by Becky Shay, *Billings Gazette,* February 24, 2002.

## February 23, 2002

*Magistri-Null meeting:* Magistri, Null.

*Terms of the deal:* Magistri.

## February 26, 2002

*If you give them the Kentucky Derby:* Author was present at senior staff meeting.

*Ridge team had grown to eighty:* Neely.

*Schumer's staff had heard from Customs officials about how wrong they were:* Member of Schumer's staff.

*Bonner had wanted to be Attorney General:* Senior customs official close to Bonner. Bonner does not deny this.

## February 27, 2002

*Schumer-Daniels meeting:* Daniels, Schumer.

*Meeting on student visas:* Author was present. However, I was asked to leave when the subject of preventing students from taking certain advanced science courses started to become detailed. I subsequently obtained a copy of a summary of the meeting, including a summary of that aspect of the meeting.

*Peterman was thinking:* Peterman.

*"Medical and Public Health Preparedness" meeting:* Minutes of meeting obtained by author.

*Lawlor frustrated:* One of Lawlor's senior staff people.

*Consensus required:* Two senior Ridge staff people.

*Raytheon meeting in Vice President's conference room:* Author was present. However, I left just before the meeting adjourned and obtained an account of that part of it from Levinson and Woollen.

*Where do I sign up? Peterman thought:* Peterman.

## February 28, 2002

*Ashcroft angry:* Senior member of Justice Department staff, senior Justice Department budget officer who heard it from another Ashcroft aide.

*Ashcroft September 10 budget submission to Daniels:* Copy obtained by author.

*"Policy time":* Two senior White House officials.

*Homeland Security Council agenda on this day:* Two Ridge aides.

## March 2, 2002

*Feinberg push back from Justice:* Feinberg, Lefkowitz, Greenspan.

**March 4, 2002**

*Iacono's business:* Iacono.

*What shoeshine men were told:* One of the men.

*New York City lost 132,000 jobs:* "Worst Job Loss for New York in a Decade," by Leslie Eaton, *New York Times,* March 6, 2002.

*Lindemann hears good news:* Lindemann, Hall.

**March 5, 2002**

*Removal of temporary roadway:* Brian Lyons; and coverage on New York One (local cable news channel).

*Lyons was determined to be there:* Brian Lyons, Elaine Lyons.

*Wedding band found:* Elaine Lyons.

*Realtor asked about escrow account:* Elaine Lyons, Brian Lyons.

*Ridge had met Bloomberg:* Ridge.

*Bloomberg gets call from Ridge:* Bloomberg.

**March 6, 2002**

*Data on Northwest bank of flights:* Cox; before-after comparison of Northwest flight schedules.

**March 7, 2002**

*Simon's numbers:* Simon showed author her calculations.

*Meeting re Empire State Development Corporation:* Bart; summary of meeting prepared by someone who was there.

**March 11, 2002**

*Jennie Farrell to Washington:* Farrell.

*Cartier disenchanted:* Michael Cartier, Farrell.

*Meetings with Bloomberg:* Michael Cartier, Farrell, Bloomberg.

*White House meeting on color alert system:* Ridge, Abbot, Neely, two senior White House aides.

**March 12, 2002**

*Raytheon war room and preparations to bid on contract:* Woollen, Shea, Poza; personal visit by author.

*1,200 people to be used:* Poza.

*TSA thinking of tinkering with RFP:* Null.

*Bush calls Ashcroft and Ridge:* Comstock, Neely, Ziglar, Peterman.

*"We had crammed it down at a middle-management level":* Ridge staff person involved in INS issues.

*Ridge worried about TSA:* Ridge, Abbot, Jackson.

*Meeting about "trusted traveler" program:* McHale; summary of meeting obtained by author.

*Strachan deposition and his cover note:* Deposition transcripts and discovery exhibits obtained by author.

*Strachan's note that he doodled to himself:* Discovery exhibits obtained by author.

*Memos in Silverstein's broker's files:* Discovery exhibits obtained by author.

*Notes of Nashville conference call:* Discovery exhibits obtained by author.


## March 17, 2002

*Lyons finds tool and possible remains:* Brian Lyons.

*Conversation with Elaine:* Brian Lyons, Elaine Lyons.


## March 19, 2002

*Justice Department leads:* Federal prosecutor involved in Buffalo terror cell investigation; local investigator involved in terror cell investigation in New Jersey.


## March 21, 2002

*Rumsfeld announcement:* Department of Defense transcript.

*CSIS scenario and report of tabletop session:* CSIS Greater Washington, D.C., crisis planning workshop, March 21, 2002, report; summary of session prepared by Ridge's office, obtained by author.

*Some on Ridge's staff believed:* Neely, Lawlor.

*Indictment of Michigan man:* "A Nation Challenged: Fraud; 23 Accused of Taking Money Meant for Sept. 11 Victims," by Robert F. Worth, *New York Times,* March 22, 2002; "22 Charged in Post-Attack Fraud; Alleged False Reports of Sept. 11 Deaths Netted $760,000," by Lena H. Sun, *Washington Post,* March 22, 2002; "Cheating Charity; DA: 23 Charged with Falsifying Claims in Attacks," by Karen Freifeld, *Newsday,* March 22, 2002.

*Red Cross records:* Records read and summarized to author by Chlopak.

*Ridge proposal to merge Customs and INS:* Ridge, Card, Falkenrath.

*Card discussion with Bush:* Card.


## March 26, 2002

*Government looking for witnesses in Moussaoui death penalty phase:* Text posted on Give Your Voice website—*www.giveyourvoice.com.*

*Patrick Cartier, Sr., experience auditioning as death penalty witness:* Patrick Cartier, Sr., Farrell.

*Simon experience:* Simon.

*Whole thing was Ashcroft's idea:* Senior Justice Department official involved in Moussaoui prosecution, government prosecutor who works in a United States attorney's office.

*Hall, Lindemann learn INS will proceed with disciplinary action:* Hall, Lindemann, France.

## March 31, 2002

*Ninety-person Raytheon team worked through the weekend:* Shea, Poza.

*Poza background and confidence:* Poza.

*Woman who headed the actual writing effort—neither Poza nor Woollen ever actually read the full text of the drafts—was the woman who had managed the FAA contract:* Poza, Woollen.

## April 1, 2002

*Ridge marveled at Loy:* Ridge.

*How Loy solved problem:* Internal Office of Homeland Security memo, obtained by author.

*Lindh hearing:* Author was not present and did not read transcript. These accounts come from articles in *Washington Post* and *New York Times* on April 2, 2002 ("Prosecutors Concede Limits of Their Case Against Lindh; Government Has No Evidence He Shot at U.S. Citizens," by Brooke A. Masters, and "A Nation Challenged: The American Prisoner; No Need to Tie Lindh to Deaths, Judge Rules," by Katharine Q. Seelye, respectively), and, then, from interviews with Brosnahan, West, and Lewis.

*Repaving in New York City:* Weinshall.

*Jaffri put on the plane without belongings:* Facts, as alleged, in suit filed against government by Jaffri's pro bono liberal legal activist lawyers.

## April 2, 2002

*Detroit Free Press published report:* "Two Border Agents Still Face Penalty," by Tamara Audi, *Detroit Free Press,* April 2, 2002.

*Magistri sells shares:* SEC InVision disclosure filings.

## April 3, 2002

*Lindemann's sector chief called:* Lindemann.

*Ziglar knew about and supported the decision to go ahead with the discipline:* Strassberger.

*Grassley called Ziglar:* Grassley aide.

*No INS media policy statement by year-end:* Strassberger.

**April 4, 2002**

*Lyons's old boss called him:* Brian Lyons.

*Byrne was asked about report in newsletter:* The author was the one who asked Byrne.

*Story about AGILE:* McGraw-Hill's *Homeland Security & Defense*, April 3, 2002. (Like Byrne, author would never have known about AGILE without reading this article.)

*Six months later, AGILE's director would say:* Coty.

*Lawlor felt even more strongly:* Lawlor.

*Situation Room meeting re TSA:* PowerPoint presentation of meeting seen by author; Mineta, Jackson, Magaw, Daniels.

**April 5, 2002**

*Decision to set up group to study new Department of Homeland Security:* Card.

*Card, Ridge discussion:* Card, Ridge.

*Falkenrath began writing memo:* Falkenrath.

**April 7, 2002**

*Simon flies home, opens mail:* Simon.

**April 8, 2002**

*Terrorism insurance event at White House:* "Bush Pushes Bill to Protect Insurers from Terrorism Losses," by Stephen Labaton with Joseph B. Treaster, *New York Times,* April 9, 2002; "Bush Pushes Congress to Revive Stalled Terrorism Insurance Bill," by Michael Schroeder, *Wall Street Journal,* April 9, 2002; "Bush Presses Senate to Act on His Agenda," by Dana Milbank, *Washington Post,* April 9, 2002; Crane, Lindsey.

*Cartier gets word:* Michael Cartier.

**April 9, 2002**

*First meeting of small group:* Two people who were present.

*Raytheon's and other proposals submitted to TSA:* Copies obtained and read, or seen and read, by author.

**April 11, 2002**

*Cox walks a visitor through the airport:* Author was the visitor.

*Scene in Oklahoma City training facility:* Author was present.

*Rossides's role in planning training and curriculum:* Magaw, Rossides.

*Iacono encounter with Bloomberg:* Iacono, Bloomberg.

*Two hours later Iacono's phone working:* Iacono.

*Iacono needed to sign Seedco papers:* Bart e-mail to Seedco and Seedco e-mail to Bart, obtained by author.

## April 12, 2002

*Schumer meeting with Cartiers:* Schumer, Michael Cartier, Patrick Cartier, Jr., Farrell.

*Smallpox exercise in Oklahoma City:* Memo about this written by one of the observers, obtained by author; aide to Lawlor.

## April 14, 2002

*Cartiers get word of remains found:* Farrell, Michael Cartier.

## April 15, 2002

*Detention and release of Palestinian in Detroit:* Strassberger, Lindemann.

## April 16, 2002

*Ridge visit to Detroit:* Weeks.

*C-TPAT:* Bonner; Customs Service press releases.

*Not more than a half mile from the Ambassador Bridge:* Author's personal observation; see text for April 26.

## April 17, 2002

*To Schumer it was part of a pattern:* Schumer.

*Null got first reports:* Null, Hardt; proposals were also read by author, who agrees with these assessments.

*The staff member who had come up with the 28,000 estimate had left out:* See account in text from October 11.

*Jackson had told Magaw, Rossides, and others not to tell airport officials:* Magaw, Rossides, Hardt—and confirmed by Jackson.

## April 18, 2002

*Threat matrix briefing:* As noted in a footnote to the text, this account comes mostly from an article entitled "For Two Tense Days, Bush Team Wrestled with Vague Terror Threat," by Jeanne Cummings and Gary Fields, in the May 17, 2002, issue of the *Wall Street Journal.* I got it confirmed from Ridge, Larry Thompson, and two people on Ridge's staff, who filled in a few details.

*CNN programming:* Watched by author.

**April 19, 2002**

*Rossides's day, office moved, etc.:* Rossides.

**April 22, 2002**

*"Can they do that?":* Senior Justice Department official.

*McCabe gets new VACIS, refines criteria:* McCabe, Hegler.

*Bonner knew of McCabe:* Bonner.

*One of the lawyers working on the Silverstein side says, "We haven't found one yet":* Interview with author.

**April 23, 2002**

*Ziglar in Australia, unaware of White House change in position:* Ziglar.

*PEOC session:* Four people who were there.

**April 24, 2002**

*Magistri activities:* Magistri, Mattson.

*Top lobbyist for American Association of Airport Executives meeting with Rogers:* Hauptli, Efford.

**April 26, 2002**

*Boats dock in Detroit:* Author's personal observation.

*Border Patrol agents on duty at the time:* France.

*Letter to Sensenbrenner:* From Department of Justice, July 26, 2002, released on Judiciary Committee website.

*Flaherty-Jackson friendly game:* Flaherty, Jackson.

**April 27, 2002**

*Elaine Lyons gets form letter:* Read by author.

*What Lyons was concerned about:* Lyons.

**April 30, 2002**

*Scene at Baltimore/Washington Airport:* Author was there.

**May 1, 2002**

*Entry-exit meeting:* Summary of meeting obtained by author.

**May 2, 2002**

*Assessment of Raytheon and other proposals to TSA:* Hardt, Null, Schambach.

*Coalition of high-tech companies from New Mexico:* Kline.

*Murray lobbied by New Mexico coalition and InVision:* Kline, McCann.

*Ridge's office helps with Interior Department/FAA arrangement:* Summary of meeting obtained by author.

## May 3, 2002

*Woollen considered RFP delay an advantage:* Woollen.

*"How can the numbers be that bad?":* Rossides.

*Pearson problems:* Jackson, Rossides, Hardt; acknowledged by Hackenson of Pearson, though he did add, accurately, that these problems were later resolved.

*Article got to Ridge:* Neely.

## May 7, 2002

*PEOC meeting:* Four people who were there.

*Ridge's view of trusted traveler programs:* Ridge, Lawlor.

*Meeting on trusted traveler:* Summary of meeting obtained by author; Jackson.

*Prior meetings over student visas:* Summaries obtained by author; author present at one meeting.

*Coalition wrote to Ridge:* Copy of letter obtained by author.

## May 8, 2002

*Circumstances of Padilla arrest:* Taken from subsequent court filings describing the arrest.

*Feds' decision bitterly opposed:* Two FBI field agents, one federal prosecutor.

*Reasons for early arrest:* Senior Justice Department official.

*Padilla's lawyer not allowed to say anything publicly:* Newman.

*Entry-exit meeting:* Minutes of meeting obtained by author.

## May 12, 2002

*McCabe thought Schumer got it right:* McCabe.

*Lyons looking for a job:* Lyons.

## May 14, 2002

*Iacono-Bart conversation:* Iacono, Bart.

*Baumeister had gathered sixty clients, talking to Beamer:* Baumeister; this could not be confirmed with Beamer, who declined to be interviewed.

*Feinberg San Francisco session:* Author was present.

*Padilla finally allowed to see lawyer:* Newman.

**May 15, 2002**

*Brosnahan eager to question Army intelligence agents, had investigators working on FBI agent:* Brosnahan, Lewis, West.

*PEOC meeting:* Five people who were there.

**May 16, 2002**

*Smallpox meeting:* Two people who were there; summary obtained by author.

*Some on Ridge's staff:* Three staff members.

*Chemical industry safety meeting:* Summary of meeting obtained by author.

*Republicans on Ridge's staff agreed the liberal environmental groups' concerns were reasonable:* Four members of Ridge's staff.

**May 17, 2002**

*Rossides gets update:* Rossides.

*Cox's budget and rates:* Cox.

*Raytheon reaction to TSA decision:* Poza, Woollen, Shea.

**May 20, 2002**

*FBI-Pentagon meeting:* Summary obtained by author.

**May 21, 2002**

*Cartier quoted:* "Kin Uniting on Memorial Agree on 7 Acres at WTC Site," by Greg Gittrich, *New York Daily News,* May 21, 2002.

*Cartier had mixed feelings:* Cartier.

*Family's anger:* Michael Cartier, John Cartier, Farrell.

*Woollen review:* Woollen, Shea.

*Article on Social Security cards:* "Foreigners Obtain Social Security ID with Fake Papers," by Robert Pear, *New York Times,* May 20, 2002.

*Ridge staff's resentment:* Two staff members.

*PEOC meeting:* Five people who were there.

*Ridge-Bush conversation:* Someone whom Ridge told about it immediately after it happened, senior White House official.

*Ridge's hint of reluctance surprised Bush's advisors:* Two senior White House officials.

*Ridge of two minds:* Ridge, Holman.

**May 22, 2002**

*Morale high at InVision:* Visit by author.

*To the extent that analysts were asked about it:* Author interviews with three analysts.

*Magistri estimated to a reporter today:* Interview with author.

*Jackson and Null had no plans to buy InVision equipment beyond current orders:* Jackson, Null.

*Raytheon demonstration of command vehicle:* Woollen, one law enforcement official who was there.

## May 23, 2002

*InVision lobbyist made the rounds:* McCann, Magistri.

## May 24, 2002

*Burnham letter:* Copy obtained by author.

*Jackson reaction to letter:* Jackson, Null, Shea.

*PEOC meeting:* Five people who were there.

## May 27, 2002

*Simon family situation:* Simon.

*Lyons families go to memorial service:* Elaine Lyons, Brian Lyons.

## May 29, 2002

*Everything plotted out meticulously:* Copy of rollout schedule obtained by author.

*Letter to Mineta:* Copy obtained by author.

New York Times *article about letter to Mineta:* "Airports Urge Delay in New Security Rules," by Matthew L. Wald, *New York Times,* June 2, 2002.

*Magistri tells lobbyist to join forces:* Magistri.

*Ground Zero ceremony:* "Last Steel Column from the Ground Zero Rubble Is Cut Down," by Charlie LeDuff, *New York Times,* May 29, 2002; "Farewell at Ground Zero; New York Concludes Its 8½-Month Recovery and Cleanup Operation," by Lynne Duke, *Washington Post,* May 31, 2002; "Ceremony Tonight at WTC Site," by Greg Gittrich, *New York Daily News,* May 28, 2002.

## May 30, 2002

*Romero was asked:* Interview with author.

*Strategy on Magaw:* Flaherty, Jackson.

*Magaw conversation with Mineta:* Senior Transportation Department official.

*Rossides's reaction to Loy appointment:* Rossides.

*Schumer activities and speech:* Author was with Schumer.

*Cartier had changed his mind:* Cartier.

**May 31, 2002**

*Feinberg-Kreindler meeting:* Feinberg, Lee Kreindler.

*Fund statistics:* Fund website.

*Feinberg getting restless:* Feinberg.

*Service centers empty:* Visits by research assistant Louise Story.

**June 1, 2002**

*Job fair:* Paige, Mohammed.

**June 5, 2002**

*Red Cross received $967 million:* Red Cross website.

*Policy time decision:* Senior White House official, member of Ridge's staff, written summary of decision obtained by author.

*Feinberg tries to edit the form:* Feinberg.

*Simon plans for filing:* Simon.

*Elaine Lyons view on filing:* Brian Lyons.

*Patrick Cartier, Sr., view on filing:* Patrick Cartier, Sr., Michael Cartier.

*Card meetings with cabinet members:* Card, Mineta, senior White House official.

*Specifics of Card meeting with Ashcroft:* Three senior White House aides.

**June 6, 2002**

*Rollout of Department of Homeland Security events:* Internal summary obtained by author.

**June 7, 2002**

*Schumer thoughts:* Schumer.

*Rossides contemplates FLETC job:* Rossides, Jackson.

*Cox gets flights back:* Cox.

*Cox trip to Dallas:* Cox.

*Preparing Padilla arguments:* Newman, two government lawyers involved in the case.

*Boeing team to meet on Saturday:* Stephens.

**June 10, 2002**

*Backstory of wording of Ashcroft announcement:* Justice Department public affairs aide, senior White House official, White House Communications Office aide.

*Wolfowitz didn't need encouragement:* White House aide involved in economics policy, White House Communications Office official, senior White House official.

*Ashcroft-Rumsfeld relationship:* Senior Ashcroft aide, senior White House official, civilian official in Pentagon, official in Justice Department Public Affairs Office, close friend of Rumsfeld's.

*Ashcroft's staff had complained to White House and some conservative columnists:* Justice Department public affairs aide, one columnist, senior White House official.

*Pentagon people knew that some on Ashcroft's staff seemed eager to tell reporters:* Pentagon civilian official.

*Ashcroft, Rumsfeld barely talking to each other:* Two senior White House officials, one of whom volunteered the information, the second of whom confirmed it; two senior officials in the Office of Homeland Security who heard this from Ashcroft's and Rumsfeld's key deputies. Rumsfeld's spokesperson declined any comment on Rumsfeld's relationship with Ashcroft.

*One of Ashcroft's closest aides was asked a few days later:* Senior Ashcroft aide involved in this and all other Ashcroft policy decisions.

*McCabe exasperated:* McCabe.

*President's meeting with congressional leaders:* Daschle, senior Ridge aide.

*Soundings taken by staff:* Falkenrath, two White House aides.

*Ridge began to get the sense:* Ridge.

## June 12, 2002

*Simon and flag:* Simon.

*Ridge meets with members of Congress, tells reporters:* "Bioterror Defense Bill Signed; Bush Says Goal Is to Counter 'Most Dangerous Weapons,' " by Bill Miller, *Washington Post,* June 13, 2002; "Traces of Terror: Domestic Security; Support for a New Agency but Concern About the Details," by David Firestone, *New York Times,* June 13, 2002.

*Ridge's outlook:* Ridge, Neely, Holman.

## June 14, 2002

*Erikenoglu encounter with state troopers:* Erikenoglu.

*Lindemann hears about a problem in new homeland security department proposal:* Lindemann, Hall; union website.

## June 17, 2002

*McCabe-Bonner encounter:* McCabe, Bonner.

*Washington Post article:* "Ashcroft's High Profile, Motives Raise White House Concerns," by Dan Eggen, *Washington Post,* June 17, 2002.

*Ashcroft furious:* Two senior Ashcroft aides.

*Aide said Rumsfeld and Ridge jealous:* Senior Ashcroft aide.

*Ashcroft hands out quotes from the scriptures:* Author's repeated visits to Attorney General's office suite.

### June 18, 2002

*Suit over Condé Nast building:* "Ruling Allows Mortgage Holders to Require Terrorism Insurance," by Peter Grant, *Wall Street Journal,* June 21, 2002.

*Rossides's reaction to Louisville incident:* Rossides.

*Cox chortled, told the story to anyone:* Cox.

### June 19, 2002

Washington Post *article:* "Separate Personnel System Envisioned for Homeland Security," by Stephen Barr. *Washington Post,* June 19, 2002.

*Rossides's reaction to hearings and bad press:* Rossides.

*Jackson and Flaherty view that Magaw had lost credibility:* Flaherty.

### June 22, 2002

*Cartier funeral service:* Author attended.

### June 23, 2002

*McCabe rehearsals:* McCabe, two other Customs people who were present.

### June 24, 2002

*Agreement between Customs and INS:* Summary of meeting obtained by author.

*Tolstoi, Canada, as source of foot and vehicle traffic into U.S.:* Visit by author, Delaquis.

*Lawlor and staff sense that something is different:* Three Office of Homeland Security staff members.

*Scene at Bush appearance in Elizabeth:* Author was there.

*Bush-McCabe conversation:* McCabe, Bonner.

*Poza tapped to run Raytheon unit:* Poza, Shea, Burnham.

### June 25, 2002

*Swiss Re mock trials:* Ostrager.

*Question of whistle-blowers had never come up:* Five people involved in the PEOC meetings.

*Lindemann thought Border Patrol would be able to fire him instantly:* Lindemann.

*Cox receives fax:* Copy obtained by author.

### June 26, 2002

*Schumer's sense of Anti Nuclear Terrorism Act's prospects:* Schumer.

### June 27, 2002

*Ridge-Raytheon meeting:* Woollen, Burnham, three other people who were there.

*It was frustrating:* Woollen.

**June 28, 2002**

*Iacono gets business interruption claim paid:* Bart.

*I'm going to buy you the best champagne:* Geerdes.

*Cox receives phone call:* Cox.

**June 29, 2002**

*September 11th Fund e-mail:* Copy obtained by author.

*All from McKinsey blueprint:* McKinsey plan read by author.

*ACLU encounter session:* Romero, Weber, two members of ACLU staff.

*Lyons's new job:* Lyons.

**July 3, 2002**

*Interview of surgeon:* West, Harris.

*Interview with Army intelligence officer:* Brosnahan, Harris.

**July 4, 2002**

*Coordinating center activities for July 4:* Office of Homeland Security internal memo obtained by author.

**July 5, 2002**

*Cox assessment of Lockheed people:* Cox.

**July 8, 2002**

*Feinberg meeting with Trial Lawyers Care group:* Feinberg, Stewart.

**July 9, 2002**

*Boeing team at Memphis airport:* Cox.

*Obey letter:* Public document, obtained by author.

*Ridge's staff reaction to letter:* Falkenrath, Lawlor.

*Fine meets with Fernandez:* Chatterjee, Brosnahan, Harris, Fernandez.

*Rene Cruz's specifics:* Chatterjee. The Justice Department refused comment on anything having to do with the Cruz case or how it might have affected its negotiations in the Lindh case.

**July 10, 2002**

*Homeland security expo:* Author was present.

*Magistri saw same security gap:* Magistri.

*Ancore being assessed by TSA:* Jackson.

*Ancore being tested in El Paso:* Ancore exhibit sales material.

*Ridge testimony:* Author was present.

*War room:* Falkenrath, Neely.

*War room's assessment:* Falkenrath, senior White House official.

*Lindemann and Hall in Senate cafeteria:* Author was present.

*Ridge and his staff had begun to believe they made a mistake:* Neely, Holman, Ridge, senior White House aide.

*Ridge's thoughts:* Ridge, Neely, Holman.

*Falkenrath and Holman increasingly frustrated:* Ridge, Falkenrath.

*Schumer view on Homeland Security Department union issue:* Schumer.

*Schumer hadn't read the full text of the Lieberman proposal:* Schumer.

*Insurance settlement discussion:* Transcript obtained by author.

## July 12, 2002

*Feinberg-plaintiffs conference call:* Schiavo, Feinberg.

*Brosnahan-government settlement discussions:* Brosnahan, Harris, West. The government would not comment beyond the assessment of one senior Justice Department official in a position to know that the details were "essentially accurate." Ashcroft said in an interview that he had "no recollection" of whether credibility problems concerning FBI agent Reimann had anything to do with the plea bargain in the Lindh case.

## July 15, 2002

*Brosnahan thought the system had been made to work, but considers Ashcroft "dangerous":* Brosnahan.

*Cox in Washington:* Cox.

*Ashcroft and staff grasped significance of Fine inquiry:* Two aides in Ashcroft's office.

## July 16, 2002

*"What we got was what was there before":* "Visions of Ground Zero: The Overview; Six Plans for Ground Zero, All Seen as a Starting Point," by Edward Wyatt, *New York Times,* July 17, 2002.

## July 17, 2002

*By now Cox wasn't that worried:* Cox.

## July 18, 2002

*Mineta staff meeting:* Mineta, Rossides.

*Rossides-Jackson conversation:* Rossides, Jackson.

*INS, State Department agree to work with Virginia Department of Motor Vehicles:* Summary of meeting obtained by author.

*Simon experience with interview:* Eileen Simon, Brittany Simon; author viewed aired version of interview.

## July 19, 2002

*Loy staff meeting:* Rossides.

## July 20, 2002

*Bloomberg theory:* Bloomberg.

*Javits Center meeting:* Research assistants Claire Miller and Elise Jordan watched tapes of the July 20 meeting, and Claire Miller attended the July 22 meeting.

*Concept of potential Silverstein deal and resolution of Trade Center rebuilding issues:* Childs, lawyer involved in Silverstein litigation on Silverstein side (but not Wachtell), senior aide to Bloomberg, two members of Lower Manhattan Development Corporation.

## July 24, 2002

*Rossides's bad news and worse news:* Rossides.

*Plan to supplement Pearson:* Rossides, Hardt.

## July 26, 2002

*Policy argument made by airline security company lobbyists:* Two of the lobbyists.

*Letter to Sensenbrenner:* Released on Judiciary Committee website.

## July 27, 2002

*Simons go to birthday party:* Eileen Simon.

*Ridge summer plans:* Ridge, two senior aides to Ridge.

*Magistri-Jackson meeting:* Magistri, Jackson.

*Real purpose of the meeting:* Jackson.

*Raytheon may try to get back into airport security:* Poza.

*Raytheon Olympics project:* Poza.

## July 31, 2002

*TSA meeting with airport directors:* Cox, Jackson, Rossides.

*Padilla hearing:* "Movement in Suit on Custody," by Benjamin Weiser, *New York Times,* August 1, 2002; Newman; author was not at the hearing and did not get a transcript. These quotations are from the *New York Times.*

## August 1, 2002

*To Schumer the proposal was his way of recalibrating thoughtfully:* Schumer.

*Lyons vacation:* Brian Lyons.

**August 7, 2002**

*Simon's decision about going to Ground Zero:* Simon, friend of hers in her widows group.

**August 9, 2002**

*Rossides's stress test:* Rossides.

**August 11, 2002**

*Cartier family vacation:* Michael Cartier, Jennie Farrell.

**August 13, 2002**

*Cox's worries:* Cox.

*US Airways bankruptcy:* "Uncertain Skies—US Airways, Hit Hard by Terror, Files Chapter 11," by Susan Carey, *Wall Street Journal*, August 12, 2002.

*Hamdi hearing:* "Judge Skewers U.S. Curbs on Detainee," by Tom Jackman, *Washington Post*, August 14, 2002; author was not there and did not read a transcript. These quotations are taken from the *Washington Post*.

**August 14, 2002**

*Lindemann's view of the fight:* Lindemann.

*Aides in the White House thought this should now be a political fight:* Holman, Ridge, two senior White House aides.

**August 15, 2002**

*Cartier family view of suit against Saudis:* Michael Cartier, Patrick Cartier, Sr.

**August 16, 2002**

*Ashcroft saw this as battle between us and them:* Two senior Justice Department officials.

*Ashcroft believed:* Ashcroft.

*Lindemann thrilled:* Lindemann.

**August 19, 2002**

*Simon and others on the beach:* Simon, one of the other women.

*Cox-Thompson meeting:* Cox, Thompson.

**August 20, 2002**

*Schumer family in Italy:* Weinshall, Schumer.

*Port Elizabeth tabletop drill:* McCabe.

## August 24, 2002

*Byrne hears about, sees Raytheon First Responder:* Byrne.

*No one at Raytheon knew:* Woollen, Poza, Shea.

Wall Street Journal *article:* "Improving Communications for Rescuers After Disasters," by Anne Marie Squeo, *Wall Street Journal,* August 28, 2002.

*Woollen gets congratulations:* Woollen.

*Raytheon had only sold two vehicles:* Shea.

*Simon family at wedding:* Simon.

## August 27, 2002

*Announcement worth $6,000 to Iacono, but a catch:* Bart.

## August 28, 2002

*Details of Detroit cell indictment:* From affidavit filed by FBI agent who made initial arrests, and from the indictment.

*One of the defendants' lawyers:* Ernst.

## September 1, 2002

*Cox chuckled:* Cox.

*Memphis airport evacuated:* "Security Scare Ties Up Flights, Travelers," by Chris Conley, *Commercial Appeal,* September 2, 2002; Cox.

*Cox's people took Thompson aside:* Thompson, Cox.

Dallas Morning News *article:* "Navigating the New Security; Trek Spanning 9 Airports Finds Smoother Process," by Terri Langford, *Dallas Morning News,* September 1, 2002.

*Pearson doing excellent screening job:* Rossides.

## September 2, 2002

*Customs inspectors start in Rotterdam:* Bonner, Dennis Murphy, McCabe.

*Bonner about to promulgate:* Bonner, Dennis Murphy. These regulations were, in fact, promulgated in November 2002.

## September 3, 2002

*Ridge state of mind:* Ridge, Holman, Neely, two senior White House officials.

## September 4, 2002

*Meeting about visa backlogs:* Summary of meeting obtained by author.

Yale Daily News *article:* "Visa Delays Keep Yalies Abroad," by Naomi Massave, *Yale Daily News,* September 6, 2002.

New York Times *article:* "Threats and Responses: Immigration; New Policy Delays Visas for Specified Muslim Men," by Raymond Bonner, *New York Times,* September 10, 2002.

*Backlog eased:* Peterman.

## September 5, 2002

*Rossides trip to St. Louis:* Rossides.

## September 9, 2002

*Faruq beginning to talk:* One FBI official, one senior White House official; also an article in the *New York Times* reported Faruq's capture and interrogation in greater detail: "Threats and Responses: Embassies; Plan to Attack Embassies Cited," by Raymond Bonner, *New York Times,* September 11, 2002.

*Same group called back to a White House meeting:* Two people who were there.

## September 10, 2002

*Whole series of steps followed changing of the alert status:* Neely.

*Extra shifts for McCabe:* McCabe.

*Simon's indecision:* Simon, friend of Simon's, Scott Simon.

## September 11, 2002

*Traffic data at Memphis airport:* Supplied by airport officials.

*Cox confidence and willingness to give TSA benefit of doubt:* Cox.

*Thermostats:* Cox.

*McCabe meeting at Coast Guard:* McCabe, Dennis Murphy.

*ABC story:* Transcript of website version; author watched the program.

*Customs' efforts to rebut story:* Dennis Murphy, McCabe.

*Customs' version of what had happened with container ABC tried to ship:* McCabe, Dennis Murphy, Bonner.

*Feinberg activities:* Feinberg.

*Feinberg review of firemen's cases:* Feinberg.

*Substance of firemen's cases:* Barasch, Feinberg; author obtained and reviewed sample case workups by Barasch.

*Cruz-Santiago case:* "The Price of Survival," by Jim Oliphant, *Legal Times,* September 23, 2002; Feinberg.

*Feinberg view of Cruz-Santiago case:* Feinberg.

*Feinberg NBC appearance:* Transcript of tape.

*"You deserve a medal":* Feinberg, Brokaw.

*Ashcroft activities:* Department of Justice Office of Public Affairs.

*Buffalo-area case:* The indictment and transcript of press conference.

*Buffalo case got some help from voluntary interviews:* Federal prosecutor knowledgeable about the case.

*Buffalo case was in part the result of use of USA Patriot Act:* Two Justice Department prosecutors involved in the case.

*Cartier family activities:* Farrell and Cartier.

*Schumer activities and scene near Ground Zero:* Author was present.

*Scene in tent:* Author was present.

*Simon activities:* Eileen Simon, Scott Simon, Brittany Simon.

## Epilogue: January 2003

*Simon's situation:* Simon.

*Status of Memphis airport and Cox:* Cox.

*Bush White House pushes terrorism/tort reform compromise through:* Schumer.

*Brian Lyons's job:* Lyons.

*Elaine Lyons's new home:* Brian Lyons, Elaine Lyons.

*Schumer not invited to signing of terrorism insurance bill:* Schumer.

*Schumer's optimism regarding legislative prospects:* Schumer, two members of his staff.

*Romero and ACLU activities:* Romero, ACLU press releases.

*ACLU membership statistics:* Romero.

*Raytheon business statistics:* Poza, Shea.

*Jackson talked about as cabinet material:* Two senior White House officials.

*Rossides asked to speak:* Rossides.

*Victims fund statistics:* Fund website.

*How logjam was broken:* Feinberg, Lee Kreindler, Baumeister.

New York Times *story about Feinberg fund delaying decision making:* "Victims' Kin Find Fault with Overseer of 9/11 Fund," by David W. Chen, *New York Times,* November 13, 2002.

New York Times Magazine *article about the victims fund:* "Just Money," by Lisa Belkin, *New York Times Magazine,* December 8, 2002.

*Patrick Cartier, Sr., expects to file:* Michael Cartier, Patrick Cartier.

*InVision financials:* InVision January 2003 public statements to stock analysts and prior SEC filings.

*Magistri's r&d spending and outlook on his business:* Magistri.

*Iacono thinks he'll make it:* Iacono.

*McCabe staff increases and electronic reports:* McCabe, U.S. Customs Office of Public Affairs.

*Ashcroft comfortable, energized:* Ashcroft.

*Almost as many entrances to New York City subway system:* New York City Metropolitan Transportation Authority Office of Public Affairs.

# Index

689

# About the Author

Steven Brill, a graduate of Yale College and Yale Law School, is the author of the bestselling *The Teamsters*. He founded *The American Lawyer* magazine in 1979, which expanded into a chain of legal publications. In 1991 he founded cable television's Court TV. After selling his interests in those businesses in 1997, he founded *Brill's Content,* a magazine about the media, which closed in 2001. After September 11th, Brill became a columnist for *Newsweek* and an analyst for NBC on issues related to the aftermath of the terrorist attacks. A winner of the National Magazine award, Brill lives in New York City with his wife and three children.

| DATE DUE | | |
|---|---|---|
|  |  |  |
|  |  |  |
|  |  |  |
|  |  |  |
|  |  |  |
|  |  |  |
|  |  |  |
|  |  |  |
|  |  |  |
|  |  |  |
|  |  |  |
|  |  |  |

3/04